*Also in the Variorum Collected Studies Series:*

**WILFERD MADELUNG**
Studies in Medieval Muslim Thought and History

**WILFERD MADELUNG**
Religious and Ethnic Movements in Medieval Islam

**DEVIN DEWEESE**
Studies on Sufism in Central Asia

**MARIBEL FIERRO**
The Almohad Revolution
Politics and Religion in the Islamic West during the Twelfth–Thirteenth Centuries

**DAVID S. POWERS**
The Development of Islamic Law and Society in the Maghrib
Qadis, Muftis and Family Law

**RICHARD M. FRANK**
Philosophy, Theology and Mysticism in Medieval Islam
Texts and Studies on the Development and History of Kalam, Vol. I

**RICHARD M. FRANK**
Early Islamic Theology: The Mu'tazilites and al-Ash'ari
Texts and Studies on the Development and History of Kalam, Vol. II

**RICHARD M. FRANK**
Classical Islamic Theology: The Ash'arites
Texts and Studies on the Development and History of Kalam, Vol. III

**NORMAN CALDER**
Interpretation and Jurisprudence in Medieval Islam

**PATRICIA CRONE**
From Kavad to al-Ghazali
Religion, Law and Political Thought in the Near East, c.600–c.1100

**FEDWA MALTI-DOUGLAS**
Power, Marginality, and the Body in Medieval Islam

**MICHAEL BRETT**
Ibn Khaldun and the Medieval Maghrib

VARIORUM COLLECTED STUDIES SERIES

# Studies in Medieval Shi‘ism

Wilferd Madelung

# Studies in Medieval Shiʿism

Edited by
Sabine Schmidtke

ROUTLEDGE
Routledge
Taylor & Francis Group
LONDON AND NEW YORK

First published 2012 by Ashgate Publishing

Published 2016 by Routledge
2 Park Square, Milton Park, Abingdon, Oxon OX14 4RN
52 Vanderbilt Avenue, New York, NY 10017

*Routledge is an imprint of the Taylor & Francis Group, an informa business*



**British Library Cataloguing in Publication Data**
Madelung, Wilferd.
Studies in medieval Shi'ism.
– (Variorum collected studies series ; CS1015)
1. Shiah – Doctrines – History – To 1500. 2. Islamic law – History – To 1500.
I. Title II. Series III. Schmidtke, Sabine.
297.2'042–dc23

ISBN 9781409450115 **(hbk)**

**Library of Congress Control Number:** 2012938512

ISBN 13: 978-1-4094-5011-5 (hbk)

VARIORUM COLLECTED STUDIES SERIES CS1015

# CONTENTS

This volume contains xii + 312 pages

**PUBLISHER'S NOTE**

*The articles in this volume, as in all others in the Variorum Collected Studies Series, have not been given a new, continuous pagination. In order to avoid confusion, and to facilitate their use where these same studies have been referred to elsewhere, the original pagination has been maintained wherever possible.*

*Each article has been given a Roman number in order of appearance, as listed in the Contents. This number is repeated on each page and is quoted in the index entries.*

# PREFACE

This volume complements the selections of Wilferd Madelung's articles previously published as *Religious Schools and Sects in Medieval Islam* (Variorum, 1985) and *Religious and Ethnic Movements in Medieval Islam* (Variorum, 1992). It brings together his articles dealing with Shīʿism that were not included in the two earlier volumes or that have appeared since.

The first two studies examine legal and political aspects of early Shīʿism. In article **I** Madelung shows the significant impact of the teachings of the Prophet's paternal cousin ʿAbd Allāh b. ʿAbbās (d. 68/686–7) on early Shīʿite religious and legal doctrine despite the otherwise ambiguous attitude of the later Imāmī Shīʿite tradition towards him. The early Shīʿites specifically adopted some of his legal doctrines such as permitting temporary marriage (*mutʿa*), rejecting the validity of divorce through triple repudiation at a single time, rejecting the automatic release of the *umm al-walad*, repudiating the practice of wiping over the shoes instead of washing or wiping the feet in the ritual ablution, or paying the alms tax directly to one's Qurʾānic recipients. Article **II** examines the character of the early *shīʿat ʿAlī* in the times of the Rightly-Guided Caliphs and argues that Shīʿism at the time of ʿAlī already meant recognition of his claim to a prior right to the succession to Muḥammad – and this against the common Sunni view according to which this evolved only after his death (usually being ascribed to ʿAbd Allāh b. Sabāʾ).

The next group of articles relates to Zaydī intellectual history and elaborates on some aspects of Madelung's seminal study *Der Imam al-Qāsim ibn Ibrāhīm und die Glaubenslehre der Zaiditen* (Berlin: de Gruyter, 1965). In article **III** Madelung discusses the literary legacy of the Imām Abū Ṭālib al-Nāṭiq bi-l-Ḥaqq (d. ca. 424/1033) as it is preserved in the various European collections of Yemeni manuscripts and suggests a relative chronology of al-Nāṭiq's preserved writings. In addition, Madelung discusses the identity of Ms. *Ambrosiana X 96 SUP*, a treatise which advocates Basran Muʿtazilite doctrines and which was copied in 499/1105 in Ṣaʿda, and suggests that it is a copy of the *Mabādiʾ al-adilla* of al-Nāṭiq bi-l-ḥaqq. Articles IV and V address the doctrinal views of the Zaydī Imām al-Qāsim b. Ibrāhīm al-Rassī (d. 246/860), providing further evidence that, contrary to the view of Rudolph Strothmann and later scholars who adopted the latter's opinion unquestioningly or argued on the basis of writings falsely attributed to al-Qāsim, the Imām was by no means associated with Muʿtazilism. In article **IV** Madelung draws on the evidence of the anti-

Mu'tazilite Kūfan Zaydī scholar Muḥammad b. Manṣūr al-Murādī who was personally associated with al-Qāsim and very familiar with the latter's thought. Al-Murādī provides a detailed account of al-Qāsim's views that were at variance with those of the Mu'tazilites and reports that the Imām publicly condemned Mu'tazilite notions. In article **V** Madelung traces the doctrinal origins of al-Qāsim's theological notions, which were shaped as it seems during his time in Egypt where he engaged in disputations with Christians and atheists. Comparing al-Qāsim's thought with the writings of his Christian contemporaries, the Nestorian 'Ammār al-Baṣrī, the Melkite Theodore Abū Qurra, the Jacobite Abū Rā'iṭa, and the Jewish author al-Muqammiṣ, a former student of the Christian Nonnus of Nisibis, Madelung shows that al-Qāsim was not only familiar with a wide range of Christian theological literature but also formatively influenced by it and that his doctrinal thought structurally resembles that of Abū Qurra in most instances. Article **VI** investigates the by and large mixed responses of Zaydī scholars towards Sufism and traces the earliest manifestations of Zaydī sympathy for early Sufi ascetic piety in the writings of the Caspian Zaydī Imām al-Mu'ayyad bi-llāh (d. 411/1021). Besides Caspian Zaydism, the article discusses the often tense relationship between Yemeni Zaydis and Sufism since the 7th/13th century which became increasingly hostile over the following centuries, culminating in the persecution of Sufi orders down into the 20th century by the imams of Yemen.

The final group of ten articles focuses on the Ismā'īliyya, their social and political history and aspects of their religious thought. Articles **VII** and **X** are based on Madelung's PhD dissertation, submitted in 1957 to the University of Hamburg. Article **X** is a slightly revised translation of his 'Fatimiden und Baḥrainqarmaṭen', published in *Der Islam* 34 (1959), pp. 34–88, while Article **VII**, the second part of his dissertation, is published here in the German original. These two articles form the basis of some of his later studies on the Ismā'īliyya most of which are included in this volume. Articles **VIII** and **IX** are devoted to the dogmatic views of the Ismā'īlī author Abū Ya'qūb al-Sijistānī (d. after 360/971). In article **VIII** Madelung reassesses Abū Ya'qūb's notion of metempsychosis as formulated in his *Kashf al-maḥjūb* and his *Risāla al-Bāhira*, placing it in the overall development of his doctrinal thought during his life. In article **IX** Madelung presents the seven faculties described by Abū Ya'qūb in his *Kitāb al-Yanābī'*. His main concern is with the seventh faculty, which is commonly given as *al-ghayba* in the preserved manuscripts and in Corbin's edition of the text. Madelung argues that this is a misreading of *al-ghunya*, self-sufficiency. Article **XI** contains a meticulous analysis of the anti-Fāṭimid as against the official Fāṭimid accounts about Ḥamdān Qarmaṭ b. al-Ash'ath (d. 321/933), an Ismā'īlī *dā'ī* and founder of the Ismā'īlī movement in Iraq, establishing that Ḥamdān Qarmaṭ (as he is called in the anti-Fāṭimid sources) was the former name of the Fāṭimid *dāʿī* Abū ʿAlī Ḥasan b. Aḥmad (as he is exclusively named in the official Fāṭimid accounts). In article **XII**, Madelung sketches the religious policy of the Fāṭimids towards their Sunnī subjects in the Maghrib and the developments that eventually led to the massacre of the remaining small Ismāʿīlī communities there in 407/1016–17 towards the end of the Fāṭimid reign. Article **XIII** is devoted to the *Kitāb Tathbīt al-imāma* by the third Fatimid caliph al-Manṣūr bi-llāh Ismāʿīl (r. 334/946–341/953), in which the latter affirms the divine right of the Fāṭimid caliphs to rule, without addressing the esoteric Ismāʿīlī doctrine on the imamate. In article **XIV**, Madelung analyses a hitherto largely ignored commentary by the fifth Ismāʿīlī Ṭayyibī *dāʿī muṭlaq* of Yemen, Sayyidnā ʿAlī b. Muḥammad b. al-Walīd (d. 612/1215), on Ibn Sīnā's *ʿAyniyya* poem. In article **XV**, the extant writings of Shahriyār b. al-Ḥasan, a contemporary of al-Muʾayyad fī l-Dīn al-Shīrāzī (d. 470/1078) and *dāʿī* of Fārs and Kirmān who was later active in Yemen, are analyzed, viz. his treatise countering the denial of the spiritual world and his tract on the transgressions committed by the prophets. Article **XVI** contains a study of the basic structure of Muḥammad b. Aḥmad al-Nasafī's (d. 332/943) cosmogony as outlined in the *Kitāb Kawn al-ʿālam* (al-Nasafī's authorship is likely yet not certain) a manuscript of which has only recently become accessible.

Misprints and minor errors in the articles have, as far as possible, been corrected. I wish to express my gratitude to the editors and publishers of the journals and books in which these articles first appeared for their kind permission to republish them here.

SABINE SCHMIDTKE

*Wassenaar*
*April 2012*

# ACKNOWLEDGEMENTS

Grateful acknowledgement is made to the following institutions and publishers for their kind permission to reproduce the papers included in this volume: Peeters Publishers, Leuven (for articles I, V and VIII); State University of New York Press, Albany, NY (II); Walter de Gruyter GmbH, Berlin (III, VII); the Swedish Research Institute in Istanbul, Beyoglu (IV); Koninklijke Brill NV, Leiden (VI, XIII); Cambridge University Press (IX, X); THESA Publishing, St Petersburg (XI); Presses de l'Université Paris-Sorbonne (XII); I.B. Tauris & Co. Ltd, London (XIV); Leiden University Press (XV); and the Center for Middle Eastern Studies, University of Chicago (XVI).

Every effort has been made to trace all the copyright holders, but if any have been inadvertently overlooked the publishers will be pleased to make the necessary arrangement at the first opportunity.

I

# ʿABD ALLĀH B. ʿABBĀS AND SHIʿITE LAW

ʿAbd Allāh b. ʿAbbās b. ʿAbd al-Muṭṭalib (d. 68/686-7), paternal cousin of the Prophet Muḥammad and of ʿAlī b. Abī Ṭālib, is in modern Islamic studies generally acknowledged as one of the founders of religious scholarship in Sunnite Islam[1]. Ibn ʿAbbās is known to have been one of the collectors of the Qur'ān, and his variant readings were later recorded in the *Kutub al-Maṣāḥif* of the Qur'ān experts. His role as the father of Qur'anic exegesis is not disputed, although his exact contribution to it is at present difficult to assess[2]. In religious law he is recognized as the chief authority of the school of Mekka from among the Companions of the Prophet[3].

His part in Shiʿite Islam has received less attention. The attitude of Imāmī Shiʿite tradition towards him is ambiguous. He is commonly recognized as a companion of Imam ʿAlī. Al-Kaššī in his book on Shiʿite transmitters (*riǧāl*) quotes both favourable and unfavourable testimonies about him. In one of his reports Imam Muḥammad al-Bāqir narrates that a man complained to his father, Imam ʿAlī Zayn al-ʿĀbidīn, about ʿAbd Allāh b. ʿAbbās who claimed that he had knowlegde of every verse of the Qur'ān, of the day when it was sent down, and of what occasioned it. Imam Zayn al-ʿĀbidīn sent him to Ibn ʿAbbās to ask him about three Qur'anic verses, but Ibn ʿAbbās was unable to identify the persons described in them. The Imam then identified the person called "blind and incapable of accepting sincere advice" in two of the verses as ʿAbd Allāh's father ʿAbbās, and the persons ordered in the third verse to be steadfast as the Imam's fathers and family. He went on to describe Ibn ʿAbbās as a treacherer who coveted what was beyond him. From among his off-spring would come forth men who would depart from the religion of God and stain the earth with the blood of the Family of

[1] See L. Veccia-Vaglieri, *ʿAbd Allāh b. al-ʿAbbās, EI²*.

[2] See C. Gilliot, *Les débuts de l'exégèse coranique, REMMM* 58, 1990, pp. 82-100; C.H.M. Versteegh, *Arabic Grammar and Qurānic Exegesis in Early Islam,* Leiden 1993, esp. pp. 203-4.

[3] See H. Motzki, *Die Anfänge der islamischen Jurisprudenz: Ihre Entwicklung in Mekka bis zur Mitte des 2./8. Jahrhunderts,* Stuttgart 1991, esp. pp. 256-7.

Muḥammad (*Āl Muḥammad*)[4]. The report evidently reflects the Shiʿite experience of persecution and oppression under the ʿAbbāsid caliphate. In another report quoted by al-Kaššī, however, Imam Ǧaʿfar al-Ṣādiq describes his father Muḥammad al-Bāqir as very fond of Ibn ʿAbbās and as regularly paying him visits in his boyhood together with the other boys of the Banū ʿAbd al-Muṭṭalib[5]. Yet whatever the attitude of later Imāmī Shiʿites to Ibn ʿAbbās, they could not recognize him as sharing the priviledged religious knowledge of the Āl Muḥammad, the imams.

There is good evidence, however, that the teaching of Ibn ʿAbbās had a significant impact on early Imāmī Shiʿite religious and legal doctrine. Several Qur'anic readings of Ibn ʿAbbās deviating from the ʿUṯmānic standard text were adopted and utilized in Imāmī Shiʿism. Imāmī Shiʿites thus read in Qur'ān 22: 52: "We have not sent before you any messenger (*rasūl*) or prophet *(nabī)*" with the addition "or one spoken to *(wa-lā muḥaddaṯ)*" found in the codex of Ibn ʿAbbās[6]. The term *muḥaddaṯūn*, interpreted as "those to whom an angel speaks", was commonly applied by Imāmī Shiʿites to their imams and became a key term in their concept of the imamate. It allowed for a form of inspiration below that of *waḥy* which was in common Islamic dogma reserved to messengers and prophets. The *muḥaddaṯ* imams were believed to hear the angel speak to them, but, unlike prophets, not to see them[7].

In Qur'ān 5: 6, where the basic rules of ablution for the ritual prayer are defined, Ibn ʿAbbās read: *fa-ġsilū wuǧūhakum wa-aydiyakum wa-msaḥū bi-ru'ūsikum wa-arǧulikum,* "wash your faces and your hands and wipe over your heads and feet", instead of the Sunnite standard reading *wa-arǧulakum* requiring the washing *(ġasl)* of the feet. According to his client ʿIkrima he maintained that God had commanded two instances of washing and two instances of wiping and had argued that this is corroborated by the second part of the Qur'anic verse, where *tayammum*, wiping with sand instead of washing, is mentioned only with

[4] Al-Kaššī, *Iḫtiyār maʿrifat al-riǧāl,* ed. MAHDĪ AL-RAǦĀʾĪ, Qumm 1404/(1983) pp.273-5.

[5] Al-Kaššī, p. 277. Muḥammad al-Bāqir, born in 57/676-7, was ten or eleven years old when Ibn ʿAbbās died in 68/687-8.

[6] See A. JEFFERY, *Materials for the History of the Text of the Qur'ān,* Leiden 1937, p. 202. The codex of Ubayy b. Kaʿb contained the reading *wa-lā nabiyyin muḥaddaṯin,* thus qualifying prophets as "spoken to." Ubayy's reading was adopted by the Baṣran Abu l-Mutawakkil ʿAlī b. Dāwūd al-Nāǧī. JEFFERY, *Materials* p. 148.

[7] For a full discussion see E. KOHLBERG, The Term *Muḥaddath* in Twelver Shiʿism, in *Studia Orientalia memoriae D.H. Baneth dedicata,* Jerusalem 1979, repr. in *Belief and Law in Imāmī Shīʿism,* Variorum, 1991. On the term *muḥaddaṯ* in Sunnite and Aḥmadī usage see Y. FRIEDMANN, *Prophecy Continuous: Aspects of Aḥmadī Religious Thought and its Medieval Background,* London etc. 1989, esp. pp. 86-92.

respect to the faces and hands[8]. When confronted with a *ḥadīṯ* according to which the Prophet had washed his feet in ablution, he observed, it seems incredulously: "The people will not accept anything but washing; yet in the Book of God we find wiping[9]." Reports transmitted by the Baṣran Ḫālid al-Ḥaḏḏā' (d. 141-2/758-60) on the authority of 'Ikrima that Ibn 'Abbās read *arǧulakum* in accordance with the Sunnite standard reading are probably secondary and unreliable[10]. The reading *arǧulikum* and the practice of wiping, rather than washing the feet in the ritual ablution were consistently upheld by the Shi'ite imams[11].

In Sunnism, attitudes were at first more divided. The Baṣran Maṭar al-Warrāq (d. *ca.* 140/757-8) still affirmed that many scholars of the law *(fuqahā')* held wiping of the feet to be obligatory[12]. Prominent among those who insisted that washing of the feet was obligatory were the caliph 'Umar and his son 'Abd Allāh[13]. The Companion Anas b. Mālik residing in Baṣra maintained that the Qur'ān had come down with the commandment of wiping the feet, but that the sunna required washing[14]. Various *ḥadīṯs* described the Prophet as practicing and prescribing the washing of the feet. Eventually all Sunnite legal schools affirmed the obligation of washing the feet, and *'ġsilū... arǧulakum,* "wash... your feet", became the standard reading of the Qur'ān.

Imāmī Shi'ite law followed the teaching of Ibn 'Abbās in permitting temporary marriage (*mut'a*). Ibn 'Abbās read in Qur'ān 4: 24: "give them (i.e. the women) their rewards for what you have enjoyed of them", *fa-mā 'stamta'tum bihī minhunna fa-ātūhunna uǧūrahunna*, with the addition: "for a specified time", *ilā aǧalin musamman,* after *min-*

[8] 'Abd al-Razzāq b. Hammām al-Ṣan'ānī, *al-Muṣannaf,* ed. Ḥabīb al-Raḥmān al-A'ẓamī, *Maǧlis Ilmi*, n.d., I 19, nrs. 54 and 55. The statement of Ibn 'Abbās was quoted from Ibn Māǧa's *Sunan* by R. Strothmann, *Kultus der Zaiditen,* Strassburg 1912, p. 30, who understood it as supporting Muslim consensus against the plain meaning of the Qur'ān. This was certainly not the intention of Ibn 'Abbās.

[9] 'Abd al-Razzāq, *Muṣannaf,* I 22, nr. 65; Ibn Abī Šayba, *Muṣannaf Ibn Abī Šayba fī l-aḥādīṯ wa l-āṯār,* ed. Sa'īd al-Laḥḥām, Beirut 1989, I 32, nr. 14.

[10] See Ibn Abī Shayba, *Muṣannaf,* I 21, nr. 8; al-Ṭabarī, *Ǧāmi' al-bayān fī tafsīr al-Qur'ān,* Cairo [1321/1903], VI 72. Both reports were transmitted by the Baṣran Ḫālid al-Ḥaḏḏā' b. Mihrān from 'Ikrima. Ḫālid al-Ḥaḏḏā' (d. 141-2/158-60) was a government official and was considered unreliable by some *ḥadīṯ* experts (Ibn Ḥaǧar, *Tahḏīb al-tahḏīb,* Hyderabad 1325-27/1907-9, III p. 120-2).

[11] Al-Kulaynī, *al-Kāfī,* ed. 'Alī Akbar al-Ġaffārī, Tehran 1968-71, III 29-31. The Zaydīs, in contrast, agreed with the Sunnite position (Strothmann, *Kultus,* pp. 26, 29).

[12] 'Abd al-Razzāq, *Muṣannaf,* I 19, nr. 54.

[13] Ibn Abī Šayba, *Muṣannaf,* I 31; al-Ṭabarī, *Ǧāmi',* VI 72.

[14] Al-Ṭabarī, *Ǧāmi',* VI 73.

*hunna*[15]. This addition to the ʿUṯmānic text was also found in the codices of Ubayy b. Kaʿb and ʿAbd Allāh b. Masʿūd[16]. It had presumably been part of the Qur'ān and was omitted in the official recension because of the subsequent prohibition of the practice. Ibn ʿAbbās maintained that *mutʿa* had been practiced in the time of the Prophet and during the caliphate of Abū Bakr and the early part of the caliphate of ʿUmar; then ʿUmar had prohibited it. According to ʿAṭāʾ b. Abī Rabāḥ, Ibn ʿAbbās said: "May God have mercy on ʿUmar. *Mutʿa* was but an indulgence on the part of God and a mercy for the Community of Muḥammad. If he had not forbidden it, no one but a wretch (*šaqī*) would feel a need for fornication[17]." ʿAbd Allāh b. ʿUmar strongly opposed Ibn ʿAbbās in this matter. When informed that Ibn ʿAbbās declared *mutʿa* licit, he first expressed disbelief. Then he commented that Ibn ʿAbbās would not have dared to say this in the time of ʿUmar. In his, Ibn ʿUmar's, view *mutʿa* was nothing but fornication (*sifāḥ*)[18]. ʿAlī, according to a report ascribed to his son Muḥammad b. al-Ḥanafiyya, had backed the prohibition of temporary marriage and reminded his cousin Ibn ʿAbbās that the Prophet had proscribed it on the Day of Ḫaybar[19]. According to another report ʿAlī remarked during his caliphate in Kūfa: "If it were not for the opinion (*raʾy*) of ʿUmar that preceded, I would order (permission of) *mutʿa*. No one but a wretch would then commit fornication[20]." Imāmī law thus upheld the teaching of Ibn ʿAbbās rather than the practice of ʿAlī.

Other agreements between Imāmī law and the teaching of Ibn ʿAbbās follow a similar pattern. Imāmī law, as is known, forbids the practice of repudiation of the wife called *ṭalāq al-bidʿa*, whose validity was accepted in Sunnite law although it is morally condemned. A triple repudiation pronounced on a single occasion is thus considered in Imāmī law as a single revocable repudiation[21]. The repudiation becomes irrevocable only after three declarations pronounced in separate menstrual periods of the wife. Ibn ʿAbbās reported that this was the law in the time of the Prophet and during the caliphate of Abū Bakr and some years of the caliphate of ʿUmar. The Prophet had occasionally asked a husband to

[15] JEFFERY, *Materials* p. 198.
[16] JEFFERY, *o.c.* pp. 36, 126.
[17] ʿAbd al-Razzāq, *Muṣannaf,* VII 496-7, nr. 14021.
[18] ʿAbd al-Razzāq, *Muṣannaf,* VII 502, nr. 14035.
[19] ʿAbd al-Razzāq, *Muṣannaf,* VII 501, nr. 14032; Ibn Abī Šayba, *Muṣannaf,* III 389, nr. 1.
[20] ʿAbd al-Razzāq, *Muṣannaf,* VII 500, nr. 14029.
[21] Al-Kulaynī, *Kāfī,* VI 70-1.

take back his wife even though he had pronounced triple repudiation[22]. Then ʿUmar recognized the triple repudiation at a single time as valid and irrevocable. According to Ibn ʿAbbās, ʿUmar did not approve of the practice, but observed that the people were hastening in a matter in which they ought to act with deliberation (*inna l-nāsa ʿstaʿǧalū amran kānat lahum fīhi anātun).* He addressed them: "You have done a lot of loose talking in repudiation. Whoever says something shall be bound by what he has said (*qad akṯartum fī hāḏā l-ṭalāq, fa-man qāla šayʾan fa-huwa ʿalā mā takallama bih*[23]. ʿUmar thus hoped to induce husbands to act more responsibly in repudiating their wives by sanctioning *ṭalāq al-bidʿa.* In fact, however, the morally condemned form of repudiation became the standard Sunnite practice.

Clearly upholding the ruling of his father, ʿAbd Allāh b. ʿUmar is quoted as stating: "Whoever pronounces triple repudiation has divorced his wife (irrevocably) and has disobeyed his Lord[24]." Although reporting that ʿUmar had changed the law in respect to triple repudiation, Ibn ʿAbbās did not, according to the Sunnite reports, expressly deny the validity of the caliph's reform. According to one report, he merely used to hint when asked about triple repudiation: "If you fear God, He has created an escape for you[25]." In another report he is quoted as telling someone who had pronounced triple divorce: "You have disobeyed your Lord and have divorced you wife (irrevocably)[26]." The Shiʿite imams, in rejecting the validity of the triple repudiation, adopted the legal practice which, according to Ibn ʿAbbās, had prevailed under the Prophet.

Another significant point of difference between early Sunnite and Shiʿite law concerned the status of the *umm al-walad,* the slave woman who had given birth to a child of her master. Imāmī Shiʿite law considered her as retaining her slave status and being subject to sale by her master. This agreed with the pre-Islamic practice in Arabia which was not modified by the Qurʾān and prevailed under the Prophet, Abū Bakr, and during the early years of ʿUmar's caliphate[27]. Then ʿUmar, according to various reports, proscribed the sale of such slave mothers, arguing that it was unacceptable for the mother of a free child to be

[22] ʿAbd al-Razzāq, *Muṣannaf,* VI 390-1, nrs. 11334-5.
[23] ʿAbd al-Razzāq, *Muṣannaf,* VI 391-3, esp. nrs. 11336 and 11338; Ibn Ḥanbal, *Musnad,* [Cairo] 1313/1895, I 314.
[24] ʿAbd al-Razzāq, *Muṣannaf,* VI 395, nr. 11344.
[25] ʿAbd al-Razzāq, *Muṣannaf,* VI 396, nr. 11346.
[26] ʿAbd al-Razzāq, *Muṣannaf,* VI 397, nr. 11352.
[27] ʿAbd al-Razzāq, *Muṣannaf,* VII 287-8, nrs. 13210-11.

sold[28]. ʿUmar's ruling was upheld by his successor ʿUṯmān. ʿAlī, however, reversed it during his reign and ruled that the *umm al-walad* does not automatically gain liberty when she gives birth to her master's child[29]. He is reported to have stated: "ʿUmar consulted me about the sale of the *umm walad,* and I and he were of the opinion (*ra'y*) that she becomes free when she gives birth. ʿUmar judged accordingly during his lifetime and so did ʿUṯmān after him. When I took over the rule, I came to the view that I should treat her as a slave." ʿUbayda al-Salmānī, who reported this, told ʿAlī: "Your and ʿUmar's opinion in union is preferable to me to your single opinion in schism (*furqa*)." ʿAlī, according to ʿUbayda, merely laughed[30].

ʿAbd Allāh b. ʿAbbās, according to ʿAṭā' b. Abī Rabāḥ, held that the *umm walad* does not become free until her master expressly manumits her. He said: "By God, she is in the same (legal) position as your camel and your sheep[31]." Less reliable appears another report according to which he placed the *umm walad* in the portion of her child's inheritance from the father (and thus presumably considered her free after his death)[32]. Patently forged is a *ḥadīṯ* that Ibn ʿAbbās is alleged to have narrated: "The Messenger of God said: 'The slave girl of any man who gives birth to a child from him shall be free after his death (*ʿan duburin minhu*)[33].'" ʿAbd Allāh b. ʿUmar, in contrast, strongly supported the

[28] ʿAbd al-Razzāq, *Muṣannaf,* VII 287, nr. 13210. See in general the article on *Umm al-walad* in *EI* by J. SCHACHT. In this article Schacht described the ordinance of ʿUmar forbidding the sale of the *umm al-walad* as "certain from numerous accounts." Dealing with the subject in his much later *Origins of Muḥammadan Jurisprudence* (Oxford 1950), Schacht does not refer to the article and comments: "Because the ancient resistance to an improvement in the status of the *umm al-walad* happened to be expressed in a tradition from ʿAlī, in pointed opposition to traditions from ʿUmar and Ibn ʿUmar, the Shiʿites, when they came to elaborate their own legal doctrine, insisted on considering the *umm al-walad* as a slave who could be sold or otherwise alienated by her master" (p. 265). This formulation reflects Schacht's new theory that discussion of legal questions began only in the later Umayyad age and that opinions reported from Companions of the Prophet were ascribed to them without historical foundation at a secondary stage.

[29] ʿAbd al-Razzāq, *Muṣannaf,* VII 290-1, nr. 13221.

[30] Ibn Abī Šayba, *Muṣannaf,* V 184, nr. 2; ʿAbd al-Razzāq, *Muṣannaf,* VII 291-2, nr. 13224. In his testament ʿAlī stipulated that those of his slave women who had a child by him should be treated as a portion of the inheritance of the child (and thus become free). His childless slave girls should be freed on his death (ʿAbd al-Razzāq, *Muṣannaf,* VII 290, nrs. 13216, 13218). Ibrāhīm al-Naḫaʿī reported that ʿAlī told an *umm walad,* who came to him: "Surely, ʿUmar has set you (plur.) free" (Ibn Abī Šayba, *Muṣannaf,* V 185, nr. 6; ʿAbd al-Razzāq, *Muṣannaf,* VII 293, nr. 13231.

[31] ʿAbd al-Razzāq, *Muṣannaf,* VII 290, nrs. 13216-18.

[32] Ibn Abī Šayba, VIII 186, nr. 11.

[33] Ibn Abī Šayba, *Muṣannaf,* V 184, nr. 1; ʿAbd al-Razzāq, *Muṣannaf,* VII 290, nr. 13219. The forger of the *ḥadīṯ* was probably Ḥusayn b. ʿAbd Allāh (b. ʿUbayd Allāh

position of his father. When told that ʿAbd Allāh b. al-Zubayr allowed the sale of slave mothers, he told his interrogators pointedly: "But Abū Ḥafṣ ʿUmar b. al-Ḫaṭṭāb, the Commander of the Faithful — do you know him? — did not permit their sale but freed them." ʿUmar, he affirmed, had ruled that they may not be sold, or given away, or be inherited. "Their master may enjoy her as long as he lives; but when he dies, she becomes free[34]."

The Shiʿite imams opposed the ruling of ʿUmar. When asked about the *umm walad*, Muḥammad al-Bāqir said: "She is a slave girl (*ama*) who may be sold, inherited, and given away. Her status (*ḥadd*) is that of a slave girl." ʿAlī, according to al-Bāqir, had stated that a slave woman with or without a child would be freed only if manumitted by her master. If the master died without freeing her, the Book of God (stipulating inheritance) had precedence with respect to her. If she had a child and the master left money, she should be put in the share of inheritance of her child. The expectation was evidently that the child would free the mother without decrease of the portion of inheritance of the other heirs. ʿAlī, also according to al-Bāqir, had been called to judge in the case of a slave mother whose daughter was still minor but was able to speak. When the daughter declared her mother free, while the kin (*mawālī*) of her father claimed possession of her, ʿAlī had ruled in favour of the daughter who had manumitted the slave mother[35].

Sharply disputed between Sunnites and Shiʿites was the practice of wiping over the shoes (*al-masḥ ʿala l-ḫuffayn*) instead of washing or wiping the feet in the ritual ablution[36]. The legitimacy of the practice was vigourously upheld by Sunnites and categorically repudiated by Shiʿites and Ḫariǧites. Imam al-Bāqir or al-Ṣādiq is quoted as stating that it was one of three practices concerning which he would never employ dissimulation (*taqiyya*)[37]. Sunnite creeds, on the other hand, declared acceptance of the practice as in accordance with the *sunna* a matter of faith[38]. The practice was first justified by reports of Compan-

b. ʿAbbās) who related it on the authority of ʿIkrima from Ibn ʿAbbās. According to Ibn Ḥanbal, Ḥusayn b. ʿAbd Allāh (d. 140-41/ 757-9) transmitted "objectionable things" (*ašyā' munkara*), and Ibn Maʿīn considered him weak (*ḍaʿīf*) in *ḥadīṯ* (Ibn Ḥaǧar, *Taḏhīb*, II 341-2).

[34] ʿAbd al-Razzāq, *Muṣannaf*, VII 292-3, nrs. 13225-9; Ibn Abī Šayba, *Muṣannaf*, V, nr. 3.

[35] Al-Kulaynī, *Kāfī*, VI 191-2, nrs. 1 and 3.

[36] See in general STROTHMANN, *Kultus*, pp. 34-46.

[37] Al-Kulaynī, *Kāfī*, III 32.

[38] A.J. WENSINCK, *The Muslim Creed*, Cambridge 1932, pp. 158-60.

ions that they had seen the Prophet exercising it on various occasions. Opponents based their rejection on the argument that Qur'ān 5: 4, laying down the rules of ablution, does not mention it. They maintained that any early permission of the practice was abrogated by the Qur'anic revelation. Countering this argument, supporters highlighted a report of Ǧarīr b. ʿAbd Allāh, who was known to have converted to Islam only after the revelation of the Qur'anic verse, that he had seen the Prophet practicing *masḥ ʿala l-ḫuffayn*[39]. The practice, however, remained disputed. ʿAbd Allāh b. ʿUmar reported that he saw Saʿd b. Abī Waqqāṣ in the time of his governorship of Kūfa under ʿUmar wiping over his shoes and reproached and questioned him about it. Saʿd insisted that it was licit and later asked the caliph in the presence of ʿAbd Allāh to give his ruling in the matter. ʿUmar confirmed the legitimacy of the practice[40]. His son thenceforth strongly backed it.

When Ibn ʿAbbās was informed of Ibn ʿUmar's report concerning Saʿd b. Abī Waqqāṣ, he exclaimed: "If you (plur.) were saying this concerning remote travel and extreme cold!", clearly indicating his general disapproval[41]. According to his client ʿIkrima, Ibn ʿAbbās stated: "The Book has precedence over (the wiping of) the shoes (*sabaqa l-kitābu l-ḫuffayn)*", thus unambigously repudiating the practice. The report of ʿIkrima with his Ḫariǧite credentials is significant for the rejection of *masḥ ʿala l-ḫuffayn* by the Ḫariǧites. Upon being informed of ʿIkrima's report, ʿAṭāʾ b. Abī Rabāḥ claimed that ʿIkrima was lying and that he, ʿAṭāʾ, had seen Ibn ʿAbbās wiping over his shoes[42]. Ibn ʿAbbās' disapproval of the practice is confirmed, however, by a report of Saʿīd b. Ǧubayr according to which he remarked that in his view there was no difference whether he wiped over his shoes or the back of his camel (*mā ubālī masaḥtu ʿala l-ḫuffayn aw masaḥtu ʿalā ẓahr buḫtī hāḏā*[43].

Ibn ʿAbbās' unequivocal rejection of *masḥ ʿala l-ḫuffayn* became universal Shiʿite doctrine. The Sunnite Ibn Abī Šayba quoted Imam Muḥammad al-Bāqir, on the authority of his son Ǧaʿfar al-Ṣādiq, ascribing to ʿAlī the very words: "The Book has precedence over the shoes",

[39] ʿAbd al-Razzāq, *Muṣannaf,* I 194-5, nrs. 706-9; Ibn Abī Šayba, *Muṣannaf,* I 203, nrs. 5-6.

[40] ʿAbd al-Razzāq, *Muṣannaf,* I 195-7, nrs. 760-63, 765; Ibn Abī Šayba, *Muṣannaf,* I 205, nr. 20, p. 207, nrs. 34-5.

[41] ʿAbd al-Razzāq, *Muṣannaf,* I 197-8, nr. 768; Ibn Abī Šayba, *Muṣannaf,* I 213, nr. 5.

[42] Ibn Abī Šayba, *Muṣannaf,* I 213, nr. 8; see also *ibid.,* I 208, nr. 44, and ʿAbd al-Razzāq, *Muṣannaf,* I 198-9, nr. 772.

[43] Ibn Abī Šayba, *Muṣannaf,* I 213, nr. 6.

which ʿIkrima had related from Ibn ʿAbbās[44]. Other Sunnite reports, however, describe ʿAlī as approving and performing the practice and as affirming that he had seen the Prophet do so[45].

Time limits prohibit the discussion of further examples here. Only one issue may still be raised because of its political significance: The question of whether the alms tax (*zakāt, ṣadaqa*) should be paid to the government or directly to the poor and others entitled to it according to the Qur'ān. The question had posed itself acutely at the time of the foundation of the caliphate by Abū Bakr and the War of Apostacy. Abū Bakr had declared any Muslim refusing payment of the alms tax to him an apostate whose blood could be shed. Some of the major Companions of the Prophet had had misgivings about this policy, and ʿUmar is reported to have confessed that he would give anything to have asked the Prophet concerning someone who withholds his alms (from the authorities) and says: "I place them in their proper place", whether he should be fought[46]. ʿUmar, according to another report, had confronted Abū Bakr with the question of how he could fight these people when the Prophet had stated: "I have been ordered to fight the people until they say: 'There is no god but God'; when they say this, they protect their blood and property from me except for legal claims (*illā bi-ḥaqqihā*), and their account is with God." Abū Bakr answered that he would fight anyone who made a distinction between prayer and paying the alms tax. The alms tax was a legal claim on property. He would fight them even for a cobble-cord which they used to pay to the Prophet and now withheld from him, Abū Bakr. ʿUmar commented that he then realized that God had dilated Abū Bakr's chest for fighting and that this was rightful[47].

It was thus established that the alms tax must be paid to the caliph in succession to the Prophet. The Baṣran Muḥammad b. Sīrīn (d. 110/728) stated: "The alms were paid in the age of the Prophet to the Messenger of God and to whomever he put in charge of them, and likewise in the age of Abū Bakr, ʿUmar, and ʿUṯmān. Then the Companions of Muḥammad differed concerning them. Some held that they should be paid to the authorities, and others held that one should distribute them himself (to those entitled)[48]." The chief protagonists of the two opposite

[44] Ibn Abī Šayba, *Muṣannaf,* I 213, nr. 3.

[45] ʿAbd al-Razzāq, *Muṣannaf,* I 194, nr. 755; Ibn Abī Šayba, *Muṣannaf,* I 208, nrs. 42-3.

[46] ʿAbd al-Razzāq, *Muṣannaf,* IV 43, nr. 6915.

[47] ʿAbd al-Razzāq, *Muṣannaf,* IV 43-4, nr. 6916.

[48] ʿAbd al-Razzāq, *Muṣannaf,* IV 47, nr. 6926; Ibn Abī Šayba, *Muṣannaf,* III 47, nr. 7. From Ibn Sīrīn's further comment quoted in the version of Ibn Abī Šayba it is apparent that he was generally in favour of paying to the government.

views were ʿAbd Allāh b. ʿUmar and ʿAbd Allāh b. ʿAbbās. Questioned by Ibn Ǧurayǧ as to whether the alms may be given directly to the legitimate recipients or must be paid to the governors, ʿAṭāʾ reported that he had heard Ibn ʿAbbās stating: "There is nothing wrong if you place them in their proper places, as long as you do not give something to anyone whom you sustain as a dependent (*taʿūluhū*). Ibn ʿUmar, in contrast, used to say: "Pay the *zakāt* to the governors." When someone countered: "But surely they do not place it in its proper places", Ibn ʿUmar replied: "Even if (they do not do so.)[49]." On a further question by Ibn Ǧurayǧ, ʿAṭāʾ affirmed that the alms must be paid to the authorities as long as these spend them in their proper places. Ibn ʿAbbās had merely meant that they could be paid directly to the recipients if the rulers failed to do so. The alms of the feast day (*zakāt al-fiṭr*) and the alms tax on livestock and crops could legitimately be paid to the rulers, who would then be responsible for what they did with them, while the taxpayer would receive his religious reward[50].

Ibn ʿUmar is quoted stressing the obligation to pay the alms tax to unjust rulers with extreme formulations. Payment must be made to them even if they were to use the money in order to eat the flesh of dogs at their tables, to buy with it lynxes and falcons (for hunting), or precious clothes and perfume[51]. Presumably in the early days of the counter-caliphate of Ibn al-Zubayr, Ibn ʿUmar learned that ʿAbd Allāh b. Muṭīʿ said: "I shall not pay the alms from my property to Ibn al-Zubayr so that he feeds them to his horses and gives them to his slaves to eat." Ibn ʿUmar sent to him and reproached him that he was wrong and did not fulfil his legal obligation. Even if he were to give alms in the same amount (to the poor), it would not be accepted from him. He was commanded (by the law) to pay the alms tax to the ruler, whether the latter was pious or a sinner[52]. It should be noted that Ibn ʿUmar himself refused to pledge allegiance to ʿAbd Allāh b. al-Zubayr since it was his principle not to support either side in inter-Muslim War[53].

It was only natural that Shiʿites, who considered the caliphs and their officials as unjust oppressors, adopted the position of Ibn ʿAbbās that the

[49] ʿAbd al-Razzāq, *Muṣannaf,* IV 44, nr. 6917.

[50] ʿAbd al-Razzāq, *Muṣannaf,* IV 45, nr. 6920.

[51] ʿAbd al-Razzāq, *Muṣannaf,* IV 46-7, nrs. 6924, 6927; Ibn Abī Šayba, *Muṣannaf,* III 47, nrs. 3-4.

[52] ʿAbd al-Razzāq, *Muṣannaf,* IV 45, nr. 7619.

[53] Al-Balāḏurī, *Ansāb al-ashrāf,* V, ed. S.D. Goitein. Jerusalem 1936, 188. ʿAbd Allāh b. Muṭīʿ al-ʿAdawī, of Ibn ʿUmar's clan ʿAdī of Quraysh, at first withheld his pledge of allegiance from Ibn al-Zubayr (see *ibid.).* Later, however, he became a prominent supporter of the counter-caliph, who appointed him governor of Kūfa.

*zakāt* be paid directly to its Qur'anic recipients. The Kūfan legal authority Sufyān al-Ṯawrī mentioned Imam Muḥammad al-Bāqir together with Ibn ʿAbbās among those who taught that the alms tax should not be paid to those who acted unjustly with it (*lā tu'addū l-zakāta ilā man yağūru fīhā*)[54]. Sufyān went on to name the Shiʿite imam among those who held that whatever was seized by the authorities by force could be taken into account in the payment of alms. A report quoted by Ibn Abī Šayba according to which al-Bāqir, when asked by the Sunnite ʿAbd Allāh b. Ḥabīb[55] about the propriety of paying *zakāt* to the rulers (*wulāt*), told him to pay them, must, if authentic, be viewed as an example of *taqiyya*[56]. In the relevant reports gathered by the Shiʿite al-Kulaynī, the view that the alms tax should be paid not to the oppressive authorities but to the legitimate recipients is taken for granted. Imams al-Bāqir and al-Ṣādiq are quoted as allowing the faithful to take into account what is extorted by the rulers as *zakāt* or *ḫarāğ* in their voluntary payments. Imam Ğaʿfar said: "Whatever the Banū Umayya seize from you, take it into account, but do not pay anything to them as far as you can. For the property does not remain as it is if you pay the legal alms on it twice[57]."

Imāmī Shiite theological, ritual, and legal doctrine thus agreed in a number of distinctive and controversial points with what according to the Sunnite sources was the teaching of ʿAbd Allāh b. ʿAbbās. The early Shiʿite texts endorsing such views and rules do not refer to him. Only in later apologetic Shiʿite works is there occasional mention that this or that point of Imāmī doctrine was in accordance with his views. Imāmī law certainly did not systematically follow the opinions of Ibn ʿAbbās. Among the numerous opinions of his quoted by ʿAbd al-Razzāq b. Hammām in his *Muṣannaf*, many do not agree with early Shiʿite doctrine or have no equivalent in it. It was evidently specific cases, where Ibn ʿAbbās relied upon a variant reading of the Qur'ān or where he claimed to uphold the practice of the Prophet against changes introduced after his death, especially by the caliph ʿUmar, that were taken up by the founders

[54] ʿAbd al-Razzāq, *Muṣannaf*, IV 48, nr. 6932. Others named by al-Ṯawrī were Saʿīd b. al-Musayyab, al-Ḥasan al-Baṣrī, and the Kūfans Ibrāhīm al-Naḫaʿī and Ḥammād b. Abī Sulaymān. The view of Saʿīd b. al-Musayyab, generally a loyalist supporter of government, seems to have differed from that of the others named. He held that it was licit to pay the alms tax directly to its Qur'anic recipients only if it did not weaken government and prevent its necessary expenditure on military stipends (*aʿṭiya*) and defence of the Muslim border towns (*ṯuġūr*). ʿAbd al-Razzāq, *Muṣannaf*, IV 45-6, nr. 6921.

[55] The Kūfan ʿAbd Allāh b. Ḥabīb b. Abī Ṯābit al-Asadī (Ibn Ḥağar, *Tahḏīb*, V 183) is probably meant.

[56] Ibn Abī Šayba, *Muṣannaf*, III 47, nr. 9.

[57] Al-Kulaynī, *Kāfī*, III 543.

of systematic Shiʿite law. His personal practice and legal reasoning (*iǧtihād)* were of little interest to them.

Early Shiʿite religious thought was, it must be kept in mind, based on the emphatic claim that Islam, including its ritual and law, had been fully revealed in the lifetime of the Prophet in accordance with the Qur'anic pronouncement (5: 3): "Today I have perfected for you your religion and have completed my bounty upon you." Any change or addition to Islam after Muḥammad's death by the Companions including the caliphs, not to mention the opinions and legal reasoning of later scholars, were thus illicit innovations. The imams of the Family of the Prophet themselves had no competence and authority to change or add to the law. Their religious teaching authority rather rested on their perfect knowledge of the original text of the Qur'ān and of the *sunna* of the Prophet which was based on it and agreed with it[58]. This explains also why Imāmī Shiʿite law paid little attention to the actual practice of ʿAlī during his caliphate as reported in the Sunnite sources and at times, as noted, preferred the teaching of Ibn ʿAbbās to it. Imam al-Bāqir explained the discrepancy between ʿAlī's practice and Shiʿite doctrine by stating that ʿAlī was loath to be accused of contravening the precedents set by Abū Bakr and ʿUmar[59]. ʿAlī thus could be seen as acting with a kind of *taqiyya* forced upon him by the popularity of the first two caliphs among his supporters. The authentic teaching of Islam presumably rested rather on the knowledge handed down by him to the imams among his off-spring.

The teaching activity of Ibn ʿAbbās, its attraction to Kūfan Shiʿites in the time of the second Inter-Muslim War (*fitna),* and its unorthodox character are independently confirmed. According to a report of ʿAṭā', the counter-caliph ʿAbd Allāh b. al-Zubayr accused ʿAbd Allāh b. ʿAbbās, together with his brother ʿUbayd Allāh, of striving to raise the banner of Abū Turāb (ʿAlī) after God had lowered it and that they were gathering the misguided (*ḍullāl)* of the people of Iraq around themselves. Ibn al-Zubayr threatened to chastize him if he would not cut his ties to these people. ʿAbd Allāh b. ʿAbbās defended himself, suggesting

[58] That this was the general view upheld by the early Imāmiyya has been forcefully argued by T. Bayhum Daou in her Ph. D. thesis: *The Imāmī Shīʿī Conception of the Knowledge of the Imām and the Sources of Religious Doctrine in the Formative Period from Hishām b. al-Ḥakam to Kulīnī,* SOAS, London 1996. A similar view was endorsed by the Zaydī Imam al-Qāsim b. Ibrāhīm as one of the five basic principles of Islam (see Madelung, *Der Imam al-Qāsim ibn Ibrāhīm,* Berlin 1965, p. 104).

[59] See Ibn Šabba, *Ta'rīḫ al-Madīna al-munawwara,* ed. Fahīm Muḥammad Šaltūt, Qumm 1410/[1989-90], p. 217.

that they were visited only by men seeking religious knowledge or hospitality (*ṭālib fiqh aw ṭālib faḍl*). The Shiʿite Companion Abū Ṭufayl ʿĀmir b. Wāṯila then reproached Ibn al-Zubayr in a poem for trying to prevent Ibn ʿAbbās and the clan (*rahṭ)* of the Prophet from teaching the religion brought by their kinsman[60]. Ibn al-Zubayr, it should be noted, was stridently anti-Hāšimid. Among the most serious charges against him was, according to al-Zuhrī, that he omitted mention of the Messenger of God in his sermons and, when questioned about this, said: "Surely, he has a family of small, evil men (*inna lahū uhayla sūʾin)* who, whenever he is named, claim to be tall and stretch their necks at his mention[61]." The Kūfan ʿAbd Allāh b. Abi l-Huḏayl al-ʿAnazī, himself an ʿUṯmānid[62], reported that, when he visited Mekka, the Kūfans gave him written questions to submit to Ibn ʿAbbās[63]. Some of the ritual practice and legal doctrine that later became distinctive of Shiʿite versus Sunnite religious law thus came to Kūfa already in the early Umayyad age. Its subsequent endorsement and adoption by Imams Muḥammad al-Bāqir and Ǧaʿfar al-Ṣādiq into Imāmī Shiʿite school law was evidently facilitated by the fact that it was already well established among the Kūfan Shiʿites. The teaching of ʿAbd Allāh b. ʿAbbās critical of the early caliphate thus came to shape Shiʿite religious thought and law just as the loyalist teaching of ʿAbd Allāh b. ʿUmar came to shape Sunnite religious thought and law.

[60] Abu l-Farağ al-Iṣfahānī, *al-Aġānī*, [Būlāq 1285/1868], XIII 168.
[61] Al-Balāḏurī, *Ansāb*, V 372.
[62] Ibn Ḥağar, *Tahḏīb*, III 62.
[63] ʿAbd al-Razzāq, *Muṣannaf*, IV 459-60, nr. 8453.

# II

## SHĪ^cISM IN THE AGE OF THE RIGHTLY-GUIDED CALIPHS

The Shīʿah as a religious movement emerged, according to the conventional modern Western view, after the death of ʿAlī. There was, to be sure, a *Shīʿat ʿAlī* during the First Inter-Muslim War (*Fitnah*), but they were simply the active supporters of ʿAlī's caliphate, just as there was a *Shīʿat ʿUthmān* composed of all those seeking revenge for ʿAlī's predecessor murdered in Madinah. The conflict between the two Parties was, in modern terms, strictly political. ʿAlī himself sought the caliphate after ʿUthmān's violent death on the same basis as his three predecessors. He faced, however, strong opposition, first from ʿĀʾishah and the Makkan Quraysh, and then from Muʿāwiyah and the Syrians. It was only after the murder of ʿAlī and the abdication of his son Ḥasan in favor of Muʿāwiyah that some of his Kufan partisans, disappointed by the failure of their cause and resentful of the transfer of the sovereign power to Syria, began to build up the idea of a special right of the *ahl al-bayt*, Muḥammad's Family, to rule the Muslim community. In order to raise ʿAlī's status they now ascribed to him a superior knowledge of Islam which he had received from the Prophet and sometimes also supernatural qualities. In due time the more radical of his partisans claimed that only ʿAlī and a line of his descendants were entitled to the religious and political leadership of the community and that ʿAlī's predecessors as well as the later caliphs were illegitimate usurpers. The further removed from political reality, the more the Shīʿah became prone to religious radicalism.

A different portrait of the origins of Shīʿism was offered, as is well known, by the early Kufan historiographer Sayf ibn ʿUmar in the early Abbasid age. According to his account, the Shīʿah was founded by ʿAbd Allāh ibn Sabaʾ, a converted Jew from Yaman. His activity began during the caliphate of ʿUthmān when he travelled from Hijaz to Syria, stirring up unrest and rebellion in Egypt, Basrah, and Kufah and inciting to the murder of the caliph by the Egyptian rebels. He preached that every prophet had a *waṣī*, a legatee, and that

ʿAlī was the divinely-appointed *waṣī* of Muḥammad. Just as Muḥammad was the seal of the prophets, ʿAlī was the seal of the legatees.[1] Ibn Sabaʾ was also responsible for the outbreak of fighting between the armies of ʿAlī and ʿĀʾishah at Basrah. According to other Sunnī and Shīʿī sources, after ʿAlī's death he taught ideas later associated with the Shīʿī extremists (*ghulāt*): that ʿAlī had not died but was riding in the clouds and would return to establish justice on earth. Sayf ibn ʿUmar was long rejected as a credible source by modern Western historians, beginning with Wellhausen. He has recently been rehabilitated by some, but his story of ʿAbd Allāh ibn Sabaʾ has not found favor. It too closely resembles similar stories about the origins of heterodox sects not to be recognized as a typical orthodox black legend. In one point, however, the modern Western view and the black legend of Ibn Sabaʾ agree. This is the assertion that ʿAlī himself had nothing to do with the rise of religious Shīʿism and its doctrine. Instead ʿAlī is said to have repudiated Ibn Sabaʾ's teachings and to have banished him from Kufah to al-Madāʾin.

In order to examine the character of the *shīʿat ʿAlī* in the time of the Rightly-Guided Caliphs it is necessary to turn to the Kufan historical tradition aside from Sayf. ʿAwānah ibn al-Ḥakam al-Kalbī reports, on the authority of al-Shaʿbī, an account of the Kufan Jundab ibn ʿAbd Allāh al-Azdī about his activity in support of ʿAlī at the beginning of ʿUthmān's reign. Jundab was, according to his own account, present in Madinah at the time of ʿUthmān's election. He visited al-Miqdād ibn ʿAmr (al-Aswad), a strong backer of ʿAlī disappointed by the election of ʿUthmān, and heard him arguing with ʿAbd al-Raḥmān ibn ʿAwf, who had played a vital role in the election. He then visited ʿAlī and offered to appeal to the people in his home town of Kufah for support for his cause. ʿAlī answered him that it was not yet time. After his return to Iraq, Jundab did, however, speak out for ʿAlī. He met for the most part with opposition and was denounced to ʿUthmān's governor of Kufah, al-Walīd ibn ʿUqbah ibn Abī Muʿayṭ, who imprisoned him. He was interceded for, and released.[2]

Probably not much later, according to Abū Mikhnaf, ʿAmr ibn Zurārah ibn Qays and Kumayl ibn Ziyād ibn Nahīk, both of the Banū al-Nakhaʿ of the Yamanite tribe of Madhḥij, began to call openly for the deposition of ʿUthmān and for allegiance to ʿAlī. ʿAmr ibn Zurārah told the people that ʿUthmān had

---

[1] Muḥammad Ibn Jarīr al-Ṭabarī, *Taʾrīkh al-rusul wa-al-mulūk*, ed. M.J. de Goeje and others, 4 vols. in 13 tomes (Lugd. Bat.: E.J. Brill, 1879-1901), I, 2942-2943.

[2] ʿAbd al-Ḥamīd ibn Hibat Allāh Ibn Abī al-Ḥadīd, *Sharḥ Nahj al-balāghah*, ed. Muḥammad Abū al-Faḍl Ibrāhīm, 20 vols. (Cairo: Dār Iḥyāʾ al-Kutub al-ʿArabīyah, 1378-1384/1959-1964), IX, 56-58. Jundab ibn ʿAbd Allāh, known as Jundab al-Khayr, was, according to Kalbī, the one who killed the magician whose tricks amused the governor al-Walīd. He was then imprisoned by al-Walīd, but escaped. According to other sources, the killer was rather Jundab ibn Kaʿb al-Azdī (Aḥmad ibn Yaḥyā al-Balādhurī, *Ansāb al-ashrāf V*, ed. Shlomo Goitein [Jerusalem: Hebrew University Press, 1936], 31-32). The latter identification seems more reliable. Jundab ibn ʿAbd Allāh's son ʿAbd al-Raḥmān was a widely-quoted informant on events in early Kufan Shīʿī history.

abandoned the truth although he knew it, had made the pious among them subject to persecution, and appointed the worst of them to rule.

When the governor al-Walīd learned of this he at first intended to ride out against them, but he was warned that the matter was serious and that he should beware lest he kindle rebellion. Mālik ibn al-Ḥārith al-Ashtar, chief of the Banū al-Nakhaᶜ, offered to intervene and easily calmed his people, warning them against sedition. Subsequently al-Walīd wrote ᶜUthmān about the affair, and the caliph instructed him to exile ᶜAmr ibn Zurārah, whom he described as a "boorish bedouin" (*aᶜrābī jilf*), to Syria. It should be noted that ᶜAmr was in fact the son of the leader of the delegation of the Banū al-Nakhaᶜ which visited the Prophet not long before his death to make their submission to Islam and that ᶜAmr himself was considered a Companion of Muḥammad.[3] As he left Kufah, ᶜAmr was escorted by al-Ashtar and two men of al-Nakhaᶜ, al-Aswad ibn Yazīd ibn Qays and ᶜAlqamah ibn Qays ibn Yazīd. The escorts then returned to Kufah. Qays ibn Qahdān ibn Salamah of the Banū al-Baddāʾ of Kindah commented on the incident in two lines of poetry, swearing that he would depose Abū Wahb (al-Walīd) and his master, the 'cave of error' ᶜUthmān ibn ᶜAffān.[4] Most of these men are known to have been prominent among the Shīᶜah during the reign of ᶜAlī and, if they survived as did Kumayl ibn Ziyād, in the generation after ᶜAlī's death.

When ᶜUthmān replaced al-Walīd ibn ᶜUqbah by Saᶜīd ibn al-ᶜĀṣ, he ordered the new governor to treat the people gently, and Saᶜīd drew the Qurʾān readers and prominent local leaders into his company and spent the evenings with them. Abū Mikhnaf names a fair number, and many appear again later as active supporters of ᶜAlī and prominent figures in the Shīᶜī movement. Among them were, besides al-Ashtar, Ṣaᶜṣaᶜah and Zayd, sons of Ṣūḥān of ᶜAbd al-Qays; Ḥurqūṣ ibn Zuhayr of Saᶜd Tamīm and Shurayḥ ibn Awfā of ᶜAbs, both of whom became Khārijīs and were killed at al-Nahrawān; Jundab ibn Zuhayr al-Azdī; Kaᶜb ibn Dhī al-Ḥabakah al-Nahdī, a pietist ascetic; ᶜAdī ibn Ḥātim, chief of the Banū Ṭayyiʾ; Ziyād ibn Khaṣafah of the Banū Taym Allāh of Rabīᶜah; and Yazīd ibn Qays al-Arḥabī. It was in one of these evening gatherings in the governor's palace that Saᶜīd ibn al-ᶜĀṣ made his memorable remark that the *sawād* was merely "a garden of Quraysh," provoking a brawl in which the police chief was manhandled. Saᶜīd ibn al-ᶜĀṣ wrote ᶜUthmān complaining that with al-Ashtar and his companions, who were called Qurʾān readers but were really insolent troublemakers, he had no control over Kufah.

---

[3] Ibn Ḥajar al-ᶜAsqalānī, *Kitāb al-iṣābah fī tamyīz al-ṣaḥābah*, 8 vols. (Cairo: Maṭbaᶜat al-Saᶜādah, 1323-1325/1905-1907), IV, 297, where ᶜAmr ibn Zurārah is described as having been "the first to depose ᶜUthmān." It is uncertain if he was alive during ᶜAlī's caliphate. The delegation of Banū al-Nakhaᶜ is said to have consisted of two hundred men who arrived in Madinah in Muḥarram 11/April 632. They had previously pledged allegiance to Muᶜādh ibn Jabal in the Yaman. Zurārah ibn Qays is said to have been a Christian before accepting Islam. Muḥammad Ibn Saᶜd, *Kitāb al-ṭabaqāt al-kubrā*, ed. Eduard Sachau, 9 pts., 15 vols. (Leiden: E.J. Brill, 1905-1940), pt. 1, vol. II, 77.

[4] Balādhurī, *Ansāb V*, 30.

ʿUthmān instructed him to exile them to Syria and sent al-Ashtar a letter of reprimand. Saʿīd sent al-Ashtar; the brothers Zayd and Ṣaʿṣaʿah; ʿĀʾidh ibn Ḥamalah al-Ṭuhawī of Tamīm, later a supporter of Ḥujr ibn ʿAdī; Kumayl ibn Ziyād; Jundab ibn Zuhayr; al-Ḥārith ibn ʿAbd Allāh al-Aʿwar al-Hamdānī; Yazīd ibn al-Mukhaffaf al-Nakhaʿī; Thābit ibn Qays al-Nakhaʿī; and Aṣʿar ibn al-Ḥārith al-Ḥārithī, leader of the Banū al-Ḥārith at the Battle of Qādisīyah, into exile in Damascus.

A group of Qurʾān readers now wrote ʿUthmān a letter of protest. The names of a few of them may be noted: Maʿqil ibn Qays al-Riyāḥī; Yazīd ibn Qays al-Arḥabī; Ḥujr ibn ʿAdī, later killed by Muʿāwiyah for his pro-ʿAlid attitude; ʿAmr ibn al-Ḥamiq al-Khuzāʿī, mentioned as being among the Egyptian rebels besieging ʿUthmān's palace in Madinah; Sulaymān ibn Ṣurad al-Khuzāʿī, later leader of the Shīʿī Penitents (Tawwābūn); Kaʿb ibn Dhī al-Ḥabakah; and Ziyād ibn al-Naḍr al-Ḥārithī, prominent leader in the Battle of Ṣiffīn. The letter assured the caliph of their loyalty as long as he obeyed God, but warned him that his reliance on oppressors such as Saʿīd was dividing the community. The letter was not signed, and ʿUthmān hastened to press the messenger, Abū Rabīʿah al-ʿAnazī, to reveal the names of the writers by beating and imprisoning him. ʿAlī, however, intervened by arguing that Abū Rabīʿah was merely a messenger conveying what he had been entrusted with. Kaʿb ibn Dhī al-Ḥabakah, who had written a separate, signed letter, was on ʿUthmān's instructions given twenty lashes by Saʿīd ibn al-ʿĀṣ and exiled to Rayy. He was later murdered as an ʿAlid sympathizer at Tathlīth, north of Yaman, by Muʿāwiyah's general Busr ibn Abī Arṭāh when the latter raided the Hijaz and Yaman in the last year of ʿAlī's caliphate.[5]

The exiles to Damascus stayed in the house of ʿAmr ibn Zurārah, who had already been deported under al-Walīd ibn ʿUqbah. Muʿāwiyah at first treated them well. Eventually, however, there were sharp words between him and al-Ashtar and al-Ashtar was imprisoned. ʿAmr ibn Zurārah reminded Muʿāwiyah that al-Ashtar had supporters, and was also imprisoned. The rest of the group too warned Muʿāwiyah to respect their rights as neighbors, but then kept silent. Muʿāwiyah asked them why they would not speak. Zayd ibn Ṣūḥān answered: "What good would speaking do? If we have been wrongdoers, we repent to God, and if we have been wronged, we ask God for well-being." Muʿāwiyah praised Zayd and allowed him to return to Kufah, writing a letter of recommendation for him to the governor Saʿīd ibn al-ʿĀṣ. Zayd thanked Muʿāwiyah who, at his request, released those whom he had imprisoned. Shortly thereafter, however, he learned that some of the people of Damascus were associating with al-Ashtar and his companions. He wrote ʿUthmān warning that the men he had sent to him in exile might corrupt his own subjects. ʿUthmān instructed him to send them on to Ḥimṣ, ruled by Muʿāwiyah's governor ʿAbd al-Raḥmān ibn Khālid ibn al-Walīd.[6]

---

[5] Ibid., 40-43.
[6] Ibid., 43.

Soon afterwards general rebellion erupted in Kufah. Saʿīd ibn al-ʿĀṣ had been called to Madinah for a conference of governors. The Kufans had hoped he would be replaced on the basis of the complaints. When they learned that he was to return, they rose in revolt. Al-Ashtar took control of the town without bloodshed on the basis of a general agreement of the Kufan leaders that they would not allow Saʿīd ibn al-ʿĀṣ to reenter. Al-Ashtar set up Abū Mūsā al-Ashʿārī, who had earlier been dismissed by ʿUthmān as governor of Basrah, in Kufah, and ʿUthmān had no choice but to appoint him governor. About a year later ʿUthmān was besieged in his palace in Madinah by Egyptian rebels. Rebel groups from Kufah under al-Ashtar and from Basrah under Ḥukaym ibn Jabalah al-ʿAbdī also came to Madinah but, heeding the warnings of ʿAlī and ʿĀʾishah against violence, did not join the siege and the subsequent fighting in which ʿUthmān was killed. While the Egyptian rebels seem to have inclined toward Ṭalḥah as their candidate, al-Ashtar evidently played a major role in securing the succession of ʿAlī to the caliphate.

The early proto-Shīʿah in Kufah thus was led by religious activists, Qurʾan readers quite a few of whom were also tribal leaders of considerable military distinction. They were highly dissatisfied with ʿUthmān and his Umayyad governors, though basically loyal to the established caliphate. Why they were particularly attached to ʿAlī among the senior Companions of Muḥammad is not evident. Their relations with ʿAlī were at this time probably not very close. He must have been aware of them and their sympathies, but certainly did not act as their teacher or control their actions. His own position was difficult, since he was on the one hand severely critical of ʿUthmān's conduct and on the other, as the closest kinsman of ʿUthmān among the senior Companions of Muḥammad, specially obliged to protect him. It was only shortly before the death of the Caliph that ʿAlī, seeing the firm grip of ʿUthmān's Umayyad kin on him, virtually cut his relations with him.

ʿAlī's caliphate was dominated by the first *Fitnah*. His conflict with Quraysh led by ʿĀʾishah, Ṭalḥah, and al-Zubayr is usually interpreted as essentially personal, ʿĀʾishah being motivated by a long-term grudge and Ṭalḥah and Zubayr by ambition. His conflict with Muʿāwiyah, on the other hand, is commonly seen as regional, reflecting the rivalry between Syria and Iraq for hegemony after the decline of Madinah. In both cases, revenge for the murdered caliph served as a rallying slogan.

Whatever the underlying motives and slogans in the conflict, religious overtones soon came to the fore. During the Battle of the Camel ʿAlī's opponents spoke of the "*dīn ʿAlī*," the religion of ʿAlī. ʿAmr ibn Yathribī of the Basran Banū Ḍabbah, who were among the most vigorous supporters of ʿĀʾishah, killed three of ʿAlī's followers, among them Zayd ibn Ṣūḥān al-ʿAbdī. In *rajaz* verse he proclaimed:

> If you kill me, I am Ibn Yathribī,
> who killed ʿIlbāʾ and Hind al-Jamalī,
> and then Ibn Ṣūḥān, followers of the religion of ʿAlī (*ʿalā dīn ʿAlī*).

Ibn Yathribī was captured and brought before ʿAlī. The Commander of the Faithful ordered him to be killed, the only captive not pardoned by him. When later questioned about this, ʿAlī is reported to have said that Ibn Yathribī had killed three men who, he claimed, were "followers of the religion of ʿAlī." The religion of ʿAlī, ʿAlī added, was the religion of Muḥammad.[7]

ʿAlī's son Muḥammad ibn al-Ḥanafīyah narrated that at one point he had charged an opponent, but when he was about to pierce him with his lance, the man said: "I am of the religion of ʿAlī ibn Abī Ṭālib." Muḥammad understood what he meant and let him go. According to another report, the Basran Azd, when forced to flee, called out in order to save their lives: "We are the followers of the religion of ʿAlī ibn Abī Ṭālib."[8]

What could *dīn ʿAlī* mean at this time beyond acceptance of his caliphate? An indication may be provided by two other lines of battle poetry recited by an anonymous shaykh of ʿAdī. The Basran Banū ʿAdī of the tribal confederation of al-Ribāb were, like the Banū Ḍabbah, staunch backers of ʿĀʾishah, and many of them were killed defending her camel litter. Holding the halter of ʿĀʾishah's camel, the shaykh recited:

> We are ʿAdī; carrying lances and Mashrafī swords,
> helmets, and twisted iron rings (of mail), we kill
> whomever opposes the legatee (*man yukhālifu al-waṣīyā*).

G. Levi della Vida, who first made known and translated these two lines quoted in Balādhurī's *Ansāb al-ashrāf*, glossed the term *waṣī* as referring to ʿAlī.[9] He apparently did not notice the incongruence of a Basran partisan of ʿĀʾishah claiming that he and his tribesmen were killing opponents of ʿAlī. The story and poetry were, moreover, narrated by a well-known scholar of the Banū ʿAdī who must have been well aware of the history of his people. It is inconceivable that he would have slipped a piece of pro-ʿAlid poetry into it. The Banū ʿAdī were, in the words of the shaykh, "seeking ʿAlī with their lances and swords" in order to call him to account for the murder of the caliph ʿUthmān. The *waṣī* whose opponents they intended to kill was not ʿAlī, but Abū Bakr, whose daughter they were now defending.

Abū Bakr is not commonly called Muḥammad's legatee. The use of the term for him is evidently polemical, aiming to counter the claim of the followers of ʿAlī that the Prophet's cousin was his *waṣī*. It had nonetheless a good basis in the argumentation of the supporters of Abū Bakr's prior title to the caliphate. They commonly asserted that Muḥammad's order for Abū Bakr to lead the communal prayers during his last illness constituted an indirect

---

[7] Abū Bakr Muḥammad ibn al-Ḥasan Ibn Durayd, *al-Ishtiqāq*, ed. ʿAbd al-Salām Muḥammad Hārūn, 2d. rev. ed. (Baghdad: Maktabat al-Muthannā, 1399/1979), 413.

[8] ʿAbd Allāh ibn Muḥammad Ibn Abī Shaybah, *al-Kitāb al-muṣannaf fī al-ḥadīth wa-al-āthār*, ed. Saʿīd Muḥammad al-Laḥḥām, 9 vols. (Beirut: Dār al-Fikr, 1409/1989), VIII, 711; Ṭabarī, *Taʾrīkh*, I, 3189-3190.

[9] "Il califfato di ʿAlī secondo il Kitāb Ansāb al-Ašrāf di Al-Balāḏurī," *Rivista degli studi orientali* 6 (1913): 444.

appointment as his successor to the leadership of the community, a view consistently propagated by ʿĀʾishah.

That ʿAlī's followers during his caliphate commonly called him the *waṣī* of Muḥammad is broadly attested in contemporary poetry in praise of him.[10] ʿAlī does not seem to have applied the term to himself, but he certainly must have approved of it. It signified his claim to have been specifically entitled to succeed Muḥammad as leader of the Muslim community and thus was bound to arouse the resentment of the admirers of Abū Bakr's and ʿUmar's caliphates. Those who tried to ridicule this claim called it "the religion of ʿAlī."

In Shīʿī tradition ʿAlī's title as the legatee of Muḥammad is commonly attested by the event at Ghadīr Khumm where the Prophet is reported to have declared to the assembled Muslims: "He whose patron I am, ʿAlī is also his patron." In her article on Ghadīr Khumm in the *Encyclopedia of Islam* (2d ed.), L. Veccia Vaglieri points out that this *ḥadīth* in view of its broad transmission in Sunnī sources cannot simply be considered a late Shīʿī fiction. She does, however, mention an aspect of the *ḥadīth* which is of particular significance in the present context. Many of the quotations of it in Sunnī sources such as Ibn Ḥanbal's *Musnad* are introduced by a report that ʿAlī once appealed to the Muslims gathered in the *raḥābah*, the plaza in front of the mosque of Kufah, asking those who had heard the words of the Prophet at Ghadīr Khumm to witness. Twelve or thirteen Companions of Muḥammad came forward and testified that they had heard these words. It is evident that ʿAlī himself was intent on propagating the *ḥadīth* which implied that he was the chosen successor of the Prophet.

In general, however, ʿAlī did not base his right to the succession on an implied appointment by Muḥammad. Rather he claimed to have had the best title on the basis of both his early and outstanding service to the Prophet and the cause of Islam and his close kinship with Muḥammad. He was in religious merit the most excellent of men after Muḥammad. This view was consistently upheld in speeches and letters by himself and by his governors such as Qays ibn Saʿd ibn ʿUbādah and Muḥammad ibn Abī Bakr in Egypt. It was not a secondary thesis developed by the Shīʿah after his death but an essential part of his message during his reign.

What then was ʿAlī's attitude to his predecessors? He had full praise for the conduct of Abū Bakr and ʿUmar as leaders of the Community and for their achievements for the cause of Islam. There is reason to think that he particularly admired ʿUmar's personal austerity and sincere devotion to Islam. He did not usually blame Abū Bakr and ʿUmar for having deprived him of his prior right to the succession but rather reproached the community in his sermons for having turned away from him after the Prophet's death. On the other hand, he harshly criticized the conduct of ʿUthmān who, in his view, had provoked the rebellion of the people by his innovations and arbitrary acts. While not expressly condoning the murder of the Caliph, he also refused to

[10] See the quotations of poetry collected by Ibn Abī Ḥadīd, *Sharḥ*, I, 143-150.

condemn the rebels. He distanced himself from any involvement in the conflict after his failure to persuade ʿUthmān to change his ways.

In the later years of his caliphate after the disappointment of Ṣiffīn, the arbitration, and the Khārijī schism, ʿAlī seems to have made a special effort to teach his most devoted followers. Abū Ayyūb al-Anṣārī is reported to have addressed the Kufans at this time, encouraging them to rally around ʿAlī: "The cousin of your Prophet has descended among you teaching you religion (*yufaqqihukum*), guiding you on the right path, and summoning you to where your [ultimate] happiness lies."[11] There is a report going back to Jundab ibn ʿAbd Allāh al-Azdī, who had fought for ʿAlī in the Battles of the Camel and Ṣiffīn, that five men, ʿAmr ibn al-Ḥamiq, Ḥujr ibn ʿAdī, Ḥabbah ibn Juwayn al-ʿUranī al-Bajalī, al-Ḥārith al-Aʿwar al-Hamdānī, and ʿAbd Allāh ibn Wahb ibn Sabaʾ al-Hamdānī came to see ʿAlī when he was in a state of despondency and sadness about the conquest of Egypt by Muʿāwiyah and ʿAmr ibn al-ʿĀṣ. They asked him his opinion of Abū Bakr and ʿUmar. ʿAlī reproached them:

> Is your mind free for such things when Egypt has just been conquered and my followers (*shīʿatī*) have been killed there? I shall bring forth a letter to you in which I describe what you are asking about, and I ask that you preserve of my right what you have lost [before]. Read it therefore to my *shīʿah* and the helpers unto the truth.

According to Balādhurī's report, he then gave them a letter to be read at all times to his followers for their benefit. Ibn Sabaʾ had a copy, but he altered it. Balādhurī himself suppresses the text of the letter, commenting that it did ʿAlī no good.[12]

The text of the letter is preserved, however, in the *Kitāb al-ghārāt* of Ibrāhīm ibn Muḥammad al-Thaqafī.[13] Whether this text is the original or the version which, according to Balādhurī, was altered by Ibn Sabaʾ is not clear. The contents, however, do not substantially differ from what is known about ʿAlī's views from other letters and speeches. He affirms that he was greatly disturbed after the Prophet's death to find the people turning away from his family and flocking to Abū Bakr to pledge allegiance to him. He, ʿAlī, had abstained for a time from doing so, holding that he had a better right to the position of the messenger of God than anyone else. Finally the apostasy of some of the people had induced him to put the cause of Islam above his own interest, and he pledged allegiance to Abū Bakr and assisted him with sincere advice. While he had not been convinced that Abū Bakr would eventually turn the reign, which he had disputed with him, over to him, neither had he been without hope that he might do so. He believed that, had it not been for the special bond between Abū Bakr and ʿUmar, Abū Bakr would not have prevented him from ruling after him. However, when Abū Bakr died he called

[11] Balādhurī, *Ansāb al-ashrāf II*, ed. Muḥammad Bāqir al-Maḥmūdī (Beirut: Muʾassasat al-Aʿlamī lil-Maṭbūʿāt, 1394/1974), 478.

[12] Ibid., 382-383.

[13] Ed. Jalāl al-Dīn al-Muḥaddith (Tehran: Intishārāt-i Islāmī, 1395/1975), 302-322.

ʿUmar instead and appointed him to succeed. ʿAlī obeyed, sincerely backing ʿUmar, and ʿUmar's conduct was pleasing and blessed by good success. When ʿUmar was about to die, ʿAlī was again confident that he would not divert the rule from him, but ʿUmar only made him one of six candidates, and these people turned out to be most opposed to his reign. The reason was that he, ʿAlī, had argued with Abū Bakr, telling Quraysh: "We, the Prophet's Family, have a better right to this matter than you as long as there is among us one who recites the Qurʾān, knows the *sunnah*, and adheres to the religion of the truth." The members of the electoral council thus feared that if ʿAlī were to rule they would obtain no share in the reign for their lifetime, and they agreed unanimously to appoint ʿUthmān and to deprive ʿAlī of the reign in the hope that they might get it in turn. They told ʿAlī that he must pledge allegiance to ʿUthmān or they would fight him, and he had done so under constraint.

ʿAlī continues the letter by praying for God's help against Quraysh who had cut their kinship bonds to him, defrauded him of his due, lowered his high station, and colluded to dispute a right to which he had title prior to any of them. When he had looked around he could not find anyone prepared to help or defend him except for his own family, that is the clan of Hāshim. Wary of bringing ruin down upon them, he suppressed his anger.

Next he reminds the faithful how they had become enraged against ʿUthmān and had come to Madinah and killed him. They had then approached ʿAlī in order to pledge allegiance to him. He had at first resisted, but in the end they had pressed him hard, assuring him that they would be satisfied with none but him, and he had accepted. He goes on to relate the story of his caliphate, the rebellion of Ṭalḥah and al-Zubayr, the refusal of the Syrians to respond to his summons, the mutiny of his army at Ṣiffīn, the failure of the arbitrators to judge in accordance with the Qurʾān, the revolt of the Khārijīs, and the desertion of most of the Kufans from his second campaign against the Syrians. Finally ʿAlī appeals to his followers to do their duty in defense of Islam, as their enemies are seizing their cities, killing his *shīʿah*, and raiding their lands.

Shīʿism in the time of ʿAlī thus entailed more than merely support for him as the fourth caliph. It meant recognition that ʿAlī had been entitled to the succession to Muḥammad after his death as leader of the Muslim community on the basis of his outstanding merits and his close kinship with the Prophet. This title would, moreover, continue to belong to Muḥammad's Family so long as one of them "recited the Qurʾān, knew the *sunnah*, and adhered to the religion of the truth." This most basic Shīʿī thesis did not evolve among the Shīʿah only after ʿAlī's death and the transfer of the caliphate to Damascus. Sayf ibn ʿUmar's story about the origins of the Shīʿah is sound insofar as it places the belief that ʿAlī was the legatee of Muḥammad at the centre of their teaching. His distortion consists in turning ʿAbd Allāh ibn Sabaʾ into the originator of this belief, suggesting that ʿAlī, a Companion just like his predecessors, had nothing to do with it. In reality, ʿAlī himself was the first and foremost teacher of the Shīʿah, a historical fact largely unacceptable to Sunnīs. Hence the black legend of ʿAbd Allāh ibn Sabaʾ.

The latter does not seem to have been a member of the earliest Shīʿah. He is mentioned for the first time in connection with ʿAlī's letter, which can be dated around Rab. I 38/Aug. 658. There is apparently another mention of him in Balādhurī,[14] not much later, when he is said to have received the pledge of allegiance of a thousand men for a renewed campaign of ʿAlī against Muʿāwiyah. Three other Shīʿī leaders, Ḥujr ibn ʿAdī, Ziyād ibn Khaṣafah, and Maʿqil ibn Qays al-Riyāḥī, are named together with him as successfully recruiting Kufans for the campaign. If Ibn Sabaʾ was, as later Shīʿī tradition has it, exiled by ʿAlī to al-Madāʾin for deviant teaching, it must have been towards the end of ʿAlī's reign. More likely his deviant teaching, entailing in particular the denial of ʿAlī's death and the expectation of his and his followers' return (*rajʿah*) to rule the earth, began only after ʿAlī's death. That he was a converted Jew is most likely part of the black legend, although Judaism was not rare among Yamanites before Islam. It seems quite unlikely that he was a client of Hamdān as has recently been suggested.[15] As a client he would at that time hardly have been able to recruit a thousand men for ʿAlī's campaign. He may well have been a regular tribesman of Hamdān without much previous distinction. Through his teaching he was to become the founder of messianic and extremist Shīʿism as it first came to the fore in the movement of al-Mukhtār. His part in the main body of the early Shīʿah was marginal.

---

[14] Balādhurī, *Ansāb II*, 478. ʿAbd Allāh ibn Wahb al-S-m-nī is obviously a corruption and should presumably be read al-Sabaʾī.

[15] Heinz Halm, *Die islamische Gnosis. Die extreme Schia und die ʿAlawiten* (Zurich: Artemis Verlag, 1982), 35.

III

# Zu einigen Werken des Imams Abū Ṭālib an-Nāṭiq bi l-Ḥaqq

Die Schriften des Imams Abū Ṭālib Yaḥyā b. al-Ḥusain al-Buṭḥānī an-Nāṭiq bi l-Ḥaqq (gest. um 424/1033), eines der bedeutendsten Gelehrten der kaspischen Zaiditen, haben noch wenig Anerkennung in der modernen Islamwissenschaft gefunden. Nur seine *Amālī*, eine Sammlung von vorwiegend erbaulichen Traditionen, sind mit seinem Namen in der Rezension des Jemeniten Qāḍī Ǧa'far b. Aḥmad b. 'Abd as-Salām (gest. 573/1177) veröffentlich worden[1]. Sein *Kitāb ad-Di'āma fī taṯbīt al-imāma*, eine Darstellung der zaiditischen Imamatslehre, ist bereits zweimal nach einer anonymen Handschrift als ein Werk des Wesirs aṣ-Ṣāḥib Ibn 'Abbād unter dem Titel *Nuṣrat maḏāhib az-Zaidīya* erschienen[2]. Fu'ād Sayyid und, ihm folgend, Fuat Sezgin identifizieren die Handschrift als eine Schrift von an-Nāṭiq's Bruder, dem Imam Aḥmad b. al-Ḥusain al-Mu'aiyad bi llāh[3]. Weiterhin unveröffentlicht ist an-Nāṭiqs *Kitāb Ǧawāmi' al-adilla*, ein Kompendium (*muḫtaṣar*) der Rechtsgrundlagenlehre, von dem mehrere Handschriften vorliegen[4]. Der zweite Band seines ausführlicheren Werkes über die Rechtsgrundlagenlehre, *Kitāb al-Muǧzī fī uṣūl al-fiqh*, ist wahrscheinlich, nach der weitgehenden Übereinstimmung in der Anlage und teilweise im

---

[1]) *Taisīr al-maṭālib fi Amālī al-Imām Abī Ṭālib, ta'līf as-Sayyid Yaḥyā b. al-Ḥusain . . . li-muḫarriǧih wa-rāwīh al-Qāḍī . . . Ǧa'far b. Aḥmad b.'Abd as-Salām*, Ed. Yaḥyā 'Abd al-Karīm al-Faḍīl, Beirut 1395/1975.

[2]) Ed. Nāǧī Ḥasan, Bagdad 1977 und Beirut 1981. Die Edition basiert auf der Handschrift Kairo, Dār al-Kutub 1567 *'ilm al-kalām*, bei der das Titelblatt fehlt. Eine vollständige Handschrift des *K. ad-Di'āma* ist Ms. Ṣan'ā', al-Ǧāmi' al-Kabīr 232 *'ilm al-kalām*, von der ein Mikrofilm in Kairo, Dār al-Kutub, vorliegt. Vgl. *Qā'ima bi l-maḫṭūṭāt al-'Arabīya al-muṣawwara bi l-mīkrūfīlm min al-Ǧumhūrīya al-'Arabīya al-Yamanīya*, Kairo 1967, S. 18.

[3]) F. Sayyid; *Fihris al-maḫṭūṭāt al-muṣawwara*, I, Kairo 1954, S. 136; GAS I 571.

[4]) Ambros. B 49, vgl. O. Löfgren und R. Traini: *Catalogue of Arabic Manuscripts in the Biblioteca Ambrosiana*, II, Vicenza 1981, S. 84. Wien, Glaser 205, vgl. W. Madelung: *Der Imam al-Qāsim ibn Ibrāhīm*, Berlin 1965, S. 179.

Wortlaut zu schließen, in einer Handschrift des Vatikans erhalten. G. Levi della Vida, der auf diese Übereinstimmungen aufmerksam machte, hielt es jedoch, offenbar in Unkenntnis der Titelliste der Schriften an-Nāṭiqs, für ein Bruchstück des *Kitāb al-Ḫilāf bain aš-šaiḫain* des Qāḍī 'Abd al-Ǧabbār[5]). M. Hamidullah andererseits meinte, es sei vielleicht mit dem *Kitāb al-'Umad* Qāḍī 'Abd al-Ǧabbārs zu identifizieren[6]). Es scheint, daß noch ein weiteres, bisher unbekanntes Werk an-Nāṭiqs in einer Handschrift in Mailand verborgen ist.

Cod. Griffini 27 (= X 96 SUP) enthält auf den ersten 67 Blättern ein Kompendium mu'tazilitischer Theologie, dessen Anfang verloren ist. O. Löfgren, der im Katalog der arabischen Handschriften der Ambrosiana ihren Inhalt kurz beschreibt, nennt als mutmaßlichen Verfasser Qāḍī 'Abd al-Ǧabbār oder einen seiner Schüler, Abū Rašīd an-Naisābūrī und Ibn Mattawaih[7]). Die beiden letzteren müssen sogleich ausscheiden, da der Verfasser offenbar ein Schüler Abū 'Abd Allāh al-Baṣrīs (gest. 369/979) war, den er regelmäßig mit seinem Ehrentitel aš-Šaiḫ al-Muršid nennt. An einer Stelle gibt er an, daß er sich nicht mehr an die Meinung Abū 'Abd Allāhs zu einer bestimmten Frage erinnere[8]). An anderer Stelle stellt er fest: „Aš-Šaiḫ al-Muršid, möge Gott ihm barmherzig sein, pflegte zu sagen . . .[9])" Weder Abū Rašīd an-Naisābūrī noch Ibn Mattawaih waren Schüler Abū 'Abd Allāh al-Baṣrīs. Ihr Lehrer, Qāḍī 'Abd al-Ǧabbār, wird nirgends im Text genannt.

Qāḍī 'Abd al-Ǧabbār selbst war Schüler Abū 'Abd Allāh al-Baṣrīs und erwähnt seine Meinungen gelegentlich in seinen Schriften. Bei eingehender Lektüre des Texts wird jedoch deutlich, daß der Verfasser, obwohl er allgemein von den mu'tazilitischen Theologen als „unseren Šaiḫs" spricht, selbst wahrscheinlich Zaidit war. Er nennt als Beispiel dafür, daß das Wort *'ilm*, Wissen(schaft), im Sinne von *ma'lūm*, Wissensinhalt, gebraucht werde, die Wissenschaften der Zaiditen und der Mu'tazila (*'ulūm az-Zaidīya wa l-Mu'tazila*)[10]). Er macht sich die These zu eigen, daß die Mu'taziliten ihre theologische Lehre von 'Alī und seinen Nachkommen übernahmen. Wāṣil b. 'Aṭā', der Gründer der Mu'tazila, war Schüler Muḥammad b. al-Ḥanafīyas, der ihn wie einen Sohn behandelte und ihn zusammen mit sei-

---

[5]) *Elenco dei Manoscritti Arabi Islamici della Biblioteca Vaticana*, Città del Vaticano 1935, S. 145–6.

[6]) Einleitung zu Hamidullahs Edition von Abu l-Ḥusain al-Baṣrīs *K. al-Mu'tamad fī uṣūl al-fiqh*, Damaskus 1965, S. 11, 18.

[7]) Löfgren und Traini: *Catalogue*, I, Vicenza 1975, S. 156–7.

[8]) Fol. 63 a.

[9]) Fol. 67 a: *wa-qad kāna š-Šaiḫ al-Muršid raḥimahu llāh yaqūl.*

[10]) Fol. 20 a.

nem eigenen Sohn Abū Hāšim aufzog. Wāṣils offenes Eintreten für die Šī'a (*iẓhār at-tašaiyu'*) in Basra sei wohlbekannt. Ebenso bekannt seien 'Alīs Bekenntnis zu den Grundthesen der Mu'tazila in seinen Predigten (*ḫuṭab*) und seine Behandlung der ḫāriǧitischen Aufrührer gegen ihn in Übereinstimmung mit der mu'tazilitischen Lehre vom Zwischenzustand (*manzila bain al-manzilatain*). Der bewaffnete Widerstand seiner Nachkommen Ḥasan, Ḥusain, Zaid, Yaḥyā b. Zaid, Muḥammad b. 'Abd Allāh and Ibrāhīm b. 'Abd Allāh gegen die Gewaltherrschaft der „Feinde Gottes" sei Anwendung des mu'tazilitischen Prinzips des „Gebietens des Billigen und Verbietens des Verwerflichen (*al-amr bi l-ma'rūf wa n-nahy 'an al-munkar*). Die Mu'taziliten, versichert der Verfasser, folgten also in ihren fünf Grundlehren den Imamen aus dem Haus des Propheten[11]). Gewiß nicht zufällig sind es die frühen Imame der Zaiditen. 'Alī, den der Verfasser nach schiitischem Brauch regelmäßig als den Herrscher der Gläubigen (*amīr al-mu'minīn*) bezeichnet und mit der Segensformal *'alaihi s-salām* beehrt, war der beste der Schöpfung Gottes nach dem Propheten[12]). In dieser Bevorzugung (*tafḍīl*) 'Alīs über Abū Bakr und 'Umar kann der Verfasser sich auf seinen Lehrer al-Muršid und auf frühere Vertreter der Bagdader Schule der Mu'tazila berufen[13]). Leider verzichtet er dann, entgegen seiner zuvor bekundeten Absicht[14]), darauf, seine Ansichten über das Imamat darzulegen. Hat er, wie die Mu'taziliten, das Imamat des Übertroffenen (*mafḍūl*) als gültig anerkannt oder, wie die Zaiditen, nur das Imamat des Vorzüglichsten (*al-fāḍil*)? Bei seinem klaren Bekenntnis zu den Zaiditenimamen ist wohl die zweite Alternative anzunehmen[15]).

Abū 'Abd Allāh al-Baṣrī hatte drei bekannte zaiditische Schüler, die Imame Abū 'Abd Allāh al-Mahdī, al-Mu'aiyad und an-Nāṭiq. Al-Mahdī kommt als Verfasser des Textes nicht in Frage, da er noch vor seinem Lehrer im Jahr 360/970 starb. Unter den Schriften al-Mu'aiyads ließ sich an ein *Kitāb at-Tabṣira* denken, das in seiner Biographie als ein feines Werk über *uṣūl* erwähnt wird[16]). Das Buch selbst ist bisher noch nicht aufgefun-

[11]) Fol. 62 b–63 a.

[12]) Fol. 34 b.

[13]) Fol. 67 a.

[14]) Fol. 49 a: *wa-la'allanā naḏkuru šai'an fī l-imāmati fī hāḏā l-muḫtaṣari fa-nūridu ṭarafan mimmā yuḥtaǧu ilayh.*

[15]) Die Tatsache, daß er die ersten drei Kalifen als *al-ḫulafā' ar-rāšidūn* bezeichnet und hervorhebt, daß Aufrührer gegen sie als Frevler (*fussāq*) anzusehen seien (fol. 63 a), spricht wohl nicht dagegen. 'Alī selbst, der rechtmäßige Imam, unterstellte sich ihnen nach zaiditischer Auffassung, um die Einheit der Muslime zu wahren.

[16]) Al-Muḥallī, *al-Ḥadā'iq al-wardīya*, II, Ms. Wien, Glaser 116, fol. 69 a: *wa-lahū fī l-uṣūl at-tabṣira.*

den worden. Doch liegt dazu ein Kommentar, *Ta'līq at-Tabṣira*, von Ismā'īl b. 'Alī ar-Rāzī vor[16a]). Nach diesem Kommentar endete al-Mu'aiyads Buch offenbar mit einem Kapitel über das Imamat nach zaiditischer Auffassung. Es kann daher nicht mit dem Text der Ambrosianahandschrift identisch sein. Andere allgemeine Schriften al-Mu'aiyads über *Kalām* werden nicht erwähnt.

Sehr viel wahrscheinlicher handelt es sich um an-Nāṭiqs *Kitāb al-Mabādi'*[17]) oder *Mabādi' al-adilla fī uṣūl ad-dīn*[18]). Der Titel „Anfangsgründe" oder „Prinzipien der Beweise in der Theologie" paßt genau auf das Werk. Der Verfasser bezeichnet es mehrfach als eine Einführung (*madḫal*)[19]) oder ein Kompendium (*muḫtaṣar*). Er will nur einige Grundlehren erklären, die dann als ein Hinweis dienen können auf das, was er nicht erwähnt[20]), und die dem Leser das Eindringen in die Werke der mu'tazilitischen Lehrmeister erleichtern[21]). Es ist offenbar als Gegenstück zu an-Nāṭiqs *Ǧawāmi' al-adilla fī uṣūl al-fiqh* gedacht, das er ebenfalls als ein *muḫtaṣar* bezeichnet.

Das *Kitāb al-mabādi'* ist andererseits offenbar lange nach dem *Kitāb Ǧawāmi' al-adilla* verfaßt. In diesem nennt er seinen Lehrer Abū 'Abd Allāh al-Baṣrī noch nicht mit seinem Ehrentitel aš-Šaiḫ al-Muršid, mit dem ihn aṣ-Ṣāḥib Ibn 'Abbād um das Jahr 367/978 auszeichnete[22]), und ohne eine seinen Tod anzeigende Segensformel[23]). Das Buch mag also noch vor diesem Jahr verfaßt sein. Der „hochwürdige Meister (*aš-šaiḫ al-ǧalīl*)", auf

---

[16a]) Vgl. Aḥmad Muḥammad 'Īsawī und Muḥammad Sa'īd al-Maliḥ: *Fihris Maḫṭūṭāt al-maktaba al-ġarbīya bi l-Ǧāmi' al-Kabīr bi-Ṣan'ā'*, Alexandrien 1398/1978, S. 146 (ms. *'ilm al-kalām* 22). Der Verfasser, Ismā'īl b. 'Alī ar-Rāzī, mag mit dem mu'tazilitischen Traditionarier und Theologen Abū Sa'd Ismā'īl b. 'Alī as-Sammān ar-Rāzī (gest. zwischen 443/1051 und 447/1056), der zaiditische Neigungen hatte, identisch sein. Über ihn vgl. *Der Imam al-Qāsim*, S. 216, und *The Spread of Māturīdisim and the Turks*, in *Actas do IV Congresso de Estudos Árabes e Islâmicos Coimbra-Lisboa 1968*, Leiden 1971, S. 114. Abū Sa'd as-Sammān überlieferte im übrigen auch von Abū Ṭālib an-Nāṭiq (vgl. Abu l-Qāsim ar-Rāfi'ī, *Kitāb at-Tadwīn fī ḏikr ahl al-'ilm bi-Qazwīn*, ms. Topkapi 12 Koğuşlar 1007, fol. 331 a).

[17]) Al-Ḥadā'iq, fol. 89 b: *lahū fī uṣūl ad-dīn al-mabādi'*.

[18]) So der Titel in der Einleitung zur Edition des *Taisīr al-maṭālib*, S. 10.

[19]) Vgl. fol. 65 b: *li-yakūna mā ḏakarnā madḫalan šāmilan li l-muta'allim.*

[20]) Fol. 5 a.

[21]) Fol. 67 b.

[22]) Vgl. J. van Ess, Art. Abū 'Abd Allāh al-Baṣrī in *E.I.*² Suppl.

[23]) Eine Ausnahme erscheint auf fol. 1 b (ms. Wien, Glaser 205) . . . *ḥakāhu šaiḫunā Abū 'Abd Allāh al-Baṣrī 'an Abi l-Ḥasan* (*al-Karḫī*) *raḥimahumā llāh*. Der Dual ist vermutlich auf einen Kopisten zurückzuführen.

dessen Anregung an-Nāṭiq das Buch abfaßte[24]), wird vermutlich sein Lehrer Abū ʿAbd Allāh selbst sein. Al-Ḥākim al-Ǧušamī erwähnt andererseits ein Werk, das an-Nāṭiq für den Wesir al-Ḥasan al-Muṣʿabī schrieb und das deshalb als *Muḫtaṣar al-Muṣʿabī* bezeichnet wurde. Dies könnte mit dem *Kitāb mabādiʾ al-adilla* identisch sein. Die Widmung wäre offenbar in dem verlorenen Anfang der Handschrift enthalten gewesen. Al-Muṣʿabī war Wesir des Ziyāriden Falak al-Maʿālī Manučihr, der von 403/1012 bis 420/1029 herrschte. Das Buch wäre also über drei Jahrzehnte nach Abū ʿAbd Allāh al-Baṣrīs Tod verfaßt. Dazu paßt, daß der Verfasser sich nicht mehr recht an eine seiner Lehren erinnern kann.

Beachtung verdient noch das Datum der Handschrift. Sie wurde vollendet am 30. Rab. I 499/9. Nov. 1105 in Ṣaʿda[25]). An-Nāṭiqs Buch ist also noch vor dem Imamat al-Mutawakkil Aḥmad b. Sulaimāns (532–566/1137–1170), unter dem der Großteil der Literatur der kaspischen und kufischen Zaiditen im Jemen eingeführt wurde[26]), dorthin gelangt. Es muß al-Mutawakkil selbst bei der Abfassung seines *Kitāb Ḥaqāʾiq al-maʿrifa* vorgelegen haben. Seine Angaben über die Abhängigkeit der frühen Muʿtazila von der Lehre der Prophetenfamilie und über die späteren Muʿtaziliten, die ʿAlīs Überlegenheit gegenüber den ersten drei Kalifen anerkannten, sind offensichtlich unmittelbar an-Nāṭiqs Buch entnommen[27]). Die Liste der Muʿtaziliten, die ʿAlīs Vorrang lehrten, nämlich die Bagdader wie Ǧaʿfar b. Ḥarb, Ǧaʿfar b. Mubaššir, al-Ǧāḥiẓ und al-Muršid, stimmt genau mit der an-Nāṭiqs[28]) überein. Der Einschluß von al-Ǧāḥiẓ ist besonders überraschend, da dieser nach muʿtazilitischer Darstellung die Ansicht vertreten haben soll, die Reihenfolge der vier ersten Kalifen entspreche ihrer Reihenfolge[29]). An-Nāṭiq berichtet jedoch, daß Abū ʿAbd Allāh al-Baṣrī sich nach eigener Angabe in seinem Buch über den Vorrang ʿAlīs auf „das Buch des Abū ʿUṯmān al-Ǧāḥiẓ über den Vorrang (*kitāb Abī ʿUṯmān al-Ǧāḥiẓ fi t-tafḍīl*)" gestützt habe. Es mag sich dabei um eine unbekannte Fälschung handeln.

Einige Einzelheiten über an-Nāṭiqs Laufbahn sind noch seinen Schriften zu entnehmen. In seinen *Amālī* gibt er an, einen seiner Gewährsmänner, dessen Name in der Edition in zwei Varianten erscheint, im Jahr 350/961 gehört zu haben[30]). Wenn er, wie Ibn Isfandiyār angibt, im Jahr 340/

---

24) Vgl. *Der Imam al-Qāsim*, S. 179.
25) Fol. 67b.
26) Vgl. *Der Imam al-Qāsim*, S. 211ff.
27) Vgl. *Der Imam al-Qāsim*, S. 35f., 210f.
28) Fol. 67a.
29) *Der Imam al-Qāsim*, S. 28.
30) *Taisīr al-maṭālib*, S. 61, 415.

951 geboren wurde[31]), war er damals nur zehn Jahre alt. Vermutlich erwähnt er das Datum eben deshalb, weil es sein erstes *samā'* war. Im Jahr 365/975-6 war er in Qazwīn, wo er Abū Bakr Aḥmad b. 'Alī, genannt Ibn al-Ustāḏ, hörte[32]). Sein *Kitāb ad-Di'āma fī taṯbīt al-imāma* verfaßte er zu Lebzeiten aṣ-Ṣāḥib Ibn 'Abbāds, also nicht später als 385/995, offenbar in Raiy. Er erwähnt in der Einleitung, daß er aus den Antworten aṣ-Ṣāḥibs auf seine Fragen in dessen Diskussionskreis (*maǧlis*) viel Nutzen zog[33]). An-Nāṭiqs Lehrtätigkeit in Ǧurǧān, Astarābād und Dailam, die al-Ḥākim al-Ǧušamī erwähnt[34]), fällt offenbar in spätere Zeit. Die *Amālī* werden von zwei Ḥasaniden, Abū Ǧa'far Muḥammad b. Ǧa'far b. 'Alī Ḫalīfa und Abu l-Ḥasan 'Alī b. Abī Ṭālib b. al-Qāsim al-Ḥasanī al-Āmulī, genannt al-Musta'īn bi llāh, überliefert, die ihn im Rab. I 420/März–April 1029 und Šawwāl 421/Oktober 1030 hörten[35]). Damals lebte er wahrscheinlich in Langā in Dailam, wo er als Imam Anerkennung fand. Seine Ergänzungen, *Ziyādāt šarḥ al-uṣūl*, zum Kommentar Qāḍī 'Abd al-Ǧabbārs zu Ibn al-Ḫallāds *Kitāb al-uṣūl* und dessen Eigenkommentar stammen vermutlich auch aus der Zeit seiner späten Lehrtätigkeit, vielleicht in Ǧurǧān. Überliefert und weiter ergänzt wurde das Werk von einem Sayyid Abu l-Qāsim. Redigiert und veröffentlicht ist es von unbekannter Hand erst nach dem Tod an-Nāṭiqs und Sayyid Abu l-Qāsims[36]).

---

[31]) Vgl. *Der Imam al-Qāsim*, 178.

[32]) *Taisīr al-maṭālib*, S. 170f., 223, 321. Nach seiner Biographie in Abu l-Qāsim ar-Rāfi'īs *K. at-Tadwīn fī ḏikr ahl al-'ilm bi-Qazwīn*, ms. Topkapi' 12 Koğuşlar 1007, fol. 134a, ist Ibn al-Ustāḏ als Abū Bakr Aḥmad b. 'Alī b. 'Abd Allāh b. al-Marzubān al-Ustāḏ ad-Dailamī zu identifizieren. Er war ein Gelehrter der Koranlesekunst, des ḥanafitischen Rechts und Erbrechts (*farā'iḍ*). Sein Vater 'Alī bekehrte eine Gegend (*nāḥiya*) von Dailam zum Islam. Abū Bakr starb 371/981–2.

[33]) *Nuṣrat maḏāhib az-Zaidīya*, Beirut 1981, S. 23. Daraus ist natürlich nicht zu schließen, daß das ganze Buch ein Diktat Ibn 'Abbāds war, wie der Herausgeber in Anmerkung 1 annimmt. Daß Ibn 'Abbād bei der Abfassung noch am Leben war, geht aus der Segensformel *adāma llāhu 'ulūwah* hervor.

[34]) 'Abd al-Ǧabbār; *Faḍl al-i'tizāl wa-Ṭabaqāt al-Mu'tazila*, Ed. Fu'ād Sayyid, Tunis 1974, S. 377.

[35]) *Taisīr al-maṭālib*, S. 25, 138, 212.

[36]) Vgl. *Der Imam al-Qāsim*, S. 180 und D. Gimaret, *Les Uṣūl al-Ḫamsa du Qāḍī 'Abd al-Ǧabbār et leurs Commentaires*, in *Annales Islamologiques*, XV (1979), S. 72. Wenn der Sayyid Abu l-Qāsim, wie dort vermutet, mit Muḥammad b. Aḥmad b. Mahdī al-Ḥasanī identisch ist, dann fallen die *Ziyādāt* wahrscheinlich in die Zeit der Lehrtätigkeit an-Nāṭiqs in Ǧurǧān, wo dieser Lehrer al-Ḥākim al-Ǧušamīs bei ihm hörte (*Der Imam al-Qāsim*, S. 178).

# IV

# Imam al-Qāsim ibn Ibrāhīm and Muᶜtazilism

The *Kitāb al-Jāmiᶜ al-kāfī* of the Kufan Zaydī Abū ᶜAbd Allāh Muḥammad b. ᶜAlī al-ᶜAlawī (d. 445/1035), a massive summary of the legal doctrine of the four chief authorities of the Zaydiyya in the 3rd/9th century, contains a final section on theological doctrine[1]. In it al-ᶜAlawī reports a few views of Imam al-Qāsim b. Ibrahīm al-Rassī (d. 246/860), the grandfather of the founder of the Zaydī imamate in the Yemen, which are not derived from his writings and are significant for defining his position in relation to contemporary Muᶜtazilī doctrine. Al-Qāsim stood, as is known, alone among the Zaydī authorities of his time backing views broadly associated with the Muᶜtazila, in particular with regard to the justice *(ᶜadl)* of God. While the three other Zaydī authorities whose doctrines are regularly reported by al-ᶜAlawī, the ᶜAlids Aḥmad b. ᶜĪsā b. Zayd, al-Ḥasan b. Yaḥyā b. al-Ḥusayn b. Zayd, and the Kufan scholar Muhammad b. Manṣūr al-Murādī, vehemently opposed Qadarī teaching and maintained that good and evil are equally determined by the divine *qadar* and Will, al-Qāsim, like the Muᶜtazila, strictly dissociated God from all evil. Yet al-Qāsim's extant treatises also reflect obvious differences with the Muᶜtazilī school doctrine in approach and substance of his theological teaching.

Al-ᶜAlawī records al-Qāsim's theological views only exceptionally. Although he does not state his own opinions, he no doubt agreed in general with the anti-Muᶜtazilī tradition of the Kufan Zaydiyya. His main sources were the books of Muḥammad b. Manṣūr al-Murādī, who in turn quoted the ᶜAlid scholars with whom he had associated over a long period, and some independent Zaydī transmissions. In the chapters on the divine *qadar* and Will, on human capacity *(istiṭāᶜa)* and the creation of human acts by God *(khalq al-afᶜāl)*, where al-Qāsim could be expected to have held deviant views, he is not quoted at all. Where he is quoted, his views were clearly in basic agreement with the Kufan Zaydī tradition. They confirm al-Qāsim's deep reservations to Muᶜtazilī *kalām* and reveal, more clearly than his writings, their basic motivation.

Al-ᶜAlawī quotes al-Murādī as stating in his *Kitāb al-Masāʾil:* »I asked al-Qāsim b. Ibrāhīm«, namely about someone who says: Whoever is killed dies without appointed term *(ajal)*, and if he had not been killed he would not have died, »and I mentioned to him the statement of someone who

[1] On Abū ᶜAbd Allāh al-ᶜAlawī and his *K. al-Jāmiᶜ al-kāfī* see W. Madelung, *Der Imam al-Qāsim ibn Ibrāhīm*, Berlin 1965, pp. 80 ff. and the biographical notes by al-Sayyid Aḥmad al-Ḥusaynī in the introduction to his edition of al-ᶜAlawī's *Faḍl ziyārat al-Ḥusayn*, Qom 1403/1983. The section on theological doctrine of *al-Jāmiᶜ al-kāfī* is available to me in a microfilm of the copy of the Great Mosque of Ṣanᶜāʾ. See *Qāʾima bi-l-Makhṭūṭāt al-ᶜarabiyya al-muṣawwara bi-l-mīkrūfīlm min al-Jumhūriyya al-ᶜArabiyya al-Yamaniyya*, Cairo 1967, p. 13.

says: Surely, when he killed him he cut his appointed term. Al-Qāsim reproved this statement and charged anyone who said this with disgrace *(aqbala ʿalā man qāla bihī bi l-makrūh)*. I asked him (further) about whoever said this, and he said: He is doomed to perdition *(hālik)*.«[2]

The immutability of man's life span appointed by God was a dogma held vital by the Muslim determinists, and al-Murādī must have been gratified to be able to quote al-Qāsim's apparent backing of their view. Al-Qāsim obviously could not have agreed with the wider doctrine of the determinists that the unlawful killing of the man occurred in accordance with the Will of God and must have restricted God's relation to the life span to His foreknowledge. This was also the position of the majority of the Muʿtazila, who, according to al-Ashʿarī held that the *ajal* was the time known to God at which a human being would die or be killed. If the person thus was killed, he was killed at his *ajal* and if he died a natural death, he died at his *ajal*. Only a few of them, described by al-Ashʿarī as being »of their ignorant«, maintained that the time until which a person according to God's knowledge would have lived if he had not been killed was his *ajal* rather than the time of his murder[3].

More problematic is al-Qāsim's condemnation of someone who states that the killer cuts the *ajal* of the victim. Did he wish to affirm that, if the person had not been killed, God would have caused him to die at the same *ajal*? This was the position of the determinists, consistent with their view that the *ajal* is not only known but also willed by God. Among the Muʿtazila, Abu l-Hudhayl is reported to have held it also, but it is difficult to see how he would have justified it. Some of the Muʿtazila of the school of Baghdad affirmed, on the contrary, that the person would definitely have continued to live, while the majority of the later Muʿtazila maintained that he might either have died or continued to live[4]. Al-Qāsim b. Ibrāhīm, who expressly dissociated God from acts forbidden by Him[5], would also have found it difficult to explain an *ajal* fixed to coincide with the failed murder. It seems more likely that he did not intend to offer any positive doctrine in the matter but rather condemned the statement, which dealt with a hypothetical question, as an example of that discussion of the *qadar* which he, in agreement with the traditionalist position, held to be forbidden[6]. In either case, his polemic is definitely anti-Muʿtazilī.

In his *Kitāb Aḥmad (b. ʿĪsā)* al-Murādī reported on the authority of an informant whom he considered trustworthy that al-Qāsim was asked concerning »the pain *(alam)* which strikes children: How can God, praise be to Him, be other than unjust in regard to what befalls them, yet if anyone else were to do this to them he would be unjust?« Al-Qāsim answered: » . . . The difference in this is for anyone who judges fairly more evident than all explanation, because God, the Powerful and Exalted, is the benefactor of every blessing in the children and is not subject to command or prohibition in anything of that kind. Thus thanks are due to God for every blessing and benefaction in them, and they have no title to any blessing incumbent *(wājiba)* on God. In every pain and harm that reaches them from God, there is a spiritual lesson *(mawʿiẓa)* for people of insight *(uli l-nuhā)*

[2] *Al-Jāmiʿ*, fol. 301b.
[3] Al-Ashʿarī, *Maqālāt al-islāmiyyīn* ed. H. Ritter, Istanbul 1929–1933, p. 256.
[4] Al-Ashʿarī, *Maqālāt*, p. 257, including footnote.
[5] *Der Imam al-Qāsim*, p. 118.
[6] *Der Imam al-Qāsim*, p. 118.

and an indication of the power of God. If that could be subject to any blame of injustice or oppression, it would even more so attach to their death which is the most painful of pains, and likewise it would attach to the death of the righteous *(abrār)* who are older than children. There is, praise be to God, no question in this from which any censure *(taʿnīf)* could follow, and only the perplexed *(kull mutaḥayyir)* will use it as an argument.«[7]

The »perplexed« to whom al-Qāsim alludes are clearly the majority of the Muʿtazila. They held that God is obliged to provide a recompense *(ʿiwaḍ)* to children, and even animals, for any pain inflicted upon them. This was a major aspect of the Muʿtazilī doctrine of divine justice, unanimously upheld by the later Muʿtazila[8]. According to al-Ashʿarī, there were some among the early Muʿtazila who disagreed with the majority and held that God inflicts pain on children for no reason *(ʿilla)*. They denied that He would recompense them for it, though they also denied that He would torment them in the hereafter. The majority, however, held that God inflicts pain on them only as a lesson *(ʿibra)* for the mature and would recompense them. If not, his infliction of pain would constitute injustice *(ẓulm)*[9]. Al-Ashʿarī does not name any of the deviators. The later Muʿtazilī sources, however, mention that ʿAbbād b. Sulaymān maintained that it was good of God to inflict pain without recompense if the purpose of it was to provide a lesson[10].

Al-Qāsim brushes aside this aspect of the Muʿtazilī concept of divine justice. The blessings of God completely outweigh for him any pains. Thanks are due to God for his blessings in children, and they »have no title to any blessing incumbent upon God« on account of pains suffered. He agreed, however, with ʿAbbād and the majority of the Muʿtazila that God inflicts pain on children only as a lesson for people of insight. While there is thus a similarity between his and ʿAbbād's view, it is unlikely that he was influenced by the latter, who was probably considerably younger and whose reasons for denying divine compensation were different[11]. His concept of the justice of God was essentially confined to strict dissociation of God from any evil human acts and the assertion of human free will[12].

Most revealing about the difficulty of maintaining doctrinal unity within the Zaydī movement in the 3rd/9th century and al-Qāsim's awareness of it is al-ʿAlawī's lengthy chapter on the doctrine of the creation of the Qurʾan[13]. The question of the nature of the Qurʾan, which was turned into a burning political issue by the *miḥna* under the caliph al-Maʾmūn and his successors, evidently also divided the Zaydiyya deeply. There were those, among the ʿAlid leaders as well as their potential supporters, who held the Qurʾan to be uncreated and others who considered it created. Openly admitting their division, Muḥammad b. Manṣūr al-Murādī stressed the need of »sticking to the gist *(jumal)*«, that is the generally agreed principles,

7 *Al-Jāmiʿ*, fol. 304b.

8 See, for instance, ʿAbd al-Jabbār, *al-Mughnī*, XIII, ed. I. Madkūr and A. ʿAfīfī, Cairo 1382/1963, pp. 226–568; Mānakdīm (pseudo-ʿAbd al-Jabbār) *Sharḥ al-uṣūl al-khamsa*, ed. ʿA. ʿUthmān, Cairo 1384/1965, pp. 483–507.

9 *Maqālāt*, p. 253.

10 Mānakdīm, *Sharḥ*, p. 489.

11 For ʿAbbād's argument see Mānakdīm, *Sharḥ*, p. 490. For the dates of his life see my art. ʿAbbād b. Salmān in *Encyclopaedia Iranica*, ed. E. Yarshater, 1:1, London . . . 1982, pp. 70f.

12 *Der Imam al-Qāsim*, pp. 117–120.

13 *Al-Jāmiʿ*, fol. 305b–308b.

while avoiding to express support for either controversial position and abstaining from any accusation of unbelief and from dissociation from the opposite camp. He affirmed: »The inquisition concerning the Qur'an is in our opinion a (reprehensible) innovation *(fa-inna l-miḥna ʿindanā fi l-Qurʾān bidʿa).*«

At the extreme end of those opposed to the doctrine of the creation of the Qur'an stood the Ḥasanid ʿAbd Allāh b. Mūsā b. ʿAbd Allāh b. al-Ḥasan (d. 247/861)[14]. According to reports which al-ʿAlawī received from informants other than al-Murādī, he affirmed that »the Qur'an is the speech of God, it is not created *(laysa bi-makhlūq)*«, and that »anyone who asserts that the Qur'an is created is an infidel, because God, the Powerful and Exalted, says: If one of the polytheists asks your protection, grant him protection until he hears the speech of God (Qur'an IX 6).« Ibrāhīm b. Maysara asked ʿAbd Allāh what he said about the Qur'an, and ʿAbd Allāh answered: »The speech of God and His book.« Ibrāhīm said: »There are people among us *(ʿindanā)* who say that it is created and that whoever does not say it is created is an infidel.« ʿAbd Allāh b. Mūsā answered: »They are more worthy of unbelief.«

Al-Murādī reported that ʿAbd Allāh b. Mūsā, when questioned by him, denied that he had met anyone of his family who held that the Qur'an is created. Al-Murādī adds that ʿAbd Allāh loathed discussion *(kalām)* of this and other questions which people had innovated *(aḥdatha)*. According to another report, al-Qāsim b. Ibrāhīm wrote ʿAbd Allāh b. Mūsā asking him about the Qur'an and ʿAbd Allāh answered: »We are of the opinion that the discussion about the Qur'an is an innovation *(bidʿa)* in which the questioner and the replier share. The questioner raises a question that he is not entitled to raise, and the replier takes upon himself what he is not obliged to undertake. Betake yourself and those who disagree about the Qur'an to its names with which God named it, and you will be among the rightly guided. Do not name the Qur'an with names made up by you, or you will be of those 'who deviate from the straight path concerning His names; they shall be recompensed for what they have been doing (Qur'an VII 180)'.«

Some of the most active partisans and *dāʿīs* of ʿAbd Allāh b. Mūsā were, however, backers of the doctrine of the creation of the Qur'an. Al-Murādī mentions that one of them, ʿAmr b. al-Haytham al-Murādī, was a prominent follower of the earlier Zaydī theologian Sulaymān b. Jarīr and held that the Qur'an was created[15]. Although ʿAmr strongly insisted on this doctrine *(shaddada fīh)*, yet he condemned the Muʿtazilī chief *qāḍī* Ibn Abī Du'ād for his furtherance of the *miḥna* about the Qur'an saying: »May God have no mercy on Ibn Abī Du'ād. The people were united on a general sentence *(jumla)* which conveyed them to God, but he cast division between them.« Al-Murādī goes on to relate that ʿAmr[16] b. al-Haytham, Bishr b. al-Ḥasan, and Muḥammad b. Yaḥyā al-Ḥajarī were all three *dāʿīs* for ʿAbd Allāh b. Mūsā and were at one about the doctrine of the creation of the Qur'an. Yet ʿAbd Allāh b. Mūsā sent his two sons[17], or one of them, together with Bishr b. al-Ḥasan to the *amīr* Ṭāhir b. al-

[14] See on him *Der Imam al-Qāsim*, index s.v.

[15] Sulaymān b. Jarīr seems to have taught that the Qur'an is partly created and partly uncreated. See al-Ashʿarī, *Maqālāt*, p. 586, and *Der Imam al-Qāsim*, p. 65-66.

[16] Ms.: ʿUmar.

[17] Ibn ʿInaba, *ʿUmdat al-ṭālib*, ed. M.Ḥ. al-Ṭālaqānī, Najaf 1380/1961, p. 116, mentions at least five sons of ʿAbd Allāh b. Mūsā.

Ḥusayn (d. 207/822) in order to invite him to support the imamate of ʿAbd Allāh *(yadʿūhu ilā hādhā l-amr)*, although ʿAbd Allāh was aware of Bishr's opinion on the Qurʾan and Bishr knew of ʿAbd Allāh's principle of »holding on to the general sentences *(al-qawl bi l-jumal)*«. Al-Murādī adds: »I did not see anyone of these profess dissociation *(barāʾa)* from those who disagreed with him in doctrine.« When Muḥammad b. Yaḥyā al-Ḥajarī was mentioned after his death to ʿAbd Allāh, he said of him: »He was my sincerest friend among the people of Kufa.«

Potential support for the Zaydī cause could also come from the Muʿtazila, in particular those of the school of Baghdad, who were sometimes described as the Zaydiyya of the Muʿtazila[18]. Al-Murādī mentions that Muḥammad b. ʿAbd Allāh al-Iskāfī (d. 240/854), in spite of his upholding of the creation of the Qurʾan, told him: »When this matter (i.e. the rising in support of the legitimate imam) occurs, we shall write on the flags: There is no god but God, Muḥammad is the Messenger of God, the Qurʾan is the speech of God. By this we want[19] to bring about concord and unanimity and to leave behind disagreement and division.« Al-Murādī goes on to state that he, al-Murādī, had associated with numerous chiefs of the Muʿtazila, among them Jaʿfar b. Ḥarb (d. 236/850–1), Jaʿfar b. Mubashshir al-Qaṣabī (d. 234/848–9), and al-Iskāfī. None of them ever questioned him about the matters on which the people disagreed, the Qurʾan and human capacity *(istiṭāʿa)*, or sought to uncover his opinion *(kashafūnī)* about any of this. »Abū Sahl al-Khurāsānī informed me that he was the messenger of Sahl b. Salāma[20], one of the eminent men and the worshippers *(ʿubbād)* of the Muʿtazila, to ʿAbd Allāh b. Mūsā to invite him to take over this matter (the imamate) and (to assure him) that Sahl would be his helper in it *(yakūnu Sahl ʿawnan lahū ʿalayh)*.«

The Ḥusaynid Aḥmad b. ʿĪsā b. Zayd, whose views al-Murādī valued most particularly, took a more uncommitted position than ʿAbd Allāh b. Mūsā concerning the nature of the Qurʾan. Al-Murādī reports that he witnessed him asking God's mercy *(yataraḥḥam)* for those who held the Qurʾan to be created and for those who did not. »In his view, the upholding of the general sentences *(al-akhdh bi l-jumal)* and abstaining from whatever was a source of division was praiseworthy. This was in his view meant by following the pious ancestors *(ittibāʿ al-salaf)*.« ʿAlī b. Aḥmad al-Bāhilī consulted Aḥmad b. ʿĪsā about the disagreement among the people about the creation of the Qurʾan. Aḥmad answered that both groups were wrong in attacking each other with pronouncements of dissociation. According to al-Murādī, Aḥmad said in commenting on the discord in religion among the people: »I fear for the imam if he were to rise. If he would go out pretending to each group that they held the truth, he would be the first to cause his own damnation, and if he joined one group, he would spoil the rest for himself.« When Muḥammad b. ʿAbd Allāh b. Sulaymān wrote Aḥmad b. ʿĪsā asking him about the Qurʾan and other questions disputed among the people, Aḥmad answered: »You have

[18] *Der Imam al-Qāsim*, pp. 41–42, 211.

[19] Reading *nurīdu*. The unpointed word could also be read *yurīdu* meaning: he (al-Iskāfī) desired.

[20] My thanks are due to Professor J. van Ess for suggesting that this Sahl b. Salāma may be identical with the Khurāsānian Abū Ḥātim Sahl b. Salāma al-Anṣārī mentioned by al-Ṭabarī (*Taʾrīkh*, ed. M. de Goeje and others, Leiden 1879–1901, III 1008–12, 1023–26, 1034–36) as the leader of a popular movement to suppress lawlessness in Baghdad in 201–2/816–8. On closer examination, this identity appears almost certain. I hope to discuss its implications for the history of that age elsewhere.

mentioned the disagreement of the people concerning the Qur'an, but they do not disagree that it is from God.« Al-Murādī comments that by this he wanted to point to the need of accepting the apparent meaning *(ẓāhir)* of the Qur'an and the general, agreed sentences *(al-jumal al-mujtamaᶜ ᶜalay-hā)*. The followers *(rijāl)* of Aḥmad b. ᶜĪsā indeed disagreed in their view about the Qur'an. Among them there was Ḥasan b. Hudhayl, who adhered to the doctrine of Abu l-Jārūd, while ᶜAbd al-Raḥmān b. Maᶜmar openly professed the doctrine of the (created) Qur'an and did not conceal it. Then there was Mukhawwal b. Ibrāhīm and his like who disagreed with these[21]. Aḥmad b. ᶜĪsā, however, did not take the side of any of these groups.

Al-Ḥasan b. Yaḥyā b. al-Ḥusayn b. Zayd was also opposed to any theological discussion of the nature of the Qur'an and to mutual accusations of infidelity by those holding opposite views in the question. Al-Murādī states that he had been connected with al-Ḥasan b. Yaḥyā for forty years, or close to that[22], and had found him associating with various kinds of pious people attached to different doctrines *(yuᶜāshir ḍurūban min al-mutadayyinīn al-mukhtalifīn fi l-madhāhib)*. Holding on to the gist *(maᶜa l-qawl fi l-jumla)* and loathing division, al-Ḥasan had never questioned anyone about his religious views nor flaunted his own. Rather he had given sincere advice to all and offered them kind companionship, and had prayed for God's mercy for all who had passed away of his ancestors and members of his family irrespective of whether he agreed or disagreed with their views. Concerning the Qur'an he said that the family of the Prophet unanimously held that God was the Creator of everything and that the Qur'an was His speech, His inspiration and His revelation *(tanzīl)* and that it should be called only by the names with which God had named it. This was also the view of the early generations of Muslims until the *kalām* theologians deviated relying on their personal reasoning *(ra'y)*.

The criticism directed at the *kalām* theologians indicates that al-Ḥasan was primarily opposed to the doctrine of the creation of the Qur'an. This is confirmed by a report of Yaḥyā b. Abī ᶜAṭā' al-Bazzāz, quoted by al-ᶜAlawī with an *isnād* independent of al-Murādī, that he heard al-Ḥasan say: »It (the Qur'an) is not a created thing *(laysa bi-mahkhlūq)*.« This was presumably in answer to a pointed question. Al-ᶜAlawī goes on to report: »Al-Ḥasan said according to what al-Ṣabbāḥ related from him, and that is also the doctrine of Muḥammad (b. Manṣūr al-Murādī) in the *Masā'il*, when both were asked about those who say the Qur'an is created or uncreated, they both said: The Qur'an is the speech of God, His inspiration, and His revelation. We say concerning this what God has said and do not go beyond it. God is the Creator of everything, the First before everything

21 Al-Ḥasan b. Hudhayl is mentioned as a follower of al-Ḥusayn b. ᶜAlī Ṣāḥib Fakhkh and later as a participant in the rebellion of Abu l-Sarāyā (Abu l-Faraj al-Iṣfahānī, *Maqātil al-Ṭālibiyyīn*, ed. A. Ṣaqr, Cairo 1949, pp. 438, 441-2, 527, 543). Mukhawwal b. Ibrāhīm was a follower of Yaḥyā b. ᶜAbd Allāh (C. van Arendonk, *De Opkomst van het Zaidietische Imamaat in Yemen*, Leiden 1919, p. 291).

22 On the basis of the present text, my statement in *Der Imam al-Qāsim* (p. 84) that al-Murādī does not seem to have transmitted from al-Ḥasan b. Yaḥyā must be modified. It would seem that al-Murādī did not mention al-Ḥasan's doctrine in his books written during the lifetime of the latter, presumably in order to protect him from suspicion of the authorities. Al-Ḥasan b. Yaḥyā was considerably younger than Aḥmad b. ᶜĪsā and al-Qāsim b. Ibrāhīm. He is said to be the author of a book on the doctrine of al-Qāsim and Aḥmad b. ᶜĪsā entitled *al-Jāmiᶜ ᶜalā madhhab al-Qāsim wa-Aḥmad b. ᶜĪsā* (M.T. Dānishpazhūh, *Do mashīkhahā-ye Zaydī* in *Nāma-ye Mīnovī*, Tehran 1350, p. 166).

and its Creator, and the One Remaining after everything and its Heir[23]. Everything which is below *(dūna)* God is created.«

At the other extreme end, among those holding the Qur'an to be created, stood al-Qāsim b. Ibrāhīm. He kept this view concealed, however, and like the other Zaydī ʿAlids of his time, stuck to the formulation that the Qur'an was the speech of God without qualification. Al-Murādī reported in his *Kitāb al-Jumla*: »I asked al-Qāsim b. Ibrāhīm about the Qur'an. He said: The speech of God, His inspiration, and His revelation. We do not go beyond this to anything else. Likewise did our ancestors.« Al-Murādī adds: »He upheld the creation of the Qur'an but concealed that *(wa-kāna yaqūlu bi-khalqi l-Qur'āni yuḍmiru dhālik).* Al-Qāsim told me: We ask those who say the Qur'an is created: Does God not know that it is created? If they say yes, they should be told[24]: Does not God know that it is created, yet He contented Himself *(ijtaza'a)* in respect to the creation with telling them that it is rendered *(majʿūl,* Qur'an XLIII 3*)*? When they say[25] yes, they are to be told: Then why do you not content yourselves in respect to His creation with what He was content with towards them?« Al-Murādī comments: »This was an incitation on his part to uphold the general sentences *(al-qawl bi l-jumal)* and to forego disagreement and division.«

According to a report independent of al-Murādī, Bunayn (?) b. Ibrāhīm said to al-Qāsim: »Ibn Manṣūr (al-Murādī) has told me about you that you have said: Whoever asserts that the Qur'an is created commits an innovation *(ibtadaʿa).*« He answered: »Yes, these are two innovations. It has not reached us that (the pious ancestors) said created or uncreated. Rather we say: The speech of God and His inspiration.« Aḥmad b. Sallām, a well-known transmitter from al-Qāsim[26], reported that he asked him about the Qur'an quoting to him a statement related from Zayd b. ʿAlī: »We do not liken *(nushabbih)* to God anyone and we do not say of the speech of God (that it is) created.« Al-Qāsim answered: »I say likewise.«

Al-Murādī praises al-Qāsim for praying for God's mercy for his brother Muḥammad b. Ibrāhīm, figurehead of a Zaydī rebellion in the region of Kufa, with whom he disagreed in theological doctrine[27]. »I heard al-Qāsim b. Ibrāhīm mention his brother Muhammad. He said: May God have mercy upon him and be pleased with him. I hope that he may have on the Day of the Resurrection a position about which he will rejoice, even though he upheld something of anthropomorphism *(ʿalā annahū kāna yaqūlu bi-shay'in min al-tashbīh).* Al-Murādī explains, evidently dissociating himself from this accusation: »That was in their view because he did not uphold the creation of the Qur'an *(wa-dhālika ʿindahum annahū lā yaqūlu bi-khalqi l-Qur'ān)*«. In the light of al-Qāsim's own position, this is probably to be understood as meaning that Muḥammad openly backed the doctrine of the uncreated nature of the Qur'an. Al-Murādī goes on to mention that al-Qāsim prayed for mercy for his brother »innumerable times« and composed an elegy for his death which al-Murādī wrote down from him. He stresses that al-Qāsim b. Ibrāhīm had wide support among the ʿAlids as a potential candidate for the imamate even though he held

23 Reading *wārithuhū* for *w-rāthuhū.*
24 Reading *qālū . . . lahum* for *qāla . . . lahū.*
25 Omitting *lahum.*
26 *Der Imam al-Qāsim*, p. 93.
27 The disagreement of al-Qāsim with his brother Muḥammad is mentioned by Abu l-Faraj, *Maqātil*, p. 553, on the authority of al-Murādī. The specific point of the disagreement, however, is not given there. See *Der Imam al-Qāsim*, p. 89.

the Qur'an to be created. ʿAbd Allāh b. Mūsā expressed his wish to al-Murādī that al-Qāsim would rise to claim the imamate promising that he, ʿAbd Allāh, would be the first to pledge allegiance to him. ʿAbd Allāh b. Mūsā added that it was said that al-Qāsim upheld the creation of the Qur'an but that he had not heard it from him.

Al-Qāsim b. Ibrāhīm's position in the contemporary conflict about the creation of the Qur'an thus emerges clearly. Within his strictly unitarian theology he could not admit the coeternity of the Qur'an with God. Everything aside from Him, including the Qur'an, must be created. He held, however, that the Qur'an should not be called »created«, but should be named only with designations taken from the Qur'an itself. In his writings he did not discuss the controversial question at all[28]. In this attitude he was motivated partly by solidarity with the majority of contemporary Zaydīs and the desire of not splitting their ranks by adopting controversial formulations and partly by his veneration for the Qur'an which occupied an outstanding place in his piety and religious thought. He did not wish to associate himself in the question with the Muʿtazila and other upholders of the creation of the Qur'an and certainly had no sympathy for the *miḥna* against their opponents instituted by al-Ma'mūn and his successors.

* * *

The information provided by Abū ʿAbd Allāh al-ʿAlawī on al-Qāsim's theological views substantially confirms the analysis of his extant authentic works[29]. Al-Qāsim cannot be considered as essentially influenced by Muʿtazilī school doctrine and as attempting to introduce it among the Zaydiyya. He agreed with the Muʿtazila on several of their basic principles. In one of them, the affirmation of human free will, this involved a radical break with the predominant doctrinal tradition within the early Zaydiyya which espoused divine determinism. His stand in this question was clearly a matter of deep religious conviction. He was reluctant to deviate from the Zaydī tradition and had no desire to associate with the Muʿtazila. It is evident from his discussions and formulations that he tried to minimize his disagreement with the Zaydī tradition. Quite in general he attempted to avoid Muʿtazilī concepts and terminology in his theological treatises. His treatment of the divine attributes differs substantially from Muʿtazilī teaching, and he repudiated major aspects of the Muʿtazilī concept of divine justice as well as the Muʿtazilī principle of the intermediate position of the grave sinner[30].

Al-Qāsim saw himself, and acted, primarily as a religious leader, not as a systematic theologian. In his writings, he repeats certain basic principles and themes with great conviction while ignoring wide areas of contem-

[28] *Der Imam al-Qāsim*, pp. 124-125.

[29] I take the occasion to correct my suggestion (*Der Imam al-Qāsim*, p. 168) that al-Qāsim did not transmit the *ḥadīth* attributed to the Prophet condemning the Rāfiḍa as polytheists. Al-ʿAlawī quotes the *ḥadīth* on the authority of Aḥmad b. ʿĪsā transmitted by al-Qāsim with his family *isnād*, followed by a comment of al-Qāsim affirming that the Rāfiḍa were polytheists in various respects (*al-Jāmiʿ*, fol. 320a). Al-ʿAlawī then quotes another report of al-Qāsim about a statement of his father, Ibrāhīm b. Ismāʿīl, made to him in which he severely censured the Rāfiḍa and their imams. These texts reflect the vehement anti-Imāmī sentiments of al-Qāsim (see *Der Imam al-Qāsim*, pp. 145-148).

[30] *Der Imam al-Qāsim*, pp. 109-114, 121-122.

porary theological interest. In his presentation, he often relies more on emotional preaching on the basis of Qur'anic texts than on cool rational argument. A few of the gaps left in his treatises, but only a few, were treated in answers to specific questions from his followers. The lack of over-all cohesion and consistency made it difficult to build a school tradition on his teaching. It was only natural that after his death his grandson Yaḥyā al-Hādī ila l-Ḥaqq led his followers to much closer association with Muʿtazilī school doctrine. Yet al-Qāsim b. Ibrāhīm would most likely have disapproved of this development.

This analysis must be reaffirmed in view of a different interpretation of al-Qāsim's theological teaching and its relationship to Muʿtazilī doctrine recently advanced by B. Abrahamov[31]. Abrahamov sees al-Qāsim as »influenced to a large extent by Muʿtazilism«. He bases this view on the acceptance of the authenticity of a number of treatises attributed to al-Qāsim which was contested in my book on him for a variety of reasons[32]. Abrahamov is aware that some of these treatises are much more definitely Muʿtazilī in their concepts, vocabulary and doctrine than the others and in some cases contradict positions upheld in these. This discrepancy is explained by him as a shift of al-Qāsim towards more outright Muʿtazilī doctrine in his later life. He does not explain why al-Qāsim, after having carefully distanced himself from the Muʿtazila and elaborated his own positions in his earlier treatises, would have abandoned these in his old age, when he had gained a wide following among the Zaydiyya, in order to write mediocre Muʿtazilī treatises in faulty Arabic.

Among the treatises accepted by Abrahamov as authentic works of al-Qāsim is the *Kitāb al-ʿAdl wa-l-tawḥīd,* in which the Qur'an, and all other scriptures of God, are expressly described as created *(makhlūq)* and those who do not affirm this are charged with denial of God and polytheism[33]. Abrahamov thus concluded that al-Qāsim openly taught, like the Muʿtazila, that God does not speak, but creates His speech[34]. The information provided by Muḥammad b. Manṣūr al-Murādī about al-Qāsim's position does not leave room for any doubt that this is not the case. It is hardly conceivable that al-Murādī, a long-time associate of al-Qāsim and the foremost authority of his age on the doctrine of the Zaydī ʿAlids, would not have been aware if al-Qāsim had affirmed the creation of the Qur'an in one of his writings or that he would have chosen to ignore it. The *Kitāb al-ʿAdl wa-l-tawḥīd*, which is arranged according to, and backs, the five basic principles of the Muʿtazila rather than those elaborated by al-Qāsim, is no work of his. It was erroneously attributed to him at a time when the Zaydīs had adopted Muʿtazilī theology in every respect except for the doctrine of the imamate and was only then included in the collection *(majmūʿ)* of his treatises[35].

Here is not the place to discuss Abrahamov's arguments for the authenticity of al-Qāsim's other disputed treatises. Suffice it to say that the case

[31] See his dissertation *The Theological Epistles of al-Ḳāsim Ibn Ibrāhīm* (in Hebrew), Tel-Aviv University 1981; »Al-Ḳāsim Ibn Ibrāhīm's Argument from Design« in *Oriens* 29-30 (1986), pp. 259-284; »Al-Ḳāsim Ibn Ibrāhīm's Theory of the Imamate« in *Arabica* XXXIV (1987), pp. 80-105.

[32] Abrahamov considers all treatises ascribed to al-Qāsim as authentic with the exception of the *Kitāb al-Kāmil al-munīr. Arabica* XXXIV, p. 84.

[33] See the edition of the text in *Rasā'il al-ʿadl wa-l-tawḥīd*, ed. Muḥammad ʿImāra, I, Cairo 1971, pp. 109, 111.

[34] *The Theological Epistles*, Engl. Abstract, p. VII.

[35] *Der Imam al-Qāsim*, p. 97.

for the authenticity of each one of them is hardly more convincing than that for the *Kitāb al-ʿAdl wa-l-tawḥīd*. For all that is known, al-Qāsim remained in his later life as reserved towards Muʿtazilism as he had ever been.

# V

# AL-QĀSIM IBN IBRĀHĪM AND CHRISTIAN THEOLOGY

Al-Qāsim b. Ibrāhīm al-Rassī (d. 246/860), Medinan Zaydī imam and grandfather of the founder of the Zaydī imamate in the Yemen, is the earliest Muslim *kalām* theologian of whose treatises a broad range is extant. Representing sectarian doctrine, his writings were not apt to have any influence on the development of general Muslim theological thought and could soon have been lost like those of so many of his predecessors and contemporaries. Among the Zaydīs, however, both in the Yemen and in the Caspian provinces, they became authoritative and thus have been faithfully preserved until the present. Within the Zaydī theological tradition, al-Qāsim's influence countered the predestinarian tendencies of the early Kūfan school doctrine and opened the door for the close identification of Zaydī imams with Mu'tazilite school doctrine apparent in the works of al-Qāsim's grandson al-Hādī ila l-Ḥaqq and, even more so, among some of the Caspian imams like the Buṭḥānī brothers Abū l-Ḥusayn al-Mu'ayyad bi'llāh and Abū Ṭālib al-Nāṭiq bi'l-Ḥaqq. It was thus only natural for R. Strothmann, the first western scholar to examine al-Qāsim's teaching, to describe him as essentially a representative of Mu'tazilite thought.[1] Strothmann's view was henceforth generally adopted by other scholars who published some of al-Qāsim's treatises or dealt with aspects of his doctrine.

Later Zaydīs, to be sure, did not generally see al-Qāsim as favouring Mu'tazilite theological thought. In fact some of those vigourously opposed to the influence of Mu'tazilite school doctrine among the Zaydīs, like the Sayyid Ḥumaydān b. Yaḥyā (7th/13th century), liked to point to, and quote, him as a main representative of ancient Zaydī, non-Mu'tazilite *kalām*. Ḥumaydān stressed the simplicity of the teaching of the ancient Zaydī authorities, their keeping aloof from discussion of the *daqīq al-kalām*, the subtle, non-essential points which took up broad space in Mu'tazilite *kalām* works.[2] Much earlier, the anti-Mu'tazilite Kūfan Zaydī scholar Muḥammad b. Manṣūr al-Murādī, who had personally associated with al-Qāsim b.

[1]Strothmann, R., "Die Literatur der Zaiditen", *Der Islam*, II (1911), 53.

[2]See Madelung, W., *Der Imam al-Qāsim ibn Ibrāhīm und die Glaubenslehre der Zaiditen*, (Berlin, 1965), 218-19.

Ibrāhīm over a long time and knew his doctrines intimately, could report views of his which were distinctly at variance with, and critical of, the Mu'tazilite view of divine justice. According to him, al-Qāsim also, while privately agreeing with the Mu'tazilite doctrine of the created nature of the Qur'ān, refused to uphold it in public and condemned equally those who affirmed or denied it.[3]

In al-Qāsim's biography, nothing points to his having had a Mu'tazilite teacher or his having associated with Mu'tazilites. Medina, where he grew up, was no centre of Mu'tazilism or of *kalām* in general. His teachers in *ḥadīth*, Abū Bakr b. Abī Uways and his brother Ismā'īl, were nephews of Mālik b. Anas and belonged to his school.[4] Through his family al-Qāsim was, no doubt, familiar with basic Zaydī beliefs. His theological thought, however, was probably not formed before he, in his twenties, went to Egypt, presumably to al-Fusṭāṭ. There he engaged in *kalām* debates with Christians and atheists and wrote his first theological treatises, among which were probably his *Refutation of the Zindīq Ibn al-Muqaffa'* and *Refutation of the Christians*. Al-Fusṭāṭ, unlike Medina, was in the age of the caliph al-Ma'mūn a centre of debate between Muslims and representatives of other religious communities. Inter-Islamic dispute, on the other hand, does not seem to have occupied al-Qāsim at this stage.

There were no well-known Mu'tazilite theologians in Egypt at this time. The most prominent *mutakallim* was the predestinarian Ḥafṣ al-Fard, whose presence at one of his debates is mentioned by al-Qāsim.[5] Yet Ḥafṣ al-Fard clearly cannot have been his teacher. Al-Qāsim was, moreover, already viewed as a religious leader, especially after the Zaydī revolt of his elder brother Muḥammad b. Ibrāhīm in 198-9/814-5. His theological views, insofar as they were at variance with the Zaydī tradition and those of his brother,[6] were probably formed in active study of the views of religious opponents, in debating their views and reading their books.

If contemporary Mu'tazilite theology thus did not have a formative influence on al-Qāsim's thought, in what context is it to be located? In my book on him I suggested some points of Christian influence without, however, attempting to trace specific sources.[7] Progress in our knowledge

[3]See Madelung, W., "Imam al-Qāsim ibn Ibrāhīm and Mu'tazilism", in *On Both Sides of al-Mandab: Ethiopean, South-Arabic and Islamic Studies presented to Oscar Löfgren on his ninetieth birthday*, (Stockholm, 1989), 29-46.

[4]*Der Imam al-Qāsim*, 131-2.

[5]*Der Imam al-Qāsim*, 89.

[6]See *Der Imam al-Qāsim*, 89; "Imam al-Qāsim ibn Ibrāhīm", 45.

[7]*Der Imam al-Qāsim*, 110-111.

both of al-Qāsim's doctrine and of contemporary Christian theology expressed in Arabic may now facilitate a resumption of the question. On the Christian side, the works of the Nestorian 'Ammār al-Baṣrī have become available in addition to those of the Melkite Theodore Abū Qurra and the Jacobite Abū Rā'iṭa. Recently edited is, moreover, the Arabic text of the slightly later theological work of the Jewish author al-Muqammiṣ who was, as is known, a pupil of the Christian Nonnus (Nānā) of Nisibis. The editor of the work, Sarah Stroumsa, has noted numerous detail points of similarity between the doctrine of al-Muqammiṣ and al-Qāsim b. Ibrāhīm.[8]

Among these four non-Muslim authors, al-Qāsim's theology stands structurally closest to that of Abū Qurra. It is noteworthy that Abū Qurra is at the same time the one least influenced by Mu'tazilite doctrine of the four. Both Abū Qurra and al-Qāsim thus completely ignore the basic Mu'tazilite distinction between eternal attributes of essence and temporal attributes of act of God. The other three authors adopted this distinction and adapted it for their purposes. 'Ammār al-Baṣrī recognises two essential divine attributes: life (*ḥayāt*) and speech (*nuṭq*), or wisdom (*ḥikma*), and identifies them with the Holy Spirit and the Son, or Logos (*kalima*), respectively, in order to establish the doctrine of the Trinity for the Muslim opponent. Other divine attributes admitted by the Muslims, he maintained, are either reducible to these two, or are caused by them (*ma'lūlāt*) and refer to God's acts (*fa'ālīl, ṣanā'i'*) and intentions (*himam*) after the creation.[9] This latter category, which includes justice (*'adl*), mercy (*raḥma*), generosity (*jūd*), bounty, forgiveness (*maghfira*),[10] evidently corresponds to the Mu'tazilite attributes of action (*ṣifāt af'āl*). In arguing for the reality of the hypostases of the Trinity, 'Ammār naturally seeks to show the absurdity of the thesis that God is ever living and wise without having a life and a wisdom, with which the Mu'tazilites tried to maintain the simple unity of God.[11] Quite similar are the arguments of Abū Rā'iṭa.[12] The Jew al-Muqammiṣ, on the other hand, adopted the Mu'tazilite position that God is eternally living and knowing by His mere essence, not through life and knowledge,[13] arguing

[8]Stroumsa, S., *Dāwūd Ibn Marwān al-Muqammiṣ's Twenty Chapters ('Ishrūn Maqāla)*, (Leiden, 1989), 129, 159, 160, 166, 172-3, 197, 204, 240, 255.

[9]'Ammār al-Baṣrī, *Apologie et Controverses*, Hayek, M., (ed), (Beirut, 1977), Arab. text 46-56, 148-69.

[10]'Ammār, 53.

[11]'Ammār, 46-7, 153-5.

[12]Graf, G., *Die Schriften des Jacobiten Ḥabīb b. Ḫidma Abū Rā'iṭa*, (Louvain, 1951), Arab. text 1-11.

[13]*Twenty Chapters*, 186-205. S. Stroumsa suggests that the position of al-Muqammiṣ differed

that the opposite Christian doctrine leads to sheer polytheism.[14] It may be noted that the identification of the Word and the Spirit with the divine attributes of wisdom and life had already been made by the Nestorian Patriarch Timothy in his *Apology* before the caliph al-Mahdī.[15] Neither Abū Qurra nor al-Qāsim mention this identification.

Central to al-Qāsim's theology is the concept that God is absolutely different from everything created. He even describes this dissimilarity as the basic attribute of God in regard to existence and essence.[16] His somewhat awkward nominal formulation that God is the dissimilarity of things (*khilāf al-ashyā'*) is literally matched by al-Muqammiṣ, who affirms that the Maker of the World is *khilāf al-'ālam* in every respect.[17] G. Vajda and S. Stroumsa observed on this passage that "al-Muqammiṣ is here preparing the ground for his debate with Christianity."[18] This is true for both al-Muqammiṣ and al-Qāsim insofar as they nominally posit an absolute and unqualified dissimilarity between God and creation. The Christian theologians of the time, while generally stressing the dissimilarity of God and the created world, also admitted an aspect of similarity. The motive behind this admission was not, as their opponents tried to imply, to accommodate the human nature of Christ, but to give a foundation to the divine attributes which could equally, if imperfectly, be predicated of man. Abū Qurra based his doctrine of divine attributes on the concept that every perfection apparent in creation must also be predicated of the Creator. The initial similarity between creation and God is then negated at a second stage by the realization that the attributes of perfection in God are unrestricted and eternal in contrast to those in man.[19] The quantitative difference is in reality

from that of the Mu'tazila (introd. 28-9; 190 n. 18). It is true that al-Muqammiṣ criticizes the formulation of the Mu'tazilite Abū l-Hudhayl. His own formulation, however, is the same as that of the majority of the Mu'tazila. Stroumsa's further comment that al-Muqammiṣ does not seem to distinguish the *ṣifāt al-af'āl* from *ṣifāt al-dhāt* (187 n. 12) is also incorrect. His formulation that "God is the living who does not live by virtue of life ..." but "He is the generous in His acts and the just in His judgment" (186-7) clearly recognises the distinction.

14 *Twenty Chapters*, 192.

15 Mingana, A., "Timothy's Apology for Christianity", in *Woodbrooke Studies*, II, (Cambridge, 1928), 23.

16 *Der Imam al-Qāsim*, p. 112.

17 *Twenty Chapters*, 159: *Fā'il al-'ālam khilāf al-'ālam min kull wajh.* Al-Qāsim's son Muḥammad used the same formulation in his *K. al-Waṣiyya*: *ḥaqīqat al-īmān bih* (scil. *Allāh*) *annahū huwa l-ladhī khilāf al-ashyā' kullihā*. Quoted by Ḥumaydān b. Yaḥya, ms. Brit. Mus. Or. 3727, fol. 79a-b.

18 *Twenty Chapters*, 159 n. 29.

19 *Mayāmir Thāūdūrus Abī Qurra Usquf Ḥarrān*, al-Bāshā, Q., (ed), (Beirut, 1904), 78-80. Trans. Graf, G., *Die arabischen Schriften des Theodor Abū Qurra, Bischofs von Ḥarrān*, (Paderborn, 1910), 162-5.

a qualitative one.

Al-Qāsim's concept of divine attributes is, in spite of his initial insistence on the absolute dissimilarity of God and creation, structurally the same. He defines the Qur'ānic description of God as *al-ṣamad* as meaning the ultimate end of goodness and of everything praiseworthy.[20] Concerning the attribute of power (*'izz*) al-Qāsim argues that the power of every powerful one witnessed by us is partial and mixed with impotence (*dhull*). From this we gain certain knowledge that there must be a King who owns all power and has no partner in that power. For only someone whose power is not shared is powerful without impotence.[21]

Distinctly apparent is the structural similarity between Abū Qurra's and al-Qāsim's proofs of God's existence. Both set out with an epistemological discussion of the various possible ways of knowing things. In his *Mīmar* on the way to knowledge of God, Abū Qurra specifies four ways: by eye-witnessing (*'iyān*), by an effect or trace (*athar*), by similarity (*shibh*), and by dissimilarity (*khilāf*). Of these he rejects the first one, eye-witnessing, and affirms the other three as leading to knowledge of God.[22] Al-Qāsim's scheme in his *Kitāb al-Dalīl* is more elaborate. He mentions sensual perception (*ḥiss*), apprehension by the soul (*idrāk nafs*), imagination (*wahm*), conjecture (*ẓann*), proof (*dalīl, dalāla*), and finally dissimilarity to everything perceived or comprehended by reason (*ma'qūl*). Concerning apprehension by the soul he notes that the "philosophers of the Rūm", probably meaning Christian apologists, assert for the soul, especially when it is divested of the body, an apprehension which is other than sensual perception or apprehension by imagination. From his elaborations elsewhere it is evident that he meant by apprehension of the soul emotions such as shame, fear, joy, sadness, patience, anxiety, pleasure, and disgust.[23] Out of all these various ways to knowledge he rejects all but the last two, by proof and by dissimilarity to all things. The way of proof consists for al-Qāsim, as for

[20]See *Der Imam al Qāsim*, 110-111.

[21]*Der Imam al-Qāsim*, 114; Abrahamov, B., *Al-Ḳāsim b. Ibrāhīm on the Proof of God's Existence: Kitāb al Dalīl al-Kabīr*, (Leiden, 1990), 136.

[22]*Mayāmir*, 75; trans. Graf, 160.

[23]See *Der Imam al-Qāsim*, 108 n. 69. In the *Kitāb al-Dalīl* (Abrahamov, 72) he rejects the possibility of the soul apprehending God because of its composite nature and perishability. He notes in this respect various faculties (*quwā*) of the soul: imagination, thought, memory, and intuition. Here he evidently understands the soul as including the intellect which he initially separated from it. In affirming the perishability of the soul, al-Qāsim clearly deviates from the Christian position of Abū Qurra who affirms that the soul, in contrast to man, does not die (*al-nafs lā tamūt*, *Mayāmir* 107, 110).

Abū Qurra, of the evidence or traces (*āthār*) of wisdom in the creation,[24] the cosmological proof, which he then elaborates at length on the basis of Qur'ānic quotations. He does not refer to Abū Qurra's third way, similarity, clearly excluding it by his accentuation of God's dissimilarity. His *Kitāb al-Dalīl* can thus perhaps be seen as an Islamic response to Abū Qurra's proof. It is evident, however, that al-Qāsim was also familiar with other relevant Christian works.

In contrast, 'Ammār al-Baṣri's proof of the existence of God lacks an epistemological introduction. It proceeds from the mutual opposition (*taḍādd*) among the four elements, earth, water, fire, and air, which require a powerful creator to force them into composition of the world and the human body.[25] The extant writings of Abū Rā'iṭa do not contain a proof of God's existence. The proof of al-Muqammiṣ is based on the argument that the world consists of substances (*jawāhir*) and accidents, both of which are created in time and thus require a creator.[26] This proof is relatively close to the traditional one of Mu'tazilite *kalām*, except that al-Muqammiṣ does not define *jawāhir* as atoms and describes accidents in terms of the Aristotelian categories.

Christian theological influence on al-Qāsim is evident in his affirmation of human free will and of the essential goodness of God, where he most radically deviated from the Kūfan Zaydī belief in predetermination. In his *Refutation of the Crypto-Manichaean (zindīq) Ibn al-Muqaffa'*, perhaps his earliest extant work, he asserts that goodness is of the essence of God. Out of this goodness (*jūd*) and generosity (*karam*) God, however, created the world by His free choice (*ikhtiyār*), not by necessity.[27] God's goodness is the basis of His justice by which He created man free to choose (*mukhayyar*) between obedience and disobedience, so that this obedience by free choice would be a good act (*iḥsān*), while disobedience would be a true act of disobedience.[28]

Here again al-Qāsim's argument structurally resembles that of Abū Qurra in his *Mīmar* on human free will. Abū Qurra questions the opponent who holds that man is compelled to do whatever good or evil he does, on whether or not he affirms that God is just. The answer, no doubt, being yes, he argues that justice means that the just will respond with equal measures

[24]Abrahamov, 64, 76.
[25]'Ammār, 95-7.
[26]*Twenty Chapters*, chapters 3-7.
[27]Guidi, M., *La lotta tra l'islam e il manichéismo*, (Rome, 1927), Arabic text, 32.
[28]*La lotta*, Arabic text, 33.

to equal conditions (*an yunzila l-'ādilu min nafsihi l-ashyā'a l-mustawiyata fī ḥāli stiwā'ihā*).[29] God in His justice will thus treat all men equally in accordance with their freely chosen acts. Later Abū Qurra affirms that God's foreknowledge does not negate the freedom with which He had endowed human nature out of His generosity (*karam*) and goodness (*jūd*),[30] employing the same terms as al-Qāsim. After his assertion of human free will Abū Qurra immediately turns to attack Mani and his dualist determinism of good and evil in the world. The problem of human free will versus determinism was evidently closely associated at the time with the fight against the crypto-Manichaeans, which had been officially sponsored by the 'Abbāsid caliph al-Mahdī. Al-Qāsim may have been partly influenced to adopt the Christian theological doctrine of human free will out of anti-dualist considerations. H.S. Nyberg has noted that most of al-Qāsim's anti-Manichaean arguments had been employed before him by Christian apologists, especially prominent theologians of the Syrian Church.[31]

None of the earlier and contemporary Mu'tazilite refutations of dualists and Manichaeans are extant for a comparison. It is evident, however, that they can hardly have been at the base of al-Qāsim's argumentation. The Mu'tazilites viewed goodness, generosity and justice as divine attributes of action rather than of essence.[32] They derived these attributes, at least in their later teaching, from God's being all-knowing, wise, and self-sufficient (*ghanī*) by His essence. God was proved to be generous because He was in no need of anything. The goodness of God was not central in their theological system as it was in Christian theology and for al-Qāsim.

A basically Christian theological perspective in al-Qāsim's view of human free will is also consistent with his criticism of relevant Mu'tazilite doctrine. Thus he is quoted as sharply rebuking those who said either: "Whoever is killed dies without an appointed term (*ajal*), and if he had not been killed he would not have died", or: "Surely, when he killed him he cut his appointed term." Some Mu'tazilites questioned the common Muslim belief that God sets the life term of man and insisted that God's foreknowledge of man's lifetime does not mean that He fixes it, or wills it, especially of a man murdered by another.[33] In the extant contemporary works of Christian theologians the question of God's determination of the lifespan of man is

[29] *Mayāmir*, 10.
[30] *Mayāmir*, 19.
[31] See *OLZ*, XXXII (1929), col. 431.
[32] See *Der Imam al-Qāsim*, 109-10.
[33] "Imam al-Qāsim ibn Ibrāhīm and Mu'tazilism", 39-40.

apparently not discussed. The Syrian Orthodox bishop of Mosul, Moshe bar Kepha, writing in Syriac one or two generations after al-Qāsim, affirmed that the term of man's life is fixed and determined by God, the Lord of life.[34] This position may reflect strong pressure of Muslim determinist doctrine in this question, since earlier Jacobite tradition had upheld the opposite thesis.[35]

Al-Qāsim also scornfully dismissed the question, evidently inspired by Mu'tazilite thinking: "How can God be considered other than unjust in inflicting pain (*alam*) on children while anyone else doing this would be unjust?" The Mu'tazilites answered the question by arguing that God is obliged to provide compensation (*'iwaḍ*) to children, and even animals, for any pain or harm inflicted on them by Him. Al-Qāsim, in contrast, basically maintained that the blessings and benefaction of God for children far outweighs any pain that reaches them.[36] This disagreement reflects a deep difference between the concept of justice in Christian and Mu'tazilite theology. The Christian concept was essentially that of distributive justice. As formulated by Abū Qurra, God, to be just, must treat all men alike under the same circumstances. Since Christian theology defined God as good and generous in essence, it attempted to justify whatever pain and harm befell man by denying that God could be held responsible for it and asserting the overwhelming preponderance of His bounties and blessings on man. Among al-Qāsim's Christian contemporaries 'Ammār al-Baṣrī offers the most thorough exposition of the relevant traditional Christian teaching. He maintains that man is inevitably aware that he owes God thanks and praise for His bounty in merely creating him and giving him life.[37] Diseases and illnesses[38] in children are not created as such by God, but are caused by improper nourishment or other harmful human conduct. A question of compensation does not arise anywhere in his discussion.

The Mu'tazilites, in contrast, espoused a concept of material justice, justice requiring compensation for harm and pain suffered. On this basis they elaborated a system of ethics which inevitably applied on equal terms to man, animals, and to God, a system far removed from both Christian theological thought and the philosophical tradition. It is characteristic that the Mu'tazilite theory of justice could be depreciated by a modern Christian

[34]Griffith, S., "Free Will in Christian Kalām", *Le Muséon*, 100 (1987), 149.
[35]Ibid. n. 23.
[36]"Imam al-Qāsim ibn Ibrāhīm and Mu'tazilism", 40-1.
[37]'Ammār, 105-6.
[38]Reading *amrāḍ* for *a'rāḍ*, 'Ammār, 120-1.

theologian like W. Montgomery Watt as measuring God's justice by human standards,[39] while arousing the interest and admiration of a Christian philosopher like G. Hourani.[40]

Al-Qāsim's familiarity with contemporary Christian theology is naturally most evident in his *Refutation of the Christians*. Notable are the lengthy quotations from the gospels. Al-Qāsim also cited the Bible in other treatises of his, and apparently was not worried by the Qur'ānic charges that the *Ahl al-Kitāb* had corrupted their scriptures. In the *Refutation of the Christians* he quotes some passages from the gospels of Matthew and John in order to establish that they agreed with "sound belief" as understood by Muslims, as against the Christian belief in the divinity of Christ.[41] At the end of the *Refutation* he quotes the first chapters of Matthew at length without commentary.[42] These quotations contain the rhymed prose characteristic of al-Qāsim's style and are evidently not directly copied from an Arabic translation of the Bible.

The Christian terminology, concepts, and doctrine mentioned in al-Qāsim's *Refutation* all match with the works of the contemporary Christian theologians. Here, too, the resemblances to Theodore Abū Qurra's Arabic treatises are most common, yet nowhere close enough to prove a direct dependence. In describing the doctrine of the Trinity, al-Qāsim, like Abū Qurra, prefers the term *ṭabīʿa*, nature,[43] to express the unitary aspect, although he also mentions the term *jawhar*, substance,[44] used by ʿAmmār and Abū Rā'iṭa. He prefers the term *shakhṣ* (pl. *ashkhāṣ*),[45] avoided by the three Christian authors and expressly repudiated by ʿAmmār,[46] for the three persons, while also noting the term *uqnūm* (pl. *aqānīm*)[47] preferred by the Christian authors. He ignores, however, Abū Qurra's alternative term, *wujūh*. He mentions the Christian analogies of the sun, its light, and its warmth, and of man, his soul, body, life and speech (*manṭiq*) with the

[39]See, for instance, Watt, W.M., *Free Will and Predestination in Islam*, (London, 1948), 68.

[40]Hourani, G., *Rationalism in the Ethics of ʿAbd al-Jabbār*, (Oxford, 1971).

[41]Di Matteo, I., "Confutazione contro i Cristiani dello Zaidita al-Qāsim b. Ibrāhīm", *RSO*, IX (1921-23), 321-5.

[42]"Confutazione", 325-31.

[43]"Confutazione", 314.

[44]"Confutazione", 318.

[45]"Confutazione", 314-15.

[46]ʿAmmār, 161-2. Contrary to Hayek's remark (introd., 29) that Abū Rā'iṭa is fond of using the term *shakhṣ*, Abū Rā'iṭa consistently uses *uqnūm* in respect to the Trinity. Only in one passage (Graf, *Die Schriften*, Arabic text, 11) does he use *al-ashkhāṣ*, immediately glossing it with *ay al-aqānīm*. The other references given by Hayek (29 n. 7) for Abū Rā'iṭa's use of *shakhṣ* do not concern the Trinity as such.

[47]"Confutazione", 315.

Trinity.[48] The former is used in Timothy's Apology,[49] by 'Ammār[50] and Abū Rā'iṭa,[51] the latter by Abū Qurra.[52] In connection with the doctrine of the Trinity, too, al-Qāsim mentions that the Christians applied three names to things, names denoting essence and substance (*asmā' dhātiyya jawhariyya*), names denoting persons (*asmā' shakhṣiyya uqnūmiyya*), and names denoting temporal, accidental aspects (*asmā' ḥāditha 'araḍiyya*).[53] Abū Qurra speaks of the first two categories as names indicating natures (*asmā' dalīla 'ala l-ṭabā'i'*) and names indicating aspects (*asmā' dalīla 'ala l-wujūh*).[54] He does not mention the third category. 'Ammār al-Baṣrī, on the other hand, speaks in his parallel discussion of four categories of things, rather than names: substance (*jawhar*), person (*qunūm*), faculties (*quwā*) like the heat of fire and the rays of the sun, and accident (*'araḍ*).[55] Al-Qāsim's description of the Christian doctrine of the original sin of Adam and the redemption by Christ[56] is relatively close to, but more detailed than, that of Abū Qurra.[57] 'Ammār's relevant elaborations[58] differ in structure.

A close comparison of al-Qāsim's theological thought with the extant writings of contemporary Christian authors thus reveals their basic similarity. Al-Qāsim was not only thoroughly familiar with the Christian theology of his time, he was also formatively influenced by it. Where he deviated from traditional Zaydī doctrine, it was most likely under this influence of Christian theology. It seems safe to assume that he was acquainted with the Arabic treatises of Theodore Abū Qurra and related both positively and negatively to them. If he knew the works of 'Ammār al-Baṣrī and Abū Rā'iṭa, he was evidently less impressed by them. Written probably somewhat later than those of Abū Qurra, they may not have been available when al-Qāsim began his examination of Christian doctrine. It is certain, however, that al-Qāsim had abundant other sources of information, both oral and written, about Christian theological teaching.

48"Confutazione", 315.
49"Timothy's Apology", 22.
50'Ammār, 49.
51Graf, *Die Schriften*, Arab. text, 16, 30; trans. 19.
52Mayāmir, 45. Abū Qurra speaks here of man, his word (*kalima*), and his spirit (*rūh*). 'Ammār (49) uses the analogy of the soul, its life and word (*kalima*). Abū Rā'iṭa also mentions the soul and its connection with the intellect (*'aql*) and speech (*nuṭq*) (Graf, *Die Schriften*, Arab. text, 16).
53"Confutazione", 318-19.
54*Mayāmir*, 331; trans. Graf. 144.
55'Ammār, 51.
56"Confutazione", 317.
57*Mayāmir*, 67; trans. Graf, 219.
5*Ammār*, 254-63.

# VI

## ZAYDĪ ATTITUDES TO SUFISM

The relationship between the religious movement of the Zaydiyya and organized Sufism has been predominantly antagonistic throughout their history. At the root of the conflict was a clash about authority in religion. As a Shii sect, the Zaydiyya recognized the ultimate religious authority of the Family of the Prophet (*ahl al-bayt*). The Zaydī imams demanded obedience from their followers not just as political rulers but also as teachers and guides in religious matters. Unlike the imams of the Twelver Shia and the Ismāᶜīliyya, however, they were not endowed with impeccability and infallibilty (*ᶜiṣma*) and their religious authority could be challenged. The Sufi shaykhs, who were mostly Sunni, demanded absolute personal obedience from their disciples, though not from their community at large.

Apart from this clash concerning leadership, there were also profound differences in religious motivation which were never bridged. Zaydī Islam was essentially sober, sharia-oriented, legalistic, and rationalist. It lacked and repudiated any dimension of ecstatic intuition, esoteric knowledge and gnosis, and any form of mystical approach to the world of the divine. The Twelver Shia and Ismāᶜīliyya shared such features with Sufism, leading Henry Corbin to his view that Sufism itself was in essence a Shii phenomenon. Zaydīs vigorously condemned antinomian and laxist tendencies in Sufism. They took offence at, and strictly forbade, Sufi practices which aimed at inducing states of ecstasy, such as the *samāᶜ*, singing, music, dancing, and gazing upon beautiful youths. They totally rejected the speculative mysticism of Ibn al-ᶜArabī and his school. Rationalist, anti-mystical Muᶜtazilī theology was adopted by the Zaydiyya more consistently than by the Twelver Shia and evidently suited them better. In agreement with the Muᶜtazila they generally restricted the possibility of miracles to prophets and denounced claims of miracles by Sufi shaykhs as sheer fraud.

There was, however, an aspect of Sufi piety which could be fully appreciated by the Zaydiyya. Like early Sufism in particular, Zaydī religious devotion contained a strong element of asceticism, i.e. rejection of this world — both its attractions and iniquities — and of a preoccupation with, and preparation for, the world to come. A popular Zaydī movement like the Muṭarrifiyya in the Yemen, which summoned to withdrawal from the world in *hijras*, to repentance, to ascetic exercises, purification and meditation, can certainly be described as analogous to early Sufism, although there is no evidence of direct Sufi influence on it. Zaydī imams and scholars, however, did not hesitate to praise early ascetic Sufis such as al-Fuḍayl b. ᶜIyāḍ, Bishr al-Ḥāfī, al-Junayd and Dhū'l-Nūn al-Miṣrī. Indeed they cited their sayings and held them up as individuals who had led exemplary religious lives.

This positive attitude towards early Sufi ascetic piety, together with some reserve, is reflected in the *Risālat siyāsat al-murīdīn* of the Caspian Zaydī Imam Aḥmad b. al-Ḥusayn al-Muʾayyad bi'llāh (d. 411/1021).[1] The *Risāla* apparently represents the earliest extant Zaydī literary reaction to Sufism, written by an imam otherwise known as an author on Muᶜtazilī Zaydī *kalām* and Zaydī (Hādawī) *fiqh*. The title, *Management of the Desirous*, employs Sufi terminology. Al-Muʾayyad begins by observing that he has found all (religious) disciplines thriving in his time except for the discipline of *muᶜāmala*, i.e. devotional practice, which had become neglected and abandoned. He goes on to quote al-Junayd's characteristic praise of ᶜAlī as the potential master in this field. Al-Junayd says: 'God shall call to account those who turned the attention of our master', meaning ᶜAlī, 'away from us through (the battles of) the Camel and Ṣiffīn. If he had not been preoccupied with these wars, he would have set forth for us what we are incapable of accomplishing with regard to these disciplines (*mā lā qibala lanā bih*)'.

The first station of devotion, al-Muʾayyad explains, is repentance (*tawba*), and the foundation of repentance is fear. The *murīd* must therefore instill fear into his own heart, especially by imagining the woes and pains of death. Repentance is followed by desire (*irāda*), which is defined as seeking to turn to God exclusively while cutting oneself loose from everything else (*ṭalab al-inqiṭāᶜ ilā'llāh min kull mā siwāh*). Here al-Muʾayyad quotes *in extenso* a lengthy exhortation (*waṣiyya*) of al-Junayd, stressing the great benefit which the *murīd* may draw from it. Throughout the *Risāla*, al-Muʾayyad cites the prophets, members of the Prophet's Family such as ᶜAlī, Zayd b. ᶜAlī, Muḥammad al-Bāqir, Jaᶜfar al-Ṣādiq, and al-Qāsim b. Ibrāhīm, and Sufis such as al-Fuḍayl b. ᶜIyāḍ, Dāwūd al-Ṭāʾī, Abū Sulaymān

---

1 Ms. Ambrosiana C 186.

al-Dārānī, Dhū'l-Nūn al-Miṣrī, Abū'l-Ḥusayn al-Nūrī, and Ruwaym b. Aḥmad; but he also warns of the defects of Sufism. The Sufi Ruwaym is quoted as saying: 'This our path consists of expenditure of the spirit (*badhl al-rūḥ*). If you are capable of it, good; but if not, do not occupy yourself with the farces of the Sufis (*turrahāt al-ṣūfiyya*)'.

The search for closeness to God requires constant exertion (*mujāhada*). Yet the enemy, Satan, attempts to delude the *murīd* by suggesting that reaching the goal is simply a gift from God and that effort and struggle in fact place a veil between God and the servant. This delusion affects in particular those who associate with the Sufis (*man yuʿāshir ahl al-taṣawwuf*). The Enemy may also suggest to the *murīd* that practices contrary to the sharia may bring him closer to his goal, practices such as listening to singing, dancing, and amusing oneself with games like backgammon and other forms of entertainment. He may encourage him to neglect his religious duties and even to abandon the obligatory prayers while making him believe that he has reached a noble and distinguished station. Al-Muʾayyad adds that he had met an old shaykh from among the ignorant Sufis (*min jahalat al-ṣūfiyya*) who used to lament about the long years (of his vain struggle) since he had not reached the goal, and who now thought that this would come about by merely removing the screen between himself and God. Al-Muʾayyad expresses shock at such monstrous ignorance. He also refers with disgust to the class of Sufis who call themselves the blameworthy (*ahl al-malāma*). They claim that by involving themselves in evil situations and committing reprehensible acts they abase their ego, yet in reality they fall from the state of repentance and may well revert to being offenders (*fussāq*). Al-Muʾayyad ignores any mystical states beyond that of *irāda*. Instead he concludes his treatise with a chapter on worship (*ʿibāda*) and holds up as examples the Prophet and ʿAlī Zayn al-ʿĀbidīn who spent their lives in strenuous and never-ceasing worship.

Al-Muʾayyad's treatise set the guidelines for later Zaydī attitudes to Sufism. It was brought to the Yemen together with his major works and is quoted at length in his biography in Ḥumayd al-Muḥallī's *al-Ḥadāʾiq al-wardiyya*, the large Yemenite collection of the lives of the early Zaydī imams.[2] The guidelines did not entirely prevent internal Zaydī controversy with respect to later develop-

---

2 See W. Madelung, *Arabic Texts concerning the History of the Zaydī Imams of Ṭabaristān, Daylamān and Gīlān* (Beirut 1987) 293-305.

ments in Sufism. Some time after 560/1165, a Zaydī pretender to the imamate, Muḥammad b. Ismāᶜīl al-Dāwūdī, was active in the Caspian region. He had written a book entitled *al-Wasīla ilā 'l-faḍīla* which is described as similar to al-Ghazālī's *al-Munqidh min al-ḍalāl*. His followers were accused of being negligent with regard to the sharia. The Caspian Zaydī community was split concerning him, and his opponents backed a counter-candidate, ᶜAlī b. Muḥammad al-Ghaznawī, for the imamate. The conflict continued for thirty years.[3] The prominent religious figure of al-Ghazālī and his Sufism evidently evoked a mixed response among Zaydīs. His espousal of a strong ethical dimension in the sharia appealed to many of them. The more esoteric aspects of his Sufism and his defence of the practice of *samāᶜ* mostly met with opposition.

In the eighth/fourteenth century the Caspian Zaydī community came under the rule of an ᶜAlid dynasty, which lasted until the community's absorption into Twelver Shiism in the early Safavid period. The founder of the dynasty, Sayyid ᶜAlī Kiyā b. Amīr Kiyā al-Malāṭī, was the leader of a Sufi movement of 'penitents' (*tāʾibān*). The Zaydī scholars of Lāhījān, according to Ẓahīr al-Dīn Marᶜashī's account, recognized him as the imam, testifying that he possessed all five qualifications required by Zaydī law for the imamate. Only one of them, Yaḥyā b. Muḥammad al-Ṣāliḥī, dissented and went into exile in Rasht.[4] At present nothing further is known about the Sufism and religious policy of the dynasty.

In the Yemen, conflict between the Zaydiyya and Sufis did not arise until the seventh/thirteenth century.[5] The Zaydīs seem to have kept Sufism out of the highlands from Ṣaᶜda to Ṣanᶜāʾ and Dhamār where they were dominant, and there is little mention of Sufism in the writings of the early Yemenite imams. Organized Sufism spread in the Sunni, mostly Shāfiᶜī, lowlands, Tihāma, Zabīd, and Taᶜizz from the fifth/eleventh century on.[6] As Zaydī imams sought to extend their domination into the lowlands, Sufi shaykhs, who wielded

---

3 W. Madelung, *Der Imam al-Qāsim ibn Ibrāhīm und die Glaubenslehre der Zaiditen* (Berlin 1965) 217-8.

4 Ẓahīr al-Dīn Marᶜashī, *Tārīkh-i Gīlān wa Daylamān*, ed. M. Sutūdeh (Tehran 1347/1969) 16, 41.

5 The following account is based in part on the study of ᶜAbd Allāh Muḥammad al-Ḥabshī (al-Ḥibshī), *al-Ṣūfiyya wa'l-fuqahāʾ fi 'l-Yaman* (Ṣanᶜāʾ 1396/1976). My thanks are due to Mr. Bernard Haykel for making available some of the literature used in this study and for valuable advice.

6 al-Ḥabshī, op. cit. 12.

considerable influence over the local populace, put up resistance. The Zaydī Imam al-Mahdī li-dīn Allāh Aḥmad b. al-Ḥusayn, who ruled from 646-656/1249-1258, wrote a letter to Abū'l-Ghayth b. Jamīl (d. 651/1253), the most prominent Yemenite Sufi shaykh — at that time active in the village of Bayt ᶜAṭāᵓ in Wādī Surdud — and summoned him politely to unite with him in 'ordering what is proper and forbidding what is reprehensible'. Abū'l-Ghayth replied to him with equal politeness, assuring him that if God supported al-Mahdī no one could overcome him. He, Abū'l-Ghayth, had heard and was following the summons of the Truth (*ḥaqq*), God, and after that there was no room left to respond to the summons of any creature.[7]

The surface politeness concealed the deep aversion of the Sufi to the pretense of the Zaydī imam. It was at this time, or perhaps on an earlier occasion when a Zaydī imam intended to invade the lowlands, that Abū'l-Ghayth wrote to another Sufi shaykh, Muḥammad b. Ismāᶜīl al-Ḥaḍramī, proposing that they both depart from Yemen because of the spread of civil strife (*ẓuhūr al-fitan*) there. Al-Ḥaḍramī, who was active in al-Ḍaḥī near al-Mahjam, replied that he was unable to leave because of his many dependents and close relatives and suggested that each one of them protect his region. Abū'l-Ghayth also decided to stay in the Yemen.[8]

Abū'l-Ghayth's rejection of Imam al-Mahdī's overture did not lead to a serious deterioration of the relations between Zaydīs and Sufis. Muḥammad b. al-Ḥasan al-Daylamī, a Zaydī scholar who came to the Yemen from the Caspian region, does not deal with the Sufis among the heretics and opponents of the Prophet's Family in his large *Kitāb qawāᶜid Āl Muḥammad* completed in 707/1307.[9] In his *Kitāb al-ṣirāṭ al-mustaqīm bi'l-dīn al-qawīm*, written a year later, he endorses Sufi ethics and ascetic practice, describing fear of God, *taqwā*, as the only condition for salvation. He names al-Ghazālī's *Iḥyāᵓ ᶜulūm al-Dīn* and 'other books of the ascetics' as works in which all errroneous opinions are rejected. Occasionally he refers to Imam al-Muᵓayyad's *Risālat siyāsat al-murīdīn*, to the Shii imams

---

7 al-Ḥabshī, op. cit. 53-4.

8 al-Sharjī, *Ṭabaqāt al-khawāṣṣ ahl al-ṣidq wa'l-ikhlāṣ* (Beirut 1406/1986) 280. Al-Ḥabshī seems to interpret the passage incorrectly in suggesting that Abū'l-Ghayth was at this time active in the highlands and proposed to move to Tihāma (op. cit. 55). Abū'l-Ghayth had been active in the highlands at an earlier stage (al-Sharjī, op. cit. 407), but when he wrote his letter to al-Ḥaḍramī he was certainly living in the Tihāma.

9 Ms. Ṣanᶜāᵓ, Great Mosque; see al-Sayyid al-Ḥusaynī, *Muᵓallafāt al-Zaydiyya* (Qumm 1413/1993) ii, 357.

Ja<sup>c</sup>far al-Ṣādiq and al-Qāsim b. Ibrāhīm, but most often he cites Sunni Sufis.[10] His *Kitāb al-taṣfiya ʿan al-mawāniʿ al-murdiya al-muhlika*, a work on religious ethics, was later read and quoted by Zaydīs inclining to Sufism.[11]

The Zaydī Imam al-Muʾayyad bi'llāh Yaḥyā b. Ḥamza, who reigned from 729-749/1328-1349, maintained good relations with the well-known Yemenite Sufi shaykh and historian ʿAfīf al-Dīn ʿAbd Allāh b. Asʿad al-Yāfiʿī (d. 768/1376-7) residing in Mekka. Al-Yāfiʿī notes in his large history *Mirʾāt al-janān wa-ʿibrat al-yaqẓān* that the imam appreciated a *qaṣīda* in which al-Yāfiʿī extolled the Sufis in general and his shaykh ʿAlī b. ʿAbd Allāh al-Ṭawāshī in particular, using metaphors (*istiʿārāt*) which were censured by some Sunni scholars. While on a raid against the Ismāʿīlīs of Ḥarāz, al-Muʾayyad asked a pilgrim on his way to Mecca to bring back from the latter city some of the writing (*kalām*) of al-Yāfiʿī, stating that he admired two of his *qaṣīda*s, one of them in praise of his shaykh. Al-Yāfiʿī expresses astonishment that the metaphors in his *qaṣīda* should be appreciated by one of the opponents (of Sunnism) who deny the stations (*maqāmāt*) of the mystics, while they were denounced by a Sunni.[12]

Imam Yaḥyā b. Ḥamza, a prolific author, wrote a large book on religious ethics and etiquette entitled *Taṣfiyat al-qulūb min daran al-awzār wa'l-dhunūb*. It may well have been patterned on al-Ghazālī's *Iḥyāʾ ʿulūm al-Dīn* as has repeatedly been suggested.[13] The work reflects Yaḥyā b. Ḥamza's lack of sectarian zeal and his openness to Sunni learning. Hardly anything is said about the religious rank of the *ahl al-bayt* as is common in Zaydī works. In the section about the death of the Prophet and the early caliphs, Abū Bakr, ʿUmar and ʿUthmān are treated virtually on a par with ʿAlī. Al-Muʾayyad Aḥmad b. al-Ḥusayn's *Siyāsat al-murīdīn* is not mentioned. While there are few citations of ʿAlī and his descendants, quotations from early Sufis, including Ibrāhīm b. Adham, al-Ḥārith al-Muḥāsibī, Abū

---

10 See Madelung, *Der Imam al-Qāsim* 220.

11 *Muʾallafāt* i, 290-1. The Zaydī Sufi Ibrāhīm al-Kaynaʿī (d. 793/1391) owned a copy of the book and quoted from it (Yaḥyā b. al-Mahdī, *Ṣilat al-ikhwān*, Ms. Ambrosiana D 222, fol. 26a).

12 al-Yāfiʿī, *Mirʾāt al-janān* (Hyderabad 1347-49/1919-21) iv, 315; al-Ḥabshī, op. cit. 63-4. Al-Muʾayyad is called by al-Yāfiʿī *imām al-Zaydiyya al-ʿallāma al-fāḍil Yaḥyā b. Ḥamza*.

13 al-Ḥabshī, op. cit. 65; Ismāʿīl b. Aḥmad al-Jirāfī, introduction to his edition of *Taṣfiyat al-qulūb* (Ṣanʿāʾ 1408/1988).

Yazīd al-Bisṭāmī and al-Shiblī, abound. The author points out that the Sufi shaykhs (*mashyakhat al-ṭarīq fī 'l-taṣawwuf*) had much to say about the reality of good ethics (*ḥaqīqat ḥusn al-khuluq*), though they said more to explain its norms and the way to achieve its fruits than about its nature and definition.[14]

Yaḥyā b. Ḥamza is adamant, however, that singing belongs to the evils of the tongue. The masters of the *ahl al-bayt* and the imams from among them are agreed that it is prohibited and reprehensible, that it is contrary to virtue and religion, and that its practice invalidates legal testimony and integrity. This was also the view of Sunni jurists such as Abū Ḥanīfa, al-Shāfiᶜī, Mālik, Sufyān al-Thawrī and others. The deviant opinion of Abū Ḥāmid al-Ghazālī that it is permitted and recommended deserves no consideration. Al-Ghazālī's evidence in support of his opinion was tenuous and based on statements of men without authority, which should be seen as an outrage and baseness in religion. Al-Ghazālī, Yaḥyā b. Ḥamza adds, surely could have dispensed with lending support to the permissibility and promotion of singing and have avoided discussing it in his religious books, not to mention arguing in favour of it.[15] Imam Yaḥyā evidently had strong feelings on the subject, for he also wrote a shorter book entitled *ᶜIqd al-laʾāliʾ fī'l-radd ᶜalā Abī Ḥāmid al-Ghazālī* in which he specifically refuted al-Ghazālī's chapter on *samāᶜ* in the *Iḥyāʾ ᶜulūm al-Dīn*.[16]

Sufism is not expressly mentioned in Imam Yaḥyā's condemnation of singing. In a chapter on the delusion (*ghurūr*) of various religious and social groups, however, the Sufis (*ahl al-taṣawwuf*) occupy a prominent position. Imam Yaḥyā describes the kinds (*ṣinf*) of delusion to which Sufis commonly fall victim. These range from their dress and speech, in which the 'would-be Sufis of our time (*mutaṣawwifat ahl zamāninā*) imitate the true Sufis such as al-Junayd, al-Shiblī, al-Bisṭāmī and others, to fraudulent claims of gnosis, antinomian libertinism, and false hopes of having reached the ultimate goal (*wuṣūl*)'.[17]

Imam Yaḥyā b. Ḥamza, it should be noted, also espoused the Muᶜtazilī theological doctrine of the school of Abū'l-Ḥusayn al-

---

14 *Taṣfiyat al-qulūb* 37.

15 *Taṣfiyat al-qulūb* 139. The passage is quoted by al-Manṣūr al-Qāsim b. Muḥammad in his *Ḥatf anf al-āfik* (ms. in a private collection in Ḍaḥyān) 63-4. Al-Manṣūr omits the mention of al-Ghazālī.

16 al-Ḥabshī, op. cit. 65; al-Ḥusaynī, *Muʾallafāt* ii, 272.

17 *Taṣfiyat al-qulūb* 498-501.

Baṣrī which, in contrast to the doctrine of the school of Abū Hāshim al-Jubbāʾī previously prevalent among the Zaydiyya, upheld the possibility of *karāmāt*, miracles of non-prophets including Sufi saints.[18] His teaching evidently furthered the emergence of an indigenous order of moderate Sufism in the Yemenite Zaydī community. Substantial information about this development is furnished by the sayyid Yaḥyā b. al-Mahdī b. Qāsim b. Muṭahhar al-Zaydī al-Ḥusaynī in his hagiographical account of the life of his shaykh and founder of a Sufi order, Ibrāhīm b. Aḥmad al-Kaynaᶜī (d. 793/1391), entitled *Ṣilat al-ikhwān fī ḥilyat barakat ahl al-zamān*. There is some evidence for an influence from the Caspian Zaydī community, where Sufi currents had been strong for a long time. Yaḥyā b. al-Mahdī mentions the sayyid Aḥmad b. Amīr [b. al-Nāṣir al-Ḥasanī] al-Jīlānī, who came to the Yemen from the country of the Jīl and Daylam intending to visit Imam al-Muʾayyad Yaḥyā b. Ḥamza. When he arrived al-Muʾayyad had already died, and he visited his successor, Imam al-Mahdī ᶜAlī b. Muḥammad (750-73/1359-71) in Ṣaᶜda and al-Mahdī's son and later successor, al-Nāṣir Ṣalāḥ al-Dīn Muḥammad b. ᶜAlī, who at that time was teaching Koran-reading in Maṣnaᶜat Banī Qays. This sayyid, according to Yaḥyā b. al-Mahdī, was the author of books on devotion and asceticism, among them one entitled *Ṣafwat al-ṣafwa fī zuhd al-ṣaḥāba*.[19]

When Yaḥyā b. al-Mahdī visited Sayyid Aḥmad b. Amīr al-Jīlānī in Mekka, he found the qadi[20] al-Ḥasan b. Salmān with him. This Yemenite from Wādī'l-Ḥār near Dhamār is described by Yaḥyā as the first person to practice the worship of the Sufis (*ahl al-ṭarīqa*) in the land of the Zaydiyya and the first to dress in their garb. At the same time he was an erudite scholar in religious law, *ḥadīth*, and Koranic exegesis. In particular he was an expert in the legal doctrine of the Caspian Zaydī imam al-Nāṣir li'l-Ḥaqq.[21] He may well have been introduced to this subject by the Jīlānī sayyid.[22] Al-Ḥasan b.

---

18 *Der Imam al-Qāsim* 222 and note 456

19 *Ṣilat al-ikhwān* 19b-20a. Aḥmad b. Amīr al-Jīlānī was later remembered among the Yemenite Zaydiyya as the one who brought the six-volume *Kitāb al-jāmiᶜ al-kāfī* of Abū ᶜAbd Allāh al-ᶜAlawī on early Kūfan Zaydī *fiqh* to the Yemen and presented it to Imam al-Mahdī ᶜAlī b. Muḥammad (see *Der Imam al-Qāsim* 88, note 236).

20 The title *qāḍī* was in Yemenite usage of the time often applied to non-ᶜAlid scholars, who were not necessarily judges.

21 Yaḥyā b. al-Mahdī, *Ṣilat al-ikhwān* 19a.

22 The Nāṣirī religious law was not practiced in the Yemen and presumably not normally taught. Yaḥyā b. al-Mahdī does not provide any information about al-Ḥasan b. Salmān's teachers. It is to be noted, however, that he must have been well-known as a Sufi ascetic

Salmān was an active supporter of Imam al-Mahdī urging the people to join his *jihād* against the opponents of the Zaydiyya and to pay their alms-tax to him.[23] The *hijra* which he founded in Wādī'l-Ḥār is still thriving under his name.[24]

Yaḥyā b. al-Mahdī refers to al-Ḥasan b. Salmān as the shaykh and model in piety of Ibrāhīm al-Kaynaᶜī, who later continued to visit him every year. More important, however, as al-Kaynaᶜī's teacher seems to have been ᶜAlī b. ᶜAbd Allāh b. Abī'l-Khayr [al-Ṣāyidī],[25] whom Yaḥyā also designates as his shaykh in asceticism and his model in words and deeds. Ibn Abī'l-Khayr was a prominent Zaydī scholar at the time, learned in religious law, legal methodology and theology, and author of books on many subjects, including refutations of the predestinarians (*mujbira*), Islamic sects, and Ismāᶜīlīs (*malāḥida*). He also wrote on the sciences of Sufi devotion, asceticism, and the stories (*ḥikāyāt*) of the Sufis, the praiseworthy as well as the reprehensible.[26] Probably late in his career, he personally became engaged in Sufi practice and devotion. In 773/1371-2 he was initiated into the practice of *dhikr* by Aḥmad b. Muḥammad al-Nassākh who in turn had been initiated by Yūsuf [b. ᶜAbd Allāh b. ᶜUmar al-Kurdī] al-Kūrānī (d. 768/1367), an Egyptian shaykh well-known for his special practice of *dhikr* which he propagated among his followers in many countries.[27] Al-Kūrānī traced his *silsila* back through Abū'l-Najīb al-Suhrawardī (d. 563/1168) to Jaᶜfar al-Ṣādiq and ᶜAlī b. Abī Ṭālib.[28]

In spite of his involvement with Sufism, Ibn Abī'l-Khayr upheld the critical attitude of the Zaydiyya to some aspects of Sufi belief and practice. Yaḥyā b. al-Mahdī quotes his treatise *al-Muqaddima wa'l-waẓā'if fī ṭarīq al-murīd wa'l-ṭā'if* in which, after describing

---

already before al-Jīlānī's arrival since Yaḥyā reports that the latter went to visit him when he arrived in the Yemen (*Ṣilat al-ikhwān* 20a).

23 *Ṣilat al-ikhwān* 19b, 34b. Al-Ḥasan b. Salmān is said to have reached an age of more than 130 years.

24 Hijrat Ḥasan Salmān; see al-Qāḍī Ismāᶜīl b. ᶜAlī al-Akwaᶜ, *al-Madkhal ilā hijar al-ᶜilm wa-maᶜāqilihī fī 'l-Yaman* (Beirut 1415/1995) 82.

25 Ṣāyid is a branch of Hamdān.

26 *Ṣilat al-ikhwān* 46a. On extant works by Ibn Abī'l-Khayr see *Mu'allafāt* iii, 227-8, where he is listed under three different names: ᶜAlī b. ᶜAbd Allāh Abī'l-Khayr, ᶜAlī b. ᶜAbd Allāh al-Ṣā'idī, and ᶜAlī b. ᶜAbd Allāh b. Abī'l-Khayr.

27 On Yūsuf al-Kūrānī see Ibn Ḥajar, *al-Durar al-kāmina* (Hyderabad 1350/1931-2) iv, 463. Aḥmad b. Muḥammad al-Najrī al-Nassākh was, according to Ibn Abī'l-Rijāl (*Maṭlaᶜ al-budūr*, ms., s.v.), a religious scholar from Khubbān (Khabbān?) with whom the Zaydī imam Ibn al-Murtaḍā read al-Zamakhsharī's Koran commentary *al-Kashshāf*.

28 *Ṣilat al-ikhwān* 48b-49a. On Abū'l-Najīb al-Suhrawardi see GAL i, 436, S i, 780.

the obstacles on the path to spiritual perfection, he specifically warns against the belief of some Sufis that contravention of the sharia is permissible once one has reached a high station, against false doctrines like anthropomorphism, determinism, and *irjāʾ*, against refusing *jihād* on behalf of the Prophet's Family and failure to respond to their summons, and against listening to music, dancing and ecstatic love (*wajd*).[29]

Ibrāhīm al-Kaynaᶜī received the *dhikr* and his Sufi frock (*khirqa*) from Ibn Abī'l-Khayr.[30] The Banū'l-Kaynaᶜī, his family, were local chiefs and owned castles one day's journey (*barīd*) west of Dhamār. Ibrāhīm was fully trained in Zaydī religious law and theology. He became closely associated with Imam al-Nāṣir Ṣalāḥ al-Dīn Muḥammad b. ᶜAlī (ruled 773-793/1371-1391) and participated in some of his campaigns against the Ṭayyibī Ismāᶜīlīs,[31] who at this time were closely allied with the Sunni Rasūlids ruling in Taᶜizz and were the major rivals of the Zaydīs in the highlands. The imam backed him and used to visit him annually in Dhamār, seeking the blessing of his prayer. During al-Kaynaᶜī's stay in Ṣanᶜāʾ, al-Nāṣir would visit him monthly or every second month for a solitary session with him. Al-Kaynaᶜī received material help for his Sufi brethren from the imam, who, at his request, gave a house confiscated from the Ismāᶜīlīs in Ṣanᶜāʾ to one of them.[32] According to Yaḥyā b. al-Mahdī, al-Kaynaᶜī stated that he had met no one better informed about the practices and disciplines of the mystics than Imam al-Nāṣir. He had seen in the imam's library rare books on the sciences of the ascetics and stories about the saints which he had not seen anywhere else, among them al-Ghazālī's *Kīmiyāʾ al-saᶜāda* and parts of his *Iḥyāʾ ᶜulūm al-dīn*.[33]

Al-Kaynaᶜī founded Sufi communities all over northern Yemen which he visited regularly, in Dhamār, Maᶜbar, Maṣnaᶜat Banī Qays, Khubbān (?), Ṣanᶜāʾ, Thulā, Ḥūth, Waᶜra, Qāra, Ẓafār, and Ṣaᶜda.[34] He established *hijras* for retreat and devotion, among them Hijrat Maᶜbar in Jahrān, Hijrat ᶜArām and Hijrat al-Washal in Wādī Zubayd and the region of Dhamār. One of his followers, al-Ḥasan b.

---

29 *Ṣilat al-ikhwān* 47b.

30 *Ṣilat al-ikhwān* 49a. Yaḥyā b. al-Mahdī in turn obtained his initiation and *khirqa* from al-Kaynaᶜī.

31 *Ṣilat al-ikhwān* 36b.

32 *Ṣilat al-ikhwān* 29a-b.

33 *Ṣilat al-ikhwān* 36b-37a; al-Ḥabshī, op. cit. 62-3.

34 *Ṣilat al-ikhwān* 19a, 66b.

Mūsā al-Awṭānī, founded Hijrat al-Awṭān in Bilād Madhḥij.[35] The qadi ᶜAbd Allāh b. Ḥasan al-Dawwārī (d. 800/1397-8) invited him to come to Ṣaᶜda in order to spread his blessings there. Many of the local inhabitants responded to his call and began to practice asceticism and *dhikr* and to read books of devotion in the mosque of Imam al-Manṣūr in the desert of Ṣaᶜda (*barriyyat Ṣaᶜda*). Their leader in worship was another Caspian immigrant to the Yemen, Dāwūd b. Muḥammad al-Jīlānī, known for his great miracles and as the author of books on Sufi devotional sciences.[36]

Al-Kaynaᶜī evidently represented a Zaydī form of ascetic Sufism which found favour with Imam al-Nāṣir Ṣalāḥ al-Dīn because it supported the Zaydī imamate and repudiated the Sufi practices generally condemned by the imams. In contrast, the uneasy truce which had prevailed between the Zaydīs and the Sunni Sufis was shattered towards the end of al-Nāṣir's reign due to a particular incident. Aḥmad b. Zayd al-Shāwirī, a Shāfiᶜī scholar of the law and Sufi shaykh active in the region of Ḥajja,[37] at that time just outside Zaydī territory, used to denounce the Zaydī creed and doctrine, and wrote a short book in which he raised the call to support Sunnism and warned against innovation.[38] In 793/1391 Imam al-Nāṣir raided his area with a strong army. The house of the shaykh was attacked, and he, his son Abū Bakr, and several of his companions were killed, although they had not put up any armed resistance. As a result of the conquest, the people of the region converted from Shāfiᶜī Sunnism to Hādawī (Zaydī) Shiism.[39] The violent death of the respected shaykh provoked a strong Sunni reaction. The prominent Shāfiᶜi scholar and poet Ismāᶜīl b. Abī Bakr al-Muqrī, who belonged to al-Shāwirī's people, composed a lengthy elegy on his death in which he sharply condemned the imam for his transgression.[40] Ismāᶜīl al-Muqrī, it should be noted, later became a vociferous Sunni critic of Sufism, in particular of the school of Ibn al-ᶜArabī.[41] At this time he was evi-

---

35 al-Akwaᶜ, *al-Madkhal* 82.

36 *Ṣilat al-ikhwān* 66b-67a. A *Kitāb al-Maqāṣid al-ukhrawiyya al-muntazaᶜ min kitāb al-anwār al-muḍiyya* by him is extant in part (*Muʾallafāt* iii, 44).

37 The region of Ḥajja is named in the account of al-Sharjī. Yaḥyā b. al-Ḥusayn b. al-Mu'ayyad speaks of the Banū Shāwir in Bilād Lāᶜa and Bilād Qaṭāba [*Anbāʾ al-zaman*, quoted in Muḥammad b. Muḥammad Zabāra, *Aʾimmat al-Yaman* (Taᶜizz 1372/1952) i, 277].

38 al-Sharjī, op. cit. 78. According to al-Ḥabshī, op. cit. 55, note 3, the book was refuted by Muḥammad b. Yūsuf al-Faḍlī in his *al-Inṣāf fī 'l-radd ᶜalā ahl al-zaygh wa'l-iᶜtiṣāf*.

39 Zabāra, *Aʾimmat al-Yaman* i, 277.

40 al-Sharjī, op. cit. 78; al-Ḥabshī, op. cit. 55-6.

41 al-Ḥabshi, op. cit. 135-42; Alexander Knysh, 'Ibn ᶜArabī in the Yemen', *Journal of*

dently still attracted to the Sufis.

Al-Nāṣir Ṣalāḥ al-Dīn's first successor, overthrown and imprisoned after only one year, was Imam al-Mahdī Aḥmad b. Yaḥyā al-Murtaḍā (d. 840/1437), author of the massive Zaydī theological and legal encyclopaedia *al-Baḥr al-zakhkhār*. In the eleventh book of the encyclopaedia, entitled *Takmilat al-aḥkām wa'l-taṣfiya ʿan bawāṭin al-āthām*, Ibn al-Murtaḍā dealt with religious ethics in a Sufi fashion. He provided a large commentary to it under the title *Thamarāt al-akmām*. The book, according to al-Ḥabshī, was widely studied among Yemenite Sufis. As late as the eleventh/seventeenth century commentaries and supplements to it were written by the Zaydī scholar Ṣalāḥ b. ʿAbd al-Khāliq al-Jaḥḥāf (d. 1053/1643),[42] as well as al-Ḥasan b. Aḥmad al-Jalāl (d. 1084/1673)[43] and others. Ibn al-Murtaḍā furthermore composed some smaller treatises on Sufi topics such as his *Ḥayāt al-qulūb fī iḥyāʾ ʿibādat ʿallām al-ghuyūb* and *al-Zahra al-zāhira bi-taḥqīr al-dunyā wa-taʿẓīm al-ākhira*.[44] Yet he also wrote a book which refutes those scholars who allowed amusements and the use of musical instruments, entitled *Kitāb al-qamar al-nawwār fī 'l-radd ʿalā 'l-murakhkhiṣīn fī 'l-malāhī wa'l-mizmār*. Here he quotes at length the *ḥadīth*s condemning musical instruments, singing, the purchase of singing slave girls, etc., which Imam al-Manṣūr ʿAbd Allāh b. Ḥamza (d. 614/1217) had collected in his *Kitāb al-shāfī*.[45] In a *Qaṣīda qāfiyya* Ibn al-Murtaḍā censured those who 'proscribed the books of right guidance and allowed the tambourine and the flute (*mizmār*) in the markets', whose enemies were the scholars (*ʿulamāʾ*) and whose friend was the dancing and clapping would-be Sufi (*al-mutaṣawwif al-raqqāṣ al-ṣaffāq*).[46]

---

*the Muhyiddin Ibn ʿArabī Society* ix (1992) 50-6; Ṭāhā Aḥmad Zayd, *Ismāʿīl al-Muqrī: ḥayātuhū wa-shiʿruhū* (Beirut 1996).

42 *Nihāyat al-afhām li-maʿānī Takmilat al-aḥkām*; see *Muʾallafāt* iii, 132.

43 *Talqīḥ al-afhām bi-ṣaḥīḥ al-kalām ʿalā Takmilat al-aḥkām*; see *Muʾallafāt* i, 325.

44 al-Ḥabshī, op. cit. 65-6.

45 This section of Ibn al-Murtaḍā's *al-Qamar al-nawwār* is quoted by al-Manṣūr al-Qāsim b. Muḥammad in his *Ḥatf anf al-āfik* 34-7. In the edition of al-Manṣūr ʿAbd Allāh b. Ḥamza's *Kitāb al-shāfī* (Ṣanʿāʾ 1406/1986) the text is found in vol. i, 221-3. ʿAbd Allāh b. Ḥamza reports these *ḥadīths* in the context of his censure of the behaviour of the ʿAbbāsid caliphs, not as anti-Sufi polemics. By contrast, the Amīr al-Nāṣir li-Dīn Allāh al-Ḥusayn b. Muḥammad b. Aḥmad b. Yaḥyā (d. 662/1261) in his *Kitāb al-yanābīʿ al-ṣaḥīḥa*, after citing the traditions forbidding play and amusements, adds a warning for the seeker of right guidance not to be deceived by the Ṣūfiyya and the empty rhetoric of the Ḥashwiyya (*al-Yanābīʿ al-ṣaḥīḥa*, facsimile edition by Aḥmad Muḥammad Ḥajar, Ṣanʿāʾ n.d., 352). The passage is quoted by al-Manṣūr al-Qāsim b. Muḥammad in his *Ḥatf anf al-āfik* 42-3.

46 Quoted by al-Manṣūr al-Qāsim b. Muḥammad, *Ḥatf anf al-āfik* 40-1.

Another book on religious ethics entitled *Kanz al-rashād wa-zād al-maᶜād* was written by Imam al-Hādī ᶜIzz al-Dīn b. al-Ḥasan al-Yaḥyawī (ruled 879-900/1474-1495).[47] ᶜIzz al-Dīn deals with the reprehensible character traits which must be avoided and the sound ones which the worshipper should strive to acquire. In the introduction he mentions his having read books encouraging asceticism (*kutub zuhdiyya*) and treatises of 'the people of the approved path (*ahl al-ṭarīq al-marḍiyya*)'.[48] At the end, however, he stresses that he never pursued the path and apologizes to those readers who believe that only those who have reached a high rank travelling the path themselves ought to write about the subject.[49] In the course of his exposition he frequently quotes from Sunni *ḥadīth*-collections. He praises al-Ghazālī for his powerful discourse in condemning man's attachment to worldly chattels,[50] but rarely mentions any other Sufi.[51]

ᶜIzz al-Dīn's predecessor, Imam al-Mutawakkil al-Muṭahhar b. Muḥammad b. Sulaymān al-Ḥamzī (ruled 840-879/1436-1474), was evidently more hostile to Sufism. Al-Manṣūr al-Qāsim b. Muḥammad in his *Ḥatf anf al-āfik* quotes some lines of poetry in which this imam derides the doctrines of a people whose religion consists of play and who dance and clap in the darkness of night. They end up in the intoxication of ecstasy deprived of their minds. Never has any *sunna* supported this practice, nor does the Book of God justify it.[52]

Systematic persecution of Sufis was initiated by Imam al-Mutawakkil Sharaf al-Dīn Yaḥyā b. Shams al-Dīn, who ruled from 912 to 965/1506-1558. In his *Kitāb al-athmār*, a popular abridgement of Ibn al-Murtaḍā's *Kitāb al-azhār*, Sharaf al-Dīn accused the Sufis of generally furthering hostility to the ᶜAlids (*naṣb*). Some of them maintained that the Family of Muḥammad (*āl Muḥammad*) consisted of all followers (*atbāᶜ*) of the Prophet.[53] Al-Manṣūr quotes

---

47 The book was completed in 897/1492. *Kanz al-rashād* (Ṣanᶜāʾ 1392/1972) 138.

48 *Kanz* 21.

49 *Kanz* 137-8.

50 *Kanz* 71.

51 al-Ḥabshī, op. cit. 66. Al-Ḥabshī erroneously states that Imam ᶜIzz al-Dīn in his introduction warns against the ecstatic sciences (*ᶜulūm shaṭḥiyya*) of the Sufis and quotes a *qaṣīda* criticizing them. This introduction is, however, by the modern editor of the text, ᶜAbd al-Wāsiᶜ b. Yaḥyā al-Wāsiᶜī, not by the imam.

52 al-Manṣūr, *Ḥatf anf al-āfik* 46.

53 See the quotation in al-Ḥabshī, op. cit. 57.

Imam Sharaf al-Dīn's response to someone asking him about the Ṣūfiyya:

'This sect (*firqa*) which in our time and before it has been called the Ṣūfiyya has no foundation in religion on which they can rely and no proof (*burhān*) in reason or in the law of religion (*sharᶜ*) to which they can refer. Rather, their affairs are based upon false fancies, empty rhetoric, deceptive illusions, and claims remote from truth and veracity. Whoever enters into these fancies to any extent departs from Islam and embraces unbelief (*kufr*) without any doubt. He becomes a corporealist and a denier of divine attributes in the recognition of the Omniscient King. This is well-known to every scholar who peruses their books and to every wise learned man who takes cognizance of their secrets. It is therefore incumbent upon every Muslim not to affiliate himself with them, nor to wear any of their emblems, nor to imitate (*yatashabbah*) any one of them; for it has come down in tradition that whoever imitates a people is counted as one of them. The rules for charging someone with unbelief and grave immorality (*aḥkām al-takfīr wa'l-tafsīq*) are based on this'.[54]

Imam Sharaf al-Dīn thus clearly branded the practice of Sufism as potentially constituting infidelity. According to Ibn Abī'l-Rijāl, he forbade adherence to Sufism and entering upon their path from the beginning of his reign. As a result, all public display of Sufi ceremonial practices disappeared, and Sufi dancing, clapping, and singing became concealed in houses.[55] In 939/1532 he summoned several Sufis, among them the qadi Muḥammad b. ᶜAṭf Allāh al-ᶜAbsī,[56] to a debate concerning their religious beliefs. After the debate Sharaf al-Dīn threatened to treat qadi Muḥammad as an apostate, to force him to relinquish his spouses, and, after a period of grace, to execute him if the latter did not renounce his Sufism. Qadi Muḥammad recanted after having been beaten and tortured and wrote a declaration in which he explained his renunciation of Sufism. The others also repented.[57] A sayyid ᶜAbd Allāh b. al-Qāsim was likewise forced by Imam Sharaf al-Dīn to sever his ties with Sufism. The sayyid had been enticed to the heresy by the shaykh ᶜAlī al-Jabartī who had visited al-Ẓahrayn in the region of Ḥajja, and had accompanied him on his travels. When his Sufi proclivities be-

---

54 al-Manṣūr, *Ḥatf* 41-2. Al-Manṣūr adds that the text of the response is much longer and invites anyone interested to read it in the original.

55 Ibn Abī'l-Rijāl, quoted by al-Ḥabshī, op. cit. 58. Al-Ḥabshī is evidently mistaken in suggesting (57) that Sharaf al-Dīn's hostility to Sufism was the result of the Sufi support of the Ottoman Turks and their forsaking him in his struggle against the invaders. From the account of Ibn Abī'l-Rijāl and other sources it is clear that Sharaf al-Dīn began to persecute the Sufis long before the Ottoman invasion in 945/1538.

56 Thus the name given by al-Ḥabshī, op. cit. 57. In Zabāra, *Aʾimmat al-Yaman* i, 408, the name appears as Muḥammad b. ᶜAbd Allāh al-ᶜAnsī.

57 al-Ḥabshī, op. cit. 57-8; *Aʾimmat al-Yaman* i, 408.

came apparent, the imam imprisoned him in the fortress of al-ᶜArūs and reprimanded him. He was only released after writing a declaration in which he dissociated himself from the teaching of the Sufis.[58]

Less fortunate was another Sufi shaykh, Ḥasan b. ᶜAlī al-Jadr, who espoused the Sufism of the practitioners of ecstatic utterances (*shaṭṭāḥūn*) and attracted many followers. The imam disdained to debate with him at the time of his debate with other Sufis since he considered him deficient in religious learning. When the forces of the imam seized Ṣaᶜda in 940/1533, a letter of Ḥasan al-Jadr was found in which he encouraged the Sufis there to remain faithful to their convictions, assuring them that the words and rebukes of the imam did not frighten him. The imam wanted to kill him, but the imam's son, Shams al-Dīn, persuaded him to have him imprisoned. Ḥasan al-Jadr then swore that he had renounced Sufism both in secret and in public and that his letter had been written before the repentance of Qāḍī Muḥammad al-ᶜAbsī. The imam accepted his excuses, and had him released. Some time later, however, it became apparent that Ḥasan al-Jadr still secretly adhered to his Sufi doctrines. He was executed in Ṣanᶜāʾ in Ṣafar 942/Aug. 1535 at the order of the imam.[59]

Anti-Sufi polemics reached their climax with Imam al-Manṣūr al-Qāsim b. Muḥammad (ruled 1006-1029/1598-1620), the founder of the Qāsimī imamate. Al-Manṣūr's reign was dominated by his relentless struggle against the Ottoman occupation of the Yemen. The Yemenite Sufis had initially welcomed the Ottoman invasion, and they were in turn courted by the Turkish governors.[60] Al-Manṣūr's fierce attack on Sufism was in part a reaction to this alliance. Early during his reign al-Manṣūr composed a sixty-line poem entitled *al-Kāmil al-mutadārik fi bayān madhhab al-ṣūfī al-hālik* together with brief explanatory notes. The poem opens with a complaint about the rejection (*rafḍ*) of Muḥammad's Family by the majority of the Muslim community ever since the death of the Prophet, which has resulted in its split into numerous sects; he then exposes the heresies of the Sufis and in particular accuses them of gross sexual debauchery.[61] He is said to have sent the poem to his son,

---

58 al-Ḥabshī, op. cit. 58.

59 al-Ḥabshī, op. cit. 58-9; Ibn al-Mu'ayyad, *Ghāyat al-amānī* 680-1.

60 al-Ḥabshī, op. cit. 52-3.

61 Ms. Brit. Mus. Or. 3851, 101b-105. Al-Manṣūr mentions three Sufi sanctuaries, one of them in the region of Dhamār in which women allegedly acted as prostitutes, and claims that the Yemenite Sufis regularly engaged in a communal sexual orgy lasting three nights

probably Muḥammad, who was then engaged in fighting the Turks. Al-Manṣūr's biographer, al-Ḥasan b. Muḥammad al-Jurmūzī quotes another anti-Sufi *Risāla* followed by a *Qaṣīda* which the imam addressed to all the Muslims it could reach. In the *risāla*, as in *al-Kāmil al-mutadārik*, al-Manṣūr describes the Sufis as a sect of the Bāṭiniyya whose religion was founded on the remnants of the Zoroastrians (*mujūs*) when they recognized they could not fight Islam openly. He accuses them of equating their lord with beautiful women and beardless youths while denying the real Lord of the world, and of adopting the singing of love poetry, music, and pleasant diversions as their religion. When they feared for their lives, they would mix exclamations of *lā ilāha illā 'llāh* into these diversions and celebrate the Prophet's birthday (*mawlid al-nabī*) in order to deceive the ignorant. It was the duty of all Muslims to declare licit the shedding of their blood and the seizure of their property because they were infidels and polytheists. Indeed their polytheism was greater than that of the polytheists whom the Prophet had fought in holy war because those had affirmed the existence of God while associating idols as partners with him, whereas these consider only beautiful women and beardless youths as their gods and do not recognize any other lord. In the *Qaṣīda* al-Manṣūr repeats these accusations and calls Muslims to allegiance to the Family of the Prophet.[62]

The Turks evidently took note of this. Sinān Pasha, then commander of the Ottoman forces in the Yemen and later governor, ordered the sayyid Muḥammad b. ᶜAbd Allāh (d. 1008/1599-1600)[63], a grandson of Imam Sharaf al-Dīn known as a poet and man of letters (*adīb*), to compose a refutation of the *al-Kāmil al-mutadārik*. Earlier in 994/1586, Sinān's master, the Ottoman governor Ḥasan Pasha, had rounded up the most prominent descendants of Imam Sharaf al-Dīn and deported them to Istanbul, Sayyid Muḥammad was not among them, but he was evidently frightened into submission to Ottoman domination.[64] He complied with the order by composing a poem in which, besides defending moderate Sufism and the practice of music, he sang the glory of the Ottoman Sultan Mehmet III and

---

during the month of Rabīᶜ al-awwal. Two Sufi works which al-Manṣūr quotes to illustrate objectionable Sufi doctrine are *al-Lumᶜa al-nūriyya* (of Abū'l-ᶜAbbās Aḥmad b. ᶜAlī al-Būnī, d. 622/1225, GAL i, 497) and *Rayḥān al-qulūb fī 'l-tawassul ilā 'l-maḥbūb* (of Yūsuf b. ᶜAbd Allāh al-Kūrānī, GAL, ii 205, the shaykh through whom Ibrāhīm al-Kaynaᶜī traced his *silsila*)

62 al-Jurmūzī, *al-Nubdha al-mushīra* [facsimile edition (Ṣanᶜāʾ ca. 1981?)] 31-2.

63 *Ghāyat al-amānī* 782.

64 In his response to Sayyid Muḥammad's *qaṣīda*, al-Manṣūr suggested that Sayyid Muḥammad had been compelled by Sinān to write it. *Ḥatf* 2-3.

praised Sinān Pasha as well.

Some time after the death of both Sayyid Muḥammad and Mehmet III, but while Sinān Pasha still held the governorship, al-Manṣūr responded with another poem and a commentary on it entitled *Kitāb Ḥatf anf al-āfik fī jawābihi ʿalā 'l-Kāmil al-mutadārik*.[65] From the outset, he again pursued the line of accusation that Sufism was derived from Zoroastrianism and Mazdakism, addressing his opponent as:

'O you who have departed from the religion of the Family of Muḥammad
by entering into the Khurramī religion of the Magians'.
(*yā khārijan ʿan dīni āli Muḥammadin bi-dukhūlihim fī dīni 'l-mujūsi 'l-khurmadī*).

In his commentary he explains that the root of the Bāṭiniyya was the religion of the Mujūs and that Khurramdīn, a Persian word, had become a name for them. This was the old accusation against the Ismāʿīliyya that their religion was a Mazdakite conspiracy to undermine Islam — which was now being applied to the Sufis.

By way of justifying his accusation, al-Manṣūr quotes the *Kitāb al-irshād* of ʿAbd Allāh b. Zayd al-ʿAnsī, a prominent Zaydī scholar writing in 632/1234, who had described the Bāṭiniyya, meaning the Ismāʿīliyya, as the most dangerous heresy in Islam founded by descendants of the Mujūs and remnants of the Khurramiyya with the aim of destroying Islam. Some of the Bāṭiniyya had infiltrated the Imāmiyya and the Ṣūfiyya, and had lured them away from Islam. Al-Manṣūr approves of this interpretation and comments that the Ismāʿīliyya, in contrast to the Sufis, were universally condemned by Muslims as infidels, although both groups were equally Bāṭinī. The reason was that the Ismāʿīlīs cursed the Companions of the Prophet, and many religious schools (meaning the Sunnis) were more inclined to get angry at insults to their ancestors than at insults to God. Thus without adverse reaction they would listen to these Sufis proclaiming their doctrine of incarnation and their denial of the prohibitions of God and the Prophet.[66]

Later in his commentary al-Manṣūr quotes at length the fatwas of the Caspian Zaydī imams and scholars against the Bāṭiniyya in which they authorized the execution of Ismāʿīlīs as apostates without allowing the option of repentance.[67] These fatwas reflected the fierce

---

65 al-Manṣūr's response is thus to be dated between Mehmet III's death in 1012/1603 and the end of Sinān's governorship in 1016/1607.

66 *Ḥatf* 43-4.

67 *Ḥatf* 69-74. The text is quoted from al-Manṣūr ʿAbd Allāh b. Ḥamza's *al-Risāla al-ʿĀlima bi'l-adilla al-ḥākima*, published in Madelung, *Arabic Texts concerning the History of*

and bloody conflict between Zaydīs and Ismāʿīlīs in Daylamān and Gīlān and were certainly not meant by their authors to be applied to the Sufis with whom they had no serious quarrel. Al-Manṣūr's adroit transfer of them to the Sufis placed the latter in the highly dangerous position of heretics and apostates. Although there is no evidence that these fatwas were actually applied to Sufis in the Yemen, the Sufis certainly felt they were under extreme pressure to conceal their beliefs.

Al-Manṣūr brushes aside the somewhat feeble defense of Sayyid Muḥammad that not all Sufis upheld dancing, incarnation (*ḥulūl*), and union (*ittiḥād*) of the mystic with God, as al-Manṣūr had indiscriminately accused them of doing. In fact moderate Sufis, Sayyid Muḥammad had argued, charged those who followed these doctrines with unbelief. Al-Manṣūr counters that this was the usual manoeuvre of the Bāṭiniyya: whenever they were reproached for their doctrines, they ascribed them to others. Yet one of the learned had already replied to Sayyid Muḥammad's *Qaṣīda* pointing out that he had read the *Tāʾiyya* of Ibn al-Fāriḍ, the *Dīwān* of Ibn al-Ḥakkāk, and the writings of Ibn al-ʿArabī only to find they contained the most shocking unbelief. Elsewhere al-Manṣūr singles out for condemnation the *Fuṣūṣ* of Ibn al-ʿArabī, whom he describes as the chief of the incarnationist Sufis (*kabīr al-ṣūfiyya al-ḥulūliyya*). In this work Ibn al-ʿArabī praises idols, justifies all the accursed men who have pretended to divinity such as Pharaoh, and virtually allows all forbidden acts.[68]

In refuting the arguments of his opponent, al-Manṣūr relies on a wide range of citations from Zaydī imams and scholars, as well as on non-Zaydī authors. Thus he quotes at length from anti-Sufi writings of two Zaydī authors active in the time of Imam al-Mutawakkil Sharaf al-Dīn, a response about Sufism by Muḥammad b. Aḥmad b. Yaḥyā b. al-Muẓaffar (d. 925/1519)[69] and a treatise by the qadi Muḥammad b. Yaḥyā Bahrān (d. 957/1550), probably *al-Kashf wa'l-bayān fī 'l-radd ʿalā 'l-mubtadiʿa min mutaṣawwifat al-zamān.*[70] He quotes the anti-Sufi remarks of the Muʿtazilī Koranic exegete al-Zamakhsharī from the latter's comments on Koran 3/31 and 5/54 and

---

*the Zaydī Imams* 163-70.

68 *Ḥatf* 7.

69 For other works by him see *Muʾallafāt* iii, 240, s.v. Muḥammad b. Aḥmad al-Ḥamdī.

70 *Muʾallafāt* ii, 385. An equally anti-Sufi *dhayl* to Muḥammad b. Yaḥyā Bahrān's treatise was written by Yaḥyā b. Muḥammad b. Ḥumayd al-Miqrāʾī (d. 990/1582). It is partly extant in Ms. Ambrosiana D 222, 102a-110.

the polemics against alleged Sufi miracles by the sayyid ᶜAbd al-Ṣamad b. ᶜAbd Allāh al-ᶜAlawī al-Dāmaghānī (tenth/sixteenth century), author of a critical assessment of the doctrines of the various *madhāhib* in Islam.[71] There are long excerpts from an anti-Sufi *Qaṣīda* of the previously mentioned Shāfiᶜī scholar Ismāᶜīl al-Muqrī,[72] followed by excerpts from the equally anti-Sufi response to it by the Zaydī sayyid Jamāl al-Dīn al-Hādī b. Ibrāhīm b. al-Murtaḍā (al-Wazīr; d. 822/1419).[73]

At the end of his treatise al-Manṣūr directs his attack against the Turks and the Ottoman sultan in response to Sayyid Muḥammad's eulogy of them. The Turks are the people whose 'faces were like shields covered with skins (*majānn muṭraqa*)', about whose advent the Prophet had warned the Muslims in well-known apocalyptic *ḥadīths*. Pretense to the sultanate (*tasalluṭ*) is not a sign of salvation (*saᶜāda*) as Sayyid Muḥammad described it, but rather a sign of damnation (*shaqāwa*). The sultan's possession of the House of God in Mekka was no valid argument for his being the legitimate protector of the Holy Cities. The polytheists and idol worshippers had been able to force the Prophet to emigrate from Mekka, and to prevent him from visiting the Sanctuary. Similarly, the innovations and Sufi practices which the sultan had introduced there were a sign of his damnation rather than his salvation. God had already responded to Sayyid Muḥammad's prayer on behalf of the sultan by causing both Sayyid Muḥammad and Mehmet III to perish. Al-Manṣūr concludes his poem by calling upon God to destroy Sinān and to defeat the Turks, and by invoking blessings on the Prophet, his Family and Companions, and forgiveness for himself and the faithful.

Al-Manṣūr al-Qāsim b. Muḥammad's harshly anti-Sufi position set the pattern for the later imams of the Qāsimī dynasty. His son Imam al-Mutawakkil Ismāᶜīl b. al-Qāsim in 1073 or 1074/1662-3 gave the order for Ibn al-ᶜArabī's *Fuṣūṣ al-ḥikam* to be burned because of the 'pure unbelief' contained in it.[74] Not much later Ṣāliḥ b. Mahdī al-Maqbalī (d. 1108/1696-7) in his *al-ᶜAlam al-shāmikh* observed with

---

71 *Ḥatf* 46-52. The work of al-Dāmaghānī quoted by al-Manṣūr is presumably *al-Jawhara al-khāliṣa ᶜan al-shawā'ib fī 'l-ᶜaqā'id al-manqūma ᶜalā jamīᶜ al-madhāhib*, *Mu'allafāt* i, 387; GAL, S ii, 966.

72 *Ḥatf* 52-5. A different anti-Sufi *Qaṣīda* by Ismāᶜīl al-Muqrī is quoted by Ṣāliḥ b. Mahdī al-Maqbalī, *al-ᶜAlam al-shāmikh fī īthār al-ḥaqq ᶜalā 'l-ābā' wa'l-mashāyikh* (Cairo 1328/1910) 504-8.

73 On the author see al-Sakhāwī, *al-Ḍaw' al-lāmiᶜ* (Cairo 1353-55/1934-36) x, 206.

74 al-Ḥabshī, op. cit. 60, quoting Ibn al-Mu'ayyad's *Bahjat al-zaman*.

satisfaction that 'God has granted us in the Yemen the extinction of this stuff (Sufism) in the mountains through the action of the imam reigning there. One of the best things he has done there is to prevent swinging and dancing as an amusement, for their (the imams') doctrine entails the proscription of singing'.[75] Persecution of Sufi orders by the imams continued down to the twentieth century. After the departure of the Ottoman Turks from the coastal regions of the Yemen in 1918, Imam Yaḥyā Ḥamīd al-Dīn (1322-1367/1904-1948) took repressive measure against the Fāsiyya Shādhiliyya brotherhood there, detaining the son of its shaykh as a hostage. Under Yaḥyā's son and successor al-Nāṣir Aḥmad (1367-1382/1948-1962), the shaykh of the brotherhood Muḥammad b. Ḥisān was himself imprisoned and several of his followers were accused of anti-state activities and beheaded. Muḥammad b. Ḥisān died in prison.[76] Al-Ḥabshī notes that al-Nāṣir Aḥmad ordered the destruction of the tomb of the Sufi shaykh Aḥmad b. ᶜAlwān in Yafrus and of other tombs of Sufis in al-Ḥudayda and Taᶜizz.[77] These actions, however, may have been triggered more by Wahhābī influence than by traditional Zaydī doctrine.

Briefly mentioned may be here the pro-Sunni school within the Zaydiyya which, founded by the sayyid Muḥammad b. Ibrāhīm al-Wazīr (d. 840/1436), became progressively more influential over time and with Muḥammad b. ᶜAlī al-Shawkānī (d. 1250/1834), chief judge under several imams, came to dominate the religious establishment of the imamate. The school was primarily influenced by Sunni traditionalism, Ḥanbalism and Ibn Taymiyya. Thus for the most part it shared the negative outlook on Sufism of the Shii Zaydīs. In his *al-ᶜAwāṣim wa'l-qawāṣim fi 'l-dhabb ᶜan sunnat Abī'l-Qāsim*, Ibn al-Wazīr defended other Sunni school doctrines which the Zaydiyya rejected but not Sufism.[78] The next major representa-

---

75 *Al-ᶜAlam al-shāmikh* 481.

76 See F. De Jong, 'Les confréries mystiques musulmanes au Machreq arabe', in A. Popovic et G. Veinstein (eds.), *Les ordres mystiques dans l'islam: Cheminements et situation actuelle* (Paris 1989) 232.

77 al-Ḥabshī, op. cit. 60.

78 In the context of his anti-Muᶜtazilī polemics, Ibn al-Wazīr quotes poetry of the Ṣūfiyya *arbāb al-dhawq wa'l-aḥwāl al-rafīᶜa* and refers to the spiritual poems *(raqāʾiq)* of Ibn al-Fāriḍ with evident admiration [*al-ᶜAwāṣim wa'l-qawāṣim*, ed. Shuᶜayb al-Arnāʾūṭ (Amman and Beirut 1405-12/1985-92) vi, 127-9]. While criticizing as baseless Ibn al-ᶜArabī's arguments in his *Fuṣūṣ* in favour of *ittiḥād* (vii, 107), he praises Shihāb al-dīn ᶜUmar al-Suhrawardī, calling him *al-shaykh al-ṣāliḥ al-ᶜārif al-ṣūfī*, because of his repudiation of the claims of extremist Sufis that they were mere tools of God's action in their violations of the

tive of the school, Ṣāliḥ al-Maqbalī, was, as noted, hostile to Sufism and in his *al-ʿAlam al-shāmikh* quoted many pages of Sunni anti-Sufi polemics, especially against Ibn al-ʿArabī and his school.[79] Muḥammad b. Ismāʿīl al-Amīr (d. 1182/1768-9), a poet and a prolific writer on religious subjects, produced a refutation of the doctrine of the unity of being (*waḥdat al-wujūd*) entitled *Nuṣrat al-maʿbūd fī 'l-radd ʿalā ahl waḥdat al-wujūd*, and denounced this doctrine in others of his writings as well.[80] A short polemical treatise *Taṭhīr al-iʿtiqād ʿan adrān al-ilḥād*, in which he denounces the veneration of tombs and the false claims to gnostic knowledge by Sufis who disregard the law of the Koran and Sunna has recently been published.[81] Al-Shawkānī, too, shared the general traditionalist aversion to Sufism, although he disapproved of some Wahhābī excesses in criticizing Sufi visitation of saints' tombs. In his youth he wrote a treatise *al-Ṣawārim al-ḥidād al-qāṭiʿa li-ʿalāʾiq arbāb al-ittiḥād* in which he condemned the proponents of *waḥdat al-wujūd*, quoting extensively from Ṣāliḥ al-Maqbalī's *al-ʿAlam al-shāmikh*.[82] Before his death, however, he retracted his criticism and stated that he now abstained from judging the religious status of the followers of Ibn al-ʿArabī.[83]

---

religious law (vii, 140).

79 *Al-ʿAlam al-shāmikh* 490-510.

80 al-Ḥabshī, op. cit. 103. According to al-Ḥabshī, the *Nuṣrat al-maʿbūd* is lost.

81 *Taṭhīr al-iʿtiqād ʿan adrān al-ilḥād*, ed. Muḥammad Ṣubḥī Ḥasan al-Ḥallāq (Ṣanʿāʾ 1411/1990).

82 Al-Shawkānī, *al-Ṣawārim al-ḥidād al-qāṭiʿa li-ʿalāʾiq arbāb al-ittiḥād*, ed. Muḥammad Ṣubḥī Ḥasan al-Ḥallāq (Ṣanʿāʾ 1411/1990).

83 al-Ḥabshī, op. cit. 103.

VII

# Das Imamat in der frühen ismailitischen Lehre*

## Die vorfatimidische Zeit

Die Geschichte der Ismailiten als einer selbständigen Bewegung beginnt mit dem Streit um das Erbe des Imamats Ǧaʿfar aṣ-Ṣādiqs. Ǧaʿfar hatte Ismāʿīl, seinen zweiten Sohn, unter Übergehung des Erstgeborenen, ʿAbd Allāh al-Afṭaḥ, zu seinem Nachfolger ernannt[1]). An der Wirklichkeit dieser Ernennung, auf die sich der Anspruch der Ismailiten auf das wahre Imamat gründet, kann nach den Ausführungen Saʿd b. ʿAbd Allāhs[2]) nicht gezweifelt werden. Saʿd b. ʿAbd Allāh glaubt selbst an die Rechtmäßigkeit der Nachfolge eines Bruders Ismāʿīls, Mūsā, und er gesteht nicht ausdrücklich ein, daß Ǧaʿfar Ismāʿīl ernannt hatte. Er berichtet aber, daß nach dem Tode Ismāʿīls eine Reihe von Ǧaʿfars Anhängern abfielen mit der Begründung, er könne nicht der Imam sein, da der von ihm ernannte Nachfolger vor ihm gestorben sei: Der von Gott geleitete Imam dürfe doch nicht lügen[3]). Die Abtrünnigen warfen Ǧaʿfar vor, er hätte sich mit der Erklärung aus der Schlinge ziehen wollen, Gott habe seinen Ratschluß hinsichtlich des Imamats Ismāʿīls geändert. Nach den Ismailiten versicherte Ǧaʿfar freilich gerade das Gegenteil[4]).

Tatsächlich gestehen die Zwölferschiiten, die das Imamat nach Ǧaʿfar über Mūsā al-Kāẓim weiterführen, im allgemeinen zu, daß Ǧaʿfar zunächst Ismāʿīl zu seinem Nachfolger bestimmte. Darauf kann

---

* Vgl. Islam XXXIV S. 34—88.

[1]) Die Idee, daß die Nachfolge durch Ernennung des Imams durch seinen Vorgänger legitimiert sein müsse, dürfte schon aus der Zeit Muḥammad al-Bāqirs, Ǧaʿfars Vater, stammen. Vgl. M. G. S. Hodgson, How did the early Shīʿa become sectarian, JAOS, 1955, S. 10.

[2]) Abū 'l-Qāsim Saʿd b. ʿAbd Allāh al-Ašʿarī al-Qummī (gest. 300/913) ist nach den Untersuchungen Abbas Iqbals als Verfasser der in den bisherigen Ausgaben dem al-Ḥasan b. Mūsā an-Naubaḫtī zugeschriebenen Schrift über die Sekten der Šīʿa anzusehen, vgl. Oriens VII S. 204. Die Schrift wird im folgenden nach der Ausgabe H. Ritters zitiert als Saʿd.

[3]) Saʿd S. 55. [4]) Vgl. unten S. 45.

sich auch der Ismailit Ǧaʿfar b. Manṣūr al-Jaman in seiner Auseinandersetzung mit ihren Thesen berufen[5]). Sie versicherten freilich, Ismāʿīl sei von seinem Vater wegen seines unsittlichen Lebenswandels der Nachfolge verlustig erklärt worden[6]). Nach der Darstellung Saʿd b. ʿAbd Allāhs, unserer ältesten, ausführlichsten und sicherlich zuverlässigsten Quelle, ist diese Behauptung zu verwerfen. Die Berichte von der Trunksucht Ismāʿīls und seiner Verfluchung durch den Vater, die später von Zwölferschiiten überliefert wurden[7]), dürften Zweckerfindungen sein.

Sicher ist, daß Ǧaʿfar nach dem Tod Ismāʿīls keinen anderen Nachfolger mehr ernannte. Denn als Ǧaʿfar starb, vertraten gleichzeitig drei Brüder Ismāʿīls den Anspruch auf die Nachfolge. Keiner von ihnen konnte sich aber auf eine Ernennung durch den Vater berufen. Die große Mehrheit der Anhänger Ǧaʿfars, unter ihnen die bedeutendsten Gelehrten, schloß sich zunächst ʿAbd Allāh an, nicht Mūsā, wie im allgemeinen angegeben wird. ʿAbd Allāh freilich starb schon ungefähr siebzig Tage nach seinem Vater kinderlos. Seine Anhänger erkannten nun Mūsā als Imam an[8]).

Die Anhänger Ismāʿīls haben sich offenbar erst nach dem Tode Ǧaʿfars von dessen übriger Anhängerschaft getrennt. So jedenfalls stellt es Saʿd b. ʿAbd Allāh dar[9]). Da Ǧaʿfar tatsächlich nichts tat, was zur Nachfolge Ismāʿīls in Widerspruch gestanden hätte[10]), bestand für sie kein Anlaß, ihm die Treue zu kündigen. Ǧaʿfar aber stand in seiner Haltung sichtlich unter dem Eindruck der Berechtigung der Argumente, welche die erwähnten Abtrünnigen nach dem Tod Ismāʿīls gegen ihn vorbrachten. Nach den Ismailiten soll er sogar erklärt haben, Gott könne in allem seinen Ratschluß und seinen Willen ändern, außer

[5]) Asrār an-nuṭaqā', in Rise, Texte S. 81. Nach ihm gestanden die Zwölfer sogar zu, daß Ismāʿīl in Gegenwart seines Vaters seinen Sohn Muḥammad zum Nachfolger ernannte. Das ist freilich kaum glaubhaft. Die Zwölfer lehrten aber auch, daß das Imamat erst im letzten Augenblick vor dem Tod eines Imams auf den Nachfolger überging, vgl. al-Kulīnī, uṣūl al-kāfī, Ed. al-Āḫūndī, Teheran 1375, I 284f. Nach dieser Theorie war der Anspruch Ismāʿīls hinfällig.

[6]) Vgl. Origins S. 38. [7]) Origins S. 38f.

[8]) Saʿd S. 65. Während die Mehrheit Mūsā nunmehr zum einzig rechtmäßigen Nachfolger Ǧaʿfars erklärte, hielten einige am Imamat ʿAbd Allāhs fest und betrachteten Mūsā als seinen Nachfolger.

[9]) Saʿd S. 57.

[10]) Das betont der Ismailit Abū Ḥātim ar-Rāzī: „. . . viele erklärten sich für sein (Ismāʿīls) Imamat zu Lebzeiten Ǧaʿfars. Er aber verwies ihnen das nicht, so daß manche Leute sagten: Ismāʿīl ist nicht zu seinen Lebzeiten gestorben. Ǧaʿfar hat ihn aus Sorge um ihn verborgen . . ." Abū Ḥātim ar-Rāzī, Kitāb az-zīna, Ms. der Muḥammadī Hamdānī Sammlung S. 233.

in bezug auf das Imamat[11]). Was anderes konnte das bedeuten, als daß Ismāʿīl der einzige rechtmäßige Nachfolger Ǧaʿfars sei? Die Qarmaṭen zitierten Ǧaʿfar nach Saʿd b. ʿAbd Allāh sogar so: „Ich sehe keine Änderung des Ratschlusses Gottes bezüglich Ismāʿīls[12]).“

Die Anhänger Ismāʿīls schlossen daraus, daß Ismāʿīl nicht wirklich gestorben sei. Sie erklärten, sein Begräbnis sei eine Täuschung Ǧaʿfars gewesen, der ihn aus Furcht um ihn vor den Menschen verborgen habe[13]). Ǧaʿfar habe auf Ismāʿīl als seinen Nachfolger hingewiesen. Der Imam aber sage nur die Wahrheit. Als dann Ismāʿīl scheinbar starb, hätten sie daher erkannt, daß Ǧaʿfar wahr gesprochen habe, und daß Ismāʿīl der Qāʾim sei und nicht wirklich gestorben[14]).

Saʿd b. ʿAbd Allāh bezeichnet die Vertreter dieser Lehre als die „reine Ismāʿīlīja“ (al-ismāʿīlīja al-ḫāliṣa)[15]). Gleich danach beschreibt er eine andere Sekte, die Muḥammad, den Sohn Ismāʿīls, als den Imam nach Ǧaʿfar aṣ-Ṣādiq(s Tod) anerkannte: Ismāʿīl sei zu Lebzeiten seines Vaters der wahre Imam gewesen und nach seinem Tod sein Sohn Muḥammad der einzig rechtmäßige Nachfolger, da das Imamat nach dem Falle von al-Ḥasan und al-Ḥusain nicht vom Bruder dem Bruder vererbt werden könne. Diese Sekte nennt Saʿd b. ʿAbd Allāh die Mubārakīja, angeblich nach einem Freigelassenen Ismāʿīls, der ihr Oberhaupt gewesen sei[16]).

---

[11]) Ǧaʿfar b. Manṣūr al-Jaman, asrār an-nuṭaqāʾ, in Rise Texte S. 81. Nach dem Verfasser überlieferten auch die Zwölfer diese Aussage Ǧaʿfar aṣ-Ṣādiqs. Nach dem Tod Ismāʿīls sagten sie jedoch: „Nie ist Gott so zu einer Änderung seines Ratschlusses geleitet wie im Falle Ismāʿīls, als er ihn zu Lebzeiten seines Vaters zu sich nahm.“ (Im Text, S. 81, ist qultum vor mā badā ausgefallen, vgl. Texte S. 94.) Dieser Satz wird von Zwölfern verschiedentlich Ǧaʿfar aṣ-Ṣādiq zugeschrieben, vgl. Goldziher, EI Artikel Badāʾ.

[12]) Saʿd S. 62. Der Text ist hier m. E. gegenüber der vom Herausgeber in der Anmerkung vorgeschlagenen Lesung korrekt. Dem widerspricht scheinbar, daß Saʿd b. ʿAbd Allāh unmittelbar zuvor als Auffassung der Qarmaṭen wiedergibt, Gott habe seinen Ratschluß hinsichtlich des Imamats Ǧaʿfars und Ismāʿīls geändert und es dem Muḥammad b. Ismāʿīl vermacht. Dies ist jedoch offensichtlich eine Spitze des Verfassers gegen die Ansicht der Qarmaṭen, daß das Imamat zu Lebzeiten Ǧaʿfars auf Ismāʿīl übergegangen sei, nicht deren tatsächliche Lehre.

[13]) So beschreibt schon der Zaiditenimam al-Qāsim b. Ibrāhīm ihre Lehre, Kitāb ar-radd ʿalāʾr-rawāfiḍ min aṣḥāb al-ġulūw, Ms. Berlin Glaser 101, fol. 104r. Diese Abhandlung ist verfaßt zwischen 219/834 und 246/860, vgl. R. Strothmann, Das Staatsrecht der Zaiditen, Straßburg 1912, S. 48.

[14]) Saʿd S. 57. [15]) Saʿd S. 58.

[16]) Saʿd S. 58. Ganz ähnlich ist die Einteilung bei al-Ašʿarī, maqālāt S. 26f. (al-ismāʿīlīja und al-mubārakīja), und bei aš-Šahrastānī, Ed. Cureton S. 128 (al-ismāʿīlīja al-wāqifa und al-mubārakīja). Nach der Darstellung aller drei

Gegen diese Darstellung bestehen gewisse Bedenken. Ivanow konnte zeigen, daß al-Mubārak wahrscheinlich der Beinamen Ismā'īls selbst war: Der ismailitische Autor Abū Ja'qūb as-Siğistānī nennt ihn mehrfach bei diesem Namen[17]). Unter der Mubārakīja sind danach ursprünglich die Verkünder des Imamats Ismā'īls zu verstehen. Wenn später allgemein als Mubārakīja die Anhänger des Muḥammad b. Ismā'īl bezeichnet werden, darf man annehmen, daß die Masse der Anhängerschaft Ismā'īls sich nach dem Tod Ğa'fars in Abwesenheit des wahren Imams um seinen Sohn Muḥammad scharte. Muḥammad fand dann bald Anerkennung als Imam, und Ismā'īl mußte nachträglich zum Imam zu Lebzeiten seines Vaters erhoben werden[18]). Dies läßt sich auch aus der frühesten erhaltenen Erwähnung der Ismailiten in einer Abhandlung des Zaiditenimams al-Qāsim b. Ibrāhīm herauslesen: „Eine Gruppe behauptete, Ğa'far habe seinem Sohn Ismā'īl die Nachfolge zugesprochen. Ismā'īl starb vor Ğa'far. Sie aber behaupteten, er sei nicht gestorben. Das Begräbnis, das Ğa'far veranstaltete, sei Schwindel gewesen. Vielmehr hätte ihn Ğa'far aus Furcht um ihn verborgen. Sie führten die Nachfolge auf seinen Sohn weiter (qādū'l-waṣījata ilā waladih). Sie werden die Mubārakīja genannt[19])." Eine Ismā'īlīja erwähnt al-Qāsim b. Ibrāhīm nicht.

Mubārakīja ist also der Name, unter dem die Ismailiten zuerst bekannt wurden, dessen Bedeutung freilich schon bald in Vergessenheit

---

Autoren wäre die fatimidisch-ismailitische Gemeinde als aus der Mubārakīja, nicht aus der ursprünglichen Ismā'īlīja hervorgegangen anzusehen. Der Ismailit Abū Ḥātim ar-Rāzī (gestorben 322/934) andererseits beschreibt in seinem Kitāb az-zīna (Ms. S. 232f.) die Lehre der Ismā'īlīja ausführlich mit der Sympathie des Anhängers. Die Erwartung der Wiederkehr Ismā'īls als Qā'im erwähnt er nicht, sondern führt das Imamat ohne weiteres in Muḥammad b. Ismā'īl fort. Die Mubārakīja läßt er in der Ismā'īlīja aufgehen, vgl. unten S. 47, Anm. 20. Mit der Ismā'īlīja, deren Anhänger „sich täglich mehren", meint er zweifellos die fatimidische Gemeinde, entgegen der Ansicht H. F. al-Hamdanis, On the genealogy of the Fatimid caliphs, Kairo 1958, S. 21.

17) The alleged Founder S. 111. Ivanow äußert Zweifel daran, ob sullam annağāt zurecht Abū Ja'qūb zugeschrieben wird. Abū Ja'qūb nennt aber auch in seinem iṯbāt an-nubūwāt Ismā'īl mit dem Namen al-Mubārak. Er zählt dort die Imame nach Muḥammad al-Bāqir in folgender Reihenfolge auf: aṣ-Ṣādiq, al-Mubārak (= Ismā'īl), al-Qā'im (= Muḥammad b. Ismā'īl). Ms. der Muḥammadī Hamdānī Sammlung S. 318f.

18) Die späteren Ismailiten, die Ismā'īl als Imam zählen, gehen im allgemeinen nicht auf die daraus erwachsende Problematik ein: Entweder gab es gleichzeitig zwei Imame oder Ğa'far verlor das Imamat nach der Ernennung Ismā'īls. Konsequent ist die von Sa'd b. 'Abd Allāh (S. 62) beschriebene Lehre der Qarmaṭen, nach der Ğa'fars Imamat mit der Ernennung Ismā'īls endete und auf Ismā'īl überging.

19) Ar-radd 'alā'r-rawāfiḍ, fol. 105r.

geriet[20]). Die zuverlässigen Nachrichten über ihre Geschichte und Lehre aus dieser Zeit sind äußerst dürftig. Der erwähnte Imam al-Qāsim b. Ibrāhīm weiß von ihnen: „Sie fasten zwei Tage vor Ramaḍān, brechen das Fasten zwei Tage vor dem Fastenbrechen und behaupten, der Monat daure von einem Verschwinden des Mondes bis zum nächsten[21]).“ Dies zeigt, daß die frühen Ismailiten dem religiösen Gesetz im allgemeinen nicht so ablehnend gegenüberstanden, wie manche der späteren Häresiologen glauben machen möchten. Es deutet auch darauf, daß das fatimidisch-ismailitische Gesetz mit seinen Sonderheiten alte Wurzeln hat[22]).

Sa'd b. 'Abd Allāh ist sichtlich bemüht, den Einfluß der von den Häresiologen allgemein als extremistisch klassifizierten Ḫaṭṭābīja auf die ismailitische Gemeinde darzulegen. Er behauptet geradezu: „die Ismā'īlīja, das ist die Ḫaṭṭābīja“, erklärt dann freilich gleich, eine Gruppe der Anhänger Abū 'l-Ḫaṭṭābs habe sich (nach dessen Tod) der Gemeinde des Muḥammad b. Ismā'īl angeschlossen[23]). Im Grunde

[20]) Auch die Ismailiten vergaßen früh seinen Ursprung. Abū Ḥātim ar-Rāzī bezeichnet (az-zīna Ms. S. 233) als al-Mubārakīja eine Gruppe, die schon zu Lebzeiten Ǧa'far aṣ-Ṣādiqs dessen Enkel Muḥammad b. Ismā'īl als Imam anerkannt hätte mit der Behauptung, Ǧa'far habe ihnen das befohlen. Den Namen leitet er von dem legendären Freigelassenen Ismā'īls ab. Die Sekte sei dann in der Ismā'īlīja aufgegangen. All dies ist offensichtlich eine Konstruktion, durch die der Name irgendwie untergebracht werden soll.

[21]) Kitāb ar-radd 'alā'r-rawāfiḍ, fol. 105r.

[22]) Die Fatimiden bestimmten Anfang und Ende des Ramaḍān nicht wie die übrigen Muslime nach der Sicht des Neumondes, sondern durch Berechnung (vgl. REI 1935, S. 178). Dadurch konnte es ohne weiteres vorkommen, daß sie den Fastenmonat zwei Tage vor jenen begannen und beendeten, wenn dies auch nicht beabsichtigt war, wie al-Qāsim es erscheinen läßt. Ebenso beruht es auf einem Mißverständnis, wenn er meint, die Ismailiten sähen das Verschwinden des Mondes als maßgeblich für den Monatsanfang an. In der Berechnung rücken zwar Verschwinden und Neuerscheinen des Monds zusammen. Das fatimidische Gesetz bestimmte jedoch, daß der Gläubige, wenn das Wort des Imams ihn nicht erreicht, sich nach der Sicht des Neumonds zu richten hat (Qāḍī an-Nu'mān, da'ā'im al-islām, Ed. A. A. A. Fyzee, Kairo 1951, I 322). Übrigens hielten sich die Fatimiden nicht ganz streng an die Berechnung, sondern zählten Ramaḍān grundsätzlich dreißig Tage, vgl. al-maǧālis al-mustanṣirīja, Ed. M. Kamil Husain, Kairo o. J., S. 131, 215ff.

[23]) Sa'd S. 59f. Abū Ḥātim ar-Rāzī berichtet, Abū 'l-Ḫaṭṭāb habe sich zunächst für das Imamat Ismā'īls erklärt. Nach dessen Tod habe er das Imamat Ǧa'fars vertreten, der ihn jedoch wegen seiner extremen Theorien verfluchte. Nach Abū 'l-Ḫaṭṭābs Tod schloß sich eine Gruppe seiner Anhänger Muḥammad b. Ismā'īl an, auf Befehl Abū 'l-Ḫaṭṭābs, wie sie behaupteten. Sie vertraten bezüglich Muḥammad b. Ismā'īls ähnlich extreme Ansichten wie über die anderen Imame (Kitāb az-zīna Ms. S. 234). Abū Ḥātim hatte zweifellos Anlaß, solche Ansichten als „schweren Unglauben“ zu verdammen.

möchte er mit der überspitzten Bemerkung die ismailitische Bewegung seiner Zeit treffen, die im Gegensatz zu den vielen anderen „häretischen" Sekten, die er beschreibt, damals eine intensive Propaganda trieb und sich, auch auf Kosten der Gemeinde der Glaubensgenossen Saʿd b. ʿAbd Allāhs, rasch ausbreitete.

Tatsächlich wird man den Einfluß der Anschauungen jener Gruppe von Anhängern Abū 'l-Ḫaṭṭābs auf die Lehre der Ismailiten nicht allzu hoch einschätzen dürfen[24]). Nach Saʿd b. ʿAbd Allāh glaubten sie, der Geist Ǧaʿfars sei auf Abū 'l-Ḫaṭṭāb und nach seinem Verschwinden auf Muḥammad b. Ismāʿīl übergegangen[25]). Das unterschied sie jedoch deutlich von der Mubārakīja. Die spätere ismailitische Imamatslehre baut aber auf der der Mubārakīja auf, Abū 'l-Ḫaṭṭāb wird im allgemeinen nur als Häretiker genannt.

Muḥammad b. Ismāʿīl verließ seine Vaterstadt Medina nach dem Tode seines Großvaters[26]) und verschwand aus dem Gesichtskreis seiner Anhänger. Die „Zeit der Verborgenheit" begann. Aber auch die weiteren Schicksale der Gemeinde seiner Anhänger sind uns verhüllt. Erst ein Jahrhundert später fanden sie plötzlich allgemeine Aufmerksamkeit, unter anderem Namen, aber immer noch in Erwartung ihres verschwundenen Meisters.

Den Angaben über die Ḫaṭṭābīja-Gruppe, die sich der Anhängerschaft des Muḥammad b. Ismāʿīl anschloß, läßt Saʿd b. ʿAbd Allāh unmittelbar eine Darstellung der Lehre der „Qarmaṭen" folgen[27]). Die Qarmaṭen, so berichtet er, sind aus der Mubārakīja hervorgegangen, indem sie die Zahl der Imame nach dem Propheten auf sieben beschränkten. Der letzte von ihnen ist Muḥammad b. Ismāʿīl, der nicht gestorben ist, sondern im Lande der Rum lebt. Er ist der rechtgeleitete Qā'im (al-qā'im al-mahdī), der von Gott mit einem neuen Gesetz gesandt wird, welches das Gesetz Mohammeds ablöst. Er ist mit dem „Siegel der Propheten" im Koran[28]) gemeint.

Bei der Aufzählung der Imame der Qarmaṭen gerät Saʿd b. ʿAbd Allāh in Widersprüche. Einmal beginnt er mit ʿAlī b. Abī Ṭālib, dem er aber als Imamgesandten (imām rasūl) eine Doppelstellung zuteilt. Um die vorgeschriebene Zahl nicht zu überschreiten, übergeht er Ismāʿīl, den Vater des siebten Imams. An anderer Stelle aber erklärt er, nach Auffassung der Qarmaṭen sei das Imamat zu Lebzeiten des Ǧaʿfar b. Muḥammad (aṣ-Ṣādiq) auf seinen Sohn Ismāʿīl übergegangen,

---

[24]) Vgl. Ivanow, The alleged Founder S. 138ff.

[25]) Saʿd S. 61.

[26]) Vgl. Ivanow, The alleged Founder S. 157f.

[27]) Saʿd S. 61ff. [28]) Koran 33, 40.

wie auch das Amt des Gottesgesandten von Mohammed noch zu seinen Lebzeiten auf Ali übergegangen sei.

Mit dem besonderen Rang Alis als Imamgesandten stimmt überein, daß er unter den sieben „Standhaften" (ūlū'l-'azm) angeführt wird. Denn im Koran, aus dem der Begriff übernommen ist, wird er als Attribut von Propheten gebraucht[29]). Und nach Sa'd b. 'Abd Allāh sind die sieben „Standhaften" in der Lehre der Qarmaṭen: Noah, Abraham, Moses, Jesus, Mohammed, Ali und Muḥammad b. Ismā'īl[30]).

Wie ist es zu verstehen, daß Ali in dieser Reihe von Propheten mitgezählt wird, obgleich es doch dem Muḥammad b. Ismā'īl vorbehalten blieb, Mohammeds Gesetz durch ein neues zu ersetzen? Sa'd b. 'Abd Allāh spricht nicht ausdrücklich von einer Offenbarung Alis, die ihn als Gottesgesandten legitimieren würde. Aus seinen weiteren Ausführungen läßt sich jedoch unschwer erraten, daß sie in der Enthüllung des „inneren Sinnes" (al-bāṭin), des Kernstücks der ismailitischen Religion, bestanden haben muß. Nach den Qarmaṭen, so weiß Sa'd b. 'Abd Allāh darüber zu berichten, haben alle Gebote, die Gott seinen Knechten auferlegt und sein Prophet festgesetzt hat, ein Äußeres und ein Inneres. Die Bücher und der religiöse Brauch, durch die Gott äußerlich von den Menschen Verehrung fordert, sind Gleichnisse, unter denen der Sinn verborgen liegt. Nach diesem inneren Sinn aber muß der Mensch handeln. „In ihm ist die Rettung, im Handeln nach dem Äußeren aber das Verderben und die Qual. Es ist ein Teil der irdischen Strafe, mit der Gott Menschen heimsucht, die die Wahrheit nicht kennen und nicht bekennen[31])." Ali ist also der Bringer des inneren Sinnes, der zwar das Gesetz Mohammeds noch nicht aufgehoben hat, aber seine wahre Bedeutung offenbarte[32]).

Die scharf antinomistische Gesinnung, die hierin Ausdruck findet, läßt erwarten, daß auch das Gesetz, das Muḥammad b. Ismā'īl bringen sollte, von besonderer Art sei. Sa'd b. 'Abd Allāh gibt dazu an, daß nach den Qarmaṭen „Muḥammad b. Ismā'īl das Paradies Adams" besitze. Die Bedeutung davon aber sei nach ihnen „die Freistellung der ver-

---

[29]) Koran 46,35.

[30]) Sa'd S. 62. [31]) Sa'd S. 64.

[32]) Da Ali in der Darstellung Sa'd b. 'Abd Allāhs diese Sonderstellung eingeräumt wird, ist es nur folgerichtig, daß der Verfasser nicht die strenge Einteilung der Weltgeschichte in die sieben Ären (adwār, sing. daur) kennt, die zum mindesten für die fatimidische Lehre so charakteristisch ist. Denn sie gründet sich auf eine Parallelität im Verlauf der ersten sechs Ären: Jede von ihnen wird von einem Propheten oder Sprecher (nāṭiq) durch Verkündung eines Gesetzes eröffnet. Ihm folgen der Vollstrecker (waṣī) oder Schweiger (ṣāmit), der den inneren Sinn des Gesetzes enthüllt, und die Imame.

botenen Dinge und alles auf der Erde Geschaffenen[33])." Der Qā'im Muḥammad b. Ismā'īl soll, in anderen Worten, die gesetzlose Urreligion des Vaters der Menschheit wiederherstellen.

Leider verrät Sa'd b. 'Abd Allāh nichts über die Quellen seiner Darstellung, hier so wenig wie anderswo. Von Interesse aber ist der Nachsatz: „Ihre Anzahl ist groß, aber sie haben weder Kampfesmut noch Kraft. Am meisten verbreitet sind sie in der Umgebung von Kufa und im Jemen. Es mögen ihrer um hunderttausend sein[34])." Dies kann nur die Lage vor dem Jahre 286/899 beschreiben[35]). Denn damals eroberte Abū Sa'īd al-Ǧannābī al-Aḥsā und gründete einen unabhängigen Qarmaṭenstaat in al-Baḥrain. Drei Jahre später begannen die Qarmaṭenaufstände in Syrien. Dann muß aber der Bericht aus der Zeit vor dem Auseinanderbrechen der einheitlichen, von Salamīja aus geleiteten ismailitischen Bewegung stammen, denn deren Einheit bestand bis zum Jahr 286/899. Tatsächlich nennt Sa'd b. 'Abd Allāh neben den Qarmaṭen keine Gruppe, die man als unmittelbare Vorläuferin der fatimidischen Ismailiten ansehen könnte.

Die Überlieferung der religiösen Literatur der Ismailiten beginnt ziemlich abrupt mit der Herrschaftnahme der Fatimiden. Zur Zeit der ersten Kalifen ihrer Dynastie schrieben die ältesten Autoritäten, deren Werke zum guten Teil erhalten sind: Qāḍī an-Nu'mān, Ǧa'far b. Manṣūr al-Jaman, Muḥammad b. Aḥmad an-Nasafī (an-Naḫšabī)[36]), Abū Ḥātim ar-Rāzī, Abū Ja'qūb as-Siǧistānī. Auf ihre Werke allein verweist schon Ḥamīd ad-Dīn al-Kirmānī als Voraussetzung für die Lektüre seines im Jahre 411/1020 verfaßten Kitāb rāḥat al-'aql[37]). Sie selbst nennen aber ihre geistigen Ahnen im allgemeinen[38]) nicht.

Über die vorfatimische Literatur der Ismailiten ist daher nur wenig bekannt. Man darf annehmen, daß bei der ständig bedrohten Lage der Gemeinde die Lehre aus Gründen der Vorsicht im wesentlichen mündlich verbreitet wurde. Daneben gab es wohl eine Anzahl meist anonymer Abhandlungen und Aufzeichnungen, die aber nur wenigen Eingeweihten, deren Zuverlässigkeit außer Zweifel stand, zugänglich gemacht wurden. Indem man peinlich die Nennung von Namen vermied

---

[33]) Sa'd S. 63. [34]) Sa'd S. 64.

[35]) P. Kraus datierte nach dieser Stelle das Buch als zwischen 266 und 297 H. verfaßt, Beiträge zur islamischen Ketzergeschichte, RSO XIV S. 366, Anm. 5.

[36]) Sein Kitāb al-maḥṣūl ist nach 'Ārif Tāmir, ḫams rasā'il ismā'īlīja S. 16, erhalten.

[37]) Al-Kirmānī, Kitāb rāḥat al-'aql, Ed. Muḥammad Kāmil Ḥusain und Muḥammad Muṣṭafā Ḥilmī, Leiden 1955, S. 22.

[38]) Abgesehen von ein paar Hinweisen auf 'Abdān, vgl. Fatimiden und Baḥrainqarmaṭen, Islam XXXIV S. 38, Anm. 5.

und gefährliche Aussagen unter einem Mantel unbestimmter Andeutungen verbarg, versuchte man die Schriften für Außenstehende, in deren Hände sie trotz aller Vorsichtsmaßnahmen fallen mochten, möglichst unverständlich zu halten. Nach dem Aufstieg der Fatimiden verloren sie rasch an Interesse, teils, weil sie sich neben den phantasievollen und großzügig angelegten Werken der Meister zu dürftig ausnahmen, teils offenbar aber auch, weil sie als veraltet und nicht mehr ganz der Lehre entsprechend angesehen wurden.

Trotzdem sind einzelne Werke aus der „Zeit der verborgenen Imame", wie man die Vorgeschichte der Fatimiden später zu nennen pflegte, erhalten geblieben. So wird der unter dem Namen Manṣūr al-Jaman bekannte al-Ḥasan b. Ḥaušab, der seit dem Jahr 268/981 im Jemen als ismailitischer Missionar tätig war, als Verfasser eines heute noch verbreiteten Kitāb al-ʿālim wa'l-ġulām[39]) genannt. Demselben Manṣūr al-Jaman wird auch ein in Bruchstücken erhaltenes Kitāb ar-rušd wa'l-hidāja[40]) zugeschrieben. Wenn auch diese Verfasserschaft nicht bewiesen werden kann, so ist nach dem Inhalt beider Werke doch nicht zu bezweifeln, daß sie noch vor dem „Erscheinen" (ẓuhūr) der Fatimiden geschrieben sind. Ihre Verwandtschaft in Stil, Ideen und Terminologie ist nach Ivanow eng genug, daß man sie wenigstens der gleichen Schule zusprechen darf, wenn sie nicht tatsächlich aus der Feder desselben Verfassers stammen[41]).

Das Kitāb ar-rušd wa'l-hidāja besteht aus im Ausdruck unbeholfener, in Methodik und Inhalt echt ismailitischer Koranauslegung. Sie wird weitgehend von einer einzigen Idee beherrscht: dem Kommen des Mahdi. Die zyklische Äreneinteilung der Geschichte ist klar vorgezeichnet[42]). Es gibt sieben Sprecher-Propheten. Jeder bringt ein Gesetz, das verschieden ist von dem seines Vorgängers[43]). Jeder braucht

[39]) Besprochen von Ivanow, Studies in Early Persian Ismailism², Bombay 1955, S. 61ff.

[40]) Hsgb. von M. Kamil Husain, Collectanea I, Leiden 1948, S. 189ff., englische Übersetzung von Ivanow, Studies S. 32ff.

[41]) Studies S. 62.

[42]) Ivanow, Studies S. 26, weist darauf hin, daß statt des späteren daur der Ausdruck waqt (Zeit) gebraucht wird.

[43]) Collectanea S. 197. Ivanow meint, der siebte sei davon ausgenommen, Studies S. 24. Das wird aber nirgends ausdrücklich gesagt. Die Stelle Collectanea S. 198, Z. 12ff., bezieht Ivanow fälschlich auf Mohammed, Studies S. 43. Sie ist m. E. so zu übersetzen: „. . . als Hinweis darauf, daß er (der Mahdi) alles erfüllt, was vor ihm in den offenbarten Gesetzen war, und daß es nach ihm kein Gesetz gibt, auf das er hinweisen wird, so wie die Sprecher einer auf den andern hingewiesen haben." Vgl. Kitāb al-ʿālim wa'l-ġulām, Studies S. 80f., wo betont wird, daß die Offenbarung Mohammeds nicht die endgültige gewesen sei.

einen Vollstrecker, der seine Stellung vervollkommnet[44]), indem er den inneren Sinn der Offenbarung deutet[45]). Außerdem folgen jedem sieben Imame[46]). Nur der Mahdi, der siebte Sprecher, vereinigt in sich den Rang des Prophetentums und den Rang des Vollstreckers[47]). Nach ihm gibt es keine allegorische Ausdeutung (ta'wīl)[48]). Er ist der letzte der Sprecher und der Imame[49]). Sein Name ist Muḥammad[50]).

Im Gegensatz dazu, was Sa'd b. 'Abd Allāh von den Qarmaṭen berichtet, wird hier der Mahdi nicht mit Muḥammad b. Ismā'īl identifiziert. Das geht deutlich hervor aus der Feststellung, der siebte Sprecher sei „der zehnte von Mohammed und Ali an. Die sieben Imame aus ihrer Nachkommenschaft sind Vollender, ... und er der achte nach den Vollenderimamen (al-a'imma al-mutimmūn)[51])." Die Namen der sieben Imame werden nirgends genannt, aber zweifellos ist die Reihe von al-Ḥasan bis Muḥammad b. Ismā'īl gemeint[52]). Die Vollenderimame bilden überhaupt eine feste Heptade. Ivanow meint, daraus entstehe der Eindruck, daß die Schrift noch vor Ablauf ihrer Herrschaft, das heißt noch im 2./8. Jahrhundert, abgefaßt sei[53]). Der Mahdi, als der achte Imam, müsse entweder 'Abd Allāh, der Sohn des Muḥammad b. Ismā'īl, oder sein Enkel Aḥmad sein[54]). Aber Ivanow gesteht selbst ein, daß all dies nicht sehr überzeugend sei[55]). Die Eingenommenheit des Verfassers von der Erwartung des Mahdi läßt vielmehr schließen, daß die Zeit der sieben Vollenderimame bereits abgelaufen war. Die Beschränkung der Zahl der Imame auf sieben entspricht der Lehre der Qarmaṭen. Sie erwarteten freilich die Wiederkehr des siebten Imams, Muḥammad b. Ismā'īl, als Mahdi. Der Verfasser des Kitāb ar-rušd begnügt sich demgegenüber damit, daß der Mahdi ein Nachkomme des Propheten sein werde[56]). Wann er kommt, weiß niemand[57]).

Enge Verwandtschaft in Terminologie und Anschauungen mit dem Kitāb ar-rušd weist das Kitāb al-kašf betitelte frühismailitische Werk

---

[44]) Collectanea S. 197. [45]) S. 204. [46]) S. 189.

[47]) S. 198. Insofern ist es nicht inkonsequent, wenn der Verfasser von den sieben Vollstreckern spricht, S. 198.

[48]) Collectanea S. 199, offensichtlich da in seiner Offenbarung äußerer und innerer Sinn zusammenfallen.

[49]) Collectanea S. 198. [50]) S. 199. [51]) S. 199.

[52]) Ivanow räumt ein, daß al-Ḥasan vielleicht nicht gezählt wurde, Studies S. 25. Das wäre aber eine bemerkenswerte Abweichung von allen bekannten frühismailitischen Werken.

[53]) Studies S. 15. [54]) Studies S. 25. [55]) Studies S. 31.

[56]) Collectanea S. 194.

[57]) Collectanea S. 201.

auf[58]). Es besteht aus einer Sammlung von sechs Abhandlungen über verschiedene Themen, die ursprünglich offensichtlich unabhängig voneinander verfaßt worden sind. Stammen sie alle vom gleichen Verfasser, so sind sie doch jedenfalls unter verschiedenen Voraussetzungen geschrieben. Die ismailitische Tradition schreibt das Buch Manṣūr al-Jamans Sohn Ǧaʿfar zu[59]). Er kann jedoch nicht der Verfasser sein[60]), da dieser, wie aus seinen eigenen Angaben in einer der Abhandlungen hervorgeht, schon einige Zeit vor dem Erscheinen der Fatimiden zu den fortgeschrittenen Eingeweihten der Gemeinde gehörte[60a]). Wahrscheinlich sind alle Abhandlungen noch in vorfatimidischer Zeit geschrieben. Ǧaʿfar b. Manṣūr al-Jaman mag sie aus dem Jemen nach Nordafrika mitgebracht und zu einem Buch vereinigt herausgegeben haben. Dann dürften auch die erklärenden Glossen, mit denen das Werk, vor allem die fünfte Abhandlung, in frühfatimidischer Zeit versehen worden ist, von ihm stammen. Wo der Kommentator in den Text, der ohnehin recht fehlerhaft erhalten ist, im einzelnen eingegriffen hat, läßt sich leider nicht immer mit Sicherheit feststellen.

Wie im Kitāb ar-rušd spielt die Erwartung des siebten Sprecherpropheten, des Mahdi oder Qā'im[61]), eine bedeutende Rolle. Sein Zeitalter ist schon angebrochen, oft wird er „Herr der Zeit" (ṣāḥib az-zamān) genannt, aber sein Erscheinen steht noch aus. Durch sein Gesetz werden alle Gesetze vollendet, er wird den inneren Sinn vollstän-

---

[58]) Herausgegeben von R. Strothmann, Islamic Research Association Series No. 13, 1952. Wie im Kitāb ar-rušd wird die Bezeichnung asās für den waṣī nicht gebraucht. Daur findet sich nur einmal, sonst stattdessen zaman, atimmā' anstelle von mutimmūn zweimal, alle drei im gleichen Abschnitt, S. 15f. Zur Terminologie des Kitāb ar-rušd im Vergleich zu der der persischen Schule vgl. Studies S. 9ff. In Übereinstimmung mit den beiden Ibn Ḥaušab zugeschriebenen Werken fehlt im Kitāb al-kašf auch jegliche Spur der ismailitischen Philosophie hellenistischen Ursprungs, vgl. etwa die Theologie der zweiten Abhandlung.

[59]) Idrīs b. al-Ḥasan, gest. 872/1468, nennt ihn als Autoren, Rise, Texte S. 64.

[60]) P. Kraus, R. E. I. 1932 S. 486, hielt den Stil dem anderer Werke Ǧaʿfars konform. Für die Ähnlichkeit der Terminologie und Ideologie der früheren Werke Ǧaʿfars und des Kitāb al-kašf erscheint sein Verhaften in der jemenitischen Tradition hinreichende Erklärung. In seinem späteren Kitāb ta'wīl az-zakāt verwendet Ǧaʿfar in vollem Maße auch die Termini und Ideen der persischen Schule.

[60a]) Vgl. unten S. 55, Anm. 71.

[61]) Der Gebrauch ist in den einzelnen Abhandlungen verschieden: In der dritten und fünften wird er überwiegend als Qā'im, in der sechsten ausschließlich als Mahdi bezeichnet; in der ersten schwankt die Anwendung.

dig offenbaren[62]). Aber er wird vor allem auch das Schwert führen[63]). Wie im Kitāb ar-rušd wird er als der letzte der Imame und Sprecher bezeichnet[64]). Er besiegelt die Epochen und Zeitalter[65]).

Auffallend ist, daß die Heptade der Vollenderimame, die im Kitāb ar-rušd als fester Begriff immer wieder erwähnt wird, hier im technischen Vokabular fast völlig fehlt. Nur an zwei Stellen, in der zweiten und sechsten Abhandlung, ist von sieben Imamen ohne nähere Bestimmung die Rede[66]). In der ersten Abhandlung heißt es andererseits bei der Exegese des Koranverses 7,142: „Mit den dreißig (Nächten) meint er die Ḥuǧǧas. ... Zwischen jedem Sprecher bis zum anderen gibt es sechs Vollender. Also sind es sechs von Adam bis Noah, und so fort bis Aḥmad, das heißt Mohammed, den Apostel Gottes. ... Sechs mal fünf aber ergibt dreißig Vollender. Mit ihnen vollenden sich die Legate[67])." Daß hier nur sechs Vollender erwähnt werden, steht nicht im Widerspruch zur alten Lehre, nach welcher der siebte Vollender der Sprecher der neuen Ära wird. Gegen sie verstieß vielmehr der Verfasser des Kitāb ar-rušd, indem er den siebten Sprecher als den achten Vollender bezeichnete. Dazu heißt es in der Fortsetzung der Exegese des Verses: „‚Wir vollenden sie mit zehn', die Ḥuǧǧas von Aḥmad (d. h. dem Propheten des Islam) bis Muḥammad (den Mahdi) finden ihre Vollendung in acht. Diese sind die Träger des Thrones[68]). Der Thron ist das Wissen, und das Wissen besteht in der allegorischen Ausdeutung. ... Mit den acht Vollendern und Aḥmad und Muḥammad ist die Zehn vollständig[69])." Ist die Zahl hier gegenüber dem Kitāb ar-rušd noch um eins erhöht, oder wird Ali, gegen die Regel, einfach als Vollender (mutimm) mitgezählt? Vielleicht spricht für die zweite Annahme, daß Ali überhaupt nicht erwähnt wird, während er doch ohne Schwierigkeiten an Stelle des Propheten, der gar nicht in die Reihe paßt, hätte aufgenommen werden können[70]).

Einige bemerkenswerte, aber nicht leicht zu klärende Andeutungen enthalten die dritte und die fünfte Abhandlung, die enger als die

---

[62]) Kitāb al-kašf S. 110. [63]) S. 160. [64]) S. 114. [65]) Z. B. S. 33, 77, 135.

[66]) S. 50, 169. Zahid Ali, maḏhab S. 130, zitiert eine weitere Stelle, die im gedruckten Text fehlt. Da heißt es ausdrücklich, daß es zwischen zwei aufeinanderfolgenden Sprechern sieben Imame gäbe.

[67]) Kitāb al-kašf S. 15. Al-waṣājā, gemeint ist das Amt des waṣī.

[68]) Koran 69,17. [69]) Kitāb al-kašf S. 16.

[70]) Ǧa'far b. Manṣūr al-Jaman deutet in seinem Kitāb al-farā'iḍ wa-ḥudūd ad-dīn bei der Exegese desselben Verses die zehn Nächte als Mohammed, Ali, die sieben Imame aus seiner Nachkommenschaft und den Mahdi. Die Deutung der dreißig Nächte ist dort verschieden. Ms. der Muḥammadī Hamdānī Sammlung S. 175f.

anderen zusammengehören. Der Verfasser zitiert mehrfach einen „Weisen" (ḥakīm), dessen Schülerkreis er angehört hat[71]). Die Segensformel, die seiner Nennung meist folgt, zeigt, daß er als Nachkomme des Propheten angesehen wurde. Und er selbst wird bei der Deutung des Wortes rafaṯ, Obszönität, so zitiert: „Das ist die Enthüllung des Geheimnisses der Familie Mohammeds ... Darum achtet auf Geheimhaltung, bis das anvertraute Gut von euch verlangt wird. Denn wir sind die Eigentümer, und bestimmt werden wir euch eines Tages danach fragen[72])." Demnach muß er ein naher Verwandter des derzeitigen Meisters der Sekte oder dieser selbst gewesen sein.

Dieser Meister nahm den Rang eines Ḥuǧǧa ein. Das geht aus folgender Aussage am Ende eines Abschnittes in der fünften Abhandlung hervor, der von den Ḥuǧǧas in den verschiedenen Prophetenären handelt: „Der Ḥuǧǧa in unserer Zeit ist unser Herr und unser Scheich, der Herr jedes und jeder Gläubigen[73])." Ob der Verfasser selbst oder sein Lehrer, der Weise, hier spricht, ist nicht klar. Das Folgende aber stammt zweifellos von dem späteren Kommentator: „Der Hinweis darin erfolgte zur Zeit des Imams Muḥammad b. Aḥmad. Er verbarg nämlich anfangs seine Identität aus Vorsicht (li't-taqīja) vor den Heuchlern[74]) und gab sich den Ḥuǧǧarang. Er wies auf den Imam hin und wies (damit in Wirklichkeit) auf sich selbst. Das aber wußten nur wenige seiner vertrauten Sendboten[75])." Für das Alter dieser Glosse spricht, daß in der Reihe der verborgenen Imame, der der vierte Fatimidenkalif al-Mu'izz Anerkennung zu verschaffen suchte[76]), und die den späteren Darstellungen der Vorgeschichte der Fatimiden meist zugrunde gelegt wurde, ein Muḥammad b. Aḥmad keine Aufnahme fand. Nach ihr folgten dem Muḥammad b. Ismā'īl die Imame 'Abd Allāh, Aḥmad und al-Ḥusain, der Vater 'Ubaid Allāhs, in direkter Deszendenz[77]). Aber 'Ubaid Allāh selbst hatte noch erklärt, daß sein Vorgänger als Imam nicht sein Vater al-Ḥusain, sondern sein Onkel war, den die spätere Version nur noch als seinen Vormund im Auftrag des

---

[71]) Vgl. S. 93: sa'altu... qāla'l-ḥakīm, S. 112. Daß der Verfasser selbst Fragen stellte, deutet auf einen gewissen Rang seinerseits, vgl. S. 72.

[72]) Kitāb al-kašf S. 121. [73]) S. 98.

[74]) Munāfiqīn, damit pflegte man Verräter innerhalb der Gemeinde zu bezeichnen. Vgl. etwa istitār S. 96.

[75]) Kitāb al-kašf S. 99. [76]) Vgl. unten S. 74f.

[77]) Unter dem fünften Fatimiden, al-'Azīz (365—386/975—996), nennt sie der Verfasser des istitār al-imām. Um die gleiche Zeit änderte Aḫū Muḥsin, der an anderer Stelle (ḫiṭaṭ I 395) angibt, zahlreiche ismailitische Bücher gelesen zu haben, die Genealogie der Fatimiden gegenüber seiner Hauptquelle, Ibn Rizām, im gleichen Sinn.

verstorbenen Imams al-Ḥusain gelten ließ. Nach ʿUbaid Allāh hieß der Onkel Muḥammad b. Aḥmad[78]). Er ist hier wohl gemeint. Das würde gut zu dem Eindruck passen, daß das Werk nicht lange vor dem politischen Aufstieg der Fatimiden verfaßt wurde[79]).

Der so vieldeutige Terminus Ḥuǧǧa wird im selben Abschnitt so erklärt: „Durch den Ḥuǧǧa gelangst du in Verbindung zum erhabenen ʿAin, das ist der Imam[80]).“ Mit dem Imam ist aber, wie aus den Angaben über die anderen Prophetenären hervorgeht, der Sprecher, das heißt hier der Mahdi, gemeint[81]). Und in Fortsetzung der Exegese heißt es: „. . . er (Gott) machte den Ḥuǧǧa zum Imam, der das Gesetz erfüllt, und auf den Sprecher hinweist.“ Der Sprecher seinerseits aber „ist ein schweigender Imam, bevor er zum sprechenden Imam wird[82]).“

Was diese geheimnisvolle Erhebung des Ḥuǧǧas in den Rang eines Imams, den der Meister der Sekte nach dem Kommentator zunächst nicht für sich in Anspruch zu nehmen gewagt hatte, für die heilsgeschichtliche Zukunft bedeuten sollte, wird gleich danach bei der Exegese von Koran 9,3 klar. Da heißt es: „Der Gebetsruf deutet auf den, der den Menschen ihre Zeit (für das Gebet) und Gebetsrichtung bekannt macht. Es ist in seiner Zeit der ehrwürdige Imam: Und dieser ist Muḥammad, unser Meister und Herr, der das Schwert führt (al-qāʾim bi's-saif). Er ist der öffentliche Sprecher seines Zeitalters (nāṭiq ʿaṣrihī ẓāhiran) in der wahren Lehre, welcher das Schwert führt zusammen mit der Lehre.“ Der Kommentator meint hierzu: „Diese Beschreibung bezieht sich auf den Imam al-Qāʾim bi-Amr Allāh Muḥammad Abū 'l-Qāsim[83]).“ Dies ist jedoch offensichtlich eine spätere Interpretation. Allem Anschein nach ist ursprünglich jener Meister der Sekte gemeint, den der Kommentator selbst zuvor als den Imam Muḥammad b. Aḥmad identifizierte. Dieser hatte wohl gehofft, noch selbst als der erwartete Imam in Erscheinung treten zu können. Aber

---

[78]) Vgl. unten S. 71. Er ist der Abū' š-Šalaʿlaʿ der Polemiker. Bei Ibn Rizām heißt dieser Aḥmad b. Muḥammad, fihrist S. 265, bei Aḫū Muḥsin Muḥammad b. Aḥmad, ittiʿāẓ S. 13. Der Verfasser des istitār nennt ihn Saʿīd al-Ḫair. Da andererseits ʿUbaid Allāh anfänglich Saʿīd genannt wurde, konnte dies leicht zu ungewollten oder gewollten Verwechslungen führen. Nach Idrīs b. al-Ḥasan hieß Muḥammad b. Aḥmad auch Abū ʿAlī al-Ḥakīm, ʿujūn al-aḫbār V 119.

[79]) Muḥammad b. Aḥmad dürfte nach den Untersuchungen Ivanows, Rise S. 31, um das Jahr 283/896 gestorben sein. [80]) Kitāb al-kašf S. 97.

[81]) Das erhabene ʿAin wird im Folgenden definiert als das „erhabenste Ziel“ (al-ġāja al-ʿuẓmā), als Hinweis auf den Schöpfer, der sich in „seinen Gebetshäusern“ (bujūtuh, Koran 34,36), nämlich den sieben Sprecherpropheten, manifestiert. Kitāb al-kašf S. 102ff. [82]) Kitāb al-kašf S. 99.

[83]) S. 103. Abū 'l-Qāsim ist doch wohl gegen beide Handschriften (Muḥ. b. al-Qāsim, vgl. Vorwort S. 11) zu lesen.

dazu kam es nicht. Darum bezieht der Kommentator die Beschreibung auf den zweiten Fatimidenkalifen, auf den sie im Rückblick besser paßte.

Der im „Gebetsruf" symbolisierte Imam weist die Menschen auf die „größte Wallfahrt" hin[84]), die nunmehr so ausgedeutet wird: „Die größte Wallfahrt, sie ist der heute Schweigende, das heißt der noch nicht erschienen ist, um auf Gottes Befehl zu sprechen. Er ist der siebte Sprecher, seine Zeit ist das Ende der Zeiten. Er ist das erhabenste seiner (Gottes) Mittel (asbāb), das erhabene ʿAin . . ."[85])

Die endzeitliche Erwartung, die sich in der von Saʿd b. ʿAbd Allāh beschriebenen Lehre in der Wiederkehr Muḥammad b. Ismāʿīls, im Kitāb ar-rušd im Auftreten des achten nach den sieben Vollenderimamen als Qā'im oder siebter Sprecher verbildlichte, erhält hier ein neues Gesicht. Sie verwirklicht sich in zwei Stufen. Zunächst — so nahe, daß der Verfasser in der Gegenwartsform spricht — tritt der zum Imam erhobene Ḥuǧǧa mit dem Schwert und der Lehre auf. Er wird schon fast wie der Qā'im selbst beschrieben[86]). Aber doch weist er die Menschen noch auf einen, der nach ihm am Ende der Zeiten kommt, den siebten Sprecher[87]).

Wenn der Meister der Sekte, wie der Kommentator versichert, sich zunächst den Rang eines Ḥuǧǧa gegeben und zur Gefolgschaft des verborgenen Imams aufgefordert hatte, so mußten diese in die verschwommene Sprache der bāṭinitischen Koranauslegung gekleideten Eröffnungen einer schwerwiegenden Veränderung der Lehre gleichkommen. Und wie um seine Thesen zu festigen, kommt der Exeget noch einmal auf den „Gebetsruf" zurück und erklärt: „. . . er ist der Meister der Lehre und verdient, die Stelle Abrahams[88]) einzunehmen." Das aber heißt: „. . . es muß (immer) einen Imam geben, der zur Gefolgschaft des Imams (nach ihm) und des Sprechers aufruft . . . Der 'Gebetsruf' ist gleich dem Imam, der zur Gefolgschaft des Sprechers aufruft und auf ihn hinweist." Der Kommentator erklärt hierzu: „Wie klar ist diese Rede für den, der ein Herz hat. Versteh', Frager, und be-

---

[84]) Vgl. S. 109, 110. [85]) Kitāb al-kašf S. 103.

[86]) *Al-qā'im* bi's-saif . . . *nāṭiq* ʿaṣrih. Vgl. auch die ganz ähnliche Beschreibung des „Imams in jedem Zeitalter" an-nāṭiq bi'l-ḥikma aẓ-ẓāhir bi's-saif (so statt šaraf zu lesen) wa'd-daʿwa, was wieder auf „unsern Meister, den Meister jedes und jeder Gläubigen" bezogen wird. S. 118.

[87]) Dasselbe Bild wird auch an einer Stelle in der dritten Abhandlung entworfen, S. 62: „. . . Der Imam (nämlich der Qā'im) sendet vor sich einen, der das Schwert führt und die Menschen vor seiner Kraft und der Härte seiner Strafe warnt. Dann kommt er, nachdem die Erde für ihn frei gemacht und vorbereitet ist." [88]) Maqām Ibrāhīm, Koran 2, 125.

greife Gottes Absicht in dieser Rede, damit du weißt, daß der Schöpfer in allen Dingen, in ihrem Äußern wie in ihrem Innern, gerecht ist. Denn er hat die Menschen durch den Vorhandenen, und nicht durch den nicht Vorhandenen, gefordert und ihnen einen Gebetsrufer ernannt, der sie zur Erkenntnis Gottes ruft und ihnen sein verborgenes Geheimnis deutet. Wer diesem Gebetsrufer und dem Sprecher Folge leistet, der ist glücklich[89]).“

Mit der Erhebung zum Imam ist der Meister der Sekte auf den höchsten Rang der Hierarchie gerückt. Wohl weist er die Menschen auf den siebten Sprecher hin, aber dieser ist vorläufig „nicht vorhanden“. Das Imamat aber ist eine dauernde Institution, solange die Welt besteht. Es wird verständlich, warum die Zahl der Imame nun keine Rolle mehr spielt.

Fast achtzig Jahre nach der Herrschaftnahme der Fatimiden, dem Ende der „Zeit der Verborgenheit“, verfaßte der Scherif Aḫū Muḥsin seine Schrift gegen die Ismailiten[90]). Sein Anliegen dabei war, wie er am Anfang seines Buches erklärt, „die Sache Ismāʿīl b. Ǧaʿfars ... und seiner Nachkommen aufzuklären, da über seinen Sohn Muḥammad viel geredet, und seiner Nachkommenschaft zugeschrieben wird, wer seiner Familie nicht angehört. Man benützt ihn als ein Tor zu Betrug und List, um Einfluß über die Betrogenen zu gewinnen. Er hat damit aber nichts zu tun[91]).“ Neben einer ausführlichen Geschichte der ismailitischen Bewegung fügte Aḫū Muḥsin seinem Buch auch einen Abriß der Lehre bei[92]).

In der dritten Stufe der Einführung, so berichtet er[93]), versichert der Sendbote seinem Zögling, daß der Schöpfer die Zahl der Imame auf sieben festgelegt hat, so wie er sieben Planeten, sieben Himmel und sieben Erden geschaffen habe. Der siebte von ihnen ist der Qāʾim, der Herr der Zeit, Muḥammad b. Ismāʿīl. Da Aḫū Muḥsin, wie auch Saʿd b. ʿAbd Allāh, Ali als Imam zählt, gerät er in dieselben Schwierigkeiten. Einige von den Bekennern, so meint er, ließen Ismāʿīl b. Ǧaʿfar aus, andere aber zählten auch ihn[94]). Doch trägt der erste Imam jedes Propheten jeweils den Titel sūs[95]). In der vierten Stufe lernt der Neube-

---

[89]) Kitāb al-kašf S. 110f.

[90]) Vgl. Fatimiden und Baḥrainqarmaṭen S. 68f.

[91]) Ibn ad-Dawādārī VI 5.

[92]) Bei an-Nuwairī übersetzt von de Sacy, Exposé, Introd. Ḫiṭaṭ I 391ff., übersetzt von Casanova, La doctrine secrète. [93]) Ḫiṭaṭ I 393.

[94]) In der vierten Stufe geht die Rechnung auf, da hier Muḥammad b. Ismāʿīl erst nach den sieben Schweigern gezählt wird.

[95]) Diese Bezeichnung für den waṣī ist mir in keinem ismailitischen Werk begegnet.

kehrte dann, daß Muḥammad b. Ismā'īl der siebte Sprecherprophet sei, der alle Gesetze, die vor ihm bestanden, aufhebt. Er aber wurde der Erbe des Wissens der Alten (intahā ilaih 'ilm al-awwalīn), er hat den inneren Sinn der Dinge eröffnet.

Am Schluß seiner Ausführungen bezeichnet Aḫū Muḥsin die von ihm dargestellte Lehre als die ursprüngliche der Ismailiten[96]). Die Bewegung habe sich dann in verschiedene Zweige gespalten. „Man änderte besonders die Anschauung über Muḥammad b. Ismā'īl, für den man zunächst Anerkennung als den Imam forderte, und setzte an seine Stelle einen Abkömmling des 'Abd Allāh b. Maimūn al-Qaddāḥ, dessen Nachkommen im Maġrib, Ägypten und Syrien regiert haben[97])." Damit sind die Fatimiden gemeint.

„Ursprünglich war diese abscheuliche Lehre zugunsten des Muḥammad b. Ismā'īl b. Ǧa'far. Man behauptete, er sei der Mahdiimam, der am Ende der Zeit erscheint und dem Recht Geltung verschafft. Ihm gebühre die Huldigung, und der Sendbote nehme sie den Leuten für ihn ab. Was man an Geldern sammle, werde für ihn bewahrt, bis er erscheine. So währte die Lehre zugunsten des Muḥammad b. Ismā'īl, bis Sa'īd, der 'Ubaid Allāh genannt wird, von Salamīja nach dem Maġrib floh, sich den Beinamen al-Mahdī zulegte, selbst der Imam wurde, und seine Genealogie auf Ismā'īl b. Ǧa'far zurückführte. Da stellten sie die Propaganda auf ihn um . . ."[98])

An anderer Stelle berichtet Aḫū Muḥsin über die Vorgänge, die zum Abfall Ḥamdān Qarmaṭs führten: „Qarmaṭ korrespondierte mit den Verführern in Salamīja. Als derjenige seiner Zeit gestorben war, und sein Sohn den Platz nach ihm einnahm, schrieb er einen Brief an Ḥamdān Qarmaṭ. Als der Brief bei ihm eintraf, und er ihn las, mißbilligte er etwas in ihm und fand darin Ausdrücke, die anders waren als bisher, und etwas, das der früheren Anordnung nicht entsprach. Da geriet er in Zweifel und argwöhnte, daß etwas vorgefallen sei. Qarmaṭ befahl nun Ibn Māliḥ, einem seiner Sendboten, auszugehen und die Sache zu erkunden. Dieser weigerte sich aber und entschuldigte sich. Da sandte er jemanden, um den Sendboten 'Abdān aus seinem Gebiet zu holen. Als er eingetroffen war, schickte er ihn fort, damit er in Er-

---

[96]) Wenn das auf die Imamatslehre weitgehend zutrifft, so muß es wahrscheinlich in anderer Hinsicht eingeschränkt werden: Die philosophischen Spekulationen, von denen in Stufe sechs bis neun die Rede ist, stammen wohl aus späterer Zeit. Vgl. S. M. Stern, Art. Abū Ya'qūb al-Sidjzī in EI².

[97]) Fatimiden und Baḥrainqarmaṭen S. 69.

[98]) An-Nuwairī, Ms. Paris 1576, fol. 58. Vgl. itti'āẓ S. 106, wo die hier als ursprünglich bezeichnete Lehre ausdrücklich als die von Ḥamdān Qarmaṭ verbreitete geschildert wird.

fahrung bringe, was sich in dieser Angelegenheit ereignet habe, und den Grund für die Änderung erkunde. ʿAbdān machte sich darum auf den Weg, und als er ankam, erfuhr er von dem Tod des Verführers, mit dem sie in Briefwechsel gestanden hatten. Er traf sich mit dem Sohn und fragte ihn nach dem Ḥuǧǧa, und wer der Imam nach ihm sei, zu dessen Gefolgschaft er aufrufe. Da fragte der Sohn: 'Und wer ist der Imam?' ʿAbdān sprach: 'Muḥammad b. Ismāʿīl b. Ǧaʿfar, der Herr der Zeit, zu dessen Gefolgschaft dein Vater aufgerufen hat und dessen Ḥuǧǧa er war.' Da leugnete er dies und sagte: 'Muḥammad b. Ismāʿīl gibt es gar nicht (lā aṣl lah). Niemand war der Imam außer meinem Vater, der ein Nachkomme des Maimūn b. Daiṣān ist, und ich nehme seinen Platz ein.' Da begriff ʿAbdān die Geschichte. Er ging der Sache auf den Grund und erfuhr, daß Muḥammad b. Ismāʿīl in Wirklichkeit gar nichts mit dieser Affäre zu schaffen habe, daß man vielmehr die Leute mit ihm hinters Licht führe; und daß jener gar nicht ein Nachkomme des ʿAqīl b. Abī Ṭālib sei[99]). ʿAbdān kehrte darauf zu Qarmaṭ zurück und berichtete ihm. Da ließ Qarmaṭ die Sendboten versammeln und teilte ihnen den Sachverhalt und was man erfahren hatte mit. Er befahl, die Propaganda abzubrechen, und ʿAbdān führte das aus. Die Mission wurde in ihrem Gebiet abgebrochen. Es war ihnen aber nicht möglich, sie auch außerhalb desselben abzubrechen. Sie hatte sich nämlich auch in den anderen Ländern ausgebreitet ...“[100])

Diese Darstellung geht zweifellos auf einen qarmaṭischen Bericht zurück[101]). Aḫū Muḥsin und seine Quelle, Ibn Rizām, geben vor, genau über Genealogie und Geschichte der Herren in Salamīja Bescheid zu wissen. Hätten sie den Bericht nach eigenem Ermessen zurechtgemacht, so dürften doch wenigstens die Namen nicht fehlen. Auch wäre ihnen kaum der Fehler unterlaufen, von Vater und Sohn zu sprechen. Nach ihren eigenen Abgaben muß es doch der Onkel ʿUbaid Allāhs gewesen sein, der vor ihm Großmeister war und nun starb. Der Berichterstatter aber, der aus dem Lager Qarmaṭs für die Schilderung des Hergangs durchaus unnötige Einzelheiten beifügt, weiß davon nichts: Eine Folge der strengen Geheimhaltung, mit der sich die Meister der Bewegung aus Vorsicht umgaben. In den vorfatimidischen ismailitischen Werken werden ihre Namen grundsätzlich nicht genannt. Hier wird nicht einmal einem Sendboten von so hohem Rang

---

[99]) Auf ihn sollen die Vorfahren der Fatimiden zunächst ihren Stammbaum zurückgeführt haben. Vgl. ittiʿāẓ S. 12.

[100]) An-Nuwairī fol. 59. Gekürzt ittiʿāẓ S. 114.

[101]) Vgl. Fatimiden und Baḥrainqarmaṭen S. 59 Anm. 1.

wie Ḥamdān Qarmaṭ vom Tod des Oberhauptes Mitteilung gemacht. ʿAbdān erfährt davon erst nach seinem Eintreffen in Salamīja[102]).

Die Veränderungen der Lehre, die Aḫū Muḥsin aufzuzeigen sucht, entsprechen wesentlich dem, was wir den vorfatimidischen Quellen entnehmen konnten. Die ursprüngliche Lehre vom Imamat, die er beschreibt, stimmt nahezu vollkommen mit der von Saʿd b. ʿAbd Allāh den Qarmaṭen zugeschriebenen überein. Hier wie dort ist der siebte Imam, Muḥammad b. Ismāʿīl, der erwartete Qāʾim. Er wird im Kitāb ar-rušd durch den achten Imam, und im Kitāb al-kašf, in Übereinstimmung mit den Angaben Aḫū Muḥsins, durch den Meister der Sekte ersetzt. Dieser hatte sich bisher als Ḥuǧǧa bezeichnet, der die Menschen zum Gehorsam des noch verborgenen Imams aufruft.

Um das Wesen dieser Veränderung zu verstehen, bedarf es einer Untersuchung der Bedeutung des Wortes Ḥuǧǧa und seiner Rolle in der Entwicklung der Lehre. Das Wort bedeutet eigentlich Argument, Beweis, oder Zeugnis. In diesem Sinne heißt es im Koran: „Gottes ist das endgültige Argument[103]).“ Die Schiiten, die den Koran so gründlich nach Beweisen für ihre Theorie vom Imamat durchforschten, zogen das Wort schon mindestens seit Ǧaʿfar aṣ-Ṣādiq für ihre Zwecke heran und personifizierten es. Sie erklärten, die Welt könne zu keiner Zeit ohne ein Zeugnis Gottes sein. Das Zeugnis Gottes ist aber, in Abwesenheit des Propheten, der Imam[104]). Die Zwölferschiiten gebrauchten den Ausdruck Ḥuǧǧa in der Bedeutung von Imam[105]).

Auch die Ismailiten benutzten das Wort in diesem ursprünglichen Sinn. So heißt es im Kitāb al-kašf: „In jedem Zeitalter gibt es einen Ḥuǧǧa Gottes, sei er Prophet, Gesandter (mursal) oder Imam[106]).“ So wird auch Mohammed als Ḥuǧǧa Gottes bezeichnet[107]). Aber vor allem stellte der Ḥuǧǧa in den ismailitischen Texten einen Rang in der

102) Dies wirft Zweifel auf die Richtigkeit der Angabe der sīrat Ǧaʿfar, S. 109, daß der alte Imam allen Sendboten die Nachfolge ʿUbaid Allāhs vor seinem Tod mitgeteilt habe und sie den Treueid auf ihn schwören ließ. Daß der qarmaṭischen Darstellung hier eher zu trauen ist, zeigt sich gerade auch darin, daß nach ihr ʿUbaid Allāh sich als Sohn seines Vorgängers ausgab. Da das Imamat nach der ismailitischen Theorie nur in direkter Deszendenz vererbt werden konnte, hatte ʿUbaid Allāh guten Grund, zu verheimlichen, daß jener sein Onkel war.

103) Koran 6, 149: li'llāhi'l-ḥuǧǧatu'l-bāliġa.

104) Gegen diese Imamatslehre polemisiert der Zaidit al-Qāsim b. Ibrāhīm (gest. 246/860) in seinen beiden Streitschriften gegen die Rāfiḍa. Das sind bei ihm die Anhängerschaft Ǧaʿfar aṣ-Ṣādiqs und alle aus ihr hervorgegangenen Gruppen. Ms. Berlin Glaser 101 fol. 104ff., fol. 111ff.

105) Ivanow, Studies S. 17, Hodgson, How did the early Shīʿa become sectarian S. 13.

106) Kitāb al-kašf S. 12. 107) Kitāb al-kašf S. 60.

Hierarchie der religiösen Würdenträger dar. Dann wird er in Verbindung mit den zwölf Provinzen (ǧazā'ir) gebracht, in die die Welt sich aufteilt: In jeder Provinz gibt es einen Ḥuǧǧa[108]). In der Stufenleiter der Ränge folgt er, jedenfalls in den älteren Systemen, unmittelbar dem Imam. Das deutet auf die Ableitung der neuen Bedeutung aus der älteren: Wenn die Welt zu keiner Zeit ohne „Zeugnis" Gottes sein konnte, so mußte in der Zeit der Verborgenheit des Imams dessen Vertreter Gottes Willen manifestieren. Hierauf gibt ein Ausspruch des Imams al-Mu'izz einen Hinweis: „Der Ḥuǧǧa vertritt den Imam. Wenn er (der Imam) verborgen ist, so handelt er als sein Vertreter und nimmt seine Stellung ein[109])." Und aš-Šahrastānī schreibt den Ismailiten die Lehre zu: „Wenn der Imam sichtbar ist, so mag sein Ḥuǧǧa verborgen sein. Wenn der Imam verborgen ist, so müssen sein Ḥuǧǧa und seine Sendboten sichtbar sein[110])."

In dritter Bedeutung steht Ḥuǧǧa für den ernannten Nachfolger des Sprechers oder Imams vor dessen Tod. So ist Ali der Ḥuǧǧa Mohammeds zu dessen Lebzeiten und der Imam derjenigen, die den Propheten überlebten[111]). Der Imam ist ein Ḥuǧǧa, bevor er Imam wird, und der Ḥuǧǧa wird Imam nach seinem Imam, weiß das Kitāb ar-rušd[112]). Nach dem Kitāb al-kašf ist es der „größte Huǧǧa (al-ḥuǧǧa al-kubrā), der in den Rang des Imamats nach dem Imam seiner Zeit nachfolgt[113])." Und Ǧa'far b. Manṣūr al-Jaman erklärt, es gäbe in jeder Ära sieben große Ḥuǧǧas, die nach dem Tod ihres Imams an seine Stelle treten[114]).

Vielleicht gehört dieser letzte Teil der Lehre schon zu den „Veränderungen" des Dogmas, welche Ḥamdān Qarmaṭ und seine Anhänger ablehnten. In der Darstellung Sa'd b. 'Abd Allāhs und Aḇū Muḥsins findet sich jedenfalls keine Andeutung davon[115]). Um so bestimmter

---

[108]) So schon bei Sa'd b. 'Abd Allāh S. 63.

[109]) Ta'wīl aš-šarī'a in maḏhab S. 309.

[110]) Aš-Šahrastānī II 28.

[111]) Kitāb al-kašf S. 55, 60.

[112]) Kitāb ar-rušd S. 201. [113]) Kitāb al-kašf S. 119.

[114]) Kitāb al-farā'iḍ wa-ḥudūd ad-dīn, Ms. der Muḥammadī Hamdānī Sammlung S. 52. Abū Ja'qūb as-Siǧistānī meint in seiner wohl späten Abhandlung tuḥfat al-mustaǧībīn, es gäbe in jeder der sieben Regionen (aqālīm) einen Ḥuǧǧa, während in den zwölf Provinzen (ǧazā'ir) je ein lāḥiq residiere. Lāḥiq wird in der frühen persischen Schule für den Ḥuǧǧa gebraucht, vgl. Ivanow, Studies S. 19. Abū Ja'qūb erklärt zunächst, die beiden Ausdrücke seien gleichbedeutend. Die sieben Ḥuǧǧas, die er dann neben die zwölf lāḥiqs stellt, sind wie diese für ihn örtliche Vertreter der Imame, nicht Nachfolger.

[115]) Nach Sa'd b. 'Abd Allāh erklärten die Qarmaṭen, daß Mohammed, nachdem er das Gesandtenamt an Ali abgetreten hatte, durch ihn „bezeugt" wurde,

sind die Angaben des Kitāb ar-rušd und des Kitāb al-kašf. Nach dem Kitāb al-kašf gehören vier Rangstufen der Hierarchie dem Haus des Propheten an: Sprecher, Vollstrecker, Imam und Ḥuǧǧa. Drei gehören ihm nicht an: Bāb, Dā'ī und Mu'min[116]).

Immerhin läßt die Herkunft der Bezeichnung Ḥuǧǧa als dem notwendigen „Zeugnis" Gottes auf Erden erkennen, daß dessen religiöser Rang weit über den eines obersten Provinzsendboten hinausging, als der er nach der Darstellung Sa'd b. 'Abd Allāhs und Aḇū Muḥsins erscheinen möchte. Vielmehr war er, in Abwesenheit des Imams, von Anfang an dessen vollberechtigter Statthalter und letzte religiöse Autorität[117]). Das nimmt der schwerwiegenden Reform der verborgenen Meister etwas von ihrem revolutionären Charakter und macht erklär-

---

S. 62: an-nabī ... kāna ... maḥǧūǧan bih. Diese Vorstellung ist aber wohl eher auf die erste als auf die dritte Wortbedeutung zurückzuführen.

[116]) Kitāb al-kašf S. 133f. Damit wird ein dem Ǧa'far aṣ-Ṣādiq zugeschriebener Ausspruch gedeutet: „Diese Angelegenheit gründet sich auf sieben: vier von uns und drei nicht von uns." Dies Wort spielte in dem Streit über die Genealogie und Vorgeschichte der Fatimiden eine Rolle, vgl. unten S. 111f. Die Zahlen vier und drei erscheinen hier gegenüber der sonst überlieferten Form des Ausspruchs vertauscht.

[117]) Versucht man, aus der Entwicklung des Ḥuǧǧa-Begriffs bei den Ismailiten auf die Frühgeschichte der Bewegung zurückzuschließen, so wäre anzunehmen, daß die Leitung in Abwesenheit des Imams zunächst in den Händen einer Gruppe lag, deren Mitglieder offenbar an verschiedenen Orten residierten. Ihre Zwölfzahl ist dabei wohl nur ideal anzusehen. Später hätte sich einer der Ḥuǧǧas, vielleicht schon von Anfang an primus inter pares, als alleiniger Meister durchgesetzt. Aus dem Bericht über die Unterredung 'Abdāns in Salamīja gewinnt man den Eindruck, daß es nur noch einen Ḥuǧǧa gab. Die höchsten Sendboten, wie Ibn Ḥaušab im Jemen und Abū 'Abd Allāh im Maġrib, werden nicht als Ḥuǧǧas bezeichnet. Wohl zu Recht bezieht daher Gateau, Sur un dinar Fatimide, Hesperis 1945, das (balaġat ḥuggat Allāh), das Abū 'Abd Allāh auf seine Dinare prägen ließ, auf 'Ubaid Allāh.

In fatimidischer Zeit läßt sich ein bestimmtes Ḥuǧǧaamt nicht feststellen. Den ersten Rang in der Propagandaorganisation nimmt seit al-Ḥākim der dā'ī ad-du'āt ein, vgl. A. M. Magued: Institutions et Cérémonial des Fatimides en Egypte, Kairo 1953—54, I 182. Magueds Angabe, daß der oberste dā'ī vorher, in der Zeit des Erscheinens der Imame, Ḥuǧǧa, in der Zeit der Verborgenheit, ḥāǧib (gemeint ist wohl ḥiǧāb) hieß, ist nicht begründet. Wenn später Ḥamīd ad-Dīn al-Kirmānī häufig ḥuǧǧat al-'irāqain genannt wird, so ist das mit Ivanow, Naṣir-i Khusraw and Ismailism, Bombay 1948, S. 44, als ehrender Beinamen, nicht als Amtsbezeichnung aufzufassen. Ähnliches gilt für die Bezeichnung Naṣir-ī Ḫusraus als Ḥuǧǧa von Ḫurāsān. In der Liste der „zwölf Provinzen", die Ivanow, Rise S. 20 Anm. 1, nach 'Alī b. al-Ḥusain b. al-Walīd (gest. 554/1159) anführt, finden sich die beiden genannten bezeichnenderweise nicht. Die Liste stimmt fast völlig mit der überein, die Ǧa'far b. Manṣūr al-Jaman in seinem Kitāb al-adilla wa'š-šawāhid gibt, zitiert am Ende des Kitāb

lich, warum sie nicht auf allgemeineren Widerstand unter den Anhängern stieß.

Auch in anderer Hinsicht gibt die Darstellung Aḫū Muḥsins Anlaß zu Kritik. Es klingt kaum überzeugend, wenn ʿUbaid Allāh damals ʿAbdān persönlich verkündet haben soll, er sei ein Nachkomme des „Maimūn b. Daiṣān". Zu deutlich läßt sich hier Aḫū Muḥsin vom Angeklagten selbst die These bestätigen, um deretwillen er sein Buch ver-

---

al-farāʾiḍ wa-ḥudūd ad-dīn S. 184. Nur anstelle der Dailam nennt Ǧaʿfar die Nubier. Aber die Listen selbst sind gewiß als reine Spekulation ohne praktische Bedeutung anzusehen.

Bei dem neuerlichen Verschwinden des rechtmäßigen Imams in spätfatimidischer Zeit mußte das Bedürfnis nach einem Ḥuǧǧa wiederaufleben. So widmete der jemenitische Sendbote al-Ḫaṭṭāb b. al-Ḥasan(gest. 533/1138) das erste Kapitel seiner Schrift ġājat al-mawālīd, in der er sich mit den Folgen des kurz vorhergegangenen Verschwindens des Imams aṭ-Ṭajjib auseinandersetzte, dem „Nachweis der Ḥuǧǧas in den zwölf Provinzen". Er erklärte die Königin des Ṣulaiḥidengeschlechts al-Malika al-Ḥurra zum derzeitigen Ḥuǧǧa des Jemens. Vgl. Rise S. 20f. Später gab es den Ḥuǧǧa in der jemenitischen Hierarchie anscheinend nicht mehr, vgl. Zahid Ali, maḏhab S. 109f. Unter den Anhängern des Imamats Nizārs nahm nach dessen „Verschwinden" Ḥasan-ī Ṣabbāḥ den Titel Ḥuǧǧa für sich in Anspruch. Vgl. Ḥātim b. ʿImrān, Risālat al-uṣūl, in ḫams rasāʾil ismāʿīlīja, S. 100, Hodgson, The Order of Assassins, Haag 1955, S. 67f.

In der dritten Bedeutung wird das Wort Ḥuǧǧa in einer Legende gebraucht, die offenbar die Nachfolge des dritten Fatimiden, al-Manṣūr, legitimieren soll. Ǧūḏar berichtet, Abū 'l-Qāsim al-Qāʾim habe ihm beim Begräbnis ʿUbaid Allāhs erklärt: „Es ist dem Ḥuǧǧa nach dem (Tod des) Imams nicht gestattet, den Imam zu begraben, bevor er einen Ḥuǧǧa für sich ernannt hat." Darauf teilte er ihm insgeheim mit, daß er seinen Sohn Ismāʿīl (al-Manṣūr) zu seinem Ḥuǧǧa und Thronfolger ernenne. Sīrat al-ustāḏ Ǧūḏar, Ed. M. K. Husain und M. A. Šuʿaira, Kairo 1954, S. 39f. Nach Qāḍī an-Nuʿmān versicherte dagegen al-Manṣūr selbst, sein Vater habe ihn unmittelbar nach dem Tod ʿUbaid Allāhs zum Nachfolger ernannt. Niemand außer al-Manṣūr sei darin eingeweiht worden. Vgl. sīrat Ǧūḏar S. 156 Anm. 28. Nach ʿAbd al-Ǧabbār, fol. 254r, hatte Abū 'l-Qāsim seinen Sohn (al-)Qāsim, der sich in Bildung und Rittertum auszeichnete, zunächst zu seinem Nachfolger ernannt. Er starb jedoch vor dem Vater. In al-Qairawān spottete man über diese falsche Voraussage. Al-Muʿizz erwähnt in einem Brief an Ǧūḏar, Qāsim habe ein Zerwürfnis zwischen ʿUbaid Allāh und Abū'l-Qāsim verursacht, sīrat Ǧūḏar S. 115. Dies bezieht sich wahrscheinlich darauf, daß Qāsim im Jahr 316/928 seinem Vater hinterbrachte, ʿUbaid Allāh wolle Abū'l-Qāsims Bruder Abū ʿAlī Aḥmad an seiner Stelle zum Thronfolger ernennen. Abū'l-Qāsim soll deshalb einen Feldzug vorzeitig abgebrochen haben. Vgl. bajān I 193, sīrat Ǧūḏar S. 171, M. Canard, Vie de l'Ustadh Jaudhar, Algier 1958, S. 174 Anm. 391. Al-Muʿizz fügt in seinem Brief hinzu, großes Unheil sei aus dem Zerwürfnis entstanden und Qāsim deshalb „entfernt geblieben" (baqija bi-maʿzil). Das scheint zu bestätigen, daß er als Nachfolger vorgesehen war.

faßte[118]). Zwar erklärte ʿUbaid Allāh tatsächlich, wie sich noch zeigen wird, Nachkomme eines Maimūn zu sein, aber nach ihm war dies der Deckname eines Imams aus dem Hause des Propheten[119]). Auch dürfte die Veränderung des Dogmas nicht so plötzlich vorgenommen worden sein, wie es bei Aḫū Muḥsin geschildert wird. Wenn unsere Interpretation des Kitāb al-kašf richtig war, so wurden schon unter jenem Muḥammad b. Aḥmad, dessen Nachfolge ʿUbaid Allāh damals antrat, Lehren verbreitet, die nach Auffassung der Qarmaṭen häretisch sein mußten.

Diese Unstimmigkeiten berühren aber kaum die grundlegende Richtigkeit der Darstellung. Die Beziehungen zwischen Ḥamdān Qarmaṭ und Salamīja scheinen schon vor dem Bruch nicht sehr eng gewesen zu sein, wie der Bericht selbst zeigt. Offenbar bestanden viel engere Bande zwischen den Meistern und anderen Gemeinden, wie der im Jemen. Ḥamdān Qarmaṭ hatte seinen eigenen Missionsmeister in ʿAbdān, der wohl weitgehende Freiheit in Ausbildung und Verbreitung der Lehre genoß und eigene Bücher verfaßte. Unter diesen Umständen ist es durchaus verständlich, wenn offensichtlich schon einige Zeit zwischen der Lehre Salamījas und der ʿAbdāns gewisse Differenzen bestanden. Saʿd b. ʿAbd Allāh kennt, obwohl seine Darstellung die gesamte Bewegung meint, nur ihren Führer Qarmaṭawaih[120]) und weiß nichts von den Meistern in Salamīja oder ihrer Stellung. Sein Bild der Lehre entspricht mehr den Anschauungen, die die Qarmaṭen im Iraq vertreten haben müssen, als denen des Kitāb ar-rušd und des Kitāb al-kašf. Trotzdem erkannte Ḥamdān Qarmaṭ die Meister in Salamīja in ihrer Stellung als Ḥuǧǧas, nicht als Imame, an, bis ʿUbaid Allāh dann offen das Imamat des Muḥammad b. Ismāʿīl leugnete und es für sich selbst in Anspruch nahm. Den besten Beweis dafür, daß die Fatimiden es waren, die die Lehre veränderten, bietet aber die fatimidische Literatur selbst.

## ʿUbaid Allāhs Reform der Lehre

Als ʿUbaid Allāh nach seinem triumphalen Einzug in Raqqāda im Jahr 297/910 den Namen al-Mahdī annahm, lag darin nicht nur der Anspruch auf einen Herrschernamen, wie er unter den Abbasiden zu den festen Insignien des Kalifenamtes gehörte. Es lag darin auch der Anspruch auf die politisch-religiöse Stellung des erwarteten Mahdi. Sein Wegbereiter Abū ʿAbd Allāh aš-Šīʿī hatte dem Berberstamm der

[118]) Vgl. oben S. 58.
[119]) Vgl. unten S. 71.
[120]) Vgl. Fatimiden und Baḥrainqarmaṭen S. 45 Anm. 3.

Kutāma das nahe bevorstehende Erscheinen des Mahdi angekündigt und von ihm behauptet, er werde die Toten zum Leben erwecken, die Sonne zurückdrehen und die ganze Welt beherrschen[121]). Als er dann ʿUbaid Allāh aus seiner Haft in Siǧilmāsa befreit hatte, konnte er seinen Anhängern erklären: „Dies ist mein und euer Herr, euer Gebieter und Imam der rechten Leitung. Er ist der von euch erwartete Mahdi, von dem ich gekündigt habe[122]).“

Aber schon vor Ablauf eines Jahres kamen Abū ʿAbd Allāh Zweifel an der Rechtmäßigkeit seines Meisters, und er begann, unter den Anführern der Kutāma Stimmung gegen ihn zu machen. ʿUbaid Allāh erfuhr jedoch von seinem Verrat und ließ ihn ermorden. Kurz danach, Ende Šaʿbān oder Anfang Ramaḍān 299/Apr.—Anf. Mai 912, ernannte er seinen Sohn Abū 'l-Qāsim, dem er schon bei seinem Einzug in Raqqāda einen eigenen Palast zugewiesen hatte[123]), zum Thronfolger[124]). Nach dem Kitāb al-ʿujūn gab er ihm damals den Namen al-Qā'im und ließ die Briefe in seinem Namen senden[125]). Dazu berichtet ein anderer Chronist: „Abū 'l-Qāsim ritt in den Tagen seines Vaters mit dem Sonnenschirm[126]). In seinem Namen wurden die Briefe und Urkunden gesandt. Die Gesuche wurden zu ihm eingereicht, und die Gesandtschaften suchten ihn auf[127]).“ „al-Qā'im leitete zu Lebzeiten ʿUbaid Allāhs die Regierung und die Glaubenspropaganda,“ erklärt Ibn al-Abbār[127a]).

In der alten Lehre waren die Bezeichnungen Mahdi und Qā'im gleichmäßig für den Erwarteten gebraucht worden. Außer dem Beinamen al-Qā'im trug der neuernannte Thronfolger aber auch noch den Namen des Propheten: Abū 'l-Qāsim Muḥammad b. ʿAbd Allāh[128]), wie dies alte Traditionen vom Mahdi geweissagt hatten. Das zeigt gerade die religiöse Bedeutung der Ernennung. Offenbar erkannte ʿUbaid

---

[121]) Ittiʿāẓ S. 34.

[122]) An-Nuʿmān b. Muḥammad, iftitāḥ ad-daʿwa, Ms. der Muḥammadī Hamdānī Sammlung S. 240. [123]) Bajān I 158.

[124]) Ibn al-Aṯīr VIII 41, ittiʿāẓ S. 41, al-Maqrīzī, al-muqaffā, übers. von Fagnan, Centenario della Nascita de Michele Amari, Palermo 1910, S. 41.

[125]) Kitāb al-ʿujūn, Ms. Berlin Wetzstein II 342, fol 80 v: ʿahada'l-Mahdī ilā'bnihī Abī'l-Qāsim wa-sammāhū'l-Qā'im wa-aǧrā kutubahū bi'smih ... Ähnlich iftitāḥ ad-daʿwa S. 271.

[126]) Das gehörte zum offiziellen Zeremoniell des fatimidischen Kalifats.

[127]) Ibn Ḥammādū S. 14. Vgl. bajān I 208.

[127a]) Ibn al-Abbār, al-ḥulla as-sijarā', in M. J. Müller, Beiträge zur Geschichte der westlichen Araber, München 1866—1878, S. 289.

[128]) ʿAbd Allāh statt ʿUbaid Allāh schreiben die Ismailiten durchweg. Auch auf seinen Münzen heißt er ʿAbd Allāh, vgl. Gateau, Sur un Dinar Fatimide, Anm. 22.

Allāh, daß er die Erwartungen, die seine Anhänger in ihn gesetzt hatten, nicht erfüllen konnte, und hoffte, Abū 'l-Qāsim werde dazu in irgendeiner Weise besser in der Lage sein. Die religiöse Propaganda wurde nun ganz auf Abū 'l-Qāsim ausgerichtet, und ihre Organisation ihm übertragen. In dem Bericht des Kitāb al-ʿujūn über den falschen Mahdi, den die Anführer der Kutāma kurz nach der Ernennung anerkannten, heißt es, daß sie Sendboten für ihn aufstellten gleich denen *Abū 'l-Qāsims*[129]). In einem Gedicht, das Abū'l-Qāsim während seines zweiten Feldzuges nach Ägypten (307-309/919-921) an die ägyptische Bevölkerung richtete, forderte er zu seinem Gehorsam auf, ohne auf ʿUbaid Allāh hinzuweisen[129a]). Ein Schiit aus Šīrāz, der im Jahre 315/927, also zu Lebzeiten ʿUbaid Allāhs, in Bagdad wegen verräterischer Korrespondenz mit Abū Ṭāhir angeklagt war, erklärte: „Unser Imam ist der Mahdi *Muḥammad*, Urenkel des Muḥammad b. Ismāʿīl b. Ǧaʿfar aṣ-Ṣādiq, der im Maġrib residiert[130])." Abū Ḥātim ar-Rāzī, der selbst im Todesjahr ʿUbaid Allāhs (322/934) starb, soll sein Kitāb az-zīna dem Imam al-Qā'im vorgelegt haben[131]). Der Kommentator des Kitāb al-kašf bezog die Ankündigung des „Sprechers seines Zeitalters" auf den Imam al-Qā'im bi-Amr Allāh Muḥammad Abū 'l- Qāsim[132]).

Als Versuche, die Hintergründe dieser bedeutsamen Erhebung des Thronfolgers zu erhellen, erscheinen gewisse Aussagen der antiismailitischen Polemiker. Ibn Rizām weiß zu berichten, Saʿīd b. al-Ḥusain, wie ʿUbaid Allāh bei ihm heißt, habe zunächst sich selbst als fatimidischen Aliden ausgegeben. Als ihm das nach seiner Ankunft im

[129]) Kitāb al-ʿujūn fol. 80 v.

[129a]) Vgl. ʿArīb S. 80ff. Nach Ibn al-Abbār sandte er das Gedicht an die Einwohner von Mekka, al-ḥulla as-sijarā' S. 268. Auch aṣ-Ṣūlī berichtet, Abū'l-Qāsim habe an die Einwohner von Mekka geschrieben und sie zu seinem Gehorsam aufgefordert, vgl. ʿArīb S. 84.

[130]) Ibn al-Aṯīr VIII 127 nach Ṯābit b. Sinān, vgl. Origins S. 80. De Goeje, Carmathes S. 162 Anm. 4, bemerkt dazu: „. . . Il se peut pourtant qu'Obaidallah ait donné son fils el Caim . . . pour le véritable Maitre de l'époque."

[131]) Ivanow, A creed of the Fatimids, Bombay 1936, S. 5f. nach ʿujūn al-aḫbar. Ivanow folgert, es müsse bald nach Abū'l-Qāsims Thronfolge geschehen sein. Dazu vgl. A. H. al-Hamdani, Actes du XXIe Congrès international des Orientalistes, S. 293, und Abū Ḥātim ar-Rāzī, Kitāb az-zīna, Ed. H. F. al-Hamdani, Kairo 1957, Einl. S. 24. A. H. al-Hamdani hält das Werk für älter. Seine Annahme, das Kitāb az-zīna sei Quelle Saʿd b. ʿAbd Allāhs (oder an-Naubaḫtīs), erscheint freilich kaum haltbar. Die größere Ausführlichkeit der Darstellung Saʿds wie auch die Anzeichen für ein höheres Alter seines Werks, als al-Hamdani ansetzt (Anfang 4. Jh. H.), weisen eher auf eine Abhängigkeit in umgekehrter Richtung hin.

[132]) Oben S. 56. Der Kommentar dürfte allerdings erst nach dem Tode ʿUbaid Allāhs verfaßt sein.

Maġrib nicht geglaubt wurde, habe er einen jungen Mann vorgestellt und behauptet, dieser sei ein Nachkomme des Muḥammad b. Ismāʿīl. Es war al-Ḥasan Abū 'l-Qāsim, der zweite Fatimidenkalif[133]). Nach Ibn Rizāms Darstellung erscheint Abū 'l-Qāsim nicht als Sohn ʿUbaid Allāhs[134]). Etwas abweichend schreibt Aḫū Muḥsin: ,,Saʿīd sagte von Muḥammad (Abū 'l-Qāsim), er sei ein Pflegesohn unter seiner Obhut (rabīb fī ḥiǧrih) und ein Nachkomme des Muḥammad b. Ismāʿīl b. Ǧaʿfar. Der Grund dafür war die Schwäche seiner Lage am Anfang. Darum wird Muḥammad b. ʿUbaid Allāh 'der Waisenknabe des Lehrers' genannt[135])." Am ausführlichsten ist die Darstellung ʿAbd al-Ǧabbārs[136]). Auch nach ihm hieß ʿUbaid Allāh ursprünglich Saʿīd. In Siǧilmāsa, also noch bevor er an die Macht gelangte, nahm er den Namen Abū Muḥammad ʿUbaid Allāh an und behauptete, aus einer begüterten Familie in al-Ahwāz zu stammen. Von seinem Sohn ʿAbd ar-Raḥmān[137]) sagte er denjenigen, denen er traute, er sei ein Waisenknabe unter seinem Schutz aus der Nachkommenschaft des Ismāʿīl b. Ǧaʿfar aṣ-Ṣādiq. Er nannte ihn damals al-Ḥasan. Als ʿUbaid Allāh dann an die Herrschaft gelangte, erklärte er, jener sei Alide und sein Sohn. Er nannte ihn nun Abū 'l-Qāsim Muḥammad[138]).

Unabhängig von diesen Quellen berichtet der Cordovaner Geschichtsschreiber Aḥmad b. Muḥammad ar-Rāzī (gest. 344/955), manche Leute sähen Abū'l-Qāsim als ʿAbd ar-Raḥmān, den Sohn ʿUbaid Allāhs an, andere aber als Muḥammad, seinen Pflegesohn. Es werde gesagt, ʿUbaid Allāh sei ein Nachkomme al-Ḥasan b. ʿAlīs, Abū'l-Qāsim stamme dagegen von al-Ḥusain b. ʿAlī über Ismāʿīl b. Ǧaʿfar ab[138a]).

---

[133]) Fihrist S. 265.

[134]) Vgl. Stern, Heterodox Ismailism at the time of al-Muʿizz, BSOAS XVII S. 21 Anm. 1. [135]) Ittiʿāẓ S. 14.

[136]) ʿAbd al-Ǧabbār fol. 252r, 254r, und Zitat bei Abū'l-Maḥāsin II 446.

[137]) So wird Abū'l-Qāsim auch von den Chronisten al-Kindī, S. 277, und ʿAbd Allāh b. Aḥmad al-Farġānī, vgl. Wüstenfeld, Fatimiden S. 4, genannt.

[138]) Damit steht ʿAbd al-Ǧabbārs eigene Behauptung in Widerspruch, Abū 'l-Qāsim habe den al-balāġ al-akbar zu Lebzeiten seines Vaters an Abū Ṭāhir gesandt, da sein Vater ihn als alidischen Waisenknaben bezeichnete, vgl. Fatimiden und Baḥrainqarmaṭen S. 71. Abū Ṭāhir gelangte keinesfalls vor 305/917—918 an die Herrschaft. ʿAbd al-Ǧabbār ergänzt hier in seinem Eifer wohl, wie auch sonst nicht selten, seine Quellen aus eigener Phantasie.

[138a]) Vgl. al-ḥulla as-sijarāʾ S. 279. Aḥmad b. Muḥammad ist wohl eher mit dem von Ibn al-Abbār zitierten ar-Rāzī gemeint als sein Sohn ʿĪsā (gest. 379/989). Die Zitate aus Abū Bakr al-Bāqillānī und Ibn Abī Ṭāhir (ʿUbaid Allāh b. Aḥmad b. Ṭaifūr), die zwischen den beiden Zitaten aus ar-Rāzī (S. 278 und 279) eingeschoben sind, stammen nicht aus seinem Werk.

Die widersprechenden Darlegungen der antiismailitischen Polemiker stimmen darin überein, daß sie das Motiv für ʿUbaid Allāhs Erklärungen zugunsten Abū ʾl-Qāsims in wirklichen oder befürchteten Zweifeln an der Echtheit der zeitweise von ihm selbst beanspruchten alidischen Abstammung suchen. Tatsächlich ist der Streit um die Genealogie ʿUbaid Allāhs seit dem Abfall Ḥamdān Qarmaṭs und ʿAbdāns bis heute nicht abgebrochen. Zahllos sind die Varianten, in denen sie entweder auf Ali oder auf jenen Maimūn zurückgeführt wird, der schon in der folgenschweren Unterredung ʿUbaid Allāhs mit ʿAbdān[139]) erwähnt ist und dessen Sohn ʿAbd Allāh in der Darstellung der Gegner der Ismailiten die ungeheuerlichste Verschwörung zur „Sprengung des Islams von innen" anstiftete[139a]). ʿUbaid Allāh hat seine Genealogie gegenüber der Öffentlichkeit nie ausgewiesen. Im Freitagsgebet ließ er seit seinem Einzug in Raqqāda sich selbst als ʿAbd Allāh Abū Muḥammad oder ʿAbd Allāh b. Muḥammad segnen und ließ seine Väter nur als Gottes rechtgeleitete Stellvertreter bezeichnen[140]). Aber in einem Schreiben an die ismailitische Gemeinde im Jemen, dessen Inhalt Ǧaʿfar b. Manṣūr al-Jaman in seinem Kitāb al-farāʾiḍ wa-ḥudūd ad-dīn mitteilt, legte ʿUbaid Allāh seinen Stammbaum dar, wie er ihn von seinen Anhängern bekannt wissen wollte. Die Analyse dieses Schreibens, das kürzlich von H. F. al-Hamdani nach dem Auszug Ǧaʿfars veröffentlicht wurde[141]), scheint der Klärung des Verhaltens ʿUbaid Allāhs gegenüber Abū ʾl-Qāsim und mancher anderer umstrittener Fragen näherzuführen.

ʿUbaid Allāh erklärt in seinem Brief, der gegenwärtige Herr (walī)

---

[139]) Vgl. oben S. 59f.

[139a]) Die eifrigen Nachforschungen, die man in Bagdad nach dem ersten Einfall der fatimidischen Heere in Ägypten (301/914) über die Herkunft des Aufrührers anstellte, führten noch zu einem anderen Ergebnis, vgl. ʿArīb S. 51f.: Aṣ-Ṣūlī (gest. 335/946) ließ sich von dem Ägypter Abū'l-Ḥasan ʿAlī b. Sarrāǧ, einem Kenner der Geschichte der Šīʿa, berichten, ʿUbaid Allāh sei der Sohn des ʿAbd Allāh b. Sālim, dem Nachkommen eines Freigelassenen des Polizeipräfekten Zijād b. Abīhs. Diese Version der Genealogie übernahm auch der Chronist ʿUbaid Allāh b. Aḥmad b. Abī Ṭāhir Ṭaifūr, der die Geschichte Bagdads seines Vaters bis in die erste Zeit der Herrschaft al-Muqtadirs (295—320/908—932) fortsetzte, vgl. al-ḥulla as-sijarāʾ S. 279.

[140]) ʿAbd Allāh Abū Muḥammad in der von Qāḍī an-Nuʿmān, iftitāḥ ad-daʿwa S. 244, überlieferten Segensformel. Ibn al-Ḫaṭīb, der die Segensformel fast wörtlich gleich zitiert, schreibt Abū Muḥammad ʿUbaid Allāh, Centenario Michele Amari II 448. Richtig ist vielleicht ʿAbd Allāh b. Muḥammad, vgl. unten S. 71. Aber ʿUbaid Allāh nannte sich zweifellos auch Abū Muḥammad.

[141]) Husayn F. al-Hamdani, On the Genealogy of Fatimid Caliphs, Kairo 1958.

— nämlich er selbst — sei ʿAlī b. al-Ḥusain b. Aḥmad b. ʿAbd Allāh b. ʿAbd Allāh b. Ǧaʿfar (aṣ-Ṣādiq) ...[142]) Er versichert also, Alide zu sein. Aber nicht auf Ismāʿīl b. Ǧaʿfar und seinen verschwundenen Sohn Muḥammad führte er seine Abstammung zurück, sondern auf Ǧaʿfars ältesten Sohn ʿAbd Allāh[143]), der in Wahrheit sein rechtmäßiger Nachfolger gewesen sei. Dies mußte freilich eine aufsehenerregende Eröffnung für seine Anhänger sein, denen nach der alten Lehre die Wiederkehr Muḥammad b. Ismāʿīls heiligster Glaubenssatz war. Und ʿUbaid Allāh muß einen Teil seines Schreibens der Frage widmen, wie es zu diesem „Mißverständnis" kommen konnte. Er erklärt, nur wenige Eingeweihte hätten gewußt, daß ʿAbd Allāh der rechtmäßige Imam nach Ǧaʿfar aṣ-Ṣādiq war. Aus Vorsicht (taqīja) verheimlichten sie ihr Wissen. ʿAbd Allāh aber nahm den Namen Ismāʿīl an. Wenn man nun lehrte, der Mahdi heiße Muḥammad b. Ismāʿīl, so sollte dies bedeuten, daß er Muḥammad aus der Nachkommenschaft ʿAbd Allāhs, der sich Ismāʿīl nannte, sei. Jeder der Imame nach ʿAbd Allāh aber nahm den Namen Muḥammad an. Und so war mit dem Hinweis in der Lehre auf Muḥammad b. Ismāʿīl jeder Imam nach ʿAbd Allāh b. Ǧaʿfar in seiner Zeit gemeint, bis Muḥammad, der „Herr des Erscheinens" (ṣāḥib aẓ-ẓuhūr), erscheint, und die „Vorsicht" endet[144]).

Diese Erklärungen ʿUbaid Allāhs in seinem Schreiben bestätigen die Richtigkeit des qarmaṭischen Berichts über seine Begegnung mit ʿAbdān. ʿUbaid Allāh bestritt nicht nur, daß Muḥammad b. Ismāʿīl der erwartete Mahdi sei, sondern versicherte, er habe überhaupt nie rechtmäßigen Anspruch auf das Imamat gehabt. In deutlicher Anspielung auf Ḥamdān Qarmaṭ und seine Anhänger bemerkt er in seinem

---

[142]) A. a. O. arab. Text S. 11 f. M. E. zu Unrecht ergänzt der Herausgeber hier wie auch auf S. 10 Ibn Muḥammad zwischen den beiden ʿAbd Allāhs. Zwar würde die Genealogie so besser mit den Angaben der späteren Autoren übereinstimmen, aber gerade deshalb erscheint es unwahrscheinlich, daß der Name durch Unachtsamkeit eines Kopisten zweimal ausgefallen sei. Al-Hamdanis Bemerkung (S. 13 Anm. 16), im Schreiben selbst werde Muḥammad b. ʿAbd Allāh erwähnt, ist unrichtig. Sie beruht auf seiner Übersetzung (S. 13 oben): "... for Muḥammad was the son of ʿAbdullāh, who was called Ismāʿīl." Der Text ist jedoch so zu übersetzen: „... denn er (nämlich der Mahdi) ist Muḥammad und er ist aus der Nachkommenschaft ʿAbd Allāhs, der sich den Namen Ismāʿīl gab." Daß Muḥammad als der Deckname jedes Imams nach ʿAbd Allāh b. Ǧaʿfar zu verstehen sei, das sagt der Verfasser danach klar genug. — Dagegen streicht der Herausgeber zu Recht Ibn ʿAlī nach al-Ḥusain: Ǧaʿfar b. Manṣūr al-Jaman erklärt selbst (S. 11), in Übereinstimmung mit den meisten übrigen Quellen, ʿUbaid Allāh sei der Neffe Muḥammad b. Aḥmads, nicht sein Großneffe.

[143]) Über ihn vgl. oben S. 44.

[144]) On the Genealogy, arab. Text S. 9 f.

Schreiben: „Eine Gruppe aber, die zu der Lehre berufen war, übte Verrat. Sie erwähnten Ismā'īl und Muḥammad b. Ismā'īl, die doch gar nicht (mehr) existierten, während die rechtmäßigen Herren wohlbehalten und sicher waren[145])." Die Übereinstimmung der Erklärungen 'Ubaid Allāhs in seinem Schreiben und der ihm von den Qarmaṭen zugeschriebenen geht noch weiter. 'Ubaid Allāh versichert, die wahren Imame nach Ǧa'far aṣ-Ṣādiq hätten aus Furcht vor Verrätern andere Namen angenommen. „Sie setzten aber ihre Namen für die Glaubenspropaganda in den Rang der Ḥuǧǧas und nannten sich Mubārak (gesegnet), Maimūn (verheißungsvoll) und Sa'īd (glücklich) wegen des guten Omens in diesen Namen[146])." Die Imame bezeichneten sich also nach 'Ubaid Allāh in der Lehre als Ḥuǧǧas und gaben sich Decknamen wie Mubārak, Maimūn und Sa'īd. Als den Imam nannten sie dagegen Muḥammad b. Ismā'īl. Dies war aber auch nur ein Deckname, und in Wirklichkeit meinten sie sich selbst. Genau dasselbe hatte 'Ubaid Allāh schon 'Abdān in jener Unterredung erklärt, wie sie Aḫū Muḥsin mit gewissen Auslassungen und Entstellungen schildert.

'Ubaid Allāh hatte jedoch 'Abdān gegenüber mit Erfolg eine Blöße in seinen persönlichen Ansprüchen auf das Imamat verheimlicht, die ihm erhebliche Sorgen bereiten mußte. Während er sich in seinem Schreiben als Sohn al-Ḥusain b. Aḥmad b. 'Abd Allāhs ausweist, nennt er bei der Aufzählung der verborgenen Imame Muḥammad b. Aḥmad nach Aḥmad b. 'Abd Allāh[147]). In Übereinstimmung damit bemerkt Ǧa'far b. Manṣūr al-Jaman, Muḥammad b. Aḥmad habe den Sohn seines Bruders entsprechend dem Ratschluß Gottes zu seinem Nachfolger gemacht[148]). 'Ubaid Allāh folgte also seinem Onkel nach. Sein Vater al-Ḥusain war offenbar nie Meister der Bewegung gewesen[149]). Aber nach einem alten Glaubenssatz, zu dem sich weite schiitische Kreise bekannten, konnte das Imamat nach dem Falle al-Ḥasans und al-Ḥusains nur vom Vater auf den Sohn vererbt werden. Die Mubārakija hatten die Nachfolge Muḥammad b. Ismā'īls eben damit zu beweisen gesucht, daß das Imamat nach al-Ḥusain nicht vom Bruder auf den Bruder übergehen könne[150]).

'Ubaid Allāh konnte rechtmäßig also nicht das Imamat von seinem Onkel erben. In seinem Schreiben erklärt er daher, sein öffentlicher Name sei 'Abd Allāh b. Muḥammad[151]), denn er sei spirituell (fi'l-

145) A. a. O. S. 10. 146) S. 9. 147) S. 10. 148) S. 11.

149) So auch nach der Darstellung Ibn Rizāms, fihrist S. 265.

150) Vgl. oben S. 45.

151) Danach ist der Name 'Abd Allāh Abū Muḥammad, wie sich 'Ubaid Allāh nach Qāḍī an-Nu'mān im Freitagsgebet nennen ließ, vielleicht zu berichtigen. Vgl. oben S. 69 Anm. 140.

bāṭin) der Sohn Muḥammad b. Aḥmads[152]). Die Schwäche des Anspruchs, den ʿUbaid Allāh selbst auf das Imamat geltend machen konnte, war anscheinend auch einer der Gründe, weshalb er seinen Sohn Abū 'l-Qāsim schon so früh zu seinem Nachfolger ernannte und ihn gleichzeitig im religiösen Rang über sich selbst erhöhte. Muḥammad b. Aḥmad hatte ʿUbaid Allāh, als er ihn zu seinem Nachfolger bestimmte, seine Tochter zur Frau gegeben. Aus dieser Ehe ging Abū 'l-Qāsim hervor[153]). Er war also der direkte Nachkomme des rechtmäßigen Imams, wenn auch nur über seine Tochter.

Über Abū 'l-Qāsim eröffnet ʿUbaid Allāh in einem Teil seines Schreibens, dessen Wortlaut Ǧaʿfar b. Manṣūr al-Jaman, wie er erklärt, nicht behalten hatte und sinngemäß in eigenen Worten wiedergibt:[154]) „Mit ihm (ʿUbaid Allāh) erschien unser Herr Abū 'l-Qāsim, dessen Name Muḥammad ist. Damit bewahrheitete sich die Weissagung von dem rechtgeleiteten Qā'im[155]) Muḥammad b. ʿAbd Allāh Abū 'l-Qāsim, dem zum Ruhme des Glaubensreiches und zum heiligen Krieg mit den Fahnen der Gläubigen erwarteten Imam." Nicht ʿUbaid Allāh selbst also, sondern Abū 'l-Qāsim war der erwartete Imam, der „Herr des Erscheinens". Während ʿUbaid Allāh erklärte, jeder der Imame nach ʿAbd Allāh b. Ǧaʿfar habe den Namen Muḥammad angenommen, legte er ihn sich selbst nicht zu. Und vielleicht wählte er in seinem Schreiben mit Bedacht den neutralen Ausdruck walī[156]) anstelle von Imam, um seinen eigenen Rang zu bezeichnen[157]).

Die antiismailitischen Polemiker haben die Hintergründe der Erhöhung Abū 'l-Qāsims durch ʿUbaid Allāh im wesentlichen falsch gedeutet. Es waren nicht Zweifel an seiner eigenen alidischen Abstammung, die ʿUbaid Allāh dazu veranlaßten. Er hat immer an dieser Abstammung festgehalten. Auch hat er nie Abū 'l-Qāsim als einen Nachkommen des Muḥammad b. Ismāʿīl bezeichnet. Vielmehr war Abū 'l-Qāsim nach ihm in gewissem Sinne selbst Muḥammad b. Ismāʿīl. Aber seine Abstammung führte er wie die eigene über ʿAbd Allāh b. Ǧaʿfar zurück, nicht über Muḥammad b. Ismāʿīl. Davon erwähnen die Polemiker nichts[158]).

---

[152]) On the Genealogy, arab. Text S. 12.

[153]) Vgl. sīrat Ǧaʿfar S. 109. Ähnlich eine alte Biographie ʿUbaid Allāhs, sīrat al-imām al-Mahdī bi'llāh, die Idrīs b. al-Ḥasan, ʿujūn al-aḫbār V 119, zitiert.

[154]) On the Genealogy, arab. Text S. 11.

[155]) Al-qā'im al-mahdī, die Ergänzung von Ibn vor al-mahdī durch den Herausgeber erscheint mir nicht gerechtfertigt. [156]) Vgl. oben S. 69f.

[157]) Öffentlich ließ er sich jedoch seit seiner Herrschaftnahme immer als Imam bezeichnen. Auch Ǧaʿfar b. Manṣūr al-Jaman nennt ihn so.

[158]) Dagegen weiß Ibn Ḥazm, ǧamharat ansāb al-ʿarab, Ed. Lévi-Provençal,

ʿUbaid Allāh versuchte, seinen Anspruch auf die Nachfolge durch seine „spirituelle" Abstammung von Muḥammad b. Aḥmad zu begründen. Nach der strengen ismailitischen Imamatslehre war dies unzulässig. Nach ihr hatte auch Abū 'l-Qāsim kein Anrecht auf das Imamat, da es nur vom Vater auf den Sohn, nicht aber auf die Tochter vererbt werden konnte. Die spätere offizielle Darstellung der Vorgeschichte der Fatimiden hat daher nachträglich ʿUbaid Allāhs Vater al-Ḥusain b. Aḥmad zum rechtmäßigen Imam erhoben und seinen Bruder Muḥammad zum Usurpator abgestempelt[159]). Vielleicht wollte ʿUbaid Allāh mit seiner Degradierung Muḥammad b. Ismāʿīls gerade auch die ismailitische Imamatslehre treffen, die ihre scharfe Fassung in der Apologetik für dessen Imamat erhalten hatte. Nach Beseitigung des Satzes, daß das Imamat nach al-Ḥasan und al-Ḥusain nur vom Vater auf den Sohn vererbt werden könne, mochte ʿUbaid Allāh auf das Vorbild der Familie des Propheten selbst zur Legitimierung seiner und Abū 'l-Qāsims Nachfolge hinweisen: Ali, der Schwiegersohn Mohammeds, wurde sein „Vollstrecker". Alis Söhne al-Ḥasan und al-Ḥusain, Enkel Mohammeds über seine Tochter, wurden die ersten Imame. Gleichsam im Mittelpunkt der heiligen Familie aber stand Fatima, die Tochter des Propheten. Ob es damit zusammenhing, daß ʿUbaid Allāh das von ihm gegründete Kalifat als fatimidisches bezeichnete?[160])

Die bisherige Darstellung ist von der Voraussetzung ausgegangen, daß Abū 'l-Qāsim der leibliche Sohn ʿUbaid Allāhs war. Dies bedarf einer Rechtfertigung gegenüber den Angaben und Andeutungen einiger ismailitischer Schriften, nach denen Abū 'l-Qāsim nicht der Sohn ʿUbaid Allāhs gewesen wäre. B. Lewis, der zuerst auf solche Andeutungen aufmerksam gemacht hat, schloß auf die Existenz einer doppelten Linie von Imamen seit Muḥammad b. Ismāʿīl. Maimūn al-Qaddāḥ und seine Nachkommen hätten das Imamat als ein Depositum

---

Kairo 1948, S. 53, daß die Fatimiden zuerst ihre Genealogie auf ʿAbd Allāh b. Ǧaʿfar zurückführten. Als sie dann einsehen mußten, daß ʿAbd Allāh außer einer Tochter keine Kinder hatte, hätten sie Ismāʿīl b. Ǧaʿfar zu ihrem Stammvater erklärt. — H. F. al-Hamdani hat keine Bedenken gegen die Richtigkeit der Angaben ʿUbaid Allāhs über seine Abstammung von ʿAbd Allāh b. Ǧaʿfar aṣ-Ṣādiq, vgl. On the Genealogy S. 16f. Dies scheint jedoch mit den Berichten über die Nachfolge nach Ǧaʿfar nicht zu vereinbaren.

[159]) Vgl. unten S. 74f.

[160]) Der Schwiegervater ʿUbaid Allāhs hieß Muḥammad. Sich selbst nennt ʿUbaid Allāh in seinem Schreiben ʿAlī. Nach den Polemikern gab er Abū 'l-Qāsim, der eigentlich ʿAbd ar-Raḥmān hieß, eine Zeitlang den Namen al-Ḥasan.

(wadīʿa) innegehabt. Mit Abū 'l-Qāsim kehrte es wieder in die alidische Linie zurück[161]). Die gleiche Ansicht vertreten H. I. Hassan und T. A. Sharaf in ihrer Biographie ʿUbaid Allāhs, mit gewissen Abweichungen in Einzelheiten der beiden Genealogien[162]). H. F. al-Hamdani in seinem Kommentar zu ʿUbaid Allāhs Schreiben hält diesen für den Vetter des rechtmäßigen Imams, des Vaters Abū 'l-Qāsims[163]).

Nach der Darstellung Ibn Rizāms[164]) erscheint Abū 'l-Qāsim tatsächlich nicht als der Sohn ʿUbaid Allāhs. Nun ist zwar seine Behauptung, ʿUbaid Allāh habe nach seinen anfänglichen Schwierigkeiten irgendeinen jungen Mann als Nachkommen des Muḥammad b. Ismāʿīl vorgestellt, leicht als böswillige Entstellung zu entlarven: ʿUbaid Allāh hatte Abū 'l-Qāsim auf seinem Weg nach dem Maġrib mit sich geführt und ihm gleich nach dem Einzug in Raqqāda einen Palast zugewiesen. Aber Ibn Rizāms Aussagen lassen doch vermuten, daß auch seine Gewährsmänner, die in östlichen Qarmaṭenkreisen zu suchen sind, Abū 'l-Qāsim nicht als Sohn ʿUbaid Allāhs ansahen. Und aus Angaben Qāḍī an-Nuʿmāns in seinem Kitāb al-maǧālis wa'l-musājarāt geht hervor, daß unter dem Fatimiden al-Muʿizz gewisse Kreise seiner Anhängerschaft die Anschauung vertraten, das Imamat sei von einem alidischen Imam auf Maimūn al-Qaddāḥ übergegangen, später aber wieder in die alidische Linie zurückgekehrt[165]).

An-Nuʿmāns Bericht läßt nicht erkennen, mit welchem Imam die alidische Linie die Herrschaft wieder übernahm. S. M. Stern bringt jedoch, aller Wahrscheinlichkeit nach zu Recht, den Bericht in Verbindung zu den Angaben Ibn Rizāms und der Drusenschriften, nach denen ʿUbaid Allāh, nicht aber Abū 'l-Qāsim, ein Nachkomme Maimūns war. Al-Muʿizz verwirft diese Ansichten, da das Imamat doch nicht auf Nichtaliden übergehen könnte. Er gesteht nur zu, daß es innerhalb der Familie des Propheten vorübergehend anderen als den direkten Nachkommen als ein Depositum übertragen werden möge. Diese seien dann zur Rückgabe an den wahren Erben verpflichtet. Als Beispiel weist er auf ʿUbaid Allāhs Onkel Muḥammad b. Aḥmad[166]) hin, der nach ihm

---

[161]) Origins S. 44ff.

[162]) In einer neueren Darstellung, ta'rīḫ ad-daula al-fāṭimīja, Kairo 1958, hält H. I. Hassan diese Ansichten nicht mehr aufrecht.

[163]) On the Genealogy S. 19f.

[164]) Vgl. oben S. 67f.

[165]) Stern, Heterodox Ismailism S. 19.

[166]) Er wird an dieser Stelle nicht namentlich genannt. Aber die Legende wird von Qāḍī an-Nuʿmān und später häufig zitiert und auf den Onkel ʿUbaid Allāhs bezogen. Šarḥ al-aḫbār in Rise, Texte S. 15, istitār al-imām S. 95f., vgl. Heterodox Ismailism S. 23 Anm. 1.

das Imamat nur als Depositum innehatte. Er ernannte seine eigenen nächsten Verwandten, einen nach dem andern, zum Nachfolger, aber sie starben alle vor ihm. Da gab er das Depositum an seinen wahren Eigentümer (ʿUbaid Allāh) zurück[167]).

In den zu Anfang des 5./11. Jahrhunderts verfaßten Schriften des Drusenkanons finden sich diese Anschauungen von der Abstammung der beiden ersten Fatimiden deutlich wiedergespiegelt. Ismāʿīl b. Muḥammad at-Tamīmī bezeichnet ʿUbaid Allāh als Saʿīd b. Aḥmad b. al-Ḥusain b. Muḥammad b. ʿAbd Allāh b. Maimūn al-Qaddāḥ[168]). Doch war al-Qaddāḥ selbst Alide[169]). Saʿīd war der Mahdi. „Er war der Thron (nämlich der Gottes, Koran 2,255, da al-Qā'im die Manifestation des Herrn ist) und derjenige, dem der Herr al-Muʿill das Depositum übergab und befahl, unserem Herrn al-Qā'im zu dienen[170])." Ḥamza nennt ihn den Ḥuǧǧa al-Qā'ims[171]) und den erhabensten Schleier unseres Herrn[172]). Er nimmt die höchste Rangstufe in der Hierarchie ein, indem man ihn Vater des Qā'im nennt[173]). Er „hat mit seinem eigenen Mund gesagt und in seiner Zeit gestanden, daß er der Diener und Sklave unseres Herrn al-Qā'im, des Wissenden und Herr-

---

[167]) H. I. Hassan und T. A. Sharaf führen zur Unterstützung der These, daß Abū 'l-Qāsim nicht ʿUbaid Allāhs Sohn sei, folgende Erzählung des al-Muʿizz aus an-Nuʿmāns al-maǧālis wa'l-musājarāt an: Die Gattin al-Mahdīs sagte nach seinem Tod zu seinen Kindern und Frauen: „Diese Sache (gemeint ist das Imamat) hat diesen Palast, d. h. den Palast des al-Mahdī bi'llāh, verlassen, und wird nie wieder zu ihm zurückkehren. Sie ist auf jenen Palast, d. h. den Palast des al-Qā'im bi-Amr Allāh, übergegangen und wird innerhalb der Nachkommenschaft seines Besitzers bleiben, solange die Erde besteht." (Al-Muʿizz li-Dīn Allāh S. 13, 140.) Es ist jedoch auszuschließen, daß an-Nuʿmān seinen Herrn zugunsten einer Lehre zitierte, die er an anderer Stelle im selben Werk scharf verurteilte. Die Absicht der Erzählung ist sicher anders. Sie mag gegen Hoffnungen gewisser Nachkommen ʿUbaid Allāhs und anderer Verwandter gerichtet sein, zwischen denen und den fatimidischen Kalifen erbitterte Feindschaft herrschte. Vgl. darüber die sīrat Ǧūḏar.

[168]) Taqsīm al-ʿulūm, Ms. Tübingen M. a. VI 131 fol. 91 v. Daselbst bezeichnet ihn at-Tamīmī aber auch als Sohn aš-Šalaʿlaʿs. Damit ist offensichtlich, wie eine Glosse bestätigt, Saʿīds Onkel gemeint, den die Polemiker Abū 'š-Šalaʿlaʿ nennen, vgl. oben S. 56 Anm. 78.

[169]) So sagt at-Tamīmī vom Urgroßvater Saʿīds, Muḥammad b. ʿAbd Allāh, „dem man im geheimen den Namen al-Mahdī gab", er stamme von al-Qaddāḥ ab und sei aus der Nachkommenschaft al-Ḥusains. Taqsīm al-ʿulūm, fol. 94r, de Sacy I 35.

[170]) Taqsīm al-ʿulūm, fol. 94v, de Sacy I 81.

[171]) Ar-radd ʿalā'n-nuṣairī, de Sacy I 78 Anm. Text hsgb. von R. Strothmann, Drusenantwort auf Nusairi-Angriff, Islam XXV, S. 279.

[172]) An-naqḍ al-ḫafī, Ms. Berlin Wetzstein 1870, fol. 34r.

[173]) An-naqḍ al-ḫafī, fol. 26v, de Sacy I 38 Anm.

schenden sei[174]).“ Al-Qā'im aber ist die erste Manifestation des Herrn auf Erden mit königlicher Würde[175]). Als solche aber ist seine Genealogie ohne Belang, denn der Herr ist immer der gleiche[176]). Doch sagt Ḥamza klar genug, daß der Herr sich selbst von al-Mahdī manifestierte[177]).

In die Lehre der Drusen sind Glaubenssätze und Bilder aus verschiedenen, sich widerstreitenden Quellen eingeflossen. Manche der hier vorgeführten Anschauungen läßt sich auf fatimidische Vorlagen zurückführen. So wohl die Auffassung, ʿUbaid Allāh sei der Ḥuǧǧa al-Qā'ims gewesen[178]). Die Auffassung, ʿUbaid Allāh habe das Imamat nur als ein Depositum verwaltet, entspricht seinen eigenen Aussagen. Ein Zugeständnis an die fatimidischen Versicherungen ist es auch, wenn Maimūn al-Qaddāḥ als Alide angesehen wird. Aber hier zeichnet sich doch auch deutlich genug jene heterodoxe Lehre ab, nach der die Führung einst von einem Imam auf ʿAbd Allāh b. Maimūn al-Qaddāḥ übergegangen und mit Abū 'l-Qāsim wieder in alidische Hände zurückgekehrt wäre[179]).

---

[174]) Bad' at-tauḥīd in de Sacy I 38 Anm. 1 und S. 77. De Sacys Übersetzung von (al-qā'im) mit l'existant oder le chef verdeckt den Sinn. Ein späterer drusischer Autor malt die Angaben Ḥamzas weiter aus: „Wenn (al-Qā'im) im Geleit ausritt . . ., schritt Saʿīd al-Mahdī vor ihm her, rief und sagte: 'Ich bin ein Diener und Sklave unseres Herrn al-Qā'im. Bei mir war eine Sache deponiert, und er hat sie von mir genommen.'“ H. Guys, Théogonie des Druses, Paris 1863, S. 58.

[175]) Taqsīm al-ʿulūm, fol. 94v, de Sacy I 38, und as-sīra al-mustaqīma (Ḥamza), Ms. Berlin Wetzstein 1870, fol. 100v, de Sacy I 71.

[176]) Vgl. de Sacy I 40ff., 46.

[177]) Aẓhara 'l-maulā ǧalla ḏikruhū nafsahū minhū, ar-radd ʿalā 'n-nuṣairī, de Sacy I 78, Drusenantwort S. 279.

[178]) Bahā' ad-Dīn verweist auf den Satz, daß der Ḥuǧǧa des Qā'im vor diesem komme, at-tanbīh wa't-ta'nīb, Ms. Berlin Orient. Quart. 819 fol. 26r. Der Satz wird im Kitāb al-kašf verbildlicht, vgl. oben S. 57. Auch später begegnet er in fatimidischen Texten. Vgl. etwa al-maǧālis al-mustanṣirīja, S. 32, wo er natürlich auf den künftigen Qā'im am Ende der Zeit bezogen ist.

[179]) Lewis geht in der Deutung der Drusentexte wohl zu weit, wenn er in dem Herrn al-Muʿill, der ʿUbaid Allāh das Depositum übergab, den wahren Vater Abū 'l-Qāsims zu erkennen sucht. Der Stammbaum müßte sich dann konsequenterweise in den früheren Manifestationen unseres Herrn, ʿAljā', Abū Zakarījā' und al-Bār, fortsetzen. Und welche irdische Persönlichkeit mag dem Herrn, als er unter dem Namen al-Muʿill zur Zeit des Imams Muḥammad b. ʿAbd Allāh „im Lande von Palmyra und den Provinzen des Ostens unter dem Äußern eines Kaufmanns erschien“ (taqsīm al-ʿulūm in de Sacy I 35), als Hülle gedient haben? Al-Muʿill ist ja kein Personenname. Es handelt sich offensichtlich um eine Personifizierung des (muʿill ʿillat al-ʿilal) „des Verursachers der Ursache der Ursachen“, wie Gott in den Drusentexten häufig genannt wird,

Die Auffassung, daß Abū 'l-Qāsim nicht der Sohn ʿUbaid Allāhs sei, fand aber auch in Schriften maßgebender Lehrmeister der nachfatimidischen Gemeinde im Jemen Eingang[180]). Al-Ḫaṭṭāb b. al-Ḥasan weiß in seinem wenige Jahre nach der Ermordung des Imams al-Āmir (524/1130) verfaßten Werk ġājat al-mawālīd von einem vierten verborgenen Imam nach der gewöhnlichen Reihe der drei Verborgenen zu berichten. Dieser ʿAlī b. al-Ḥusain war es, der den Sendboten Ibn Ḥaušab nach dem Jemen schickte[181]). „Durch ihn ging die Sonne auf." Aber auf dem Weg nach dem Maġrib, wo Abū ʿAbd Allāh ihm den Boden bereitet hatte, starb er und ernannte seinen Ḥuǧǧa Saʿīd al-Ḫair, der al-Mahdī genannt wird, zum Nachfolger. Ob dieser irgendwie mit Maimūn al-Qaddāḥ verwandt sein soll, der vorher als Ḥuǧǧa des Ismāʿīl b. Ǧaʿfar erwähnt wurde, macht der Verfasser nicht klar. Als al-Mahdī aber starb, „gab er das Depositum an seinen festen Ort zurück. Muḥammad b. *ʿAlī* al-Qā'im bi-Amr Allāh übernahm es, und das Imamat setzte sich in seiner Nachkommenschaft fort ..."[182])

Die Absicht al-Ḫaṭṭābs liegt in seinen Ausführungen klar zutage: Es soll die Notwendigkeit eines Stellvertreters im Falle der Minderjährigkeit des rechtmäßigen Imams bewiesen werden. In diesem Falle verwaltet der Ḥuǧǧa des Vaters das Imamat als Depositum[183]). Dafür sucht al-Ḫaṭṭāb historische Beispiele. Und eines fand er in Abū 'l-Qāsim, den ʿUbaid Allāh selbst als den wahren erwarteten Imam hingestellt hatte. Einer alten Quelle mochte er auch entnehmen, daß Abū 'l-Qāsims Name Muḥammad b. ʿAlī b. al-Ḥusain sei. Er übersah dabei, daß ʿUbaid Allāh sich selbst als ʿAlī b. al-Ḥusain bezeichnet hatte. Dies ist verständlich, da er längst nur noch nach seinem „öffentlichen" Namen ʿAbd Allāh genannt wurde. ʿAlī b. al-Ḥusain mußte dann ein vierter verborgener Imam gewesen sein.

Wie wenig die Darstellung al-Ḫaṭṭābs mit den Angaben der fati-

---

vgl. de Sacy II 77. Dies entspricht der Personifizierung anderer Namen Gottes, wie al-Bār, al-ʿAlī al-Aʿlā, und der ganzen Reihe der Prinzipien der höheren Welt, die man aus der ismailitischen Kosmologie übernahm.

[180]) Sie mögen in der Ausbildung ihrer Theorien von der Vorgeschichte der Fatimiden aus al-Mu'ajjads Abhandlung iṯbāt al-imāma Nutzen gezogen haben, wie H. F. al-Hamdani (On the Genealogy S. 7 Anm. 4) annimmt. Auch Imam al-Mustanṣir selbst scheint gewisse Enthüllungen über die Geschichte ʿUbaid Allāhs gemacht zu haben, vgl. Rise S. 37. Aber es ist schwerlich anzunehmen, daß sie von dem Gründer des Fatimidenreiches lehrten, er sei nicht der Stammvater der Dynastie gewesen.

[181]) Rise, Texte S. 36. [182]) Rise, Texte S. 37.

[183]) Da diese Notwendigkeit zur Zeit der drei Verborgenen nicht bestand, ist die Annahme einer Reihe von stellvertretenden Imamen von Maimūn bis Saʿīd ʿUbaid Allāh ausgeschlossen.

midischen Quellen zu vereinbaren war, zeigen die Schwierigkeiten, die sie drei Jahrhunderte später dem belesenen Idrīs b. al-Ḥasan bereitete. Seinem exoterischen Geschichtswerk ʿujūn al-aḫbār legte Idrīs die offizielle Version der Vorgeschichte der Fatimiden zugrunde, nach der al-Ḥusain b. Aḥmad, al-Mahdī und al-Qā'im Imame einer Linie sind[184]). In dem esoterischen Gegenstück, zahr al-maʿānī, gerät er bei dem Versuch, diese Version mit der al-Ḫaṭṭābs zu vereinigen, in unauflösbare Zweideutigkeiten. Imam al-Ḥusain b. Aḥmad soll es gewesen sein, der den Sendboten Ibn Ḥaušab nach dem Jemen schickte[185]). Aber schon die Angabe, daß der Imam, Herr der Zeit — den Namen verschweigt Idrīs, da er einen ʿAlī b. al-Ḥusain nicht unterzubringen weiß — auf dem Weg nach dem Maġrib gestorben sei, verrät die Vorlage von al-Ḫaṭṭābs Schrift. Denn al-Ḥusain ist nach der offiziellen Version, der man hier wahrscheinlich Glauben schenken darf, schon lange vorher gestorben[186]). Wie bei al-Ḫaṭṭāb soll der sterbende Imam die Vormundschaft über seinen Sohn einem Saʿīd al-Ḫair übertragen haben. Aber Saʿīd al-Ḫair ist auch der Bruder des Imams, was wiederum der offiziellen Version entspricht. Nach dem alten istitār al-imām gab al-Ḥusain seinen Sohn al-Mahdī in die Vormundschaft seines Bruders Saʿīd al-Ḫair[187]). Im folgenden Abschnitt aber vermeidet der Verfasser geschickt die Nennung von Namen, so daß sie der Leser je nach seinen Vorkenntnissen einsetzen kann[188]).

Doch ist al-Mahdī der vierte Imam der zweiten Heptade[189]), wenn auch sein Name vorsichtshalber unerwähnt bleibt. Al-Qā'im heißt Muḥammad b. ʿAbd Allāh und ist „sein Sohn, ihm wegen seiner Erziehung und Lehre zugeschrieben[190])." Al-Mahdī hat auf seinen hohen

---

[184]) Rise S. 37f.

[185]) Rise, Texte S. 65. Dagegen zitiert er in ʿujūn al-aḫbār (V 119) die sīrat al-imām al-Mahdī bi'llāh, nach der Muḥammad b. Aḥmad, ʿUbaid Allāhs Onkel, Ibn Ḥaušab entsandte.

[186]) Nach der sīrat al-imām al-Mahdī, die Idrīs selbst in ʿujūn al-aḫbār (V 119) zitiert, starb ʿUbaid Allāhs Vater, als dieser acht Jahre alt war.

[187]) Istitār S. 95. H. I. Hassan und T. A. Sharaf, ʿUbaid Allāh S. 90, lesen (Saʿīd al-Ḫair) im Genitiv statt im Nominativ, wodurch er als Bruder al-Mahdīs erscheint. Das ist aber nach dem weiteren Verlauf der Darstellung nicht zulässig: „Damals war sein (al-Ḥusains) Sohn im Kindesalter." Dies im Gegensatz zu seinem, nämlich al-Ḥusains, Bruder.

[188]) Ivanow, Rise S. 258, übersetzt zu Unrecht den Ausdruck (waladuhū' l-qā'im min baʿdihī) "... his ... son ... al-Qā'im, who had to be the Imam after him." Es soll einfach heißen: Sein Sohn, der ihm nachfolgte.

[189]) Rise, Texte S. 57.

[190]) Waladuhū 'l-muntasibu ilaihī bi-taʿlīmihī wa-ifādatihī, Ivanows Übersetzung, S.260, ist hier unzulässig.

Rang hingewiesen[191]). Er war der Träger des Depositums und hat es an seinen „festen Ort" zurückgegeben. Al-Qā'im stand zu ihm im gleichen Verhältnis wie Ali zu Mohammed[192]).

Die Bilanz dieser Aussagen spricht nicht gerade dafür, daß Abū 'l-Qāsim nicht der Sohn ʿUbaid Allāhs war. Zwar hat sich gezeigt, daß gewisse ismailitische Kreise Abū 'l-Qāsim als Nachkommen des Muḥammad b. Ismāʿīl anerkannten, während sie ʿUbaid Allāh als Sproß Maimūn al-Qaddāḥs ansahen. Aber ʿUbaid Allāh selbst hat sicher nie von Abū 'l-Qāsim gesagt, er sei nicht sein Sohn. Das behaupten auch die Gründer der Drusenreligion nicht. Ebensowenig ist anzunehmen, daß einer der späteren Fatimiden ʿUbaid Allāh nicht als seinen Stammvater bezeichnet hat[193]). Daraus kann man nur schließen, daß jene Kreise ʿUbaid Allāhs Eröffnungen nach ihren älteren Anschauungen interpretierten. Sie hatten die Vorfahren der Fatimiden als Nachkommen des Maimūn al-Qaddāḥ angesehen[194]). Sie schenkten den Beteuerungen ʿUbaid Allāhs, Maimūn sei ein Deckname des rechtmäßigen Imams gewesen, keinen Glauben. Aber sie waren bereit, seine Erklärungen zugunsten Abū 'l-Qāsims anzunehmen, und erkannten diesen als den erwarteten Imam aus der Nachkommenschaft des Muḥammad b. Ismāʿīl an.

In den Berichten der Chronisten über die Herrschaft ʿUbaid Allāhs deutet nichts darauf hin, daß Abū 'l-Qāsim nicht sein Sohn gewesen sein könnte. Tatsächlich ist es schwer vorzustellen, daß ein Herrscher, der so skrupellos die Glaubenslehre für seine Herrschaftsinteressen einsetzte und veränderte, zeitenweise sogar ihre Bekenner verfolgte, einen anderen als seinen Sohn zum Nachfolger gemacht hätte. Auch nachdem er Abū 'l-Qāsim zum erwarteten Imam erklärt hatte, behielt er die Zügel der Macht ausschließlich in den eigenen Händen. Es konnte sogar das Gerücht aufkommen, er wolle Abū 'l-Qāsim wieder von der Thronfolge ausschließen und sie auf einen anderen Sohn übertragen. Abū 'l-Qāsim glaubte, das Gerücht ernst nehmen zu müssen[195]). Nach den Andeutungen des Idrīs b. al-Ḥasan wäre ʿUbaid Allāh

---

[191]) Rise, Texte S. 66, 70. [192]) Rise, Texte S. 70.

[193]) Al-Manṣūr, der Sohn Abū 'l-Qāsims, bezeichnete in der Rede, in der er seinen Anhängern und den Kutāma den Tod seines Vaters mitteilte, ʿUbaid Allāh als seinen Großvater und Nachkommen des Propheten, sīrat Ǧūḏar S. 58. Aber auch in einem privaten Brief an den Thronfolger al-Muʿizz spricht er von den Kindern „deiner beiden Ahnen (ǧaddaika) al-Mahdī bi'llāh und al-Qā'im bi-Amr Allāh." Sīrat Ǧūḏar S. 63.

[194]) Im Unterschied zu den Gemeinden im Jemen und Nordafrika, die zweifellos ʿUbaid Allāh, wie schon vor ihm seinen Onkel, als Aliden anerkannten.

[195]) Vgl. oben S. 63 Anm. 117, letzter Absatz.

unter den unsicheren Verhältnissen zunächst als der Erwartete bezeichnet worden, um Feinde und Verräter vom wahren Herrn fernzuhalten. In Wirklichkeit aber wurde Abū 'l-Qāsim immer wieder mit den gefährlichsten Kriegszügen beauftragt, während ʿUbaid Allāh nie an einer Schlacht teilgenommen hat.

Nicht nur in den Mängeln seiner Genealogie mußte ʿUbaid Allāhs Anspruch, der erwartete Mahdi zu sein, auf Schwierigkeiten stoßen. Nach den Chronisten hat Abū ʿAbd Allāh den Aufruhr gegen seinen Herrn mit dem Hinweis auf die göttlichen Zeichen entfacht, mit denen der Mahdi sich zu legitimieren habe[196]). Er mochte dabei seine alten Anhänger daran erinnern, was er ihnen vom Kommen des Mahdīs geweissagt hatte. ʿUbaid Allāh konnte auch nicht hoffen, diesen Makel durch die Erhebung seines Sohnes zum erwarteten Imam auszuräumen. Es war vorauszusehen, daß der weitere Verlauf der Geschichte der Fatimidendynastie die hochgespannten Hoffnungen ihrer Anhänger noch mehr enttäuschen würde. Der Mahdī, so hatte man früher gelehrt, werde als der siebente Sprecherprophet die Gesetze aller Propheten aufheben, den „inneren Sinn" öffentlich verkünden und das vollkommene Gesetz bringen, in dem es keinen Unterschied zwischen äußerlicher Bedeutung und verborgener Wahrheit gibt. Aber gegenüber der feindseligen Haltung der Masse der Bevölkerung im Maġrib mußten die Fatimiden nicht nur ihre Missionstätigkeit aufs äußerste einschränken, sondern auch ihre Anhänger zur strengen Einhaltung der Gesetze des Islams zwingen. Der Mahdī sollte ferner unumschränkt die ganze Welt regieren, über die Menschheit zu Gericht sitzen und dem Rechte Geltung verschaffen, wo vorher Willkür und Unterdrückung herrschten. Die fatimidischen Heere aber steckten nach anfänglichen Erfolgen Niederlage auf Niederlage ein bei dem Versuch, Ägypten zu erobern. Wie wenig man selbst das maġribinische Reich in der Gewalt hatte, erwies der schreckliche Aufstand des Ḫāriǧiten Abū Jazīd, der fast das ganze Reich Abū 'l-Qāsims erobern konnte und ihn selbst in der Hauptstadt mehrere Monate lang belagerte. Schließlich aber sollte der Mahdi nach der Lehre auch der Herr der Auferstehung sein, der Letzte der Propheten und Imame, mit dem die Welt endet.

ʿUbaid Allāh gelang es durch sein entschlossenes und geschicktes Durchgreifen, die Aufstände der enttäuschten Anhänger in den ersten Jahren seiner Herrschaft niederzuschlagen. Aber die Entwicklung der äußeren Umstände konnte nicht ohne nachhaltige Wirkung auf die Lehre bleiben. Ihre Meister waren vor die schwierige Aufgabe gestellt,

[196]) Vgl. bajān I 161.

sie den neuen Gegebenheiten anzupassen und dabei doch den Schein der Kontinuität zu wahren.

Erste Schritte in dieser Richtung ging schon ʿUbaid Allāh selbst, wie die Zitate Ǧaʿfar b. Manṣūr al-Jamans aus seinem Schreiben[197]) an die ismailitische Gemeinde im Jemen zeigen. Nach ʿUbaid Allāh wurde Imam Ǧaʿfar aṣ-Ṣādiq einmal von einem Anhänger gefragt, ob denn aus seiner Familie nur ein einziger Mahdi am Ende der Zeit hervorgehen werde, da so viele Umajjaden und Abbasiden als Könige geherrscht hätten. Ǧaʿfar antwortete darauf, Gott hätte den Rang der Familie des Propheten niedrig gemacht, wenn aus ihr nur ein Mahdi hervorgehen solle. Der erwartete Mahdi werde das Recht zugunsten der Prophetenfamilie und ihrer Anhänger wiederherstellen. Nach ihm werden aus seiner Nachkommenschaft viele rechtgeleitete Leiter mit göttlicher Unterstützung bis zur letzten Stunde herrschen. „Von uns ist der Mahdi, von uns der Hādī und von uns der Muhtadā bih." „Wenn du aber denjenigen meinst, von dem der Gesandte Gottes gesagt hat: ʻDie Auferstehung wird kommen, wenn die Herrschaft der Welt in den Händen eines Mannes aus meiner Nachkommenschaft, aus der Nachkommenschaft al-Ḥusains sein wird. Er ist es, hinter dem Jesus, der Sohn der Maria, beten wirdʼ: dies wird aber sein zur Zeit des Erdbebens und des Versagens der Werke. Niemand möge ihn darum herbeiwünschen[198]), der nicht auf sein Wissen vertrauen kann."[199])

Dies Zitat Ǧaʿfar aṣ-Ṣādiqs soll offensichtlich den Glaubenssatz widerlegen, der Mahdi sei der letzte der Imame und der Herr der Auferstehung[200]). Die Aufgabe des Mahdi und seiner nächsten Nachkom-

[197]) Der Herausgeber geht von der Annahme aus, alle Zitate stammten nur aus einem Schreiben. Aber Ǧaʿfar selbst erwähnt offenbar ein zweites Schreiben, On the Genealogy, arab. Text S. 14 Anm. 5. Auch vorher sind seine Angaben über die Herkunft der Zitate unbestimmt. Wahrscheinlich erinnerte er sich selbst nicht mehr genau. Mit Sicherheit bildeten jedoch die Erklärungen über Vorgeschichte und Genealogie der Fatimiden eine Einheit. Die Zuverlässigkeit der Angabe Ǧaʿfars, ʿUbaid Allāh habe diese Erklärungen nach seiner Ankunft in al-Mahdīja (308/920) abgegeben, scheint mir zweifelhaft. Sie stehen in deutlichem Zusammenhang mit der Erhöhung Abū 'l-Qāsims zehn Jahre vorher. Es scheint schwer vorstellbar, daß ʿUbaid Allāh so lange mit der Unterrichtung der jemenitischen Gemeinde wartete. Ǧaʿfar mochte im Rückblick mit der Ankunft in al-Mahdīja den Einzug in Raqqāda meinen, zumal er sich bis nach dem Tode ʿUbaid Allāhs noch im Jemen aufhielt.

[198]) Fa-lā jatamannahū in der Handschrift ist wohl gegen die Änderung des Herausgebers vorzuziehen.

[199]) On the Genealogy, arab. Text S. 12f.

[200]) Dieselbe Absicht liegt der nächsten Erklärung ʿUbaid Allāhs zugrunde, arab. Text S. 13: Zwischen je zwei aufeinanderfolgenden Sprechern muß es einen Imam geben, der mit offener Macht und dem Schwert herrscht. Das be-

men beschränkt sich darauf, dem Recht mit dem Schwert Geltung zu verschaffen. Damit war der Fatimidendynastie ein Platz in der Heilsgeschichte eingeräumt.

ʿUbaid Allāh hatte auch eine Antwort auf die Frage, wieso die Zahl seiner Vorfahren seit Ali größer sein könne als sieben, während doch in der Lehre die Anzahl der Imame zwischen je zwei Sprechern auf sieben festgesetzt war. Er versicherte, gemeint seien sieben Rangstufen, die im Kreislauf wiederkehrten wie die Tage der Woche. Es gibt aber in diesen Rängen so viele Imame, wie Gott wünscht, bis plötzlich der Sprecher erscheint, wenn Gott will[201]).

Ganz auf ʿUbaid Allāhs neuer Lehre vom Mahdi und seinem Amt baute der gelehrte Autor und Qāḍī an-Nuʿmān b. Muḥammad (gest. 363/974) in der Sammlung von Traditionen über den Mahdi auf, die er in seinem unter al-Muʿizz[202]) verfaßten Werk šarḥ al-aḫbār zusammengestellt und kommentiert hat[203]). An-Nuʿmān bezieht die Traditionen, die zum größten Teil dem Propheten und den Imamen zugeschrieben werden, auf ʿUbaid Allāh und seine Nachkommen. Schon in seinem unter Abū ʾl-Qāsim verfaßten Gedicht al-urǧūza al-muḫtāra hatte er den Mahdititel auch auf seinen derzeitigen Herrn ausgedehnt, nicht ohne auf dessen Namen Abū ʾl-Qāsim Muḥammad hinzuweisen[204]). Nun werden die Taten und Eigenschaften des Mahdi ʿUbaid Allāh und den Imamen aus seiner Nachkommenschaft bis zum jüngsten Tag zugeschrieben. Zu der Weissagung, daß der Qāʾim alle Gegner der Šīʿa, die den wahren Glauben trotz Aufforderung nicht annähmen, entweder töten oder zur Zahlung der Kopfsteuer zwingen werde, erklärt an-Nuʿmān: „Dies ist noch nicht geschehen von seiten der bisherigen Imame. Es wird aber geschehen unter demjenigen von ihnen, der herrscht, wenn die Welt untertan, seine Sache stark und der Glaube einer ist, wie Gott versprochen hat[205]).“

Freilich muß sich an-Nuʿmān immer wieder gleichsam entschuldigen für seine offensichtliche Willkür. So meint er, Gott habe auch sein Versprechen gegenüber dem Propheten, die wahre Religion triumphieren zu lassen (Koran 9,33), zunächst nur teilweise erfüllt und werde es

---

deutet, daß zwischen Mohammed und dem Herrn der Auferstehung der Mahdi kommt. Hier wird zugleich die Lehre getroffen, der Mahdi sei der siebte Sprecher, der ja Mohammeds Gesetz aufheben sollte.

[201]) On the Genealogy, arab. Text S. 14.

[202]) Wahrscheinlich wurde es zwischen 350/961 und 360/971 fertiggestellt, vgl. Ivanow, Rise S. 12.

[203]) Rise, Texte S. 1—31, übersetzt und kommentiert S. 61—65, 96—122.

[204]) Maḏhab S. 175.

[205]) Tradition 6.

durch die Imame aus seiner Nachkommenschaft ganz erfüllen[206]). Ǧaʿfar aṣ-Ṣādiq sagte: „Wenn ich euch etwas in bezug auf einen von uns erzähle, es ist aber nicht in ihm, so wird es nach ihm in seinem Sohn sein[207]).“ Als Bestätigung seiner Auffassung zitiert an-Nuʿmān schließlich seinen Herrn al-Muʿizz: Al-Mahdī habe einmal auf die Frage, ob er wirklich der erwartete Mahdi sei, geantwortet, die Gnade Gottes sei groß. Er selbst habe wesentlichen Anteil daran, aber auch die nach ihm kämen, seien von ihm begnadet. Al-Mahdī, so schließt al-Muʿizz daraus, sei der Schlüssel zum Schloß der Gnade gewesen, aber sie daure in seiner Nachkommenschaft fort, bis Gottes Versprechen eingelöst sei[208]).

Daneben führt an-Nuʿmān einige Traditionen an, nach denen der Mahdi mehrere Nachfolger haben sollte. In einer davon heißt es, ʿAlī (Zain al-ʿĀbidīn) b. al-Ḥusain habe gesagt: „Der Qā'im wird von uns hervorgehen, und nach ihm werden zwölf Mahdis kommen[209]).“ Nach einer andern hat der Mahdi allerdings nur sieben Nachfolger[210]). Nach einer dritten aber sollte es zwölf Kalifen aus der Familie des Propheten geben, bevor die Welt untergeht. Einer von ihnen werde vierzig Jahre, ein anderer dreißig Jahre herrschen[211]). Ivanow nimmt an, daß diese Traditionen erst in der Fatimidenzeit entstanden sind[212]).

Auch die Auswahl selbst ist charakteristisch: Ivanow weist auf das Fehlen der Traditionen hin über die Wunder, die der Mahdi wirken sollte[213]). Dagegen spielen die politischen Erwartungen, vor allem die Eroberungen, eine prominente Rolle. Auch erscheint der Mahdi als der Neubeleber und Wahrer des Islams.

Hierher gehört an-Nuʿmāns Kommentar zu der Tradition: „Der Islam begann in der Fremde (bada'a ġarīban) und wird in die Fremde zurückkehren, wie er begann. Heil also denen, die in der Fremde sind.“ Imam Ǧaʿfar erklärte sie so: Ein Rufer von uns wird einen neuen Ruf beginnen, wie der Prophet gerufen hat. „Ebenso hat al-Mahdī einen neuen Ruf zu Gott begonnen, nachdem die religiösen Bräuche verändert worden waren, (ketzerische) Neuerungen überhand nahmen, die Imame des Irrtums an die Macht gelangten, und die Imame der rechten Führung in Vergessenheit gerieten.“ Dieselbe Tradition hatten

[206]) Traditionen 3 und 5.

[207]) Trad. 5. Diese Tradition wird schon von dem Zwölferschiiten al-Kulīnī (gest. 329/941) überliefert, uṣūl al-kāfī I 535.

[208]) Trad. 28.

[209]) Trad. 42.

[210]) Trad. 45.

[211]) Trad. 43.

[212]) Rise S. 103. [213]) Rise S. 122.

die Qarmaṭen als Beweis für die Aufhebung des islamischen Gesetzes angeführt[214]).

Auffällig ist, daß an-Nuʿmān die endzeitliche Erwartung, die sonst so eng mit dem Mahdi verknüpft ist, in seiner Traditionensammlung nicht zu Worte kommen läßt. Nur bei der Erklärung des dem Propheten zugeschriebenen Wortes: „Durch uns wird der Glaube beschlossen, wie er durch uns eröffnet worden ist," erwähnt er das Ende der Welt und die Auferstehung[215]), die sich im Zeitalter eines Imams aus der der Nachkommenschaft al-Mahdīs ereignen werde[216]).

Besondere Schwierigkeiten mußte die Anpassung der Lehre bei der allegorischen Exegese bereiten. In ihr vor allem fand die ismailitische Theorie der Heilsgeschichte Ausdruck, in ihr suchte sie ihre Rechtfertigung. Hier lag aber ein wohldurchdachtes System mit festen Proportionen vor, die man nicht willkürlich verändern konnte, ohne dem Ganzen seine eigentliche Überzeugungskraft zu nehmen. Dies gilt besonders von der Anschauung der zyklischen Weltalter und der Bedeutung, die der Zahl Sieben darin zukommt. Die Ordnung, die, wie gezeigt wurde, noch in vorfatimidischer Zeit ins Wanken geraten war, konnte mit der Fortdauer des fatimidischen Anspruchs auf das Imamat nur durch einen drastischen Eingriff wiederhergestellt werden. In seinem Buch über „die Grundlage der Auslegung" (asās at-taʾwīl) bietet an-Nuʿmān folgende Lösung an, auch hier gestützt auf die Erläuterungen ʿUbaid Allāhs: „Nach jedem Sprecher führen in seiner Ära Imame in Heptaden sein Gesetz durch, die Gnade aber gelangt zum siebten. Der sechste vor ihm wird Vollender (mutimm) genannt, denn die Offenbarung (bajān) endet vor ihm, von ihm erfolgt keine Offenbarung. Dann bringt der siebte die Offenbarung, und die Macht der (göttlichen) Unterstützung wird in ihm sichtbar. Wenn die Zeit gekommen ist, daß er ein Gottgesandter werde, und die Ära des Sprechers vor ihm vollendet ist, so wird er ein Sprecher. Wenn sie noch nicht gekommen ist, so läuft nach ihm eine gleiche Heptade ab, bis die Zeit dafür kommt. Gott hat aber das Gesandtenamt und das Prophetenamt mit Mohammed abgeschlossen ... Die Imame folgen also einander in der Ära Mohammeds, wie das in der Ära jedes Sprechers geschehen ist. Aber keiner von ihnen ist ein Gottgesandter oder Prophet, da Gott das Prophetenamt in Mohammed als besonderen

---

214) Saʿd S. 62f. Wie an-Nuʿmān selbst erwähnt, wird die Tradition auch von Sunniten überliefert. Vgl. Wensinck, Concordance et Indices de la Tradition Musulmane I 148.

215) Ivanows Übersetzung, Rise S. 99, von (al-qijāma) mit "religious revolution" ist hier nicht zulässig. 216) Trad. 18.

Vorzug abgeschlossen hat, ohne daß sein Gesetz durch ein (anderes) Gesetz aufgehoben würde oder sein Gesandtenamt durch einen (anderen) Gesandten[217]).“

Durch Einführung neuer Heptaden kann an-Nu'mān den „verborgenen Imamen“ und den Fatimidenkalifen einen festen Platz in der Kette der von Gott eingesetzten Lenker und Herren der Menschheit zuweisen. Aber dem Mahdi wird seine eigentliche Bedeutung genommen. 'Ubaid Allāh, Abū 'l-Qāsim, Ismā'īl al-Manṣūr unterscheiden sich im Rang nicht von den Imamen vor ihnen. Auch der siebte Imam nach Ali, sei er nun der wirkliche oder der vermeintliche Muḥammad b. Ismā'īl, kann keine besondere Rolle spielen. Die sechste Ära, die des Propheten des Islams, ist nicht abgeschlossen. An-Nu'mān, selbst Verfasser des maßgebenden fatimidischen Rechtswerkes da'ā'im al-islām, wird auch in seinen esoterischen Werken nicht müde zu versichern, daß die äußeren Gesetze und der innere Sinn gleichberechtigt nebeneinander stehen[218]).

Doch übernimmt an-Nu'mān die Idee des letzten Qā'im aus der alten Lehre. In seinem ta'wīl da'ā'im al-islām erklärt er, die Wallfahrt, das Siegel der Pflichten des Gläubigen, sei das Symbol Mohammeds, des Siegels der Propheten. „Nach der Wallfahrt bleibt von den Säulen des Islams nur noch der heilige Krieg. Er ist das Symbol des siebten Imams, der der siebte ihrer letzten Heptade ist, der Herr der Auferstehung[219]).“ Nach ihm wird es keine Vollstrecker und keine Imame mehr geben[220]). Er wird den inneren Sinn offen verkünden, der vorher in der Zeit der Propheten bei deren Ḥuǧǧas verborgen war. Die äußerlichen Gesetze wird er aufheben[221]). An-Nu'mān zählt seinen Herrn al-Mu'izz als den siebten Imam der zweiten Heptade und läßt einmal durchblicken, daß vielleicht dieser das Siegel der Imame und der Herr der Auferstehung sei. Aber sogleich fügt er vorsichtig hinzu: „Es wird aber auch gesagt, der dritte vom siebten an, der Nachfolger des Nachfolgers, der auf ihn folgt (ṯānī ṯānīhi'llaḏī jatlūhū min ba'dihi) sei das Siegel[222]).“ Der Drusenlehrmeister Bahā' ad-Dīn bezog das, durchaus berechtigt, auf al-Ḥākim[223]).

[217]) Asās at-ta'wīl in maḏhab S. 140. [218]) Vgl. maḏhab S. 144.

[219]) Al-maǧālis al-mustanṣirīja S. 160, muntaḫabāt ismā'īlīja, Ed. 'Ādil al-'Awwā, Damaskus 1958, S. 10.

[220]) Ta'wīl da'ā'im al-islām in dīwān al-Mu'ajjad, Ed. M. K. Ḥusain, Kairo 1949, S. 333.

[221]) Asās at-ta'wīl in maḏhab S. 140.

[222]) Ta'wīl da'ā'im al-islām in maḏhab, Einl. S. Nūn. Vgl. maḏhab S. 452.

[223]) Īḍāḥ at-tauḥīd, Ms. Berlin Orient. Quart. 814 fol. 199. Ebenso ein späterer ismailitischer Kommentator, vgl. maḏhab Einl. S. Nūn.

In den hier beschriebenen Lehren Qāḍī an-Nu'māns finden sich kaum Anschauungen, die der sunnitische Islam als extrem (ġulūw) kennzeichnen würde. Mochte man an-Nu'māns Dogma von der Notwendigkeit des gottgeleiteten Imams verwerfen, mochte man seinen Begriff des „inneren Sinnes" als abscheuliche Spekulation abtun, so konnte man ihn doch nicht beschuldigen, den Boden des Islams irgendwo grundsätzlich verlassen zu haben. Hierin unterscheidet sich die Dogmatik an-Nu'māns sichtlich von der mancher vorfatimidischer Lehrmeister.

Diese Reform der Lehre war ganz wesentlich das Werk 'Ubaid Allāhs. Sie war, soviel läßt sich wohl sagen, staatspolitisch weise, ja unumgänglich, wenn die ismailitische Lehre jemals tatsächlich zur Staatsreligion erhoben werden sollte. Es mag müßig sein, die Frage aufzuwerfen, ob die Masse der Bevölkerung des Maġrib, Ägyptens und Syriens für ein „gemäßigtes" Schiitentum hätte gewonnen werden können. Unzweifelhaft war aber eine spekulative Lehre, die den Islam als überholt und seine Gebote als aufgehoben betrachtete, dazu nicht geeignet. Ihre Anhänger schlossen sich von selbst aus der muslimischen Gemeinschaft aus[224]). Auch innerhalb des Fatimidenreiches konnten sie nichts als eine Geheimsekte bilden.

Aber dies Bild der Lehren an-Nu'māns ist nicht vollständig. Ein anderes Bild entsteht aus einer Schrift, die er vielleicht nicht allzu lang vor seinem Tod verfaßte[225]). Es weicht so stark von dem ersten ab, daß man von einer neuen Reform der Lehre sprechen kann. Der Urheber dieser Reform war, wie sich zeigen wird, an-Nu'māns letzter Herr, der Imam al-Mu'izz.

## Die Reform des al-Mu'izz

An-Nu'māns Schrift ar-Risāla al-muḏhiba[226]) ist ein Antwortschreiben auf die Fragen offenbar eines Sendboten über dogmatische Probleme. Die Fragen lassen vermuten, daß der Sendbote seine religiöse Ausbildung nicht in der offiziellen fatimidischen Lehre empfangen hatte. Wahrscheinlich gehörte er einer jener östlichen ismailitischen

[224]) Die Ähnlichkeit der Situation mit der der Nizārīs nach der Proklamation der „Auferstehung" im Jahr 559/1164 liegt auf der Hand, vgl. die Darstellung Hodgsons, The Order of Assassins, S. 156f.

[225]) Jedenfalls nach dem Jahr 354/965, da er das in diesem Jahr verfaßte Schreiben des al-Mu'izz an den Sendboten Ǧalam b. Šaibān (vgl. unten S. 110) erwähnt. Ar-Risāla al-muḏhiba in ḫams rasā'il ismā'īlīja, Ed. 'Ārif Tāmir, S. 56.

[226]) Zum Namen vgl. S. 28: Sie soll die Einflüsterungen des Teufels vertreiben.

Gemeinden an, wo noch unter al-Muʿizz manche heterodoxe Theorien fortlebten. An-Nuʿmān hatte mit ihm schon mehrere Schreiben gewechselt[227]). In Fragen und Antworten begegnen Begriffe und Vorstellungen einer gnostischen Kosmologie, von der sich in den bisher untersuchten Texten keine Spur fand. Auch ihren Ursprung darf man in östlichen Gemeinden suchen. Al-Muʿizz übernahm sie und formte sie zu einem eigenen System aus.

Ein großer Teil der Fragen beschäftigt sich mit dem Qā'im, seinem Rang, seinem Erscheinen in der körperlichen Welt und seiner Erhöhung in der geistigen. An-Nuʿmān beschreibt zunächst die verschiedenen Theorien der Kenner der Traditionen der Imame über den Qā'im[228]). Die eine Gruppe von ihnen behauptete, er sei körperlich, ohne göttliche Unterstützung. Sie meinten, er werde nur in die Spuren seines Ahnen, des Propheten, treten, von seinem Wissen zehren, und nach seinen Geboten richten. An-Nuʿmān verwirft diese Ansicht, da Gott doch dem Qā'im einen höheren Rang als irgendeinem Menschen gegeben habe. Eine andere Gruppe, die große Menge, behauptete, er sei spirituell, unabhängig von seiner körperlichen Erscheinung. Als Beispiel erwähnt er die Anhänger des Imams Muḥammad al-Ǧawād[229]), die von ihm sagten, er sei spirituell geworden wie Ali, und werde spirituell die Welt regieren und das Recht auf Erden herstellen. An-Nuʿmān fragt, wie das möglich sei, da die Erde den körperlichen Wesen gehöre. Eine weitere Gruppe — zu ihr sind wohl die Anhänger Ḥamdān Qarmaṭs zu rechnen — sagte, der Qā'im sei der siebte von sieben von Adam und der achte von achten von Ali an. Ihnen wirft an-Nuʿmān vor, sie hätten übersehen, daß Gott Mohammed vor seinen Vorgängern bevorzugt habe, indem er ihm „sieben Wiederholte und den erhabenen Koran" gab (nach Koran 15,87). Das bedeutete, wie an-Nuʿmān an anderer Stelle erklärt[230]), daß die Heptade der Imame nach Mohammed sich wiederholen sollte, während sie sich bei seinen Vorgängern nicht wiederholte.

Eine letzte Gruppe vertrat die Auffassung, der Qā'im trete sowohl körperlich als auch spirituell auf. Sie begründete dies damit, daß die Auferstehung in zwei Schritten vor sich gehe: Zuerst werden die Gläubigen belohnt und die Ungläubigen bestraft. Dazu erscheint der Qā'im in körperlicher Gestalt. Schließlich wird aber Gott die Erde erben, und dann wird der Qā'im über die spirituellen Wesen herrschen. An-Nuʿmān

---

[227]) Vgl. S. 64. [228]) S. 45ff.

[229]) An-Nuʿmān erwähnt ihn nicht namentlich. Er ist es jedoch, der im Jahr 220 (835) in Bagdad starb.

[230]) Ar-Risāla al-muḏhiba S. 70,56.

äußert zu dieser Theorie keine Meinung[231]). Sie kommt seiner später vorgetragenen Lehre am nächsten, ist aber nicht vollständig.

Der Qā'im, erklärt an-Nu'mān, hat drei Grade (ḥudūd): den Grad des Körperlichen, den Grad der Auferstehung in der geistigen Welt und den Grad der Abrechnung (des jüngsten Gerichts). Er hat ferner zwei Stufen: die der Geheimhaltung und die der Offenbarung. Der Qā'im ist aber das äußerste Ende des körperlichen Grades und daher hat er zwei (körperliche) Grade erhalten: den Grad der Sprecher in der Ära der verborgenen Imame und den Grad der rechtgeleiteten Stellvertreter (al-ḫulafā' ar-rāšidīn). ,,Er ist mit seiner Enthüllung erschienen, dann hat er sich verborgen ... um mit der Vollendung seiner Sache zu erscheinen[232]).'' Wann der Qā'im den Grad der Sprecher erreicht hat, wer die rechtgeleiteten Stellvertreter sind, und wie er wieder erscheinen wird, das erläutert an-Nu'mān gegen Ende seines Schreibens, um, wie er angibt, seinem Partner eine zusammenfassende Erklärung für seine Probleme zu geben: ,,Sein Erscheinen in der körperlichen Ära ist am Ende der Ära der sechs Sprecher und der sieben Imame. Er setzt achtzehn Stellvertreter für sich ein, die verborgen sind in der Zeit der Vorsicht[233]) und erscheinen in der Zeit der Enthüllung. Durch den letzten von ihnen wird das Ende eintreten. Dann wird er erscheinen in der Ära der Gestirnwelt (daur al-ǧirm) ... Er wird die feste Zuteilung in das Paradies oder das Feuer bestimmen[234]).''

Der Qā'im ist also am Ende der sieben Imame in Muḥammad b. Ismā'īl erschienen, in ihm erreichte er seinen ersten Grad. An-Nu'mān nennt ihn zwar nicht namentlich[235]). Aber er folgt auch hier gewiß seinem Herrn al-Mu'izz, der gegen die Erklärungen 'Ubaid Allāhs seinen Stammbaum über Muḥammad b. Ismā'īl zurückführte[236]). Muḥammad b. Ismā'īl war der siebte Sprecher, er brachte die Enthüllung, aber da er in der Zeit der Verborgenheit gekommen war, blieb auch sie verborgen. Darum setzte er Stellvertreter für sich ein, und in ihnen erreichte der Qā'im seinen zweiten Grad in der körperlichen Welt. Auch die ersten der Stellvertreter waren verborgen, aber mit 'Ubaid Allāh traten sie in die Zeit des Erscheinens. Durch sie wird der

---

[231]) Ebenso auch al-Mu'izz nicht, vgl. maḏhab S. 137.

[232]) Ar-Risāla al-muḏhiba S. 71.

[233]) At-taqīja zu lesen anstatt al-baqīja. [234]) S. 79.

[235]) An-Nu'mān zählt in all seinen Schriften die Imame nach Ǧa'far aṣ-Ṣādiq bis 'Ubaid Allāh als verborgene und nennt sie nie namentlich, vgl. maḏhab S. 163ff. Auch in ar-Risāla al-muḏhiba verweigert er dem Fragesteller jegliche Auskunft über sie, vgl. S. 57. Dies ist ursprünglich in den Erklärungen 'Ubaid Allāhs begründet, nach welchen schon Ǧa'far aṣ-Ṣādiq den Namen seines Nachfolgers ('Abd Allāh) verborgen hätte. [236]) Vgl. unten S. 92.

Qā'im die über ihn geweissagten Taten vollbringen[237]). Denn Muḥammad b. Ismā'īl wird nicht wiederkehren. Seine Stellvertreter werden bis zum Ende der körperlichen Welt herrschen. Der letzte von ihnen ist der Ḥuǧǧa des Qā'im[238]). Er ist wohl auch der „Herr der Ära unter den Stellvertretern", durch den Jesus erscheinen wird, um das Kreuz zu zerbrechen und das Schwein zu töten[239]). Dann aber wird der Qā'im einen neuen Grad erreichen, in der Welt der Gestirne erscheinen und zu Gericht sitzen. Und schließlich wird er aufsteigen, sich mit der Weltseele verbinden und über alle Grade der Hierarchie herrschen[240]).

An-Nu'mān erläutert auch, worin die Enthüllung besteht, die der Qā'im bringen soll. Der Qā'im „hebt alle Gesetze auf, er offenbart ihren Sinn und übersetzt sie[241])." Mit dem Qā'im „schließt Gott die Ära des Werks ab und eröffnet die Ära des Wissens und der Vergeltung[242])." Diese Enthüllung konnte zur Zeit der ersten Verkörperung des Qā'im in Muḥammad b. Ismā'īl nicht wirksam werden, da er in einer Periode völliger Verborgenheit gekommen war. Aber nach dem Erscheinen der Fatimiden, seiner Stellvertreter, bestand kein Anlaß mehr, daß seine Offenbarung den Gläubigen vorbehalten werde. Die Frage des Sendboten, ob etwas von den äußeren Werken mit dem Wissen ihres inneren Sinnes hinfällig werde, erscheint natürlich, ja sogar überflüssig.

Und doch antwortet an-Nu'mān entrüstet, nichts von den religiösen Pflichten sei aufgehoben, oder würde aufgehoben bis zum jüngsten Gericht: Erst dann werde die Ära Mohammeds enden[243]). Hier wird ein innerer Zwiespalt in dem neuen Lehrsystem deutlich, der in der Meditation der nachdenklicheren Gläubigen auf einen Ausgleich nach der einen oder der anderen Richtung drängen mußte. Der Qā'im war am Ende der sieben Imame gekommen, seine Ära hatte begonnen, und seine Stellvertreter waren erschienen, um seine Offenbarung des inneren Sinnes der Gesetze zu enthüllen. Aber die Ära Mohammeds dauerte fort, die Stellvertreter des Qā'im waren „die sieben Wiederholten", die zweite Heptade von Imamen, die Gott Mohammed allein

---

[237]) Damit begegnet an-Nu'mān der Frage seines Partners, wie der Qā'im der Vollender der Sprecher sein könne, da er doch erschienen und „aufgestiegen" sei, aber nichts neues gebracht habe. An-Nu'mān bestätigt, daß der Qā'im der letzte der Sprecher sei, aber dies wird erst am Ende, durch die „Wiederholten" Mohammeds wirksam, da zuvor finstere Nacht herrschte. S. 56.

[238]) Vgl. S. 66.

[239]) Hierin wird nach an-Nu'mān die „Auswanderung" (hiǧra) Jesu bestehen, die ihm als einzigem unter den Propheten abging. S. 68f.

[240]) Vgl. S. 74f. [241]) S. 70.

[242]) S. 83. [243]) S. 75.

unter den Propheten gegeben hatte, und sein Gesetz würde bis zum jüngsten Gericht seine Geltung behalten.

Es ist wohl keine leere Redensart, wenn an-Nu'mān seinem Fragesteller versichert, daß er die Antworten auf seine Fragen nicht aus sich selbst schöpfe, sondern daraus, was er „den edlen Wissenden, deren die ganze Schöpfung bedarf, entlehnt" habe[244]). In mehreren seiner Bücher erwähnt er, wie stark sein Herr al-Mu'izz sich dafür interessierte, was an-Nu'mān schrieb, wie er sich alles vorlegen ließ, überprüfte und Anregungen gab. Für al-Mu'izz war die Glaubenslehre, wie für 'Ubaid Allāh, ein Instrument der Politik. Aber wenn Realismus und Staatsräson 'Ubaid Allāh schließlich veranlaßten, gegen die zu phantastischen Vorstellungen seiner Anhänger von ihm Stellung zu nehmen, so trieb seinen Urenkel der maßlose Ehrgeiz seiner politischen Ziele dazu, seinen eigenen religiösen Rang bis zur Schwärmerei zu übersteigern.

Einen Eindruck von seiner hochgespannten Konzeption vom Imamat gibt der lange Exkurs in seinem Brief an den Qarmaṭen al-Ḥasan al-A'ṣam[245]). Der gleiche Geist spricht aus der „geheimen Zwiesprache" (munāǧāt), die ihm von den syrischen Ismailiten zugeschrieben wird[246]). In den „Gebeten der sieben Tage"[247]) entwirft er ein Bild der Heilsgeschichte, in dem er die Fatimiden auf den Gipfel der Menschheitsentwicklung stellt, in ihrem Erscheinen geradezu den Sinn der Geschichte erkennt. Die sieben Ären der Sprecherpropheten sind hier auf die sieben Tage der Woche verteilt, und, beginnend mit dem Sonntag[248]), wird an jedem Tag der Woche für einen von ihnen und seine Nachfolger gebetet. „Oh Gott, segne unseren Vater Adam, den du erhöht und geehrt hast ... und segne seine Pforte (bāb) und seinen Vollstrecker Seth b. Adam und die Imame seiner Ära. Es sind sechs, wie die Grade (ḥudūd) von allem, was Grade hat. Denn jeder Sprecher hat in seiner Ära sechs Grade. Der siebte aber wird ihm selbst gleich." Dann nennt al-Mu'izz die sechs Imame namentlich. Die folgenden Gebete entsprechen dem ersten fast wörtlich, doch wird die Aufhebung des „Äußeren" des vom jeweiligen Vorgänger geoffenbarten Gesetzes erwähnt.

Nach Aufzählung der sechs Imame in der Ära Mohammeds — der

---

[244]) S. 52.

[245]) Vgl. die Zitate in Fatimiden und Baḥrainqarmaṭen S. 86f.

[246]) Hrsgb. von S. Guyard, Fragments relatifs a la doctrine des Ismaëlis, Paris 1874, S. 48ff. Echt ?

[247]) Angeführt mit Kürzungen in maḏhab S. 91ff., tārīḫ S. 543f.

[248]) Vgl. tārīḫ S. 543. In den Gebeten selbst deutet anscheinend nichts auf diese Einteilung.

letzte ist Ismā'īl b. Ǧa'far — heißt es dann: „... Oh Gott, gewähre uns die Begegnung[249]) mit dem Erscheinen dessen, der das Recht ausführt (al-qā'im bi'l-ḥaqq), der die Offenbarung enthüllt ... Lenke die natürliche Welt durch die sieben Sprecher, die sieben Fundamente, die sieben Vollender und die sieben Edlen[250]). ... Oh Gott, segne die sieben spirituellen Grade und segne, oh Herr, die sieben körperlichen ... Und segne, oh Herr, den Bruder deines Propheten, den Herrn der auserwählten Vollstrecker, und Fatima, die Leuchtende, die Herrin der Frauen der Welten, und seine beiden Enkel al-Ḥasan und al-Ḥusain. Segne den, der das Recht ausführt, und die Wahrheit verkündet (al-qā'im bi'l-ḥaqq an-nāṭiq bi'ṣ-ṣidq), den neunten seit seinem Ahnen, dem Propheten, den achten seit seinem Vorvater, dem Kauṯar[251]), den siebten seit seinen Vätern, den Imamen, den siebten der Gesandten seit Adam, den siebten der Vollstrecker seit Seth, den siebten der Imame aus seiner (des Propheten) rechtschaffenen Familie. Wie du gesagt hast: 'Wir haben die Himmel und die Erde in sechs Tagen gleichmäßig (sawā'an) für die Suchenden geschaffen. Dann richtete Er sich (istawā) zum Himmel auf[252]).' Es ist dies der Ausgleich (istiwā') der Sache der Sprecher mit dem siebten, dem Qā'im. Wie wir es zuvor erwähnt haben, den du erhöht und geehrt und herrlich gemacht hast, durch den du die natürliche Welt beschlossen hast, durch den du das Äußere des Gesetzes Mohammeds aufgehoben hast[253]), und durch den du die Erde mit Gerechtigkeit und Redlichkeit füllst, wie sie mit Unrecht und Unterdrückung erfüllt war. Wie dein Prophet von ihm verkündete, als er sagte: 'Der Mahdi ist von uns, der Prophetenfamilie. Er ist ein Mann mit schöner Adlernase und schwarzen Augen, der die Erde mit Gerechtigkeit und Redlichkeit füllt, wie sie mit Unterdrückung und Willkür erfüllt war[254]).' Er ist der Übersetzer und Erklärer des Korans, der seine Beweiskraft offenbart und ihn erleuchtet. Er ist der Qā'im der Auferstehung[255]), der Wiederbelebung, der Ent-

[249]) Talāqina, vgl. jaum at-talāqi, Koran 40,15, der letzte Tag.

[250]) An-nuǧabā', vielleicht sind damit hier die Stellvertreter gemeint.

[251]) Koran 108,1. Eigentlich die Fülle. Traditionsgemäß als ein Fluß im Paradies interpretiert. Hier ist Ali gemeint.

[252]) Freie Vereinigung und Umdeutung von Koran 50,38 und 41,9—10.

[253]) Ivanows Übersetzung, Rise S. 245, mit „purified" verfälscht den Sinn.

[254]) Vgl. šarḥ al-aḫbār, Rise, Texte S. 9, Tradition 13, die an-Nu'mān auf 'Ubaid Allāh bezieht.

[255]) Die Übersetzung folgt hier zahr al-ma'ānī, Rise, Texte S. 56. Zahid Ali liest, nach mehreren Handschriften, (wa-hūa jaum al-qijāma) er ist der Tag der Auferstehung. Idrīs b. al-Ḥasan mag das Wort (qā'im) nur als Erläuterung interpoliert haben. Jedoch ist nicht anzunehmen, daß al-Mu'izz damit die Auferstehung überhaupt leugnen wollte. Vgl. unten S. 93.

scheidung, der Übervorteilung[256]), der Auferweckung, 'des Tags, da den Frevlern ihre Ausrede nichts nützt[257])' ... der Herr der Entstehung (ṣāḥib an-nušū'), den die Menschen nicht erkennen, die Vollendung des Wortes, der erste Gedanke, die Lotusblume von al-muntahā[258]), bei welcher der Garten von al-ma'wā[259]), der Bezwinger der Tyrannen, der Helfer der Frommen, der Qā'im des Glaubens, al-Mahdī bi'llāh, der Herrscher der Gläubigen. Und segne seine rechtgeleiteten Stellvertreter (ḫulafā'), die nach dem Recht richten und durch es redlich handeln. Oh Gott, gib ihnen Heil und Erfolg, und hilf ihnen, die offenbare Wahrheit, die sie geheimhielten, zum Siege zu führen."

Al-Mu'izz nennt Muḥammad b. Ismā'īl nicht mit Namen. Da er jedoch zuvor Ismā'īl als den sechsten Imam der Ära des Propheten bezeichnete, kann mit dem „neunten nach Mohammed, dem achten nach Ali und dem siebten nach den Imamen" niemand anderes gemeint sein. In Übereinstimmung damit wird al-Mu'izz auch die folgende Sinndeutung zugeschrieben: „Der Gebetsruf besteht aus fünfzehn Wörtern. Sie deuten auf das Fundament, sechs Vollender und sieben Stellvertreter. Das fünfzehnte ist ein Hinweis auf den Qā'im[260])." Da nur sechs Vollenderimame genannt sind, muß der letzte ihrer Heptade, Muḥammad b. Ismā'īl, der Qā'im sein. So stellt al-Mu'izz ferner fest: „Die zweimalige Wiederholung des Satzes 'Allāhu akbar' ... weist darauf hin, daß, am Ende der Sache der Vollenderimame, die Stellvertreter die Lehre des Qā'im mit Unterstützung der beiden Urprinzipien[261]) vertreten[262])."

Nun aber erklärt al-Mu'izz: „Dann spricht er (der Gebetsrufer) einmal: Es gibt keinen Gott außer Allah; das heißt: Es gibt keinen Qā'im außer dem Imam der Zeit, und es gibt keinen Herrn des Zeitalters außer dem, der den inneren Sinn der Gesetze unvermischt, rein und ohne Äußerlichkeit vertritt (al-qā'im bi-bāṭin aš-šarā'i' ...) ...[263])." Dies klingt fast wie eine Polemik gegen diejenigen, die die leibliche Wiederkehr des Muḥammad b. Ismā'īl, des wahren Herrn der

---

[256]) At-taġābun, Koran 64,9. Nämlich der Ungläubigen durch die Gläubigen.

[257]) Koran 40,52.

[258]) Koran 53,14. Von den Kommentaren als eine Lotusblume an der Schwelle des siebten Himmels ausgelegt.

[259]) Koran 53,15. Die Kommentare verstehen darunter einen Garten des Paradieses.

[260]) Ta'wīl aš-šarī'a in ad-Dailamī, bajān maḏhab al-bāṭinīja, S. 43.

[261]) Al-aṣlān, d. h. der Vorgänger (as-sābiq) und der Folger (at-tālī), die beiden ersten Geschöpfe. [262]) Ta'wīl aš-šarī'a in maḏhab S. 134f.

[263]) Maḏhab S. 135. Auf S. 401, 408 und 632 lautet das Zitat allerdings (lā imām) anstatt (lā qā'im), aber gegen Zahid Alis Übersetzung S. 135.

Zeit, erwarteten. Die Fatimiden, die doch die Stellvertreter des Qā'im sind, übernehmen sein Amt vollkommen uneingeschränkt, indem sie die reine Lehre des inneren Sinnes vertreten. In seinen Gebeten geht al-Mu'izz so weit, den Rang des siebten Gesandten, des Qā'im, von Muḥammad b. Ismā'īl, dem er ihn zuerst zuspricht, auf 'Ubaid Allāh zu übertragen: Der neunte nach Muḥammad, der Qā'im, ist niemand anders als al-Mahdī bi'llāh, amīr al-mu'minīn, d. h. der erste Fatimidenkalif[264]). Die Wiederkehr des Muḥammad b. Ismā'īl wird spirituell umgedeutet. Denn al-Mu'izz will nicht sagen, 'Ubaid Allāh sei der körperlich zurückgekehrte Muḥammad b. Ismā'īl. So erklärt er an anderer Stelle, Gott habe seine Religion über die anderen Religionen triumphieren lassen „durch den vierten einer Heptade von den Heptaden der Imame Mohammeds, nämlich al-Mahdī bi'llāh. Der vierte der sieben Imame mag der mächtigste sein, wie der vierte Sprecher (Moses) der mächtigste war. Denn er ist die Mitte zwischen je dreien, wie die Sonne, welche der mächtigste der sieben Planeten ist[265])."

Der Zug zur Spiritualisierung der Lehre ist auch sonst unverkennbar. In seinem Gebet ruft al-Mu'izz die „sieben spirituellen Grade" an, die von der Geistessphäre die Welt regieren[266]). Der Mahdi, der nach seinem Kommen die Welt beenden sollte, hat die „natürliche Welt" ('ālam aṭ-ṭabā'i') abgeschlossen. Man darf wohl ergänzen, er hat die geistige Welt eröffnet. Dies ist jedoch als teilweise Vorwegnahme zu verstehen und bedeutet nicht, daß al-Mu'izz den jüngsten Tag im überkommenen Sinn, als Ende des irdischen Daseins überhaupt, gänzlich leugnen wollte. Nach den Drusenlehrern erklärte er jedenfalls: „Ich bin der siebte in der zweiten Heptade ... Nach mir wird es keine (vollständige) Heptade mehr geben[267])."

Der siebte Sprecher hat das Äußere des Gesetzes Mohammeds aufgehoben. Aber er bringt kein neues Gesetz, vielmehr ist er der Übersetzer und Erklärer des Korans. Anderswo drückt sich al-Mu'izz deutlicher aus: „Der Qā'im hebt mit seinem Gesetz alle Gesetze auf, die vorausgegangen sind. Er aber schafft kein neues Gesetz, sondern bringt

---

[264]) Zahid Ali bezieht in Übereinstimmung mit der später traditionellen Interpretation die Aussagen über den Mahdiqā'im in den Gebeten nur auf Muḥammad b. Ismā'īl. Aber al-Mahdī bi'llāh amīr al-mu'minīn war für die Zeitgenossen gewiß 'Ubaid Allāh, und die Taten, die al-Mu'izz ihm hier zuschreibt, werden von Ǧa'far b. Manṣūr al-Jaman eindeutig auf 'Ubaid Allāh, nicht auf Muḥammad b. Ismā'īl bezogen.

[265]) Ta'wīl aš-šarī'a in maḏhab S. 19.

[266]) Die Vorstellung des al-Mu'izz von ihnen gibt wohl an-Nu'mān, ar-Risāla al-muḏhiba S. 52f., wieder.

[267]) Ḥamza, an-naqḍ al-ḫafī, fol. 31r, Bahā' ad-Dīn, al-ǧuz' al-awwal, fol. 11v, de Sacy I 69.

den inneren Sinn der Gesetze und Schriften (ṣuḥuf), rein und unvermischt. So aber war seine Lehre ... Er lehnt das äußere Werk ab, nicht aber die vernunftsgemäßen Dinge (al-ʿaqlījāt) ..." Wenn der Prophet zum Beispiel anordnete, daß dreißig Tage gefastet werde, nicht etwa vierzig, oder daß zwei Beugungen mit der ersten Sure und einer anderen zusammen, zwei Beugungen aber mit der Sure al-ḥamd allein gebetet würden, so sind dies Symbole; ,,der Qā'im erklärt den Zweck darin, bringt aber nichts dergleichen[268])."

Andererseits wirft die tatsächliche Lage der Fatimiden manche Schatten auf das allgemeine Bild des Optimismus. Ein großer Teil der Anhänger des al-Muʿizz lebte außerhalb der Grenzen des fatimidischen Reiches, noch immer der ,,Willkür der Gewalthaber" ausgesetzt. Nicht zum wenigsten für ihren Gebrauch waren gewiß die Gebete bestimmt. Al-Muʿizz aber hegte die Hoffnung, Bagdad, ja Konstantinopel zu erobern. So erklären sich die Bitte nach der ,,Begegnung mit dem Erscheinen des Qā'im", obwohl al-Muʿizz gleich danach deutlich macht, daß er schon erschienen ist, und die Bitte um den Sieg der Wahrheit, die so lange geheim geblieben ist.

Ähnlich wie bei Qāḍī an-Nuʿmān fand die Reform des al-Muʿizz ihren Niederschlag in den späteren Werken Ǧaʿfar b. Manṣūr al-Jamans. Über Ǧaʿfars Leben ist nur wenig bekannt. Nach Ibn Mālik al-Jamānī hielt er allein unter seinen Brüdern nach dem Tod des Vaters (302/914—915) ʿUbaid Allāh die Treue, als dieser einen anderen Sendboten als Haupt der Gemeinde im Jemen bestätigte. Ǧaʿfar begab sich dann zu Abū 'l-Qāsim nach dem Maġrib[269]). Nach dem Abbruch der erfolglosen Belagerung al-Mahdījas durch Abū Jazīd feierte er den fatimidischen Sieg in einem Gedicht[270]). Im Monat Šaʿbān 335/März 947 nahm er an einer Schlacht al-Manṣūrs gegen Abū Jazīd teil[271]). Unter al-Muʿizz besaß er ein Haus in der Hauptstadt al-Manṣūrīja (Ṣabra). Als er in Geldschwierigkeiten kam, ließ ihm al-Muʿizz seinen besonderen Schutz angedeihen[272]). Öffentliche Ämter hat er, im Gegensatz zu an-Nuʿmān, im Maġrib offenbar nicht bekleidet, sondern widmete sich ganz der Abfassung von Werken über die allegorische Exegese. Wann er starb, ist nicht bekannt[273]). Später wird

[268]) Ta'wīl aš-šarīʿa in maḏhab S. 137f.

[269]) Ibn Mālik, kašf asrār al-bāṭinīja, S. 40.

[270]) Idrīs, ʿujūn al-aḫbār V 301.

[271]) ʿUjūn al-aḫbār V 407.

[272]) Sīrat Ǧūḏar S. 126.

[273]) Er kann natürlich das Kitāb asrār an-nuṭaqā' nicht erst um das Jahr 380/990 verfaßt haben. Wenn das Werk also von ihm stammt, was sehr wahrscheinlich erscheint, so sind die hundertzwanzig Jahre, die seit dem Verschwin-

Ǧaʿfar als die höchste Pforte (bāb al-abwāb) seines Herrn al-Muʿizz bezeichnet und im Rang noch über Qāḍī an-Nuʿmān gestellt[274]).

Es war Ǧaʿfar, der in seinem Kitāb al-farā'iḍ wa-ḥudūd ad-dīn das Schreiben ʿUbaid Allāhs an die Gemeinde im Jemen zitierte. Und ʿUbaid Allāhs Lehren sucht Ǧaʿfar bei seiner Exegese hier wie auch in seinem Kitāb aš-šawāhid wa'l-bajān[275]) Ausdruck zu geben. Die sieben Imame sind ein feststehender Begriff, unentbehrlich für die Deutung des inneren Sinnes. In aš-šawāhid wa'l-bajān meint Ǧaʿfar zunächst, Gott habe zwischen je zwei aufeinanderfolgende Sprecher sieben Vollenderimame gesetzt[276]). Aber gegen Ende des Werkes[277]) erklärt er, wenn die Zahl der Imame sieben erreiche, so beginne ihre zweite Ära, bis der Sprecher erscheine, wann Gott will. Der Beweis dafür sei, daß zwischen Moses und Jesus 1050 Jahre und zwischen Jesus und Mohammed 500 Jahre verstrichen seien, ohne daß Gott sich an eine den Menschen erkennbare Zahl von Imamen hielt. Das Imamat aber könne zu keiner Zeit unterbrochen werden.

Der Qā'im oder Mahdi ist der siebte Sprecher, der achte von acht Nachkommen Alis. Sein Namen ist Muḥammad[278]). Vor seinem Erscheinen rufen sieben Imame zu seiner Gefolgschaft auf[279]). Man wird auch diese Angaben im Sinne der Erklärungen ʿUbaid Allāhs auslegen müssen. Mohammed ist das Siegel der Propheten und Gesetze, nach ihm wird es kein weiteres Gesetz geben. Der siebte Sprecher aus seiner Nachkommenschaft ist nur der „Übersetzer des Korans Mohammeds, der Vollender seiner Sache, und der Offenbarer seines Lichts[280])."

Großartiger ist das Bild des Qā'im, das Ǧaʿfar in seinem Kitāb ta'wīl az-zakāt entwirft. Er verfaßte diese Schrift unter al-Muʿizz, den er als Herrscher der Gläubigen bezeichnet[281]), vielleicht erst in den

---

den des letzten Imams der Zwölferschiiten vergangen sein sollen (vgl. Rise S. 18 Anm. 2), eine seiner nicht seltenen Leichtfertigkeiten mit Zahlen oder die „Berichtigung" eines frühen Kopisten.

[274]) Vgl. maḏhab Einl. S. Sīn und Ġain/6, H. F. Hamdani: Some unknown Ismaili Authors, JRAS 1933, S. 371.

[275]) In der Terminologie und dem Fehlen der philosophischen Begriffe sind die beiden Schriften eng mit dem Kitāb al-kašf verwandt.

[276]) Aš-šawāhid wa'l-bajān, Ms. der Muḥammadī Hamdānī Sammlung, S. 11.

[277]) S. 133.

[278]) Aš-šawāhid wa'l-bajān S. 20.

[279]) Al-farā'iḍ wa-ḥudūd ad-dīn, Ms. der Muḥammadī Hamdānī Sammlung, S. 10, 175.

[280]) Aš-šawāhid wa'l-bajān S. 21.

[281]) Ta'wīl az-zakāt, Ms. Leiden 2613, S. 213. Die zahlreichen, aber im allgemeinen leicht durchsichtigen Fehler der Handschrift werden im folgenden verbessert, ohne auf sie im einzelnen einzugehen.

Jahren 364—365/975 — Anfang 976[282]). Mohammed, so sagt Ǧaʿfar, ist der vorzüglichste der Gottesgesandten und das Siegel der Prophe-

[282]) Diese Annahme stützt sich auf folgende Andeutung Ǧaʿfars, taʾwīl az-zakāt S. 213: „Wenn zwei Fundamente und ein Vollender in einem Zeitalter zusammenkommen, ernennen sie einen Folger über die Hierarchie, um die Lehre in ihrem Namen zu vertreten (aqāmū lāḥiqan ʿalā'l-ḥudūd li-iqāmat ad-daʿwa bi'smihim) ... Nur in fünf Zeitaltern aber kamen zwei Fundamente und ein Vollender zusammen zu gleicher Zeit. Der Hinweis darin erübrigt die Erklärung, und in der Anspielung darauf findet sich die Niederschrift für denjenigen, der darüber nachdenkt und es versteht." Die fünf Zeitalter werden dann als die Abrahams, Moses', Mohammeds, des Ǧaʿfar aṣ-Ṣādiq und al-Muʿizz angegeben. Ein Vergleich mit Ǧaʿfars Darstellung der Nachfolge für Imam Ǧaʿfar aṣ-Ṣādiq in seinem Werk asrār an-nuṭaqāʾ, Rise, Texte S. 96ff., zeigt, daß wohl auch hier auf gewisse Unregelmäßigkeiten in der Nachfolge angespielt wird. In asrār an-nuṭaqāʾ führt Ǧaʿfar dieselben biblischen Parallelen an: Abraham ernannte zuerst Lot als seinen Schweiger (ṣāmit), später aber machte er Ismael zu seinem Fundament. Ebenso ernannte Moses erst Josua, dann Aaron. Mohammed ernannte erst Ubai b. Kaʿb und später, so darf man ergänzen, ʿAlī b. Abī Ṭālib. Nach einem Hinweis auf Salomon und David meint der Verfasser, Ǧaʿfar aṣ-Ṣādiq sei genau so verfahren. Wie dies zu verstehen ist, macht er an anderer Stelle (S. 82) klar: Als Ismāʿīl b. Ǧaʿfar zu Lebzeiten seines Vaters starb, vermachte er das Imamat seinem Sohn Muḥammad und ernannte einen Stellvertreter für ihn (dies ist offenbar im Text zu ergänzen), um seine Sache zu verbergen, wie Aaron Josua zum Stellvertreter seines Sohnes ernannt hatte. — Von al-Muʿizz ist bekannt, daß er seinen Sohn ʿAbd Allāh zum Nachfolger ernannt hatte, dieser aber am 9. Ǧum. I 364/25. Jan. 975 vor ihm selbst starb (Wüstenfeld, Fatimiden S. 130, sīrat Ǧūdar S. 139 und Anm. 134). Nach der ismailitischen Lehre aber durfte eine Ernennung nicht zurückgenommen und, nach dem Fall der Enkel des Propheten, auf den Bruder übertragen werden. Vielmehr mußte das Imamat auf den Sohn ʿAbd Allāhs übergehen. Ein Sohn ʿAbd Allāhs wird zwar in den Quellen nicht ausdrücklich genannt. Aber die Angabe Ibn al-Abbārs (al-ḥulla as-sijarāʾ S. 291f., ähnlich Ibn Hammādū S. 47), daß al-Muʿizz seinen ältesten Sohn Tamīm bei der Ernennung zur Nachfolge deshalb überging, weil er keinen Sohn hatte, ist durchaus glaubhaft. Selbst wenn sie nur auf ein Gerücht zurückginge, setzte sie voraus, daß ʿAbd Allāh einen Sohn hatte. (Zu Unrecht schließen die Herausgeber des Dīwān Tamīm b. al-Muʿizz, Kairo 1957, Einl. S. Mīm, aus der kunja Tamīms, er müsse einen Sohn gehabt haben. An der Beilegung einer kunja vor Geburt eines Sohnes ist nichts ungewöhnliches, vgl. für die Fatimiden daselbst Einl. S. Zāʾ. Daß Tamīm zunächst für die Thronfolge vorgesehen war, wird von fatimidischer Seite bestätigt in dem Sendschreiben īqāʿ ṣawāʿiq al-irġām, in al-hidāja al-āmirīja, Ed. A. A. A. Fyzee, Oxford University Press 1938, arab. Text S. 36. Hier wird erklärt, al-ʿAzīz sei zum Imamnachfolger ernannt worden, nachdem bereits zwei andere vor ihm erwähnt worden waren. Andererseits hatte Nizār (al-ʿAzīz Abū Manṣūr), den al-Muʿizz nach dem Tod ʿAbd Allāhs zum Thronfolger bestimmte, damals noch keinen Sohn. Sein ältester Sohn Manṣūr (al-Ḥākim) wurde erst im Jahr 375/985 geboren. Die Andeutungen Ǧaʿfars sollen also offenbar die Thronfolge Nizārs legitimieren, aber zugleich auf den recht-

ten[283]). Der Qā'im al-Mahdī bi'llāh ist der Herr der Ära der Vergeltung (ṣāḥib daur al-ǧazā'), der die Ären abschließt. Er ist der letzte Grad (āḫir al-ḥudūd), der Besiegler der Ären und der Gesetze, nach ihm erfolgt die wirkliche Auferstehung (wa-innamā ba'dahū ǧiddat an-nušūr wa'l-ba'ṯ)[284]). Er schließt die Ära des Diesseits und öffnet die Pforte des Jenseits. Er hebt alle Gesetze auf, macht das „Äußere" der Sprecher ungültig und offenbart die Wissenschaft der allegorischen Exegese[285]). Seine Ära ist eine Ära des Wissens ohne Werk[286]). Freilich weiß Ǧa'far auch, daß man den Neubekehrten nichts vom inneren Sinn eröffnen darf, was ihr Fassungsvermögen überschreitet[287]). Das Äußere benötigt das Innere, das Innere aber bedarf des Äußern nicht, es sei denn, um es erkennbar zu machen, denn es (das Innere) kann nur durch feste Gelübde (gemeint ist der Initiationseid) erlangt werden[288]). Trotzdem „ist das Äußere allein Unglaube und Polytheismus und ebenso das Innere allein Ketzerei in bezug auf die Zeichen Gottes und Übertretung seiner Gebote; denn das Äußere verhält sich zum Inneren wie der Körper zum Geist[289])."

In diesen anscheinend unauflösbaren Widersprüchen tritt derselbe Zwiespalt wie in der späten Lehre Qāḍī an-Nu'māns zutag. Er ist offenbar das Ergebnis des Zusammenstoßes der Theorie und der ganz anderen Wirklichkeit. In Ǧa'fars Terminologie übersetzt, könnte man sagen, die Endzeit, das Jenseits hat bereits begonnen, aber gleichzeitig dauert die alte Ära, das Diesseits, noch fort. Ǧa'far interpretiert die „Leute der Höhle" im Koran[290]) als die sieben Imame aus der Nachkommenschaft Alis[291]). Ihr Schlaf deutet auf die Zeit der Verborgenheit, „bis die Religion Gottes zu ihrem Recht gelangte und aus der Verborgenheit und der Geheimhaltung offenbar wurde mit dem Erscheinen des Qā'im am Ende von dreihundert und neun Jahren seit der Zeit als sie sich verbarg, und die Ungläubigen die Oberhand gewannen[292])." Diese Zahl von Jahren ist natürlich auch aus der Erzählung im Koran[293]) übernommen, und der Versuch wäre verfehlt, sie auf geschichtliche Ereignisse anzuwenden. Ǧa'far geht auch nicht so weit wie Ḥamīd ad-Dīn al-Kirmānī, der behauptet, al-Mahdī sei im Jahre

mäßigen Nachfolger, den Sohn 'Abd Allāhs, hinweisen. Nizār al-'Azīz ernannte dann später freilich seinen eigenen Sohn zum Nachfolger.

[283]) Ta'wīl az-zakāt S. 32.

[284]) Ta'wīl az-zakāt S. 35. [285]) S. 103.

[286]) Ta'wīl az-zakāt S. 36, 39, vgl. sarā'ir an-nuṭaqā' in maḏhab, Einl. S. Mīm Anm. 5, Ǧīm.

[287]) Ta'wīl az-zakāt S. 27. [288]) S. 99. [289]) S. 101.

[290]) Koran 18,9: Die Siebenschläfer. [291]) Ta'wīl az-zakāt S. 76.

[292]) Ta'wīl az-zakāt S. 77. [293]) Koran 18, 25.

309 (921) im Maġrib erschienen[294]). Aber Ǧa'far gibt hier in aller Klarheit dem Leser zu verstehen, daß der Qā'im bereits erschienen sei. Und doch kann er an anderer Stelle sprechen von „... den gegenwärtigen Imamen, die sich im Zeitalter des Propheten (Mohammed) befinden, und den erwarteten Imamen, den Inhabern der Ränge (aṣḥāb al-marātib) beim Erscheinen des Qā'im, zur Zeit seines Kommens und der Trennung von Körper und Seele[295])." Dies wird nur verständlich auf der Grundlage der von an-Nu'mān dargelegten Theorie, nach der sich der Qā'im in mehreren Graden offenbart.

Hatte Ǧa'far in seinen früheren Werken die Rolle des Mahdi deutlich unter die Mohammeds gesetzt, so hob er ihn und seine Stellvertreter nun im Rang weit über die Sprecherpropheten. Dies wird bei seiner Interpretation der acht Träger von Gottes Thron[296]) deutlich. Damit sind die sieben Imame gemeint, die zur Nachfolge des Herrn des achten Ranges, des Mahdiqā'im, aufrufen[297]). Diese acht sind gefeit vor dem Ungehorsam (gegen Gott), denn über ihren Rängen gibt es keinen höheren, nach dem ihre Seelen verlangen könnten und damit ungehorsam wären. Im Gegensatz dazu sind die begnadeten Propheten (al-mu'ajjadūn min ar-rusul) nicht sündlos, sondern verfallen dem Ungehorsam, da ihre Seelen nach höheren Rängen verlangen[298]).

Die sieben Imame sind auch hier für Ǧa'far ein fester Begriff, den er immer wieder ohne nähere Erklärung benutzt[299]). Aber er weiß auch, daß al-Mu'izz der siebte zweier Heptaden und der vierte von vieren ist[300]). Dies stimmt durchaus mit der Zählung der Imame überein, die bei an-Nu'mān begegnete und sich später allgemein durchsetzte. An anderer Stelle[301]) spricht Ǧa'far sehr unklar von „den sieben, mit denen Gott die Regelung der Dinge des Diesseits abschließt und die Regelung der Dinge des Jenseits eröffnet." Der erste dieser sieben ist anscheinend der erste der verborgenen Imame, der Sohn des Muḥammad

---

[294]) Maḏhab S. 172. Ebenso 'Alī b. Muḥammad b. al-Walīd (gest. 612/1215), dāmiġ al-bāṭil, vgl. L. Massignon, Les sept dormants d'Ephèse en Islam et en Chrétienté, REI 1954, S. 73. Massignon meint, es handle sich um die Vollendung der fatimidischen Hauptstadt al-Mahdīja. Diese Ansicht ist aber offenbar nicht aus den Texten begründet, und 'Ubaid Allāh verlegte seine Residenz schon im Jahr 308/920 nach al-Mahdīja. [295]) Ta'wīl az-zakāt S. 366.

[296]) Koran 69,17. [297]) Ta'wīl az-zakāt S. 241.

[298]) Ta'wīl az-zakāt S. 243. Vgl. H. Corbin, Épiphanie divine at naissance spirituelle dans la gnose ismaélienne, Eranos-Jahrbuch XXIII S. 195f.

[299]) Auch sieben Vollender genannt. S. 283 definiert der Verfasser den Vollender (mutimm) als den sechsten Imam jeder Ära. Aber sein Wortgebrauch stimmt damit wohl nicht immer überein.

[300]) Ta'wīl az-zakāt S. 214.

[301]) S. 365f.

b. Ismāʿīl. Ǧaʿfar bricht aber sogleich ab, um zu erklären, daß Muḥammad b. Ismāʿīl der siebte der Imame von al-Ḥasan an sei. Ali, als das Fundament des Propheten, wird nicht gezählt, denn im Koranvers 15,87: „Wir gaben dir die sieben wiederholten (Verse) und den erhabenen Koran“, entspricht er dem Koran. Al-Ḥasan ist also der erste Imam und am weitesten unter ihnen vom Jenseits entfernt. Der Sohn des Muḥammad b. Ismāʿīl ist der erste Imam der zweiten Heptade[302]) und der dem Jenseits nächste. „Mit den sieben Nächsten (al-aqrabūn) vollendet Gott siebzig[303]) Vollender. Dies ist die Zahl der siebzig Steine, die in Minâ geworfen werden[304]).“

Leider erklärt Ǧaʿfar hier nicht, wer die sieben dem Jenseits nächsten Imame sind. Aber er bezeichnet einmal den Mahdiqā'im als den achten der Stellvertreter (ṯāmin al-ḫulafā')[305]). Auch kehrt er gegen Ende seines Werkes noch einmal zu der Interpretation der Höhle zurück und erklärt, die Jünglinge[306]), die in ihr Zuflucht suchen, seien die sieben Vollender und die sieben Stellvertreter, die „Wiederholten“ (maṯānī) des Propheten[307]). Da er aber unmittelbar zuvor noch einmal versicherte, am Ende von 309 Jahren sei der Herr der Enthüllung (ṣāḥib al-kašf) erschienen, und habe die Höhle der Geheimhaltung (kahf at-taqīja) ihr Ende gefunden, so kann die Heptade dieser Stellvertreter nicht mit der in al-Muʿizz endenden Heptade von Imamen gleichgesetzt werden, die die Tradition später als die sieben Stellvertreter bezeichnet[308]), obwohl auch Ǧaʿfar eine Heptade mit al-Muʿizz enden läßt. Die Zitate, die Zahid Ali aus anderen Werken Ǧaʿfars[309]) gesammelt hat, bestätigen dies.

„Wir sagen, daß die Ären sieben sind. Die erste von ihnen ist die Ära Adams ..., und die sechste Ära ist die Mohammeds und seines Fundaments, des Herrschers der Gläubigen (Ali) und sechs Imamen ... Die siebte Ära aber ist die des Qā'im Muḥammad b. Ismāʿīl und seiner Stellvertreter. Ihr siebter ist der Mahdi, mit dem das Diesseits endet und das Jenseits beginnt[310]).“ „Sie wußten nicht, daß er dies ihnen an-

---

[302]) Ms.: awwal as-sabʿa al-a'imma aṯ-ṯānī, vielleicht al-maṯānī zu lesen.

[303]) Diese Zahl erklärt sich offenbar nur aus dem folgenden.

[304]) Das Steinwerfen ist eine Zeremonie bei der Wallfahrt nach Mekka.

[305]) Ta'wīl az-zakāt S. 242.

[306]) Koran 18,10. [307]) Ta'wīl az-zakāt S. 427.

[308]) Die dritte Heptade, von al-ʿAzīz bis aṭ-Ṭajjib, wird nach H. F. Hamdani, IC 1937, S. 216, al-ašhad, nach Ivanow, Studies S. 15, al-abdāl genannt.

[309]) Die Zitate aus dem Kitāb al-fatarāt wa'l-qirānāt schließe ich wegen der Bedenken aus, die P. Kraus, REI 1932, S. 486, und M. K. Husain, Dīwān al-Mu'ajjad S. 7, gegen Ǧaʿfars Autorschaft erhoben haben.

[310]) Al-adilla wa'š-šawāhid in maḏhab S. 129.

deutete: Wenn dem Muḥammad b. Ismāʿīl sieben Imame und acht Stellvertreter erfüllt sind, dann müßt ihr eure Herrschaft verbergen, denn die Herrschaft geht auf sie über. Die sieben Tage sind aber die Imame und die acht Nächte die Stellvertreter. Von ihnen sprach das Buch in der Geschichte Hūds: 'Er ließ ihn (den Sturm) sieben Nächte und acht Tage von ununterbrochenem Schrecken wüten[311].' Ebenso wird nach Vollendung dieser sieben Imame und der acht Stellvertreter die körperliche Sache Mohammeds vollendet und die geistige Ära (ad-daur ar-rūḥānī) eröffnet[312]."

Der Beginn des „Jenseits" und der „geistigen Ära" ist gewiß auch hier auf nichts anderes bezogen als das Ende der natürlichen Welt im Gebet des al-Muʿizz: Auf das Erscheinen des erwarteten Mahdi, ʿUbaid Allāh. Die Stellvertreter des Qā'im, Muḥammad b. Ismāʿīl, füllen also die Lücke zwischen ihm und dem ersten Fatimiden[313]). Zugleich zeigt die Unstimmigkeit, nach der der Mahdi einmal der siebte, dann der achte, ja der neunte der Stellvertreter sein sollte, wie sehr dies alles Spekulation ist, und wie wenig sich eine feste Theorie über die dunkle Zeit der Verborgenheit hatte bilden können.

Die Änderungen, die al-Muʿizz an der Lehre seines Urgroßvaters vornahm, lassen sich in folgenden Hauptpunkten zusammenfassen:

1. Er setzte Ismāʿīl b. Ǧaʿfar und Muḥammad b. Ismāʿīl wieder anstelle von ʿAbd Allāh b. Ǧaʿfar in die Linie der rechtmäßigen Imame ein. Damit erhöhte er zugleich die Zahl der Ahnen der Fatimiden um eins und wurde der siebte zweier Heptaden.

2. Um der strengen ismailitischen Deszendenzlehre bezüglich des Imamats Genüge zu tun, erklärte er ʿUbaid Allāhs Vater al-Ḥusain zum rechtmäßigen Imam und ʿUbaid Allāhs Onkel Muḥammad, der tatsächlich der Meister der Bewegung gewesen war, zum Usurpator oder bestenfalls stellvertretenden Imam.

3. Er sprach Muḥammad b. Ismāʿīl, als dem siebten Imam, wieder den Rang des Mahdiqā'im, des siebten Sprechers, zu.

4. Da Muḥammad b. Ismāʿīl aber in einer Zeit völliger Verborgenheit gekommen war, sollten die Handlungen des Qā'im von seinen Stellvertretern nach der Enthüllung ausgeführt werden. Diese Stellvertreter, die Fatimiden, stehen daher im Rang nicht etwa unter dem Qā'im, sondern sind eine weitere Verkörperung seines Prinzips.

---

[311]) Koran 69,7. [312]) Sarā'ir an-nuṭaqā' in maḏhab S. 124.

[313]) Wenn an-Nuʿmāns Feststellung, daß der Qā'im für sich achtzehn Stellvertreter in der Zeit der Verborgenheit und der Enthüllung einsetzte (oben S. 88), mit seiner zuvor ausgesprochenen Erwartung von elf herrschenden Mahdiimamen in Verbindung zu bringen ist (ar-Risāla al-muḏhiba S. 57), so zählte auch er sieben Stellvertreter in der Zeit der Verborgenheit.

5. Er führte in die fatimidische Lehre eine gnostische Kosmologie ein.

Diese Änderungen bedeuteten gegenüber der Reform ʿUbaid Allāhs teilweise eine Rückkehr zu der älteren Lehre. Mit der Wiedereinsetzung des Muḥammad b. Ismāʿīl in die Rolle kehrte al-Muʿizz zu dem Kerndogma der ursprünglichen Lehre zurück. Durch dessen Leugnung oder Umdeutung hatte ʿUbaid Allāh die Abfallbewegung Ḥamdān Qarmaṭs und ʿAbdāns ausgelöst und damit die Einheit der Bewegung gesprengt. Hier wird das Motiv für die neue Reform des al-Muʿizz deutlich. Seine Vorgänger, al-Qāʾim und al-Manṣūr, waren durch die Anstrengungen zur Wahrung der fatimidischen Herrschaft im Maġrib so stark beansprucht, daß sie sich um dogmatische Fragen und die Beziehungen zu den östlichen ismailitischen Gemeinden wenig kümmern konnten. Dies erklärt, wie zur Zeit des al-Muʿizz auch in Gemeinden von Anhängern der Fatimiden mit deren Lehre völlig unvereinbare Anschauungen fortleben konnten. Als al-Muʿizz nach Festigung seiner Herrschaft im Maġrib seine imperialen Pläne der Eroberung des Orients entwickelte, mußte ihn die Existenz dieser Gemeinden verlocken, sie sich für seine Zwecke dienstbar zu machen. Es ist bekannt, wie er Abgesandte seiner östlichen Anhängergemeinden empfing, ihnen Anweisungen erteilte und ihre dogmatischen „Irrtümer" vorsichtig berichtigte[314]). Darüber hinaus mußte al-Muʿizz aber auch bemüht sein, die von den Fatimiden abgefallenen Gemeinden wiederzugewinnen, unter denen sich ein so schlagkräftiger potentieller Vasall wie der Staat der Baḥrainqarmaṭen befand. Dies war offenbar nur möglich, wenn man die Erklärungen ʿUbaid Allāhs, die zu dem Abfall geführt hatten, zurücknahm und der anderen Seite auf dogmatischem Gebiet entgegenkam. Unter al-Muʿizz setzten sich die fatimidischen Lehrmeister wieder mit den wirklichen oder vermeintlichen Lehren ʿAbdāns auseinander und fanden Lob für ihn[315]). Und im Rahmen dieser Versuche, die ursprüngliche Einheit der ismailitischen Bewegung wiederherzustellen, ist auch der lange Brief zu sehen, den al-Muʿizz an den Qarmaṭen al-Ḥasan al-Aʿṣam schrieb[316]).

## Die persische Schule

Die Reform des al-Muʿizz ist also aus der Auseinandersetzung mit den Lehren der östlichen ismailitischen Gemeinden hervorgegangen. Auch dort war die Lehre in ihrer alten Form nicht einfach bewahrt

[314]) Vgl. Stern, Heterodox Ismailism.

[315]) Vgl. Fatimiden und Baḥrainqarmaṭen S. 38 Anm. 5.

[316]) Vgl. Fatimiden und Baḥrainqarmaṭen S. 85ff.

worden, sondern schöpferische Lehrmeister hatten ihr ein neues Gesicht gegeben. Ohne einheitliche Führung waren diese Gemeinden sicher auch in dogmatischen Fragen mehr und mehr auseinandergetrieben. Über diese Entwicklung läßt sich im einzelnen vorläufig nur wenig feststellen. Aber die Lehre dreier ismailitischer Autoritäten, die in frühfatimidischer Zeit in Persien wirkten, ist, wenigstens in den Grundzügen, zu erkennen[317]).

Anscheinend der erste Meister der persischen Schule, der die Lehre nicht nur in Wort, sondern auch in Schrift propagierte, war Muḥammad b. Aḥmad an-Nasafī (hingerichtet 332/943—944). S. M. Stern sieht in ihm den Begründer der ismailitischen Philosophie[318]). Noch in vorfatimidischer Zeit oder während der Herrschaft ʿUbaid Allāhs verfaßte er ein Kitāb al-maḥṣūl, eine Summa seiner Lehre[319]). Da sein Buch, jedenfalls vorläufig, nicht zugänglich ist, muß seine Lehre aus den Zitaten und Diskussionen späterer Autoren wiedergewonnen werden.

Auch an-Nasafī sah die Geschichte als Ablauf der Ären der sieben ismailitischen Sprecherpropheten. Der Sprecherprophet bringt ein Gesetz und gibt ihm eine Grundlage, indem er das „Fundament" (asās) einsetzt[320]). Dem Fundament folgten als Abschluß der Ära sechs Vollenderimame. Nach ihnen kam der Sprecher der neuen Ära[321]).

Dies Bild trifft jedoch für die erste und die siebte Ära nicht zu. Adam hat nach an-Nasafī kein Gesetz gebracht[322]). Er lehrte vielmehr die Einheit Gottes (at-tauḥīd) ohne das Werk[323]). Dies war auch nicht nötig, da Adam der erste war und das einzelne Wesen nicht der Schlechtigkeit (ḫasā'is) verfällt, bis es sich mit einem anderen vermischt. Erst als mit dem Kommen Noahs Seinesgleichen sich zu ihm gesellte, be-

---

[317]) Über das wenige, was von ihren Lebensumständen und der Geschichte der frühen ismailitischen Mission in Persien bekannt ist, vgl. S. M. Stern, The Early Ismaili Missionaries in North-West Persia and in Khurasan and Transoxania, BSOAS 1960, S. 56ff. [318]) Missionaries S. 79.

[319]) Da Abū Ḥātim ar-Rāzī, der es zu berichtigen suchte, wahrscheinlich 322/934 starb, muß es vor diesem Datum verfaßt sein. Ivanows Zweifel an der Verfasserschaft an-Nasafīs, Studies S. 89, erscheinen nicht genügend begründet.

[320]) An-Nasafī war es anscheinend, der den Begriff asās für den waṣī einführte. Er verstand darunter das Fundament des Gesetzes, nicht des Imamats, wie Ivanow, Studies S. 12, das Wort erklärt. Vgl. das Zitat bei Abū Ḥātim ar-Rāzī, al-iṣlāḥ, Ms. der Muḥammadī Hamdānī Sammlung S. 83: (Nūḥ) ... awwalu man assasa'š-šarīʿata wa-aqāma'l-asās. Adam brachte kein Gesetz und setzte darum kein Fundament ein. [321]) Al-iṣlāḥ S. 315.

[322]) Jesus ähnelte nach an-Nasafī Adam darin, daß er kein Gesetz brachte. Er ließ das Gesetz Moses unverändert fortbestehen, al-iṣlāḥ S. 252.

[323]) Al-iṣlāḥ S. 81.

durfte es des Äußeren und der Abfassung eines Gesetzes. Adam hatte darum kein Fundament: Seth war seine Pforte für die Offenbarung seiner Identität[324]).

Hier wird eine antinomistische Tendenz deutlich, die an die von Sa'd b. 'Abd Allāh den Qarmaṭen zugeschriebene Lehre erinnert. Wie dort sollte offenbar der siebte Sprecher, Muḥammad b. Ismā'īl, den gesetzlosen Urzustand und die reine Lehre der Einheit Gottes ohne Werk wiederherstellen. Von ihm erklärte an-Nasafī, daß er wie Jesus verschwunden sei und wiederkehren werde[325]). Diese Wiederkehr stand noch aus. Was an-Nasafī über die Zwischenzeit vor der Wiederkehr aussagte, ist leider vorläufig nicht sicher festzustellen[326]). Aber aus dem Nachdruck, mit dem Abū Ḥātim ar-Rāzī in seiner Berichtigung versicherte, die Ära Mohammeds sei noch nicht abgeschlossen, darf man vielleicht schließen, daß nach an-Nasafīs Darstellung die siebte Ära angebrochen war. In dieser Ära herrschten nicht mehr die Vollenderimame, sondern die Herren der zwölf Provinzen der Welt[327]). Ein anderer Rang war den Vorfahren der Fatimiden in seiner Lehre wohl nicht zugebilligt. 'Ubaid Allāh seinerseits hat offenbar nicht nur an-Nasafīs Lehre vom Qā'im, sondern auch all seine philosophische Spekulation grundsätzlich abgelehnt[328]).

Der Berichtigung der Irrtümer an-Nasafīs widmete Abū Ḥātim ar-Rāzī ein umfangreiches Buch. Versucht man zu ergründen, was ihn zu diesem unter Glaubensbrüdern, die in schwierigsten äußeren Verhält-

---

[324]) Al-iṣlāḥ S. 83. [325]) Al-iṣlāḥ S. 245, Studies S. 118.

[326]) Abū Ḥātims al-iṣlāh ist nur unvollständig erhalten, vgl. Ivanow, Studies S. 92. Außer dem Anfang fehlt auch das Ende. Wahrscheinlich behandelte Abū Ḥātim in dem fehlenden Teil noch die Zwischenzeit.

[327]) Die Institution der zwölf Folger (lawāḥiq), die den zwölf Ḥuǧǧas in der jemenitischen Lehre entsprechen, kannte an-Nasafī, vgl. al-iṣlāḥ S. 315. Abū Ja'qūb as-Siǧistānī, der die Lehren an-Nasafīs im wesentlichen übernahm und ausbaute, erklärte, in der Ära der Enthüllung herrschten die zwölf Engel als Herren der Provinzen anstelle der sieben Imame, die die Herren in der Zeit der Verborgenheit seien. Andererseits herrschen nach ihm aber in der Ära des Qā'im auch dessen Stellvertreter. Da an-Nasafī von der Theorie der Stellvertreter des Qā'im anscheinend nichts wußte, möchte ich annehmen, daß das erste Bild auf ihn zurückgeht.

[328]) Im Jemen scheint man, zum mindesten in der von 'Ubaid Allāh abgefallenen Gemeinde des 'Alī b. al-Faḍl, die ismailitische Philosophie zu Anfang des 4./10. Jahrhunderts schon gekannt zu haben, vgl. C. van Arendonk, De Opkomst van het Zaidietische Imamaat in Yemen, Leiden 1919, S. 303ff. In den Maǵrib ließ sie 'Ubaid Allāh nicht eindringen. Der höchste Lehrmeister während seiner Herrschaft im Maǵrib, Abū 'Alī al-Ḥasan b. Aḥmad (gest. 321/933) verfaßte ein Buch ummahāt al-islām, in dem er unter anderem die Lehren der Philosophen widerlegte. Idrīs, 'ujūn al-aḫbār V 222.

nissen gemeinsame Ziele verfolgten, ungewöhnlichen Schritt veranlaßte, so stößt man auf Abū Ḥātims kompromißlose Ablehnung jener antinomistischen Tendenz, die in den Thesen an-Nasafīs Ausdruck fand.

Abū Ḥātim erklärt gegen an-Nasafī, es sei unvorstellbar, daß Adam die Einheit Gottes ohne Werk gelehrt habe, denn die Einheit Gottes sei nur durch die Werke, Gebote und Hinweise zu begreifen, die die Sprecherpropheten bringen[329]). Niemand dürfe glauben, daß es in der Ära Adams, die die längste aller Ären war, keine äußeren Gebote gegeben habe, da alle wahre Lehre sich auf dem göttlichen Gesetz aufbaue, und der innere Sinn der äußeren Offenbarung bedürfe[330]). Adam hat also, wie die fünf Sprecher nach ihm, ein Gesetz gebracht. Seth war sein Fundament[331]).

Doch weiß auch Abū Ḥātim, daß der siebte Sprecher kein Gesetz bringt, da er der Herr der Enthüllung ist[332]). In der siebten Ära gibt es kein Werk, in ihm wird die Welt in ihren Urzustand zurückkehren[333]). Da nun aber der siebte Sprecher in Muḥammad b. Ismā'īl, dem siebten Vollenderimam der Ära Mohammads, bereits erschienen ist, so müßte die siebte Ära ohne Werk bereits begonnen haben. Um diese Folgerung nichtig zu machen, führt Abū Ḥātim den Begriff der Zwischenzeit (fatra) ein. Er definiert sie als die Abwesenheit des Vollenderimams[334]). Die Zwischenzeit tritt notwendig am Ende jeder Ära ein[335]), nämlich nach dem Verschwinden des siebten Vollenderimams bis zum Kommen des Sprechers der nächsten Ära. In dieser Zwischenzeit herrschen die zwölf Folger (lawāḥiq, Einz.: lāḥiq). Einer unter ihnen ist aber der Stellvertreter (mustaḫlaf oder ḫalīfa) des abwesenden Vollenders. Er ist der Schiedsrichter unter ihnen. Da er jedoch im Rang nicht über ihnen steht, kann ihm sein Amt streitig gemacht werden, während der Vollenderimam einzig ist in seiner Zeit[336]).

Eine solche Zwischenzeit war auch nach dem Verschwinden Muḥammad b. Ismā'īls eingetreten. Darum ist die Ära Mohammeds noch nicht abgelaufen[337]). Der siebte Sprecher hat drei Grade: den der übrigen Vollenderimame, den der Abwesenheit und den des Erscheinens[338]). Darum ist auch die Gleichsetzung der Abwesenheit des Siebten mit der Erhebung Jesu zum Himmel falsch, da die Sache Jesu

---

[329]) Al-iṣlāḥ S. 77. [330]) Al-iṣlāḥ S. 64. [331]) S. 83.

[332]) S. 61. [333]) S. 77. [334]) S. 231, 332.

[335]) Al-iṣlāḥ S. 331. Sie kann auch inmitten einer Ära eintreten, wenn nämlich ein Vollenderimam stirbt und sein rechtmäßiger Nachfolger noch zu jung zur Übernahme seines Amtes ist.

[336]) Al-iṣlāḥ S. 14, 231, 268. [337]) S. 58. [338]) S. 127.

bei seinem Scheiden aus der Welt abgeschlossen war, während die Sache des Siebten bei seinem Verschwinden noch nicht abgeschlossen war[339]). Erst bei seiner Wiederkehr wird er den Grad der Letztheit[340]) erlangen.

Während die Vollenderimame alle Nachkommen des Sprechers und des Fundaments sind, ist der Rang der Folger und damit der Stellvertreter ausschließlich der übrigen Menschheit vorbehalten. Abū Ḥātim erklärt, Abraham habe einen seiner Söhne zum Folger machen wollen, aber Gott verwehrte ihm dies, da diese Würde der Gemeinde der Gläubigen nicht auch noch vorenthalten werden könne. Abū Ḥātim betont, daß diese Regelung Gottes in allen Ären, auch der Mohammeds, gültig sei[341]). Daraus erhellt, daß Abū Ḥātim die Vorfahren der Fatimiden, wenn er sie als die Stellvertreter Muḥammad b. Ismāʿīls ansah, keinesfalls als Aliden anerkannte[342]).

Hat Abū Ḥātim ar-Rāzī Abū 'l-Qāsim als Imam anerkannt, wie die späten Angaben des Idrīs b. al-Ḥasan[343]) andeuten? Er müßte in ihm den wiedergekehrten Muḥammad b. Ismāʿīl gesehen haben, während er seine tatsächlichen Ahnen nicht für Aliden hielt[344]). Dies ist im Hinblick auf die Angaben von ismailitischen Gemeinden, die Abū 'l-Qāsim im Gegensatz zu ʿUbaid Allāh als Aliden ansahen, nicht ohne weiteres auszuschließen. Dagegen sprechen aber gewichtige Nachrichten aus der Biographie Abū Ḥātims.

Nach Niẓām al-Mulk versprach Abū Ḥātim seinen Anhängern in Ṭabaristān das baldige Erscheinen des Imams. Als jedoch das Datum, das er ihnen genannt hatte, verstrich, ohne daß der Imam erschien, be-

---

[339]) Al-iṣlāḥ S. 245. Abū Ḥātim fügt hinzu, daß die Erhebung des Messias zum Himmel, die im Koran (4,158) erwähnt wird, vielmehr auf Ali zu deuten sei. Ali werde beim Erscheinen des Herrn der Enthüllung vom Himmel steigen und hinter ihm beten, S. 248.

[340]) Ḥadd al-āḫirīja, S. 244. [341]) Al-iṣlāḥ S. 178f.

[342]) Gelegentlich konnte in Abwesenheit des Vollenders das Gotteszeugnis statt in einem Folger in einem Depositär (mustaudaʿ) sein. Dieser stand eigentlich außerhalb der Hierarchie. Er mochte das Depositum anvertraut bekommen, wenn entweder die Zwischenzeit besonders lang war, wie vor dem Erscheinen Mohammeds (S. 333), oder der Folger, der die Hierarchie beherrschte, Unrecht tat und nach einem höheren Rang verlangte (S. 317). Depositär konnte auch ein Alide werden: Nach dem zweiten Vollender Mohammeds (al-Ḥusain) verwahrte ein Depositär getreulich das Depositum, nicht der herrschende Folger (S. 327). Mit dem Depositär ist hier offenbar Muḥammad b. al-Ḥanafīja gemeint. [343]) Vgl. oben S. 67.

[344]) ʿUbaid Allāh könnte dann die „Pforte des Siebten“, die unmittelbar vor der Enthüllung erscheint (S. 235), „der Achte“, der das Tor der Buße schließt (S. 251), sein. Dieser ist aber anscheinend auch der wiederverkörperte Ali.

drohten sie ihn, und er mußte fliehen[345]). Zuvor war Abū Ḥātim Sendbote in ar-Rajj gewesen. Diesem unterstanden, jedenfalls in späterer Zeit, die Sendboten im nördlichen Zweistromland (Mosul) und Bagdad. Sicherlich bestanden auch schon, als Abū Ḥātim in ar-Rajj residierte, enge Beziehungen dorthin. Wohl nicht zufällig nennt ihn ʿAbd al-Ǧabbār zusammen mit den Sendboten Abū 'l-Qāsim ʿĪsā b. Mūsā und den Brüdern Abū Muslim und Abū Bakr b. Ḥammād von Mosul[346]). Diese Kreise aber waren es, die das Vermächtnis ʿAbdāns hüteten und andererseits engste Beziehungen zu den Baḥrainqarmaṭen, jedenfalls bis zu dem Fiasko mit dem Isfahaner, unterhielten[347]). All dies läßt es wahrscheinlich erscheinen, daß Abū Ḥātim, wie die Baḥrainqarmaṭen, weder ʿUbaid Allāh noch Abū 'l-Qāsim als den erwarteten Imam anerkannte. Man darf dann wohl das Bild von dem ungerechten Folger, der die Hierarchie beherrscht und unterdrückt, und nach dem Rang des Sprechers verlangt, da er weiß, daß dessen Erscheinen bevorsteht[348]), für die Ära Mohammeds auf ʿUbaid Allāh beziehen[349]). Die Reform des al-Muʿizz hat dann Abū Ḥātim, wie ʿAbdān, rehabilitiert[350]).

Gegen die Angriffe Abū Ḥātims hat die Thesen an-Nasafīs Abū Jaʿqūb as-Siǧistānī in einem eigenen Buch verteidigt. Während sich mehrere andere Werke Abū Jaʿqūbs noch heute in den ismailitischen Bibliotheken finden, ist das Kitāb an-nuṣra anscheinend nicht erhalten. Aber eine Reihe von Zitaten daraus führt Ḥamīd ad-Dīn al-Kirmānī in seinem Kitāb ar-rijāḍ an, in dem er die Rolle des Schiedsrichters in dem alten Gelehrtenstreit einzunehmen versuchte.

Abū Jaʿqūb ging, so scheint es, in seiner Abwertung der Werke und der religiösen Gesetzlichkeit noch über an-Nasafī hinaus. Er fragt, wie

---

345) Vgl. Stern, Missionaries S. 64. 346) Vgl. Missionaries S. 69.

347) Über ʿĪsā b. Mūsā vgl. Fatimiden und Baḥrainqarmaṭen S. 84f. Über die Banū Ḥammād vgl. Missionaries S. 68: Wie ʿĪsā b. Mūsā sollen sie Bücher verfaßt und ʿAbdān zugeschrieben haben. Zu diesem Kreis gehörte offenbar auch der aus Bagdad stammende Literat Abū'l-Ḥasan ʿAlī b. Waṣīf, ein Freund und Gesellschafter Ibn an-Nadīms. Den größeren Teil seines Lebens verbrachte er in ar-Raqqa, später lebte er in Mosul. Auch er schrieb mehrere seiner Bücher ʿAbdān zu, vgl. fihrist, Ed. Flügel, I 139, Yāqūt, iršād, Ed. Margoliouth, V 435.

348) Al-iṣlāḥ S. 317, bezogen auf das Ende der dritten Ära.

349) Dies spricht gegen die Annahme Sterns, Missionaries S. 69, 75, daß die Baḥrainqarmaṭen ʿUbaid Allāh und seine Nachfolger nicht als Imame, aber als politische Herren anerkannten. Das erscheint mir unwahrscheinlich.

350) Nach Idrīs b. al-Ḥasan sprach sich al-Muʿizz lobend über Abū Ḥātims Kitāb az-zīna aus, vgl. Ivanow, The alleged Founder S. 87 Anm. 2. Al-Kirmānīs Hochschätzung für Abū Ḥātim (vgl. unten S. 124) beruhte auf seinem strengen Festhalten am Gesetz Mohammeds, das auch al-Kirmānī mehr galt, als der Gehorsam gegenüber den Imamen.

es dem Verfasser des Kitāb al-maḥṣūl habe unterlaufen können, einerseits zu erklären, Adam habe die Einheit Gottes ohne das Werk gelehrt, andererseits zu behaupten, die Einheit Gottes sei nur durch die Werke und die Andeutungen der Propheten zu begreifen. Dies sei abgesehen von seiner Widersprüchlichkeit grundfalsch. In der wunderbaren Weisheit der Ordnung der Welt, der Zusammensetzung der Körper und der Mischung gegensätzlicher Naturen gäbe es genügend Hinweise auf die Einheit Gottes, um die Festsetzung von Werken und verschiedenartigen Auflagen, die auf eine ohnehin klare Bedeutung hindeuten sollten, überflüssig zu machen. Viele von diesen Hinweisen, Werken und äußerlichen Ausdrücken (in den Offenbarungen der Propheten) hätten die Mehrheit der Menschen nur vom Bekenntnis der Einheit Gottes abgebracht und sie zu seiner Verähnlichung (tašbīh) mit der Schöpfung geführt, die dem niedrigsten seiner Geschöpfe unwürdig sei[351]).

Den Erklärungen Abū Ḥātims über die Notwendigkeit der religiösen Gesetze als Quelle des Wissens begegnet Abū Ja'qūb mit der Frage, ob jener meine, daß die Geschöpfe in der großen Ära (gemeint ist die Zeit vor Adam) die Einheit Gottes nicht gekannt hätten, da es bei ihnen kein äußeres Gesetz gab, und daß der Qā'im, indem er die Gesetze aufhebe, das Wissen um die Einheit zerstöre und die Menschen zur Inhaltsentleerung (ta'ṭīl) leite[352]). Abū Ja'qūb verteidigt die Lehre an-Nasafīs, daß Adam kein Gesetz gebracht habe, und erklärt, dessen habe es damals nicht bedurft, da die Geschöpfe vor und zu Adams Zeit nicht die Hierarchie mißachtet hätten oder dem Widersacher (aḍ-ḍidd) gefolgt wären[353]). Bis zur Zeit Noahs lag die Herrschaft über die Hierarchie bei den Folgern[354]). Auch sonst scheint Abū Ja'qūb das Geschichtsbild an-Nasafīs gegen Abū Ḥātim vertreten zu haben, soweit die wenigen Zitate bei al-Kirmānī darüber dies erkennen lassen. Zwischen den Sprecherpropheten, erklärt er, gibt es je sieben Imame, deren letzter, darf man wohl ergänzen, wieder ein Sprecher wird[355]). Nach dem Qā'im gibt es aber keine Imame mehr, sondern die Ära seiner Folger und Stellvertreter, die ihm in der Welt folgen, bricht an[356]). Für

---

[351]) Al-Kirmānī, Kitāb ar-rijāḍ, Ms. der Muḥammadī Hamdānī Sammlung S. 194. [352]) Ar-rijāḍ S. 200. [353]) S. 187.

[354]) Ar-rijāḍ S. 218. Im Gegensatz dazu erklärt Abū Ja'qūb an anderer Stelle, wie al-Kirmānī ihm zu Recht vorwirft, Adam seien sechs Imame in seiner Ära gefolgt, S. 209.

[355]) Die fatra definiert er in iṯbāt an-nubūwāt (S. 317) als einen Schwächezustand der Teilseelen in der körperlichen Welt, durch den sie eine Zeitlang am Empfang der göttlichen Unterstützung gehindert sind, nicht als Abwesenheit des Imams wie Abū Ḥātim. [356]) Ar-rijāḍ S. 209.

Abū Jaʿqūb, wie für an-Nasafī, hatte die Ära Mohammeds mit dem Kommen des Qā'im, Muḥammad b. Ismāʿīl, geendet[357]).

Äußerungen solch radikaler Abwertung der prophetischen Offenbarungen bedeuteten in einer bei allen Widersprüchen eminent religiösen Gesellschaft ein Wagnis. Vielleicht wollte Abū Jaʿqūb gefährlicher Kritik begegnen, als er sein „Buch der Bestätigung des Prophetentums" (iṯbāt an-nubūwāt) verfaßte. Er beteuert darin, nicht zu denen zu gehören, die sich auf die Sinndeutungen (ta'wīlāt) ohne Befolgung der religiösen Gebote verließen[358]). Er qualifiziert sorgfältig, was von den religiösen Gesetzen durch den Qā'im aufgehoben werden könne und was nicht. Manche Gebote, erklärt er, sind vernunftgemäß (ʿaqlī), wie das Verbot des Tötens. Diese können niemals aufgehoben werden, da das Wohl der Menschheit von ihnen abhängt. Andere Gebote sind einfach gesetzt (waḍʿi), wie die Bestimmungen über rituelle Reinheit, Gebet und Almosen. Diese Bestimmungen sind festgesetzt wegen der in ihnen verborgenen Hinweise. Die gesetzten Gebote können auch nicht mehr vollständig aufgehoben werden, da sie sich den vernunftgemäßen angenähert haben, insofern sie für die menschliche Ordnung und das Wohl des Körpers erforderlich sind. Aber ihre Einzelvorschriften können geändert oder aufgehoben werden. Dies aber steht nur dem Qā'im zu. Jeder andere, der es sich anmaßt, setzt sich dem Fluch Gottes aus[359]). Am Schluß seiner Erörterung meint Abū Jaʿqūb jedoch, auf die Frage, ob die Gebote auf einmal oder eines nach dem anderen aufgehoben würden, sei zu antworten, weder der Qā'im noch seine Stellvertreter höben sie auf, sondern die Völker selbst, Stück für Stück. Wenn dann der Qā'im erscheine, sei nichts mehr in ihren Händen[360]).

Das sechste Kapitel, in dem Abū Jaʿqūb seine Lehre der Heilsgeschichte ausführlich darstellte, ist leider bis auf einige kurze Bruchstücke verloren. Aber aus den erhaltenen Teilen ist soviel zu entnehmen, daß er seine in Unterstützung an-Nasafīs vorgetragenen Ansich-

---

[357]) Darin wie in anderen Fragen, modifizierte er später seine hier vertretenen "extremen" Ansichten. In seinem kašf al-maḥǧūb, Ed. H. Corbin, Teheran 1949, S. 53, bezeichnet er Mohammed als „Herrn unserer Ära".

[358]) Kitāb iṯbāt an-nubūwāt, Ms. der Muḥammadī Hamdânī Sammlung S. 79.

[359]) S. 300ff. Unter dem Qā'im sind auch seine Stellvertreter zu verstehen, da sie seine Handlungen ausführen. Als Beispiel eines aufzuhebenden Gebots nennt Abū Jaʿqūb die Wallfahrt nach Mekka. Das Haus Gottes in Mekka sei ein Hinweis auf den von Gott eingesetzten Imam in der Zeit der Herrschaft der falschen Imame. Wenn der wahre Imam seine Herrschaft über die ganze Welt ausgebreitet habe und kein Gegner ihm das Imamat und das Kalifat mehr streitig mache, müsse das Gebot aufgehoben werden. S. 300f.

[360]) S. 303.

ten im wesentlichen weiterführte. Adam hat, wie der Qā'im, kein Gesetz gebracht[361]). Zwischen den Sprechern gibt es je sieben Imame, deren siebter der nächste Sprecher wird[362]). Mohammed ist das Siegel der Propheten. In seiner Nachkommenschaft bleibt das Imamat und die Stellvertreterschaft (ḫilāfa) bis zum Tag der Auferstehung. Denn die Stellvertreter des Herrn der Auferstehung sind die sieben Wiederholten, die Gott Mohammed gab[363]). Und diese Stellvertreter bezeichnet Abū Ja'qūb jetzt, im Gegensatz zu seinen Erklärungen in dem Kitāb an-nuṣra, als Imame[364]). Sie sind es, die die Taten des Qā'im vollbringen[365]).

Unverkennbar nähert sich Abū Ja'qūb hier der Reformlehre des al-Mu'izz. Die Anklänge sind so stark, daß man eine unmittelbare Abhängigkeit zwischen ihnen annehmen muß. Leider läßt anscheinend nichts in den erhaltenen Teilen von Abū Ja'qūbs Buch das Datum seiner Abfassung erkennen. Übernahm er hier die neue Lehre des Fatimiden oder war er ihr eigentlicher Schöpfer? Auch wenn manches für die erste Alternative spricht, darf man annehmen, daß al-Mu'izz seinerseits bei seiner Reform wesentlich auf der älteren Lehre Abū Ja'qūbs aufbaute. Sicher ist auch, daß Abū Ja'qūb, zum mindesten seit der Zeit der Abfassung des Kitāb iṯbāt an-nubūwāt, die Fatimiden als Imame anerkannt hat[366]).

---

[361]) S. 215. [362]) S. 282, 278.

[363]) S. 6. Von den sieben Stellvertretern, die nach den sieben Vollendern kommen, spricht Abū Ja'qūb auch in seinem Kitāb al-janābī', Ms. der Muḥammadī Hamdānī Sammlung, S. 16. In der kurzen Abhandlung Risālat tuḥfat al-mustaǧībīn erklärt er unbestimmt, nach dem Qā'im, Muḥammad b. Ismā'īl, folgten seine Stellvertreter sieben auf sieben (sab'a bi-sab'a) bis zur Vollendung der Zahl. Ähnlich waren in den früheren Ären sechs auf sechs Imame dem Sprecher gefolgt, bis am Ende der Ära der siebte zum Sprechergrad aufstieg. Ḫams rasā'il ismā'īlīja, S. 152f. Die Abhandlung mag später als die vorgenannten Werke, vielleicht erst unter al-'Azīz verfaßt sein.

[364]) Iṯbāt an-nubūwāt S. 300. [365]) S. 311.

[366]) Über seine frühere Haltung läßt sich vorläufig nichts sicheres sagen. In an-Nasafīs Kitāb al-maḥṣūl hatte anscheinend nichts auf eine Anerkennung der Fatimiden als Herren der Gläubigen gedeutet. Andererseits wurde nach Ibn an-Nadīm (wohl Ibn Rizām) der zweite Sendbote in Ḫurāsān, Abū Sa'īd aš-Ša'rānī, von 'Ubaid Allāh geschickt, vgl. Missionaries S. 77. Nach Ibn ad-Dawādārī VI 66 (Aḫū Muḥsin) wurde vielmehr sein Vorgänger, Abū 'Abd Allāh al-Ḫādim, ursprünglich ein Diener (ḫādim) 'Ubaid Allāhs im Maġrib, von ihm gesandt, und er war es, der aš-Ša'rānī für die Lehre gewann. Aus diesen Angaben wäre zu schließen, daß die Mission in Ḫurāsān, im Gegensatz zu der in Westpersien, den Fatimiden unterstand. Dann hätten an-Nasafī und nach ihm Abū Ja'qūb, die Fatimiden als Herren anerkannt, allerdings in heterodoxer Lehre als Stellvertreter Muḥammad b. Ismā'īls, nicht als Imame. Daß der von 'Ubaid Allāh ge-

Der Begriff der Stellvertreter (ḫulafā') des Qā'im gibt noch einige Fragen auf. Im ältesten Bestand der ismailitischen Lehre ließ er sich nicht feststellen. Er begegnete am frühesten bei Abū Ḥātim ar-Rāzī[367]), für den der Stellvertreter der erste unter den zwölf Folgern (lawāḥiq) war und den abwesenden Imam vertrat. Er war also einer der Ḥuǧǧas, kein Imam. Darüber hinaus betonte Abū Ḥātim, daß der Rang des Folgers, und damit des Stellvertreters, keinesfalls von einem Angehörigen der Familie des Propheten eingenommen werden könne. Es ist nicht zu beweisen, daß Abū Ḥātim als erster den Begriff in die Lehre eingeführt hat. Aber wahrscheinlich entspricht sein Gebrauch von ihm ungefähr der ältesten mit ihm verbundenen Vorstellung.

Ähnliche Vorstellungen waren später unter Anhängern des Imams al-Mu'izz in as-Sind verbreitet. Al-Mu'izz mußte sich mit ihnen in einem 354/965 abgefaßten Schreiben an seinen dortigen Sendboten, Ǧalam b. Šaibān, auseinandersetzen[368]). Al-Mu'izz beschreibt ihre Lehre so: Nach Muḥammad b. Ismā'īl gibt es keinen Imam. Er ernannte als seinen Stellvertreter 'Abd Allāh b. Maimūn al-Qaddāḥ. Die Zahl der Stellvertreter, die ihren jeweiligen Nachfolger ernennen, ist auf sieben beschränkt. Nach dem siebten erwarteten sie anscheinend die Wiederkunft des Muḥammad b. Ismā'īl in Glorie[368a]). Al-Mu'izz

---

schickte Lehrmeister solche Lehren vertrat, ist nicht anzunehmen. Wenn aber schon ein derartiger Bruch in der Tradition der Lehre der Ḫurāsāner Mission anzunehmen ist, so mochte er freilich ebensogut zu einem Abfall von den Fatimiden geführt haben. S. M. Stern identifiziert den Abū Ja'qūb, der nach Ibn Rizām um 320—330/932—942 die Mission in Westpersien leitete, mit as-Siǧistānī, Missionaries S. 68. Ist diese Identifikation richtig, so dürfte as-Siǧistānī ursprünglich kein Anhänger der Fatimiden gewesen sein. Zwar mochte die Mission in Westpersien die Beziehungen zu den Baḥrainqarmaṭen nach dem verheerenden Ausgang der Episode mit dem Isfahaner abgebrochen haben. Aber die Bezeichnung jenes Sendboten Abū Ja'qūb als Stellvertreter des Imams deutet darauf hin, daß man die Fatimiden nicht als Herren anerkannte. Denn Imame gab es in der heterodoxen Lehre nach Muḥammad b. Ismā'īl nicht mehr. Sein Stellvertreter war nun aber offenbar jener Abū Ja'qūb.

[367]) Die Idee selbst dagegen ist älter. Nach Sa'd b. 'Abd Allāh, S. 68, waren einige Anhänger des Mūsā b. Ǧa'far, die seinen Tod leugneten, der Ansicht, daß 'Alī ar-Riḍā und seine Nachfolger nicht Imame seien, sondern seine Stellvertreter, bis er wieder erscheine.

[368]) Vgl. Stern, Heterodox Ismailism S. 11ff.

[368a]) Dieselbe Lehre ist in einem leider sehr gekürzten Zitat Ibn al-Ǧauzīs, al-muntaẓam V 119, aus ungenannter antiismailitischer Quelle zu erkennen: Die Anhänger 'Abd Allāh b. Maimūns „sagten, der jeweilige Vorgänger von ihnen ernenne bei seinem Tod einen Stellvertreter, und alle seien sie Stellvertreter des Muḥammad b. Ismā'īl ... Zu den Sendboten, die zur Gefolgschaft des Imams aufrufen, gehören auch Ma'add Abū (abā statt ibn zu lesen)

lehnt in seiner Stellungnahme diese Befristung (tauqīt) des Erscheinens des Qā'im ab. Noch stärker wehrt er sich dagegen, daß das Imamat je unterbrochen werden könne, und daß Muḥammad b. Ismā'īl einen gewöhnlichen Menschen zu seinem Nachfolger hätte ernennen können.

Aber die Vertreter dieser Lehre, die den Meistern nach Muḥammad b. Ismā'īl nur den Rang von Stellvertretern, nicht von Imamen, zubilligten, erkannten, wie Stern dargelegt hat, die drei Fatimiden al-Qā'im, al-Manṣūr und al-Mu'izz als Aliden an. Dies wird durch die Angabe an-Nu'māns bestätigt, wonach jene sich auf das Ǧa'far aṣ-Ṣādiq zugeschriebene Wort bezogen: „Die Vollendung unserer Sache ist in dreien von uns und vieren, die nicht von uns sind[369]).“ An-Nu'mān erklärt dazu, sie hätten Ursprung und Sinn des Wortes mißverstanden. Gemeint seien mit den „drei von uns“ Ǧa'far selbst, sein Sohn (Ismā'īl), und sein Enkel (Muḥammad b. Ismā'īl). Und die „vier, die nicht von uns sind“, identifiziert an-Nu'mān natürlich nicht mit 'Ubaid Allāh und seinen drei verborgenen Ahnen[370]).

Noch eine andere Interpretation des Ausspruchs Ǧa'fars läßt die Form erkennen, in der ihn der ein Jahrhundert später schreibende Sendbote Muḥammad b. 'Alī aṣ-Ṣūrī[371]) überliefert. Nach ihm soll Imam Ǧa'far gesagt haben: „Drei von uns werden sich selbst vergraben und sich verbergen. Durch sie ist die Vollendung unserer Sache. Es werden ihnen vier folgen (oder: vier werden ihre Stellvertreter sein), die nicht von uns sind. Dann wird sich der Sohn erheben, der begnadete Herr und Gebieter[372]).“ Aṣ-Ṣūrī erklärt, dieser sei, kein Zweifel, der Qā'im der Auferstehung, nämlich aus der Nachkommenschaft des Fatimiden al-Mustanṣir. Aber die Quelle, der er die Weissagung entnahm, sah in dem begnadeten Herrn und Gebieter wohl eher Abū 'l-Qāsim, den zweiten Fatimiden. Die drei Vollender waren dann Ǧa'far, sein Sohn und sein Enkel, wie an-Nu'mān versicherte. Die vier Stellvertreter aber waren offenbar 'Abd Allāh b. Maimūn und seine Nachfolger bis 'Ubaid Allāh.

Leider ist diese Quelle aṣ-Ṣūrīs nicht zu ermitteln. Nur soviel läßt sich annehmen, daß der Ausspruch in diese Form schon zu Zeiten 'Ubaid Allāhs oder Abū 'l-Qāsims gebracht worden ist. Später wurde er mit der Veränderung der Dogmen immer wieder neu interpretiert. Die Anhänger des al-Mu'izz in as-Sind schoben die „drei von uns“ an

---

Tamīm und sein Vater (abāhu statt ibnahū, vgl. die Textherausgabe de Somogyis, RSO XIII 265) Ismā'īl, die über den Maġrib herrschen.“

369) Ar-Risāla al-muḏhiba S. 56. 370) Ar-Risāla al-muḏhiba S. 72.

371) Über ihn vgl. unten S. 128.

372) Aṣ-Ṣūrī, al-Qaṣīda aṣ-ṣūrīja, Ed. Arif Tamir, Damaskus 1955, S. 69.

den Schluß, um auf sieben Stellvertreter zu kommen. An-Nuʿmān suchte zu zeigen, daß die vier Nichtaliden nicht zu den Vorfahren der Fatimiden gehörten. Ǧaʿfar b. Manṣūr al-Jaman und der Drusenlehrer at-Tamīmī[373]) zählten die drei Aliden erst nach Muḥammad b. Ismāʿīl, um eine Heptade vor ʿUbaid Allāh oder Abū 'l-Qāsim zu erfüllen.

Es ist nunmehr möglich, den Charakter jenes Kitāb as-sijāsa[374]), das ein geschickter Fälscher als das Produkt des zynischen Libertinismus eines ismailitischen Lehrmeisters verbreitete, etwas näher zu bestimmen. Die spätere antiismailitische Polemik legte die Schrift ganz unberechtigt ʿUbaid Allāh oder Abū 'l-Qāsim zur Last. Sie stellt vielmehr eine auf genauer Kenntnis beruhende Satire auf die neue Lehre des al-Muʿizz dar.

„Wenn du mit einem Philosophen zu tun bekommst," schreibt der Meister an seinen Sendboten, „so wisse, daß die Philosophen unsere Stütze sind. Wir und sie sind uns darin einig, was die Gesetze der Propheten anbelangt, und im Dogma der Ewigkeit der Welt ...[375])" „Wenn dir ein Dualist zuläuft, so ist die Sache ausgezeichnet, denn du hast einen gewonnen, der dir äußerst nahe steht. Du führst dich bei ihm ein, in dem du die Einheit Gottes leugnest und von dem Vorgänger und dem Folger[376]) redest[377])."

Es war al-Muʿizz, der die Ideen neuplatonischer Philosophie in die fatimidische Lehre aufnahm. Aber das bedeutet nicht, daß er sich dem Dualismus näherte. Wie der Fälscher der Schrift zu dem an sich durchaus unberechtigten Vorwurf vom Dogma der Ewigkeit der Welt kommt, erhellt aus einer anderen Stelle. Dem Adressaten wird geraten, zum Beweis für dies Dogma seinen fortgeschrittenen Schülern beizubringen, daß es vor Adam schon viele Menschen gegeben habe[378]). Tatsächlich findet sich die Ausweitung der in die sieben Prophetenären eingeteilten Weltgeschichte zu einem größeren System des Wechsels von Zeiten der Verborgenheit (satr) und der Enthüllung (kašf), wie es von späteren ismailitischen Verfassern ausgemalt wurhe, schon bei den Lehrmeistern der Zeit des vierten Fatimiden angedeutet. Aber es waren geistige Wesen, nicht Menschen, die die Welt vor Adam bevölkerten. So erklärt Ǧaʿfar b. Manṣūr al-Jaman: „Adam war der Ursprung dieses Zyklus[379]). Vor ihm gab es Zyklen, die unsergleichen nicht

---

[373]) Vgl. unten S. 117. [374]) Vgl. Fatimiden und Baḥrainqarmaṭen S. 69ff.

[375]) Ad-Dailamī S. 79. Al-Baġdādī S. 177: „... die Ablehnung der Gesetze ...' [376]) Vgl. oben S. 92 Anm. 261. [377]) Ad-Dailamī S. 73.

[378]) De Sacy I, CLIX, vgl. dazu B. Lewis, An Ismaili Interpretation of the Fall of Adam, BSOAS IX, S. 697.

[379]) Kaur im Gegensatz zu daur, Ära eines Propheten.

erforschen kann, da sie spirituell waren[380])." „Vor Adam hat es kein Werk gegeben, wie es nach dem Qā'im kein Werk gibt[381])."

Dagegen werden die Anhänger des Muḥammad b. Ismā'īl mit einiger Sympathie, als die eigentlich Betrogenen gezeichnet. Manche Konvertiten soll der Sendbote nur bis zu dem Glauben führen, jener sei der Imam und lebe noch. Ihnen gegenüber ist es angeraten, die größte Verachtung von Gold und Silber an den Tag zu legen. Man fordert sie auf, Lüge, Unzucht, Sodomie und Wein zu meiden, und bricht sie, indem man ihnen eine übergroße Zahl von Gebeten auferlegt. Dann werden sie zu absolut verläßlichen Anhängern und sind bereit, ihr gesamtes Hab und Gut zu opfern[382]).

„Nur einer kleinen Zahl solcher, die du für fähig hältst, weiter in die Kenntnis unseres Systems eingeführt zu werden, wirst du lehren, daß der Qā'im tot sei, daß er in spiritueller Weise auf die Erde zurückkehrt, und daß die Menschen zu ihm zurückkehren durch die Vereinigung mit den geistigen Bildern (aṣ-ṣuwar ar-rūḥānīja), daß er die Scheidung unter den Menschen trifft nach dem Befehl Gottes, der Rache nimmt an den Ungläubigen für diejenigen, die an die spirituellen Bilder glauben. Das wird dir ausgezeichnete Dienste leisten gegenüber denen, die du für die Lehre gewonnen hast, um das Dogma von der Auferstehung und dem Hervorkommen der Toten aus ihren Gräbern zu zerstören ...[383])"

Damit ist die unter al-Mu'izz von den Sendboten verbreitete Lehre gut getroffen. Weniger glaubhaft ist die folgende Anweisung: „Diejenigen, die du bis zu diesem Grad (der Leugnung Gottes) geführt hast, kannst du wissen lassen, wie wir dich selbst wissen ließen, was in

---

[380]) Sarā'ir an-nuṭaqā', in maḏhab S. 57. Das Zitat aus al-Buṯḥānīs Streitschrift (vgl. Fatimiden und Baḥrainqarmaṭen S. 72), das Zahid Ali hier heranzieht, stützt sich natürlich unmittelbar auf die Darstellung des Kitāb as-sijāsa. Über die spätere Weltzeitentheorie vgl. etwa H. F. al-Hamdani, IC 1939, S. 216ff., maḏhab Kap. 3.

[381]) Ta'wīl ṣūrat an-nisā' in maḏhab S. 136. Qāḍī an-Nu'mān antwortet auf die Frage, ob es vor Adam Menschen gegeben habe, vorsichtig mit dem Hinweis auf das Wort, Adam sei der Erwählte. Ar-Risāla al-muḏhiba S. 79. Abū Ja'qūb as-Siǧistānī lehrte, vor Adam sei die Herrschaft über die Hierarchie bei den zwölf Folgern, nicht den Imamen gelegen. An-Nuṣra, zitiert in ar-rijāḍ S. 192. In iṯbāt an-nubūwāt widmete er im verlorenen sechsten Teil ein Kapitel den Ären vor Adam, vgl. S. 126. In al-janābī' sucht er nachzuweisen, daß die Menschheit nicht von einem einzigen Menschen abstamme, sondern Gott sie auf einmal geschaffen habe, S. 47ff. Daß es vor Adam Menschen gab, erklärt klar der Kommentator der Qaṣīda des Abū 'l-Haiṯam al-Ǧurǧānī. Vgl. Commentaire de la Qaṣīda Ismaélienne d'Abū 'l-Haitham Jorjānī attribué à Moḥammed Ibn Sorkh de Nishapour, Ed. H. Corbin et M. Moin, Bibl. Iran. IV 47, 80.

[382]) De Sacy I CLIVff.

[383]) De Sacy I CLVIIf.

Wirklichkeit der Imam ist, und ihnen eröffnen, daß Ismāʿīl und Muḥammad, sein Sohn, nur Pforten sind, die zu ihm führen. Dann kannst du ihnen gegenüber leicht das angebliche Imamat Alis zerstören und offen erklären, wem das Imamat wirklich gehört[384]).“ Hier findet die These der Qarmaṭen Ausdruck, die Fatimiden hätten ihre Genealogie gefälscht.

Die so scharf gegen die Fatimiden gerichtete Spitze legt die Vermutung nahe, daß die Schrift in den fünfziger oder sechziger Jahren des 4. Jahrhunderts der Hidschra/961—980 entstanden ist, als man die Gefahr der Fatimiden im Orient als unmittelbare Bedrohung empfand, während die Qarmaṭen an Schreck verloren hatten und in die Dienste Bagdads traten. Sie ist wohl als eine Antwort auf den intensiven Propagandafeldzug anzusehen, den al-Muʿizz zur Stützung seiner Eroberungspolitik führte. Ibn Rizām hat sie offenbar noch nicht gekannt. Ibn an-Nadīm und Aḫū Muḥsin geben an, sie selbst gelesen zu haben.

## Die Spaltung der Gemeinde unter al-Ḥākim

Durch seine Reform der Lehre war es al-Muʿizz gelungen, einen Teil der abgefallenen östlichen ismailitischen Gemeinden in das fatimidische Lager zurückzuführen. Aber seine Bestrebungen, die äußere Einheit der Bewegung wiederherzustellen, leiteten ihn zu bedenklichen Zugeständnissen und teilweise Toleranz gegenüber heterodoxen Lehren. Sein Schreiben an den Sendboten Ǧalam b. Šaibān und Angaben Qāḍī an-Nuʿmāns zeigen, wie vorsichtig er war, nicht durch Aufzwingen seiner Lehren gegen althergebrachte Glaubenssätze sich irgendwelche Anhänger zu entfremden[385]). Darüber hinaus offenbarte sich in seiner eigenen Lehre ein tiefer Zwiespalt, in dem sich das Nebeneinander seiner hohen Hoffnungen und ehrgeizigen Ansprüche und der kargeren Wirklichkeit wiederspiegelte. All das mußte eine schwere Bedrohung für die Fortdauer der inneren Einheit der Bewegung darstellen. Dies um so mehr, als die großen Erwartungen, die al-Muʿizz in Unterstützung seiner Thesen unter seinen Anhängern genährt hatte, nur zu bald enttäuscht wurden. Der fatimidische Vormarsch nach dem Osten lief sich in Syrien hoffnungslos fest. Auf religiösem Gebiet übte al-ʿAzīz eine Politik der Toleranz. Für die spekulative ismailitische Theologie scheint er überhaupt keinen Sinn gehabt zu haben.

Unter al-Ḥākim kam es dann zur Spaltung. Bezeichnenderweise wurden nun gerade die Sinnlosigkeit seiner Handlungen, seine Launen-

---

[384]) De Sacy I CLX. [385]) Vgl. Heterodox Ismailism S. 15.

haftigkeit und seine Brutalität von der extremen[386]) Richtung seiner Anhänger als Zeichen seiner Göttlichkeit ausgelegt. Auch hinsichtlich des religiösen Gesetzes gingen die Gründer der Religion der Drusen über das von al-Mu'izz gezeichnete Idealbild hinaus: Nicht nur das „Äußere", sondern auch das „Innere" der Gesetze ist mit der Manifestation Gottes auf Erden in königlicher Würde aufgehoben. Wie sehr man dabei aber auf der Gedankenwelt der Ismailiten aufbaute, zeigt die Theorie der Heilsgeschichte der Drusenlehrer.

Ḥamza b. ʿAlī, der eigentliche Gründer der Drusenreligion, legte sein Geschichtsbild im wesentlichen in der im Jahr 410/1019 verfaßten Schrift as-sīra al-mustaqīma[387]) dar. Zu der Zeit, als Adam aṣ-Ṣafā[388]) am Anfang unseres Zyklus unter dem Namen Šaṭnīl erschien, manifestierte sich der Herr in menschlicher Gestalt unter dem Namen al-Bār. In Adam-Šaṭnīls Gesetz[389]) gab es weder Pflichten noch Anbetung des Kalbs. Es war ein feines Gesetz, das die Einheit Gottes lehrte (šarīʿa laṭīfa tauḥīdīja). Ḥamza läßt durchblicken, daß er es seinen Anhängern wiedergebracht habe. Als die Menschen jedoch dem Polytheismus verfielen, zürnte der Herr und nahm die Gnade seiner Manifestation von ihnen. Er schickte ihnen Noah mit einem Gesetz, das die Anbetung des Nichts und die Einheit des Götzen lehrte (ʿibādat al-ʿadam wa-tauḥīd aṣ-ṣanam). Gleicher Art waren auch die Gesetze, die Abraham, Moses, Jesus und Mohammed brachten. Am Ende der Ära Mohammeds erschien ein weiterer Sprecher, Muḥammad b. Ismāʿīl, der die Gesetze besiegelte und vollendete. In seiner Ära kamen die „drei, deren vierter Saʿīd b. Aḥmad al-Mahdī ist ... und drei Stellvertreter vor (oder: von) ihnen[390]). Damit waren es sieben, die die Ära

---

[386]) Extrem auch hier im Sinne der sunnitischen Auffassung von ġulūw.

[387]) Ms. Berlin Wetzstein 1870, fol. 88—107.

[388]) Nach Ḥamza gibt es drei Adam: Ādam aṣ-Ṣafā' al-kullī, Ādam al-ʿĀṣī al-ǧuzwī und Ādam an-Nāsī al-ǧirmānī. Am Anfang unseres Zyklus manifestierte sich der erste in Šaṭnīl = Adam, der zweite in Henoch (Aḫnūḫ), und der dritte in Šarḥ = Seth (Šaiṯ), den Adam zu seinem Fundament erkor. Nach at-Tamīmī wird außerdem Noah als der zweite Adam (Ādam aṯ-ṯānī) bezeichnet, weil das Volk des Gesetzes durch ihn zu Menschen wurde (ta'addamū, taqsīm al-ʿulūm fol. 91r.

[389]) Nach der späteren Lehre der Drusen war es Henoch (Ādam al-ʿĀṣī), der dieses spirituelle und lobenswerte Gesetz brachte, vgl. Seybold, Die Drusenschrift al-Noqaṭ wad-dawā'ir, Tübingen 1902, S. 44, 72.

[390]) In der zwei Jahre früher (408/1017) verfaßten Schrift an-naqḍ al-ḫafī (fol. 34r) bezeichnete Ḥamza andererseits Saʿīd als den vierten der Stellvertreter und den letzten der Ära der Verborgenheit. Hier findet der Unterschied zwischen der Bezeichnung der zweiten Heptade von Imamen (die Ḥamza natürlich als solche nicht anerkennt) als Stellvertreter und der Theorie einer Heptade

Muhammad b. Ismā'īls vollendeten. Ihr letzter war 'Abd Allāh al-Mahdī[391]), der der Sklave unseres Herrn war. Da nahm der Herr den Namen al-Qā'im an. Dies ist aber der Namen seines Sklaven (nämlich der Ḥamzas) ... Er nannte sich aber al-Qā'im, da er sich zum ersten Mal der Welt in königlicher Würde und Menschengestalt in den Tagen der Sprecher der polytheistischen Gesetze manifestierte." „Nun aber ist die Umdrehung der Perioden abgeschlossen und hinfällig, was in allen Zeitaltern war. Nichts ist geblieben vom Feuer des polytheistischen Gesetzes als Flackern und Funken. Seine Hitze wird erlöschen und die Mangelhaftigkeit zerrinnen. Denn der Ruhepunkt hat zu erscheinen begonnen mit der Verkündung der Einheit unseres Herrn ..."

Ādam aṣ-Ṣafā' ist für Ḥamza das erste der Urprinzipien, der universelle Intellekt. Er hat sich in Ḥamza, dem Qā'im, wiederverkörpert. Aber er ist auch schon in siebzig Zyklen vor unserem Zyklus erschienen[392]). Jeder dieser Zyklen bestand aus siebzig Wochen, jede Woche aus siebzig Altern ('ām), und jedes Alter aus tausend Jahren (sana). In jedem dieser Zyklen haben sich der Herr, der universelle Intellekt und der Widersacher (aḍ-ḍidd) manifestiert[393]). Adam-Šaṭnīl erschien unter einem Volk ('ālam), das Ǧinn genannt wurde und das Nichts anbetete. Ḥamza betont, daß er Vater und Mutter hatte[394]).

Davon unterscheidet sich das Geschichtsbild, das Ḥamzas Schüler Ismā'īl at-Tamīmī in seiner Schrift taqsīm al-'ulūm wa-iṯbāt al-ḥaqq wa-kašf al-maknūn[395]) entwirft, fast nur durch größere Ausführlichkeit. Auch nach ihm lehrten die Sprecherpropheten von Noah bis

---

von Stellvertretern zwischen Muḥammad b. Ismā'īl und Abū 'l-Qāsim (oder 'Ubaid Allāh) Ausdruck. Ḥamza lehrte damals noch, Sa'īd al-Mahdī habe, am Ende von sieben Imamen und drei Stellvertretern, die Ära Mohammeds abgeschlossen, nicht Muḥammad b. Ismā'īl. Er zählte Sa'īd als den siebten Sprecher von Adam an und Qaddāḥ (!) als den siebten Vollstrecker. Bahā' ad-Dīn greift dies in al-ǧuz' al-awwal min as-sab'a aǧzā' auf und erklärt, Sa'īd habe das siebte äußere Gesetz gebracht und sein Fundament Qaddāḥ at-ta'wīlī das siebte innere Gesetz. Vgl. de Sacy I 82.

391) Die Verbesserung in 'Ubaid Allāh, die de Sacy I 80 vorschlägt, ist nicht berechtigt. Vgl. oben S. 66 Anm. 128.

392) Im Gegensatz zu Ādam al-'Āṣī und Ādam an-Nāsī, die erst am Anfang unseres Zyklus erschaffen wurden, sabab al-asbāb, hrsgb. von E. von Döbeln, MO III, S. 108.

393) Kašf al-ḥaqā'iq in Seybold, Drusenschrift S. 84. Ḥamza verspricht, ihre Namen in einer anderen Schrift zu nennen. Dazu ist er wohl nicht mehr gekommen, vgl. de Sacy I 18ff. Später heißt der Herr in seinen Manifestationen während der ersten siebzig Zyklen al-'Alī al-A'lā, vgl. etwa Seybold, Drusenschrift S. 42ff., 71, wo diese vorgeschichtliche Zeit ausführlich dargestellt wird.

394) As-sīra al-mustaqīma, der Vater hieß Dānīl.

395) Ms. Tübingen M. a. VI 131 fol. 87—97.

Muḥammad b. Ismāʿīl nur die Einheit des Nichts. In ihren Ären kannte man nur das erste Urprinzip, nicht den Herrn. „Die Weisheit des Herrn gestattete ihm nicht, sich unter diesen Völkern zu manifestieren, die den Toten glichen." Nach Muḥammad b. Ismāʿīl kamen die Stellvertreter, die das Depositum innehatten (al-ḫulafā' al-mustaudaʿūn). At-Tamīmī zählt sie dann namentlich als die „sieben Himmel" auf[396]). Auch hier heben sich die vier letzten von den drei ersten ab: ʿAbd Allāh, der vierte Himmel, heißt zwar Sohn Aḥmads (des dritten), stammt aber von Maimūn al- Qaddāḥ ab[397]). Saʿīd al-Mahdī kommt aber, im Gegensatz zu den Angaben Ḥamzas, erst nach den sieben Verborgenen, er ist der achte. Zur Zeit des dritten Himmels aber erschien der Herr in Gestalt eines Menschen, aber ohne königliche Würde, und nannte sich Abū Zakarījā'. Danach manifestierte er sich noch zweimal, unter dem Namen ʿAljā' und al-Muʿill, bevor er in al-Qā'im in königlicher Würde erschien.

Es erübrigt sich, auf die fatimidischen und anderen ismailitischen Vorlagen dieser Lehren im einzelnen einzugehen. Gerade auch die Ungereimtheiten des Gesamtbildes, das etwa de Sacy aus Schriften des Drusenkanons zog, gehen zu einem guten Teil auf Widersprüche in den älteren Theorien zurück[397a]). Je nach dem Bedarf des Augenblicks griff man das eine oder das andere Vorbild auf, ohne die Gegensätze auszugleichen. Die Gründe für das Zustandekommen dieser widerspruchsvollen Vorbilder begriff man längst nicht mehr, sie waren auch bedeutungslos geworden.

Dabei waren es ganz wesentlich die uneingelösten Versprechen der alten Lehrmeister, die die Drusenlehrer zur Ausbildung ihrer Thesen ermutigten. Immer wieder zitiert Bahā' ad-Dīn in seiner Apologetik die Schriften der fatimidischen Missionsmeister, um den Anhängern der nunmehr veralteten Lehre vom inneren Sinn zu beweisen, daß sie den „versprochenen Termin" versäumt hätten. Mochte er dabei manches willkürlich nach seinen Anschauungen auslegen, so konnte er doch ganz berechtigt auf die Erklärung einer so maßgeblichen Autorität wie Qāḍī an-Nuʿmān hinweisen, daß der Nachfolger des Nachfolgers des al-Muʿizz der Herr der Enthüllung sein werde[398]).

Für Ḥamza mußten sich diese alten Versprechen konkret in der irdischen Wirklichkeit erfüllen. Sein Hauptgegner war im Grunde jene

---

[396]) Übersetzung bei de Sacy I 33ff. [397]) Vgl. auch oben S. 75f.

[397a]) Das verkennt Ivanow, wenn er meint, Ḥamza und Bahā' ad-Dīn hätten keine solchen „Absurditäten" reden können, und sie als spätere „Berichtigungen" zu verstehen sucht. The alleged Founder, 2. Aufl., Bombay 1957, S. 140.

[398]) Vgl. oben S. 85.

von al-Mu'izz in die fatimidische Lehre eingeführte spekulative Philosophie, die drohte, das ganze Heilsgeschehen in spirituelle, „unsichtbare" Sphären zu verlegen und die Versprechungen ihrer irdischen Bedeutung zu entkleiden. Daher rührt sein besessener Kampf gegen die Anbetung des Nichts und gegen die Propheten, die die Menschen zur „Verehrung dessen anleiteten, der nicht mit Augen gesehen werden kann, und die Einheit dessen lehrten, der nicht zu erkennen ist[399])."

Man kann die ursprüngliche Lehre der Drusen weitgehend als eine Materialisierung und Mythisierung der spiritualisierten, von der Philosophie bestimmten Anschauungen ihrer fatimidisch-ismailitischen Vorgänger ansehen. Die symbolischen Entsprechungen zwischen der Hierarchie der irdischen Rangstufen und den göttlichen Emanationen, ihren Vorbildern in der geistigen Welt, genügen nicht mehr. „Die Symbole wurden hinfällig mit dem Erscheinen der symbolisierten Dinge"[400]), so beschreibt ein Druse die Enthüllung. Aus den Begnadeten, aus der Masse durch unmittelbare göttliche Unterstützung (ta'jīd) hervorgehobenen Menschen werden nun Verkörperungen, Manifestationen der Wesen der höheren Welt. Die Krönung des neuen Systems bildet der Glaube, daß der höchste Gott selbst sich auf Erden manifestiert hat, derselbe Gott, um dessen für die Vernunft unfaßbare Einheit zu wahren, die ismailitische Theologie alle seine koranischen Attribute, ja sogar den Namen Allāh, auf seine Schöpfung übertrug. Nun sagt Bahā' ad-Dīn: „... Aber in Wahrheit, nach der Art wie die (Anhänger der Gesetze und der früheren Religionen) es verstehen, daß Gott frei von allen diesen Attributen ist, bedeutet dies, daß er nicht existiert und daß die Augen ihn nicht wahrnehmen können. Wenn er aber, ihrer Meinung entsprechend, nicht existierte, so wäre dies kein Ruhmestitel für ihn, daß die Augen ihn nicht wahrnehmen könnten — denn es wäre nur der Mangel seiner Existenz, der ihn nicht wahrnehmbar für die Augen machte — und daß ihre Augen ihn wahrnähmen, wenn ihm eine Existenz zukäme, und nicht ohnmächtig wären, ihre Funktion ihm gegenüber auszuüben. Dies ist ihre Lehre, und es wäre ihnen kein Vorwurf zu machen, wenn die Augen ihn nicht wahrnehmen könnten. Aber, bei Gott, was seine Macht am höchsten erhebt, und der unwiderleglichste Beweis seiner Göttlichkeit ist, daß er inmitten seiner Geschöpfe existiert, und daß jedes von ihnen seine Einheit und seine Existenz, frei von jeglichem Attribut, bekennt, im Verhältnis zu

---

[399]) Jad'ūn an-nās ilā 'ibādat man lā jušāhad wa-tauḥīd man lā ju'raf, as-sīra al-mustaqīma.

[400]) Baṭalat al-amṯāl bi-ẓuhūr al-mamṯūlāt, Seybold, Drusenschrift S. 49.

dem Maß an Wahrheit, das sich mit ihm identifiziert hat[401]), und dem Licht, das ihm Gott mitgeteilt hat[402]).“

Dieser Aufstand gegen die spekulative Theologie, der zu einer für den Charakter der Religion so tiefgreifenden Umbildung führte, wurde offenbar von dem Verlangen weiterer Kreise der fatimidischen Anhängerschaft getragen. Die Einführung der philosophischen Spekulation, die es ermöglicht hatte, die so konkrete alte Lehre wenigstens scheinbar zu rechtfertigen und sie gleichzeitig zu einer Kosmologie erweiterte, machte sie zu abstrakt, um die Menge der Gläubigen zu befriedigen. Ḥamza und seine Schüler konkretisierten sie wieder, unter Beibehaltung des erweiterten Systems und seiner Terminologie. Seine Lehre fand zunächst weite Verbreitung innerhalb und außerhalb des fatimidischen Reiches[403]).

Die Bewegung blieb jedoch, trotz der Unterstützung, die al-Ḥākim ihr zeitenweise zukommen ließ, eine Häresie. Von seiten der offiziellen Lehrmeister der Gemeinde in Kairo und gewiß auch anderswo stieß sie auf schärfste Ablehnung. „Wenn die Anhänger al-Hādīs (Ḥamzas) die Anhänger Ḫattigīns, des höchsten Missionsmeisters (dāʿī ad-duʿāt) trafen, verfluchten sie sich gegenseitig, und jede Partei erklärte die andere zu Ungläubigen[404]).“ Zur Zeit der größten Wirren kam Ḥamīd ad-Dīn al-Kirmānī, der als Sendbote in Bagdad und Basra tätig gewesen war, in die ägyptische Hauptstadt[405]). In seinem Sendschreiben mabāsim al-bišārāt bi'l-Imām al-Ḥākim schildert er die Lage der Ge-

[401]) De Sacy bemerkt hierzu: „Les verités sont, dans la système des Druses, des émanations substantielles de la divinité, lesquelles s'identifient et s'incarnent, pour ainsi dire, dans celui qui en reçoit la connaissance.“

[402]) Ar-Risāla al-mausūma bi'š-šāfija li-nufūs al-muwaḥḥidīn, übersetzt in de Sacy I 9f.

[403]) Vgl. P. Hitti, The Origins of the Druze People and Religion, New York 1928, S. 11. [404]) Jaḥjā b. Saʿīd, Kitāb aḏ-ḏail, Ed. L. Cheikho, S. 223f.

[405]) Nach Idrīs, ʿujūn al-aḫbār, hätte ihn al-Ḥākim selbst berufen, vgl. ar-Risāla al-wāʿiẓa, Ed. M. K. Husain, Maǧallat kullījat al-ādāb XIV, S. 5. K. Husain nennt als Jahr der Ankunft 408/1017. Zahid Ali dagegen meint, die in Kairo verfaßte Risālat mabāsim al-bišārāt sei schon 402/1010—1011 geschrieben, maḏhab S. 205. Die Stelle, auf die er sich dabei stützt, maḏhab S. 212, muß aber wohl verdorben sein. Al-Kirmānī nennt das Jahr 1326 der Ära Alexanders als gegenwärtiges Datum, vgl. das Zitat (nach Idrīs, ʿujūn al-aḫbār) in P. Kraus, Hebräische und syrische Zitate in ismailitischen Schriften, Islam XIX, S. 254, übersetzt S. 256. (Danach ist die Jahreszahl 1327, die Zahid Ali, maḏhab S. 211, in seiner Übersetzung der Stelle angibt, zu berichtigen, da es bis zum Jahr 1336 noch neun Jahre sein sollen.) Das entspricht dem Jahr vom 1. Okt. 1014—30. Sept. 1015 = Rab. II 405 — Rab. II 406. Zum gleichen Ergebnis führt die Angabe, daß bis zur Vollendung des 40. Lebensjahres al-Ḥākims (geb. 3. Rab. I 375/13. Aug. 985) noch neun Jahre verstreichen sollten, maḏhab S. 211.

meinde in den schwärzesten Farben. Die allgemeine Ungewißheit, Schwierigkeiten in der Verbreitung der wahren Lehre, Uneinigkeit und Gerüchte bedrängen die Gläubigen[406]).

Aber al-Kirmānī hat ihnen eine frohe Botschaft zu künden. Al-Ḥākim wird das ganze islamische Reich unter seiner Herrschaft vereinigen. Er ist es, der mit dem Tag des Sieges im Koran[407]) gemeint ist. In neun Jahren wird seine Sache triumphieren, wie auch aus einer Prophezeiung Daniels hervorgeht[408]). Nach der Zeit der Schwäche, die über die Anhänger der wahren Lehre gekommen ist, wird Gott sein Versprechen erfüllen und die Einheit des Islams unter dem rechten Imam wie zur Zeit des Propheten wiederherstellen. Wenn das wahre Imamat einmal in einer Person festgestellt und bewiesen ist, fügt al-Kirmānī hinzu, so darf man nicht nach seinen Taten urteilen, wenn sie auch bar jeder Weisheit erscheinen. Denn diesen Taten muß ein tiefer Sinn zugrunde liegen, wenn er auch unbekannt ist. Das Imamat ist ein heiliger Rang, dem Gottes Unterstützung zuteil wird. Es ist auf Unfehlbarkeit gegründet[409]).

Zugleich gibt al-Kirmānī eine Warnung kund: Wenn in einem der Imame himmlische Kraft und göttliche Unterstützung offenbar werden, so darf man nicht glauben, er sei der Herr der größten Auferstehung. Sie wird erst nach Ablauf aller „Grade" der Ära Mohammeds erfolgen[410]). Dies stellte eine Kampfansage an die Extremisten noch ohne Namensnennung dar. Aber bald sah sich al-Kirmānī veranlaßt, unmittelbar in den Streit der Parteien einzugreifen. Im Monat Ǧum. II 408/Nov. 1017 verfaßte er ein „mahnendes Sendschreiben" in Antwort auf einen Brief des al-Ḥasan al-Farġānī al-Aḫram[411]), eines der Künder der Göttlichkeit al-Ḥākims. Wie al-Kirmānī erwähnt, hatte al-Aḫram schon früher ähnliche Schreiben an ihn gerichtet. Al-Kirmānī hatte ihn von seiner Ketzerei abzubringen versucht, aber vergebens.

Nun warnt er ihn noch einmal eindringlich vor den Folgen seines Beharrens im Unglauben. Gott ist vor den Blicken der Menschen verborgen. Sie vermögen ihm gegenüber nichts, als um seine Gnade und Vergebung ihrer Fehltritte zu bitten. In seiner umfassenden Barm-

---

406) Ar-Risāla al-wā'iẓa S. 5f. 407) Koran 32,29.

408) Daniel 12,12. Vgl. Kraus, Islam XIX, S. 254ff.

409) Maḏhab S. 307ff. 410) Ar-Risāla al-wā'iẓa S. 23 Anm. 2.

411) Nach Ibn Ẓāfir, Wüstenfeld, Fatimiden S. 204, trat al-Aḫram erst Raǧab 409/Nov.—Dez. 1018 mit seiner Lehre auf. Dies bezieht sich offenbar nur auf die öffentliche Verkündigung. Im Ramaḍān 409/Januar 1019 wurde er ermordet. In welchem Verhältnis er zu Ḥamza stand, ist nicht klar. Zu den Drusenlehrern gehört er nicht. Nach den Angaben al-Kirmānīs zu schließen, lehrte er nur die Göttlichkeit al-Ḥākims, nicht der übrigen Fatimiden.

herzigkeit hat er die Propheten, Vollstrecker und Imame unter sie als Botschafter zwischen sich und ihnen geschickt. Sie bitten um Gnade bei ihm für diejenigen, welche sie um Gnade bitten, und Gott vergibt ihnen. Zur Zeit des Propheten waltete dieser selbst des Amts der Fürbitte (Koran 4,64). Nach ihm ging es auf die Imame über, und nun ist der Herrscher der Gläubigen al-Ḥākim bi-Amr Allāh damit betraut. Nach ihm werden es andere Imame übernehmen bis zum jüngsten Tag. Wer aber die Zerstörung der Moscheen, die Schließung der Tore der Gottesverehrung und Zunichtemachung der Mittel zum Erlangen der Seligkeit fordert, der strebt nach Unmöglichem. Nichts gedeiht ihm daraus denn Enttäuschung und der Zorn des Barmherzigen[412]).

Dann geht al-Kirmānī auf den Brief al-Aḫrams ein. Er wirft ihm vor, daß er, indem er die gebräuchliche Namensnennung Gottes und den Segenswunsch für den Propheten und die Imame ausgelassen, gegen das Gebot al-Ḥākims verstoßen habe, als dessen Anhänger er sich brüste. Al-Ḥākim selbst pflege diese Sitte in seinen Erlassen, Briefen und Reden[413]). Al-Aḫram stellte in seinem Schreiben die Behauptung auf: ,,Wer von euch den Imam seiner Zeit kennt, der ist besser als jeder von den hingeschiedenen Generationen, sei er auch Prophet, Vollstrecker oder Imam.'' Er suchte aus dem Namen Allāh zu beweisen, daß Gott menschliche Gestalt habe, da der Buchstabe Alif der Länge entspreche, Lām der Breite und Hā' der Tiefe. Al-Kirmānī deckt die Unsinnigkeit dieser Argumente auf und führt mit der ihm eigenen Umständlichkeit den Nachweis, daß Gott kein Körper sein könne[414]).

Nun folgt das Kernstück der Auseinandersetzung. Wenn al-Aḫram der ismailitischen Gemeinde zurief: ,,Eure Auferstehung ist erfolgt, und eure Ära der Verborgenheit ist abgelaufen'', so sprach er damit keine Neuerung der Lehre aus. Von Anfang an hatten die Ismailiten die Hoffnung auf die Auferstehung und das Ende der Verborgenheit mit dem Erscheinen des Mahdi verbunden. Al-Mu'izz und die großen Lehrmeister seiner Zeit hatten das gleiche gesagt, wenn sie auch vor den Konsequenzen zurückschreckten. Al-Kirmānī aber nimmt ebenso fest Stellung wie sein Gegner. Seine Antwort läßt erkennen, wieviel realer ihm bei aller Vorliebe für die philosophische Spekulation das ,,Äußere'' des Geschehens als sein ,,innerer Sinn'' war. ,,Die Rede, die des Beweises entbehrt, ist eine Art von Faselei. Wie denn soll die Auferstehung erfolgt sein, da ihr doch Bedingungen und Zeichen eigen sind, die der Herr der Propheten, der Gesandte des Herrn der Welten,

---

412) Ar-Risāla al-wā'iẓa S. 11—14. 413) Ar-Risāla al-wā'iẓa S. 14f.
414) Ar-Risāla al-wā'iẓa S. 17f.

Mohammed ... deutlich gemacht hat, nichts aber von ihnen erschienen ist? Oder wie soll die Ära abgelaufen sein, da doch die Gebote der Offenbarung und des Gesetzes gewahrt und durch das Auge der Ewigkeit bewacht sind bis zum jüngsten Tag? Da der wahrhafteste aller Sprechenden spricht: 'Wahrlich, wir haben die Ermahnung hinabgesandt und wir sind gewiß ihr Hüter'[415])? ... Wenn du aber wüßtest, in welch einem Verhältnis du zu der Ära stehst, so würdest du von deinem Gefasel ablassen. Aber indem du deiner subjektiven Meinung gefolgt bist, konnte deine zum Bösen antreibende Seele dir eingeben, was sie dir an Irrtum und übler Rede eingegeben hat. Aber weit gefehlt, weit gefehlt: 'Diese (die nicht glauben) werden von einem fernen Platz gerufen'[416]) (und hören darum nichts). Wo stehst du zu dem, was wir in unserem Sendschreiben mabāsim al-bišārāt andeuteten, daß Gott für Mohammed, seinen Gesandten, durch seinen Vertrauten auf der Erde, den Herrscher der Gläubigen al-Ḥākim bi-Amr Allāh seinem Gesetz Geltung verschaffen, seine Anordnungen und seine Sunna unterstützen werde, und daß er die Macht erneuern werde in demjenigen, der nach ihm seinen Platz einnimmt ...? Wo stehst du zu dem achtzehnten Imam und seinen Taten in der Ära des Propheten, den Taten des einundzwanzigsten, des fünfundzwanzigsten ... und des fünfunddreißigsten ...? Wo stehst du vielmehr vom hundertsten, der herrschen wird, ermächtigen, wen er will, und demütigen, wen er will, mit der Erlaubnis Gottes, des Herren der Welten? Nein, du befindest dich in offenbarem Irrtum. Wahrlich, ein Mensch, der die Auflösung der Gebote des Glaubens für möglich hält oder das Ablassen der Menschen von der Verehrung Gottes für erlaubt, solange die Himmel und die Erde währen, dessen Verstand ist schwach, und dessen Phantasie ist krank".[417])

Auf die Frage al-Aḫrams, was denn die Grundbedingungen des Islams seien, antwortet al-Kirmānī: Das Zeugnis, daß es keinen Gott außer Gott allein, ohne Teilhaber, gebe, daß Mohammed sein Diener und Prophet sei, daß Paradies und Hölle wahr seien, daß die Stunde (des letzten Gerichtes) komme, und daß die Toten auferweckt würden[418]). Die Verehrung Gottes besteht in zweierlei, Wissen und Werk[419]). In der Vergötterung al-Ḥākims aber sieht al-Kirmānī krassen Polytheismus[420]).

In al-Kirmānīs großem Werk rāḥat al-ʿaql, in dem er die Summe seiner Weltanschauung darstellt, kommt seine Neuordnung der Lehre in aller Klarheit zum Ausdruck. Gleich im ersten Kapitel betont der

[415]) Koran 15,9. [416]) Koran 41, 44. [417]) Ar-Risāla al-wāʿiẓa S. 21ff.
[418]) Ar-Risāla al-wāʿiẓa S. 24. [419]) Ar-Risāla al-wāʿiẓa S. 25. [420]) S. 27.

Verfasser, daß der Leser seines Werkes zuerst sein Selbst von den niederen Trieben der Natur befreien müsse, indem er die Zeremonien des Islams ausübe und die gesetzlichen Vorschriften befolge. Nur dann kann das Wissen, das sein Werk vermittelt, ihm zu Vollkommenheit und ewigem Glück verhelfen. „Denn da die Laster schneller von der Seele, indem sie sich in der Welt der Natur befindet, Besitz ergreifen als das Feuer vom Erdöl, und einzig das Gesetz und seine Bestimmungen diese Laster von ihr fernhalten können, so ist derjenige, der am Gebot festhält und seine Seele durch Unterwerfung unter seine Lasten übt, unser Bruder in Wahrheit. Wahrlich, er verspürt bei jeder Station (seines Fortschritts) eine Lust in seiner Seele. Wer aber von ihm abirrt, indem er einen Teil erfüllt und einen Teil unterläßt, oder indem er es ganz unerfüllt läßt, der schadet allein sich selbst. Gott wird tun, was sein Fall erfordert, und er ist schnell in der Abrechnung. Also möge der Leser dieses Buches in sich gehen und den aufrichtigen Rat annehmen[421])." Zu diesem Thema kehrt der Verfasser immer wieder zurück.

Es ist nicht viel mehr als ein Lippenbekenntnis, das al-Kirmānī den „Altmeistern der Lehre" (šujūḫ ad-daʿwa) zollt, „deren Zuverlässigkeit in der Methodik bekannt ist", und wenn er auf das Kitab taʾwīl aš-šarīʿa des al-Muʿizz und die Werke des Ǧaʿfar b. Manṣūr al-Jaman verweist[422]). Er weiß nichts vom Wechsel der Perioden von Verborgenheit und Enthüllung, von materiellen und geistigen Zeitaltern. Adam ist für ihn der Vater der Menschheit[423]) und der Bringer des ersten Gesetzes[424]). Und er legt großen Wert darauf, daß die Vergeltung der Taten im Jenseits Wirklichkeit sei. Schon in früheren Schriften habe er die Fehlerhaftigkeit der Ansicht nachgewiesen, daß die Vergeltung im Diesseits erfolge[425]). Wenn al-Kirmānī als Vertreter dieser Ansicht neben dem Erzketzer Razes (Muḥammad b. Zakarījāʾ ar-Rāzī) die „Extremisten und Anhänger der Lehre von der Wiederkehr"

---

[421]) Rāḥat al-ʿaql, Ed. M. K. Husain und M. M. Hilmi, Leiden 1953, S. 17.

[422]) Rāḥat al-ʿaql S. 22. Von den Werken an-Nuʿmāns führt er sechs nament lich auf. Sie lagen ihm gewiß näher.

[423]) Rāḥat al-ʿaql S. 146. In der al-Kirmānī zugeschriebenen Risālat usbūʿ daur as-satr, die Arif Tamir, arbaʿ rasāʾil ismāʿīlīja S. 59ff., nach einer syrischen Handschrift veröffentlicht hat, wird Adam der „Anfang der Ära der Verborgenheit und das Ende der Ära der Enthüllung" genannt, S. 63. Die Verfasserschaft al-Kirmānīs erscheint aber schon aus anderen Gründen unwahrscheinlich: Der Stil entspricht nicht dem so ausgeprägten al-Kirmānīs, der Inhalt steht einige Stufen unter seinem Niveau. In der Sammlung von al-Kirmānīs Sendschreiben, welche die Mustaʿlīer bewahren, gibt es keines diesen Namens.

[424]) Rāḥat al-ʿaql S. 191.

[425]) Allerdings läßt al-Kirmānī zu, daß ein Teil der Vergeltung durch den Qāʾim im Diesseits erfolge, rāḥat al-ʿaql S. 368ff.

nennt[426]), so liegt darin eine scharfe Absage an gewisse Kreise der eigenen Gemeinde.

Tatsächlich hat sich al-Kirmānī in einem anderen Werk, Kitāb ar-rijāḍ[427]), sehr gründlich mit einigen Theorien der älteren Meister der ismailitischen Lehre, freilich unmittelbar nur der persischen Schule, auseinandergesetzt. Zum Anlaß nahm er den alten Streit zwischen Abū Ḥātim ar-Rāzī und Abū Ja'qūb as-Siğistānī um die Thesen des Kitāb al-maḥṣūl an-Nasafīs. Wie zu erwarten, stellt er sich dabei meist hinter Abū Ḥātim gegen Abū Ja'qūb. Und ähnlich wie Abū Ja'qūb in der Abwertung der Werke und der äußeren Gesetzlichkeit über an-Nasafī hinausging, treibt al-Kirmānī ihre Verteidigung über die Abū Ḥātims hinaus. Adam hat ein Gesetz gebracht, das Wissen und Werk vereinigte. Als Beweis dafür genügt die Einsicht, daß Gott ihn als Lehrer und rechten Leiter seinem Volk gesandt hat. Denn die rechte Leitung der Menschen besteht in nichts anderem als den Geboten der Anbetung (qawānīn al-'ibāda), eben dem Gesetz[428]). Gegen Abū Ja'qūbs These, daß in der Ordnung der Welt genügend Hinweis auf die Einheit des Schöpfers offenbar werde, reagiert al-Kirmānī scharf: Dies würde bedeuten, daß die Sendung der Propheten überflüssig sei. Es sei ihm unverständlich, wie Abū Ja'qūb dies behaupten konnte, da doch völlig klar sei, daß die Ordnung der Welt nicht ausreiche, um auf die Einheit Gottes hinzuweisen, daß dafür vielmehr Lehrer von hohem Wissen notwendig seien, die aus der Erkenntnis dieser Ordnung Nutzen zögen. Diese Lehrer aber seien die von Gott eingesetzte Hierarchie. „Zusammenfassend (ist zu sagen), daß diese Meinung, die zur Aufhebung der Grade der Hierarchie führt, nicht zu unserem Glauben und nicht zur Lehre unserer Herrn gehört. Vielleicht haben die Widersacher diese Behauptung in das Buch (Abū Ja'qūbs) eingefügt, damit sie dem Verfasser zugeschrieben werde. Gott weiß es am besten[429]).“

---

[426]) Rāḥat al-'aql S. 364.

[427]) Besprochen von Ivanow, Studies in Early Persian Ismailism. Al-Kirmānī scheint einige seiner Werke mehrmals herausgegeben und dabei Verweise auf andere inzwischen fertiggestellte Schriften ergänzt zu haben. Nur so ist zu erklären, daß in rāḥat al-'aql auf ar-rijāḍ und in ar-rijāḍ auf rāḥat al-'aql mit Inhaltsangaben verwiesen wird, vgl. Studies S. 106. Daß es sich um Ergänzungen eines Kopisten handelt, erscheint unwahrscheinlich. Auch in anderen seiner Schriften finden sich Verweise, die erst nach der ersten Veröffentlichung beigefügt sein müssen. Vgl. ar-Risāla ad-durrīja ... wa-Risālat an-nuẓum, Ed. M. K. Husain, Maṣājif, Einl. S. 8f.

[428]) Kitāb ar-rijāḍ, Ms. der Muḥammadī Hamdānī Sammlung S. 173.

[429]) Ar-rijāḍ S. 195f. Zu dieser Meinung konnte al-Kirmānī offenbar kommen, da Abū Ja'qūb in seinen späteren Werken die hier vertretene Ansicht wesentlich

Darum ist auch der Glaube, daß der Qā'im die Gesetze aufhebe, fehlerhaft[430]). Nicht dafür kommt er in die Welt, sondern um die verflossenen Ären abzuschließen. Er wird die Grade der Hierarchie beseitigen, da ihre Lehre nun nicht mehr gebraucht wird[431]). Denn die zweite Schöpfung[432]) ist nunmehr vollständig, das Wissen ist aktuell (bi'l-fi'l) und allgemein, das Unwissen potentiell (bi'l-qūwa). Abū Ja'qūb hatte völlig Unrecht mit der Behauptung, daß nach dem Qā'im eine Zeit des Wissens ohne Werk und Gesetz beginne, wie es in der großen Ära vor Adam nur das reine Wissen gegeben habe. Vielmehr herrschte unter den Wesen vor Adam das reine Unwissen, sie kannten die Grade der Hierarchie nicht, und darum sandte Gott Adam[433]). Und nach dem Qā'im wird das Unwissen allmählich wieder aktuell und das Wissen potentiell, da der Qā'im die Lehrhierarchie beseitigt hat[434]). Die Umwertung der Werte gegenüber Abū Ja'qūb ist damit vollständig.

Die ganz andere Auffassung al-Kirmānīs vom Verhältnis zwischen dem „Äußeren" und dem „inneren Sinn" erhellt auch aus den Regeln, die er für die Exegese aufstellt. Einmal hält er Abū Ja'qūb vor: „Dieser Koranvers gehört nicht zu den gleichnishaften, die man auf ihren Sinn zurückführt und dann ihren äußeren Wortlaut vernach-

---

modifizierte. Auch an anderer Stelle (S. 218) meint al-Kirmānī, der Text seiner Kopie müsse wohl verdorben sein. Er gibt dafür die Schuld dem geringen Interesse an der Religion und der Nachlässigkeit der Kopisten, die es versäumten, ihre Abschriften den Gelehrten zur Überprüfung vorzulesen.

430) Zu Unrecht erklärt daher ein späterer ismailitischer Autor, al-Kirmānī habe in seinem Kitāb ar-rijāḍ gegenüber den meisten Lehrautoritäten, die nur verallgemeinernd von der Aufhebung der Gesetze durch den Qā'im sprachen, den wahren Sachverhalt dargelegt: Der Qā'im wird nur die Lasten (at-takālīf), nicht aber die vernunftbedingten Gesetze aufheben. Vgl. R. Strothmann, Gnosistexte der Ismailiten, Göttingen 1943, S. 91 und 10. Dies hatten vielmehr al-Mu'izz und Abū Ja'qūb in seinem iṯbāt an-nubūwāt gelehrt. Al-Kirmānī kannte zwar auch den Unterschied zwischen immer notwendigen Geboten, wie denen über Nahrung, Talion, Ehe, Erbschaft, Bestattung, und den Geboten der Gottesverehrung, die zeitweise, wie vor der Sendung Adams, unvollständig oder überhaupt nicht vorhanden sein können, S. 189ff. Aber der Qā'im hebt davon nichts auf, er stellt vielmehr die Gesetze in ihrer ursprünglichen Form wieder her, rāḥat al-'aql S. 435 Z. 8. 431) Ar-rijāḍ S. 205.

432) Al-ḫalq aṯ-ṯānī. Die erste Schöpfung ist die des Körpers. Die zweite Schöpfung erreicht der Mensch durch die ständige Übung von Werk und Wissen. 433) Ar-rijāḍ S. 198.

434) S. 203, 206, 212. Dies ist so zu verstehen, daß der Qā'im die wissenden Seelen in sich vereinigt hat und mit ihnen in die geistige Welt aufgestiegen ist, vgl. rāḥat al-'aql S. 379ff., 431f. Die Wesen, die auf der Erde zurückbleiben, verfallen der Unwissenheit, wie sie vor der Sendung Adams herrschte.

lässigen darf[435])." Ein anderes Mal erklärt er: „Diese Sinndeutung (Abū Ja'qūbs) ist nicht von der Art, daß sie die Tatsächlichkeit des äußeren Wortsinnes nicht zuließe. Vielmehr bestätigt sie seine Tatsächlichkeit[436])." Als Grundregel stellt er aber auf: „Die Summe der Rede aber ist dies, daß jegliche Exegese, die zur Erlaubnis dessen, was Gott verboten hat, oder zum Verbot dessen, was Gott erlaubt hat, oder zu einer Änderung der Rangstufen der Hierarchie der Religion Gottes führt, oder einen Tadel gegen das Gesetz darstellt und zum Unterlassen des Handelns nach ihm auffordert, fehlerhaft ist[437])."

Die Vielzahl der Imame, die durch die Fortdauer der Ära Mohammeds zustande kommt, bringt al-Kirmānī durch Einführung kleiner Ären in die großen der Sprecher in seinem System unter. Dem siebten Imam ist jeweils eine besondere Kraft und bedeutende Unterstützung vom Himmel eigen, da er einer edlen Zahl entspricht. Er ist der Vollender einer kleinen Ära, das heißt einer Heptade von Imamen, innerhalb einer großen[438]). Da al-Kirmānī an der Siebenzahl der Vollender festhält, muß er zu der Summe von neunundvierzig Imamen in der großen Ära kommen. Diese Anschauung findet mehrere Male Ausdruck: „... in der (großen) Ära gibt es zehn Grade; der erste von ihnen ist der Sprecher, dann der Vollstrecker und sieben Vollender, die die kleinen Ären vollenden. Der zehnte ist derjenige, welcher den Platz des Sprechers in seiner Ära einnimmt und dann mit einer neuen Sache in einer neuen Ära auftritt[439])." Wie sehr das jedoch auch für ihn selbst eine neue Spekulation war, erhellt daraus, daß er früher vom hundertsten Imam in der Ära Mohammeds gesprochen hatte.

Die Erwartung der Endzeit ist damit zum ersten Mal in die weite Ferne gerückt und der gefährlichen Spekulation um sie, durch die so viele Anhänger der Imame zu ketzerischen Ansichten über Mohammed und die Gültigkeit seines Gesetzes verführt worden waren, der Boden entzogen[440]). Erst wenn alle fünfzig Grade der Ära Mohammeds erfüllt

---

435) Ar-rijāḍ S. 172.

436) Ar-rijāḍ S. 191.

437) Ar-rijāḍ in maḏhab S. 400.

438) Rāḥat al-'aql S. 424.

439) Rāḥat al-'aql S. 126. Ähnlich S. 124, 180, 187, 427, ar-rijāḍ S. 212.

440) Al-Kirmānī weiß natürlich gut, daß er damit gegen die Lehren der alten, von ihm als maßgebliche Autoritäten anerkannten Lehrmeister und Imame verstieß. So meint er zu der Feststellung Abū Ja'qūbs, daß in der Ära des Qā'im das Wissen herrsche, dies sei richtig, soweit er damit das Bild der Lehre meine, wonach die Ära der Stellvertreter des Qā'im nach Vollendung der Ära Mohammeds und vor dem Erscheinen des Qā'im sei. (in kāna murādahū mā 'alaihī ṣūratu'd-da'wati min kaun ...).

sind, wird Gott die „reine Seele", den Herrn der Auferstehung erscheinen lassen, der die großen und die kleinen Ären beschließt[441]).

In al-Kirmānī erreichte das philosophische Denken der Ismailiten einen Höhepunkt. Aber es setzte sich zugleich seine Schranken. Am Ende seiner Summa verurteilt er die Philosophen mit bitteren Worten, stellt sie neben die religiösen Extremisten (al-ġulāt), und droht ihnen mit der ewigen Verdammnis[442]). Ihr Irrtum liegt darin, daß sie sich nur auf die eigene Vernunft verlassen, Gottes Gebote nicht befolgen und die von ihm eingesetzte Lehrhierarchie mißachten. Denn die menschliche Vernunft ist von Natur aus unzulänglich. Nur durch die Berührung mit der höheren Vernunft kann sie zum rettenden Wissen gelangen. Die Vermittler dieser höheren Vernunft sind aber nur die Grade der Hierarchie, an ihrer Spitze die Propheten und die Imame. Darum muß die menschliche Vernunft sich bescheiden, wo ihr die Handlungen des rechtmäßigen Imams unbegreiflich erscheinen. Es ist die Zeit Imam al-Ḥākims.

## Die fatimidische Lehre zur Zeit al-Mustanṣirs

Al-Kirmānīs These der Fortdauer der Ära Mohammeds und der Gültigkeit seines Gesetzes wurde für die Anhänger der Fatimiden nach dem Tod al-Ḥākims verbindlich. Ḥamza und seine Schule erkannten ihn ohnehin als die letzte Verkörperung Gottes an und stellten sich damit in Gegnerschaft zu seinen Nachfolgern auf dem ägyptischen Thron. Innerhalb der fatimidisch-ismailitischen Gemeinde setzte sich aber die gemäßigte Richtung durch.

Freilich übernahm man nicht allgemein die radikal neue Imamatslehre, die al-Kirmānī in seinen Schriften entwickelt hatte[443]). Hier griff man weiterhin auf die Bilder und Anschauungen der frühen Fatimidenzeit zurück, deren vorzüglichsten Vertretern, wie al-Mu'izz und Ǧa'far b. Manṣūr al-Jaman, ja auch al-Kirmānī das Zeugnis der Orthodoxie hatte ausstellen müssen. Vor allem behielt die Interpretation der sieben wiederholten Verse im Koran mit den Imamheptaden nach Moham-

[441]) Rāḥat al-'aql S. 427. Es ist offenbar nur ein versehentlicher Rückgriff auf einen abgelegten Begriff, wenn al-Kirmānī, rāḥat al-'aql S. 261, einmal die Stellvertreter des Qā'im erwähnt. Der Qā'im wird ja die Hierarchie beseitigen, und vor ihm kommen nicht seine Stellvertreter, sondern die Imame der Ära Mohammeds. Sonst gebraucht er das Wort ḫulafā' im Sinne der Ḥuǧǧas in den Provinzen, vgl. S. 415, 426.

[442]) Rāḥat al-'aql S. 436ff.

[443]) Sie spielt eine Rolle in den späten masā'il maǧmū'a, Gnositexte arab. Texte S. 100.

med noch unter den Lehrmeistern der Zeit al-Mustanṣirs (427—487/1036—1094), des achtzehnten Imams, ihre Beliebtheit.

Muḥammad b. ʿAlī b. Ḥasan aṣ-Ṣūrī war in dieser Zeit als Sendbote in Syrien tätig. In seinem langen Gedicht, al-Qaṣīda aṣ-ṣūrīja, in dem er seine Weltanschauung darlegt, nimmt er wieder die Idee auf, daß Adam eine gesetzlose Zeit voraufgegangen sei[444]). Die Zahl der Imame in den vorangegangenen Prophetenären nennt er nicht. Aber diejenigen der Ära Mohammeds zählt er einzeln auf. In den Heptaden ist der siebte der vorzüglichste wegen seiner Nähe vom Herrn der Enthüllung. Er ist der „Imam des Glaubens" und sein Nachfolger der Qā'im[445]). Muḥammad b. Ismāʿīl wohnte neben der Kraft der Siebenzahl auch die der Vierzahl ein[446]). Er „wurde spirituell in potentia, nachdem er körperlich gewesen war[447])." Das Amt des Mahdi und das Amt des Qā'im sind nun klar voneinander getrennt. Der eine entspricht dem Fest des Fastenbrechens, der andere dem Opferfest, dazwischen sind siebzig Tage. „Der erste von ihnen (den Tagen) ist der Mahdi, er ist schon erschienen, der letzte der Qā'im, er ist der Erwartete[448])." Die übrigen Tage sind Imame und Pforten, die zu ihrer Gefolgschaft aufrufen. Die Vollender des Gesetzes, sagt aṣ-Ṣūrī, sind nicht gleich den Stellvertretern des Vollkommenen[449]), womit offenbar Muḥammad b. Ismāʿīl gemeint ist. Al-Muʿizz ist das Siegel der „sieben Wiederholten[450])". Durch al-ʿAzīz erhoffen die Wissenden ihre Rettung, denn er ist der achte nach dem siebten[451]). Im neunten, al-Ḥākim, offenbarte sich Gottes Gebot und die Weisheit des Gerechten. Das Verborgene wurde sichtbar[452]). Seine Handlungen, wie die Zerstörung von Kirchen, Verbot von Alkohol, Ausgehverbot für Frauen, sind Andeutungen dafür, was am Ende der Ära geschehen wird. Die Kalifen aẓ-Ẓāhir und al-Mustanṣir nennt aṣ-Ṣūrī ohne Numerierung. Der Qā'im aus der Nach-

[444]) Al-Qaṣīda aṣ-ṣūrīja, Ed. Arif Tamir, S. 42.

[445]) Al-Qaṣīda aṣ-ṣūrīja S. 68, Vers 5—6.

[446]) Al-Qaṣīda aṣ-ṣūrīja S. 67, V. 10. Dies geht offenbar auf eine Theorie Abū Ḥātims zurück. Gegen die These an-Nasafīs, daß Moses als der vierte Sprecher der vollkommenste unter ihnen war wie die Sonne unter den Planeten, teilte er die ersten sechs Sprecher in zwei Gruppen von je dreien ein. Moses erneuerte das Gesetz Adams, Jesus das Noahs und Mohammed das Abrahams. Abraham und Mohammed standen damit höher als die übrigen Sprecher. Den vierten Grad erreicht aber der siebte Sprecher, dem daher die Rangstufe der Vierzahl und der Siebenzahl innewohnt. Kitāb al-iṣlāḥ S. 198ff. Da aṣ-Ṣūrī Muḥammad b. Ismāʿīl nicht als den siebten Sprecher ansieht, ist sein Rückgriff auf dieses Bild natürlich verfehlt.

[447]) Al-Qaṣīda aṣ-ṣūrīja S. 67, V. 11. [448]) Al-Qaṣīda aṣ-ṣūrīja S. 67 unten.

[449]) S. 68, V. 7. [450]) S. 68, V. 12.

[451]) S. 68, V. 17—18. Al-ʿārifūn statt al-ʿārifīn zu lesen. [452]) S. 69, V. 1—7.

kommenschaft al-Mustanṣirs, wird die Ära der Verborgenheit beenden und das Verdeckte enthüllen. Die Religion wird dann wiederum nur im Wissen ohne Pflichten bestehen[453]).

Diese Darstellung läßt erkennen, daß sich nach Ablauf der zweiten Heptade von Imamen in der Lehre ganz ähnliche Schwierigkeiten ergaben, wie nach der ersten. Wieder zwang das Festhalten an Anschauungen, die nicht in Erfüllung gegangenen Erwartungen und Versprechungen einer früheren Epoche entsprachen, zu Umdeutungen und Anpassungen an die neuen Verhältnisse. Andererseits mochte sich die ismailitische Religion, die von Anfang an so stark auf eine endzeitliche Erwartung ausgerichtet war, zu keiner Zeit bereitfinden, diese Erwartung in eine unbestimmte, ferne Zukunft zu verschieben. Diese inhärente Neigung mußte gegen die allgemeine Annahme einer Lehre wie der al-Kirmānīs wirken und immer wieder in die Versuchung führen, bestimmtere Voraussagen zu machen.

Solche Tendenzen sind auch bei dem Verfasser einer Sammlung von Lehrvorträgen, al-maǧālis al-mustanṣirīja[454]), deutlich erkennbar. „Die Imame", so meint er, „sind die Entsprechungen der ‘sieben Wiederholten’ wegen ihrer Aufeinanderfolge in der Welt: Jedesmal, wenn sieben von ihnen vorbeigegangen sind, kommen nach ihnen sieben, wie die sieben Tage. Der sechste der Imame ist ein Vollender, wie der Donnerstag, und der siebte ist von hohem Rang, wie der Freitag. Dieser Zustand wird ebenso fortdauern, bis der Qā’im der Auferstehung auftritt ... Dann wird der siebte der Imame, die an seine Ära grenzen, sein Ḥuǧǧa sein. Der Qā’im wird der achte jener Ära unter den Imamen und der siebte der durch göttliche Unterstützung und Weisheit bevorzugten Sprecher sein."

„Wisset aber, Gemeinde der Gläubigen, daß der Imam eurer Zeit der achte der machtvollen (ūlū’l-‘azm) unter den Imamen ist ... Wenn also die Zeit für das Auftreten des Qā’im schon gekommen ist ..., so ist er der Herr dieser großen Sache und der hohen, würdigen Stellung. Es wird eine Ära sein, die 50000 Jahre dauert, ohne Geheimhaltung (taqīja) und ohne Armut. Gott wird ihm alle Länder der Erde öffnen ..."[455])

Diese hohe Hoffnung spricht der Verfasser noch in mehreren anderen seiner Vorlesungen aus[456]). Er weiß natürlich recht gut, daß al-

---

[453]) S. 70.

[454]) Die ismailitische Tradition schreibt das Werk dem Wesir Badr al-Ǧamālī zu. Doch erscheint diese Verfasserschaft recht zweifelhaft, wie der Herausgeber, M. Kamil Husain, ausführt. Vgl. maǧālis S. 7ff.

[455]) Maǧālis S. 30f. [456]) Maǧālis S. 32, 36, 64.

Mustanṣir eigentlich der neunzehnte Imam nach dem Propheten ist[457]). Aber er beginnt seine Zählung kurzerhand mit den Fatimiden. Diese offenkundige Neuerung kann er mit einer älteren Theorie verknüpfen: Er nennt al-Mustanṣir den achten der Ḫulafā[458]), was bisher als Stellvertreter zu übersetzen war, hier aber die fatimidischen Kalifen meint.

Die so diesseitige Ausdeutung, die der Verfasser an der angeführten Stelle der Auferstehung gab, soll keine Leugnung der Wiedererweckung der Toten und des jüngsten Gerichts bedeuten. In einer anderen Vorlesung sieht er sich genötigt, auf ihre Wirklichkeit mit Nachdruck zu verweisen. Was die Lehre über irdische Entsprechungen für diese Dinge aussagt, widerspricht dem nicht. Denn was davon im Diesseits geschieht ist nur das Äußere, das für das Jenseits versprochene sein innerer Sinn. Die Gläubigen müssen sich aber zum Äußeren und zum Inneren gemeinsam bekennen. „Dies ist eine Stelle, an der viele Exegeten in die Irre gegangen sind[459]), wodurch mancher Hörer ins Verderben geraten ist. Darum wollten wir die Klarstellung der Sache bis zum Äußersten führen, damit dies ein anzuwendender Grundsatz und ein verläßlicher Hinweis sei. Denn jemand von geringem Verstand pflegte zu sagen, wenn immer ihm die Erwähnung des Paradieses vorkam: 'Die Auslegung des Paradieses ist die wahre Lehre.' Dies führte dazu, daß einer, dessen Wissen begrenzt war, das Paradies leugnete. Gott bewahre uns davor[460]).“

Anders muß Nāṣir-e Ḫosraus exegetisches Werk wağh-e dīn beurteilt werden. Auch Nāṣir greift auf die Anschauungen und Begriffe der frühen Fatimidenzeit zurück. Ja, seine Abhängigkeit ist offenbar sehr direkt: Yahya el-Khachab erkennt in Teilen eine reine Übersetzung aus dem Ğa'far b. Manṣūr al-Jaman zugeschriebenen Kitāb al-fatarāt wa'l-qirānāt[461]). Ebenso läßt sich Ğa'fars ta'wīl az-zakāt leicht als

---

[457]) S. 32, 36, natürlich unter Einschluß Alis. Nach der Heptadenzählung, die mit al-Ḥasan anfängt, ist er der vierte der dritten Heptade.

[458]) Mağālis S. 64, 117. [459]) Ḍalla statt dalla zu lesen.

[460]) Mağālis S. 46.

[461]) Yahya el-Khachab, Nāṣir è Ḫosraw, Kairo 1940, vor allem S. 151ff., S. 291. Wenn das späte Datum, das P. Kraus und Kamil Husain dem Werk zuschreiben, (vgl. oben S. 99 Anm. 309, nämlich Ende 5./11. Jhs.), richtig ist, müßte die Abhängigkeit in umgekehrte Richtung sein. Aber die Stellen, die für die spätere Datierung sprechen, mögen hinzugefügt sein, während ein Kern von Ğa'far stammt, wie Kraus selbst einräumt. Auch eine gemeinsame Quelle mag vorliegen. Unabhängig davon hat Ivanow über wağh-e dīn bemerkt, fast das ganze Werk zeige typische Anzeichen einer wörtlichen Übersetzung aus dem Arabischen, Notes sur l'Ummu'l-Kitāb, REI 1932, S. 421 Anm. 1, und Problems in Nāṣir-i Khusraws Biography, Bombay 1956, S. 52. Die Originalität des philosophischen und theologischen Werks Nāṣir-e Ḫosraus erscheint auch von ande-

eine seiner Vorlagen erkennen, wenn Nāṣir auch stark gekürzt und die extremeren Aussagen entfernt hat.

Die sieben Imame bilden für Nāṣir einen Begriff, den er ständig ohne nähere Erläuterung gebraucht. Dem siebten kommt der Rang der Auferstehung zu[462]. „Von den sieben Imamen tritt der siebte hervor, gibt sich selbst zu erkennen, legt Prophetentum und Gesetz fest[463].“ „Auf den Propheten folgen sechs Imame, deren Vollendung im Erscheinen des Qā'im der Wahrheit ist[464].“ Bei der Sinndeutung der „sieben Wiederholten“ verwendet er das geläufige Bild: „Sodann sagen wir, daß die Ära, in der wir uns befinden, aus zwei Abschnitten besteht. Der eine ist der erste Teil, nämlich die Ära[465] der Imame. Der andere Teil ist der Teil der Stellvertreter[466]. Dies ist die Ära der Auferstehung. Alle zwei Teile gehen auf die spirituellen Prinzipien zurück[467].“

Es kann kein Zweifel bestehen, daß Nāṣir-e Ḫosrau die orthodoxe fatimidische Lehre seiner Zeit vertrat. Aus anderen seiner Schriften, wie auch aus der Einleitung zu waǧh-e din selbst, geht hervor, daß er das Erscheinen des Qā'im der Auferstehung und die Aufhebung der Gesetze als ein zukünftiges Ereignis betrachtete[468]. Auf keine der üblichen Prophezeiungen über das Wann des großen Ereignisses läßt er sich ein. Der Zahl der Imame mißt er anderswo keine Rolle bei[469].

rer Seite in Frage gestellt. S. Pines, La longue recension de la théologie d'Aristote dans ses rapports avec la doctrine ismaélienne, REI 1954, S. 13ff., zeigt, daß Nāṣir die Stellung des göttlichen Befehls (amr) in der Kosmogonie in vier seiner Abhandlungen jedesmal verschieden darstellt. Pines meint dazu, die Annahme, es handle sich um die Entwicklung einer persönlichen Anschauung sei unwahrscheinlich, und wirft die Frage auf, ob Nāṣir nicht einfach arabische Abhandlungen ins Persische übersetzte, ohne wesentliche Änderungen vorzunehmen und ohne die Widersprüche ihrer Lehren auszumerzen. Dies schwächt die Grundlage der Annahme A. E. Bertels, Nasir-i Chosrov i Ismailizm, Moskau 1959, S. 197, der Text von waǧh-e dīn müsse Veränderungen ausgesetzt gewesen sein, wenn das Werk überhaupt von Nāṣir stamme.

[462]) Waǧh-e dīn, Ed. Kaviani, Berlin 1925, S. 88. [463]) S. 163. [464]) S. 223.

[465]) Hier gebraucht Nāṣir das Wort daur im geläufigen Sinn. Daneben kennt er aber auch große und kleine Ären. Im Gegensatz zur Vorstellung al-Kirmānīs meint er mit der großen Ära nur die Zeit des einzelnen Propheten, mit der kleinen die eines einzelnen Imams. Vgl. S. 109, 135, 293.

[466]) Hier, S. 215 Z. 8, wie noch einmal weiter unten, Z. 10, ist zweifellos ḫulafā' statt ḫalqān, zu lesen. Interessant ist S. 213 Z. 13: haft imām wa haft ḥuǧǧat, wo wiederum die ḫulafā' gemeint sind. [467]) Waǧh-e dīn S. 215.

[468]) Z. B. waǧh-e dīn S. 250f., raušanā'ī-nāma, Ed. Ivanow, Leiden 1949, 6. Kap., ḫwān al-iḫwān, Ed. el-Khachab, Kairo 1940, S. 245. Freilich stellt Nāṣir den Wert des Inneren hoch über den des Äußeren, waǧh-e dīn S. 64ff.

[469]) Sehr deutlich in Ḫwān S. 72, wo er neben den namentlich genannten Sprecher jeder Ära und sein Fundament „seinen Imam“ als eine Rangstufe setzt.

Daraus kann man nur schließen, daß Nāṣirs Ausführungen in seinem waǧh-e dīn gar nicht auf die irdische Wirklichkeit bezogen werden dürfen. An keiner Stelle nennt er auch einen seiner Imame oder den Qā'im beim Namen, noch deutet er irgendeine historische Begebenheit an. Offenbar übernahm er einfach das System der Bilder, Begriffe und Methodik der Deutung aus den heiligen Schriften der alten Lehrautoritäten als ideell gültige Wahrheit. Seine Exegese will nicht mehr sein als ein Operieren mit festen symbolischen Begriffen nach festgelegten Gesetzen. Die Rechtfertigung liegt in der Heiligkeit dieser Gesetze und Symbole selbst, sie brauchen keine Bestätigung durch die irdische Realität.

Hierin liegt ein grundsätzlicher Unterschied zu den bisher untersuchten Werken. Gewiß gab es auch da die reine Spekulation, die nur von ihren eigenen Gesetzen bestimmt ist. Dies gilt besonders von der hierarchischen Ordnung der religiösen Rangstufen, die fast in jedem Werk der allegorischen Deutung eine große Rolle spielen. Die Zahl solcher Systeme dürfte der der Abhandlungen darüber nahekommen[470]). Mit der tatsächlichen Organisation der fatimidischen Mission haben sie sicher wenig gemein[471]). Der Konservativismus, das ständige Zurückgreifen auf durch ihr Alter geheiligte Anschauungen, ist eine hervorstechende Eigenschaft der ismailitischen Literatur. Aber immer suchte man doch, die Theorie durch die Realität zu bestätigen, und, wo nötig, ihr anzupassen. Oft genug ist zwischen den scheinbar so abstrusen Gedankengebäuden ein sehr massiver politischer Zweck zu erkennen.

### Spätere Auslegung der „Gebete der sieben Tage"

Mit der Festlegung der Lehre auf die gemäßigte Richtung ergab sich die Notwendigkeit, die Stellen der älteren, weiterhin als orthodox anerkannten Texte, die nicht mit ihr übereinstimmten, neu zu interpretieren. Zahid Ali führt in seiner Untersuchung der ismailitischen Lehre einige Beispiele solcher Interpretationen der Gebete des al-Mu'izz an, denen ja, als dem Wort des Imams, besondere Bedeutung zukommen mußte. Auf sie sei hier noch kurz eingegangen, obwohl sie erst der nachfatimidischen[472]) jemenitischen Schule angehören.

---

[470]) Vgl. maḏhab Kap. 11.

[471]) Vgl. Ivanow, The Organization of the Fatimid Propaganda, JBBRAS 1939, S. 8.

[472]) Das bedeutet hier nach dem Jahre 524/1130, da die jemenitische Gemeinde die fatimidischen Kalifen nach al-Āmir bis zum Fall der Dynastie nicht als Imame anerkannten.

Ibrāhīm b. al-Ḥusain al-Ḥāmidī (gest. 557/1162) schreibt in seinem für die spätere esoterische Lehre wichtigen Werk kanz al-walad: „... Muḥammad b. Ismā'īl ist aber der Vollender seines (Mohammeds) Gesetzes, der Erfüller seiner (des Gesetzes) Rechte und Schranken, und der siebte der Gottesgesandten. Die Erläuterung davon ist in den Gebeten unseres Herrn al-Mu'izz. Er (Mohammed) legt Zeugnis für ihn (Muḥammad b. Ismā'īl) ab und für den Qā'im Muḥammad b. 'Abd Allāh al-Mahdī — denn er[473]) ist der Qā'im der mittleren Auferstehung, der Qā'im der ersten Auferstehung ist der Herrscher der Gläubigen (Ali) und der Qā'im der größten Auferstehung ist der Herr der Enthüllung — in seinem Gebetsruf mit den Worten: 'Ich bezeuge, daß Muḥammad der Gesandte Gottes ist, ich bezeuge, daß Muḥammad der Gesandte Gottes ist.' Denn die Menschen bezeugen sein (Mohammeds) Prophetentum, und er legt Zeugnis ab für den Vollender seiner Ära, seines Gesetzes und seines Systems[474])."

Al-Ḥāmidī macht sich hier die Doppeldeutigkeit des Wortes Vollendung zunutze, das auch im Arabischen sowohl Ende, als auch Vollkommenheit bezeichnet. Andererseits versucht er zu erklären, warum Muḥammad b. Ismā'īl und der zweite Fatimide in älteren Texten als der Qā'im bezeichnet werden, der doch für ihn und seine zeitgenössischen Glaubensbrüder unzweifelhaft erst in der Zukunft erscheinen konnte.

Etwas anders löst sein Zeitgenosse Muḥammad b. Ṭāhir (gest. 584/1188) dasselbe Problem. Auch er meint, das Glaubensbekenntnis des Propheten Mohammed gelte dem Muḥammad b. Ismā'īl, da es doch nicht zulässig sei, daß er für sich selbst Zeugnis ablege. Wenn das Bekenntnis im Gebetsruf wiederholt wird, so meint das erste Mohammed, das zweite Muḥammad b. Ismā'īl, „welcher der Vollender seiner Ära und der siebte Gesandte ist. Auf ihn deutete unser Herr al-Mu'izz in seinem Samstagsgebet hin, denn er ist der siebte Sprecher. Was den Qā'im der Auferstehung anbelangt, so ist seine Sache höher als dies, denn er ist nicht in die Reihe der Gesandten eingeordnet[475])."

Muḥammad b. Ṭāhir erklärt diese Auffassung an anderer Stelle noch näher. Muḥammad b. Ismā'īl ist „der potentielle Qā'im, der Herr

---

[473]) Zahid Ali ergänzt in der Übersetzung Muḥammad b. Ismā'īl. Später (S. 108) drückt er Verwunderung darüber aus, daß al-Ḥāmidī zwei Propheten nach Mohammed anerkenne. Aber das zeigt nur, wie gut al-Ḥāmidī die alte Lehre verstand, die Zweideutigkeit des Fürworts ist gewollt. Daß al-Mu'izz nur Muḥammad b. Ismā'īl als den siebten Gesandten bezeichnete, darin kann ich Zahid Ali nicht beipflichten. Allerdings nannte er den ersten, nicht den zweiten Fatimiden.

[474]) Kanz al-walad in maḏhab S. 97.

[475]) Al-anwār al-laṭīfa in maḏhab S. 98.

der ersten Enthüllung, denn der wirkliche Qā'im ist der universelle Qā'im, welcher der Herr der letzten Enthüllung und der größten Gewalt ist. Es gibt nämlich viele Auferstehungen, die erste ist der „beschränkt Autorisierte" (al-ma'ḏūn al-makfūf) . . .[476]) Die letzte ist der Qā'im der Auferstehungen. Er vertritt den Zehnten[477]) auf seinem Platz nach seiner Erhöhung aus diesem Bereich. Der Name des siebten Sprechers aber findet Anwendung auf ihn[478]), da er das göttliche Gebot ausspricht und 'Ich' sagt( ? )[479]). Denn er ist nicht in die Reihe der Sprecher der Ära der Verborgenheit eingeordnet, da er ihr widerspricht[480]). Er ist kein Vollender, ist nicht in ihre Grade eingeordnet, und ist auch kein Gesandter. Vielmehr ist er einzig in der Rangstufe der Einheit und der Göttlichkeit. Muḥammad b. Ismā'īl ist aber damit bezeichnet, weil er in die Reihe der Ränge der Ära der Verborgenheit[481]) und ihrer Sprecher eingeordnet ist." Muḥammad b. Ṭāhir erklärt dies an Hand der Aufzählung der Sprecher, Vollstrecker und Vollenderimame, wie sie al-Mu'izz in seinen Gebeten gegeben hatte. Im Auftreten des Muḥammad b. Ismā'īl „ist die Vollendung der Ära der Verborgenheit und der Beginn[482]) der Ära der Enthüllung und die Aufhebung des Gesetzes des sechsten Gesandten." Dafür kann Muḥammad b. Ṭāhir wiederum al-Mu'izz als Zeugen zitieren. Dann fügt er

[476]) Nun werden die Ränge der Hierarchie aufgeführt. (Zahid Ali läßt die Stelle aus, vgl. aber Idrīs, zahr al-ma'ānī in Rise, Texte S. 55, der hier Muḥammad b. Ṭāhir frei zitiert.) Die Vorstellung dabei ist, daß der Aufstieg zu einem höheren Grad in der Hierarchie jeweils eine Auferstehung darstellt. Vgl. Corbin, Rituel Sabéen et exegèse ismaélienne du Rituel, Eranos-Jahrbuch XIX, S. 199f., und Epiphanie . . ., Eranos-Jahrbuch XXIII, S. 184, 236.

[477]) Gemeint ist der zehnte Intellekt, der Weltenlenker. Al-'āšir statt al-'āš ist auch bei Lewis, An Ismaili Interpretation of the Fall of Adam, im arabischen Text jeweils zu lesen.

[478]) Zahid Ali bezieht das Fürwort in seiner Übersetzung, S. 100 und Anm. 2, auf Muḥammad b. Ismā'īl. Das ist zweifellos unzulässig, da danach gesagt wird, der genannte stehe außerhalb der Prophetenreihe. Von Muḥammad b. Ismā'īl heißt es dann im Gegenteil, er sei in die Reihe der Sprecher der Ära der Verborgenheit eingegliedert. Es soll hier vielmehr erklärt werden, warum der letzte Qā'im auch der siebte Sprecher genannt wird, obwohl dieser Name nach Muḥammad b. Ṭāhir eigentlich dem Muḥammad b. Ismā'īl gebührt.

[479]) Qaulihī ana, so die beiden Handschriften Zahid Alis.

[480]) Iḏ hūa bi-ḫilāfihī, nämlich als Herr der Enthüllung.

[481]) Damit ist hier der ganze Zyklus von Adam bis zum letzten Qā'im gemeint, nicht etwa die Periode der verborgenen Imame vor dem Auftreten der Fatimiden. Ivanows Ergänzung von (impending) bei der Übersetzung der Parallelstelle in zahr al-ma'ānī, Rise S. 244, ist verfehlt.

[482]) Wahrscheinlich ibtidā' statt i'tiqād zu lesen, entsprechend der Übersetzung Zahid Alis, S. 101.

aber hinzu: „Dies alles ist potentiell, nicht wirksam, denn er ist potentiell ein Qā'im[483]).“

Damit ist schließlich den Spekulationen die letzte Sprengkraft genommen. Idrīs b. al-Ḥasan, der die Ausführungen des Muḥammad b. Ṭāhir in seinem esoterischen Werk zahr al-ma'ānī stellenweise wörtlich übernimmt, sagt mit Nachdruck: „Muḥammad b. Ismā'īl hat nichts vom Äußeren des Gesetzes Mohammeds aufgehoben, sondern hat es gefestigt, und befohlen, daß nach ihm gehandelt werde. So ist der Brauch der reinen Imame, indem sie die Pflichten und die Gebote wahren ohne Konzession, ohne Nachlässigkeit, ohne Unterlassung und ohne Nichtigachtung. Der Imam al-Mu'izz meinte jedoch mit seinen Worten: '... und mit dessen Auftreten du das Äußere des Gesetzes Mohammeds aufgehoben hast', daß er, indem er seine Bedeutung offenbarte und seine Geheimnisse enthüllte und erhellte, seinen Anhängern und seinen Getreuen den Glauben an das Äußere nahm, soweit darin Inhaltsentleerung (ta'ṭīl), Verähnlichung des wahren Schöpfers mit seinen Geschöpfen, Gleichsetzung und Anthropomorphismus in bezug auf die spirituellen eingeschlossen sind ... Diesen Glauben hat er abgeschafft und erklärt, was damit gemeint ist, indem er die Wahrheiten entdeckte, die wahrhafte Erläuterung offenbarte und die Deutung unternahm, in der die göttliche Einheit in Wahrheit bekannt wurde ...“[484])

---

[483]) Bi-kaunihī qā'iman bi'l-qūwa: oder einfach '... denn er tritt potentiell auf.' Al-anwār al-laṭīfa in maḏhab S. 99f.

[484]) Zahr al-ma'ānī in Rise, Texte S. 57f., maḏhab S. 103.

# VIII

## ABŪ YA'QŪB AL-SIJISTĀNĪ AND METEMPSYCHOSIS

In his book on India, al-Bīrūnī, after describing Hindu beliefs in the transmigration of souls, states that Abū Ya'qūb al-Sijzī, known as Cottonseed (*khayshafūj*)[1], maintained in his book *Kashf al-maḥjūb* that metempsychosis occurs only within each species. This was in contrast to the view of Pythagoras and Plato who, according to John Philoponus, had held that human rational souls could transmigrate to the bodies of animals[2]. That Abū Ya'qūb al-Sijistānī, the Ismā'īlī *dā'ī* of the early Fāṭimid age[3], taught metempsychosis, is confirmed by the later Ismā'īlī missionary Nāṣir-i Khusraw in two of his works. In his *Zād al-musāfirīn*, Nāṣir speaks of those who believe that reward and punishment take place on earth. The Hindus, he states, uphold this doctrine and many of them kill or burn themselves in the hope that they would return to a better life. Abū Ya'qūb al-Sijzī likewise talked in this sense at a time when he suffered from melancholy and called the followers of the Legitimate House (Ismā'īlīs) to this doctrine in his books entitled *Sūs al-baqā'*, *Kashf al-maḥjūb*, *al-Risāla al-Bāhira*, and others. When the lord of the time (imam) learned of his teaching, he disapproved of it and said that melancholy has overcome him. Yet a group of the (Ismā'īlī) Shī'a still cling to his mistaken views[4].

More explicit are Nāṣir's statements in his *Khwān al-ikhwān*. He discusses Abū Ya'qūb's views on metempsychosis there in the context of various opinions about *barzakh* (lit. border, partition). Qur'an XXIII.100 says of the dead: "beyond them there is a border (*barzakh*) until the day when they will be resuscitated (*yub'athūn*)." *Barzakh* was thus commonly understood to mean the place or state of the dead before the Last Judgment, reward and punishment[5]. Nāṣir explains that for the exoterics (*ahl al-ẓāhir*), i.e., the ordinary Muslims, who do not distinguish sharply between body and soul, *barzakh* consists in the grave where man is subject to the torment of the grave (*'adhāb-i qabr*) and the questioning by the angels Munkar and Nakīr[6]. In regard to the Ismā'īlī esoterics, for whom the soul is the essential part of man, Nāṣir first mentions the views of Muḥammad b. Aḥmad al-Nasafī (Nakhshabī, d. 332/943), the initiator of the classical Ismā'īlī cosmology and teacher of Abū Ya'qūb. Al-Nasafī described *barzakh* as a fine light (*nūrī laṭīf*) located beyond the outermost sphere (*falak al-aflāk*) which is neither in motion nor at rest. Whereas the upper part of this light is fine and connected to the Universal Soul (*Nafs-i kull*), the lower part is dense and coarse (*sitabr*) and is connected to the (outer) sphere. Each soul which acquires any kind of knowledge is prevented by it from becoming nothing and is made permanent. If that knowledge was religious, the soul has been educated by action in accordance with the *sharīʿa* and abstention from sin. When it is separated from the body, it passes by the spheres and heavenly bodies to that light and comes to rest on the side of it which is connected to the Universal Soul. The souls of those who have done evil and deserve punishment come to rest on the side which is connected to the sphere[7]. In his *Kitāb al-Maḥṣūl* al-Nasafī affirmed that the physical world would be annihilated at the end. He did not, Nāṣir adds, teach metempsychosis and the transfer of the soul from body to body[8]. Al-Nasafī presumably held that after the advent of the Qā'im and his ultimate rise to the spiritual world the souls of the faithful would rise with him and find their permanent resting place and reward with the Universal Soul near the Intellect, while the souls of the evil would be annihilated together with the physical world.

Nāṣir next mentions Dihqān, the son of al-Nasafī and chief of the *daʿwa* of the province of Khurāsān[9] after Abū Yaʿqūb. Dihqān taught that *barzakh* was the natural soul (*nafs-i ṭabīʿī*) and that the human soul, so long as it was tied to the natural world, could not escape from *barzakh* and rise above the natures. He did not mention anything like his father's doctrine about *barzakh* and accused Abū Yaʿqūb of being an advocate of metempsychosis (*tanasukhī*)[10]. In view of his denunciation of *tanāsukh*, Dihqān's doctrine must be understood to mean that man during his lifetime could free himself through gnosis from the fetters of nature. Perhaps in reaction to Abū Yaʿqūb's radical views, he seems to have avoided the question of what would happen to the souls of either the faithful or the wicked after death before the advent of the Qā'im. Would the souls of the gnostics be released from their bodies but fail to reach their final destination in the spiritual world, while the souls of the evil would remain tied to their dead bodies? Or did Dihqān agree with his father's view without expressly endorsing it? His brother Ḥasan Masʿūd, in any case, upheld the father's doctrine about the light beyond the outer sphere[11].

After reporting some more, anonymous views, Nāṣir turns to Abū Yaʿqūb. In one place the latter defined *barzakh* as the religious laws of the prophets, calling the prophets lords of the cycle of concealment (*khudāwandān-i dawr-i satr*) and the Qā'im lord of the cycle of disclosure (*khudāwand-i dawr-i kashf*). He also referred to the Qā'im as lord of the great aeon (*kawr-i ʿaẓīm*)[12] and spoke, without sense and proof, about the time before Adam and the time after the Qā'im which would be like it. He said that the instructional souls (*nafshā-yi taʿlīmī*) came to dwell in the physical world through the power of divine support (*ta'yīd*) of the prophets and that through the power of the lord of the great aeon[13] they would become spiritual (*rūḥānī*). In another place Abū Yaʿqūb defined *barzakh* as the persons of men (*shakhṣhā-yi mardum*) and said that the souls come into the persons in this world until the advent of the lord of the resurrection (*khudāwand-i qiyāmat*), i.e., the Qā'im. At that time every soul which had done good would reach divine support and rise to the world of the Intellect (*ʿālam-i ʿaqlī*) which is paradise and each soul which had done evil would fail to receive divine support and remain in the physical world which is hell. Nāṣir adds that Abū Yaʿqūb said many good and agreeable things, but what he said in support of *tanāsukh* could not be approved by reasonable men[14]. Further on in the same chapter, Nāṣir, like al-Bīrūnī, compares Abū Yaʿqūb's doctrine of *tanāsukh* with Plato's[15]. The subject of *barzakh* with its potential implication of *tanāsukh* was evidently controversial in the time of Nāṣir, for he states that he wrote a book entitled *Kitāb al-miṣbāḥ* on it at the order of the Imam al-Mustanṣir Bi'llāh[16].

In the next chapter, Nāṣir comes back to Plato's views. According to Plato's books, human souls after their separation from the body return to animal bodies, lions, donkeys, and cows according to their nature. Some of Plato's disciples, however, said that he did not mean *tanāsukh* by this but was speaking in allusions and similitudes. According to some he held that the soul of each species could return only to its appropriate body and that the souls of the wicked would become demons. According to others he did not mean by the bodies to which the souls would return the coarse bodies (of the physical world) but rather (immaterial) bodies engendered by the coarse bodies and the actions of the soul in which they would remain forever. About the hereafter, Plato taught that the evil souls were unable to leave the physical world because the soul needed the instrument of the body to become subtle and pure. The reward consisted in the soul becoming a substance like the intellect, for the soul is potentially intellect and at that time actually becomes intellect and returns to the divine world. Nāṣir then contrasts Abū Yaʿqūb's view with Plato's. Some people said that Abū Ya'qūb does not mention an abode for the soul outside this coarse world. This, Nāṣir comments, is indeed evident in Abū Ya'qūb's elaborations in his *Kashf al-maḥjūb*. A group of his disciples, however, who claimed to know his true doctrine, said that according to him the soul, when it had become pure, would return to the higher world and remain there forever[17].

Both W. Ivanow and H. Corbin, apparently unaware of the testimony of al-Bīrūnī, have maintained that Abū Ya'qūb did not really teach metempsychosis. Ivanow suggested that Nāṣir, who also accused the orthodox Muslims of *tanāsukh*[18], meant by this term no more than the dogma of "resurrection in flesh. Nāṣir did not make this clear in order that his book should not seem outrageous to the orthodox[19]." Corbin accepted Ivanow's suggestion but offered a more qualified assessment of Abū Ya'qūb's views. While he noted that Abū Ya'qūb in the extant Persian version of *Kashf al-maḥjūb* expressly rejected *tanāsukh*, he admitted that there were sections in it which could be seen to support the idea of a *resurrectio carnis*. The word of those of his disciples who claimed to know the secret of his doctrine should be trusted. Corbin raised the question of how a resurrection of the flesh could be integrated in Abū Ya'qūb's general cosmological views. Did it imply, besides the spiritual resurrection, a gradual refinement and sublimation of matter itself as envisaged in some Ismā'īlī gnostic thought[20]? Was Abū Ya'qūb's "world of the Resurrection" the higher world to which his disciples referred? Or was it rather the future "cycle of disclosure" in this world mentioned repeatedly in *Kashf al-maḥjūb*? Corbin concluded that a clear and definite answer to these questions could not yet be given[21].

The examination of Abū Ya'qūb's controversial views is hampered by the partial loss of his relevant works. The *Kitāb Sūs al-baqā'* is not extant. The *Risāla al-Bāhira* is available in manuscript. "Reading through its pages," Ivanow stated, "one fails to discover any traces of *tanāsukh*[22]." The *Kashf al-maḥjūb* is extant in a Persian translation which is, as shown by S.M. Stern, incomplete[23]. The translation was probably, as suggested by S. Nafīsī, by Nāṣir-i Khusraw[24] who could well have omitted some passages more overtly supporting metempsychosis. Yet there is no reason to doubt that what remains reflects Abū Ya'qūb's thought faithfully enough. A careful reading may thus reveal the basis of the accusations against Abū Ya'qūb of having taught *tanāsukh*.

In Chapter 5, 3rd Inquiry, Abū Yaʿqūb, as noted by Corbin, expressly repudiates *tanāsukh*. He gives the term, however, the narrow meaning of transmigration of the human soul to an animal body. What he indignantly rejects is the mingling of species (*āmīkhtan-i anwāʿ bā yak dīgar*). In no way does he deny the possibility of a return of the human soul to earth in a human body. This closely tallies with al-Bīrūnī's statement that Abū Yaʿqūb in his *Kashf al-maḥjūb* taught "that the species are preserved (*al-anwāʿ maḥfūẓa*) and that *tanāsukh* occurred in each one of them without transgressing to another species." There is no reason to assume that he later uses the term *tanāsukh*, when denouncing it as the doctrine of the incapable and ignorant[25], in a different sense.

Abū Yaʿqūb's views on the destiny of the human soul become clear in Chapter 6, concerning *baʿth* (*bar angīkhtan*). For orthodox Muslims the terms *baʿth* and *qiyāma* are virtually synonymous, meaning the Resurrection of the dead for the Judgment at the end of the terrestrial world. The Ismāʿīlī gnostic Abū Yaʿqūb, here and in other works, clearly distinguishes between the two. *Qiyāma* means for him the imminent advent of the Qā'im, or rather his return in glory[26], in order to open the cycle of disclosure. *Baʿth*, in contrast, does not refer to a single event in time. Rather it means the resuscitation or rebirth of the individual soul through, or in the course of, gnosis. In order to maintain the distinction, only *qiyāma* will be translated here as resurrection and *baʿth* as resuscitation or rebirth[27].

In Chapter 6 of *Kashf al-maḥjūb* Abū Yaʿqūb describes *baʿth* at times as a spiritual rebirth during life and at times as a physical rebirth of the dead. The latter sense is, as noted by Corbin[28], particularly evident in the Second and Third Inquiry. In the Second Inquiry he argues against a *baʿth* in large number as implied in the orthodox belief of a universal Resurrection. If the people of all past cycles were to be resuscitated at one time, the whole earth would be used up to restore their bodies, since an increase of the earth by God would not be proper. Where would this mass of people dwell then? Abū Yaʿqūb affirms that infants and insane people lacking a sound mind are not reborn because they do not deserve a recompense for their acts. Likewise it would be incompatible with the wisdom and mercy of the Creator to resuscitate blacks, Turks, and the people of Sind living at the extremities of the earth who have not acquired any knowledge or (religious) work and thus do not merit either reward or punishment. At the same time Abū Yaʿqūb implies that the resuscitation of those who deserve it does not take place at a single time.

In the Third Inquiry Abū Yaʿqūb affirms that knowledge of the rebirth remains veiled to the individual soul. This means both that it loses the knowledge it had acquired in its previous physical figure and that it has no knowledge of its future state after rebirth. When the soul is separated from the human figure (*shakhṣ*), its gnostic knowledge (*maʿrifathā*) is deposited in a place beyond its reach. Since every age and time has different principles and derived rules of knowledge, the previous knowledge would in fact be an obstacle for the soul if it became mixed up with its new knowledge appropriate for its time. If, on the other hand, knowledge of its state after rebirth were not veiled from the soul, it would lose its incentive to acquire knowledge and good work since there would be no room for either hope or fear.

In the Fourth Inquiry, on *baʿth* consisting in the training (*riyāḍat*) of the soul, *baʿth* is at first described as a purely spiritual rebirth within life. Through the teaching of a gnostic teacher the soul may be transformed to such a degree that someone having met a person before would imagine him to be a different person. Abū Yaʿqūb insists that this resuscitation is an ennoblement of the soul rather than the body. In the last section, however, he asks: If it is possible for someone to acquire such a refined soul even in his original body, how much more will it be possible for him, after becoming joined to a body more balanced, more remote from evil, and closer to good, to pursue more intense training and to acquire further refinement[29]?

The Fifth Inquiry is entitled: That through resuscitation the unfortunate may become fortunate and the fortunate may become unfortunate. The cause of misfortune is that someone learns from a misguided and deviant teacher. Afterwards, however, he may find an intelligent and ascetic gnostic who will direct him to the right path and teach him to do good acts. When his soul is separated from his body and the time comes for his rebirth, great happiness (*saʿādathā-yi ʿaẓīm*) will reach his soul as a reward for his good effort. Likewise someone fortunate may turn negligent in observing the knowledge which he has been given and be deceived by a deviant teacher. After his soul becomes separated from his body, that misfortune which his soul deserves for his negligence and carelessness will attach itself to it and become the cause of his punishment. Abū Yaʿqūb then mentions the case of someone having died after incurring good or evil seven thousand years ago or some other lengthy time ago and asks whether his reward or punishment which he deserved would have reached him or not? If not there would not be either reward or punishment. But if their recompense has reached them, their resuscitation must already have occurred[30]. How indeed could it be otherwise and be compatible with reason? Abū Ya'qūb here evidently rejects the orthodox belief in a universal Resurrection at the end of the world. The rebirth for the recompense occurs soon after death.

In the Sixth Inquiry, *ba'th* again appears as a purely spiritual awakening. This may occur after a short or a long time, depending on whether the disciple seeking the true path finds a guiding teacher quickly or not, and whether the deviant pupil finds someone who aids him in his aberrancy. A gnostic in possession of the subtle and obscure knowledge may also be miserly with it and refuse to impart it to anyone unless he finds him fully deserving. God knows mysteries in regard to the rebirth which are veiled from the creatures of the world, and its economy is in His hand just like their return, their reward and punishment.

In the last, Seventh Inquiry, Abū Ya'qūb argues that good acts, both intellectual and those in accordance with the religious law, contribute to the maintenance of the order of the world and thus benefit those who will be reborn in the remaining cycles, while acts contrary to reason and the law harm them. The happiness and peace which derive from doing good acts as well as the grief and anxiety which are engendered by doing evil acts are not from this world but from the other, since if they were from this world the wicked would have more reason to be happy and at peace, and the good would more likely be grieved and anxious. That other world, Abū Ya'qūb affirms in conclusion, is the promise of rebirth (*wa'da-yi bar angīkhtan*).

Nāṣir-i Khusraw was evidently right in charging that Abū Ya'qūb in his *Kashf al-maḥjūb* did not mention a permanent abode of the soul outside this world. Even the Place of Return (*ma'ād*), the hereafter, is dissolved into the promise of rebirth on earth. The role of the Qā'im, the lord of the Resurrection, is also described in entirely worldly terms. He will guide the faithful to the knowledge of the Kingdom of God, revealing the truths which were hidden in the scriptures and laws of the prophets of the era of concealment. The opponents will either voluntarily join the religion of God or will be killed by the Qā'im. The human souls, which in the era of concealment were as if ill, will be healthy in the era of disclosure inaugurated by the lord of the Resurrection[31]. The other role of the Qā'im in common Ismā'īlī teaching, that of the last judge who assigns men to their permanent abode in the hereafter, is not mentioned. Abū Ya'qūb's view of sacred history as an era of disclosure preceding Adam, the initiator of the era of concealment, and another era of disclosure following the advent of the Qā'im could easily be expanded into a cyclical sequence of innumerable eras of disclosure and concealment as envisaged in later Ṭayyibī Ismā'īlī gnosis[32].

Those disciples of Abū Ya'qūb who maintained that according to his true doctrine the purified soul would ultimately return to the higher world and dwell there permanently evidently based their claim on his teaching in other works. They may not have been entirely mistaken in thus interpreting his *Kashf al-maḥjūb*. It is difficult to see how Abū Ya'qūb, basically adhering to a Neoplatonic concept of the world in which the individual human souls were part of the Universal Soul, could ever have envisaged a permanent chain of reincarnations without a final return to their spiritual home[33]. In his *al-Risāla al-Bāhira* Abū Ya'qūb describes the end of the chain of rebirths in a final judgment sentencing the souls to a permanent state of reward or punishment.

The *al-Risāla al-Bāhira* is addressed to an anonymous 'Alid in reply to a question about the reality of the Greatest Resurrection (*qiyāma kubrā*). Abū Ya'qūb insists that the Resurrection is brought about by spiritual (*nafsānī*) rather than physical (*ṭabī'ī*) influences and changes. God will not annihilate the physical structure and order of the world and sit in judgment over man as the orthodox Muslims and other religious groups believe. Rather the Qā'im, the Pure Soul, will through his presence turn the evil influences of the heavenly spheres and bodies, which will be dominant in the time preceding his advent, into beneficial influences. Through him the virtues, gnostic knowledge, and emanations of the Universal Intellect will engulf the faithful of all cycles and aeons (*adwār wa akwār*) who thus will reach their reward, while the souls of the opponents who fail to accept his light will have no abode but the fire.

The question arises of how the souls of all the bygone ages reach their state of reward or punishment at that time. Abū Ya'qūb explains that this is a matter difficult to understand except for someone with a pure soul used to grasping spiritual matters. The answer lies in the recognition of the meaning of *barzakh* as referred to in Qur'an XXIII 100. Knowledge of the *barzakhs* consists in the realization that the world is at all times filled with souls united to persons and life. When the world is emptied of some persons others like them take their place. The one who replaces will have the same form as the one who passes away (*yakūn al-mustakhlaf ṣūrata al-munqariḍ*), for we find the speech, intercourse, sciences, political conduct, professions, and crafts of those who are in the world today to be what they were endowed with from those who passed away (*ma ulbisūhu min al-munqariḍīn*). "Thus these have become the *barzakhs* of those who passed away, and the souls are only what they bequeathed to them (*laysat al-anfus illā mā awrathūhum*). Thus there arise for each group of righteous and offenders errants and rightly guided, others who take their place after them and who will bequeath what they inherited from those who passed away to those after them, so that reward and punishment shall reach the souls having acquired good and evil who remain continuously (*mawṣūlat al-ḥibāl*) until the rise of the Greatest Resurrection. At that time all will be gathered and whatever each deserves will amply be bestowed upon them." Abū Ya'qūb adds that he will not fully elaborate the discourse on this law (*qānūn*) relying on the subtlety of the understanding, the sharpness of the mind, and the lofty aspiration of his partner.

The doctrine of metempsychosis expounded in the *al-Risāla al-Bāhira* with its identification of *barzakh* with the human persons in successive generations tallies closely with the second view ascribed to Abū Ya'qūb by Nāṣir-i Khusraw. There can be little doubt that the "other place" referred to by Nāṣir is in fact the *Risāla*[34]. The ideas of the *Kashf al-maḥjūb* seem to correspond more to Abū Ya'qūb's first view described by Nāṣir. However, some details, especially the identification of *barzakh* with the religious laws of the prophets, are missing. Unless they were omitted in the translation, it would seem that Nāṣir is describing in the first view the doctrine of the lost *Sūs al-baqā'*.

Abū Ya'qūb's teaching of metempsychosis represented a passing phase in his career. He had begun his involvement with Ismā'īlī thought as a disciple of al-Nasafī, and perhaps his first work, most likely written still in the lifetime of his teacher, was his *Kitāb al-Nuṣra* in which he defended al-Nasafī's teaching against the criticism of Abū Ḥātim al-Rāzī. After al-Nasafī's death his own thought appears to have developed along more independent lines and he soon came into conflict with the followers of the school of al-Nasafī. Abu l-Qāsim al-Bustī reports that a great controversy arose among the Ismā'īlīs of Khurāsān. While al-Nasafī and his followers held that the *da'wa* should concern itself with the soul, the prophetic cycles, and the problems of creation, Abū Ya'qūb asserted that the *da'wa* must begin with the *sharī'a* and its esoteric interpretation (*ta'wīl*)[35]. Nāṣir's report about the quarrel about *tanāsukh* shows that the controversy was not, as Stern suggested, entirely concerned with missionary tactics but had also a dogmatic dimension. This conflict most likely occurred in the decade or two after al-Nasafī's death. In his later works, when he adhered to the Fāṭimid *da'wa*, Abū Ya'qūb did not endorse metempsychosis. Official Fāṭimid doctrine always seems to have disapproved of that idea. Yet Abū Ya'qūb apparently never clearly repudiated his earlier teaching. The question of *barzakh*, the fate of the soul before the advent of the Qā'im, remained unresolved in his later works.

In his *Kitāb al-Iftikhār*, for instance, Abū Ya'qūb describes the Resurrection as the advent of the Qā'im who will judge all souls in the name of God and sentence them to their permanent abode of reward or punishment. The physical world, he again insists, will not be changed or annihilated, as the exoterics hold. The Qur'anic passages which apparently describe the destruction of the physical world must be understood as referring to spiritual events. In the discussion of *ba'th*, Abū Ya'qūb becomes entangled in ambiguities. He mocks the belief of the orthodox that God will restore the flesh and bones of the dead and their expectation that all the dead will be restored to life at the same time after the annihilation of the earth. Could it not be, he asks them, that the resuscitation has occurred many times while you were not aware of it? As in his *Kashf al-maḥjūb*, he questions how it could be compatible with the justice and wisdom of God to raise someone who died ten years after Adam seven thousand years ago together with the last dead who would remain in earth only a short time. Yet he does not explain why God should restore the life of anyone before the advent of the Qā'im and his judgment. The resuscitation is in some instances clearly described in spiritual terms. If the man to be rewarded or punished were restored with his limbs and shape as he was in his former life he would again be subject to hunger, thirst, illness and death. But reward and punishment are to be permanent. God is surely able to restore man to life in the spiritual world without his disintegrated body yet with the knowledge that he is the same one who was in this world. In other places, however, Abū Ya'qūb envisages a more material rebirth. He compares it to the action of a craftsman or builder who restores his damaged or destroyed work in the same form not from exactly the same, but from similar or even different material. And he interprets Qur'an II 260 as meaning that God may revive the dead from the same four elements into which their bodies earlier disintegrated[36]. Those of Abū Ya'qūb's followers who were familiar with his *Kashf al-maḥjūb* and *al-Risāla al-Bāhira* could resolve these apparent contradictions without difficulty. Man was subject to repeated rebirths on earth before his judgment by the Qā'im and his rise to the spiritual world.

In his *Kitāb al-Maqālīd*, Abū Ya'qūb devotes a chapter (*Iqlīd* 44) to the refutation of *tanāsukh*. As in *Kashf al-maḥjūb*, however, the supporters of *tanāsukh* are for him those who teach transmigration of the spirits (*arwāḥ*) to all animals. They hold, moreover, that the spirits fell to earth because of a sin which they committed in the other world and that they remain in the terrestrial bodies until they have expiated it[37], a doctrine which Abū Ya'qūb could repudiate without denying any of the views expressed in his earlier works. In another chapter (*Iqlīd* 45) he rejects the idea of some astrologers (*ahl al-tanjīm*) that the spirits will return to their bodies in exactly the same conditions as now after a period of some 30,000 years when the heavenly sphere reaches a certain point. He mentions that he refuted their doctrine in detail in his *Kitāb al-Bishāra*[38]. He identifies *ba'th* with the final rise (*nash'a ākhira*) and argues that it is only spiritual since it will occur suddenly (*baghtatan*) and physical bodies can grow only gradually. There is no suggestion that any *ba'th* has already occurred. Yet he admits the rational possibility of a *ba'th* of both spirit and body as witnessed in natural generation[39]. The reader unacqainted with his earlier works could not find a trace of metempsychosis in his elaborations. For his followers who were familiar with his thought, however, there was nothing which clearly contradicted what he had taught there. The question of the fate of the soul after death and before the final rise is not addressed. There was thus a basis for the survival of a school of Abū Ya'qūb holding on to the belief in repeated rebirths on earth before the advent of the Qā'im in the time of Nāṣir-i Khusraw. The official Fāṭimid *da'wa* considered the matter evidently as serious enough to commission Nāṣir with writing a refutation.

## NOTES

[1] Concerning this nickname see S.M. Stern, "Arabo-Persica," in *W.B. Henning Memorial Volume*, ed. M. Boyce and I. Gershevitch, London, 1970, pp. 415-16.

[2] Al-Bīrūnī, *Kitāb Mā li'l-Hind*, ed. E. Sachau, Berlin, 1887, p. 32.

[3] For his life see in particular S.M. Stern, "The Early Ismā'īlī Missionaries in North-West Persia and in Khurāsān and Transoxania", *BSOAS* XXIII, 1960, pp. 68-70, 80-81; I.K. Poonawala, "Al-Sijistānī and his *Kitāb al-Maqālīd*," in *Essays on Islamic Civilization Presented to Niyazi Berkes*, ed. D.P. Little, Leiden, 1976, pp. 274-76, and idem, *Bio-bibliography of Ismā'īlī Literature*, Malibu, 1977, pp. 82-83. On the basis of references to the Fāṭimid caliph al-Ḥākim in two works ascribed to Abū Ya'qūb, Poonawala suggests that he was killed after 386/996. Since Abū Ya'qūb himself mentions having made the pilgrimage to Mecca in 322/934, he would have reached a high age, if the references to al-Ḥākim are not later additions. P. Walker informs me that one of the two works, the *Kitāb al-mawāzīn*, is definitely inauthentic in its extant form.

[4] Nāṣir-i Khusraw, *Zād al-musāfirīn*, ed. Muḥammad Badhl al-Raḥmān, Berlin, 1341/1923, pp. 421-22.

[5] See B. Carra de Vaux, "Barzakh," in *E.I.*, 2nd ed.

[6] Nāṣir-i Khusraw, *Khwān al-ikhwān*, ed. Qawīm, Tehran, 1338sh/1959, p. 133.

[7] Abū Ya'qūb's *Kitāb al-Maqālīd* contains a chapter (*Iqlīd* 43) entitled: "That man's imagining of the (Universal) Soul being higher than the (heavenly) sphere and the (Universal) Intellect being higher than the Soul like the water is above the earth and the air is above the water is false." He argues there that the Soul is spiritual and thus cannot spatially surround the sphere. The chapter may well have been intended to be a refutation of al-Nasafī's concept of *barzakh*.

For the *Kitāb al-Maqālīd*, a partial photocopy of the unique ms. in the possession of Dr. Abbas Hamdani was available to me through the courtesy of the Institute of Ismaili Studies in London and Mr. J. Badakhshani. A photocopy of the ms. has been presented to the Institute by the owner. For Abū Ya'qūb's *al-Risālā al-Bāhira*, a photocopy of the ms. of the Library of the Institute briefly described by A. Gacek, *Catalogue of Arabic Manuscripts in the Library of the Institute of Ismaili Studies*, Vol. one, London, 1984, p. 94, was used. My thanks are due to the Library of the Institute and Mr. Badakhshani for making these copies available to me.

[8] *Khwān*, pp. 130-31. In the text *bi-tanāsukh ... gūyad* must no doubt be read *na-gūyad*. Nāṣir clearly wants to restrict the accusation of having taught *tanāsukh* among the Ismā'īlīs to Abū Ya'qūb. Al-Nasafī's idea of *barzakh* does not envisage a return of the soul to earth. Ivanow was misled by the corrupt text into assuming that Nāṣir considered al-Nasafī's doctrine as also implying *tanāsukh* (*Nāṣir-i Khusraw and Ismailism*, Leiden and Bombay, 1948, p. 58; idem, *Problems in Nāṣir-i Khusraw's Biography*, Bombay, 1956, p. 65). Ḥamīd al-Dīn al-Kirmānī, an opponent of all forms of *tanāsukh*, located the *barzakh* at "the limit (*nihāya*) between Paradise and Hell, the highest spot of the world of nature, the surface of the skies (*ṣafḥat al-samawāt*)" (al-Kirmānī, *Rāḥat al-'aql*, ed. Muṣṭafā Ghālib, Beirut, 1967, p. 538; al-Ḥāmidī, *Kanz al-walad*, ed. M. Ghālib, Wiesbaden, 1971, p. 161). There the souls of the virtuous and of the wicked would remain until the advent of the Qā'im.

[9] For the reading Khurāsān see Stern, "Missionaries," p. 80, n. 3. Stern and, following him, Poonawala (*Biobibliography*, p. 75) identified Dihqān with Ḥasan (al-)Mas'ūd, also mentioned by Nāṣir and Abu'l-Qāsim al-Bustī as a son of al-Nasafī and head of the *da'wa* in Khurāsān. It is to be noted, however, that Nāṣir describes the doctrine of Ḥasan Mas'ūd on *barzakh* later in the chapter as identical with that of his father (*Khwān*, p. 135) in contrast to that of Dihqān. The identity of the two must thus remain doubtful.

[10] *Khwān*, p. 131.

[11] *Khwān*, p. 135.

[12] Reading *kawr* for *gūr*.

[13] Reading *kawr-i buzurg* for *gūr-i buzurg*.

[14] *Khwān*, pp. 132-33.

[15] *Khwān*, p. 135.

[16] *Khwān*, pp. 132, 136. The book seems to be lost.

[17] *Khwān*, pp. 138-39.

[18] *Zād al-musāfirīn*, pp. 420-22, 424.

[19] *Nāṣir-i Khusraw and Ismailism*, p. 59.

[20] Corbin was here presumably thinking of Ṭayyibī doctrine. See H. Corbin, *Trilogie Ismaëlienne*, Tehran, 1961, pp. 177-79.

[21] Introd. to edition of Abū Ya'qūb al-Sijistānī, *Kashf al-maḥjūb*, Tehran and Paris, 1949, pp. 16-18.

[22] *Nāṣir-i Khusraw and Ismailism*, p. 58.

[23] Stern, "Abu'l-Qāsim al-Bustī and his Refutation of Ismā'īlism", *JRAS*, 1961, p. 22.

[24] Sa'īd Nafīsī, *Ta'rīkh-i naẓm wa nathr dar Īrān dar zabān-i Fārsī*, Tehran, 1344sh/1965, I, pp. 28, 59.

[25] *Kashf*, p. 88.

[26] The Qā'im was for Abū Ya'qūb and the contemporary Persian *da'wa* the seventh

Imam Muḥammad b. Ismāʿīl, who had disappeared almost two centuries before but was expected to reappear to rule the world. See Madelung, "Das Imamat in der frühen ismailitischen Lehre," *Islam* XXXVII, 1961, pp. 106-09.

[27] The Persian translation preserves the distinction by leaving *qiyāma* untranslated (*qiyāmat*) while rendering *ba'th* by *bar angīkhtan*. Corbin, however, translated both terms as *résurrection* thus blurring the distinction for the critical reader. He translated *bar angīkhta* as *ressussité*. *Abû Ya'qûb Sejestânî: Le Dévoilement des choses cachées*, transl. H. Corbin, Lagrasse, 1988.

[28] Introd. to *Kashf*, p. 17.

[29] Corbin's translation (pp. 123-24): *Or ce que cet homme s'assimile ainsi tourne au profit de son âme subtile, certes, mais pareillement aussi au profit de son corps physique tel qu'il existait au début*, seems inaccurate. Abū Yaʿqūb wants to say that the soul can be reborn even while in the same body.

[30] The Persian text (p. 91) states the opposite: the time of (their) resuscitation has not yet come. Corbin, however, translates (p. 125): *c'est que le moment de leur résurrection est déjà advenu*. The context clearly requires this latter translation. It is evident that Abū Yaʿqūb's text has been changed either by the Persian translator or a later copyist because of objections to the implications.

[31] *Kashf*, pp. 81-83.

[32] This is not to suggest that the Ṭayyibī doctrine is derived from Abū Yaʿqūb's thought. The Ṭayyibīs uphold reincarnation on earth, even in animal bodies, only in respect to the wicked as a punishment. They believe in an eventual end of this world. Their doctrine on reincarnation seems to be derived primarily from the *al-Risāla al-Jāmi'a* of the Ikhwān al-Ṣafā and an anonymous *Risālat al-Ḥayawān* in which Qāḍī al-Nuʿmān and Ḥamīd al-Dīn al-Kirmānī are quoted. See al-Ḥāmidī, *Kanz al-walad*, pp. 34-36, 112-13, 185-89, 300.

[33] The ultimate return of the individual souls to the Universal Soul and the Intellect is described in Abū Yaʿqūb's *Kitāb al-Bishārāt*. See the quotations in *Kanz al-walad*, pp. 248-64.

[34] Nāṣir's summary is obviously more explicit than the elusive language used by Abū Yaʿqūb and evidently reflects the common interpretation of his school. Abū Yaʿqūb does not expressly state that the souls return to the persons in this world but this is clearly implied in his allusion. He does not say that the soul will rise after the Resurrection to the world of the Intellect. Rather he describes the spiritual benefits which the faithful will receive through the Qā'im in this world. They will be joined to him in spiritual companionship and become like one single soul. But he speaks then of their entering the gardens of Paradise in the vicinity of the Merciful which in Ismāʿīlī terms could legitimately be understood as the world of the Intellect. Likewise he does not expressly identify the fire to which those who reject the benefits of the Qā'im are condemned with remaining in the physical world. Yet such an interpretation is reasonable enough. Abū Yaʿqūb's elusive language obviously misled Ivanow into judging that there was not a trace of *tanāsukh* in the *Risāla*.

[35] See Stern, "Abu'l-Qāsim al-Bustī," pp. 22-23.

[36] Abū Yaʿqūb al-Sijistānī, *Kitāb al-Iftikhār*, ed. M. Ghālib, Beirut, 1980, pp. 74-91.

[37] This doctrine is upheld in the *al-Risāla al-Jāmi'a* of the Ikhwān al-Ṣafā' (ed. J. Ṣalība, Damascus 1368/1949, esp. I, pp. 298-305) where prime matter and form are defined as the *barāzikh* in which the fallen souls remain until the day of the Resurrection (*yawm yub'athūn*, I p. 300, here in the sense of the ultimate Resurrection) and was later adopted by the Ṭayyibīs (see *Kanz al-walad*, pp. 34-37, 112-13). Abū Yaʿqūb may well have had the teaching of the Ikhwān in mind.

[38] Presumably the same as his *Kitāb al-Bishārāt* of which only some excerpts are extant.

[39] *Iqlīd* 40.

# IX

## Abū Yaʿqūb al-Sijistānī and the seven faculties of the Intellect

IN THE sixteenth chapter of his *Book of Wellsprings* (*Kitāb al-yanābīʿ*), the Ismaʿili *dāʿī* Abū Yaʿqūb al-Sijistānī describes the seven faculties (*quwā*) which were, he says, originated together with the Universal Intellect all at once, and which necessarily accompany it.[1] The first among them is Eternal Time (*dahr*).[2] The proof for its coextension with the Universal Intellect is that the individual intellect, when it becomes acquisitive (*muktasib*) through the perception of an intelligible, will be permanently accompanied by that intelligible. Thus it becomes known that the absolute Eternal Time extends with the Preceder (*sābiq*=Universal Intellect) at the origination (*ibdāʿ*) and ever thereafter.

The second faculty of the Intellect is Truth (*ḥaqq*). For the truth of any intelligible coextends with the acquisitive intellect. The supposition that it could be removed from it is false, since its contrary would annihilate the intellect.[3] Thus it becomes known that absolute Truth extends with the Intellect at the origination and thereafter.

The third faculty is Joy (*surūr*). For joy is present in the acquisitive intellect whenever it comprehends an intelligible. Thus it becomes known that absolute Joy extends with the Intellect at the origination and thereafter.

The fourth faculty is Demonstration (*burhān*). For demonstration does not lag behind the acquisitive intellect when it comprehends an intelligible. Thus is becomes known that Demonstration is coextensive with the Intellect at the origination and thereafter.

The fifth faculty is Life (*ḥayāt*). Life exists with the intellect when it is set in motion by the perception of intelligibles. Thus it becomes known that absolute Life extends with the Preceder at the origination and thereafter without a delay.

The sixth faculty is Perfection (*kamāl*). Perfection does not lack behind the partial acquisitive intellect whenever it comprehends an intelligible, for in comprehension it does not imagine the intelligible in deficiency but in perfection. Thus it becomes known that Perfection extends with the Preceder at the origination and thereafter.

The identity of the seventh, and highest, faculty of the Intellect has caused some confusion among the later Isma'ili transmitters of texts and among modern scholars. In his edition of the *Kitāb al-yanābī'*, H. Corbin preserved the reading *ghayba*, absence or occultation, which he found in his manuscripts. He pointed out, however, that Nāṣir-i Khusraw in his Persian paraphrase of the text in his *Khwān al-ikhwān* rendered it by *bī-niyāzī*, needlessness or self-sufficiency, which clearly presupposed the reading *ghunya* in Arabic.[4] While admitting the plausibility of the reading *ghunya*, Corbin preferred the reading *ghayba* as the original one, noting that in both Nāṣir-i Khusraw's *Jāmi' al-ḥikmatayn* and in the Commentary to the Isma'ili *Qaṣīda* of Abu'l-Haytham al-Jurjānī, attributed to Muḥammad b. Surkh al-Nīsābūrī, the word equally appears as *ghaybat*. He argued, further, that *ghunya* does not add anything significant to the meaning of *kamāl*, perfection, the two words being a mere doublet. The reading *ghunya* would, thus, banalize the sense and deprive it of its profoundness and originality. *Ghayba*, in contrast, was a term loaded with significance in Shi'i theology,[5] as well as in Sufism. In the present context, it meant 'occultation, the hidden state, ecstatic absence from the visible world, presence in the invisible world, and as such the invisible, suprasensible dimension of a being'.[6]

A close reading of the relevant texts, however, reveals clearly that *ghunya*, self-sufficiency, rather than *ghayba*, must have originally been intended in all of them. In *Jāmi' al-ḥikmatayn*, Nāṣir-i Khusraw gives an esoteric interpretation of six of the seven terms mentioned in the *Qaṣīda* of Abu'l-Haytham.[7] Concerning *kamāl*, he explains that the human soul reaches perfection when it completely accepts the emanation (*ifāḍat*) of the Universal Intellect. The six major prophets, Adam, Noah, Abraham, Moses, Jesus and Mohammed, have over a period of nearly 7,000 years established their rule over a part of mankind by conveying the emanation of the Intellect to them. The fact, however, that they have not been able to establish their rule over all of mankind is proof that no one has yet completely accepted the Intellect. Thus the day when, according to the Qur'an (LXXXII:19), 'the Order will belong to God', has not yet come.

The sentence opening the next paragraph in the edition of the *Jāmi' al-ḥikmatayn* reads: *wa-ʿināyat-i nafs-i kullī az iḥtiyāj-i khwīsh bi-dān shakhṣ bāshad ki ifāḍat-i ʿaql-i kullī rā tamām ū padhīrad wa bar khalq bi-jumlagī ū sālār shawad.*[8] This is quite incomprehensible. The expression *az iḥtiyāj-i khwīsh* requires the reading *ghunyat-i* or, graphically more likely, the equivalent *ghanā-yi*, instead of *ʿināyat-i.* 'The self-sufficiency of the Universal Soul [of which the individual souls are parts] from the neediness of its own self will occur through that person who accepts the emanation of the Universal Intellect completely and who will become ruler over all of creation.' Nāṣir-i Khusraw goes on to explain that this person will be the last of these rulers with whom the cycle will be closed. Some people call him the Messiah, who will return, others call him the Mahdi, and still others the Qā'im. God thus says: 'About what do they question each other? About the great announcement concerning which they differ' (Qur'an, LXXVIII:1–3). It is evident, then, that Nāṣir-i Khusraw must also have read *ghunyat*, rather than *ghaybat*, in the poem of Abu'l-Haytham.[9]

The commentator of the *Qaṣīda* of Abu'l-Haytham says about the seven faculties, described as lights in the poem, that they are called 'divine emanation' (*ifāḍat-i ilāhī*). They exist with the Intellect and are concealed from the Soul. Every soul accepts them to the extent of its nobility, disposition, subtleness, and effort. Thus, it may accept one, two, or three, and the souls of prophets accept all seven.[10] The commentator describes the last, and most noble, of these emanations of the Intellect which shine upon the soul thus: 'Everyone upon whom this emanation shines becomes independent[11] of the two worlds. Self-sufficiency (reading *ghunyat* instead of *ghaybat*) consists in independence from the humiliation of posing questions, of the pain of reading, writing, and learning. He reaches a station about which God says: 'In it is what the souls long for and the eyes delight in' (Qur'an, XLIII:71). For every longing that may emerge from the soul, a means to deal with it arises from that emanation, and a response comes to him from his intellect. The soul has no longer a need of anything else.'[12] Translating this passage, Corbin commented that the *ghaybat* thus defined a privileged relationship between the individual soul and the Intellect, of which *ghunya* is merely the result.[13] Much more likely, the self-sufficiency of the soul is itself described here as the highest state it can reach. A state of ecstatic absence, as Corbin interpreted the term *ghaybat*, is not described or implied in any of the texts.

Abū Yaʿqūb's description of the seventh faculty of the Intellect can on this basis be translated thus: 'The seventh is Self-sufficiency. For self-sufficiency is in the partial acquisitive intellect, when it comprehends any intelligibles, an existent entity (*'ayn mawjūd*). Thus it becomes known that Self-sufficiency extends with the Preceder at the origination and thereafter. Among the faculties of the Intellect which were originated together with it, Self-sufficiency is certainly the most excellent and noble one. When the Preceder emanates self-sufficiency of its faculties upon anyone, this emanation is the most excellent and highest emanation.'[14]

Abū Ya'qūb goes on to explain that the lowest emanation of the Intellect is Eternal Time, even though in relation to physical matters it is of the utmost nobility because of its permanence and because God has made it the custodian of the movements of time. Each of the seven faculties branches out into countless and unlimited branches. Above them there are things which cannot be described by reason or imagined, since the Preceder alone possesses them. We do not know when he will emanate them on his effects (the human souls), so that the effects will be able to imagine, express, and establish them. They will manifest themselves in the aeons (*akwār*) and cycles (*adwār*), of which only he has knowledge. At present, they are all retained by him and are gathered in a point which is the centre of the universe (*al-'ālamīn*).[15]

Abū Ya'qūb's concept of the faculties of the Intellect is thus less mystical than Corbin had thought. It is, rather, grounded in the philosophical tradition. Some of the faculties were mentioned as attributes of the Intellect in earlier Neoplatonic texts.[16] Their confinement to seven basic qualities is probably Abū Ya'qūb's own Isma'ili contribution. There is so far no evidence suggesting that his teacher, the Transoxanian *dā'ī* Muḥammad b. Aḥmad al-Nasafī (d. 332/943), had envisaged this heptad.

The prevalence of the misreading *ghayba(t)* in all the relevant texts illustrates the deplorable current state of the Isma'ili manuscript tradition. While the correct reading was still fully available in the 5th/11th century, it was evidently later forgotten in the course of centuries of persecution and decline of learning among the Isma'ilis. *Ghunyat* is, as Corbin pointed out,[17] hardly used in Persian and was, therefore, easily replaced by *ghaybat*. But in the Arabic text of Abū Ya'qūb's *al-Yanābī'*, too, the faulty variant now established itself. Without Nāṣir-i Khusraw's Persian rendering of it as *bī-niyāzī*, it would have been difficult to recover Abū Ya'qūb al-Sijistānī's original concept of the seventh faculty of the Intellect.[18] The poor condition of the modern Isma'ili manuscript tradition must be taken into account in editing and studying these and other Isma'ili texts.

# *Al-Sijistānī and the seven faculties of the Intellect*

## NOTES

1 Abū Ya'qūb al-Sijistānī, *Kitāb al-yanābī'*, ed. and tr. H. Corbin in his *Trilogie Ismaélienne* (Tehran–Paris, 1961), Arabic text pp. 41–43.

2 The variant reading *dhihn* in the editions of Nāṣir-i Khusraw's *Khwān al-ikhwān*, containing the Persian paraphrase of Abū Ya'qūb's chapter, has been rightly rejected by Corbin (*Trilogie*, translation p. 60) as an atrocious misreading of a copyist.

3 Reading *wa-buṭlānuhu 'anhu tawahhumun bāṭilun li-anna khilāfahu mubṭilun lahu.*

4 Corbin, *Trilogie*, translation pp. 62–63.

5 See *Commentaire de la Qasida Ismaélienne d'Abu'l-Haitham Jorjani attribué à Mohammad ibn Sorkh de Nishapour*, ed. H. Corbin and M. Mu'īn (Tehran–Paris, 1955), French introduction p. 52.

6 Corbin, *Trilogie*, translation p. 62.

7 Nāṣir-i Khusraw, *Jāmi' al-ḥikmatayn*, ed. H. Corbin and M. Mu'īn (Tehran–Paris, 1953), Persian text pp. 112–122. Nāṣir-i Khusraw omits the term *burhān* taking it as part of the context. He is able to do so by separating the previous line of the poem, which speaks of seven shining lights from which every being accepts fire to the extent of its subtleness.

8 Nāṣir-i Khusraw, *Jāmi'*, Persian text p. 121 l.18 – p. 122 l.1.

9 Ibid., Persian text p. 112 l.9. Read also *ghunyat* in place of *ghaybat* in lines 6 and 14.

10 *Commentaire*, Persian text p. 19.

11 *Chāra*, glossed by Corbin in his translation (*Trilogie*, p. 63) as *bī-niyāz*. Note that the term occurs in this sense in the last line of the section of the *Qaṣīda* dealing with the seven lights (*Commentaire*, Persian text p. 19 l.13): Independence comes only to a place where there are four (*chār*); evidently the last four lights, Demonstration, permanent Life, Perfection, and Self-sufficiency. In the version of Nāṣir-i Khusraw's *Jāmi' al-ḥikmatayn*, p. 112 l.10, the text of the line differs and is probably corrupt: Independence is in the place where four do not come. This reading is consistent with Nāṣir-i Khusraw's omission of Demonstration from his list of mystical terms.

12 *Commentaire*, Persian text pp. 21–22.

13 Corbin, *Trilogie*, translation p. 63.

14 Abū Ya'qūb al-Sijistānī, *al-Yanābī'*, in *Trilogie*, Arabic text pp. 42–43.

15 Ibid., Arabic text p. 43.

16 See P. Walker, *Early Philosophical Shiism: The Ismaili Neoplatonism of Abū Ya'qūb al-Sijistānī* (Cambridge, 1993), pp. 91 and 179 n. 20.

17 Corbin, *Trilogie*, translation p. 62.

18 Another passage in Corbin's edition of the Arabic text of *al-Yanābī'* which Nāṣir-i Khusraw's Persian paraphrase helps to correct relates to the reading *shaṭriyya* on p. 71 l.17, and p. 72 l.1 and l.10. In his translation Corbin used Nāṣir's Persian text which has *dandāna*, meaning here the tooth, or bit, of a key (*Trilogie*, pp. 93 and 95 n. 185). The word in Arabic must, therefore, be read *shaẓiyya*; it is correctly preserved on p. 73 l.1 of the Arabic text.

# X

## The Fatimids and the Qarmaṭīs of Baḥrayn

### INTRODUCTORY NOTE

THE PRESENT article is a slightly revised translation of my 'Fatimiden und Baḥrainqarmaṭen' published in the journal *Der Islam*, XXXIV (1959), pp. 34–88. It substantially reflects the state of research at that time. In a few instances references to more recent studies have been added in the notes. It has not been the intention, however, to bring the article systematically up to date. My thanks are due to Madam Azizeh Azodi, Paris, for translating the main text of the article.

Among the rebellious movements of the 3rd/9th and 4th/10th centuries characterized by the Arab chronicles as 'Qarmaṭī', the one in Baḥrayn assumes a special position. Here alone the rebels succeeded in founding a powerful state which enjoyed unlimited power over a wide area. They easily managed to repel the attacks on their independence to which they were exposed at the beginning. In the following decades, they disposed of the most effective and redoubted fighting forces in the Islamic world. They became a true scourge for the caliphate of Baghdad. Plundering and assassinating, they penetrated into southern Mesopotamia in ever renewed incursions, and attacked the pilgrim caravans on their way to or from Mecca. The armies of the caliph, though often far outnumbering them, could not hold out against them. In 316/928, it was as by miracle that Baghdad escaped being conquered. A year later, they occupied Mecca, wrought a terrible massacre among the inhabitants and pilgrims, and robbed the Kaʿba of its Black Stone, a sacrilege that is unparalleled in the history of Islam. The caliph was incapable of even raising a finger to recover the relic by force. It was not until twenty-two years later that the stone was brought back to its place voluntarily, against payment of a high ransom.

The Qarmaṭīs justified their rebellion against the existing order by proclaiming the sovereignty of the Mahdi, the rightly-guided imam from the house of the Prophet who would rule over the world and establish justice and order. Two decades after the establishment of the Qarmaṭī state in Baḥrayn, another rebel, who claimed to be the expected imam of the Prophet's lineage, founded a Fatimid counter-caliphate in Raqqāda near Qayrawān. Repeated attempts at conquering Egypt and intensive anti-ʿAbbasid propaganda showed the seriousness of the claim.

The importance of the question about the relationship between the Qarmaṭī state and the rising Fatimid empire in North Africa for a proper understanding of the political history of the period is obvious. Yet to the opponents of the Fatimids, this question was interesting in another sense. For in the history of the Qarmaṭīs of Baḥrayn they believed they had found for the first time a clear confirmation of the accusations of unbelief and libertinism which they had quite generally levelled against the Bāṭinīs. Had not the Qarmaṭīs murdered thousands of defenceless pilgrims, had they not burned Qur'ans, defiled the holy city and openly blasphemed against the Lord of the Kaʿba? Did not these deeds reveal the true face of the Ismaʿili heresy, which was normally concealed under the cloak of devotion to the family of the Prophet, in order to recruit proselytes and to escape persecution at the hands of the faithful? 'Externally they feign the Shiʿi faith, internally they hide pure unbelief', was the judgement, for example, of the Qāḍī Abū Bakr al-Bāqillānī,[1] alluding to their doctrine that behind the outward text of the Qur'an and the laws of Islam, lie concealed the inner, esoteric truths of religion.

The most detailed study of the history of the Qarmaṭīs in Baḥrayn is that of M. J. de Goeje, who directed particular attention to their relations with the Fatimids. Relying on a wealth of source material, he arrived at the following conclusions: Qarmaṭīs and Fatimids had sprung from one and the same movement. Despite the secession of Ḥamdān Qarmaṭ, after whom the sect was named, and that of his brother-in-law ʿAbdān, the master of the missionary propaganda, Abū Saʿīd al-Jannābī, the head of the Qarmaṭīs of Baḥrayn, kept his allegiance to the Fatimid imams even after the establishment of their sovereignty in North Africa.[2] Under Abū Saʿīd's son Abū Ṭāhir, the collaboration between the Qarmaṭīs and their lords grew particularly close. In all important enterprises they acted on the direct command of ʿUbayd Allāh, the Fatimid caliph.[3] But the Fatimids did not dare acknowledge them publicly as allies.[4] With ʿUbayd Allāh's death, their close co-operation ended, but the Qarmaṭīs still continued acknowledging his successors as imams. The breach occurred when al-Ḥasan al-Aʿṣam gained control in Baḥrayn in 358/969. He entered the service of the ʿAbbasids and led the Qarmaṭīs to fight against the Fatimids. After the year 375/985, however, they once again returned under the sway of the Fatimids.[5]

A more recent investigation has been presented by B. Lewis.[6] For the early history of the Qarmaṭīs of Baḥrayn, he uses contradictory source material and leaves the question open whether they originally adhered to an Ismaʿili or a Ḥanafī[7] succession of imams.[8] In any case they formed a group of their own. Around the beginning of the 4th/10th century, they were won over to the Fatimid doctrine. Later they paid homage, for a short time, to a false prophet, seceded from the Fatimids and published all the secrets of the doctrine. But still later, they returned under the sway of the Fatimids until the secession of al-Aʿṣam.

W. Ivanow, on the other hand, upholds the Ismaʿili origin of the Qarmaṭīs.[9] He says that they may have issued from the defection of Aḥmad b. al-Kayyāl from the Imam ʿAbd Allāh b. Muḥammad b. Ismāʿīl, which is mentioned in the *ʿUyūn al-akhbār*, the historical work of the Ismaʿili *dāʿī* Idrīs b. al-Ḥasan.[10] Ibn al-Kayyāl may be identical with Aḥmad, the son of ʿAbd Allāh b. Maymūn al-Qaddāḥ, whom the anti-Ismaʿili historiographers consider as the founder of the Bāṭinī heresy.[11] Later, the relations of the Qarmaṭīs with the Fatimids were determined by the fact that they did not recognize the Fatimid imamate, but anticipated the return of the Imam Muḥammad b. Ismāʿīl. Whenever they were disappointed in their expectation, which was to be fulfilled on specific dates, they might turn to the Fatimids again.[12] The arguments which de Goeje had presented for the continuation of the close association between the Qarmaṭīs of Baḥrayn and the Fatimids, however, were not refuted by Ivanow.

Ḥ. I. Ḥasan and Ṭ. A. Sharaf represent the view, in their biography of the Fatimid ʿUbayd Allāh,[13] that a group of Ḥanafī Kaysānīs[14] under Ḥamdān Qarmaṭ were converted to the Ismaʿili doctrine by the ancestors of the Fatimids.[15] Later, however, Ḥamdān Qarmaṭ seceded.[16] He or a descendant of Maymūn al-Qaddāḥ, who resided in Ṭāliqān,[17] sent Abū Saʿīd al-Jannābī to Baḥrayn. Abū Saʿīd founded the Qarmaṭī state there and himself stood in opposition to the Fatimids.[18] Elsewhere the authors assume, however, that Abū Saʿīd was opposed to Ḥamdān Qarmaṭ and at first supported the Fatimids.[19] Encouraged by his success, he took more and more of a fancy to his independence. Nevertheless, he continued to recognize the Fatimid imamate nominally. Perhaps ʿUbayd Allāh, weary of Abū Saʿīd's dubious politics, had a hand in his assassination.[20] The description of the later history of the Qarmaṭīs and their relations with the Fatimids essentially follows that of de Goeje.

Here it is proposed to re-examine these very different conclusions. The general history of the Qarmaṭī movement will be discussed only as far as the context requires. On that subject the reader may still be referred to de Goeje's work.[21]

The oldest tangible event in the sources is the conversion of Ḥamdān Qarmaṭ by a missionary.[22] What Ḥamdān's earlier confession was is not stated in the reports. The new doctrine which he now adopted, and to the propagation of which he was soon to contribute considerably as a high-ranking missionary, was no doubt the one spread from Salamiyya in Syria through the ancestors of the Fatimids. Admittedly, al-Ṭabarī only mentions that after winning numerous adherents for his doctrine, the foreign missionary went to Syria, where he was never heard of again.[23] But reliable information is given in definite statements by Ibn Rizām,[24] Akhū Muḥsin,[25] and Ibn Ḥawqal.[26] Even in later times, works of ʿAbdān, Ḥamdān's brother-in-law and companion in the propagation of the doctrine, were current among the Ismaʿilis.[27]

Ḥamdān Qarmaṭ and ʿAbdān eventually quarrelled with their lord at Salamiyya and broke off the propaganda conducted in his name. In retaliation for this defection ʿAbdān was assassinated by the followers of the missionary Zikrawayh. But Ḥamdān Qarmaṭ disappeared,[28] as is reported in detail by Akhū Muḥsin.[29] De Goeje has expressed serious doubts about the accuracy of certain details of the account, but not about the fact of the defection itself.[30] In this connection the question about the date is of primary interest. Akhū Muḥsin places the events in the year 286/899.[31] But de Goeje establishes a connection with the defection of Abū ʿAbd Allāh al-Shīʿī, who had paved the way for ʿUbayd Allāh in North Africa, and of his brother. He thinks that Ḥamdān Qarmaṭ and ʿAbdān, too, had seceded after ʿUbayd Allāh had gained supremacy and proclaimed himself the expected Mahdi.[32] This view is contradicted by two sources which could hardly have been influenced by Akhū Muḥsin. The Ismaʿili work *Istitār al-imām* of Aḥmad b. Muḥammad al-Nīsābūrī, written during the caliphate of the Fatimid al-ʿAzīz (365–386/975–996), reports that the sons of Abū Muḥammad – i.e., Zikrawayh – had killed their brother-in-law, whom they accused of being a hypocrite and disobedient to the imam.[33] This is cited, in conformity with Akhū Muḥsin's account, among the events which took place between the succession of ʿUbayd Allāh and the rebellions of Zikrawayh's sons in Syria. It is highly probable, as suggested by Ivanow,[34] that the murdered person was ʿAbdān. Ibn Ḥawqal also mentions the assassination of ʿAbdān without giving a definite date. It led, however, to the assassination of Abū Zakariyyā' al-Ṭamāmī by Abū Saʿīd, which, according to all reports,[35] happened at the beginning of the latter's rule in Baḥrayn.[36]

Abū Saʿīd al-Jannābī was entrusted by Ḥamdān Qarmaṭ and ʿAbdān with the propagation of the doctrine in Baḥrayn. This is unanimously reported by such different sources as the pro-Fatimid Ibn Ḥawqal,[37] the anti-Fatimid Akhū Muḥsin,[38] and ʿAbd al-Jabbar.[39] But how did Abū Saʿīd comport himself at the defection of his teachers? De Goeje still believed that he did not let himself be influenced in his attitude towards the Fatimids and that he remained faithful to them.[40] This is contradicted by the text of the new edition of Ibn Ḥawqal, which says:[41] 'He [Abū Saʿīd] then espoused the doctrine of the one residing in the Maghrib,[42] until his master ʿAbdān was killed. Then he defected from what he had believed and killed Abū Zakariyyā' al-Ṭamāmī, a missionary who had represented the lords of the Maghrib before him.' The assassination of Abū Zakariyyā' is also mentioned in other sources,[43] although without the motivation mentioned here.

The thesis about the Ḥanafī origin of the Qarmaṭīs is based on two sources. Al-Ṭabarī describes their creed in a manner which poses several problems.[44] He does not name his informant, but begins with the statement: 'Of those Qarmaṭīs it is said,[45] among other things with respect to their doctrine, that they bring a book in which it is written . . .' There now follows a word-by-word quotation. A certain al-Faraj b. ʿUthmān from a village called Naṣrāna, 'the missionary of the Messiah, who is Jesus, who is the Word, who is the Mahdi, who is Aḥmad b. Muḥammad b. al-Ḥanafiyya, who is Gabriel' declares that the Messiah has appeared to him in human shape and has said to him: 'You are the envoy, you are the evidence (*ḥujja*), you are the she-camel (*nāqa*),[46] you are the beast (*dābba*),[47] you are the Holy Spirit, you are John, son of Zachariah.' Thereupon, he had explained to him the prayer and other prescriptions of the law. In the call to prayer, seven prophets are attested: Adam, Noah, Abraham, Moses, Jesus, Mohammed and Aḥmad b. Muḥammad b. al-Ḥanafiyya. In the prayer itself, the opening (*al-istiftāḥ*) is recited from the revelation of the seventh prophet. Al-Ṭabarī quotes this *sūra* verbatim, a primitive imitation of the Qur'an with a *bāṭinī* exegesis.[48] The law is based on the model of the Islamic *sharīʿa*, but considerably alters and simplifies the individual prescriptions.

Paul Casanova says about this report that it turns the Qarmaṭīs into a sect which is quite alien to Isma'ilism, since they acknowledged a son of Muḥammad b. al-Ḥanafiyya as the imam.[49] But this judgement must be modified to a large extent.

1. The doctrine undoubtedly shows *bāṭinī* characteristics. But it was not only the Isma'ilis who were searching for the inner meaning of the laws at the time. On the other hand, early Isma'ili doctrine seems to know nothing of a revelation by the seventh emissary of God. It was not expected until his return and was to consist, according to the doctrine of the esoterics, of the proclamation of the inner meaning. Laws and ritual prescriptions such as those described here reveal no similarity with the laws of the Fatimids, which only differed slightly from those of the Twelver Shi'is.

2. Nothing is known of a son of Muḥammad b. al-Ḥanafiyya by the name of Aḥmad.[50] This means that we are not dealing with evidence of a sect formed in a succession dispute after the death of Muḥammad b. al-Ḥanafiyya. Rather, the name and the person are freely invented in order to legitimize the mission of al-Faraj b. 'Uthmān. But then the question arises as to how the choice of this name for the seventh prophet is to be explained. Aḥmad is the prophet whose coming Jesus had prophesied according to the Qur'an.[51] This is evidently applied to the seventh prophet here. But why is he made a son of Muḥammad b. al-Ḥanafiyya? It cannot be construed as reliable evidence that the members of the sect addressed by al-Faraj had already earlier professed to a Ḥanafī succession of imams. The names and the number of the other prophets mentioned conform precisely with Isma'ili doctrine. This suggests that the Isma'ili system was altered for some reason here.[52] The reversion to a son of Muḥammad b. al-Ḥanafiyya is perhaps to be understood as a challenge to the 'Abbasid house, which traced back its own claim to the imamate to the bequest of one of his sons.

3. Al-Ṭabarī gives no information about the person of al-Faraj b. 'Uthmān. Neither the Qarmaṭī nor the Fatimid traditions know him, despite the high rank he is given in the text. Only Ibn Khaldūn explains that al-Faraj b. 'Uthmān al-Qāshānī was another name of Zikrawayh b. Mahdawayh.[53] Is he basing himself on information from an earlier source, or is this simply an attempt to explain al-Ṭabarī's account, which he quotes at length? Ibn Khaldūn's working method speaks for the second alternative.[54] The Isma'ili character of the rebellions of Zikrawayh's sons is well-known.[55] They traced their genealogy to Muḥammad b. Ismā'īl. If Ibn Khaldūn's identification were nonetheless true, it would

have to be assumed that Zikrawayh himself had brought this strange book to his followers at his last appearance. But for this conjecture there is no support.

To sum up, it seems certain that the doctrine described by al-Ṭabarī is merely evidence of a fractional sect, not that of 'the Qarmaṭīs' in general. It can further be assumed, with some likelihood, that it represents an Isma'ili heresy. But about its originator and followers nothing definite can be said. Quite unjustified is the conclusion, based on al-Ṭabarī's account, that Ḥamdān Qarmaṭ and his followers had been Ḥanafīs before their conversion to Isma'ilism.[56]

As a second source for the Ḥanafī origin of the Qarmaṭīs, B. Lewis referred to a statement by the Qāḍī 'Abd al-Jabbār b. Aḥmad.[57] According to the latter, Abū Sa'īd al-Jannābī had said of himself as early as the eighties of the third Islamic century (893–902 AD) that he was the envoy of the Imam Muḥammad b. 'Abd Allāh b. Muḥammad b. al-Ḥanafiyya, who lived somewhere in the mountains. He was the Mahdi and would appear in the year 300/912–913.

Here, too, the name and the person of the Imam-Mahdi are invented. History reports nothing about a son of 'Abd Allāh b. Muḥammad b. al-Ḥanafiyya. The anti-'Abbasid tendency, however, is quite evident. For Abū Hāshim 'Abd Allāh was widely known to have bequeathed his right to the imamate to the 'Abbasid Muḥammad b. 'Alī before he died.[58] The name of the son is also well-founded. An old tradition had it that the Mahdi would have the same name as the Prophet, Muḥammad b. 'Abd Allāh.

'Abd al-Jabbār names Abū Sa'īd as the originator of this doctrine. In this statement B. Lewis sees confirmation of Casanova's hypothesis that the Qarmaṭīs were originally Ḥanafīs.[59] But 'Abd al-Jabbār himself is among the sources that connect Abū Sa'īd with Ḥamdān Qarmaṭ.[60] Abū Sa'īd is said to have made the assertion several years after 280/893. 'Abd al-Jabbār reports it in connection with Abū Sa'īd's return after his flight and the assassination of Abū Zakariyyā' al-Ṭamāmī, which was, according to Ibn Ḥawqal, a result of his secession from the Fatimids. So, were one to trust 'Abd al-Jabbār, who is quite an unreliable source to be used with caution, one would have to consider the new doctrine too, as a result of the secession from the Fatimids.

The conflict between Ḥamdān Qarmaṭ and his masters had broken out over the question of the imamate. Ḥamdān and 'Abdān had been instructed to teach that the Imam Muḥammad b. Ismā'īl was alive and that his return as the Mahdi was imminent. Now 'Ubayd Allāh claimed the imamate for himself and denied the return of Muḥammad b. Ismāʿīl. Ḥamdān and ʿAbdān considered themselves cheated and broke off the propagation of the doctrine. All this is reported in detail by Akhū Muḥsin.[61] After the disappearance of Ḥamdān and the assassination of ʿAbdān their followers found themselves without a leader and in an ideological crisis. Even Zikrawayh and his sons, who at first pretended to remain faithful to ʿUbayd Allāh, were seized by a confidence crisis. It soon turned out that they were merely working for their own advantage.[62] For Abū Saʿīd this must have seemed a favourable opportunity to make himself completely independent. He had been appointed to his office by Ḥamdān Qarmaṭ and ʿAbdān, and he must have shared the ideological crisis with his teachers. He may very well have tried to solve it by designating another Imam-Mahdi and giving himself out to be his emissary.

Quite similar motives may have been at the origin of the doctrine of al-Faraj b. ʿUthmān. There is no reason, however, to relate them, on the basis of ʿAbd al-Jabbār's statements, to the Qarmaṭīs of Baḥrayn. For one thing, the difference in the names of the Mahdi in the two texts goes against their being connected. For another, one would have to identify al-Faraj with Abū Saʿīd, which is hardly possible.

Equally untenable is the opinion espoused by Ivanow that the Qarmaṭī movement issued from the defection of Aḥmad b. al-Kayyāl. Ivanow starts out with al-Nawbakhtī's statement that the Qarmaṭīs belonged to the followers of Muḥammad b. Ismāʿīl,[63] but subsequently let the imamate end with him and expected his return as the Mahdi.[64] He connects this statement with the report of the Ismaʿili *dāʿī* Idrīs b. al-Ḥasan about the defection of Ibn al-Kayyāl from the Imam ʿAbd Allāh b. Muḥammad b. Ismāʿīl, and says that this defection is probably identical with the break between Qarmaṭīs and Ismaʿilis,[65] i.e., the later Fatimids.

If Idrīs' report is to be trusted,[66] this defection must have occurred soon after the death of Muḥammad b. Ismāʿīl. It cannot, therefore, be identical with the secession of the Qarmaṭīs from the Fatimids. The Qarmaṭī tradition confirms the view that its leader, Ḥamdān Qarmaṭ,[67] was first converted by the Fatimids.

According to al-Shahrastānī, Ibn al-Kayyāl had also claimed the imamate for himself and asserted that he was the Qāʾim.[68] We hear nothing of this from the Qarmaṭīs. Ibn al-Kayyāl's whole doctrine has little in common with theirs.[69] Finally, Ivanow's basic assumption that the secession of the Qarmaṭīs was due to the fact that, contrary to the

Fatimids, they had the imamate end with Muḥammad b. Ismāʿīl, is debatable. To all appearances, this had long been the doctrine of the fathers of the Fatimids as well. It was only the later Fatimid theory about the imamate which elevated ʿUbayd Allāh's ancestors to the rank of imams.

Let us go back to Abū Saʿīd. Apart from Ibn Ḥawqal, the secession of Abū Saʿīd is also explicitly mentioned by Muḥammad b. Mālik al-Yamānī, a contemporary of the Fatimid caliph al-Mustanṣir (427–487/1036–1094), who had ostensibly gone over to the Bāṭinīs in order to discover their secrets.[70] According to him, the Qarmaṭī ʿAlī b. al-Faḍl who carried the mission to the Yemen together with Ibn Ḥawshab, had explained his apostasy from ʿUbayd b. Maymūn (meaning ʿUbayd Allāh) to his associate by saying that he had a precedent in Abū Saʿīd al-Jannābī. The latter had given up Maymūn and his son and carried on the mission in his own name.[71]

De Goeje, who did not know all these reports and who assumed that Abū Saʿīd had remained loyal to ʿUbayd Allāh, found it astonishing that the Qarmaṭīs of Baḥrayn had remained completely passive during the rebellions of Zikrawayh's sons. He saw an explanation in the fact that the latter gave themselves out as the awaited imam one after the other.[72] But that does not explain why no attempt was made to support ʿUbayd Allāh, the real imam, who was now in utmost danger both from the pretenders and the ʿAbbasids. Nor does it explain why ʿUbayd Allāh, if in fact offered such a nearby and secure refuge in the solidly established Qarmaṭī state, should set off on the dangerous road to an unknown future in the west, only to turn his eyes eastward again immediately after his triumph.

De Goeje found confirmation of his view in an invasion by the Qarmaṭīs of the Baṣra area in the year 300/912–913.[73] Since the Fatimids began their first eastern campaign in that year, one could assume the Qarmaṭī invasion to have been incited by ʿUbayd Allāh in his view. But an examination of the reports about the two campaigns yields the following results: Only ʿArīb b. Saʿd,[74] Ibn Miskawayh,[75] al-Hamadhānī,[76] and Ibn al-Athīr[77] mention the Qarmaṭī raid. It was evidently a very small enterprise, since Ibn Miskawayh, al-Hamadhānī and Ibn al-Athīr speak of a unit of thirty men. Abū Saʿīd certainly did not take part in it. For a dating, the end of the year 299/July – August 912, according to the accounts of Ibn Miskawayh and Ibn al-Athīr, is to be preferred, because Ibn Miskawayh reports that the governor of Baṣra had written to Ibn al-Furāt, who was vizier at the time. In the month of Dhu'l-Ḥijja/19 July–17 August, Ibn al-Furāt fell out of favour and was thrown into prison.[78] 'Arīb's mention of it among the events of the following year is perhaps to be explained by the fact that the news did not become generally known in Baghdad until then.[79] As the date for the assassination of Abū Sa'īd, the very well-informed al-Mas'ūdī mentions Dhu'l-Qa'da 300/9 June–8 July 913.[80]

The Fatimid campaign against Egypt, however, did not begin until the year 301/913–914. Admittedly, Abu'l-Qāsim, 'Ubayd Allāh's son, was sent against the rebellious city of Tripoli, which had successfully resisted a Fatimid army for several months in the year 300/912–913.[81] But after conquering the city he returned to Raqqāda.[82] In the following year Ḥubāsa b. Yūsuf set off east with further aims. He conquered Surt and Ajdābiyya. On 7 Rajab 301/6 February 914 he entered Barqa.[83] On Thursday 14 Dhu'l-Ḥijja/7 July 914 Abu'l-Qāsim followed him from Raqqāda with a large army.[84] Against his order, Ḥubāsa, without waiting for his arrival, pushed further east and invaded Alexandria on 2 Ṣafar 302/27 August 914.[85] Abu'l-Qāsim arrived there on Friday 14 Rabī' II/4 November 914.[86] In view of the weakness of the Qarmaṭī enterprise and the interval between the two campaigns – if the Qarmaṭī raid can be thus designated – there can evidently be no question of a joint strategy.[87]

It is precisely this argument which has so far been used as a significant basis to prove a specially close bond of the Qarmaṭīs under Abū Sa'īd's son Abū Ṭāhir with the Fatimid imams. The question of military co-operation is, indeed, particularly important in this respect. For no matter how painstaking the effort to conceal the secret connection between the various branches of the Isma'ili movement, the overthrow of the 'Abbasids – the supreme aim of the rebels – required that all available forces be combined and subjected to a unified strategy. How could the imams of North Africa have desisted from harnessing those formidable fighting forces so near the heart of the 'Abbasid empire to further their own aims, using them to tie up the hostile armies so that they themselves might force their way east by way of Egypt? Thus Ibn Khaldūn reports:[88] 'In the year 306[89] (918–919), Abu'l-Qāsim reached Egypt, summoned Abū Ṭāhir, the Qarmaṭī, and waited for him. But Mu'nis al-Khādim stole a march on him. He set off [for Egypt] on behalf of al-Muqtadir and defeated him. [Abu'l-Qāsim] returned to Mahdiyya. Thereupon, Abū Ṭāhir marched against Baṣra, overran it and withdrew. Baghdad was terror-stricken, and al-Muqtadir ordered that the defects of the city walls be repaired.'

This is the account on which de Goeje,[90] and Ḥasan and Sharaf,[91] base their assumption of a unified strategy between the Fatimid and Qarmaṭī armies in the second campaign against Egypt. But a closer examination proves it to be untenable.

Abu'l-Qāsim's renewed invasion of Egypt must be viewed in connection with the constant pressure exercised by the Fatimid armies on the eastern borders since Ḥubāsa's campaign, from 301/913–914 to the end of the year 311/beginning of 924. At his withdrawal from Egypt towards the end of the year 302/spring 915, Abu'l-Qāsim had left a garrison in Barqa. After his departure, however, it had been overpowered and killed by the population. Thereupon 'Ubayd Allāh had sent an army against the city under Abū Madyan b. Farrūkh al-Lahīṣī at the beginning of 303/autumn 915.[92] He was only able to conquer it after an eighteen-month siege.[93] In the month of Shawwāl 304/April 917 fugitives from Lūbiya and Marāqiya, the area east of Barqa, arrived in Alexandria. Dhukā, the governor of Egypt, transferred troops to Alexandria.[94] Under the Aghlabids, Barqa had belonged to the governorship of Egypt. It was the gateway to Egypt, and the Fatimids did not relinquish it again.[95] Its fall was the prerequisite for Abu'l-Qāsim's new campaign. For the year 305/917–918 there is only a report of Maṣāla b. Ḥabūs' activity in the service of 'Ubayd Allāh in the western part of the country. Then, strong contingents of Berbers and Arabs were concentrated in Raqqāda.

Abu'l-Qāsim set off eastward on Monday 1 Dhu'l-Qa'da 306/5 April 919.[96] On Friday 8 Ṣafar 307/9 July 919 the vanguard of the army arrived in Alexandria.[97] In the month of Jumādā 11/29 October–26 November news reached Baghdad of a battle, in which each side had lost about 4,000 men. Thereupon the caliph al-Muqtadir commissioned the eunuch Mu'nis to march on Egypt for the second time. But it was not until Ramaḍān 307/February 920 that the latter left Baghdad.[98] Nor did he give any signs of hurry on the way. He only arrived in Fusṭāṭ on Thursday 4 Muḥarram 308/26 May 920,[99] and camped in Jīza. Meanwhile, Abu'l-Qāsim had marched south, settled in Ushmūnayn and collected the land tax in the area of Fayyūm.[100] For a year the fighting went on, more by means of defamatory poetry than with the sword.[101] Only after Thamil al-Khādim had succeeded in driving out the Fatimid armies from Alexandria and joining up with Mu'nis did the joint armies of Fusṭāṭ advance and capture the city of Fayyūm on Thursday 18 Ṣafar 309/28 June 921.[102] Abu'l-Qāsim had no choice but to retreat, and arrived in Mahdiyya on Saturday 1 Rajab 309/13 November 921.[103]

During this entire period the Qarmaṭīs of Baḥrayn were entirely quiet.

For the attack recorded by Ibn Khaldūn evidently did not take place. None of the early chroniclers, such as ʿArīb, Ibn Miskawayh, nor even Ibn al-Athīr, report any activity on the part of the Qarmaṭīs in those years.[104] Al-Masʿūdī,[105] Akhū Muḥsin,[106] and ʿAbd al-Jabbār,[107] who describe the history of the Qarmaṭīs consecutively, even emphasize the fact that after the death of Abū Saʿīd they remained peaceful until Abū Ṭāhir's capture of Baṣra in the year 311/923.[108] During the invasion of that year the inhabitants of Baṣra did not even suspect that the assailants were Qarmaṭīs. They first took them for ordinary Arabs.[109] This would hardly have been possible if the Qarmaṭīs had already overrun the city four years earlier. The Qarmaṭīs, moreover, are reported to have declared to the inhabitants of the city that the removal of ʿAlī b. ʿĪsā by the caliph had motivated their campaign.[110] Yet ʿAlī b. ʿĪsā had already been in office in the year 307/919.

The first source to mention the earlier invasion is apparently Ibn al-Jawzī. He reports under the year 307/919–920 that: 'In this year the Qarmaṭīs penetrated into Baṣra. Ḥāmid was dismissed from his office as vizier, and Abu'l-Ḥasan Ibn al-Furāt took charge [of it] for the third time.'[111] The second statement evidently offers a clue to the riddle, for the removal of Ḥāmid b. al-ʿAbbās and the new tenure of Ibn al-Furāt certainly occurred in 311/923.[112] Presumably, then, the notice of the Qarmaṭī incursion also refers to that year.

The details given by Ibn Khaldūn are not very convincing either. Nowhere is there any mention of an agitation in Baghdad on account of the Qarmaṭīs before the year 311/923,[113] or of a restoration of the city walls. On the contrary, after the disaster of that year Ibn al-Furāt criticized ʿAlī b. ʿĪsā for having neglected to pay the people entrusted with the maintenance of the walls of Baṣra and for thus having attracted the Qarmaṭīs.[114] Abu'l-Maḥāsin, who mentions the invasion of the year 307/919–920 after Ibn Khaldūn, reports no more than this: 'In this year the Qarmaṭīs penetrated into Baṣra, plundered the city, murdered and robbed.'[115]

It is obvious, then, that Ibn Khaldūn's account in this passage is based on a late, faulty source, rather than on a particularly well-informed report, as one might have expected considering his precise knowledge of the relations between Fatimids and Qarmaṭīs. But even if there had really been a Qarmaṭī invasion in the year 307/919–920, his report could easily have been recognized as an unacceptable historical reconstruction. The Qarmaṭīs made no attempt to follow the alleged command of Abu'l-Qāsim to march towards Egypt. Mu'nis did not forestall them by driving the

Fatimids out of Egypt. In fact, after Mu'nis finally reached Egypt in May 920 the armies stood facing each other for over a year, while the Qarmaṭīs did not stir.[116]

In the year 310/922–923, a battle is reported between a Fatimid detachment under Falāḥ b. Qamūn and Egyptian troops near Dhāt al-Ḥumām, 38 miles west of Alexandria.[117]

A further attack by Fatimid troops on Egyptian soil took place in the year 311/April 923–March 924. Masrūr b. Sulaymān b. Kāfī raided two oasis forts in upper Egypt and defeated their governor. He occupied the place, but the outbreak of an epidemic among his soldiers forced him to retreat to Barqa. Ibn ʿIdhārī, the only source to report this event, gives no precise date for it.[118] But since news of the victory was read out publicly in Qayrawān only on Thursday 22 Muḥarram 312/29 April 924,[119] it may be assumed that the raid took place not earlier than towards the end of the year 311 AH, i.e., hardly earlier than February 924. De Goeje connects this enterprise with the invasion of Baṣra by Abū Ṭāhir.[120] But that event took place more than six months earlier, at the end of Rabīʿ I 311/beginning of July 923. If one were to compare the movements of the two 'partners' closely, it would be more appropriate to bring up Abū Ṭāhir's attack on the pilgrim caravan returning from Mecca to Iraq in Muḥarram 312/April 924. Yet, Masrūr's campaign was obviously an enterprise with limited means and limited aims. Abū Ṭāhir, on the other hand, made no signs of marching towards Egypt, although he was certainly in a position to do so.

The following decade saw the greatest activity of the Qarmaṭīs of Baḥrayn. Almost every year Abū Ṭāhir led a raid into Mesopotamia or attacked the pilgrim caravans. The end of the ʿAbbasid reign seemed imminent. Meanwhile ʿUbayd Allāh was keeping his troops busy subduing northwestern Africa. The eastern border suddenly grew quiet.[121] The favourable opportunity to seize further parts of the impotent ʿAbbasid empire or to wipe it out altogether in collaboration with the Qarmaṭīs slipped by unused. For many a contemporary who saw in the two rebellious powers in Baḥrayn and North Africa simply two arms of the same Shiʿi movement, this must have been as incomprehensible as it is for the later observer who presupposes a general imamate of ʿUbayd Allāh over all Ismaʿilis. Thus ʿAbd al-Jabbār reports about the year 316/928, when Abū Ṭāhir was threatening Baghdad itself: 'Some people thought he [Abū Ṭāhir] was waiting for the arrival of the Maghribī Qarmaṭīs, according to an arrangement between them. But when no one came, he returned to al-Aḥsā.'[122]

The next eastern advance of the Fatimids did not occur until after the impetus of the Qarmaṭī incursions had died down. It is a misunderstanding of Ḥ. I. Ḥasan and Ṭ. A. Sharaf to assume, on the basis of al-Kindī's account,[123] that already in the year 321/933 troops from the Maghrib sent by ʿUbayd Allāh were stationed in Egypt.[124] These Maghribīs under the leadership of Ḥabashī b. Aḥmad were in fact part of the Egyptian army which the powerful Muḥammad b. ʿAlī al-Mādharāʾī had contrived to use for his private purposes. They first fought against the governor Muḥammad b. Tekin, then against Muḥammad b. Ṭughj al-Ikhshīd after his nomination by the caliph.[125] Muḥammad b. Ṭughj, however, gained the upper hand, and the rebellious Maghribīs decided to retreat to Barqa at the end of the year 323/October–November 935. At the same time they wrote to Abu'l-Qāsim, who had meanwhile succeeded ʿUbayd Allāh under his regnal name al-Qāʾim bi-Amr Allāh, asking him for permission to enter his domain and calling upon him to send an army with them to Egypt, since they knew the way and were familiar with the ins and outs of warfare. Thereupon, al-Qāʾim sent an army.[126] In the month of Rabīʿ II 324/March 936 the vanguard arrived in Alexandria. But Muḥammad b. Ṭughj sent his brother al-Ḥasan with an army to meet the aggressors. He defeated them on 5 Jumādā I 324/31 March 936, reconquered Alexandria, and the remnants of the Fatimid army fled to Barqa.[127] For this year there are no reports of activities by the Qarmaṭīs.[128]

Equally unconvincing is de Goeje's view that the raids of the Qarmaṭīs of Baḥrayn on Syria at the time of the Fatimid al-Muʿizz were carried out on the latter's instructions.[129] It is well-known that after the years of their most intensive activity the Qarmaṭīs freely negotiated and concluded agreements with the ʿAbbasid viziers, Būyids and Ḥamdānids, who granted them certain tributes and rights, above all that of taxing the pilgrims to Mecca as a reward for guarding them.[130] In the year 353/964 they exacted a consignment of iron from the Ḥamdānid Sayf al-Dawla. The latter showed such zeal in fulfilling their wish that he had the gates of Raqqa pulled down and the weights of merchants and tradesmen confiscated.[131] In the same year there is a report from Egypt about a general agitation because of a Qarmaṭī march on Syria.[132] Was it perhaps a detachment sent to watch over the transportation of the iron?

At the end of the year 354/965 Arabs of the Banū Sulaym tribe attacked and robbed the pilgrims from Egypt and Syria.[133] But the plundered goods were brought back to Kāfūr, the ruler of Egypt, by the Qarmaṭīs.[134] After Kāfūr's death on Tuesday 21 Jumādā I 357/21 April 968,[135] the Qarmaṭīs again attacked Syria under the leadership of al-Ḥasan al-Aʿṣam. They conquered Damascus and defeated the governor of Syria, al-Ḥasan b. ʿUbayd Allāh b. Ṭughj, on 2 Dhu'l-Ḥijja 357/28 October 968 before Ramla. Al-Ḥasan b. ʿUbayd Allāh fled to Egypt. The Qarmaṭīs entered Ramla and plundered the town for two days. Finally, the inhabitants ransomed themselves from the plague with the sum of 125,000 Egyptian dinars, and the Qarmaṭīs left.[136] Al-Ḥasan set out from Egypt on the 1st of Rabīʿ II/22 February 969 to return to his province.[137]

Two weeks earlier, on 14 Rabīʿ I 358/5 February 969, the Fatimid army under Jawhar had set off to conquer Egypt.[138] In the letter of safety he issued for the inhabitants of Fusṭāṭ, at the beginning of Shaʿbān 358/end of June 969, Jawhar promised in the name of his suzerain to reopen and protect the routes for the Mecca pilgrims, whose life and property had been threatened by the repeated attacks.[139] This signified an open declaration of war against the Qarmaṭīs.[140] At the first Friday worship which Jawhar attended in Fusṭāṭ on 20 Shaʿbān/9 July, the preacher read out at the end of his sermon the affirmation that al-Muʿizz had sent his armies for a holy war against the infidels (Byzantium) and those who prevented the pilgrimage.[141] That same month Jawhar also wrote a general letter of safety for the inhabitants of the country and of upper Egypt, explicitly naming and cursing the Qarmaṭīs.[142]

Al-Ḥasan b. ʿUbayd Allāh, having heard of the conquest of Egypt by Jawhar, had left Damascus in Ramaḍān 358/July–August 969 and gone to Ramla, where he was preparing for a defence against the Fatimid army. Here the Qarmaṭīs again attacked and defeated him. But he was able to conclude peace with them, and also established marriage ties with them (*ṣāharahum*) in Dhu'l-Ḥijja/16 October–13 November.[143] After the Qarmaṭīs had camped near the city for thirty days, they withdrew. A detachment evidently remained, however, for the contemporary Ibn Zūlāq reports that Jaʿfar b. Falāḥ, the Fatimid general, fought and defeated the Qarmaṭīs early in the year 359/970,[144] in a battle near Ramla in which al-Ḥasan b. ʿUbayd Allāh was taken prisoner.[145] Among the prisoners whom Jawhar sent to his suzerain on 17 Jumādā II 359/27 April 970, there was, besides al-Ḥasan, a certain Ibn Ghazwān, chief of the Qarmaṭīs.[146]

It was probably at the peace treaty between al-Ḥasan and the Qarmaṭīs that the former had bound himself to an annual tribute of 300,000 dinars.[147] The loss of this tribute with the conquest of Syria by Jaʿfar b. Falāḥ is given by most sources as the cause for the Qarmaṭī attack on the Fatimid army in the following year. De Goeje's opinion that this reason is too insignificant seems tenable only if it is assumed that the Baḥrayn

Qarmaṭīs had hitherto been loyal followers of the Fatimids.[148] But it is already clear that this was by no means the case. The true motive of the Qarmaṭīs for their raids in Syria lay in their desire for booty and tribute, which had determined the policies of their, by nature, very poor state of Baḥrayn since the thirties of the 10th century AD. To the Syrians and Egyptians who had duly paid their pilgrimage taxes they were prepared to secure the return of robbed properties, as they had to do in order to preserve their good reputation as protectors of the pilgrim caravans. But the confusion which ensued in Egypt after Kāfūr's death offered them a good opportunity to gain booty. As soon as this aim was reached, they withdrew without making any attempt to introduce the Shi'i doctrine in the conquered areas or to subject them to Fatimid reign, as might have been expected if these campaigns had been carried out on the order of al-Mu'izz. When the advance of the Fatimid army cut off their new source of income, and Jawhar openly announced his intention to deprive the Qarmaṭīs of their right to pose as guardians of the pilgrim caravans, there was no alternative left to them but war.

Among the accounts of the Arab historians on which the argument for a close co-operation between Qarmaṭīs of Baḥrayn and Fatimids during the reign of al-Mu'izz is normally based, special mention must be made of Ibn Khaldūn. In a closely-written three-page report[149] he describes how the Fatimid caliphs again and again interfered from North Africa in the internal affairs of the Qarmaṭīs, until al-Ḥasan rebelled against his distant masters in the year 360/971. He does not mention his sources, but he seems to have had at his disposal an account which is no longer available to us, for he reports a series of events that are not mentioned in our other sources. On the whole, however, he gives the impression of having dealt very freely with his sources.

De Goeje has already found evidence of numerous errors in this report.[150] Nevertheless, Ibn Khaldūn is his most valuable witness in his demonstration of an understanding between the Qarmaṭī and Fatimid movements. It may, therefore, be useful to juxtapose the reports suggesting a subordination of that kind on the part of the Qarmaṭīs with the oldest available accounts.

Ibn Khaldūn writes about the events leading from Abū Sa'īd's assassination to Abū Ṭāhir's succession: 'Abū Sa'īd had destined his eldest son, Sa'īd, for the succession . . . (gap in text) . . . But his youngest brother Abū Ṭāhir[151] Sulaymān rebelled against him, killed him, and assumed the rule over them. The 'Iqdāniyya[152] swore allegiance to him, and he received 'Ubayd Allāh's letter with the investiture.'[153]

It is known that Abu'l-Qāsim Sa'īd was not killed at the time, but rather died in the year 361/972.[154] The Baghdad chronicles, which were generally copied by later historical works,[155] confirm that Abū Sa'īd had appointed his eldest son as his successor, and that Abū Ṭāhir had then forced his way to power. In addition there is another tradition which no doubt has its origin in the Qarmaṭī history by the anti-Isma'ili polemical writer Abū 'Abd Allāh Muḥammad b. 'Alī b. Rizām al-Ṭā'ī of Kūfa.[156] According to this tradition, Abū Sa'īd had provided that after his death his eldest son, Sa'īd, should first assume the succession. When Abū Ṭāhir had grown up, however, he should turn over the rule to him. Following this direction, Sa'īd had surrendered the command to his brother in the year 305/June 917–July 918.[157] Abū Ṭāhir, to be sure, must have been only ten years old at the time.[158] Similarly, Ibn Ḥawqal reports that Abū Sa'īd had instructed his elder sons to submit and be obedient to the youngest when he came of age 'for a reason which he communicated to his survivors'.[159] An intervention by 'Ubayd Allāh is nowhere mentioned.

The untenability of Ibn Khaldūn's report about the Qarmaṭī attack on Baṣra in the year 307/919–920 has already been shown. After describing the pillage of Mecca, the massacre of the pilgrims, and the seizure of the Black Stone of the Ka'ba, he writes: "Ubayd Allāh al-Mahdī wrote to him [Abū Ṭāhir] from Qayrawān, reproved, and warned, him about it. So he wrote to him that he was incapable of restoring the [killed] people and promised the return of the Black Stone.'[160] 'Ubayd Allāh's letter is known from the report of Thābit b. Sinān, who quotes a passage from it verbatim.[161] But this letter should not be interpreted as proof of the unity of the Qarmaṭīs and the Fatimids, or of the continuation of this unity. For the Black Stone was not returned until years after Abū Ṭāhir's death. De Goeje is therefore forced to assume a secret order on the part of 'Ubayd Allāh which ran counter to the public letter.[162] But it has already been shown that the way the Qarmaṭīs acted around this time by no means gives grounds for the assumption that they acted on secret orders from the Fatimids. It is certainly possible that the motive for 'Ubayd Allāh's letter was to wash himself clean of any suspicions of his complicity in the outrage.[163] For during those very years there had evidently been a widespread suspicion that the two Shi'i movements in North Africa and Baḥrayn were acting hand in glove with each other.[164]

Ibn Khaldūn goes on: 'Then he gave it [the Black Stone] back in the year 339 (951), after al-Manṣūr Ismā'īl of Qayrawān had approached him regarding its return.'[165] If de Goeje relies on this passage to substantiate his opinion that the Qarmaṭīs had returned the Black Stone on al-Manṣūr's order,[166] then Quṭb al-Dīn's statement, which he also interprets in his favour, suggests the contrary. For the latter reports that al-Manṣūr had written to Aḥmad b. Abī Sa'īd and offered him 50,000 dinars for the return of the stone, but he had refused.[167] This version of the correspondence seems the only one which is consistent with the accounts in the other sources. For as de Goeje himself explains, the return was negotiated with the 'Abbasid government and probably paid with a large tribute.[168] The account of Ibn 'Idhārī, the third of de Goeje's sources, is totally useless. According to him, al-Manṣūr had set out for the orient (*bilād al-mashriq*) in the year 339/950–951 and had brought back the Black Stone to its place in its corner of the Ka'ba.[169] Al-Manṣūr actually never left his empire.

Ibn Khaldūn then reports: 'So they brought it back. Bajkam,[170] the usurper of the power in Baghdad in the days of al-Mustakfī,[171] had offered them 50,000 gold [dinars] to restore it. But they had refused and maintained that they had taken it away by the order of their imam, 'Ubayd Allāh, and would only restore it by his order or that of his successor.' This seems to be a typical result of Ibn Khaldūn's working method. For the Qarmaṭīs' claim that they had been ordered to take the stone away and would restore it only by order actually recurs in numerous sources,[172] but a name is nowhere mentioned. This omission cannot be accidental, for if the Qarmaṭīs had really said they had acted on 'Ubayd Allāh's order, this would certainly have been handed down by the earliest chroniclers, who mostly had anti-Fatimid attitudes.

The Qarmaṭīs' motive in maintaining that they were acting on order evidently was not meant to shift the responsibility for these actions to someone else. At the root of it lay one of their essential convictions, namely, that everything that happened was precisely predestined to happen, and they alone, as the true believers, possessed the knowledge of this predestination. Through this knowledge they were infallible and invincible in their actions.[173] Al-Dhahabī clearly understood this when he explained their words by saying what they meant was predestination (*al-qadar*).[174]

About the events following Abū Ṭāhir's death in 332/944, Ibn Khaldūn reports as follows:[175] At first his brother Aḥmad assumed the power. The 'Iqdāniyya council, however, was inclined towards Sābūr, the son of Abū Ṭāhir, and wrote to the Fatimid al-Qā'im on this matter. The latter invested Aḥmad and appointed Sābūr as his successor. So Aḥmad continued ruling. It was he who restored the Black Stone.[176] In the year 358/969, Sābūr imprisoned his uncle by arrangement with his brothers. But Aḥmad's brother rebelled and freed him. Sābūr was killed, and his brothers and followers were banished to the island of Uwāl. In the year 359/970, Abū Manṣūr Aḥmad died, allegedly poisoned by Sābūr's followers. Then his son al-Ḥasan al-Aʿṣam took over the reign.

This description of the succession deviates considerably from the accounts in other sources. Aḥmad b. Abī Saʿīd is mentioned by Quṭb al-Dīn as the partner of the ineffectual correspondence with the Fatimid al-Manṣūr about the return of the Black Stone.[177] As successors of Abū Ṭāhir, however, three of his brothers are usually named: Abu'l-Qāsim Saʿīd, who was apparently the most influential, the ailing Abu'l-ʿAbbās al-Faḍl and Abū Yaʿqūb Yūsuf, who was addicted to drink.[178] Already in Abū Ṭāhir's time it can be assumed that nominally power lay jointly in the hands of Abū Saʿīd's sons, although the personality of Abū Ṭāhir secured him the decision.[179] This system came into full force after his death. The letter announcing the return of the Black Stone was written jointly by Abū Ṭāhir's brothers.[180] This exactly corresponds with the picture of the structure of the Qarmaṭī state presented by Ibn Ḥawqal.[181] It was only for warfare that a leader was agreed on. Even when al-Ḥasan al-Aʿṣam acted as the constant commander of the Qarmaṭī army during the fights against the Fatimids, the supreme power remained in the hands of Abū Saʿīd's sons. Thus Ibn al-Jawzī reports under the year 361/972:[182] 'In Jumādā II, Abu'l-Qāsim Saʿīd b. Abī Saʿīd al-Jannābī died in Hajar. After him his brother Abū Yaʿqūb Yūsuf ruled. Except for him, none of the sons of Abū Saʿīd al-Jannābī remained alive. After Abū Yaʿqūb,[183] the Qarmaṭīs transferred the authority to six of their sons jointly.'[184]

By further developing Ibn Khaldūn's account, de Goeje has tried to elucidate the background for Sābūr's rebellion which led to his imprisonment and death in the middle of Ramaḍān 358/beginning of August 969. He believed that al-Muʿizz had nominated Sābūr as successor to his father Abū Ṭāhir since he could not expect any effective support for the conquest of Egypt from Sābūr's uncle Aḥmad[185] who had contented himself with an annual tribute after his victory over al-Ḥasan b. 'Ubayd Allāh in 357/968. This hypothesis is untenable. According to Ibn Ḥawqal, Aḥmad's son al-Ḥasan al-Aʿṣam, who had led the invasion of Syria, was suspected after his return of having embezzled booty.[186] This has nothing to do with Sābūr's revolt. Nor was he immediately rehabilitated after Sābūr's death. In the second Syrian campaign, which followed two months later, two of his cousins obtained the command over the army in his place.[187]

Although the scanty sources for the history of the Qarmaṭī state in this period allow us no insight into the details of the developments, the overall balance of power leading to Sābūr's revolt appears to be quite clear. After the death of Abū Ṭāhir, who had practically ruled as an autocrat, his brothers divided the authority among themselves. The seven sons of Abū Ṭāhir enjoyed high esteem and honour, but they were excluded from power.[188] Sābūr, the eldest and most esteemed among them, was not satisfied with the situation. He demanded the rule and the command of the army on the grounds that his father had designated him as his successor.[189] Thereupon he was thrown into prison by his uncles and died. There is no reason whatsoever to assume an intervention by the Fatimids.

Ibn Khaldūn describes the events leading to the 'secession' of the Qarmaṭīs as follows: After the conquest of Damascus by Ja'far b. Falāḥ, al-Ḥasan al-A'ṣam demanded the tribute levied from the city, but this was refused. Al-Mu'izz wrote him a rude letter and engaged in intrigues on behalf of the followers and sons of Abū Ṭāhir, who had been exiled to the island of Uwāl after Sābūr's revolt. When al-Ḥasan heard of this, he renounced his allegiance to al-Mu'izz and marched towards Damascus. In the year 361/972, al-Mu'izz once again wrote to him, severely rebuked him, and deposed him.

By the second letter which Ibn Khaldūn mentions here, the letter preserved by Akhū Muḥsin must be meant.[190] In fact, al-Mu'izz wrote it only after his arrival in Cairo,[191] that is not before Ramaḍān 362/June 973. From its contents one is inclined to conclude that it was the first letter he sent to al-Ḥasan. There is no mention of a dismissal in it. On the other hand, Ibn Ḥawqal also refers to the continuation of political rivalries among the Qarmaṭīs of Baḥrayn after Sābūr's death, but without giving any definite reasons.[192]

The defectiveness of the continuation of Ibn Khaldūn's report has been sufficiently pointed out by de Goeje.[193] Yet he believed that he could follow him in supposing that the Qarmaṭīs returned to the allegiance of the Fatimids because around the year 378/988 al-Muqaddasī mentions a treasury of the Mahdi (*khizānat al-Mahdī*) in al-Aḥsā.[194] This must indeed seem surprising, because only ten years earlier the Fatimid al-'Azīz had promised the Qarmaṭīs an annual tribute to restrain them from further attacks on Syria.[195] Is de Goeje perhaps wrong here in equating the Mahdi with the Fatimids? This becomes almost a certainty when one considers Ibn Ḥawqal's report for the year 367/977 that a fifth of the revenues of the Qarmaṭī state was set aside for the 'Lord of the Time'.[196]

On the basis of de Goeje's investigations and the examples mentioned here, Ibn Khaldūn's report proves to be a late historical construction which is worthless for a critical assessment of the question regarding the connection between Qarmaṭīs and Fatimids. Here only a strict examination of the earliest sources can lead us further.[197]

Al-Mas'ūdī's report in his *Kitāb al-tanbīh wa'l-ishrāf*, written in 345/956, is only a short synopsis of his earlier, lost accounts to which he frequently refers. This is all the more unfortunate since he was exceptionally knowledgeable in Qarmaṭī affairs. He mentions that he had talked to many of their envoys and scholars.[198] He briefly points out the ideological union of the movements in Baḥrayn, the Yemen, and North Africa which he had described at length elsewhere.[199]

A consecutive history of the Qarmaṭīs was written by Thābit b. Sinān, who continued it until the year of his death, 365/976. His work was extensively used by Ibn al-Athīr.[200] He only reports definite events which he evidently considered well-authenticated and never directly deals with the connection between the Qarmaṭīs and the Fatimids. But several passages which have been pointed out by B. Lewis,[201] imply a union of this kind. An inhabitant of Baghdad who had immigrated from Shīrāz was accused of treasonable correspondence with Abū Ṭāhir and declared at his trial that his imam was the Fatimid one in North Africa.[202] The secretary of Yūsuf b. Abi'l-Sāj, who was commissioned by the caliph to fight against the Qarmaṭīs of Baḥrayn, accused his master of having secretly revealed to him that he believed in the imamate of the 'Alid in North Africa whom Abū Ṭāhir also followed.

These reports, both recorded under the year 315/927, are of great interest as regards the mental atmosphere in Baghdad at the time. Hitherto they had evidently had no suspicion of a relationship between the two Shi'i movements.[203] So the statements of the Isma'ili must have made them prick up their ears. This is perhaps the reason why the otherwise insignificant episode was recorded by the chronicler. It does not offer any certain proof for the political bonds between Baḥrayn and Qayrawān. A follower of the Fatimid imams in Baghdad might well supply Abū Ṭāhir with information in order to support him in fighting the common enemy, whether or not he knew if the latter directly served his master. He himself said that he did not know Abū Ṭāhir personally. The secretary's accusation of Yūsuf b. Abi'l-Sāj, which can easily be assumed to be a calumny,[204] springs from a similar reflection: Two Shi'i rebellions were threatening the 'Abbasid empire. What was more natural than to see a single conspiracy behind them?

Finally, Thābit mentions the letter of al-Muʿizz to al-Ḥasan al-Aʿṣam in which he reminded him 'that the doctrine is one, and that the Qarmaṭīs had summoned to allegiance to him and his fathers'.[205]

The pro-Fatimid attitude is represented by Ibn Ḥawqal in his *Kitāb ṣūrat al-arḍ*, written around the year 367/978. He also had connections with high-ranking personalities among the Qarmaṭīs. In 361/972 he had spoken to Abu'l-Ḥusayn ʿAlī al-Jazarī in Sicily, who had told him about the events leading to the alliance between the Qarmaṭīs and the ʿAbbasids.[206] From him stems the information that Abū Saʿīd was originally a follower of the Fatimids but had defected after the assassination of ʿAbdān and killed the missionary Abū Zakariyyā' al-Ṭamāmī. He curses Abū Saʿīd and Abū Ṭāhir for their atrocities for which reason de Goeje calls him a hypocrite.[207] Elsewhere he speaks in connection with Abū Zakariyyā' al-Ṭamāmī of the 'first doctrine and old rule' of the Qarmaṭīs.[208] He characterizes their doctrine at his time by the fact that they let the imamate come to an end.[209] With Shiʿi sects this normally meant that they were expecting the return of the last imam as the Mahdi. Unfortunately, he does not name the latter.

Shortly after the year 372/983, the Sharīf Akhū Muḥsin from Damascus, himself a descendant of the same Muḥammad b. Ismāʿīl to whom the Fatimids traced back their genealogy, wrote one of those polemical works intended to reveal the secrets of the Ismaʿilis and refute their doctrine from a Sunni point of view.[210] In the historical section of his work he presents a detailed history of the Qarmaṭī movement which relies on Ibn Rizām for its passages on the earlier history. He reports at great length about the secession of Ḥamdān Qarmaṭ and ʿAbdān, though without saying anything about the attitude of the Qarmaṭīs of Baḥrayn. Only in his explanation of the threatening letter which al-Muʿizz wrote to al-Ḥasan al-Aʿṣam, he reports, according to al-Nuwayrī: After his arrival in Egypt, al-Muʿizz decided to write to al-Ḥasan b. Aḥmad to let him know that they belonged to the same confession, and that the Qarmaṭīs had received their doctrine from the Ismaʿilis, who were their masters in this respect. From al-Ḥasan's reply to his threats he hoped to learn what he had up his sleeve, and whether the news of his arrival in Egypt would frighten him. 'Al-Ḥasan knew full well that the two sects were one and the same, for it was not unknown to him that the one and the other confessed to the exoteric and the esoteric doctrine. In fact, both agreed on teaching atheism and total anarchy regarding men and property, and on denying the prophetic mission. But even if agreement on the doctrine prevails, as soon as the adherents of one party have the advantage over those of another, they consider it permissible to kill them, and grant them no mercy.'[211]

Here a union of Qarmaṭīs and Isma'ilis, i.e., followers of the Fatimids, is shown not on the basis of definite political relations, but on the grounds of an ideological conformity of the most general kind. Despite this conformity they form two parties. The same Akhū Muḥsin writes at the end of that section of his book where he describes the doctrine of the Bāṭinīs: 'This original doctrine went through a few changes in the course of time, and the community split up into different branches after its dissemination in the Maghrib, Egypt and Syria. In particular, there was a change of opinion about Muḥammad b. Ismā'īl, for whom they first demanded recognition as the imam and who was then replaced by a descendant of 'Abd Allāh b. Maymūn al-Qaddāḥ, whose progeny ruled in the Maghrib, Egypt and Syria.'[212]

In Akhū Muḥsin's work we also first come across an allegedly Isma'ili writing which was to excite the minds of pious people for a long time to come. For the heresiographers and polemicists it became one of the main sources from which they drew their knowledge about the secret doctrine of the Bāṭinīs. They found in it all the atheism, libertinism and blasphemy they could have wished for to demonstrate the infamy of these heretics. It even radiated its effect towards the Christian Occident. According to L. Massignon, it is to be regarded as the first version of the legend 'de tribus impostoribus', which circulated two centuries later in the West and was finally credited to Frederic II Hohenstaufen.[213]

Akhū Muḥsin knew the work under the title *Kitāb al-siyāsa*. He states that he had read it himself and quotes two fragments from it.[214] This 'book of methodology' consists of instructions for the missionaries about the procedure of catching souls. The author speaks of seven steps of attainment (*balāgh*) through which the neophyte is gradually initiated into the atheistic doctrine.[215] Only a few years later Ibn al-Nadīm (writing in 377/987) mentions these seven degrees. The book of the first degree is destined for the general public, that of the second for the somewhat advanced, that of the third for people converted in the second year, etc. Of the 'book of the seventh attainment' (*Kitāb al-balāgh al-sābi'*) he says that he has read it himself and has found in it a great deal of libertinism and mockery of the prophets.[216] This description is characteristic and shows that it was a supplement to the 'book of methodology'. 'Abd al-Qāhir al-Baghdādī (d. 429/1038) knows the book under the title of *Kitāb al-siyāsa wa'l-balāgh al-akīd wa'l-nāmūs al-a'ẓam*, and his quotations from it bear out Ibn al-Nadīm's verdict.[217] While Akhū Muḥsin and Ibn al-Nadīm name neither the author nor a definite addressee,[218] he claims that ʿUbayd Allāh had sent the work to Abū Ṭāhir. The Qāḍī Abū Bakr al-Bāqillānī (d. 403/1013) refuted it in his lost *Kitāb hatk al-astār wa-kashf al-asrār* and seems to have named a Fatimid *qāḍī* as its author.[219] ʿAbd al-Jabbār (wrote around 400/1010) reports, however, that the Fatimid Abu'l-Qāsim had sent it to Abū Ṭāhir while his father was still alive. For ʿUbayd Allāh had first described him as an orphan from the house of ʿAlī, descending from Ismāʿīl b. Jaʿfar (al-Ṣādiq).[220] Niẓām al-Mulk (wrote in 485/1092) suggests that Abū Ṭāhir had requested it from the missionaries.[221] Abu'l-Qāsim al-Qayrawānī is also mentioned by the Yemenite Muḥammad b. al-Ḥasan al-Daylamī (wrote in 707/1308) as the author of the work, from which he quotes at length under the title of *al-Balāgh al-akbar*.[222] The Zaydī Imam Ibn al-Murtaḍā (d. 840/1437) says that Abu'l-Qāsim al-Qayrawānī had sent it to a certain Waṣīf al-Muḥammadī.[223]

Abu'l-Muẓaffar ʿImād al-Dīn Ṭāhir al-Isfarā'inī (d. 471/1078) mentions the work without naming its title, probably following al-Baghdādī.[224] Ibn al-Jawzī (d. 597/1200) quotes an excerpt, without naming the title of the book, as an instruction to the missionaries.[225] The theologian Sayf al-Dīn ʿAlī al-Āmidī (d. 631/1233) knows at least the title.[226] Ibn Taymiyya (d. 728/1328) mentions it in his legal opinion about the Nuṣayrīs.[227] The later historian ʿImād al-Dīn b. Kathīr knows it from al-Bāqillānī's refutation and tries to identify the Fatimid *qāḍī* who is alleged to have written it. He believes it was the Qāḍī ʿAbd al-ʿAzīz, the son-in-law of Jawhar, the conqueror of Egypt.[228] He means ʿAbd al-ʿAzīz b. Muḥammad b. al-Nuʿmān, the grandson of the well-known *qāḍī* under the Fatimids al-Manṣūr and al-Muʿizz and author of the most important Ismaʿili law book. But ʿAbd al-ʿAzīz was only born in the year 355/966, and Ibn Ḥajar al-ʿAsqalānī tries to correct Ibn Kathīr. The book, he says, was written by ʿAlī, the uncle of ʿAbd al-ʿAzīz, and by al-Nuʿmān, his grandfather.[229]

The Ismaʿili tradition, however, seems to know this work merely from the polemics of its opponents. Ḥamīd al-Dīn al-Kirmānī, an important author and teacher of the Fatimid Ismaʿilis (d. around 411/1020), at any rate denies, in his letter *al-Risāla al-kāfiya fī'l-radd ʿalā'l-Hārūnī al-Ḥasanī*, that it belongs to the literature of his community. His opponent, the Daylamī Zaydī Imam Abu'l-Ḥusayn al-Mu'ayyad bi'llāh Aḥmad b. al-Ḥusayn b. Hārūn al-Buṭḥānī (d. 411/1020), who had substantiated his accusations against the Ismaʿilis on the strength of the *al-Balāgh al-akbar*, is advised by him to read reliable and well-known Ismaʿili works.[230]

Already C. H. Becker saw a malevolent forgery in the work as quoted by Akhū Muḥsin,[231] and the details given by al-Daylamī and al-Baghdādī fully confirm this. It hardly seems likely that the preaching of a religion should be based on such cynicisms; and the doctrine ascribed to the Ismaʿilis here is an intentional distortion, though based on considerable knowledge, as are repeated attempts to prove that they belonged to the Dahriyya, the Naturalists, who considered the material world to be uncreated.[232]

Al-Maqrīzī, who often used Akhū Muḥsin, though usually without acknowledging his source, does not quote his commentary to the threatening letter of al-Muʿizz.[233] Instead, he adds to his account of the Qarmaṭī attack on Egypt the following quotation from a contemporary, probably the well-known man of letters and *qāḍī* Abū ʿAlī al-Muḥassin al-Tanūkhī (d. 384/994):[234] 'All this after the Qarmaṭīs had first bragged about the Mahdi and made people believe that he was the lord of the Maghrib, and that their propaganda was for him. They had exchanged letters with the Imam al-Manṣūr Ismāʿīl b. Muḥammad al-Qāʾim b. ʿUbayd Allāh al-Mahdī and revealed to their greatest friends that they belonged to his following.[235] Until their lie became obvious through the war led against them by the general Jawhar . . . '

This judgement must be understood against the background of the external situation. The Qarmaṭīs, who had hitherto given themselves out to be the followers of the Mahdi, now all of a sudden publicly embraced the cause of the ʿAbbasid caliphate. They formed the only effective fighting force which offered resistance to the further eastern advance of the Fatimids. They cursed the latter from the pulpit, although the Fatimids had claimed to represent the Mahdi.[236] From their speeches about the Mahdi, some people had taken them for vassals of the Fatimids. Now the observer concludes from their volte-face that they had formerly lied in order to lead the world astray.[237] As a proof for this, however, he can only mention an exchange of letters with al-Manṣūr,[238] of which he unfortunately does not give the content, and vague rumours.

The real difficulty in assessing the Qarmaṭī movement in Baḥrayn lies in the scarcity of sources bearing witness to their creed. While the religious literature of the Fatimids has been preserved in rich abundance through the survival of the community of their adherents, the historian has to rely in respect of Qarmaṭī views almost exclusively on the statements of their Sunni opponents. The latter, however, treated all Bāṭinīs as a unit and rarely took the trouble, in their polemic zeal, to distinguish between spatially and temporally limited phenomena. This approach was intensified by the strict secrecy in which the Bāṭinīs themselves enveloped part of their doctrine, as well as their early history. Thus, there are only very few occasional reports which definitely refer to the creed of the Qarmaṭīs of Baḥrayn. These reports indicate that the expectation of the imminent coming of the Mahdi played a significant part in their doctrine, and also that this expectation was not fulfilled by the appearance of the Fatimids.

In the year 316/928, a young Persian from Iṣfahān, ostensibly a descendant of the Persian kings, joined the Qarmaṭīs in Baḥrayn.[239] In Ramaḍān 319/September–October 931, Abū Ṭāhir surrendered the government to him. For a short time he disposed of absolute power, ordered the most senseless atrocities, and had a number of influential people killed.[240] De Goeje has translated and commented various reports about these events.[241] His explanation that the false prophet had attained his power by claiming to be an emissary of ʿUbayd Allāh[242] is unacceptable and has been rejected in more recent investigations.[243] Nor is it consistent with al-Masʿūdī's report that the Iṣfahānī had already lived with the Qarmaṭīs for years.

Remarkable, however, is the explanation in one of the reports that Ibn Sanbar had initiated the Iṣfahānī into some secrets which Abū Ṭāhir had confided to him alone and had instructed him: 'Go to Abū Ṭāhir and tell him that you are the man to whose allegiance his father and he himself have summoned the people. If he then asks you for signs and proofs, reveal these secrets to him.' Abū Ṭāhir had no doubts about the authenticity of these signs and proclaimed to his adherents: 'This is the man I have summoned you to follow, and to him belongs the command.'[244]

Particularly interesting, in spite of certain hardly credible details, is the eyewitness report of the physician Ibn Ḥamdān which Ibn Rizām added to his description of the episode. Here, too, there is a mention of a sign by which the Iṣfahānī was able to delude Abū Ṭāhir and his brothers into believing that he was the expected one.[245] Abū Ṭāhir now proclaimed to his adherents that they had all been asses so far. God in his goodness had now sent them the young Persian, who was Abū Ṭāhir's own and their Lord and God, and they were his servants. To him belonged the sovereignty, and he possessed them all. Then they picked up earth and strewed it on their heads. Thereupon, Abū Ṭāhir declared: 'Know then, community of men, that the religion has henceforth appeared. It is the religion of our father Adam, and all the belief we had was false. All the things the missionaries made you hear, their talk about Moses, Jesus and Mohammed, was falsehood and deceit. The [true] religion is in fact the original religion of Adam,[246] and those are all wily deceivers (*dajjālūn*); so curse them.' Then the people cursed them, including Abraham, Mohammed, even ʿAlī and his descendants.[247]

Here the antinomian tendency which had from the beginning more or less latently characterized a major part of the Ismaʿili movement evidently led to a drastic turn. The lawgivers, the prophets, are unequivocally condemned. The true religion is the lawless religion of Adam which is now revived by the expected one turned God. For the reform of the Iṣfahānī consisted of the abrogation of religious laws. Thus far Ibn Ḥamdān's statements can certainly be trusted.

On the basis of this report the account of ʿAbd al-Jabbār seems to require certain corrections.[248] According to him, Abū Ṭāhir had explained to his followers that the doctrines dished out to them about Muḥammad, then ʿAlī, then Ismāʿīl b. Jaʿfar, then Muḥammad b. Ismāʿīl and the Mahdi were nonsense. This was a secret which he and his predecessors had kept for sixty years and were now making public. Abū Ṭāhir ordered them to curse the 'liars', namely, the prophets, including Adam, and ordered the missionaries to reveal their secrets. So they reported the machinations of ʿAbd Allāh b. Maymūn and Muḥammad b. al-Ḥusayn,[249] as they were mentioned in the books of Ibn Rizām, a certain ʿAṭiyya, and other scholars.

From this account, taken by itself, it would be possible to deduce with B. Lewis[250] a secession from the Fatimids who were pilloried as the descendants of that very ʿAbd Allāh b. Maymūn. Yet ʿAbd al-Jabbār is too much of a secondary polemical source to be trusted without reservation as is clear from a comparison of his statements with those of Ibn Ḥamdān, one of his sources by way of Ibn Rizām.[251] Whether it was exactly at that time that 'the machinations of ʿAbd Allāh b. Maymūn and Muḥammad b. al-Ḥusayn' were made public for the first time is uncertain.[252] What is more important is the fact that the Iṣfahānī owed his success to the expectation of the Mahdi which the Qarmaṭīs of Baḥrayn had already held long before his appearance despite the Fatimids' claim to the title.

Here another aspect of the episode may briefly be discussed. The false Mahdi was a Persian and, according to al-Masʿūdī, a descendant of the Persian kings. It is a favourite theme of anti-Ismaʿili polemics that the motive of the founders of the Ismaʿili movement was a plot against Islam and the reign of the Arabs in order to re-establish the reign of the Persians and their faith. The polemicists refer above all to Muḥammad b. al-Ḥusayn Dindān, who is described as a fanatical Shuʿūbī and hater of

Arabs. According to Ibn Rizām,[253] he claimed to have discovered in the stars that the hegemony of Islam would be replaced by that of the Persians and their religion in the eighth conjunction, because of (or after) the transition of the triplicity of Scorpio, the sign of Islam, to Sagittarius, the sign of the Persian religion. A similar prediction is mentioned by al-Bīrūnī and al-Baghdādī in connection with the Qarmaṭī creed. It was predicted that the Persians would recover their hegemony in the 18th conjunction after the birth of Muḥammad.[254]

These polemic accusations are not particularly credible as regards the Isma'ili movement in general. In the Fatimid doctrine there are no reverberations of Shu'ūbī tendencies, and this is also true of the doctrine of Ḥamdān Qarmaṭ and 'Abdān, as far as we know. So here the Qarmaṭīs of Baḥrayn went their own way.[255]

The expectation of the Mahdi is also reflected in a poem, by Abū Ṭāhir, of which fragments are extant.[256] In it he warns the inhabitants of Iraq against false hopes because of his retreat to Hajar. He will return, he will inflict defeat after defeat on them and slaughter them without mercy. Then he designates himself as the one who summons to obey the Mahdi. Does he mean 'Ubayd Allāh, as Ṭ. A. Sharaf and Ḥ. I. Ḥasan assume?[257] Characteristically, they do not quote another verse where Abū Ṭāhir declares that he will live until the coming of Jesus, son of Mary. There can hardly be any doubt that he means the appearance of the expected Mahdi.[258]

De Goeje has cautiously dated the poem in 319/931, after Abū Ṭāhir's voluntary retreat from Kūfa. The verse with the astrological content, which he analyzed in detail and which prompted him to carry out a valuable investigation of the significance of astrological predictions for the Fatimids and Qarmaṭīs, is unfortunately handed down in variants and cannot be interpreted unequivocally.[259] But from the fragments of the poem transmitted by al-Dhahabī it may be inferred that Abū Ṭāhir meant his retreat after the fighting of the year 316, beginning of Sha'bān/end of September 928. In four lines[260] he mentions details of his campaigns in that year, the capture of al-Anbār, and the advance to 'Aqarqūf,[261] only four hours away from Baghdad. The context in which the poem is handed down by al-Bīrūnī and al-Baghdādī points to the same conclusion.

It was around this time, at any rate, that the expectation of the Mahdi consolidated itself into the firm conviction that his appearance was imminent. Thus al-Bīrūnī writes: 'Before the appearance of this boy [the Iṣtahanī], the Qarmaṭīs . . . had promised each other the arrival of the expected one in the seventh conjunction of the fiery triplicity.'[262] As evidence he then quotes Abū Ṭāhir's poem. The conjunction referred to occurred in the year 316/928.[263] The same is reported by al-Baghdādī, who adds that Abū Ṭāhir had set out from al-Aḥsā with this assertion, had waylaid the pilgrims, and finally overrun Mecca.[264] His statement that Abū Ṭāhir had sent the poem to the Muslims after a defeat can only refer then to the retreat of 316/928, not to the peaceful surrender of Kūfa in 319/931. Finally, ʿAbd al-Jabbār[265] adds to his description of the pillage of Baṣra and Kūfa in the years 311/923 and 312/925:[266] 'The Shiʿis . . . said: Abū Ṭāhir b. Abī Saʿīd is the friend of God, the proof of God (*walī Allāh wa-ḥūjjat Allāh*) and the deputy (*khalīfa*) of the Mahdi, who will soon appear, in Baḥrayn. Abū Ṭāhir is his deputy, who conquers the earth for him, and his [the Mahdi's] reign will be in Baḥrayn. Then a large crowd of the inhabitants of Kūfa and surroundings set out, and saying: let us emigrate to the land of the Mahdi before he appears, brought their goods and chattels and their families [to Baḥrayn].'

In his *al-Tanbīh*, al-Masʿūdī hints that there were certain reasons, evidently of a special kind, for Abū Ṭāhir's retreat in 316/928, and that he had mentioned them elsewhere.[267] Unfortunately, this passage is not extant. But it is not unlikely that these reasons were precisely the fact that the Mahdi was now to appear in Baḥrayn. Ibn al-Jawzī's report[268] is significant in this respect: 'After Abū Ṭāhir al-Qarmaṭī had returned to his country, he built an abode (*dār*), which he called "abode of emigration",[269] and summoned to the Mahdi.[270] His affair was taking on serious forms, the number of his adherents increased, and he felt tempted to attack Kūfa. The tax-collectors of the government in the cultivated land (*sawād*) fled, and his followers raided the villages, murdered and plundered.' As can be gathered from subsequent statements, what is meant by the followers is the group of Qarmaṭīs in the surroundings of Kūfa whom the chroniclers know under the name of Baqliyya.[271] They had so far remained quiet. While Abū Ṭāhir was in Syria[272] they had assembled in their 'abode of emigration' and summoned the whole population to follow them.[273] It is reported of them, too, that they summoned to the Mahdi.[274] The revolt was, however, quickly suppressed by troops of the caliph.

Since de Goeje considers these Qarmaṭīs of the Kūfa area, the former arena of Ḥamdān Qarmaṭ and ʿAbdān, as followers of ʿUbayd Allāh,[275] we may briefly go into the rather sparse reports about the Ismaʿili movement in Iraq after the death of Zikrawayh. Akhū Muḥsin reports that after the disappearance of Abū Ḥātim al-Zuṭṭī, a group of Qarmaṭīs maintained that Zikrawayh was still alive. But another group said: 'God's proof (*ḥujja*) is Muḥammad b. Ismāʿīl.'[276] Of the followers of Zikrawayh there are no reports later on. From the year 312/925 we learn, however, that near Kūfa a man appeared who pretended to be Muḥammad b. Ismāʿīl. He was able to gather around him a large number of Arabs and inhabitants of the cultivated land (*sawād*). When the matter took on a threatening aspect in Shawwāl 312/January 925, an army was sent against him from Baghdad. He was defeated, and many of his adherents were killed.[277]

In Baghdad around this time the vizier Abu'l-Qāsim al-Khāqānī tracked down those inhabitants of the town who were accused of corresponding with Abū Ṭāhir and being followers of the Ismaʿili religion. He learned of a missionary of the Qarmaṭī doctrine called al-Kaʿkī. He himself managed to avoid being arrested, but in his house they found his deputy and a few pupils. Al-Muqtadir learned that the Shiʿis usually assembled in the mosque of Barāthā,[278] and cursed the 'Companions of the Prophet'. In Ṣafar 313/May 925, thirty men were caught there at the Friday prayer, who declared their dissociation from those who recognized al-Muqtadir as their imam. They were arrested. When they were inspected, white[279] clay seals were found that had been stamped for them by al-Kaʿkī with the inscription: Muḥammad ibn Ismāʿīl, the Mahdi-Imam, the friend of God. Al-Khāqānī had the jurists issue a warrant that the mosque was a shelter for mischief, infidelity and discord among the Muslims. He testified that, unless it were destroyed, it would be a sanctuary for the missionaries and Qarmaṭīs. Then al-Muqtadir ordered its destruction.[280]

This report only mentions connections with Abū Ṭāhir, not with the Fatimids. As their imam and Mahdi the rebels named Muḥammad b. Ismāʿīl, not ʿUbayd Allāh. Two years later it caused a stir when a follower of the Fatimids was found as well. Everything thus indicates that the majority of the Ismaʿilis in Iraq co-operated closely with the Qarmaṭīs of Baḥrayn and rejected the Fatimid imamate.

After the defeat of the rebellious Baqliyya some of them joined Abū Ṭāhir on his retreat from Hīt to Baḥrayn. They were known in his army as the Ajamiyyūn.[281] At the beginning of the reign of the false Mahdi they were still in Baḥrayn.[282] The course of events and the disastrous end subsequently led to their departure. Many of the Qarmaṭī leaders defected.[283] Among them was Abu'l-Ghayth b. ʿAbda of the tribe of ʿIjl,[284] who is said to have had 30,000 men under his command and to have taken part in the Baqliyya rising.[285] In the following decades,

Qarmaṭīs are often mentioned as being in the service of Sunni rulers and generals. ʿArīb, who emphasizes the disastrous consequences of the episode with the Persian for the affairs of the Qarmaṭīs of Baḥrayn,[286] refers for the first time, evidently as an oddity, to seventy Qarmaṭīs of rank in the service of Mu'nis in 320/932.[287] Later, it was no longer considered unusual. About the origin of these Qarmaṭīs nothing is mentioned anywhere. It seems likely, however, that they were members of the Qarmaṭī Arab tribes from Iraq who, after their heavy defeats and their ideological crisis, hired themselves out to Sunni masters.

Abu'l-Qāsim ʿĪsā b. Mūsā, the nephew of ʿAbdān, was one of the leaders of the Baqliyya rising and was imprisoned. During the disturbances towards the end of al-Muqtadir's reign (320/932) he escaped. He stayed in Baghdad and won followers for his doctrine. As he is said to have ascribed books to his uncle,[288] it may be assumed that he continued teaching the imamate of Muḥammad b. Ismāʿīl. He was now an opponent both of the Fatimids and of the Qarmaṭīs of Baḥrayn. According to ʿAbd al-Jabbār, his son Abū Ṭālib 'and the likes of him' cursed Abū Ṭāhir bitterly whenever they mentioned his lapse.[289] ʿĪsā's school still existed at the time when Akhū Muḥsin was writing.[290]

After the short interlude with the Iṣfahānī, the Qarmaṭīs of Baḥrayn reverted to their old doctrine about the future advent of the Mahdi. For it is no doubt to the expected one, rather than to the Fatimids, that the reports about their later history relate, where the Mahdi is mentioned. ʿAbd al-Jabbār reports that Abū Ṭāhir now tried to collect some of his soldiers' booty for the Mahdi, as he had done before, but that they only answered him with insults.[291] As noted, according to Ibn Ḥawqal, one fifth was set aside for the 'Lord of the Time', and al-Muqaddasī mentions a treasury of the Mahdi in al-Aḥsā. There are also reports that after the death of Kāfūr, the ʿAlid ʿAbd Allāh b. ʿUbayd Allāh b. Ṭāhir, known as Akhū Muslim, sought recognition for himself as the Mahdi among the ʿAlids. When he failed to succeed, he joined the Qarmaṭīs and took part in their war against al-Muʿizz.[292] But apparently they would not acknowledge him either. A century later, Nāṣir-i Khusraw reports that the Qarmaṭīs of Baḥrayn were expecting the return of the Sharīf Abū Saʿīd which he himself had promised them.[293] Did he really understand all this correctly?

There is yet an important document to be discussed in which de Goeje rightly saw the most obvious evidence for his theory that the Qarmaṭīs remained loyal to the Fatimids until the year 358/969,[294] the letter al-Muʿizz wrote to al-Ḥasan al-Aʿṣam after his arrival in Cairo in

Ramaḍān 362/June 973. Its authenticity can hardly be questioned.[295] Formally it agrees with other letters by al-Mu'izz. The doctrines that are expounded in it fall within the framework of what is known from other Fatimid writings.

The letter was evidently made public by the recipient for propaganda purposes shortly after it had arrived. Thus 'Abd al-Jabbār reports: 'Al-Ḥasan . . . read out his [al-Mu'izz's] letter to the people and thereby showed up his false doctrine and lies.'[296] That is why Thābit b. Sinān knew and reported it already in 363/974.[297] A few years later, Akhū Muḥsin recorded it fully in his history of the Qarmaṭīs where it has been preserved in its most complete form.[298]

Al-Mu'izz begins with a long introduction about the nature of the prophets and their deputies, the imams. God has created us as spirits before the creation of the world and has equipped us with power.[299] All the things of the world, from the heavenly spheres to the innermost souls, are ours and for our sake and point to us.[300] No prophet has been sent, no executor (*waṣī*) has appeared without pointing to us.[301] 'We are the everlasting words of God, His perfect names, His shining lights, His illuminated signposts, His clear chandeliers, His created miracles, His dazzling signs and active destinies. Nothing is without relation to us (*lā yakhruju minnā amr*), no age is empty of us.'[302] Al-Mu'izz has come to Egypt at a predestined time: 'We do not lift our foot or set it down without a firm knowledge, a universally valid decision, a predestined term, a prior command and a realized destination.'[303]

Then al-Mu'izz turns to al-Ḥasan. He calls him a perjured traitor and reproaches him for apostasy from the faith of his fathers and for kindling the flame of rebellion. But his case has not remained hidden from al-Mu'izz. 'We have learned what views you have made your own (*'alā ayyi ra'yin aṣalt*), what paths you are treading. Do you not have an example in your grandfather Abū Sa'īd, a model in the actions of Abū Ṭāhir? Have you not seen their writings and their history, have you not read their enactments and their poems? Were you absent from their houses, is nothing known to you of their deeds (*mā kāna min āthārihim*)? Do you not know[304] that they were servants of ours, of great bravery, firm will, of righteousness and praiseworthy actions, toward whom our substance flowed and over whom our blessing spread? So they overcame the provinces, all the princes and governors served them, and they obtained the title of 'lords' (*al-sāda*) and ruled, as a favour from us.'[305] They spread terror everywhere, fear among the sons of 'Abbās, they defeated army upon army, 'and our eyes followed them, our support was allotted them, as God the exalted has said: Verily, We support our messengers and those who have faith in the present life . . . [306]This remained their attitude,[307] while God's eye looked upon them, until he chose, in accord with their own choice, to lead them from the realm of transitoriness to the realm of eternity, from transitory joy to lasting joy. They were praised in life and mourned when departing for peace and life in the gardens of bliss. Joy is theirs and a good end.'[308] Al-Muʿizz continues by addressing reproaches, warnings and threats to al-Ḥasan.

The letter as a whole clearly displays its essentially political purpose. It does not reveal any secrets, but rather the opponent is to be frightened with arguments that are to make the strongest impressions on him. The whole doctrine of the Qarmaṭīs was dominated by the idea of the Mahdi who commands the world, so al-Muʿizz describes his omnipotence and that of his fathers in glittering colours.[309] Abū Saʿīd and Abū Ṭāhir enjoyed the highest honour as founders of the Qarmaṭī state and of its powerful position, that is why al-Muʿizz tries to impress al-Ḥasan with the reproach that he has betrayed the faith of his fathers. The latter, however, owed their success exclusively to the favour of the Fatimids, and dire punishment was in store for al-Ḥasan.

If Abū Saʿīd and Abū Ṭāhir had really been such loyal followers of the Fatimids, why does al-Muʿizz try to prove this in so many vague words? He surely cannot suppose that al-Ḥasan does not know of their deeds, writings and poems, his questions here are quite rhetorical. On the other hand, the reference to their works clearly implies that they contained clear proof of Abū Saʿīd's and Abū Ṭāhir's loyalty. But the ancient chroniclers and polemicists who were sometimes quite well informed about the internal affairs of the Qarmaṭīs, had no concrete information to offer on this subject,[310] whereas they mention the expected Mahdi time and again in their reports. So it seems that al-Muʿizz was doing what many observers before and after him were tempted to do. He applied Abū Saʿīd's and his son's speeches and prophecies about the Mahdi to the Fatimids. Only, he was no doubt aware of his falsifying strategy.

This move is not so nonsensical as it might appear at first sight. The Qarmaṭī doctrine had insisted from its beginning that the coming of the expected one was imminent. It was even believed that the exact date for it could be read in the stars. This conviction was so firm that it had led to the fiasco with the Iṣfahānī which had shaken the order of the state in Baḥrayn to its foundations. Even now the hope of the Qarmaṭīs must have been directed towards the fulfilment of their expectations. Why not win them over to the Fatimid claim? For al-Muʿizz this would have meant an enormous increase in power, which would have brought him near the realization of his most ardent desire, the overthrow of the ʿAbbasid caliphate.[311]

In order to win over the Qarmaṭīs, al-Muʿizz had to avoid giving the lie to their most respected teachers and the founders of their power. So he tried to prove that they had in fact acted in the service of the Fatimids. The course of events shows that he failed.

## NOTES

1 Ibn Kathīr, *al-Bidāya waʾl-nihāya* (Cairo, 1932–1939), vol. 11, p. 346: *yuẓhirūnaʾl-rafḍ wa-yubṭinūnaʾl-kufraʾl-maḥḍ*. In this or a similar form the sentence was later frequently quoted as a standing phrase. See, for instance, Ibn al-Jawzī, *al-Muntaẓam* (Hyderabad, 1357–1362/1938–1943), vol. 5, p. 115, and al-Qazwīnī, *Mufīd al-ʿulūm* (Cairo, 1310/1892), p. 37.

2 M. J. de Goeje, *Mémoire sur les Carmathes du Bahraïn et les Fatimides* (2nd edn, Leiden, 1886), p. 69; henceforth quoted as *Carmathes*.

3 *Carmathes*, pp. 82–83.

4 Ibid., p. 185.

5 Ibid., pp. 194–195.

6 B. Lewis, *The Origins of Ismāʿīlism* (Cambridge, 1940), pp. 76 ff.

7 Thus termed after Muḥammad, a son of ʿAlī, called Ibn al-Ḥanafiyya after his mother.

8 The view that the Qarmaṭīs adhered to a Ḥanafī line of imams and were not Ismaʿilis at all had been proposed by P. Casanova, 'La doctrine secrète des Fatimides d'Egypte', BIFAO, 18 (1921), pp. 121–165.

9 W. Ivanow, 'Ismailis and Qarmatians', JBBRAS, NS, 16 (1940), pp. 43–85.

10 Ibid., p. 81.

11 Ibid., p. 83. This identification had already been suggested by de Goeje, *Carmathes*, p. 21. He considered Aḥmad b. al-Kayyāl, however, as an ancestor of the Fatimids.

12 *Carmathes*, pp. 82–83. In his *Brief Survey of the Evolution of Ismailism*, (Leiden, 1952), p. 10, Ivanow suggested, however, that the Qarmaṭīs who expected the return of Muḥammad b. Ismāʿīl perhaps honoured the Fatimids as his direct and genuine descendants. Perhaps they wished, Ivanow conjectured, to give them a special place in their own sect, but the repudiation of this undesired honour by the Fatimids offended the Qarmaṭīs and called forth their enmity and revenge.

13 Ḥasan Ibrāhīm Ḥasan and Ṭāhā Aḥmad Sharaf, *ʿUbayd Allāh al-Mahdī* (Cairo, 1947).

14 Kaysāniyya was the name given to the followers of Muḥammad b. al-Ḥanafiyya after one of their leaders in Kūfa.

15 Ḥasan and Sharaf, *ʿUbayd Allāh*, p. 26.

16 Ibid., pp. 93 ff.

17 The *Ṣāḥib al-Nāqa* in the presentation of L. Massignon, *La Passion d'al-Hosayn-Ibn-Mansour al-Hallaj* (Paris, 1922), vol. 2, pp. 734–735, and his 'Ḳarmaṭians', EI, vol. 2, pp. 767–772. He may be identical with Abū Muḥammad, brother of the caliph al-Mahdī, as suggested by H. Halm, 'Die Söhne Zikrawaihs und das erste fatimidische Kalifat (290/903)', WO, 10 (1979), pp. 32, 36, and his *Das Reich des Mahdi: Der Aufstieg der Fatimiden* (Munich, 1991), pp. 70, 76.

18 Ḥasan and Sharaf, *'Ubayd Allāh*, pp. 110–111.

19 Ibid., pp. 210 ff.

20 Ibid., p. 214. See also B. Carra de Vaux, 'al-Djannābī', EI, vol. 1, p. 1016.

21 For a new study of their history, valuable material would be available in al-Maqrīzī's *Itti'āẓ*, al-Mas'ūdī's *Tanbīh*, and in al-Nuwayrī's account which had been only partly translated by de Sacy.

22 The two available accounts go back to al-Ṭabarī and Akhū Muḥsin, who is probably using Ibn Rizām here as his source. See *Carmathes*, pp. 16–17.

23 Al-Ṭabarī, *Ta'rīkh al-rusul wa'l-mulūk*, ed. M. J. de Goeje et al. (Leiden, 1879–1901), III, p. 2128.

24 Ibn al-Nadīm, *Kitāb al-fihrist* (Cairo, 1348/1929–1930), p. 265. The date of the conversion is given there as the year 261/874–875.

25 Al-Maqrīzī, *Itti'āẓ al-ḥunafā'*, ed. H. Bunz (Leipzig, 1909), pp. 13, 114.

26 Ibn Ḥawqal, *Kitāb ṣūrat al-arḍ*, ed. J. H. Kramers (2nd edn, Leiden, 1938–1939), p. 295.

27 See S. M. Stern, "Abdān', EI2, vol. 1, pp. 95–96. The Fatimid Isma'ili author Ja'far b. Manṣūr al-Yaman discusses his doctrine; see Zāhid 'Alī, *Ta'rīkh-i Fāṭimiyyīn-i Miṣr* (Hyderabad, 1367/1948), p. 436 n. 3. Al-Qāḍī al-Nu'mān quotes with approval from a book of 'Abdān entitled *al-Ibtidā'* in his *al-Risāla al-mudhhiba*, in *Khams rasā'il Ismā'īliyya*, ed. 'Ā. Tāmir (Salamiyya, 1956), p. 41. Zāhid 'Alī quotes in his *Hamārē Ismā'īlī madhhab kī ḥaqīqat awr us kā niẓām* (Hyderabad, 1373/1954), pp. 548 and 615, a *Kitāb al-rusūm wa'l-izdiwāj* in his possession, which is ascribed to Abū Muḥammad 'Abdān. Ibn al-Nadīm does not name it among 'Abdān's works. A heresiographer of the 6th/12th century, however, enumerates a *Kitāb al-izdiwāj*, without mentioning its author, among the Isma'ili books read by himself; see *Kitāb al-kashf*, ed. R. Strothmann (London, etc., 1952), introduction p. *Ḥā'*. The Syrian Nizārī Isma'ili Shihāb al-Dīn Abū Firās (d. 937/1530) mentions in his *Risālat maṭāli' al-shumūs*, in *Arba' rasā'il Ismā'īliyya*, ed. 'Ā. Tāmir (Salamiyya, 1952), p. 52, 'Abdān's *Kitāb al-mīzān* among his sources. This work may be identical with the *Kitāb al-mīdān* mentioned by Ibn al-Nadīm, *al-Fihrist*, p. 267, where the title should probably be read *Kitāb al-mīzān*. Most of the books attributed to 'Abdān, however, were, as stated by Ibn al-Nadīm himself, later forgeries. His nephew 'Īsā b. Mūsā in particular is said to have been active in this regard. He composed numerous works and ascribed them to 'Abdān in order to create the impression that he was a scholar in all branches of philosophy and other sciences and was endowed with the gift of predicting future events. See Akhū Muḥsin in al-Nuwayrī, *Nihāyat al-arab*, vol. 25, ed. M. J. 'A. al-Ḥīnī and 'A. al-Ahwānī (Cairo, 1984), pp. 295–296, and al-Maqrīzī, *Itti'āẓ*, p. 130.

28 According to Ibn Mālik, *Kashf asrār al-Bāṭiniyya wa-akhbār al-Qarāmiṭa* (Cairo, 1357/1939), p. 18, he was killed in Baghdad. Ibn Mālik does not mention a date. According to Ibn Ḥawqal (p. 96), however, Ḥamdān Qarmaṭ survived and was later known under the *kunya* Abū 'Alī. This would imply that after initially defecting together with 'Abdān, he rejoined the Fatimid camp and was moved to Fusṭāṭ in Egypt from where he maintained the links between the headquarters of the movement in Salamiyya and the Isma'ili missionaries in the Yemen and the Maghrib. His son Abu'l-Ḥasan later became chief of the Fatimid treasury in the Maghrib. Ibn Ḥawqal knew Abu'l-Ḥasan personally. His information may well be reliable.

29 Silvestre de Sacy, *Exposé de la religion des Druzes* (Paris, 1838), vol. 1, introduction pp. 193 ff., and al-Maqrīzī, *Itti'āẓ*, pp. 114 ff.

30 *Carmathes*, p. 59.
31 This date refers directly only to the assassination of ʿAbdān. The account does not suggest, however, that a long time had passed since the defection. This is confirmed by the statement of Ibn Ḥawqal quoted below that Abū Saʿīd still served the Fatimids at the beginning of his career in Baḥrayn (not before 281/894; *Carmathes*, p. 34). The suggestion of Zāhid ʿAlī, *Taʾrīkh*, p. 436, that Ḥamdān since 268/August 881–July 882 was spreading a new doctrine, is thus hardly justified.
32 *Carmathes*, p. 67. By contrast, see Stern, "ʿAbdān', in EI2.
33 *Istitār al-imām*, ed. W. Ivanow, in *Majallat Kulliyyat al-Ādāb*, 4 (1936), p. 96.
34 W. Ivanow, *Ismaili Tradition Concerning the Rise of the Fatimids* (London, etc., 1942), p. 78.
35 Lewis, *Origins*, pp. 77–78.
36 Ibn Ḥawqal, p. 295. That Ibn Ḥawqal here calls the Fatimid 'the one residing in the Maghrib' (*al-muqīm biʾl-Maghrib*) is an anticipation without significance.
37 Ibn Ḥawqal, p. 295.
38 Al-Maqrīzī, *Ittiʿāẓ*, p. 107.
39 Cited in Lewis, *Origins*, p. 78. Abū Saʿīd had been converted to the doctrine at an earlier date. The contradictory information about the beginnings of his career is summed up by Lewis. See further the article 'Abū Saʿīd Jannābī' in EIR, vol. 1, pp. 380–381.
40 *Carmathes*, p. 69.
41 Ibn Ḥawqal, p. 295.
42 See note 36 above.
43 Listed in Lewis, *Origins*, pp. 77–78; see also al-Masʿūdī, *Kitāb al-tanbīh waʾl-ishrāf*, ed. M. J. de Goeje (Leiden, 1894), pp. 384, 392.
44 Al-Ṭabarī, III, pp. 2128–2129.
45 *Wa-kāna fīmā ḥakaw ʿan hāʾulāʾiʾl-Qarāmiṭa.* Casanova, 'La doctrine secrète', p. 151, considered this report as part of the statements made by the brother-in-law of Zikrawayh captured in 294/906. These statements were transmitted to al-Ṭabarī by a companion (*baʿḍ aṣḥābinā*) who is mentioned as his informant on pp. 2127 and 2130. The present text, however, belongs to a different tradition as is evident from the indefinite plural. It may refer back to the anonymous Kūfans mentioned on p. 2127.
46 The camel of the prophet Ṣāliḥ, Qurʾan, VII:73–79, is meant. See de Sacy, *Exposé*, vol. 1, introduction p. 177 n. 1.
47 The beast which God will send forth from the earth at the end of time according to the Qurʾan, XXVII:82, is meant here. See de Sacy, ibid.
48 Say: The new moons are fixed times for mankind (see Qurʾan, II:189). Their exterior is that the number of years may be recognized, the calculation, the months, and the days. Their inner meaning is My helpers who guide My servants on My path.
49 Casanova, 'La doctrine secrète', p. 151.
50 See C. van Arendonk, 'Kaisānīya', EI, vol. 2, pp. 658–659.
51 In Qurʾan, LXI:6, Muḥammad is meant.
52 There does not seem to be evidence of any group fixing the number of prophets at seven before the Ismaʿilis, certainly not with the same names. The speculations about the number seven presumably started in respect to the imamate, the central idea of the Shiʿis. Ismāʿīl b. Jaʿfar, or his son, Muḥammad b. Ismāʿīl, was the seventh imam and thus entitled to the highest rank. A son of Muḥammad b. al-Ḥanafiyya could not claim that for himself.

53 Ibn Khaldūn, *Kitāb al-ʿibar* (Cairo, 1289/1872), vol. 4, p. 84, vol. 3, p. 336. See G. Weil, *Geschichte der Chalifen* (Mannheim, 1846–1862), vol. 2, p. 495 n. 4. The statement of Ibn al-ʿIbrī in his Syriac chronicle that the first missionary of the Qarmaṭīs in Kūfa was the author of the book (ibid.; de Sacy, *Exposé*, vol. 1, introduction p. 177 n. 1) is obviously worthless.

54 This seems all the more likely since Zikrawayh is also identical with the founder of the Qarmaṭī sect in Iraq in his account. Here the first missionary, who converted Ḥamdān Qarmaṭ, Qarmaṭ himself, and Zikrawayh are all fused as a single person. The explanation that Zikrawayh was meant in the book of the Qarmaṭīs was then quite natural since al-Ṭabarī before and afterwards named Zikrawayh's brother-in-law as the source of his information about the Qarmaṭīs. But where did Ibn Khaldūn find the name al-Qāshānī? According to his account (*al-ʿIbar*, vol. 2, p. 336), this al-Faraj b. Yaḥyā, i.e., Zikrawayh, was also the one who negotiated with the *Ṣāḥib al-Zanj*. Al-Ṭabarī (III, p. 2130) rather names Ḥamdān Qarmaṭ. The brother-in-law of Zikrawayh was merely the transmitter. According to Akhū Muḥsin, however, it was the father of Zikrawayh who conducted these negotiations. He is said to have already proclaimed doctrines of his own; see al-Maqrīzī, *Ittiʿāẓ*, p. 107.

55 Lewis, *Origins*, pp. 73–74; Ivanow, *Rise*, pp. 87 ff.; Ḥasan and Sharaf, *ʿUbayd Allāh*, pp. 98 ff. See now further Halm, 'Die Söhne Zikrawaihs', pp. 30–53, who suggests that the sons of Zikrawayh did not claim descent from Muḥammad b. Ismāʿīl for themselves but were in fact proclaiming ʿUbayd Allāh as the Mahdi.

56 Thus Ḥasan and Sharaf, *ʿUbayd Allāh*, p. 26.

57 Lewis, *Origins*, p. 78; ʿAbd al-Jabbār, *Tathbīt dalāʾil al-nubuwwa*, ed. ʿAbd al-Karīm ʿUthmān (Beirut, 1966–1968), p. 379.

58 See S. Moscati, 'Il testamento di Abū Hāšim', *Rivista degli Studi Orientali*, 27 (1952), pp. 28 ff.

59 Lewis, *Origins*, p. 79.

60 ʿAbd al-Jabbār, *Tathbīt*, p. 379, and Lewis, *Origins*, p. 78.

61 Al-Maqrīzī, *Ittiʿāẓ*, pp. 106, 114.

62 This statement should now be modified in the light of the discussion of Halm, 'Die Söhne Zikrawaihs'.

63 Al-Nawbakhtī, *Firaq al-Shīʿa*, ed. H. Ritter (Istanbul, 1931), p. 61.

64 Ivanow, 'Ismailis and Qarmatians', p. 79.

65 Ibid., p. 81.

66 Ivanow evidently does not do so since he ('Ismailis and Qarmatians', p. 84) considers it possible that Idrīs simply took the name of the apostate from al-Shahrastānī. In reality, he suggests, perhaps ʿAbd Allāh b. Maymūn al-Qaddāḥ was meant.

67 He is presumably identical with the Qarmaṭawayh (Qarmaṭōē) mentioned by al-Nawbakhtī.

68 Al-Shahrastānī, *al-Milal waʾl-niḥal*, in the margin of Ibn Ḥazm, *al-Fiṣal* (Cairo, 1317–1321/1899–1903), vol. 2, p. 17.

69 Ibid., vol. 2, pp. 17–21.

70 So at least he himself claimed. He may be the brother of the Ismaʿili chief missionary and *qāḍī* in the Yemen, Lamak b. Mālik, as suggested by Fuʾād Sayyid; see al-Jaʿdī, *Ṭabaqāt fuqahāʾ al-Yaman*, ed. Fuʾād Sayyid (Cairo, 1957), p. 234 n. 3.

71 Ibn Mālik, *Kashf*, p. 33; see also p. 20: Abū Saʿīd asserted that he was the Mahdi who acts in accordance with the religion of God (*al-Mahdī al-qāʾim bi-dīn Allāh*). See

al-Jawbarī in *Carmathes*, p. 208: *iddaʿāʾl-nubuwwa.*

72 *Carmathes*, pp. 57–58.

73 Ibid., p. 69.

74 ʿArīb b. Saʿd, *Ṣilat taʾrīkh al-Ṭabarī*, ed. M. J. de Goeje (Leiden, 1897), p. 38.

75 Ibn Miskawayh, *Tajārib al-umam* (Cairo, 1914–1916), vol. 1, pp. 33–34.

76 Al-Hamadhānī, *Takmilat taʾrīkh al-Ṭabarī*, ed. A. Y. Kanʿān, in *al-Mashriq*, 51 (1955), p. 41.

77 Ibn al-Athīr, *al-Kāmil fīʾl-taʾrīkh*, ed. C. J. Tornberg (Leiden, 1851–1876), vol. 8, p. 49.

78 Al-Ṭabarī, *III*, p. 2287.

79 Al-Hamadhānī reports the event only under the year 301/913–914.

80 Al-Masʿūdī, *al-Tanbīh*, p. 394. Al-Jawbarī ( in *Carmathes*, p. 208) and ʿAbd al-Jabbār (*Tathbīt*, p. 397) also give the date as the year 300, and other sources mention 301 AH. The fact that the news reached Baghdad only at the end of the year 301/middle of 914 speaks against the early date (see *Carmathes*, p. 70). Perhaps the death was at first kept secret by the Qarmaṭīs. According to al-Masʿūdī, Abū Saʿīd was assassinated by two slaves whom he had captured in war against Badr al-Maḥallī and taken into his service. According to Akhū Muḥsin (in al-Maqrīzī, *Ittiʿāẓ*, p. 112) and ʿAbd al-Jabbār, the murderer had once been a servant of Abu'l-Faḍl al-Ghanawī. All this information does not speak for the assumption that ʿUbayd Allāh had a hand in the matter.

81 According to Ibn ʿIdhārī, *al-Bayān al-mughrib*, ed. G. S. Colin and E. Lévi-Provençal (New edn, Leiden, 1948–1951), vol. 1, p. 169, Abu'l-Qāsim left Raqqāda on Sunday 2 Jumādā I 300/13 December 912. The conversion of the Hijra dates will be based on the tables of Wüstenfeld-Mahler. Wherever the day of the week is mentioned, the dates of the Christian era have been, when necessary, adjusted. Usually the Hijra date was one or two, and occasionally up to four, days earlier than indicated by the tables. It is, thus, likely that the Christian dates in the cases where the day of the week is not specified should frequently also be moved back one or two days.

82 Ibn ʿIdhārī, *al-Bayān*, vol. 1, p. 169. The identity of the leader about whose defeat the ʿAbbasid governor of Barqa sent a report to Baghdad in this year (al-Ṭabarī, III, p. 2288) is unknown. The governor was, no doubt, Abu'l-Nimr Aḥmad b. Ṣāliḥ who had been sent by Tekin, the governor of Egypt, to Barqa with a strong army and reached Surt further west; see al-Kindī, *Kitāb al-wulāt wa-kitāb al-quḍāt*, ed. R. Guest (Leiden–London, 1912), p. 268. Perhaps the Fatimid contingent moved, after the conquest of Tripoli, further east. It was, however, hardly an attempt to reach Egypt.

83 Idrīs ʿImād al-Dīn, *Taʾrīkh al-khulafāʾ al-Fāṭimiyyīn bīʾl-Maghrib* (= *ʿUyūn al-akhbār*, vol. 5 and part of vol. 6), ed. M. al-Yaʿlāwī (Beirut, 1985), p. 193.

84 Idrīs, *Taʾrīkh*, p. 194.

85 Idrīs, *Taʾrīkh*, p. 195. According to al-Kindī, *Wulāt*, p. 269, Alexandria was taken already on Saturday 8 Muḥarram 302/31 July 914.

86 Idrīs, *Taʾrīkh*, p. 195.

87 Ibn Kathīr, *al-Bidāya*, vol. 11, p. 122, reports that the Mecca pilgrims of the year 302/915 were attacked and pillaged by Arabs and a group of Qarmaṭīs. According to Ibn al-Jawzī, *al-Muntaẓam*, vol. 6, p. 128, whose report is probably Ibn Kathīr's source, and ʿArīb (p. 54) the rebels were an ʿAlid and the sons of Ṣāliḥ b. Mudrik of the tribe of Ṭayyiʾ. The Qarmaṭīs of Baḥrayn were certainly not involved; see de Goeje, *Carmathes*, p. 76. Ṣāliḥ b. Mudrik had in Muḥarram 286/February 899 pillaged

the caravan of pilgrims returning from Mecca. At the end of the same year, January 900, he was captured during a new attack on the pilgrim caravan and was killed (al-Ṭabarī, *III*, pp. 2191–2192).

88 Ibn Khaldūn, *al-ʿIbar*, vol. 4, p. 89.

89 For *thamānīn* read *thalāthmiʾa*.

90 *Carmathes*, p. 78. De Goeje expressed some reservations since Abū Ṭāhir did not attempt to move to Egypt and since Muʾnis, according to ʿArīb, left Baghdad only in Ramaḍān 307/February 920.

91 Ḥasan and Sharaf, *ʿUbayd Allāh*, pp. 186 ff.

92 Ibn ʿIdhārī, *al-Bayān*, vol. 1, p. 173.

93 Ibid., vol. 1, p. 175.

94 Al-Kindī, *Wulāt*, p. 274.

95 After the defection of al-Muʿizz b. Bādīs under the Fatimid al-Mustanṣir, Jabbāra b. Mukhtār al-ʿArabī, governor of Barqa, submitted to the former in the year 443/1051–1052 and had the Fatimids cursed (Ibn ʿIdhārī, *al-Bayān*, vol. 1, p. 288).

96 Ibn ʿIdhārī, *al-Bayān*, vol. 1, p. 181.

97 Al-Kindī, *Wulāt*, p. 275, and al-Maqrīzī, *al-Khiṭaṭ* (Būlāq, 1270/1853–1854), vol. 1, p. 328. According to Ibn al-Athīr (vol. 8, p. 83), Abu'l-Qāsim arrived in Alexandria in Rabīʿ II 307/September 919. F. Wüstenfeld, *Die Statthalter von Ägypten zur Zeit der Chalifen* (Göttingen, 1875–1876), vol. 4, p. 14, is to be corrected here.

98 ʿArīb, *Ṣila*, p. 79.

99 ʿArīb, *Ṣila*, p. 80, but al-Kindī, *Wulāt*, p. 277, gives 5 Muḥarram, likewise as a Thursday.

100 Ibn ʿIdhārī, *al-Bayān*, vol. 1, p. 182; ʿArīb, *Ṣila*, p. 80, and al-Kindī, *Wulāt*, p. 277.

101 ʿArīb, *Ṣila*, p. 80.

102 Al-Kindī, *Wulāt*, p. 278.

103 Ibn ʿIdhārī, *al-Bayān*, vol. 1, p. 185.

104 This has been pointed out already by H. Bowen, *The Life and Times of ʿAlī Ibn ʿĪsā* (Cambridge, 1928), p. 205.

105 Al-Masʿūdī, *al-Tanbīh*, pp. 380, 391.

106 Cited in al-Maqrīzī, *Ittiʿāẓ*, p. 124.

107 ʿAbd al-Jabbār, *Tathbīt*, p. 381.

108 Al-Maqrīzī, *Ittiʿāẓ*, p. 124, erroneously mentions 310/922.

109 Ibn Miskawayh, *Tajārib*, vol. 1, p. 109.

110 See de Goeje, *Carmathes*, p. 79; and, similarly, ʿAbd al-Jabbār, *Tathbīt*, p. 381. According to him the Shiʿis wrote to the sons of Abū Saʿīd from Baghdad and asked them to make war on the caliph. They answered, however, that ʿAlī b. ʿĪsā was a good man and that they did not want to stand up against him. When al-Muqtadir deposed ʿAlī b. ʿĪsā, the Shiʿis sent the news with carrier pigeons to Baḥrayn. Bowen, *ʿAlī Ibn ʿĪsā*, p. 206, rightly points out, however, that any connection between the dismissal of ʿAlī b. ʿĪsā and the attack of the Qarmaṭīs on Baṣra is highly unlikely because of the shortness of the interval.

111 Ibn al-Jawzī, *al-Muntaẓam*, vol. 6, p. 153. Bowen, *ʿAlī Ibn ʿĪsā*, p. 205, mentions Sibṭ Ibn al-Jawzī. The latter presumably took the report from his grandfather's work.

112 ʿArīb, *Ṣila*, p. 110, and Ibn Miskawayh, *Tajārib*, vol. 1, p. 85. Ibn al-Jawzī himself mentions the events in this year once more (*al-Muntaẓam*, vol. 6, p. 173).

113 ʿArīb, *Ṣila*, p. 110.

114 Ibn Miskawayh, *Tajārib*, vol. 1, p. 109, and Ibn al-Athīr, vol. 8, p. 105.

115 Abū'l-Maḥāsin b. Taghrībirdī, *al-Nujūm al-ẓāhira*, ed. T. G. J. Juynboll and B. F. Matthes (Leiden, 1855–1861), vol. 2, p. 207. He probably took the report from al-Dhahabī, *Ta'rīkh al-Islām*, one of his main sources. Al-Dhahabī on his part is dependent on Ibn al-Jawzī. Ibn Kathīr, *al-Bidāya*, vol. 11, p. 130, quoted the report together with the information about the dismissal of Ḥāmid and the third vizierate of Ibn al-Furāt from Ibn al-Jawzī.

116 It is also uncertain whether Abū Ṭāhir was at that time already the leader of the Qarmaṭīs. Al-Mas'ūdī, *al-Tanbīh*, p. 391, mentions as his birth date Ramaḍān 294/June–July 907. This agrees with the common statement in the sources (de Goeje, *Carmathes*, pp. 73–74) that Abū Ṭāhir was seventeen years old at the time of his attack on the pilgrim caravan returning from Mecca at the beginning of the year 312/April 924. Al-Mas'ūdī goes on to state that Abū Ṭāhir took over the command of the army in Ramaḍān 310/23 December 922–21 January 923. Akhū Muḥsin, in contrast, reports, as cited in al-Maqrīzī, *Itti'āẓ*, p. 112, that Abū Ṭāhir acceded to the rule in the year 305/June 917–June 918.

117 Ibn 'Idhārī, *al-Bayān*, vol. 1, p. 187.

118 Ibid., vol. 1, p. 188.

119 Ibid., vol. 1, p. 190.

120 De Goeje, *Carmathes*, p. 78.

121 In the year 316/928, while Abu'l-Qāsim was occupied with his troops in the west, the Fatimid governor of Barqa, Faḥl b. Nūḥ al-Lahīṣī, moved to Dhāt al-Ḥumām and defeated the Egyptians under Abu'l-Nimr Aḥmad b. Ṣāliḥ. He withdrew, however, immediately; see Idrīs 'Imād al-Dīn, *'Uyūn al-akhbār*, ed. M. Ghālib (Beirut, 1973–1984), vol. 5, p. 150.

122 'Abd al-Jabbār, *Tathbīt*, p. 383.

123 Al-Kindī, *Wulāt*, pp. 281 ff.

124 Ḥasan and Sharaf, *'Ubayd Allāh*, pp. 181 ff. The authors infer from this that the unsuccessful incursion of the Qarmaṭīs in southwestern Persia in the year 321/933 was carried out at the order of 'Ubayd Allāh.

125 For details, see H. Gottschalk, *Die Mādarā'ijjūn* (Berlin–Leipzig, 1931), pp. 93 ff.

126 Al-Kindī, *Wulāt*, p. 287; Ibn Sa'īd, *al-Mughrib fī ḥula'l-Maghrib*, ed. K. C. Tallquist (Leiden, 1899), p. 14.

127 Al-Kindī, *Wulāt*, p. 288.

128 De Goeje, *Carmathes*, p. 139.

129 Ibid., p. 182.

130 *Carmathes*, pp. 138 ff., and Ḥ. I. Ḥasan and Ṭ. A. Sharaf, *al-Mu'izz li-Dīn Allāh* (Cairo, 1367/1948), p. 100.

131 Ibn Miskawayh, *Tajārib*, vol. 2, p. 203; Ibn al-Jawzī, *al-Muntaẓam*, vol. 7, p. 19, and de Goeje, *Carmathes*, p. 180.

132 Al-Maqrīzī, *al-Khiṭaṭ*, vol. 1, p. 329, and de Goeje, *Carmathes*, p. 182. According to the anonymous continuator of Eutychius, *Eutychii Patriarchae Alexandrini Annales*, ed. L. Cheikho et al. (Paris, 1909), vol. 2, p. 293, there was a Qarmaṭī revenge attack on the 'Uqaylid Mulhim (read *li-ṭalab tha'rihi min Mulhim b. Dīnār*) in Ṭabariyya on 15 Rabī' II 353/1 May 964. In the same month, a rising of the Berbers of Alexandria took place. Abu'l-Maḥāsin, *al-Nujūm*, vol. 2, p. 355, reports the same events, probably erroneously, under the year 352/963 and claims that the Berbers were sent by al-Mu'izz. This seems quite unlikely. The Berber rebellion, according to Abu'l-

Maḥāsin, prevented the Egyptians from repelling the Qarmaṭī attack.

133 Ibn Miskawayh, *Tajārib*, vol. 2, p. 215; Ibn al-Athīr, vol. 8, p. 424, and anonymous continuator of Eutychius, *Eutychii Annales*, vol. 2, p. 294. The latter source (vol. 2, p. 295) also mentions an attack of a Fatimid commander (*Ṣāḥib Abī Tamīm Maʿadd*) on the oases of upper Egypt in Ṣafar 355/February 966. This attack is probably the one mentioned also by al-Maqrīzī, *al-Khiṭaṭ*, vol. 2, p. 27, according to whom Kāfūr sent an army which expelled the Maghribīs.

134 Al-Kindī, *Wulāt*, p. 297.

135 Ibn Ẓāfir, in F. Wüstenfeld, *Statthalter*, vol. 4, p. 59, and al-Maqrīzī, *al-Khiṭaṭ*, vol. 2, p. 27.

136 Yaḥyā b. Saʿīd al-Anṭākī, *Kitāb al-dhayl*, ed. I. Kratchkovsky and A. Vasiliev (Paris, 1924–1932), p. 119.

137 Ibn Khallikān, *Wafayāt al-aʿyān* (Cairo, 1310/1892), vol. 2, p. 42.

138 Al-Maqrīzī, *Ittiʿāẓ*, p. 62.

139 Ibid., p. 68.

140 See M. Jamāl al-Dīn Surūr, *al-Nufūdh al-Fāṭimī fī bilād al-Shām wa'l-ʿIrāq* (Cairo, 1957), p. 17.

141 Al-Maqrīzī, *Ittiʿāẓ*, pp. 75–76.

142 Ibn Ḥammād, *Akhbār mulūk Banī ʿUbayd*, ed. M. Vonderheyden (Algiers–Paris, 1927), p. 42.

143 Al-Maqrīzī, *Ittiʿāẓ*, pp. 80, 131; *Eutychii Annales*, vol. 2, p. 295; Idrīs, *Ta'rīkh*, p. 694 (presumably based on Ibn Zūlāq's *Sīrat Jawhar*), and Ibn al-Dawādārī, *Kanz al-durar*, vol. 6, ed. Ṣ. al-Munajjid (Cairo, 1961) p. 122. De Goeje was unaware of this renewed invasion of the Qarmaṭīs. It has also been ignored in the more recent studies. The divergence of circumstances and the testimony of the contemporary chronicler Ibn Zūlāq (cited in al-Maqrīzī, *Ittiʿāẓ*, p. 77 l.6 and p. 78 l.12; Idrīs, *Ta'rīkh*, pp. 694–695) show that there is no confusion with the invasion of 357/968. The account of the campaign of Jaʿfar b. Falāḥ inserted by al-Maqrīzī into his report appears to have been taken from an early Syrian chronicle which is quoted again on p. 131. Since these passages do not quite agree with the account of Ibn Zūlāq and Akhū Muḥsin, respectively, they were most likely added by al-Maqrīzī.

The new campaign of the Qarmaṭīs was under the command of Kisrā b. Abi'l-Qāsim (Saʿīd) and Ṣakhr b. Abī Isḥāq (Ibrāhīm), cousins of al-Ḥasan al-Aʿṣam, since the latter was accused of having withheld some of the booty gained during the previous campaign; see Ibn Ḥawqal, p. 26. De Goeje (*Carmathes*, p. 182) identified the two invasions of Syria mentioned by Ibn Ḥawqal with those of 353/964 and 357/968. This is not tenable, since according to the account of Ibn Ẓāfir (in Wüstenfeld, *Statthalter*, vol. 4, p. 61) the campaign of 357/968 was led by al-Aʿṣam. Ibn ʿAsākir likewise states that al-Aʿṣam overcame Syria in the year 357/968 and then returned to Damascus in the year 360/971; see Ibn Manẓūr, *Mukhtaṣar ta'rīkh Dimashq* (Damascus, 1984–1990), vol. 6. p. 133.

144 Jaʿfar set out from Cairo on 18 Muḥarram 359/1 December 969 (al-Maqrīzī, *Ittiʿāẓ*, p. 78). News of the battle reached Jawhar in Egypt in Rabīʿ II/February–March 970 (Idrīs, *Ta'rīkh*, p. 695). Th. Bianquis, *Damas et la Syrie sous la domination Fatimide, 359–468/969–1076* (Damascus, 1986–1989), vol. 1, p. 40, gives the date of the battle as 7 Rabīʿ II/17 February 970 without mentioning a source. The date mentioned by al-Maqrīzī's Syrian source (*Ittiʿāẓ*, p. 81; similarly by Ibn Ẓāfir, in Wüstenfeld,

*Statthalter*, vol. 4, p. 62, and by Ibn al-Dawādārī, *Kanz*, vol. 6, p. 123), namely middle of Rajab 359/end of May 970, is too late.

145 Al-Maqrīzī, *Itti'āz*, p. 78, and Idrīs, *Ta'rīkh*, p. 695.

146 *Ṣāḥib al-Qarāmiṭa*; see al-Maqrīzī, *Itti'āz*, p. 79, and Idrīs, *Ta'rīkh*, p. 695 (Abū Ghazwān).

147 F. Wüstenfeld, *Geschichte der Faṭimiden-Chalifen* (Göttingen, 1881), p. 112, states that al-Ḥasan b. 'Ubayd Allāh after his return to Syria made peace with al-A'ṣam and committed himself to an annual tribute of 100,000 dinars in return for the undisturbed possession of his province. This is hardly correct in this form. Both Hilāl al-Ṣābi' (in Ibn al-Qalānisī, *Dhayl ta'rīkh Dimashq*, ed. H. F. Amedroz, Leiden, 1908, p. 1) and Ibn al-Athīr (vol. 8, p. 452), however, confirm that it was Ibn Ṭughj, i.e., al-Ḥasan b. 'Ubayd Allāh, who committed himself to the tribute. According to Akhū Muḥsin (in al-Maqrīzī, *Itti'āz*, p. 131) it was rather a tribute of the Ikhshīdids which had been paid from Egypt for many years. This version seems less likely in the course of the events.

148 *Carmathes*, p. 187. De Goeje's doubts based on chronological considerations are not cogent. Even if the Qarmaṭīs entered into negotiations with the 'Abbasid government already before the conquest of Damascus by Ja'far b. Falāḥ (end of 359/autumn 970), the situation was clear after the capture of al-Ḥasan b. 'Ubayd Allāh at the latest.

149 Ibn Khaldūn, *al-'Ibar*, vol. 4, pp. 88–91.

150 *Carmathes*, pp. 74, 78, 142, 144, 151, 194.

151 Read Abū Ṭāhir for *wa'l-ẓāhir*.

152 A high council which made the most important political decisions. See de Goeje, *Carmathes*, p. 74.

153 Ibn Khaldūn, *al-'Ibar*, vol. 4, p. 88.

154 *Carmathes*, p. 74, and Ibn al-Jawzī, *al-Muntaẓam*, vol. 7, p. 57.

155 Listed in *Carmathes*, p. 74.

156 'Abd al-Jabbār, for whom he is an important source, seems to have known two works by him, *al-Marātib al-khams*, and *al-Kitāb al-kabīr* (*Tathbīt*, p. 393, the text is ambiguous). Two extracts of several pages' length from his work, without any mention of a title, are extant in Ibn al-Nadīm, *al-Fihrist*, pp. 264–267 and al-Dhahabī, *Ta'rīkh al-Islām*, printed in Ibn Miskawayh, *Tajārib*, vol. 2, pp. 57–60 where he names as his informant a physician called Ibn Ḥamdān who had lived among the Qarmaṭīs in Baḥrayn. For a proper assessment of his work it is essential to recognize that his informants came from the Qarmaṭī circles of Iraq. This is evident from his statements and is only natural since he lived in Kūfa in the centre of the Iraqī Qarmaṭī movement. 'Abd al-Jabbār does in fact report (*Tathbīt*, pp. 392–393) that he mentioned a number of Qarmaṭī leaders who defected from the movement apparently after the disaster with the false prophet of the Qarmaṭīs of Baḥrayn. Among them, there was Abu'l-Ghayt al-'Ijlī who now wrote a book in which he explained that 'their (the Qarmaṭīs') matter had been unclear to him, and he had believed them to be Shi'is and followers of the Mahdi'. On the basis of these quotations it is evident that the common dating of the work of Ibn Rizām to the beginning of the 4th/10th century (I. Goldziher, *Streitschrift des Ġazālī gegen die Bāṭinijja-Sekte*, Leiden, 1916, p. 15; S. M. Stern, "Abd Allāh b. Maymūn', EI2, vol. 1, p. 48) is too early. In the extract of Ibn al-Nadīm he evidently continues his

account to the death of the Fatimid al-Manṣūr (29 Shawwāl 341/18 March 953). The dates of the later Fatimids were presumably added by Ibn al-Nadīm. Al-Mas'ūdī knew Ibn Rizām's refutation of the Qarmaṭīs in the year 345/956 (*al-Tanbīh*, p. 396, also without any mention of a title). L. Massignon's suggestion, in his 'Esquisse d'une bibliographie Qarmaṭe', in *A Volume of Oriental Studies Presented to Edward G. Browne*, ed. T. W. Arnold and R. A. Nicholson (Cambridge, 1922), p. 344, that he is identical with the *nāẓir al-maẓālim* in Baghdad in the year 329/941 mentioned by Hilāl al-Ṣābi', in *Kitāb al-wuzarā'*, ed. H. F. Amedroz (Leiden, 1904), p. 317, is probably erroneous. The *nāẓir al-maẓālim* here is most likely Aḥmad b. 'Alī al-Kūfī. Ibn Rizām's work was extensively used by the Damascene Sharīf Akhū Muḥsin Muḥammad b. 'Alī (d. 398/1008) who had met Ibn Rizām personally; see Ibn al-Dawādārī, *Kanz*, vol. 6, p. 55. Large parts of Akhū Muḥsin's work are preserved by al-Nuwayrī, Ibn al-Dawādārī, and al-Maqrīzī. He mentions the death of 'Aḍud al-Dawla in 372/983 (in al-Maqrīzī, *Itti'āẓ*, p. 15). But he deviates substantially from Ibn Rizām's account on some points; for instance, in respect to the genealogy of the Fatimids. His account is independant of that of Thābit b. Sinān, Ibn al-Athīr's source, even for the later history not covered by Ibn Rizām.

157 Al-Maqrīzī, *Itti'āẓ*, p. 112; Ibn al-Dawādārī, *Kanz*, vol. 6, p. 62; al-Dhahabī, *Ta'rīkh*, quoted in Ibn Miskawayh, *Tajārib*, vol. 2, p. 57 n. 1. The express quote from Ibn Rizām begins in the text of al-Dhahabī only afterwards. The partly literal agreement of the passage preceding it is evidence, however, that it is taken from the same source.

158 See note 116 above.

159 Ibn Ḥawqal, p. 296.

160 Ibn Khaldūn, *al-'Ibar*, vol. 4, p. 89.

161 Translated by Lewis, *Origins*, p. 81. Contrary to Lewis' suggestion, Ibn Rizām and Akhū Muḥsin apparently knew nothing of the letter. Al-Nuwayrī's quotation is from Ibn al-Athīr.

162 De Goeje, *Carmathes*, p. 83.

163 Ibid.

164 A different account of the events is provided by Quṭb al-Dīn al-Nahrawālī, *Die Chroniken der Stadt Mekka*, ed. F. Wüstenfeld (Leipzig, 1857), vol. 3, p. 165. According to him, Abū Ṭāhir gave orders for 'Ubayd Allāh to be mentioned in Mecca in the Friday prayer. When the latter heard this he cursed Abū Ṭāhir in a letter. Abū Ṭāhir then renounced his allegiance to him. This account, whose source is unknown, is less credible than that of Thābit, especially since the naming of 'Ubayd Allāh in the Friday sermon is not mentioned in any of the reports about the Qarmaṭī sacking of Mecca. A fact of such significance would surely have attracted more attention. A defection of Abū Ṭāhir at this time is quite unlikely, as will be seen. No reliability can be attributed to the report of Niẓām al-Mulk, *Siyāsat-nāma*, ed. 'A. Iqbāl (Tehran, 1320/1941), p. 279, according to whom Abū Ṭāhir sent presents to 'Ubayd Allāh after the conquest of Mecca.

165 Abū Ṭāhir is meant here. This is obviously an error for which Ibn Khaldūn, however, had a precedent in Ibn al-Athīr, vol. 8, p. 158. Abū Ṭāhir had died in Ramaḍān 322/May 944.

166 *Carmathes*, p. 145.

167 Al-Nahrawālī, *Chroniken*, vol. 3, p. 166.

168 *Carmathes*, p. 146. Here it would again be necessary to assume a secret order of the

Fatimids which the Qarmaṭīs did not carry out until they had extorted money from the ʿAbbasids. De Goeje rather suggests that al-Manṣūr wanted to win the hearts of the Muslims for himself and his dynasty by his order for the return of the Black Stone.

169 Ibn ʿIdhārī, *al-Bayān*, vol. 1, p. 220. This is presumably how de Goeje understood the passage, and E. Fagnan, *Histoire de l'Afrique et de l'Espagne intitulée: Al-Bayano'l-Mogrib* (Algiers, 1901), vol. 1, p. 320, translated it accordingly. Perhaps *rudda*, the Black Stone was returned, should be read instead of *radda*. The departure of al-Manṣūr would then refer to some campaign to the east. There is, however, no other information about such a campaign.

170 Read thus for *al-ḥkm*. See Ibn Miskawayh, *Tajārib*, vol. 2, p. 126.

171 In reality Bajkam was no longer alive at the time of the accession of al-Mustakfī; see Ibn Miskawayh, *Tajārib*, vol. 2, p. 9.

172 See, for instance, Ibn Miskawayh, *Tajārib*, vol. 2, p. 127; Ibn al-Jawzī, *al-Muntaẓam*, vol.6, p. 367; Ibn al-Athīr, vol. 8, p. 339, and al-Nahrawālī, *Chroniken*, vol. 3, p. 166.

173 This conviction is severely censured above all by ʿAbd al-Jabbār. The 'shameful scandals' (*faḍāʾiḥ*) of the Bāṭiniyya, including the Fatimids, which he constantly uncovers consisted mostly in their grandiose predictions which turned out to be nothing but lies and fraud. They had, however, a disarming answer ready: 'Whenever they were unmasked or their lying became manifest they said: There is a hidden meaning to this (*li-hādhā bāṭin*)'; see ʿAbd al-Jabbār, *Tathbīt*, p. 396.

174 Al-Dhahabī added that they were lying here since according to the Qur'an, VII:27, God does not order abomination (*Taʾrīkh al-Islām*, Ms. Paris 1581, fol. 163r, quoted by Abu'l-Maḥāsin, *al-Nujūm*, vol. 2, p. 238). When Sanbar b. al-Ḥasan b. Sanbar returned the Black Stone to Mecca he is supposed to have said: 'We took it with God's power and we brought it back with God's will.' See al-Maqrīzī, *Ittiʿāẓ*, p. 129, probably Akhū Muḥsin, and similarly al-Musabbiḥī quoted by al-Dhahabī in the footnote to Ibn Miskawayh, *Tajārib*, vol. 2, p. 137.

175 Ibn Khaldūn, *al-ʿIbar*, vol. 4, p. 90.

176 If Ibn Khaldūn meant by this that Aḥmad returned it personally, it is erroneous. That was done by Sanbar b. al-Ḥasan b. Sanbar (al-Maqrīzī, *Ittiʿāẓ*, p. 129), the head of the family which occupied the highest rank in the social order of the Qarmaṭī state after the descendants of Abū Saʿīd al-Jannābī (Ibn Ḥawqal, pp. 25–26).

177 Al-Nahrawālī, *Chroniken*, vol. 3, p. 166. Al-Maqrīzī states in his *al-Muqaffā* (in *Akhbār al-Qarāmiṭa*, ed. Suhayl Zakkār, Damascus, 1400/1980, p. 402) that Abū Ṭāhir was succeeded by his two brothers Abu'l-Qāsim Saʿīd and Abu'l-ʿAbbās (*sic*) Aḥmad.

178 De Goeje, *Carmathes*, pp. 143–144, and Ibn al-Jawzī, *al-Muntaẓam*, vol. 6, p. 336. The reports are not uniform.

179 Ibn al-Athīr, in de Goeje, *Carmathes*, p. 143.

180 Ibn Miskawayh, *Tajārib*, vol. 2, p. 127.

181 Ibn Ḥawqal, pp. 25–26.

182 Ibn al-Jawzī, *al-Muntaẓam*, vol. 7, p. 57.

183 Abū Yaʿqūb died in 366/977 (de Goeje, *Carmathes*, p. 191).

184 On the coins minted at the order of al-Ḥasan al-Aʿṣam in Ramla and Damascus in 361/972 the caliph al-Muṭīʿ and al-Ḥasan himself are named on one side and the 'reigning lords' (*al-sāda al-ruʾasāʾ*), namely, the sons of Abū Saʿīd, on the other. In the following year, the title properly appears in the singular (*al-sayyid al-raʾis*). See

Stanley Lane-Poole, 'Unpublished Arabic Coins from the Collection of the Rev. T. Calvert', *Numismatic Chronicle*, NS, 19 (1879), pp. 74 ff. On a dirham minted in Damascus, al-Ḥasan is also called *al-sayyid*, but this is perhaps an arrogation; see H. Porter, 'Unpublished Coins of the Caliphate', *Numismatic Chronicle*, 5th series, 1 (1921), p. 331.

185 De Goeje, *Carmathes*, p. 186.

186 Ibn Ḥawqal, p. 26; see note 143 above. Whether Aḥmad was still alive seems doubtful.

187 Ibn Ḥawqal, p. 26.

188 Ibid., p. 25.

189 Ibn al-Athīr, vol. 8, p. 443.

190 Al-Maqrīzī, *Itti'āẓ*, pp. 133 ff.

191 Ibid., pp. 133, 138.

192 Ibn Ḥawqal, p. 26.

193 *Carmathes*, p. 194.

194 Al-Muqaddasī, *Aḥsan al-taqāsīm*, ed. M. J. de Goeje (2nd edn, Leiden, 1906), p. 94.

195 De Goeje, *Carmathes*, pp. 192, 194. Ibn al-Qalānisī, *Dhayl*, p. 20, mentions the amount as 30,000 dinars. The leader of the Qarmaṭīs was, however, Ja'far b. Aḥmad b. Abī Sa'īd, not his brother al-Ḥasan al-A'ṣam, as Ibn al-Qalānisī and Ibn al-Athīr (vol. 8, p. 487) state. Al-Ḥasan had died on 23 Rajab 366/17 March 977 in Ramla during the siege of Jawhar (al-Maqrīzī, *al-Muqaffā*, in *Akhbār al-Qarāmiṭa*, p. 405). The tribute is said to have been paid until the death of Ja'far (or al-'Azīz?, the passage is ambiguous; Ibn al-Qalānisī, *Dhayl*, p. 21).

196 Ibn Ḥawqal, pp. 25, 27. De Goeje, *Carmathes*, p. 173, and Lewis, *Origins*, p. 89, also took Ibn Ḥawqal to mean that this amount was sent as tribute to the Fatimid imams. But in this year there was war between the Qarmaṭīs and the Fatimids. To be sure, Ibn Ḥawqal primarily knew and described the situation before the outbreak of the war and the alliance of the Qarmaṭīs with the 'Abbasid caliphate. But the uninhibitedness with which he reports on the use of the fifth suggests that he did not think that anything had changed. De Goeje, however, took this to mean that he was trying to conceal the allegiance of the Qarmaṭīs to the Fatimids. 'Lord of the Time' (*ṣāḥib al-zamān*) was a term mostly used for the expected Mahdi and sometimes more generally for the imam of the age.

197 Concerning the gradual growth of knowledge among Sunni historians of the unity of the Bāṭinī movement, see C. H. Becker, 'Zur Geschichtsschreibung unter den Fatimiden', in *Beiträge zur Geschichte Ägyptens unter dem Islam* (Strassburg, 1902–1903), vol. 1, pp. 3 ff, and Lewis, *Origins*, pp. 3 ff.

198 Al-Mas'ūdī, *al-Tanbīh*, p. 384.

199 Al-Mas'ūdī, *al-Tanbīh*, p. 392. His mention here (l.10) of 'their expectation', no doubt of the Mahdi, perhaps indicates that he meant their original unity, since at least for the followers of the Fatimids this expectation had for the time being been fulfilled with the 'appearance' of 'Ubayd Allāh.

200 Lewis, *Origins*, p. 5. Ibn Miskawayh is independent of Thābit. For the early history, he evidently used the same source as the latter, but usually quoted it more fully. See the juxtaposition in Lewis, *Origins*, pp. 80–81.

201 Lewis, *Origins*, pp. 80–81.

202 In the parallel report of Ibn Miskawayh, *Tajārib*, vol. 1, p. 181, there is no mention that the imam was 'the one residing in the Maghrib' (*al-muqīm bi'l-Maghrib*) as

specified by Thābit.

203 See de Goeje, *Carmathes*, p. 71.

204 Against de Goeje, *Carmathes*, p. 93, see Bowen, *'Alī Ibn 'Īsā*, p. 263. New light is shed on the campaign of Ibn Abi'l-Sāj by the account of Akhū Muḥsin, in al-Maqrīzī, *Itti'āẓ*, p. 126, who is using here a Kūfan source, presumably Ibn Rizām, as is evident from the exact dates for the conquests of Kūfa. He reports that Ibn Abi'l-Sāj was worried about marching through the desert to Baḥrayn with his large army. He therefore relied on a ruse and wrote to Abū Ṭāhir that their aims were the same and that he, Ibn Abi'l-Sāj, would assist him in the conquest of Baghdad. Abū Ṭāhir was deceived by this and set out with all his followers, even women and children. Al-Maqrīzī, on the other hand, reported in his *al-Muqaffā* that Yūsuf b. Abi'l-Sāj sent money to 'Ubayd Allāh and offered him military assistance. 'Ubayd Allāh advised him, however, to exercise restraint for the time being. See Ḥ. I. Ḥasan, *Ta'rīkh al-dawla al-Fāṭimiyya* (Cairo, 1958), p. 70. If this report is reliable, as Ḥ. I. Ḥasan assumes, one would have to conclude from the murder of Ibn Abi'l-Sāj by Abū Ṭāhir that the latter stood in sharp opposition to 'Ubayd Allāh at that time.

205 Lewis, *Origins*, pp. 81–82, and Ibn al-Athīr, vol. 8, p. 469.

206 Ibn Ḥawqal, p. 26.

207 *Carmathes*, p. 81.

208 Ibn Ḥawqal, p. 27.

209 This is presumably how the sentence *wa-umūruhum ka'l-wāqifa fīmā baynahum* is to be understood. *Fīmā baynahum*, among themselves, that is in contrast to the official recognition of the caliphate of the 'Abbasids, whose names were mentioned in the Friday sermons in the towns conquered by them at that time. This placed the Qarmaṭīs obviously also in ideological conflict with the followers of the Fatimids.

210 Against Becker's view (*Beiträge*, vol. 1, p. 5), he is certainly the 'pious Sharīf al-Ḥasanī of Damascus' mentioned by Ibn Ẓāfir (in Wüstenfeld, *Faṭimiden*, p. 3), as is evident from the description of his book. Al-Ḥasanī is to be corrected to al-Ḥusaynī.

211 Translated from the French rendering of de Sacy, *Exposé*, vol. 1, introduction pp. 228–229.

212 Translated from the French of de Sacy, *Exposé*, vol. 1, introduction pp. 137–138.

213 Massignon, 'Esquisse', p. 336, and his 'La legende "de tribus impostoribus" et ses origines Islamiques', *Revue de l'Histoire des Religions*, 82 (1920). See now further S. M. Stern, 'The Book of the Highest Initiation and other anti-Ismā'īlī Travesties', in his *Studies in Early Ismā'īlism* (Jerusalem–Leiden, 1983), pp. 56–83.

214 De Sacy, *Exposé*, vol. 1, introduction pp. 148–164.

215 De Sacy (*Exposé*, vol. 1, introduction p. 153 n. 2) sought to identify these steps with the degrees of initiation related from Akhū Muḥsin previously (in *Exposé*, vol. 1, introduction pp. 74–137). They are, however, different. De Sacy's proposal to read *nine degrees* instead of *seven* (*Exposé*, vol. 1, introduction p. 160) is mistaken.

216 Ibn al-Nadīm, *al-Fihrist*, p. 268.

217 Al-Baghdādī, *al-Farq bayn al-firaq*, ed. M. Z. al-Kawtharī (Cairo, 1948), pp. 177 ff. Whether books of the first six degrees actually existed seems doubtful. There are apparently no quotations from them. Ibn al-Nadīm may have deduced their existence merely from allusions to them in the work itself. The nine degrees named and described by al-Baghdādī differ from those of Akhū Muḥsin and are independent of the *Kitāb al-balāgh*. It is evident even from their names that they are

also fictitious. They were, however, the second major source of the heresiographers. Even al-Ghazālī relied on them in his refutation of the Bāṭiniyya (see Goldziher, *Streitschrift*, introduction pp. 40–41), while he does not mention the *Kitāb al-balāgh*. Nothing is known about the *Kitāb al-dars al-shāfī lī'l-nafs* mentioned by Akhū Muḥsin (cited in de Sacy, *Exposé*, vol. 1, introduction p. 159).

218 Massignon erroneously states (in his 'Esquisse', p. 331 and 'Ḳarmaṭians', EI) that Ibn al-Nadīm ascribes the book to 'Abdān.

219 See Ibn Kathīr, *al-Bidāya*, vol. 11, p. 62. Here as many as sixteen degrees are mentioned, and the title is given as *al-Balāgh al-aʿẓam wa'l-nāmūs al-akbar*. Later (vol. 11, p. 311), the title is, probably more correctly, quoted as *al-Balāgh al-akbar wa'l-nāmūs al-aʿẓam*. Al-Bāqillānī's *Kitāb fī madhāhib al-Qarāmiṭa*, quoted by Ibn Ḥazm, *al-Fiṣal*, vol. 4, p. 22, is presumably identical with his *Kitāb hatk al-astār*, as suggested by M. al-Khuḍayrī and M. Abū Rīda in their edition of al-Bāqillānī's *al-Tamhīd fī'l-radd 'alā'l-mulḥida* (Cairo, 1947), p. 259 n. 3.

220 'Abd al-Jabbār, *Tathbīt*, pp. 359 and 601, where the title is given as *al-Balāgh al-sābiʿ wa'l-nāmūs al-akbar*.

221 Niẓām al-Mulk, *Siyāsat-nāma*, p. 277.

222 Al-Daylamī, *Bayān madhhab al-Bāṭiniyya wa-buṭlānih*, ed. R. Strothmann (Istanbul, 1939), see index.

223 Ibn al-Murtaḍā, *al-Munya wa'l-amal fī sharḥ kitāb al-milal wa'l-niḥal*, ed. M. J. Mashkūr (Beirut, 1399/1979). Ibn al-Murtaḍā's source is al-Ḥākim al-Jushamī (Abū Saʿīd al-Bayhaqī), *Sharḥ 'uyūn al-masā'il*; see Stern, *Studies*, pp. 63–64.

224 Al-Isfarā'inī, *al-Tabṣīr fī'l-dīn*, ed. M. Z. al-Kawtharī (Cairo–Baghdad, 1955), p. 126. Al-Isfarā'inī evidently did not know who was meant by the alleged author 'Ubayd Allāh b. al-Ḥasan al-Qayrawānī.

225 Ibn al-Jawzī, *al-Muntaẓam*, vol. 5, pp. 114–115. The passage was recognized by J. de Somogyi, 'A Treatise on the Qarmaṭians in the Kitāb al-Muntaẓam of Ibn al-Jauzī', *Rivista degli Studi Orientali*, 13 (1932), p. 252 n. 2, as an abridged version of a section of the *Kitāb al-siyāsa*. He erroneously named Akhū Muḥsin as its author.

226 Al-Āmidī, *Abkār al-afkār*, Ms. Berlin Pet. I 233, fol. 280r. After describing the eighth degree and the allegorical exegesis he adds: *wa-hādhā huwa'l-nāmūs al-aʿẓam wa'l-balāgh al-akbar al-ladhī 'alayhi madār iʿtiqādihim*.

227 S. Guyard, 'Le Fetwa d'Ibn Taimiyyah sur les Nosairis', *Journal Asiatique*, 6 série, 18 (1871), text pp. 171–172, translation p. 191: *nihāyat al-balāgh al-akbar wa'l-nāmūs al-aʿẓam*.

228 Ibn Kathīr, *al-Bidāya*, vol. 11, p. 311; while on p. 331 he speaks of Muḥammad b. al-Nuʿmān (d. 389/999), who is made out to be the brother of 'Abd al-'Azīz. Muḥammad composed the *Balāgh* in which he tried to refute al-Bāqillānī. Is the passage corrupt or did such a refutation really exist?

229 Al-Kindī, *Wulāt*, p. 603.

230 Ivanow, *Rise*, p. 142; see also his *A Guide to Ismaili Literature* (London, 1933), pp. 41, 78. The refuted book of al-Buṭḥānī, however, is not his *Siyāsat al-murtaddīn* as suggested by Ivanow, *The Alleged Founder of Ismailism* (Bombay, 1946), p. 3 n. 3. This is rather a short treatise of mystical and paraenetic contents. The correct title is *Siyāsat al-murīdīn*. At the beginning of his *Kitāb ithbāt nubuwwat al-nabī*, al-Buṭḥānī sharply attacks the Bāṭiniyya denouncing them as the most dangerous critics of the miracles of the Prophet and states that he had elsewhere described the contents of their treatise *al-Balāgh al-sābiʿ* or *al-Balāgh al-akbar wa'l-nāmūs al-aʿẓam*; see al-Mu'ayyad

bi'llāh, *Ithbāt nubuwwat al-nabī*, ed. Kh. A. Ibrāhīm al-Ḥājj (Beirut, 1980), p. 13.

231 Becker, *Beiträge*, vol. 1, p. 7; and similarly, Massignon, 'Esquisse', p. 332.

232 See, for instance, al-Baghdādī, *al-Farq*, p. 177, and al-Daylamī, *Bayān*, p. 72.

233 Al-Maqrīzī, *Itti'āẓ*, p. 133. As a defender of the authenticity of the genealogy of the Fatimids, al-Maqrīzī omitted many of the polemical statements of Akhū Muḥsin about them and about the doctrine of the Bāṭiniyya.

234 Cited in al-Maqrīzī, *Itti'āẓ*, p. 133. Ibn al-Jawzī, *al-Muntaẓam*, vol. 6, p. 224, quotes the passage in a longer text which he attributes to al-Tanūkhī. Whether al-Maqrīzī quotes from Ibn al-Jawzī or from another source cannot definitely be established. The small additions in his text may be al-Maqrīzī's own, although he was generally more inclined to abridge his sources. The marginal note earlier in the text (*wa-aqāma . . . al-khalīfa al-'Abbāsī*) is taken from the same source. Al-Tanūkhī was generally conscientious in mentioning his informants. It thus seems likely that these were his own reflections.

235 *Yukhrijūna ilā akābir aṣḥābihim annahum min aṣḥābih*, missing in Ibn al-Jawzī.

236 Abu'l-Maḥāsin, *al-Nujūm*, vol. 2, p. 445.

237 The whole text is a commentary on the heinous crimes of the Qarmaṭīs at their sacking of Mecca. Al-Tanūkhī wants to prove that they were not really Shi'is but rather infidels (*zanādiqa*). Just before the passage quoted by al-Maqrīzī, he mentions as an argument for this thesis that Abū Ṭāhir had been in Kūfa several times but had never visited the grave of 'Alī and that he had passed by Karbalā' without paying a visit to the tomb of al-Ḥusayn. Al-Tanūkhī displayed some sympathies for the Shi'is in his works; see Rouchdi Fakkar, *At-Tanūḫi et son livre: La délivrance après l'angoisse* (Cairo, 1955), pp. 19, 109, and also for the Fatimids. But only infidel heretics could commit acts like those of the Qarmaṭīs. Their claim to represent the Mahdi, by which they compromised honest Shi'is like the Fatimids, seemed an outrageous lie to the cosmopolitan Sunni al-Tanūkhī.

238 A reference to the exchange about the return of the Black Stone mentioned in other sources?

239 According to 'Arīb, *Ṣila*, pp. 162–163, who calls him a Khurāsānī, he was among the prisoners which the Qarmaṭīs carried away on their raid of Qaṣr Ibn Hubayra in 318/931. H. Halm (*Das Reich des Mahdi*, p. 414) suggests that the reference is to the raid of Qaṣr Ibn Hubayra by Ibn Sanbar in 316/928, as reported by Ibn Miskawayh, *Tajārib*, vol. 1, p. 183.

240 Al-Mas'ūdī, *al-Tanbīh*, pp. 391–392.

241 *Carmathes*, pp. 129 ff.

242 *Carmathes*, p. 136. That the Yaḥyā b. al-Mahdī mentioned here is a different person was later recognized by de Goeje himself; see al-Mas'ūdī, *al-Tanbīh*, p. 384 n. u, and de Goeje, 'La fin de l'empire des Carmathes du Bahraïn', *Journal Asiatique*, 9 série, 5 (1895), p. 27.

243 Massignon, 'Ḳarmaṭians', EI, and Lewis, *Origins*, pp. 87 ff. They interpreted the episode as a temporary defection from the Fatimids.

244 Ibn Miskawayh, *Tajārib*, vol. 2, pp. 55–56, and de Goeje quoting *Kitāb al-'uyūn* in his *Carmathes*, pp. 131 ff. It is evident from the detail of these passages that the account is older than the book of Thābit b. Sinān. The latter abridged it and erroneously placed it in the year 326/938. Ibn al-Athīr, vol. 8, pp. 263–264, followed him in this error. For this reason the dating of the episode by de Goeje is still valid against

Bowen, *'Alī Ibn 'Īsā*, p. 358, and the doubts of Lewis, *Origins*, p. 88.

245 When he recognized that his fraud had been uncovered, he is reported to have begged that he be not immediately killed. He said that he would tend their riding animals until his father would appear, from whom he had stolen the sign, and who should judge him. In order to justify the murder of the Iṣfahānī, Ibn Sanbar then told the Qarmaṭīs: 'This young man has come with a lie which he stole from a source of truth (*ma'din ḥaqq*) and with a sign which he used fraudulently. Because of this we believed him.' (Ibn Miskawayh, *Tajārib*, vol. 2, p. 59).

246 Or: The religion of the first Adam (*dīn Ādam al-awwal*). An adamology in which several persons bear that name is not necessarily implied.

247 Ibn Miskawayh, *Tajārib*, vol. 2, p. 57.

248 'Abd al-Jabbār, *Tathbīt*, p. 386, summarized in Lewis, *Origins*, p. 88.

249 Dindān; see Lewis, *Origins*, pp. 69 ff.

250 Lewis, *Origins*, pp. 87–88.

251 'Abd al-Jabbār asserts, on the one hand, that Abū Ṭāhir received his instructions from the Fatimid Abu'l-Qāsim and, on the other, that his followers were predicting the advent of the Mahdi in Baḥrayn. Apart from this inconsistency, nothing in his account points to an allegiance of the Qarmaṭīs of Baḥrayn towards the Fatimid imams.

252 The relevant information, however, certainly came from Qarmaṭī circles. Ibn Rizām merely adapted it to his own polemical purposes; see also S. M. Stern, 'Heterodox Ismā'īlism at the time of al-Mu'izz', BSOAS, 17 (1955), pp. 20–21. Ivanow's suggestion that the Qarmaṭīs wanted to accord the Fatimids, as descendants of Muḥammad b. Ismā'īl, a special rank in their sect, but these gave them the cold shoulder, is quite mistaken. In fact the reverse was the case. The Fatimids could only regret the defection of their former adherents, and al-Mu'izz made every effort to regain their allegiance. They, however, accused the Fatimids of having forged their genealogy.

253 Cited in Ibn al-Nadīm, *al-Fihrist*, p. 267. Contrary to the assumption of Lewis, *Origins*, p. 56, the passage is almost certainly quoted from Ibn Rizām.

254 Al-Bīrūnī, *al-Āthār al-bāqiya*, ed. C.E. Sachau (Leipzig, 1878), p. 213, and al-Baghdādī, *al-Farq*, p. 172. According to his own statement (pp. 211, 213), al-Bīrūnī reported on the Qarmaṭīs in an earlier work entitled *Fī akhbār al-Mubayyiḍa wa'l-Qarāmiṭa*. This work was evidently used by al-Baghdādī who usually does not name his sources. Al-Baghdādī's information about al-Muqanna' and the Mubayyiḍa of Transoxania is probably also taken from there. Al-Bīrūnī was not particularly well informed about the history of the Qarmaṭīs. Thus he erroneously names the Iṣfahānī as Ibn Abī Zakariyyā' al-Ṭamāmī (*Āthār*, p. 213, and al-Baghdādī, *al-Farq*, p. 172). The 18th conjunction of Jupiter and Saturn occurred in the year 296/908. P. Casanova connects the prediction of Dindān with this one and proposes to read 'in the 18th conjunction' there too (*al-thāmin 'ashar* instead of *al-thāmin*); see his 'Une date astronomique dans les Epîtres des Ikhwān as-Ṣafā', *Journal Asiatique*, 11 série, 5 (1915), p. 10. Casanova rightly rejects the emendations proposed by O. Loth and de Goeje.

255 Since when did this Shu'ūbī tendency have a decisive influence on their doctrine? Abū Sa'īd al-Ḥasan b. Bahrām was of Persian origin (al-Maqrīzī, *Itti'āẓ*, p. 107). During his mission in southwest Persia he is said to have expressed strongly anti-Arab sentiments (see de Goeje, *Carmathes*, p. 33). The settled population of

Baḥrayn, formerly a province of the Persian empire, consisted largely of Persians and Jews (*Carmathes*, p. 36). Some of Abū Saʿīd's grandsons bore the names of Persian kings: Sābūr b. Abī Ṭāhir and Kisrā b. Abi'l-Qāsim (Ibn Ḥawqal, p. 26). In spite of this, it is unlikely that Abū Saʿīd and Abū Ṭāhir preached the transfer of the reign to the Persians from the beginning. From the outset of their career they relied on the support of Arab tribes and many of the leading men were of Arab descent (see *Carmathes*, p. 161). Abū Ṭāhir, moreover, could hardly have won the backing of the Qarmaṭī Arab tribes from Iraq for an extreme Shuʿūbī programme. The question rather arises as to what extent some of the relevant statements of the heresiographers are influenced by their endeavour to explain the surprising action of Abū Ṭāhir and to discover his spiritual ancestors for it. This endeavour is quite clear in the case of al-Bīrūnī. He emphasizes that the Qarmaṭīs before the advent of the Iṣfahānī espoused a Bāṭinī doctrine and were counted among the Shiʿa. He refers to an alleged ancient Persian prophecy that 1,500 years after Zoroaster the reign of the Magians would be restored. This corresponded to the end of the year 1242 of the era of Alexander (Ramaḍān 319/September 931). Al-Bīrūnī adds that the Qarmaṭīs hit on the right time, yet the reign was not transferred to the Magians. The Shuʿūbī with his astrological prediction had been equally mistaken. Al-Bīrūnī does not put him directly in connection with the Qarmaṭīs. Al-Baghdādī's vague description of him as 'a man of the Bāṭiniyya' is probably a personal elaboration.

256 Translated by de Goeje, *Carmathes*, pp. 113 ff; see also al-Baghdādī, *al-Farq*, p. 173.

257 Ḥasan and Sharaf, *ʿUbayd Allāh*, p. 230. The authors also see (p. 221) in the letter of Abū Ṭāhir quoted by Ibn Mālik, *Kashf*, pp. 34–35, which they date to around 313/925, an open declaration of his allegiance to ʿUbayd Allāh. Ibn Mālik unfortunately does not mention the source from which he took the letter. He first calls the author of the letter Saʿīd and then Abū Saʿīd, while in the letter itself the author is called Abu'l-Ḥasan (read Ibn al-Ḥasan?). Abū Ṭāhir would seem to be the most likely author. The pun on p. 351 l.10 definitely identifies the addressee as the caliph al-Muqtadir (295–320/908–932). There is, however, no good reason to assume that the vague words 'the expected imam has arisen against you like a lion' refer to ʿUbayd Allāh. The Shuʿūbī tendency in the remark that the imam has no need of the help of the Arabs could rather point to the Iṣfahānī. The year 313/925 seems to be only the earliest possible date of the letter, and it could have been written years later. The extremely insolent tenor rather speaks for a later date, whereas in 312/924 Abū Ṭāhir was still negotiating with the ʿAbbasid government about a surrender of Baṣra and Ahwāz to him (see de Goeje, *Carmathes*, p. 86). But the letter may also have been written before the advent of the Iṣfahānī without any necessity to identify the expected imam with ʿUbayd Allāh. For the Mahdi was imagined to be actually present even if not apparent. The Qarmaṭīs always claimed that they were acting on his order.

258 In another line of the poem, Abū Ṭāhir refers to himself as the one announced in the *sūra al-Zumar* (Qur'an, XXXIX:37, '*wa-man yahdi Allāhu famā lahū min muḍill*'). This should evidently not be interpreted as a claim to be the Mahdi.

259 De Goeje, *Carmathes*, p. 129.

260 Al-Dhahabī, *Ta'rīkh al-Islām*, fol. 56v. Abu'l-Maḥāsin, *al-Nujūm*, vol. 2, p. 239, quoted al-Dhahabī, but omitted these four lines.

261 See *Carmathes*, p. 97, and al-Masʿūdī, *al-Tanbīh*, p. 382.

262 Al-Bīrūnī, *al-Āthār*, p. 213.

263 *Carmathes*, p. 122. Al-Baghdādī, *al-Farq*, p. 173, states explicitly that Jupiter and Saturn were meant by the 'two stars' mentioned in the poem. This would exclude the interpretation of de Goeje, *Carmathes*, p. 123, that Jupiter and the moon were meant. The problem remains how Mars, according to al-Baghdādī's variants rejected by de Goeje as unreasonable, is to enter into conjunction with the two stars. It is evident, however, that al-Bīrūnī saw the line as alluding to the conjunction of the year 316/928.

264 Al-Baghdādī, *al-Farq*, p. 173.

265 'Abd al-Jabbār, *Tathbīt*, pp. 381–382.

266 This is no doubt the correct date of the conquest of Kūfa contrary to the view of Bowen, *'Alī Ibn 'Īsā*, pp. 249 and 250 n. 1. In al-Mas'ūdī, *al-Tanbīh*, p. 281, l.1, the date has to be read twice as 312.

267 Al-Mas'ūdī, *al-Tanbīh*, p. 385.

268 Ibn al-Jawzī, *al-Muntaẓam*, vol. 6, p. 216. Al-Dhahabī (in Ibn Miskawayh, *Tajārib*, vol. 1, p. 183), Abu'l-Maḥāsin, *al-Nujūm*, vol. 2, p. 232, and Ibn Kathīr, *al-Bidāya*, vol. 11, p. 157, are probably all dependent on him.

269 *Dār al-hijra*. De Goeje, *Carmathes*, p. 130, ignored the religious significance in suggesting that the term signified for the Qarmaṭīs merely the residence of the missionary and in arguing on that basis that the report about Abū Ṭāhir building a *dār al-hijra* as late as 316/928 must be mistaken. Medina, the *dār al-hijra* of Muḥammad, was the place of foundation of Islam. Similarly, for the Isma'ilis the *dār al-hijra* was the residence of the Mahdi and the place of foundation of his religion. The Isma'ilis attributed great significance to the well-known *ḥadīth* which Shi'is attributed to the Imam Ja'far: 'Islam began as a stranger (*gharīban*, meaning in Medina), it will return as a stranger as it began. Good tidings therefore to the strangers.' According to al-Nawbakhtī, *Firaq al-Shī'a*, pp. 62–63, the Qarmaṭīs founded their thesis of the abrogation of Islam by the religion of the Mahdi on this. The abrogation of Islam was the background of the removal of the Black Stone a year later.

270 *Da'ā ila'l-mahdī*. Abu'l-Maḥāsin: *al-mahdi'l-'Alawī*. De Goeje, *Carmathes*, p. 82 n. 2, interpreted this as referring to 'Ubayd Allāh (similarly, Weil, *Geschichte der Chalifen*, vol. 2, p. 611). Ibn Kathīr, who quotes Ibn al-Jawzī almost literally, adds as an explanation: 'who was in the Maghrib in the town of al-Mahdiyya'. Time and again the later historiographers sought to identify the Mahdi of the Qarmaṭīs in this manner. Another example is evidently Abu'l-Maḥāsin's statement, *al-Nujūm*, vol. 2, p. 238: 'Abū Ṭāhir . . . claimed that he was the missionary of the Mahdi 'Ubayd Allāh.' Yet the contemporary chroniclers and polemicists would certainly have given prominence to any public confession of Abū Ṭāhir that he was a follower of the Fatimids.

271 Thus the name in al-Mas'ūdī, *al-Tanbīh*, p. 391, and in 'Abd al-Jabbār, *Tathbīt*, p. 383. Al-Nafaliyya and al-Naqaliyya in the other sources (*Carmathes*, p. 99) must be corrected. Al-Mas'ūdī stresses that it was a religious name. The origin of the name is explained by Akhū Muḥsin (see 'Baḳliyya', in EI2). He reports that in 295/908 a certain Abū Ḥātim al-Zuṭṭī visited the followers of al-Būrānī, a missionary of 'Abdān in Ṭassūj al-Tustar (al-Maqrīzī, *Itti'āẓ*, p. 104), and taught them things 'which are accepted only by an idiot'. He forbade them to eat garlic, onions, leeks

and radishes, and to shed the blood of any animal. They were called Baqliyya (al-Maqrīzī, *Itti'āẓ*, p. 124; de Sacy, *Exposé*, vol. 1, introduction p. 210). Akhū Muḥsin adds that Abū Ḥātim stayed only one year with them. Thereafter, discord prevailed among them. It is thus uncertain whether the rebels of the year 316/928 still held on to his teaching. Perhaps only the name remained.

272 See al-Maqrīzī, *Itti'āẓ*, p. 130, and al-Mas'ūdī, *al-Tanbīh*, p. 391. The chronology of the report and of de Goeje, *Carmathes*, p. 99, must be corrected on this basis.

273 Al-Maqrīzī, *Itti'āẓ*, p. 130, and Ibn al-Athīr, vol. 8, p. 136. The eschatological character of the movement is reflected in the statement of 'Abd al-Jabbār, *Tathbīt*, p. 383: 'They said: The truth has appeared, the Mahdi has risen, the reign of the 'Abbasids, the scholars of the law, the readers of the Qur'an, and the traditionists has come to an end . . . Nothing remains to be expected, and we have not come to establish a reign, but to abolish a law.'

274 Ibn al-Athīr, vol. 8, p. 136: *wa-kānū yad'ūna ilā'l-mahdī*. De Goeje supplies 'Ubayd Allāh (*Carmathes*, p. 99). Similarly, Ibn Kathīr, *al-Bidāya*, vol. 11, p. 158, quoting the passage from Ibn al-Athīr, adds: 'who appeared in the Maghrib, the ancestor of the Fatimids'.

275 *Carmathes*, p. 99, and, likewise, Weil, *Geschichte*, vol. 2, p. 611. Since 'Īsā b. Mūsā, 'Abdān's nephew, was among the rebels, de Goeje suggested that the defection of 'Abdān was a personal affair.

276 Al-Maqrīzī, *Itti'āẓ*, p. 124.

277 Ibn al-Athīr, vol. 8, p. 115.

278 A quarter of Baghdad inhabited mainly by Shi'is. See 'Barāthā', in EI2.

279 The colour of the Isma'ilis in contrast to the black colour of the 'Abbasids. See *Carmathes*, pp. 179–180.

280 Ibn al-Jawzī, *al-Muntaẓam*, vol. 6, p. 195.

281 Al-Mas'ūdī, *al-Tanbīh*, p. 391, where the name is explained.

282 'Abd al-Jabbār, *Tathbīt*, p. 386.

283 See note 156 above.

284 The 'Ijl lived in the environs of Kūfa and had previously participated in Shi'i rebellions. In the edition of 'Abd al-Jabbār, *Tathbīt*, the name of Abu'l-Ghayth's father is given as 'Ubayda. In the manuscript, however, it appears as 'Abda.

285 'Abd al-Jabbār, *Tathbīt*, pp. 383, 392.

286 'Arīb, *Ṣila*, p. 163.

287 'Arīb, *Ṣila*, p. 168. See *Carmathes*, pp. 136–137.

288 See note 27 above.

289 'Abd al-Jabbār, *Tathbīt*, p. 392.

290 Al-Nuwayrī, *Nihāyat al-arab*, vol. 25, p. 296, and al-Maqrīzī, *Itti'āẓ*, p. 130.

291 'Abd al-Jabbār, *Tathbīt*, p. 388.

292 E. M. Quatremère, 'Vie du khalife Fatimite Möezz-li-din-Allah', *Journal Asiatique*, 3 série, 3 (1837), p. 182, and Wüstenfeld, *Faṭimiden*, p. 122. See now Th. Bianquis, 'La prise du pouvoir par les Fatimides en Egypte (357–363/968–974)', *Annales Islamologiques*, 11 (1972), pp. 63–64.

293 Nāṣir-i Khusraw, *Safar-nāma* (Berlin, 1922), p. 123.

294 *Carmathes*, p. 190.

295 Lewis, *Origins*, p. 82, and Zāhid 'Alī, *Ta'rīkh*, p. 147.

296 'Abd al-Jabbār, *Tathbīt*, p. 607.

297 See Lewis, *Origins*, p. 81.

298 Cited in al-Maqrīzī, *Itti'āẓ*, pp. 133 ff.

299 Ibid., p. 134.

300 Ibid.

301 Ibid., p. 136.

302 Ibid., pp. 137–138.

303 Ibid., p. 138.

304 Read *ta'lam* for *ta'mal*, as in al-Maqrīzī, *Itti'āẓ*, ed. Jamāl al-Dīn al-Shayyāl (Cairo, 1367/1948), p. 259.

305 Al-Maqrīzī, *Itti'āẓ*, ed. Bunz, p. 139.

306 Qur'an, XL:51.

307 Read *da'buhum* for *dānuhum*, as in al-Maqrīzī, *Itti'āẓ*, ed. al-Shayyāl, p. 260.

308 Al-Maqrīzī, *Itti'āẓ*, p. 139, read *ma'āb* for *ma'āt*, as in *Itti'āẓ*, ed. al-Shayyāl, p. 260.

309 See also al-Maqrīzī, *Itti'āẓ*, p. 134: *minnā wa-min ābā'inā'l-rāshidīna'l-mahdiyyīna'l-muntakhabīn.*

310 Characteristic is Akhū Muḥsin's commentary on the letter mentioned above. Rather than seeing in it a confirmation of the unity of the Fatimids and Qarmaṭīs, he finds it necessary to explain the motives of al-Mu'izz. They all originated, to be sure, in the same heresy, yet they form two parties.

311 See al-Maqrīzī, *Itti'āẓ*, p. 141: 'Don't you know that al-Muṭī' is the last of the sons of al-'Abbās and the last to arrogate the reign over mankind to himself?'

XI

# Ḥamdān Qarmaṭ and the Dā'ī Abū 'Alī

The history of the Ismā'īlī missionary activity before the rise of the Fāṭimid caliphate is narrated to us in the accounts of both Fāṭimid and anti-Fāṭimid sources. The anti-Fāṭimid account, as is known, goes back, aside from al-Ṭabarī, to the Kūfan Abū 'Abd Allāh Muḥammad b. 'Alī b. Rizām al-Ṭā'ī, who relied evidently on local Qarmaṭī sources and whose lost work was extensively quoted by Ibn al-Nadīm, the Damascene Sharīf Akhū Muḥsin Muḥammad b. 'Alī, and others. The official Fāṭimid account is available in particular in the *Kitāb Iftitāḥ al-da'wa* of the Qāḍī al-Nu'mān b. Ḥayyūn, the autobiographical *Sīra* of the Chamberlain Ja'far recorded by Muḥammad b. Muḥammad al-Yamānī, and the *Kitāb Istitār al-imām* of the *dā'ī* Aḥmad b. Ibrāhīm al-Naysābūrī.

Given their basically antagonistic perspective as well as the different local provenance, it is not surprising that there is both substantial agreement and disagreement between these accounts. Some of the figures playing a prominent part in one account are not mentioned at all or only marginally in the other. Sometimes the name under which the same person is known differs in the two versions. Their identification, however, is generally easy and uncontroversial, and the two accounts often complement each other.

One of the more intriguing discrepancies between the two accounts concerns the key figure in the early Ismā'īlī missionary activity in southern Iraq according to the anti-Fāṭimid version, Ḥamdān b. al-Ash'ath Qarmaṭ [1]. According to this account, Ḥamdān gave his *laqab* Qarmaṭ to the sectarian movement of the Qarāmiṭa in Iraq and elsewhere. He came from a village called al-Dūr in the district (*ṭassūj*) of Bādaqlā near Kūfa and was recruited for the Ismā'īlī movement by the *dā'ī* al-Ḥusayn al-Ahwāzī between the years 261/874—5 and 264/877—8, presumably as a very young man. After the death or departure of al-Ḥusayn al-Ahwāzī he became the leader of the *da'wa* in the cultivated land (*sawād*) of Kūfa. His chief assistant was his brother-in-law 'Abdān, a prominent *dā'ī*, originally probably from al-Ahwāz, and author of popular missionary books [2]. Ḥamdān Qarmaṭ and 'Abdān not only trained and controlled the *dā'īs* in the *sawād* but also sent out some prominent missionaries to other provinces, like Abū Sa'īd al-Jannābī to al-Baḥrayn, and Ibn Ḥawshab Manṣūr al-Yaman and 'Alī b. al-Faḍl al-Jayshānī to the Yemen [3]. Ḥamdān's headquarters were then at Kalwādhā, a small town south of East Baghdad.

Ḥamdān and 'Abdān were at this time summoning to the Ismā'īlī cause on behalf of the leaders of the movement who were residing first in al-Ahwāz and later in Salamya in Syria. When 'Abd Allāh ('Ubayd Allāh), the later Fāṭimid caliph al-Mahdī, succeeded to the leadership about the year 286/899, a crisis erupted. Suspecting that the new leader was changing fundamental doctrine, Ḥamdān Qarmaṭ sent 'Abdān to Salamya to investigate the situation. 'Abdān found that al-Mahdī was abandoning the earlier tenet that Muḥammad b. Ismā'īl was the hidden imām about to reappear as the Qā'im-Mahdī and was claiming to be himself the imām. Ḥamdān and 'Abdān now suspended the propagation of the doctrine causing a momentous schism in the movement between the supporters of the Fāṭimid house and the Qarāmiṭa. 'Abdān was soon afterwards murdered by the followers of Zakarūya b. Mihrūya, one of his *dā'īs* opposed to the discontinuation of the religious propaganda. Ḥamdān Qarmaṭ disappeared from Kalwādhā without a trace. The anti-Fāṭimid account does not mention him again thereafter.

In the Fāṭimid account Ḥamdān Qarmaṭ does not appear at all. 'Abdān, too, is not named. Al-Naysabūrī narrated, however, in his *Istitār al-imām* that the sons of Abū Muḥammad, namely the *dā'ī* Zakarūya, killed their in-law accusing him of being a hypocrite disloyal to the imām. W. Ivanow was, no doubt, right in suggesting that the murder of 'Abdān is meant here [4]. The later Fāṭimid tradition had evidently little interest in publicising the dangerous split in the movement which nearly thwarted the ambitions of the Fāṭimid house. The anti-Fāṭimid tradition, on the other hand, put Ḥamdān Qarmaṭ and 'Abdān at the centre of its story portraying them as first duped and then, as they awoke from their delusion, as victims dumped by the impious leaders of the movement.

The story could end here were it not for a curious note by the geographer Ibn Ḥawqal in his *Kitāb Ṣūrat al-arḍ*. In quoting information about the revenue of the Fāṭimid caliphs in the Maghrib which he had heard from the head of the Fāṭimid public treasury (*bayt al-māl*) in the year 336/947—8, Ibn Ḥawqal identifies this official as one Abū l-Ḥasan, the son of the *dā'ī* Abū 'Alī who had formerly been known as Ḥamdān Qarmaṭ (*al-ma'rūf kāna bi-Ḥamdān Qarmaṭ*) [5]. The notice, though not entirely overlooked by modern historians, has so far not attracted much credit or even interest. In his recent book on the rise of the Fāṭimid empire, H. Halm refers to it twice, but rejects the identity asserted by Ibn Ḥawqal first as hardly possible [6] and then, more cautiously, as doubtful [7]. Did Ibn Ḥawqal make a mistake then, or perhaps report an unfounded rumour? Ibn Ḥawqal was, as is known, distinctly pro-Fāṭimid in his political views, though probably not an Ismā'īlī. He was personally acquainted with the treasurer Abū l-Ḥasan and many other prominent men in the Ismā'īlī movement, both Fāṭimid and anti-Fāṭimid. It is difficult to assume that he either wanted to discredit Abū l-Ḥasan or was careless in reporting about his identity. There is thus initially good reason to take his notice seriously and to examine closely whether the *dā'ī* Ḥamdān Qarmaṭ, whose activity is described in the anti-Fāṭimid sources, could not, after these lost track of him by his disappearance, have had a second career as the Fāṭimid *dā'ī* Abū 'Alī. The investigation of Abū 'Alī's career is greatly aided by an obituary notice on him in the 5th volume of the *Kitāb 'Uyūn al-akhbār* by the *dā'ī* Idrīs 'Imād al-Dīn which has so far escaped the attention of modern historians [8].

The shaykh and *dā'ī* Abū 'Alī died on Thursday, 14 Rabī' I 321/14 March 933. If he, as Ḥamdān Qarmaṭ, was converted to the Ismā'īlī cause about the age of twenty, he would then have been less than eighty moon years, no unreasonable age. At the time of the schism in 286/899, when he changed his identity, he would have been about forty-two to forty-five years old. According to the anti-Fāṭimid account, he suspended the propaganda in favour of the Fāṭimid al-Mahdī, acting in concert with 'Abdān. He must then have changed his mind, absconded from Kalwādhā, and restored his allegiance to the Fāṭimid imām. The latter evidently forgave him, at least partly, for his temporary slip. He was too important a figure in the hierarchy of the *da'wa* and had too many connections to be simply dropped. Since 'Abdān, together with most of the *dā'īs* in Iraq and throughout the east, persisted in their revolt against the leadership, Ḥamdān was transferred to al-Fusṭāṭ in Egypt and provided with a new identity as Abū 'Alī.

There is one report of the chamberlain Ja'far that is incompatible with this assumption. According to Ja'far, Abū 'Abd Allāh al-Shī'ī, the *dā'ī* of the Maghrib, and his brother Abū l-'Abbās were both recruited for the Ismā'īlī cause by Abū 'Alī who lived then in their neighbourhood in Kūfa. When Abū 'Alī was transferred to Egypt, the two brothers obtained permission to join him there. It was, according to Ja'far, from Egypt that Abū 'Alī sent Abū 'Abd Allāh al-Shī'ī to Ibn Ḥawshab in the Yemen to be trained as a *dā'ī* before al-Shī'ī set out on his mission to the country of the Kutāma Berbers in the Maghrib [9]. Abū 'Abd Allāh al-Shī'ī's voyage to the Yemen is known to have taken place in 278/892, eight years before the schism in the movement.

If Abū 'Alī was transferred from Kūfa to Egypt before this date, he can hardly be identical with Ḥamdān Qarmaṭ. It might barely be possible to assume that his transfer there at this time was not final and that, at the time of the schism, he was in Iraq. This is, however, quite unlikely. If he had been associated already before this schism with a mission in Egypt, the eastern *da'wa* would hardly have lost track of him after his disappearance from Kalwādhā. Much more likely the account of Ja'far the Chamberlain, who was personally not involved in the activity of the *da'wa*, is simply mistaken. He evidently associated Abū 'Alī with Egypt, where he met him first. Narrating his story many decades after the events, he assumed that Abū 'Alī had sent Abū 'Abd Allāh al-Shī'ī from Egypt to the Yemen. This is not confirmed by any of the other sources, either Fāṭimid or anti-Fāṭimid. Moreover, Abū 'Alī is not mentioned at all when Abū 'Abd Allāh, a year later, passed through Egypt in company with a group of Kutāma pilgrims. Abū 'Abd Allāh al-Shī'ī was probably sent by Abū 'Alī, alias Ḥamdān Qarmaṭ, to the Yemen from Iraq.

For the Fāṭimid imām, Abū 'Alī was now vital primarily in order to salvage as much as possible of the *da'wa* for the Fāṭimid cause. The repentant chief *dā'ī* thus should best keep a low profile in al-Fusṭāṭ concealing his identity and whereabouts from those of his former followers who were irretrievably lost and might be prepared to murder him for his volte-face. There was no need for him to build up an Ismā'īlī community in Egypt. Rather he should maintain the ties with those of his *dā'īs* in outlying communities who still remained loyal. Abū 'Alī successfully managed the relations with Ibn Ḥawshab in the Yemen, who in turn was able to ensure the loyalty of various *dā'īs* whom he had sent to remote regions to the Fāṭimid movement. Abū 'Abd Allāh al-Shī'ī, who was gaining a broad following among the Kutāma in the Maghrib, was also controlled through Abū 'Alī. Abū 'Abd Allāh's brother Abū l-'Abbās stayed with Abū 'Alī acting as a reliable messenger between him and the residence of the imām in Salamya [10].

The obituary describes the shaykh Abū 'Alī as the *dā'ī* known as the Gate of Gates (*bāb al-abwāb*). Ḥamdān Qarmaṭ evidently retained his former position as the chief *dā'ī* in charge of the propaganda of the movement. Only his identity was entirely changed. The obituary gives his lineage as follows: Abū 'Alī al-Ḥasan b. Aḥmad b. Dāwūd b. Muḥammad b. Maymūn b. 'Amr b. 'Abd Allāh b. Muslim b. 'Aqīl b. Abī Ṭālib. As a descendant of 'Alī's brother 'Aqīl he belonged distinctly to the Hāshimite nobility. The leaders of the movement themselves, it is known, had for some time claimed descent from 'Aqīl [11]. Ibn Ḥawhab Manṣūr al-Yaman was alleged to be a descendant of Muslim b. 'Aqīl [12]. Claims of descent from 'Alī's brother were perhaps less open to public questioning than claims to be descended from 'Ali or al-

'Abbās. Muslim b. 'Aqīl, from whom Abū 'Alī traced his lineage according to this pedigree, was, however, commonly known not to have had any offspring [13]. Besides the Arab name al-Ḥasan, Abū 'Alī seems to have also used the Persian pen-name Shahriyār. He is called Sayyidunā Shahriyār Abū 'Alī Bāb al-Abwāb in an excerpt from one of his works extant in a manuscript [14].

When the imām, having left his residence in Salamya in fear for his life, arrived in 291/904 with his whole family and household in al-Fusṭāṭ, Abū 'Alī became responsible for their lodging and shelter. He instructed the *dā'ī* not to lodge him in his house or with anyone belonging to the *da'wa*. Abū 'Alī made arrangements for them to stay with Ibn 'Ayyāsh, an acquaintance of his who was not initiated [15]. The imām evidently did not wish to stay with Abū 'Alī in order not to arouse undue suspicion. Yet he probably also wanted to keep the *dā'ī*, a man whom he needed but, after his earlier indiscretion, did not fully trust, at a safe distance. The party remained a full year in al- Fusṭāṭ. At first the plan was to move on to the Yemen to Ibn Ḥawshab Manṣūr al-Yaman and to proclaim the advent of the Mahdī there. These plans were spoiled, however, by disturbing news about the conduct of the second *dā'ī* in the Yemen, 'Alī b. al-Faḍl, who acted more and more independently in defiance of the loyal Ibn Ḥawshab. The imām decided to move to the Maghrib to join Abū 'Abd Allāh al-Shī'ī. The sun was to rise from the west.

The change of direction, according to Ja'far the Chamberlain, upset Fayrūz, *dā'ī* in the company of the imām and father-in-law of Abū 'Alī. Ja'far, who was evidently not well informed about the inner working of the *da'wa*, describes him as the chief *dā'ī (dā'ī l-du'āt)* and *bāb al-abwāb*. More likely he was rather an aide of the imām through whom he conducted his relations with the *da'wa* [16]. Fayrūz absconded and went to the Yemen on his own. Ibn Ḥawshab, unaware of his treason, at first received him well. When letters informing him of the facts and ordering him to kill the turncoat *dā'ī* arrived from Egypt, Fayrūz fled and joined 'Alī b. al-Faḍl encouraging him in his rebellion against the imām. Ibn Ḥawshab later captured and killed him [17]. Abū 'Alī, on the other hand, expressed great eagerness to accompany the imām to the Maghrib. Al-Mahdī, however, ordered him to stay in Egypt [18]. Again he preferred to keep him at a distance.

Five years later, in 297/910, the chief *dā'ī* went on a formal visit (*wafada*) to the imām and Mahdī, who had just ascended his throne in Raqqāda, to pay his respects. If he had hoped that he would now be permitted to spend the evening of his life in the Fāṭimid capital with the full honours due to the chief of a triumphant *da'wa*, he was to be disappointed. The imām quickly sent him on a new dangerous mission. He was to go to the country of the Byzantines to summon to Islam and to guide the Muslims there to the teaching of the imāms. This time his long experience in working underground did not save him from getting into trouble. He was discovered and denounced to the emperor (Leo VI?) who threw him into prison. He remained there for five years when he was released "with the permission of God", as the obituary puts it. There is no word as to whether al-Mahdī made any diplomatic effort to secure his release. It may be doubted.

Abū 'Alī returned to the Maghrib to find his world changed. Abū 'Abd Allāh al-Shī'ī, the architect of the Fāṭimid reign, and his brother Abū l-'Abbās, both of whom had been won for the cause by him three decades ago, were dead, executed by the imām for spreading doubts about his being truly the Expected Mahdī. Abū 'Alī used to say that had he not been a prisoner in the country of the Rūm at that time and had he been present in the capital he would have cleared up the confusion and removed the doubt. "Our Lord", he explained, "the Commander of the Faithful is like the sun whose light is bright and blinding such that if it were not followed by the moon to moderate and cool its effects no plant could develop properly on earth and the heat would overpower it." After quoting Abū 'Alī's sun metaphor for the imām fully, the author of the obituary went on to comment that because of the strength of the knowledge of the *dā'ī* Abū 'Alī al-Ḥasan b. Aḥmad and of his trust in it he could vouch that had he been present the matter would have been straightened out and the evil would have been little.

More important for Abū 'Alī's own future was perhaps the fact that al-Mahdī had turned over the direction of the *da'wa* to his son and heir apparent al-Qā'im who seems to have fully appreciated the qualities of the old *dā'ī*. He did not send him off to remote corners again but employed him to establish the *da'wa* and to compose sound books supporting it. Abū 'Alī, according to the obituary, wrote many solid works (*ta'līfat jamma*), among them the book entitled *Ummahāt al-Islām*. In it he refuted the philosophers who deny the attributes of God (*al-falāsifa al-mu'aṭṭilīn*) and the communities opposed to Islam, and argued for the affirmation of esoteric interpretation (*ta'wīl*) and clarified the proof for its necessity.

Abū 'Alī, it is evident, was taking aim in this book at philosophical speculation and foreign religious thought of the type propagated by his murdered former colleague and brother-in-law 'Abdān as well as the Neoplatonizing thought recently propounded by the Transoxanian *dā'ī* Muḥammad b. Aḥmad al-Nasafī. The metamorphosis was complete. Abū 'Alī, "formerly known as Ḥamdān Qarmaṭ", refuted the teaching of those renegate Ismā'īlīs who were henceforth known as the Qarāmiṭa.

Abū 'Alī's guidelines were followed strictly in the early Fāṭimid *da'wa*. The extant works of the early Fāṭimid *dā'īs*, most notably Qāḍi al-Nu'mān and Ja'far b. Manṣūr al-Yaman, completely spurned the Neoplatonic speculation of the contemporary eastern *dā'īs* and were deeply committed to the *ta'wīl*, interpretation of the inner, esoteric meaning of religious texts and law. The author of the original part of the *Kitāb al-Fatarāt wa l-qirānāt*, perhaps Ja'far b. Manṣūr al-Yaman, expresses his high esteem for *ta'wīl* mentioning that he had heard the great shaykh and teacher, the *bāb al-abwāb* Abū 'Alī say: "Whoever practices the inner meaning (*bāṭin*) and the outer aspect (*ẓāhir*) belongs to us; whoever practices only the outer aspect without the inner meaning, he is worse than a dog" [19].

The sharp division between the Fāṭimid and the non-Fāṭimid eastern Ismā'īlī *da'wa* in this regard may also throw light on a controversy in the Khurāsānian community reported by the anti-Ismā'īlī Mu'tazilī Abū l-Qāsim al-Bustī to which S. Stern has first drawn attention. Stern's analysis may be quoted here:

> "Of great interest is the passage in which al-Bustī states that there was a fundamental difference of opinion between the followers of al-Nasafī and Abū Ya'qūb [al-Sijistānī] with regard to the methods to be followed in the preaching of Ismā'īlism: 'A great controversy concerning the *da'wa* occurred among the people of Khurāsān. Al-Nasafī and his followers were of the opinion that the *da'wa* must concern itself with the soul, the cycles, and the problem of creation, while according to Khayshafūj [Abū Ya'qūb] the *da'wa* must begin with the *sharī'a* and its allegorical interpretation (*ta'wīl*); there was between his followers and those of al-Nasafī much quarrelling and enmity.' The difference of opinion was not doctrinal but rather concerned missionary tactics: al-Nasafī and those who followed him laid stress on philosophical doctrines (which, we may add, were introduced into Ismā'īlism by al-Nasafī himself), while Abū Ya'qūb, while preferring (on the whole) the same doctrines, insisted that for tactical reasons the preaching of Ismā'īlism should begin with the allegorical interpretation of the Islamic law. Unfortunately we do not seem to have any information about the controversy and its background beyond al-Bustī's laconic statement" [20].

Stern, writing in 1961, was not aware of the conflict between the early Fāṭimid and the eastern Qarmaṭī *da'wa* in this question. Abū Ya'qūb al-Sijistānī, as is known, started out as a pupil of al-Nasafī who vigorously defended, in his *Kitāb al-Nuṣra*, the Neoplatonic teaching of al-Nasafī against the criticism of Abū Ḥātim al-Rāzī. Later, however, during the caliphate of the fourth Fāṭimid caliph al-Mu'izz, he joined the Fāṭimid *da'wa*. Al-Mu'izz was prepared to compromise with the eastern renegade Ismā'īlīs and to accept al-Nasafī's Neoplatonic thought on a secondary level. The Fāṭimid *da'wa*, however, still insisted on the primacy of *ta'wīl* over *falsafa*. This is reflected in the controversy in Khurāsān between the followers of al-Nasafī and Abū Ya'qūb described by al-Bustī. What was involved was not just a matter of missionary tactics, but the fundamental question of allegiance either to the concealed imām Muḥammad b. Ismā'īl, whose return as the Qā'im-Mahdī was expected, or to the Fāṭimid caliphate. As is known, the followers of Abū Ya'qūb accepting the imāmate of the Fāṭimid caliphs were to win the battle.

The controversy in Khurāsān occurred, to be sure, about three decades after Abū 'Alī's death. The *bāb al-abwāb* died just a year before his imām al-Mahdī who had appointed him, at an unknown date, chief of the public treasury (*mutawallī bayt al-māl*) [21]. The crown prince al-Qā'im bi-Amr Allāh led the funeral prayer and took charge of his burial. Al-Mahdī did not attend; perhaps he had still not entirely forgiven him his misstep. According to the author of the *Kitāb al-Fatarāt wa l-qirānāt* two eminent scholars of the *da'wa*, one of whom he merely calls his "brother" and an otherwise unknown Abū Muslim al-Khayyāṭ, washed and buried him [22]. The imām, presumably al-Mahdī, then appointed Abū 'Alī's son Abū l-Ḥasan Muḥammad b. al-Ḥasan b. Aḥmad in his place as chief *dā'ī* and put him in charge of the public treasury. Abū l-Ḥasan served the caliphs al-Mahdī, al-Qā'im, al-Manṣūr, and al-Mu'izz in these functions [23]. He evidently moved together with al-Mu'izz to Egypt. For his son Ḥasan b. Muḥammad b. Abī 'Alī al-Dā'ī became an informant of the well-known Egyptian chronicler al-Musabbiḥī narrating to him anecdotes about the imām al-Mahdī's stay in al-Fusṭāṭ and his grandfather Abū 'Alī's relations with him at that time [24]. Ibn Ḥawqal, as noted, met Abū l-Ḥasan Muḥammad as treasurer in al-Mahdiyya during the caliphate of al-Manṣūr. It was Abū l-Ḥasan who revealed the well-guarded secret of his father to posterity.

## Notes

1. See "Ḥamdān Ḳarmaṭ" in *E. I.*, 2nd. ed.
2. See "'Abdān b. al-Rabīṭ" in E. Ir. The name al-Rabīṭ attributed to 'Abdān's father in al-Mas'ūdī's *K. al-Tanbīh* (p. 391) may well be a slur in the meaning of the pimp", as pointed out to me by Iḥsān 'Abbās.
3. Ibn Ḥawshab was, according to Akhū Muḥsin's account, sent to the Yemen by the *dā'ī* Ibn Abi l-Fawāris, an assistant of 'Abdan (al-Maqrīzī, *Itti'āẓ al-ḥunafā'*, I, ed. J. al-Shayyāl, Cairo 1967, p. 166; al-Nuwayrī, *Nihāyat al-arab* XXV 245; Ibn al-Dawādārī, *Kanz al-durar* VI 63, calls Ibn Ḥawshab erroneously the son of Ibn Abī l-Fawāris).
4. W. Ivanow, *Ismaili Tradition concerning the Rise of the Fatimids*, p. 78.
5. Ibn Ḥawqal, *Ṣūrat al-arḍ*, ed. J. H. Kramers, p. 96.
6. H. Halm, *Das Reich des Mahdi*, p. 385, n. 23.

7. P. 426, n. 76.

8. Ed. Muḥ. al-Ya'lāwī, Beirut 1985, pp. 236—8. The text is missing in the edition of Muṣṭafā Ghālib (Beirut 1975).

9. Ivanow, *Rise*, p. 206.

10. *Ibid.*, p. 207.

11. Halm, *Reich*, pp. 19—20; "Les Fatimides à Salamya", *REI* 54 (1986), pp. 139—40. Halm admits the possibility that the Fāṭimids were descendants of 'Aqīl.

12. Descent from Muslim b. 'Aqīl is claimed for Ibn Ḥawshab in a letter attributed to his son Ja'far b. Manṣūr al-Yaman (ms. Munich, Glaser 154 = cod. arab. 1270, fol. 34a. About the manuscript see I. K. Poonawala, *Biobibliography of Ismā'īlī Literature*, p. 323). The letter, whether authentic or not, seems to be early. Later Yemenite Sunnite sources also mention Ibn Ḥawshab's claim of descent from 'Aqīl (see C. van Arendonk, *Les débuts de l'imamat Zaidite au Yémen*, Leiden 1960, pp. 121—2.

13. Al-Zubayrī, *Nasab Quraysh*, ed. E. Lévi-Provençal, p. 84.

14. See I. K. Poonawala, *Biobibliography*, pp. 323, 530.

15. Ivanow, *Rise*, p. 194.

16. Ja'far al-Ḥājib describes Fayrūz as the chief *dā'ī* who recruited both Abū 'Alī and Ibn Ḥawshab. His close link with the latter is confirmed by the fact that he, after deserting the imām in disobedience, first joined Ibn Ḥawshab in the Yemen. He was evidently originally from Iraq. The name Fayrūz is presumably assumed in order to hide his identity. If he is mentioned in the anti-Fāṭimid account, his name can be expected to be different there. Ḥamdān Qarmaṭ, according to the anti-Fāṭimid account, was converted by al-Ḥusayn al-Ahwāzī who died soon afterwards leaving him as the chief of the *da'wa* in Iraq. It is thus clear that Fayrūz cannot have recruited Abū 'Alī if the latter is identical with Ḥamdān. A clue to the identity of Fayrūz may be provided by the fact that Ibn Ḥawshab, according to the anti-Fāṭimid account, was sent to the Yemen by Ibn Abī l-Fawāris. The latter is most likely the same as Abū l-Fawāris, an Iraqi *dā'ī* recruited, according to the anti-Fāṭimid account, by 'Abdān (al-Maqrīzī, *Itti'āẓ*, I 155; Ibn al-Dawādārī, *Kanz al-durar* VI 47). Ibn Abī l-Fawāris would then have been drawn by the leadership to Salamya to act as an intermediary between it and the vital *da'wa* in Iraq. That he was not the chief *dā'ī* is evident from the lack of any attention paid to him in the story of the Yemenite *da'wa*.

17. Idrīs, *'Uyūn* V 152; Ivanow, *Rise* pp. 196—7. The statement of Ja'far the Chamberlain that Ibn Ḥawshab seized and killed both Fayrūz and 'Alī b. al-Faḍl is mistaken. 'Alī b. al-Faḍl survived Ibn Ḥawshab.

18. Ivanow, *Rise* p. 196.

19. Halm, "Zur Datierung des ismā'īlitischen 'Buches der Zwischenzeiten und der zehn Konjunktionen' ", *Die Welt des Orients* 8 (1975), p. 93.

20. S. Stern, *Studies in Early Ismā'īlism*, p. 308.

21. Ibn Ḥammād (Ibn Ḥamāduh), *Akhbār Mulūk Banī 'Ubayd*, p. 17.

22. Halm, "Zur Datierung", p. 93.

23. Ivanow, *Rise*, p. 196. Ibn Ḥamāduh names him as the chief of the public treasury under al-Qā'im (*Akhbār Mulūk Banī 'Ubayd*, p. 21; *b. 'Alī* read *b. Abī 'Alī*).

24. Al-Maqrīzī, *al-Muqaffā al-kabīr, tarājim Maghribiyya wa-Mashriqiyya min al-fatra al-'Ubaydiyya*, ed. Muḥ. al-Ya'lāwī, Beirut 1987/1407, pp. 82—3.

# XII

## The Religious Policy of the Fatimids toward their Sunnī Subjects in the Maghrib

On the eve of the rise of the Fatimid caliphate the Muslim population of al-Qayrawān and Ifrīqiya mostly belonged to two recognized religious schools and communities. The Mālikī school, known locally as the Medinans, had since the days of Saḥnūn (d. 240/855) come to constitute the popular majority. The school of Abū Ḥanīfa, known as the ᶜIrāqīs, were the minority, but were usually favoured by the Aghlabid ruling house. In 407/1016-17, about 110 years after the establishment of the Fatimid caliphate, popular mobs, incited by the Mālikī *ᶜulamā'*, began to massacre the small Ismāᶜīlī communities throughout Ifrīqiya.[1] This happened at a time when the local Zirid ruler al-Muᶜizz b. Bādīs was still a vassal of the Fatimid caliph in Egypt. Within a few years Ismāᶜīlism in Ifrīqiya was extinguished. The Mālikī school thus triumphed in an orgy of bloodshed and has ever since exclusively dominated religious life in the eastern Maghrib. What were the major steps in these developments?

For the situation at the beginning of the Fatimid reign, the Mālikī *Ṭabaqāt* works on the *ᶜulamā'* of Ifrīqiya as well the chronicle of the Andalusian ᶜArīb b. Saᶜd provide fairly detailed information from the Mālikī perspective.[2] From the Ismāᶜīlī perspective, there is now available, aside from the *Iftitāḥ al-daᶜwa* of Qāḍī al-Nuᶜmān, the *Kitāb al-Munāẓarāt* of the Ismāᶜīlī *dāᶜī* Ibn al-Haytham. This book, which is currently being edited by Paul Walker, describes the experiences of the author during the ten month's rule of Abū ᶜAbd Allāh al-Shīᶜī and his brother Abu l-ᶜAbbās in Raqqāda and al-Qayrawān before the arrival of the Fatimid caliph al-Mahdī.

From Ibn al-Haytham's account it is evident that there were a few old-established Shīᶜī families in Ifrīqiya. His own ancestor in the sixth generation, al- Haytham b. ᶜAbd Allāh, was a Kufan Arab of the Banū Minqar of Tamīm who came to Ifrīqiya in the year154 or 155/771-2 with the governor Yazīd b. Ḥātim and was later, on the order of the ᶜAbbasid caliph al-Hādī or Hārūn al-Rashīd, given land to settle in al-Qayrawān and extensive estates in the country. The family remained Zaydī Shīᶜī. Another Shīᶜī family were the the Banu l-Marwarūdhī or al-Marwadhī, whose ancestor had belonged to the Jund of Khurāsān and presumably arrived in Ifrīqiya in the early ᶜAbbasid age.

In contrast to the situation in Baghdad and the Mashriq, the Shīᶜa in Ifrīqiya were not a recognized, if underprivileged, religious community. They were forced to conceal their religious allegiance, were not permitted to teach their school doctrines in public, and lost all protection of the law if their beliefs became known. When engaged in a legal suit to gain his inheritance, Ibn al-Haytham, whose father had died while he was still a minor, was compelled to hide his father's unorthodox books with his aunts to protect himself from the Mālikī *qāḍī* Ḥimās b. Marwān who

---

1 See H.R. Idris, *La Berbérie orientale sous les Zīrīdes*, Paris 1962, pp. 143-9.

2 ᶜArīb's chronicle is contained in Ibn ᶜIdhārī, *al-Bayān al-Mughrib*, ed. G.S. Colin and E. Lévi-Provençal, Leiden 1948.

suspected his beliefs and had his house searched. A family friend in high office then intervened in Ibn al-Haytham's favour, warning the judge in the name of the Aghlabid emir against investigating the beliefs of the litigants before him.

Unable to study Shīʿī religious sciences, Ibn al-Haytham and a friend belonging to the Marwadhī family first studied Ḥanafī law and other subjects with the leading Ḥanafī scholar and former *qāḍī* Ibn ʿAbdūn. He then was privately introduced to Shīʿī doctrine and fiqh by an eastern Shīʿī scholar, Muḥammad al-Kūfī[3], who came to Ifrīqiya travelling via Sicily and contacted local Shīʿī families, seeking their material support. It was only through him that Ibn al-Haytham learned about other Shīʿī families.

None of these Shīʿīs were Ismāʿīlī. It is evident from Ibn al-Haytham's account that no Ismāʿīlī *dāʿīs* were active in al-Qayrawān and the other towns of Ifrīqiya before their conquest by Abū ʿAbd Allāh al-Shīʿī. The latter concentrated his efforts fully on converting the Kutāma Berber tribe and did not send out *dāʿīs* elsewhere. When Abū ʿAbd Allāh arrived in the capital Raqqāda he sought the backing of the few local Shīʿīs, who readily joined the Ismāʿīlī *daʿwa*. The young Ibn al-Haytham, then in his early twenties, according to his own account, was particularly favoured and trusted by him.

Abū ʿAbd Allāh also hoped to gain converts among the Sunnī *ʿulamā'* of al-Qayrawān by engaging in debate with them about the relative merits of the early caliphs and other religious questions. Disputation, *jadal*, on theological and legal questions was a discipline of study and had been widely practiced between Ḥanafī and Mālikī scholars, often in the presence of the Aghlabid rulers. The Sunnī scholars thus were well prepared for it. Among the Mālikīs, the elderly Abū Saʿīd b. al-Ḥaddād had achieved a high reputation as the foremost debater. He now debated with Abū ʿAbd Allāh and his brother Abu l-ʿAbbās. Later he wrote a small book about these debates in which he described himself as invariably worsting his opponents. He sent copies of it everywhere and his account is widely quoted in the Mālikī *Ṭabaqāt*. Ibn al-Haytham states that he had attended all these debates and accuses Ibn al-Ḥaddād of having added to the discussion and of lying in his pamphlet. When Ibn al-Haytham first saw it, he had refuted Ibn al Ḥaddād's claims and comprehensively criticized his arguments. This refutation is unfortunately not extant. Ibn al-Haytham, however, mentions one discussion about the meaning of *mawlā* in which he forced Ibn al-Ḥaddād to excuse himself from further discussion and to appeal to Abū ʿAbd Allāh's forbearance, while according to his own presentation he had won the argument.[4]

Lists of scholars who converted to Ismāʿīlism are given by the contemporary Mālikī al-Khushanī[5] and Ibn al-Haytham. There were only few Mālikīs among them. The great majority were Ḥanafīs. The Ḥanafīs had generally been close to the government under the Aghlabids, who favoured them. Under pressure from the popular Mālikī majority, they were evidently more ready to cooperate with the new government. Ibn al-Haytham's Ḥanafī teacher Ibn ʿAbdūn remained faithful to his Sunnī school, but he expressed his pleasure about the success of his Shīʿī pupil. The wide-spread conversion of Ḥanafī scholars to Ismāʿīlism led to the extinction of the school in Ifrīqiya.

Immediately after his arrival Abū ʿAbd Allāh imposed the introduction of the Shīʿī formula of the call to prayer including *ḥayya ʿalā khayri l-ʿamal* and the omission of the Sunnī formula *al-*

---

3 This Muḥammad al-Kūfī is most likely identical with Abū ʿAbd Allāh Muḥammad b. Sallām b. Sayyār al-Kūfī (d. 310/922-3), a pupil of the Kufan Zaydī scholar Muḥammad b. Manṣūr al-Murādī. His books *(kutub)* were a source of Qāḍī al-Nuʿmān's legal doctrine (Madelung, "The sources of Ismāʿīlī Law", *JNES* XXXV (1976), pp. 31, 35, 38, Ibn ʿIdhārī (*Bayān* I 188) gives him the *nisba* al-Barqī al-Hamadānī, probably referring to his or his family's origin before he studied in Kufa. Against my earlier assumption that the *nisba* al-Barqī refers to Barqa in Libya and that the *nisba* al-Hamadānī should be read al-Hamdānī ("Some Notes on non-Ismāʿīlī Shiism in the Maghrib", *SI* XLIV (1976), p. 97), it seems now more likely to me that he or his family came from Barqarūd near Hamadān. The *nisba* al-Barqī of several Imāmī scholars refers to this village near Hamadān.

4 Ibn al-Ḥaddād's version is quoted by al-Khushanī, *Quḍāt Qurṭuba wa ʿulamā' Ifrīqiya*, ed. ʿIzzat al-ʿAṭṭār al-Ḥusaynī, Cairo 1372 and al-Mālikī, *Riyāḍ al-Nufūs*, ed. Bashīr al-Bakkūsh, Beirut 1981-3/1401-3, II 84-5.

5 Al-Khushanī, pp. 291-5.

*ṣalātu khayrun mina l-nawm*. He ordered that in the Friday sermon a blessing of ᶜAlī, Fāṭima, Ḥasan and Ḥusayn be added to that of the Prophet.[6] This implied a ranking of ᶜAlī and the *ahl al-bayt* above all other Companions of Muḥammad in accordance with Shīᶜī belief. There is no sound evidence of cursing of any of the Companions from the pulpits.[7]

According to Ibn al-Haytham, Abū ᶜAbd Allāh soon expressed the wish to appoint him *qāḍī* of al-Qayrawān. Ibn al-Haytham declined, however, and proposed "our shaykh", Muḥammad b. ᶜUmar al-Marwadhī, father of his friend Aḥmad, as more worthy of the position. Abū ᶜAbd Allāh appointed al-Marwadhī, warning him to beware of the rancours of the past and to ignore any blood that had been shed between himself and any litigant in the Jāhiliyya, as he called the time before his arrival. At the same time Abū ᶜAbd Allāh asked Ibn al-Haytham to bring forth his Shīᶜī legal books and authorized him to debate legal matters and to render fetwas in accordance with the teaching of the Family of the Prophet. He instructed him to prevent the people from reading the books of Abū Ḥanīfa and Mālik. Public teaching of Ḥanafī and Mālikī school doctrine thus was prohibited. Ibn al-Haytham later comments that the books of Mālik and Abū Ḥanīfa were commonly sold to physicians, pharmacists and perfume dealers to be used as wrapping paper as people made light of them because of their uselessness. Other copies were shipped to Andalus and to the East. Ibn al-Haytham then persuaded Abū ᶜAbd Allāh to forbid the popular supererogatory *tarāwīḥ* prayers in Ramaḍān. When this provoked a veiled protest by the imam of the congregational mosque in his recitation of the Qurᵓān, Abū ᶜAbd Allāh appointed Ibn al-Haytham's eastern Shīᶜī teacher Muḥammad al-Kūfī preacher of the mosque.

As tensions kept growing, the first bloodshed occurred in the absence of Abū ᶜAbd Allāh while his brother Abu l-ᶜAbbās was in command in the capital. According to Ibn al-Haytham's account, two Mālikī scholars, Ibrāhīm b. al-Birdhawn and Abū Bakr b. al-Hudhayl, had asserted that Muᶜāwiya was more excellent than ᶜAlī whom they accused of wrongfully claiming the imamate and making war on Muᶜāwiya. Abu l-ᶜAbbās gave orders to execute them and to drag their bodies, tied to the tails of mules, through al-Qayrawān. Abu l-Ḥasan al-Jaᶜfarī, a local pro-Shīᶜī nobleman, intervened to save the life of Ibn al-Hudhayl, who seems to have been merely passively associated with Ibn al-Birdhawn and was generally known as a pious man. Abū Jaᶜfar al-Khazarī, an eastern *dāᶜī* who had arrived together with Abu l-ᶜAbbās and is described by Ibn al-Haytham as a fanatic, rudely rebuked al-Jaᶜfarī, and both men were killed. When Abu l-ᶜAbbās informed his brother by letter about the incident, Abū ᶜAbd Allāh is said to have severely chided him, suggesting that he had ruined the good relationship with the town and its people which they dearly needed.[8]

Behind the incident were pre-Fatimid Mālikī-Ḥanafī rancours. According to the contemporary al-Khushanī, Ibn al-Birdhawn, a pupil of Ibn al-Ḥaddād with a sharp tongue, had during the Aghlabid reign received a flogging because of his vituperative criticism of the ᶜIrāqīs. In particular he had viciously attacked and ridiculed the prominent Ḥanafī scholar Muḥammad b. al-Kalāᶜī in a book refuting the doctrine of the creation of the Qurᵓān. Ibn al-Kalāᶜī, who, according to Ibn al-Haytham, accepted the Ismāᶜīlī *daᶜwa*, and his Ḥanafī friends now brought charges against Ibn al-Birdhawn. Al-Khushanī sees these events entirely in the context of the old Mālikī-Ḥanafī quarrels and does not even explain the nature of the charges brought against Ibn al-Birdhawn.[9] The chronicler ᶜArīb, on the other hand, states that Ibn al-Kalāᶜī and his Ḥanafī companions accused Ibn al-Birdhawn and Ibn al-Hudhayl of defaming the state by putting ᶜAlī on a par with Abū Bakr, ᶜUmar, and ᶜUthmān.[10] This turned the two men into martyrs of sound Sunnī faith which the unorthodox pro-Umayyad criticism of ᶜAlī could not do.

---

6 *Bayān*, I, 151.

7 The passage *Bayān*, I, 151 l. 18 hardly implies the public cursing of the first three caliphs from the pulpits as H. Halm (*Das Reich des Mahdi*, Munich 1991, p. 119 and n. 269) interprets it.

8 *Bayān*, I, 155.

9 Al-Khushanī, pp. 281-2, 299.

10 *Bayān*, I 155.

Mālikī hagiographical fiction then took full possession of the two men. In the second half of the 4th/10th century the story of their martyrdom was narrated as follows: When ᶜUbayd Allāh arrived in Raqqāda, he sent to al-Qayrawān to have Ibn al-Birdhawn and Ibn al-Hudhayl, two virtuous scholars of the law, brought to him. Upon their arrival they found him sitting on his royal throne, to his right Abū ᶜAbd Allāh al-Shīᶜī and to his left his brother Abu l-ᶜAbbās. As they stood in front of him, Abū ᶜAbd Allāh and Abu l-ᶜAbbās, pointing at ᶜUbayd Allāh, told him: "Will you testify that this one is the Messenger of God ?" They said with a single voice: "By God besides Whom there is no god, if this one came with the sun on his right and the moon on his left, asserting that he is the Messenger of God, we would not say that he is the Messenger of God". ᶜUbayd Allāh ordered to slaughter them both and to tie them to the tails of mules.[11]

The narrator of this version was an otherwise unknown Abū ᶜAbd Allāh Muḥammad b. Khurāsān. From other tales narrated by him, it is evident that he was not a scholar but a story-teller who mixed uplifting legend with anti-Fatimid hate-mongering propaganda. The authors of the later Mālikī *Ṭabaqāt* works, beginning with Abū Bakr al-Mālikī, all quoted the story, even though they could hardly be unaware of its patent anachronism. The Mālikī scholar Muḥammad b. Saᶜdūn (d. 486/1093) included it in his extraordinary collection of anti-Fatimid calumnies which he composed "to comfort the people of al-Qayrawān *(Taᶜziyat ahl al-Qayrawān)*."[12] This and similar stories evidently served to justify the part played by the Mālikī *ᶜulamā'* in instigating the popular massacres of the Ismāᶜīlīs.

Another case illustrating the anti-Fatimid distortion in the later Mālikī martyriology is that of Abū Jaᶜfar Muḥammad b. Khayrūn, a wealthy merchant owning a large mosque and several hotels *(fanādiq)* near the prison in al-Qayrawān. His father Abū ᶜAbd Allāh, who had emigrated from Andalus, had built the mosque in 252/866,[13] and was famous as the scholar who introduced the discipline of Qur'ān recitation in the Maghrib. The son Abū Jaᶜfar had made a trip to ᶜIraq from where he brought back some books of Dāwūd b. Khalaf, the founder of the Ẓāhiriyya law school. According to information received by al-Khushanī, he had written a book for the caliph al-Mahdī on the genealogy and history of the Family of the Prophet[14] and hoped to be appointed *qāḍī*. For this reason the *qāḍī* al-Marwadhī sought to ruin him and accused him of concealing a large deposit. Abū Jaᶜfar was pressed to surrender it and died under torture.[15] Since al-Khushanī was himself in Ifrīqiya at the time of this incident, his report must be taken seriously. The caliph al-Mahdī evidently could not be pleased about the death of a scholar of distinction who had written in praise of his house. It may well have contributed to the dismissal of al-Marwadhī a year later. He, too, died under torture to press money out of him.[16]

The later Mālikī authors know nothing of Ibn Khayrūn's ambition to become *qāḍī* in Fatimid al-Qayrawān. ᶜArīb merely states that al-Marwadhī endeavoured to ruin him without mentioning a motive.[17] Al-Mālikī reports a long hagiographical legend on the authority of the renowned Mālikī scholar Abu l-Ḥasan (b.) al-Qābisī (d. 403/1022). Al-Qābisī's informant was sitting in the hall of Ibn Abī Khinzīr, the governor of al-Qayrawān, when a well-dressed and dignified shaykh entered and Ibn Abī Khinzīr began to weep. Asked about the reason, the governor said: "The ruler – meaning ᶜUbayd Allāh – sent me order that I command this shaykh to be trampled to death". Ibn Khayrūn was led to the audience room, thrown on his back, and the blacks kept jumping on him with their feet until he died. Then they carried him off and dumped him in a ditch. This was done, al-Qābisī explained, because of his *jihād* for the faith and his hatred of ᶜUbayd Allāh and his soldiers. The

11 Al-Mālikī, II, 49.

12 *Bayān*, I, 281-7.

13 *Bayān*, I, 114. *Ḥamdūn* should read *Khayrūn*.

14 Al-Khushanī (p. 229) characteristically speaks of *nasab al-shīᶜa wa-akhbārihim*. Obviously the ᶜAlids must be meant.

15 *Bayān*, I, 169.

16 *Bayān*, I, 173.

17 *Bayān*, I, 169.

tale goes on to describe the even more gruesome death of al-Marwadhī who had striven to destroy Ibn Khayrūn. Ibn Abī Khinzīr, tired of killing so many scholars and pious men delivered to him by the *qāḍī*, accused him before ᶜUbayd Allāh in al-Mahdiyya, who accepted his charges and gave him control over al-Marwadhī. Ibn Abī Khinzīr threw him on the ground in his stables and let the beasts trample him to death. Before he died, he addressed a slave girl of Ibn Khayrūn who had been appropriated by Ibn Abī Khinzīr, hoping to gain her sympathy: "You have come to be with the governor through me." She told him: "You evil shaykh, you have killed my master Ibn Khayrūn, have taken me away from him and turned me over to a pig, son of a pig *(khinzīr ibn khinzīr).*" On her command her servants slapped his face and made him eat his own filth. It was she who took charge of his torture until he perished.[18]

In the light of such gross distortion of the historical facts in the later Mālikī *Ṭabaqāt* works it is evident that they can be used only with great caution as sources for Fatimid history. Even the much more sober reports of the Cordovan ᶜArīb b. Saᶜd, written in the service of the Umayyad caliphate in Andalus, reflect a deeply hostile view, seeking to discredit the reign of the rival dynasty. These reports must be judged on the basis of what may be seen as reasonable in comparison with the Fatimid sources.

The space limits of this paper make it impossible to offer more than a summary sketch of the policy of the Fatimid caliphs towards their Sunnī subjects in the Maghrib. Al-Mahdī basically followed the guidelines set by Abū ᶜAbd Allāh al-Shīᶜī. While he relied to some extent on Sunnī officials for administrative positions, only Shīᶜī's were appointed to religious offices. *Qāḍīs*, imams, muftis, public witnesses, writers of legal documents had to be Ismāᶜīlīs or had to convert formally before they were allowed to practice.

The Sunnī *ᶜulamā'* were not only excluded from any religious offices. They were also prohibited to teach their school doctrine and to issue inofficial fetwas. Aside from humiliating them, this also struck at the means of their livelihood. The loss of their normal income and the heavier taxation imposed by the new government were certainly major factors in the quickly growing opposition to Fatimid rule. Some joined the Sufi type groups based in the *ribāṭs*, leading a life of ascetic self-denial and devotion. These groups became hotbeds of anti-Fatimid sentiment and activity.

Sunnī teaching, to be sure, could not be completely prevented. While it might be effectively banned in the major mosques, it was certainly carried on in private houses and gatherings. Al-Khushanī does not complain about having had problems in studying Mālikī *fiqh* in al-Qayrawān and Tunis in the early years of the Fatimid caliphate. He left for Andalus in 311/923, evidently not because of a sense of persecution, but in the hope of finding employment. The famous Mālikī scholar Ibn Abī Zayd studied in al-Qayrawān during the reign of al-Mahdī and composed his *Risāla*, a compendium of Mālikī law, in 327/938 under al-Qā'im.[19]

Al-Mahdī had, on the other hand, little sympathy for the Ismāᶜīlī *daᶜwa*. He had come to distrust it ever since the breakaway of ᶜAbdān and many of the eastern Ismāᶜīlī communities. This distrust was only enhanced by the disloyalty of Abū ᶜAbd Allāh al-Shīᶜī and his brother Abu l-ᶜAbbās which affected many of his Kutāma followers. Al-Mahdī was worried about both antinomian tendencies and excessive veneration and expectations concerning the Imams in the teaching of the *daᶜwa* which could foster aversion and opposition among the Sunnī population. After an outbreak of riots and street fighting in al-Qayrawān between the inhabitants and the Ismāᶜīlī Kutāma soldiers, he forbade the *daᶜwa* to teach and to proselytize for a long time. He directed the *daᶜwa* to focus its apocalyptic expectations on his son al-Qā'im and put him formally in charge of its hierarchy[20], evidently in order to deflect extremist expectations from himself, but continued to interfere in its activitity and to exert

18 Al-Mālikī, II, 53-4.

19 H. R. Idris, art. "Ibn Abī Zayd al-Qayrawānī", in *E.I.* 2nd ed.

20 Ibn al-Athīr, *al-Kāmil*, ed. C.J. Tornberg, Leiden 1851-76, VIII 41; Madelung, "Das Imamat in der frühen ismailitischen Lehre", *Isl.* XXXVII (1961), p. 66.

strict control. There are frequent reports about his severe punishment of *dāʿīs* who had provoked public offense. In 309/921-2 he ordered, according to ʿArīb, to round up 200 *dāʿīs* in al-Qayrawān, Bāja and Tūnis who had openly drunk wine and eaten pork during Ramaḍān. Most of them were left to die in prison.[21] The reports of the Sunnī sources in this regard are fully confirmed by Qāḍī al-Nuʿmān, who in his *Daʿāʾim al-Islām* describes the merciless chastisement, torture, life imprisonment and execution of *dāʿīs* with a record of long faithful service by al-Mahdī for such licentiousness.[22]

The second Fatimid caliph, al-Qā'im, followed the policies of al-Mahdī. He kept his officials, displayed extreme grief about the loss of his father, and encouraged official veneration of him as the founder of the Fatimid caliphate.[23] Sunnī polemical sources accuse him of bringing the hidden Ismāʿīlī unbelief into the open. He and the *dāʿīs* started cursing not only the Companions and wives of the Prophet, but the Prophet himself, ʿAlī and Fāṭima. They claimed that al-Mahdī was the true God, openly treated the religious law with contempt, and had intercourse with their daughters.[24] All this is plain calumny, designed to explain the support given by the Mālikī *ʿulamā'* to the Khārijī rebel Abū Yazīd against the Shīʿī dynasty. At most it could be assumed that al-Qā'im gave the *dāʿīs* a freer hand than his father had done. He certainly did not encourage violation of the religious law or public cursing of the Companions.

Sunnī backing of Abū Yazīd came mainly from the Mālikī ascetics and mystics rather than the scholars of the law. They summoned in al-Qayrawān to *jihād* against the Fatimids, claiming that these and their followers were infidels in contrast to the Khārijī leader. Abu l-ʿArab, scion of an early governor of al-Qayrawān and traditionist, encouraged them by quoting the well-known anti-Shīʿī hadith ascribed to the Prophet: "There will be people at the end of time called the Rāfiḍa. When you meet them, kill them, for they are infidels".[25] Only a month later Abū Yazīd suffered a severe defeat near al-Mahdiyya, and eighty-five of the volunteers from al-Qayrawān, including some of their leaders, were killed.[26] The popular mood quickly turned against Abū Yazīd, and he was now suspected of having the Mālikī *ʿulamā'* intentionally exposed to death in order to get rid of them.[27]

When al-Manṣūr, the third Fatimid caliph, recovered al-Qayrawān, the populace welcomed him as a liberator and backed his campaign against Abū Yazīd. Yet he was aware of their deep disaffection that had been revealed during the rebellion. Abū Yazīd had captured and killed 700 Ismāʿīlīs, including the *qāḍī* Aḥmad b. Baḥr, in the town.[28] Then he had allowed the people of al-Qayrawān to choose their own Mālikī imam and preacher[29] and encouraged them to resume teaching Mālikī fiqh in the Great Mosque.[30] Al-Manṣūr decided to break with the Fatimid practice of appointing only Ismāʿīlīs to religious office and to name a Mālikī *qāḍī* of al-Qayrawān. At first he offered the position to an old local jurist, Abū Maysara Aḥmad b. Nizār, but the latter excused

21 *Bayān*, I, 185-6.

22 Al-Nuʿmān b. Muḥammad, *Daʿā'im al-Islām*, ed. A.A.A. Fyzee, Cairo 1960-3, I 68-9.

23 *Bayān*, I, 208.

24 ʿAbd al-Jabbār, *Tathbīt dalā'il al-nubuwwa*, ed. ʿAbd al-Karīm ʿUthmān, Beirut 1966-8, pp. 341, 601; *Bayān*, I 216; Ibn al-Nadīm, *al-Fihrist*, ed. G. Flügel, Leipzig 1871-2, p. 187.

25 Al-Mālikī, II, 309.

26 Al-Mālikī, II, 345.

27 *Bayān*, I, 218.

28 *Kitāb al-ʿuyūn wa l-ḥadā'iq*, ed. ʿUmar al-Saʿīdī, Damascus 1973, p. 423.

29 The choice of the imam, Abū Ibrāhīm Aḥmad b. Muḥammad b. Abi l-Walīd, was, according to al-Mālikī (II 342), suggested by Abu l-Faḍl al-Mimmasī, one of the leaders of the revolt killed in battle (Mālikī, II 292-305). He gave fiery anti-Fatimid sermons, calling the caliph al-Qā'im an infidel Qarmaṭī who claimed divinity (Ibn Saʿdūn in *Bayān*, I 285). According to Ibn Ḥamāduh he was chosen as *qāḍī* by the people and then confirmed by al-Qā'im (sic) (Ibn Ḥammād, *Akhbār mulūk Banī ʿUbayd*, ed. M. Vonderheyden, Alger 1907, p. 21, where *b. al-Walīd* should read *b. Abi l-Walīd*). Al-Dabbāgh calls him *ṣāḥib maẓālim al-Qayrawān wa l ḥākim bihā ayyām Abī Yazīd* (al-Dabbāgh, *Maʿālim al-īmān*, ed. Ibrāhīm Shabbūḥ and others, Cairo 1968-78, III 61). He evidently had the ear of Abū Yazīd. The Fatimid al-Manṣūr must have pardoned him, and he died in 345/956-7.

30 *Bayān*, I, 217.

himself because of his frailty and blindness.[31] Then he appointed Muḥammad b. Abi l-Manẓūr al-Anṣārī, an aged scholar of Andalusian origin who had studied in Baghdad and Ṣanᶜā'. Ibn Abi l-Manẓūr is said to have stipulated that he would not have to accept gifts from the ruler, visit him for congratulations or condolences, nor accept the testimony of anyone close to his court.[32] This may exaggerate the independence of the *qāḍī*, for he led the delegation of the people of al-Qayrawān who congratulated al-Manṣūr when he returned from his victory over Abū Yazīd.[33] It is evident, however, that Ibn Abī Manẓūr was entirely free to judge according to his Mālikī school doctrine. When he died in 337/948, al-Manṣūr appointed ᶜAbd Allāh b. Hāshim, son of a Mālikī pious worshipper and public benefactor.[34]

At about the same time the caliph named the Ismāᶜīlī Abū Ḥanīfa al-Nuᶜmān *qāḍī* of his new residential town al-Manṣūriyya near al-Qayrawān and chief judge of all of Ifrīqiya and other Fatimid provinces.[35] In practice, however, jurisdiction was henceforth split in the Fatimid realm. The towns where Mālikī Sunnism prevailed had Mālikī judges and other religious officials who were in general allowed to act in accordance with Mālikī law, while Ismāᶜīlī communities were subject to Ismāᶜīlī jurisdiction. Ismāᶜīlīs anywhere presumably could appeal to the Ismāᶜīlī chief *qāḍī*, but Qāḍī al-Nuᶜmān had otherwise no control over the Mālikī judges ruling within their communities. Use of the Shīᶜī form of the call to prayer, aside from the blessing of the caliph in the sermon, was probably still generally enforced as a sign of Fatimid sovereignty. Otherwise Sunnī practice normally prevailed in most of the Fatimid territories.

A case in point is that of the *qāḍī* of Barqa, Muhammad b. Isḥāq al-Ḥablī, who was told by the governor, the Kutāmī Ibn Kāfī, that the feast of breaking the fast of Ramaḍān had been set by the caliph for the next day. This agreed with the Ismāᶜīlī practice of setting the beginning of the month by calculation rather than on the basis of sighting the new moon. The *qāḍī*, evidently not used to accepting instructions of the government, insisted on waiting for the new moon. As it was not sighted, he refused to proclaim the feast and to lead the feast day prayer. The governor asked someone else to preach and perform the feast day prayer and sent the recalcitrant *qāḍī* to the caliph. When al-Ḥablī refused to join the Ismāᶜīlī *daᶜwa*, he was tied to a mast at a gate of the mosque and exposed to the sun until he died.[36] This happened shortly before the death of al-Manṣūr in 341/953.

This case reveals the particular sensitivity of permitting separate communal practice to Muslims in respect to offical feast days and public worship. If the *qāḍī* had been allowed to set the date of the feast on the basis of sighting the new moon, the governor, the Kutāma troops and other Ismāᶜīlīs would have been compelled to have their feast separately, bringing the deep division in the ranks of the caliph's Muslim subjects into the open. The same concern is apparent in an order issued eight years later (349/960) by al-Muᶜizz, the fourth Fatimid caliph. According to Ibn ᶜIdhārī, the *qāḍī*, most likely ᶜAbd Allāh b. Hāshim, was instructed to order the imams of mosques and the muezzins not to call to prayer without the *ḥayᶜala*, to recite the *basmala* at the beginning of every *sūra* of the Qur'ān, to pronounce two *taslīmas* in the ritual prayer, to say five *takbīrs* in the funeral prayer, not to postpone the afternoon prayer nor to advance the final evening prayer.[37] Since the officially installed imams and muezzins in the predominantly Sunnī towns were now Sunnīs, and Ismāᶜīlīs were expected to pray behind them in ritual and funeral prayers, these instructions were meant to insure that the payers were valid according to Shīᶜī norms.

---

31 Al-Mālikī, II, 361-2.

32 Al-Mālikī, II, 358.

33 Ibn Ḥammād, pp. 36-7.

34 Al-Dabbāgh, III 80-1. Al-Mālikī, II, 144-52.

35 F. Dachraoui, art. "al-Nuᶜmān", *E.I.* 2nd ed.

36 Al-Mālikī, II, 404-5.

37 *Bayān*, I, 223. Two further orders were that women should not be permitted to scream behind a funeral procession and that blind men should not recite the Qur'ān on graves except at the time of burial.

In general al-Muᶜizz followed the policy of his father in keeping Mālikīs in religious office in the predominantly Sunnī regions. ᶜAbd Allāh b. Hāshim remained *qāḍī* of al-Qayrawān until his death in 363/974, a year after the Fatimid caliph had left Ifrīqiya for Egypt.[38] It may just be noted that al-Muᶜizz basically applied the same policy in Egypt. Rather than systematically replacing the Sunnī *qāḍīs* and religious officials by Ismāᶜīlīs, he left them in office and merely imposed on them the application of Ismāᶜīlī ritual and law in a few specific matters.

The transfer of the Fatimid caliphate to Egypt greatly reduced the strength of the Ismāᶜīlī communities left behind in the Maghrib. The ruling family and household, the leaders of the *daᶜwa*, including Qāḍī al-Nuᶜmān, high government officials and the bulk of the Kutāma troops departed. The *daᶜwa* in Ifrīqiya was seriously weakened. In al-Manṣūriyya a Mālikī, Muḥammad b. Isḥāq al-Tamīmī, known as Ibn al-Kūfī, succeeded Qāḍī al-Nuᶜmān as *qāḍī* of the town. The Banu l-Kūfī remained judges in al-Manṣūriyya through four generations, while in al-Qayrawān the office of *qāḍī* remained hereditary among the descendants of ᶜAbd Allāh b. Hāshim.[39]

Al-Muᶜizz left behind the Zirids, chiefs of the Berber Ṣanhāja, as his viceroys. The Ṣanhāja, in contrast to their rivals the Kutāma, never had become Ismāᶜīlīs, but were political supporters of the Fatimid caliphate, chiefly against the pro-Umayyad Zanāta in the western Maghrib. The Zirids soon turned against the *daᶜwa*, suspecting that the Fatimid government was using it to build up potential rivals to their rule. In 363/974 Buluggīn b. Zīrī appointed ᶜAbd Allāh b. Muḥammad al-Tamīmī al-Kātib, a scion of the Aghlabid house and gifted man of letters, to head the administration of al-Manṣūriyya and al-Qayrawān. ᶜAbd Allāh quickly became powerful and turned out to be an active Ismāᶜīlī who revived the practice of holding religious debates and vainly attempted to convert some Mālikī scholars and the poet Ibn al-Baqqāl.[40] In 377/987 the Fatimid caliph al-ᶜAzīz put him in charge of the *daᶜwa* in Ifrīqiya. He is said to have boasted that now he was safe from any enemy. Only a few months later the Zirid al-Manṣūr b. Buluggīn killed him with his own hands. One of the causes for his downfall was that he had facilitated the mission of the *dāᶜī* Abu l-Fahm al-Khurāsānī, who was sent from Egypt by al-ᶜAzīz to summon the Kutāma to renew their bonds of allegiance to the caliph.[41] Ignoring written instructions of the caliph not to interfere with the mission, al-Manṣūr led two campaigns against the Kutāma, who had so far been virtually independent of his rule, killing large numbers of them, their chiefs and *dāᶜīs* and devastating their land. Abu l-Fahm was tortured to death with particular cruelty. The Fatimid caliph, unable to interfere, ignored these acts of defiance of his vassal.[42] The subjugation of the Kutāma, who had first established the Fatimid caliphate in the Maghrib, set the stage for the massacres of the remaining Ismāᶜīlī communities in the towns of Ifrīqiya three decades later.

38 Idris, *Zīrīdes*, p. 556.
39 Idris, *Zīrīdes*, pp. 556-60.
40 Idris, *Zīrīdes*, pp. 48-9.
41 Idris, *Zīrīdes*, pp. 66-9.
42 Idris, *Zīrīdes*, pp. 75-9.

# XIII

## A TREATISE ON THE IMAMATE OF THE FATIMID CALIPH AL-MANṢŪR BI-ALLĀH

In the chronicles of the Fatimid dynasty, al-Manṣūr bi-Allāh Ismāʿīl, the third caliph (334–41/946–53) of the ruling dynasty, appears primarily as the glorious victor over the apocalyptic 'Deceiver' (*dajjāl*), the Khariji rebel Abū Yazīd, and as the restorer of the Fatimid reign in the Maghrib after its near collapse. Since he died only four years after the final suppression of the rebellion, at the age of forty, it was his son and successor al-Muʿizz li-Dīn Allāh who reaped most of the benefits of the restoration. During his much longer reign (341–65/953–75), al-Muʿizz was able to pursue truly imperial designs culminating in the conquest of Egypt and the transfer of the Fatimid capital to the newly founded Cairo.

Al-Manṣūr was faced, in the few years of his reign left after his military triumph, with the need to gain the loyal allegiance of his Sunni, mostly Mālikī subjects, many of whom had for a time sided with the Khariji rebel. He did so by making substantial concessions to the Mālikī *ʿulamāʾ*, who under the first two Fatimid caliphs had been completely excluded from the administration of justice and been prohibited from teaching their school doctrine of the religious law in public. Al-Manṣūr now appointed a Mālikī judge in al-Qayrawān, the old religious capital, while nominating the Ismaili Abū Ḥanīfa al-Nuʿmān judge of his new residential town al-Manṣūriyya and chief judge of the whole Fatimid realm. Official jurisdiction was in effect communally split, Mālikī Sunni law prevailing in the predominantly Sunni towns and Ismaili Shiite law being applied to Ismailis throughout Fatimid territories.[1]

The recognition of Sunni Islam as a legitimate religious and legal community by al-Manṣūr was a momentous development in Islamic government. It remained a characteristic aspect of the Fatimid state

[1] See W. Madelung, 'The religious policy of the Fatimids toward their Sunnī subjects in the Maghrib', in M. Barrucand, ed., *L'Egypte Fatimide; son art et son histoire*, Paris, 1999, 97–104.

until its overthrow. Islamic government had, ever since its origins, recognized legitimate religious communities which were allowed a degree of legal autonomy. Especially the Qur'ānic 'Peoples of the Book', Jews and Christians, enjoyed such a status, which was then extended to other non-Muslim communities. Within Islam, no separate communities were officially sanctioned. Serious religious dissent was viewed as *bidʿa*, heresy, or apostasy, to be stamped out or suppressed. Prevented from expressing and propagating their beliefs in public, the dissenters were forced underground, to teach clandestinely in private and to practise precautionary dissimulation, *taqiyya*. This was the situation of the Mālikī *ʿulamā'* under the reign of the first two Fatimid caliphs, as it had been the situation of the Shiites under the previous Sunni regime.

Al-Manṣūr's recognition of the Sunnis as a legitimate community initially strengthened Fatimid authority. Sunni sources describe him and his reign with some admiration and even praise, in marked contrast to their extreme hostility to most of the Fatimid caliphs. However, his policy of tolerance towards his Sunni subjects was not reciprocated by Sunni rulers at the time or after the decline of the Fatimid caliphate. When Sunni government was restored in the Maghrib by the Zirids, the Ismaili minority was massacred by the populace incited by the Mālikī *ʿulamā'*. In Egypt the Ismaili community did not fare much better after the restoration of Sunni government by the Ayyūbid Saladin.

Recognition of the Sunnis as a legitimate community did not imply recognition as true believers. Jewish and Christian *dhimmī*s belonged to recognised legitimate communities but, by their rejection of the Prophet Muḥammad, were unbelievers (*kuffār*). Similarly, Sunnis, by their affirmation of the prophethood of Muḥammad, were Muslims, but by their failure to recognise the rightful imam, were not believers (*mu'minūn*). Non-recognition of the Proof (*ḥujja*) of God, the rightful imam, was, according to a statement of ʿAlī quoted by Qāḍī al-Nuʿmān in his *Daʿā'im al-Islām*, the lowest degree of errancy (*ḍalāl*).[2]

Al-Manṣūr took his obligation as imam to provide religious guidance to the faithful seriously. He issued a book on religious law which was probably the first official Fatimid legal code. Superseded

[2] Abū Ḥanīfa al-Nūʿmān b. Muḥammad, *Daʿā'im al-Islām*, A.A.A. Fyzee, ed., Cairo, 1951, i, 13.

under al-Muʿizz by Qāḍī al-Nuʿmān's *Daʿāʾim al-Islām*, it seems to have been lost at an early date. Quotations from it, however, are contained in a partly preserved *Kitāb al-Yanbūʿ*, a legal compendium itself probably dating from the reign of al-Manṣūr or the early reign of al-Muʿizz.[3] Al-Manṣūr's work is cited there simply as the *Kitāb al-Imām al-Manṣūr bi-Allāh*. Al-Manṣūr seems to have set forth his rulings without referring to the pronouncements of any former imams or justifying them by legal reasoning, solely relying on his own authority as the infallible imam.

The divinely sanctioned authority of the imam in religious and legal matters was unambiguously upheld by al-Manṣūr in another work which is extant in manuscript but has not yet been examined by modern students of Fatimid history. A manuscript of this book, entitled *Tathbīt al-imāma*, is now accessible in the library of the Institute of Ismaili Studies in London.[4] The date of composition of it is not known. It must, however, express the position of al-Manṣūr in the debate about religious and political authority during his restoration of the Fatimid caliphate after the defeat of the great rebellion. Qāḍī al-Nuʿmān refers to a book on the imamate (*fī 'l-imāma*) by al-Manṣūr in his *Daʿāʾim al-Islām*.[5] It is safe to assume that the same work is meant. Unlike al-Manṣūr's legal compendium it evidently remained authoritative under his successor al-Muʿizz.

The book is addressed to an unnamed questioner, evidently a follower, who asked the author about the establishment of proof for the imamate of the Commander of the Faithful ʿAlī b. Abī Ṭālib and his title to it. Al-Manṣūr promises to provide cogent proof and asks the questioner to rely on it in rational investigation before looking

[3] The *Kitāb al-Yanbūʿ* is commonly ascribed to Qāḍī al-Nuʿmān. The reliability of this ascription has been questioned by W. Ivanow, A.A.A. Fyzee and T.S. Lokhandwalla in view of the contrast in style, contents and arrangement between it and Qāḍī al-Nuʿmān's authentic legal works. See I.K. Poonawala, *Biobibliography of Ismāʿīlī literature*, Malibu, 1977, 54; A.A.A. Fyzee, *Compendium of Fatimid Law*, Simla, 1969, xxvii–xxix; S.T. Lokhandwalla, *The Origins of Ismaili Law*, D.Phil. thesis Oxford, 1951, 36–39. The *Kitāb al-Yanbūʿ* is not mentioned in Qāḍī al-Nuʿmān's other works. A manuscript of the extant second part of it is available at the Institute of Ismaili Studies in London. See A. Gacek, *Catalogue of Arabic Manuscripts in the Library of the Institute of Ismaili Studies*, i, London, 1984, 52.

[4] MS 1120 of the Zāhid ʿAlī collection. The manuscript contains 123 folios. The quality of the text varies. Large sections are well preserved while some appear badly corrupted. Other manuscripts of the book are in private collections. Poonawala, *Biobibliography*, 45.

[5] *Daʿāʾim*, i, 48.

into the historical reports (*riwāyāt*) of the various parties who affirm the inevitable need of the people for an imam. Throughout his discussion, it is evident that al-Manṣūr, in agreement with the general Shiite position, saw the imamate as a primary necessity of reason. The reports about its institution thus had to be interpreted in the light of this rational necessity.

The discussion continues in the form of questions to be addressed to the opponents and answers to their claims and questions. The anonymous opponents are primarily the Sunni *ʿulamāʾ* who uphold the legitimacy of the imamate of Abū Bakr and ʿUmar and the validity of the historical Umayyad and Abbasid caliphate. The questions and answers no doubt closely reflect the arguments employed in the contemporary disputations about the imamate between supporters of the Fatimid caliphate and the mostly Mālikī Sunni scholars.

The opponents agreed on the essential need of mankind for an imam, but evidently did not consider the imamate as a prime obligation (*farīḍa*) imposed by God. Al-Manṣūr's first question to them is designed to bring this out. They are to be asked whether the need for the imam is something they have decided by their own opinion or a religious obligation laid down by God. If they answer that it is a religious obligation and that Abū Bakr was the one named (*manṣūṣ*) by God, they were contradicted by Abū Bakr himself when he initially proposed Abū ʿUbayda b. al-Jarrāḥ and ʿUmar b. al-Khaṭṭāb as satisfactory choices for the position, when he appealed to the Muslims: "Relieve me, relieve me" (*aqīlūnī aqīlūnī*), and when he said: "Would that I had asked the Messenger of God to whom the rule belonged after him." Abū Bakr had further stated: "Surely, the Muslims have made me the deputy (of the Prophet, *istakhlafūnī*) and were satisfied with me", and he took his daily wage of two dirhams from the treasury (*bayt māl*) of the Muslims. Likewise ʿUmar contradicted them when he told the Muslims: "If I leave you (without appointing my successor), then someone better then myself (meaning the Prophet) has left you; but if I appoint a successor, someone better than myself (meaning Abū Bakr) has appointed his successor." These and other reported statements, al-Manṣūr argues, confirm that the early Muslims, including Abū Bakr and ʿUmar, did not claim that Abū Bakr was named by God or the Prophet. If the opponents, however, acted on their own opinion in setting up Abū Bakr as the imam, how could they presume that God would not take care of the supreme need of His creation and that they were more considerate of the requirements of the community than God and His Messenger?

In al-Manṣūr's view, the imamate is the "greatest religious obligation (*farḍ akbar*) without which mankind cannot function and act righteously". Other basic religious obligations depend on it, such as the ritual prayer, legal alms, the pilgrimage to Mecca, jihad, and legal punishments (*ḥudūd*). How could it be that God would not provide for it and would leave it to the Muslim community to choose their imam? Taking the place of the Prophet, the imam must be personally nominated by God and the Prophet. How could Abū Bakr permit himself to be called the 'deputy (*khalīfa*) of the Messenger of God' when he, as he admitted, was not appointed by the Prophet as his successor?

Al-Manṣūr highlights the practical difficulties in establishing an imam if he, in accordance with Sunni belief, is not named by God. If he is to be established by election (*ikhtiyār*), who are the electors and who is obliged to accept their choice? Is a certain town privileged to make the choice which then becomes binding for the rest of the Muslim world? What is the number of electors needed to make the election legitimate? No number, even or uneven, seems naturally preferable, and one may end up admitting that the choice of a single Muslim is binding for the whole community.[6] If there is disagreement among the electors about the choice, how is it to be resolved?

Nominated by God and the Prophet, the imam must be the most excellent (*fāḍil*) among his contemporaries. Just like the Prophet, he is God's Proof and Argument (*ḥujja*) in relation to mankind in his time. God cannot permit in His religion that the excellent be ruled by the less excellent (*mafḍūl*). Al-Manṣūr argues at length against the view that the imamate of the less excellent is legitimate and that the imam, if his knowledge of the religious law is deficient, may rely on those who know it better.

Abū Bakr could not be the most excellent among his contemporaries. He had himself told the Muslims: "I have come to govern you, yet I am not the best of you." His knowledge of the Qur'ān was deficient, and the Companions, first among them ʿUmar, had opposed some of his rulings in the religious law. The Muslims thus could not rely on the soundness of his pronouncements, but had to choose between the opinions of Abū Bakr and ʿUmar and others.

[6] The opinion that a single elector was sufficient to make the choice of the imam binding for the community was upheld by al-Ashʿarī. See D. Gimaret, *La Doctrine d'al Ashʿarī*, Paris 1990, 557.

Yet the Qur'ān ordered them to refer their differences to God, His Messenger, and those in authority (*ūlī al-amr*) among them (IV:83) and to obey them (IV:59). 'Those in authority', al-Manṣūr affirms, are none other than the rightful imams.

In the absence of an authoritative imam, the opponents employed personal opinion, analogy, *ijtihād*, discretionary preference (*istiḥsān*), approximation (*taqrīb*), and conjecture to derive the law and admitted the legitimacy of difference of opinion in it. Al-Manṣūr categorically rejects all these methods as in conflict with the Qur'ānic command: "Whoever does not judge according to what God has sent down, those are the wrong-doers" (V:45). The Prophet did not use them and did not permit them to be used. The famous hadith adduced by the opponents to justify their practice, according to which the Prophet approved Mu'ādh b. Jabal's use of personal reasoning in his legal judgements if he could not find the appropriate law in the Qur'ān or the sunna of the Prophet, must be considered unsound or be interpreted so as to exclude such illicit legislation. As the Qur'ān stated, God's religion, Islam, was complete and perfect (V:3) before the Prophet's death. There was no need to add to the Qur'ān and the sunna of the Prophet. The only permanent need was for a just imam who had perfect knowledge of the religious law.

Muḥammad thus could not have been recommending Abū Bakr for the succession when he ordered him to lead the prayers during his final illness, as claimed by many of the opponents. Rather the Prophet gave instructions for the army assembled under the command of his freedman Usāma b. Zayd, which included Abū Bakr and 'Umar, to proceed with their campaign. Do the opponents claim that the Prophet did not know that God would put an end to his life and that the community was in need of Abū Bakr after his death? Abū Bakr and his supporters acted in disobedience to the Prophet's order when they failed to proceed and instead set up Abū Bakr as the imam. The sentence of the Qur'ān applied to them: "Whoever disobeys God and His Messenger, surely hellfire is his lot, to dwell therein forever" (LXXII:23).

'Alī was appointed by the Prophet as the imam to succeed him at Ghadīr Khumm. The hadith about Muḥammad's pronouncement there in his cousin's favour is broadly transmitted and cannot be rejected. The opponents vainly seek to negate its clear meaning by false interpretation. 'Alī's exclusive title to the imamate in succession to the Prophet was, however, also evident from the fact that only he fulfilled all the relevant qualifications of excellence. Adopting a common Shiite argument, al-Manṣūr maintains that there was a consensus of all groups of Muslims in respect to the other Companions that each one of them was excelled in one or the other qualification. There was no such negative consensus in respect to ʿAlī since one group, the Shia, held that he excelled in all qualifications. Among these qualifications, perfect knowledge of the religious law is discussed by al-Manṣūr at greatest length and was evidently most important in his view. He notes much more briefly that the imam must also excel in piety (*waraʿ*) and courage (*shajāʿa*).

Aside from the qualification of excellence, al-Manṣūr discusses the condition of close kinship (*qarāba*) for the rightful imam with his predecessor. He notes that this condition does not require the successor to be the closest kin or the son. He may be the brother, cousin, or nephew, anyone considered a close kinsman (*qarīb*) in ordinary speech. The requirement that the imam must be the most excellent has precedence over the closest kinship. Al-Manṣūr here ignores the standard Imami Shiite rule that after the succession of the two grandsons of Muḥammad, al-Ḥasan and al-Ḥusayn, the imamate could only be handed down from father to son among the descendants of al-Ḥusayn. His position may well take account of the early Fatimid version of the pre-history of the dynasty according to which the first Fatimid caliph, al-Mahdī, had been named by his uncle Muḥammad.[7]

Al-Manṣūr's Ismaili perspective is also apparent in his extending the concept of the imamate to the ages before the mission of Muḥammad. Imami Shiite theory generally viewed the age of the imamate as beginning only with ʿAlī, since the age of prophethood preceding it had come to its end with Muḥammad. Al-Manṣūr views the imamate as a permanent institution and maintains that Jesus had a legatee (*waṣī*) and successor from whom the legacy was handed down to a *ḥujja* or imam in the time of Muḥammad. Although the name and identity of this imam are not known, he must have pronounced the divine appointment (*naṣṣ*) of Muḥammad, since every imam names his successor, summoning mankind to him. Al-Manṣūr admits that the requirement of close kinship of the successor may have been less stringent before Muḥammad than it is now.

---

[7] See W. Madelung, 'Das Imamat in der frühen ismailitischen Lehre' in *Der Islam*, 37, 1961, 55, 71. Al-Muʿizz seems to have been the first Fatimid caliph to insist that al-Mahdī's father al-Ḥusayn was the true imam. Madelung, *Das Imamat*, 74–75.

Since the imamate implements God's government of this world, its basic nature can never change. Al-Manṣūr sharply criticises the view of those opponents who hold that the early imamate in succession to Muḥammad was divinely sanctioned, whether based on nomination or election, while the later imamate lacked legitimacy and thus does not command unconditional obedience of the faithful. Presumably he had in mind here the common Sunni theory based on a well-known hadith that the true *khilāfa* of the Prophet had lasted only thirty years, during the reign of the Rightly-Guided caliphs and that the later caliphate was merely worldly kingship (*mulk*) acquired by usurpation. In their opinion, al-Manṣūr questions these opponents, was God more considerate of mankind when He imposed on them the duty to obey the rightful imam or now that He has lifted that obligation from them? In reality their view inevitably leads to the conclusion that God has abandoned the government of this world and that disobedience to His orders and transgression of His laws now prevail.

The rightful and just imam, al-Manṣūr affirms, is owed unconditional obedience by all Muslims just as the Prophet was. Like the Prophet, he has perfect knowledge of the religious law and does not rely on judicial reasoning and analogy to derive it. As God's chosen governor of mankind, he must be impeccable, protected from error and sin (*maʿṣūm*) by Him. His knowledge of the law necessarily being superior to that of all others, he could not be known through a consensus of the Muslims, since each sect or school of them would naturally prefer one of their own group. The imam must therefore be named by his predecessor. Al-Manṣūr leaves the question open as to how the imams know their successors. It may be that the Prophet identified them by name to ʿAlī or he may have instructed him as to how to choose the successor. In any case, the imam is protected by God from error in the choice of his successor.

In spite of their being chosen by God and protected from error and sin, the imams are not equal to the Prophet. Unlike prophets, they do not receive divine revelation (*waḥy*). The Prophet ranks above them in excellence (*tafḍīl*). Their religious knowledge is derived from that of the Prophet. No abrogation (*naskh*) can occur during their reign as it occurred in the age of the Prophet. Whatever miraculous foreknowledge of events ʿAlī displayed during his imamate, it depended on information given him by Muḥammad, as he himself always stated. Al-Manṣūr disassociates himself categorically from those who ascribed knowledge of the unseen (*ghayb*) to ʿAlī, or who claimed that ʿAlī was a prophet or God, adding that he had never met anyone claiming that.[8]

Al-Manṣūr's treatise on the imamate stands distinctly in the tradition of radical Shiism. The absolute right of ʿAlī to the succession to Muḥammad, and the illegitimacy of the caliphate of his predecessors are uncompromisingly upheld. Al-Manṣūr denies claims of the opponents that ʿAlī himself recognised the legitimacy of their caliphate, although he may have been compelled to do so in precautionary dissimulation (*taqiyya*). Most of the author's arguments are familiar from earlier and contemporary Imami apologetic texts. Except for the minor instances noted, the treatise could be read as an Imami Shiite work. Its purpose was to provide arguments for the debates with the Sunni *ʿulamāʾ* on the rightful succession to Muḥammad, to refute their claims, and to affirm the divine right of the Fatimid caliphs to rule, not to explain esoteric Ismaili doctrine on the imamate. The imam is thus viewed as the divinely appointed enforcer of the religious law entitled to the obedience of all Muslims. There is no mention of the imam's task of providing the esoteric interpretation (*taʾwīl*) of the scripture and of the law brought by the Prophet, of the significance of the seventh imam and of Ismaili Mahdi expectations. Al-Manṣūr rather emphasised that all religious knowledge and authority of the imams derived from the Prophet Muḥammad.

This view of the imamate certainly reflects al-Manṣūr's priorities during his restoration of the Fatimid caliphate. Jaʿfar b. Manṣūr al-Yaman, son of the distinguished *dāʿī* of the Yemen and expert in Ismaili esoteric thought, enjoyed some favour at his court and was encouraged to compose books on *taʾwīl* for the Ismaili *daʿwa*. Like his grandfather al-Mahdī, however, al-Manṣūr sought to limit the activity of the *daʿwa* and to prevent it from spreading extremist claims, attributing supernatural qualities to the Fatimid caliphs which might scandalise their Sunni subjects. These must primarily be persuaded to recognise the divine right of the Fatimids to rule, not their authority to teach esoteric knowledge.

[8] This closely agrees with Qāḍī al-Nuʿmān's quotation of statements of al-Manṣūr denouncing those who ascribed divinity or prophethood to him and the other imams. *Daʿāʾim*, i, 69–70.

# XIV

## An Ismaili Interpretation of Ibn Sīnā's *Qaṣīdat al-Nafs*

Ibn Sīnā's *'Ayniyya* poem on the terrestrial exile of the human soul from its heavenly home has by its mystical and aesthetic qualities always appealed to a wider public than the circle of experts and students occupied with his philosophical thought. Its unusual contents and style as compared with his other works have even aroused doubts about its authenticity among a few modern scholars.[1] Over the centuries, however, Ibn Sīnā's authorship has not been questioned, and numerous commentaries, some by renowned mystics such as Ibn al-'Arabī and 'Afīf al-Dīn al-Tilimsānī, have been composed on it. They have been listed in the bibliographies of Ibn Sīnā's works by C. Brockelmann, G. Anawati, and Y. Mahdavi, but have not yet been seriously studied.[2] Entirely missing in their lists of commentaries is one composed by the fifth Ṭayyibī Ismaili *dā'ī muṭlaq* in the Yemen, Sayyidnā 'Alī b. Muḥammad b. al-Walīd (d. 612/1215), entitled *al-Risāla al-mufīda fī īḍāḥ mulghaz al-qaṣīda*. It has been registered in the bibliographies of Ismaili literature by W. Ivanow and I. Poonawala, and some excerpts from it have been published in the sixth *Risāla ramaḍāniyya* of Sayyidnā Ṭāhir Sayf al-Dīn, the fifty-first *dā'ī muṭlaq* of the Bohra community in India.[3] In Western scholarship, however, it has remained virtually unknown.

At the beginning of his treatise, Ibn al-Walīd states that one of the 'virtuous brethren', evidently a member of the Ismaili community, had come upon a *qaṣīda* ascribed to the Ra'īs Abū 'Alī b. Sīnā in which the latter obscured the meanings and hinted at esoteric mysteries (*asrār ḥaqīqiyya*). The author's purpose in doing so was, Ibn al-Walīd suggests, to reserve its noble concepts and subtle sciences for those whom God has blessed with seeking them from their owners (*arbāb*) and aiming for them through their gates (*abwāb*), while withholding them from the partisans of the satans and devils who claim the ranks they do not deserve.

By the owners and gates of the esoteric science, Ibn al-Walīd evidently means the Ismaili Imams. He is thus implying that Ibn Sīnā, or the author of the poem, was in fact a disciple of the Imams who veiled the spiritual truths so that the members of their community might discover them through the teaching hierarchy of the *da'wa*. It may be recalled here that Ibn Sīnā's father and brother had, according to his own testimony, been attracted to Ismaili teaching by a Fatimid *dā'ī*. Ibn Sīnā himself, however, had repudiated it, and in his philosophical thought rather adhered to the Peripatetic tradition.[4] The Ismaili *da'wa* did not count him as an initiate and in general ignored his philosophy and his writings. His theological views, it is true, had been radically criticised from an Ismaili perspective by Tāj al-Dīn al-Shahrastānī in his philosophical *Wrestling Match* (*Kitāb al-muṣāra'a*). The latter, however, was, in the words of al-Sam'ānī, associated with the 'people of the mountain fortresses (*ahl al-qilā'*)', the Nizārī Ismailis in Iran,[5] and Ibn al-Walīd in the Yemen most likely was not aware of his work. Ibn Sīnā's *qaṣīda* on the soul evidently was also unknown in the Ṭayyibī *da'wa*, and Ibn al-Walīd's attention was drawn to it only because of its discovery by a member of the community. How then should he react to its message? Impressed by its affinity to Ismaili esoteric thought, he could not fail to recognise its author, whoever he was, as inspired by the spiritual wisdom of the Imams. The identity of the author presumably was of not much importance to him. He does not name Ibn Sīnā again in his commentary.

When requested by the 'virtuous brother' to elucidate the subtle secrets, enigmas, and noble truths which the author had deposited in his poem, Ibn al-Walīd felt obliged to comply, obeying the maxim of the Prophet: 'Do not give wisdom to others than those worthy of it lest you wrong it, nor withhold it from those worthy of it lest you wrong them.' Thus he came to compose his treatise, entitling it *The Instructive Epistle in Elucidation of the Enigmatic in the Qaṣīda* and seeking the assistance of God and the blessing of the one whose sphere encompassed him. He adds that he would not in his exposition go beyond indication, in order to protect wisdom from falling into the hands of the ignorant rabble who do not deserve it.

Ibn al-Walīd explains the fall of the 'ash-grey dove' (*warqā'*), as Ibn Sīnā depicts the human soul, from its lofty abode, stating that this refers to the laxness (*futūr*) that occurred in a part of the spiritual world of origination (*'ālam al-ibdā'*) in its response to the divine summons, which led to its coarsening (*takaththuf*) and fall from the world of subtleness to the site of coarseness, from the space of the exalted lights to the centre of decaying bodies and the darkness of the world of generation and corruption and the abode of mixture. This statement distinctly alludes to the mythical events designated first by H. Corbin as the 'drama in heaven',[6] which had become characteristic of Ṭayyibī gnostic cosmology ever since it was described by the second *dā'ī muṭlaq* Ibrāhīm al-Ḥāmidī (d. 557/1141–1142) in his *Kanz al-walad*. According to it, the Third Intellect and Second Emanation, not identified here by Ibn al-Walīd, fell from its rank as it refused to recognise the priority of the Second

Intellect and so became the Tenth Intellect in rank, the demiurge (*mudabbir*) who governs the sublunar material world. The sublunar world was constituted by the spiritual forms, including the human souls, which had, together with the Third Intellect, repudiated the priority of the Second Intellect and remained in a state of disobedience.

Ibn al-Walīd goes on to explain that the dove's description as possessing pride and aloofness (*dhāt taʿazzuz wa-tamannuʿ*) is an allusion to the haughty refusal of the spiritual forms to submit to the one who preceded them in responding to the divine summons and their resistance to obey whomever they were ordered to obey. They became then divided into three groups, those who repented and asked for forgiveness after that had become difficult, those who doubted and remained in bewilderment and who in reality came to constitute the three elements, and those who persisted in their haughty refusal and became the centre of the earth.[7] The demiurge placed these three divisions in the proper place they deserved according to the rule of justice. The spheres and stars became the fathers (*ābā'*), the elements the mothers (*ummahāt*), in order that the realms of nature (*mawālīd*) would be borne by them. The first of these realms was that of the minerals, and their ultimate limit was the true man, who was the aim, the first thought and the last work. The demiurge arranged the macrocosm so that in the encompassing sphere, its highest, brightest, and most noble part, matter, would, because of its subtlety, almost become assimilated to its form, while in the earth, its lowest, coarsest, and darkest part, form, would almost be assimilated to matter. In between these extremities all revolving spheres and moving globes were placed higher in accordance with their subtlety and nobility or lower in accordance with their deficiency and coarseness.

Ibn al-Walīd then documents the pre-existence of the human soul from Ismaili religious literature, noting that the 'virtuous person, Author of the Epistles', that is the concealed Imam believed to have composed the *Rasā'il Ikhwān al-Ṣafā'*, had hinted at it, or upheld it explicitly, in many places. As an example he quotes a passage from the *Risāla al-jāmiʿa*, where it is explained that when the sages speak of the 'partial souls', they mean the power that emanates from the Universal Soul and falls to the low centre, being driven into the world of nature. They have fallen short of accepting the spiritual outpouring and lagged behind in the glorification and sanctification in the abode of lights and have therefore been cast into the centre, where servitude and the hardship of obedience with physical instruments and in bodily shape was imposed on them. They had been of a kind which they are not now and to which they shall return when they have repented of their sin and sought forgiveness for their stumbling. For this reason the Universal Soul inclines in compassion towards them, and God sends His Messengers to warn them, aided by His close angels. If they repent they will return to blessed repose, but if they disobey and remain haughty, they will stay in bewilderment, ever more cut up into nations in the darkness of the lowest nether world.[8]

It may be noted that this description of the human souls as an emanation of the Universal Soul stands in contrast with Ṭayyibī cosmology, which, based upon the philosophical system of Ḥamīd al-Dīn al-Kirmānī, considers them as issuing from the Third Intellect, which is identified with Nature. In the present context, however, this difference hardly required a comment from the learned *dāʿī*. He next quotes another text of the Author of the Epistles, this time from the *Jāmiʿat al-jāmiʿa*, referring to an act of disobedience on the part of the Universal Adam in the world of the Soul from which the psychic power (*quwwa nafsāniyya*) flowed to the first human individual, the partial, rebellious Adam, who was forbidden to eat from the tree.[9]

The Commander of the Faithful ʿAlī b. Abī Ṭālib, Ibn al-Walīd notes, also hinted in some of his statements, in the *Nahj al-balāgha* and elsewhere, at the pre-existence of the human soul. Thus he said: 'Let one of you look out whether he is moving forward or turning back; for from the hereafter he has come and to it he will return.' Next Ibn al-Walīd adduces Qur'an 77:30–31 and 2:36 as evidence and concludes with the verse: 'Oh you trustful soul, return to your Lord, approving and approved'. (Qur'an 89:27–28) He observes that the order to return to a place in reasonable speech is only given to someone who was there before.

In the second line of the poem Ibn Sīnā describes the dove representing the soul as hidden from every eye, yet showing itself openly and not wearing a veil. Ibn al-Walīd explains that he meant by this the aforementioned life that has fallen and has been covered by the waves of perplexity and become mixed up with the bodies in blackest darkness. It is at times termed Nature, at other times the 'pervading life' (*ḥayāt sāriya*) or the 'originational leaven' (*khamīra ibdāʿiyya*) and is meant by the word of God: 'And He is the one who brings forth what is hidden (*al-khabʾ*) in the heavens and the earth'. (Qur'an 27:25) No part of the macrocosm and its realms is bare of it, nor is any corporeal being without it. Rather it is the substance (*jawhar*) that bears its accidents, leading them to their most excellent states and most perfect purposes. Ibn al-Walīd then quotes from the first *mashraʿ* of the fifth *sūr* of al-Kirmānī's *Rāḥat al-ʿaql*, where he discusses matter and form and explains that Nature is the more noble part of them and is termed form. It is, al-Kirmānī affirms, life *in actu*, emanating from the world of sanctity, but is not independent by itself in its existence. Rather it is carried by prime matter. Al-Kirmānī goes on to explain that life pervades everything in the heavens and on earth as its active part, endowing it with its first perfection (*kamāl awwal*) and moving it on.[10]

Ibn al-Walīd then describes in some detail the action of latent life as it moves from potentiality to actuality: the spheres govern; the Mothers (= elements) become parturient; minerals, plants, and animals emerge successively, until the human being is reached, who is the intended purpose. In the minerals, life remains mostly concealed, yet its actions may be witnessed in the magnetic stone and other phenomena. As it rises through the realms of nature, its actions become more and more varied, apparent and noble. In man it constitutes the faculty of imagination, memory, thought, recollection, intelligence, artisanship, discrimination, and reflection. It continues to rise through the ranks of humanity until it reaches its ultimate end in the rank of those receiving the divine support (*ta'yīd*), who are in touch with the close angels through the subtleness of their souls, not their coarse bodies. These manifest acts of life are what in reality the bodies alone are incapable of, and are what is meant by the poet's words: 'it shows itself openly and does not wear a veil.'

The third line of the poem depicts the soul as loath to join the body and then, paradoxically, as perhaps loath to depart from it, while in agony. Ibn al-Walīd explains that this refers to its fall into this world under compulsion, involuntarily as a result of its lagging behind in the affirmation of the priority of those preceding it and of its continued unbelief and haughtiness. Therefore the darknesses of the three dimensions enveloped the souls, and divine wisdom necessitated their removal. The demiurge in charge of them knew that they could not stay in that noble luminous world and sacred spiritual abode and that they would not be cured of the disease attaching to them but through the succession of times, the motion of the spheres, and the mixture of the elements. He arranged them therefore in accordance with the requirements of justice in this world, against their will and choice, leading them to their first physical perfection which consists in the shape of the human body. Ibn al-Walīd adds that this compulsion occurs in reality between two conditions of choice, a hardship between two states of ease, yet only the knowing understand this.

With regard to the souls being loath to leave the body and being in agony, Ibn al-Walīd observes that all souls, the good and the evil, hate death. The evil do so because as they become accustomed to the natural, animal world and absorbed in the sea of dark matter, forget the noble luminous world from which they departed, and their state, origin and destination are obscured to them, and so they wish to enjoy this terrestrial transitory life and choose to stay in these decaying bodies. They hate death out of ignorance of where they are going and out of fear of what they are approaching. In contrast, the good souls, the friends of God, as they realise into what affliction they have fallen, understand the mistake and sin which necessitated that, and repent of their shortcomings, they seek to take advantage of acquiring good qualities and deeds through the tool of their body as long as they remain in the abode of acquisition (*iktisāb*). For that reason they hate death. Ibn al-Walīd again refers to the 'virtuous person, the Author of the Epistles' for corroboration of his argument. This time he quotes from the 'Sessions of Purification by Cleanliness of the Souls' (*Majālis al-tanaẓẓuf bi ṭahārat al-nufūs*), a work so far unknown. The excerpt closely resembles the Epistles of the Sincere Brethren in style and analyses at considerable length the different motives of the friends of God as well as of His enemies for hating death.

The next line repeats, in different terms, the point that the soul at first disdains her coming to this world but after joining it becomes fond of 'the neighbourhood of the desolate ruin'. Ibn al-Walīd notes that the explanation of this has already been given in the previous section. Then he points out that the Author of the Epistles told a parable relating to this theme in which he alluded to the departure of the souls from the abode of simple spiritual beings, their joining with the composite corporeal shapes, and their becoming fond of them after initial aversion and disdain. He will summarise it here because of its pertinence and its clear intimations about origin and destination. From the *Epistle in Explanation of the Belief of the Sincere Brethren* he then quotes the story about the fortunate city located on a mountain top on an island whose inhabitants live in permanent peace, concord and prosperity. A group of them travel by sea and suffer shipwreck. They are cast ashore on a wretched island with rugged mountains, dark caves, murky water and wild beasts of prey, inhabited by a race of apes. A bird of powerful constitution dominates the island and every day carries off some of the apes to eat them. The castaways live a life of hardship and misery on the island. As the apes get accustomed to them, some of the men get attracted to their females, mingle with them and reproduce. Eventually they compete eagerly for the favour of the female apes, hate and fight each other, find enjoyment in this life and desire its perpetuity. Then one of them has a dream in which he returns to his home town. When the people there hear of his arrival they come out full of joy to receive and welcome him. They see that travel and life abroad have changed him and, loath for him to enter in this state, wash him in a spring at the gates of the city, shave his hair, cut his nails, dress him in new clothes and perfume him. Then they put him on a mount and enter the town with him. All gather around him, marvelling at him and at his safe return after his/their (?) despair, while he feels happy with them and that God has rescued him from his exile, the company of those apes, and that miserable life. As he awakes and finds himself among the apes he becomes sad and averse to remaining in that wretched place, thinking about how to return to his home. He tells his dream to one of his brethren who now also remembers their home town and their people and the bounty they used to enjoy. They decide to gather wood on the island so as to build a ship and to return to their home by sea. They remind others of their brethren who had come with them of their former abode of happiness, opening their eyes to the sordid state of their present abode, and everyone joins in the task of building the ship. Then one day the bird comes and snatches one of them, flying off to eat him. When the bird notices that he is a man, not an ape as he was accustomed to, he carries on flying until he reaches the island from which he (the man) had originally come and drops him on the very roof of his house. As the man recognises his town and home he simply wishes that the bird would snatch one of his brethren every day and return him to his home. The people on the wretched island, however, weep after the bird carries him away and continue to grieve over his absence because they do not know what the bird has done with him. Yet if they only knew they would wish as he wished. This, the teller of the story observes, should be the belief of the Sincere Brethren about those whose death precedes theirs. For the lower world resembles that island, and its inhabitants resemble the apes. Death is like that bird, and the friends of God are like the shipwrecked people. The abode of the hereafter is like that other island where their home and their people are to be found.[11]

In the next lines the poet elaborates on the experiences of the soul in this world. At first she seems to forget her former stay in the 'protected enclosure' (*ḥimā*) which she was not satisfied to leave. Yet when the heavy burdens of physical existence bear down on her she weeps from eyes flowing without cease as she remembers her stay in that enclosure. Ibn al-Walīd comments only briefly, referring back to his previous explanations. Her weeping, he suggests, is an allusion to her repentance and distress about the loss of her true being and her containment in the confines of non-being. By this repentance her rise on the stairs of ascent comes about, as does her attachment to the rope of life that is extended to her through the guidance of the Imams and the ranks of the teaching hierarchy (*ḥudūd*).

Yet the dense shape of the body, the poem continues, holds her back like a cage from the lofty spacious summit and she remains tied to that which must stay behind, allied to the dust. Ibn al-Walīd comments that by the alliance to dust is meant the body's return to the earth from which it has come and from which it draws its nourishment, whereas the soul returns to her abode, and her parts join her whole, gaining salvation. He quotes one of the ranking teachers who said:

> Since every kind shall join its kind from a shell that remains in the abode of senses
> to a pearl that joins the Spirit of Holiness.

The poem continues: 'When the voyage to the protected enclosure with the wide open space draws near, the dove coos in excitement as the veil is lifted and she sees what cannot be perceived with drowsy eyes.' Ibn al-Walīd interprets the approach of the voyage as the arrival of the life that is trapped in matter at the human shape, which is the end of objective existence (*wujūd dhātī*) and the beginning of formal existence (*wujūd ṣūrī*), after it has traversed the inverted, crooked path and reached the straight path. If it is granted success and enters the gates of the gardens of bliss by ascent on the ladder of salvation it obtains the second perfection, flowing to the vast open space of holy spirituality. When the soul in her travel reaches this stage, which is the last gate of the world of generation and corruption, when she enters the circle of existence by obedience to the Imams of right guidance, takes cognisance of the ranks of the physical as well as the sacred spiritual hierarchy and opens up through the spiritual sciences, the veil is lifted for her from the hidden mysteries. At that time she awakens from the sleep of unawareness, seizes the opportunity to acquire the gnostic insights in the time of respite and speaks with the tongue of wisdom and reflection, while longing to join the righteous of her likes and her brethren. A witness to this is the statement of the Commander of the Faithful ʿAlī b. Abī Ṭālib when he said: 'If the veil were lifted my certitude could not increase', because of his full realisation of his closeness to God and of his lofty rank. ʿAlī also said, when he was struck by the sword of his murderer: 'I have won, by the Lord of the Kaʿba.' As further testimony Ibn al-Walīd quotes eight lines from a *qaṣīda* of al-Sulṭān al-Khaṭṭāb b. al-Ḥasan al-Ḥajūrī (d. 533/1138), chief of a clan of Hamdān in northwestern Yemen, *ma'dhūn* in the Ismaili teaching hierarchy, and poet. There al-Khaṭṭāb laments his long journey in this world, bidding the bodily frame that holds him back from his aims to part. Having associated with his body when a wrap covered his eye, he is, now that it has been cleared away, ready for a decisive break. Let each one of them join his kind, be it of earth or of heaven. He expects to reach his hopes as he knows, beyond all guessing, his destination when the veil is removed. The bliss that he shall find is above description by his thought and intelligence.[12]

The poet continues stating that as the dove comes to warble on the peak of a lofty height so knowledge raises the rank of the one who had not been raised. Ibn al-Walīd repeats that the soul's warbling is in response to her cognition of the divine sciences, obscure secrets, and gnostic truths and expresses her longing to join her like, who have been freed from their bodies and have left behind the rebellious opponents of the faith. The summit of the lofty height signifies her reaching the upright stature (*qāma alifiyya*) that resembles the first originational beings[13] and her rise through the ranks of the hierarchy, gaining the two perfections, the objective and the formal, and yearning to appear in the most excellent camphoric shape (*shabaḥ kāfūrī*). Ibn al-Walīd endorses, in glowing terms, Ibn Sīnā's praise of knowledge as raising the rank of the soul. How could it be otherwise, he asks, when knowledge is the greatest magnet drawing noble souls to their destination, their protector from disintegration and corruption, when it dyes them with the beautiful and splendid dye of God, joins them to the radiant lights of the highest world, removes from them evil habits and beastly traits, endows them with pleasing angelic dispositions, turns them into substances after they were counted among accidents and ordains for them permanent happiness and arrival at all goals? ʿAlī b. Abī Ṭālib stated: 'When God wishes to humiliate a servant He denies him knowledge', and the Prophet said: 'God does not give a servant knowledge but that He will rescue him some day through it.'

In the next section a certain tension becomes apparent between Ibn Sīnā's poem as conventionally understood and the Ismaili interpretation of Sayyidnā Ibn al-Walīd. There are in fact some minor but significant variants between the commonly transmitted text and that quoted by Ibn al-Walīd, highlighting the different perspective of the philosopher and the religious gnostic. Ibn Sīnā first poses the question as to why the dove may have been cast from its high summit to the bottom of the lowest depth. If God caused her to descend for a wise reason it has been hidden even from the most pious of intelligent men. For Ibn al-Walīd this cannot be a real question. He states briefly that he has already explained the fall of the soul and her imprisonment in the corporeal world by her initial failure to hold on to the one above her in rank and to obey him when summoned to obedience. This offence prevented her from gaining her share of the second perfection and necessitated her dismissal to the transitory world of decay. Yet the Intellects of the world of origination turn with compassion and affection to its fallen parts and emit noble benefits to them in order to repair their deficiency and perfect their substance. That Divine Wisdom which is hidden from the minds of mankind reaches them only through the tongues of the Friends of the Truth, and becomes known only to the deserving on whom they bestow it.

The poem now presses the question further: If the fall of the dove was a due blow to make her hear when she would not hear and to make her know every obscure matter in the two worlds, then her defect has not yet been mended. The version cited by Ibn al-Walīd turns the conditional 'if the fall was' (*in kāna*) into a categorical affirmation 'no doubt the fall was' (*lā shakka*), and the apodosis of the conditional sentence introduced by 'then' (*fa-*) is changed into a clause introduced by 'while' (*wāw ḥāliyya*). Ibn al-Walīd comments that the poet seems to refer by this to the concealed sciences and protected wisdom through which the soul obtains the perfection of her substance and nobility of her constitution and to her cognition of the mysteries of the two worlds, that of density and that of purity, before her deficiency has yet been mended by her arrival at these sciences and before she has been freed from her slavery by taking cognisance of them.

In its conventional form the poem continues: Time has cut short the path of the dove such that she 'set outside the place of rising' (*gharaba bi ghayr al-maṭlaʿ*). The cutting short of her path is naturally to be understood as referring to death, while her setting far from the place of rising suggests its finality. The anonymous commentator quoted by B. Carra de Vaux sees in it, not unreasonably, a repudiation of metempsychosis (*tanāsukh*) by Ibn Sīnā.[14] In Ibn al-Walīd's reading of the text, *bi ghayr al-maṭlaʿ* is replaced by *bi-ʿayn' al-maṭlaʿ*, implying that she declined in the very place of rising.[15] Ibn al-Walīd then interprets time's cutting short of the soul's path in the context of her cosmological voyage in exile. He suggests that the poet meant that the soul, when entering under the rule of time, among the movements of the spheres and the mixture of the elements, becomes united with the forces of the elements and in the mixture joins the first of the realms of nature, that of the minerals. That is the final stage of her descent, from where her ascent and return to the original spiritual beings begin. The poet alluded by the places of setting and rising to this stage. In confirmation of this interpretation Ibn al-Walīd cites Ḥamīd al-Dīn al-Kirmānī, who in his *Kitāb maʿālim al-dīn*[16] mentioned the first stage of the minerals, which is gypsum, stating: 'That is where Nature appears in reverse, returning to parallel the First (Intellect).' On this, Ibn al-Walīd adds, the eminent shaykh ʿAlī b. al-Ḥusayn b. al-Walīd based his treatise known as *Risālat al-ḍilʿ*,[17]

where he describes the right side (*ḍilʿ*) of a cosmological triangle drawn by him as the path of descent in objects (*dhawāt*), the left side as the path of ascent in forms, and the base of the triangle as the place of the realms of nature, which are the end of the fall and the beginning of the rise.[18] The mineral realm, which constitutes the first stage, is thus the place of both setting and rising. Similarly Sayyidnā Ḥamīd al-Dīn Abū ʿAlī Bāb al-Abwāb stated in his *Kitāb al-dhāt wa'l-ṣūra* that the world of compulsion (*ʿālam majbūr*) consists of physical objects (*dhawāt*) without form, while the world of free choice (*ʿālam mukhtār*) consists of abstract forms without objects. Whatever is between them is both objects and forms.[19] Our descent from that world to this world thus was in objects, and our ascent from this world to that world will be in forms.

The final line of the poem likens the dove, or her exile on earth, to a bolt of lightning that flashes in the enclosure and then vanishes as if it had never shone. Following its vain search for the wisdom that lies behind her exile, the poem thus seems to end on a note of pessimism or agnosticism.[20] The Ismaili gnostic, certain of possessing the key for understanding the cause of the soul's exile, reads the line rather as an admonition to the faithful. The poet, he suggests, meant by this the state of the soul when she appeared in the human mould and was embodied in the Adamic shape, her short life span, the closeness of its end and the readiness of her composite body to disintegrate. He represented all that by the flashing of the lightning and the speed of its disappearance. The poet then admonished the righteous out in front to gather provisions for the day of return, to hasten to perform good deeds and to exertion, to restrain the irascible soul from reprehensible morals and evil acts, which is the reality of jihad, to resolve upon acts of worship and the acquisition of enduring pious works, to adorn themselves with the mark of the fear of God, which consists in combining the two kinds of worship: that of knowledge and that of work, to be friends of the Friends of God and the members of the hierarchy, who are the best of mankind, so that their souls may gain eternal blessings in the hereafter, emanations of the luminous Intellects and everlasting joys. Let therefore every prudent, knowledgeable, and sensible person, every vigilant, consummate, and refined character take advantage of this short life and avail himself of the period of brief respite, which may be likened to a flash of lightning because of the speed of its passing and disappearance, before the Lender demands back His loan, lest repentance befall them when there is no time for repentance and before the One to whom destiny leads seizes the souls, when man will meet the acts he has performed and there will be no helper to be called upon. Ibn al-Walīd concludes his commentary with a prayer for himself and all believers that God might seal their lives as He seals those of His close Friends.

## Notes

1. Aḥmad Amīn held that the poem by its poetical inspiration stood in clear contrast with the generally clumsy Arabic style of Ibn Sīnā in both his prose and poetry. He suggested that the real author of the poem was the poet, philosopher and ascetic Muḥammad b. al-Ḥusayn b. al-Shibl al-Baghdādī (d. 473/1080–1081). Aḥmad Fu'ād al-Ahwānī, on the other hand, expressed doubts on Ibn Sīnā's authorship because the contents of the poem do not agree with some of his views about the human soul. Especially, he argued, the depiction of the soul at the beginning of the poem as pre-existing the body was in conflict with Ibn Sīnā's commonly upheld view that the soul originates with the body. See F. Kholeif (Khulayf), *Ibn Sīnā wa-madhhabuh fi'l-nafs* (Beirut, 1974), pp. 131–136. Kholeif rejects these doubts. He notes in particular the similarity of some of the terms and metaphors used by Ibn Sīnā in both the *'Ayniyya* and his *Risālat al-ṭayr* (pp. 155–158).

2. Notes from an anonymous commentary are provided by B. Carra de Vaux in his edition and translation of the poem, 'La Ḳaçîdah d'Avicenne sur l'âme', *JA*, 9th ser. vol. 14. It is to be noted that the reference to this article in *GAL*, SI, p. 818 is erroneously to *JA*, 9th ser. vol. 4. The mistaken reference has been copied by both G. Anawati, *Mu'allafāt Ibn Sīnā* (Cairo, 1950), p. 155 and Y. Mahdavī, *Fihrist-i nuskhahā-yi muṣannafāt-i Ibn-i Sīnā* (Tehran, 1954), p. 197. F. Kholeif gives a few quotations from four commentaries on the poem.

3. W. Ivanow, *A Guide to Ismaili Literature* (London, 1933), p. 59; I. K. Poonawala, *Biobibliography of Ismā'īlī Literature* (Malibu, CA, 1977), p. 159. The sixth *Risāla ramaḍāniyya* of Sayyidnā Ṭāhir Sayf al-Dīn, entitled *Durār al-hudā al-muḍī'a*, was published in Bombay 1341/1923. The excerpts from the *R. al-mufīda* are on pp. 44–61. The present study is based on four manuscripts belonging to The Institute of Ismaili Studies in London.

4. See W. E. Gohlman, *The Life of Ibn Sīnā* (Albany, NY, 1974), pp. 18–19.

5. Al-Subkī, *Ṭabaqāt al-shāfi'iyya al-kubrā* (Cairo, 1905–1906), vol. 4, p. 79.

6. See H. Corbin, *Trilogie Ismaélienne* (Tehran and Paris, 1961), pp. 135–136.

7. The same division of the rebellious spiritual forms is described by al-Ḥusayn b. 'Alī b. al-Walīd, the son of 'Alī b. Muḥammad and eighth *dā'ī muṭlaq*, in his *Risālat al-mabda' wa'l-ma'ād* (ed. H. Corbin in *Trilogie Ismaélienne*, Arabic text, p. 106). The repentant forms constitute the ether, the perplexed ones make up the other three elements – air, water, earth – and the recalcitrant become the rock (*ṣakhra*) at the centre of the earth.

8. *Al-Risāla al-jāmi'a*, ed. J. Ṣalībā (Damascus, 1949), vol. 2, pp. 38–39; ed. M. Ghālib (Beirut, 1974), pp. 354–355.

9. The *Jāmi'at al-jāmi'a* quoted here is a work belonging to the literature of the Ṭayyibīs and is not yet published. It differs from the *Jāmi'at al-jāmi'a* edited by 'Ārif Tāmir (Beirut, n.d.).

10. Al-Kirmānī, *Rāḥat al-'aql*, ed. M. Ghālib (Beirut, 1967), pp. 269–270. Al-Kirmānī's identification of nature with life, form, motion and soul is thoroughly analysed by D. De Smet, *La Quiétude de l'Intellect* (Leuven, 1995), pp. 324–331.

11. *Risālat bayān i'tiqād Ikhwān al-Ṣafā'* in *Rasā'il Ikhwān al-Ṣafā'*, ed. Kh. al-Ziriklī (Cairo, 1928), vol. 4, pp. 102–104.

12. Al-Khaṭṭāb's lengthy poem is edited by I. Poonawala in his *al-Sulṭān al-Khaṭṭāb: Ḥayātuh wa-shi'ruh* (Cairo, n.d.), pp. 121–129. The lines quoted by Ibn al-Walīd are on p. 124, nos. 35–42, as noted there by the editor.

13. The spiritual beings of the *ibdāʿ* world possess upright *alif* stature like the human stature. They are, however, distinguished by exceeding purity, luminosity and splendour so that they cannot be perceived by physical senses or described by corporeal attributes. See the question and answer no. 1 in R. Strothmann, *Gnosis-Texte der Ismailiten* (Göttingen, 1943), Arabic text, p. 111.

14. *JA*, 9th ser., vol. 14, pp. 164–165, 172.

15. Kholeif, *Ibn Sīnā*, p. 131 n. 4, notes the variant *bi-ʿayn* from the *Dīwān Ibn Sīnā*, ed. Ḥ. ʿA. Maḥfūẓ (Tehran, 1957).

16. The *Kitāb maʿālim al-dīn* is commonly known as *al-Risāla al-waḍīʿa fī maʿālim al-dīn*. The quoted passage is in the edition by Muḥammad ʿĪsā al-Ḥarīrī (Kuwait, 1987), on p. 127.

17. See Poonawala, *Biobibliography*, pp. 140, 146. It is alternatively known as *Risālat tuḥfat al-ṭālib wa-umniyyat al-bāḥith al-rāghib*. The author, ʿAlī b. al-Ḥusayn b. Jaʿfar b. Ibrāhīm b. al-Walīd (d. 554/1159), was an uncle and the first teacher of ʿAlī b. Muḥammad b. al-Walīd.

18. In the manuscripts of the *Risālat al-ḍilʿ* the descent appears to the onlooker in fact on the left side of the triangle and the ascent on the right side.

19. The *Kitāb al-dhāt waʾl-ṣūra* has so far been known only through a reference to it, without the name of the author, in al-Bhārūjī's *Kitāb al-azhār*, ed. ʿĀdil al-ʿAwwā, *Muntakhabāt Ismāʿīliyya* (Damascus, 1958), vol. 1, p. 198. See Poonawala, *Biobibliography*, p. 321. There is a brief quotation from it in ʿAlī b. al-Ḥusayn's *Risālat al-ḍilʿ*: 'The worshipper's raising of his hands at the *takbīr* is an indication that the world of acts (*ʿālam al-afʿāl*) will return to the world of statements (*ʿālam al-aqwāl*).' ʿAlī b. al-Ḥusayn takes the world of acts as referring to the descent and the world of statements as referring to the ascent in his cosmological triangle. The author of the *Risālat al-dhāt waʾl-ṣūra* is called by ʿAlī b. al-Ḥusayn merely Bāb al-Abwāb. The author to whom it is ascribed here by Ibn al-Walīd seems to be identical with the early Fatimid *dāʿī* Abū ʿAlī al-Ḥasan b. Aḥmad Bāb al-Abwāb (d. 321/933), who, according to Ibn Ḥawqal, had earlier been known as Ḥamdān Qarmaṭ (see Madelung, 'Ḥamdān Qarmaṭ and the Dāʿī Abū ʿAlī', in *Proceedings of the 17th Congress of the UEAI*, St. Petersburg, 1997, pp. 115–124) The name Ḥamīd al-Dīn may be an erroneous addition by an early scribe, induced by the occurrence of it a few lines before referring to al-Kirmānī, or it may have been intentionally added as an honorific title (suggestion by I. Poonawala in a letter dated 27/9/1999). It is not known if the book is extant. The terminology employed in it, contrasting *dhāt*, in the sense of a physical, corporeal object, with *ṣūra*, abstract form, is unusual in Ismaili literature. Ibn al-Walīd, however, uses it in several passages of his commentary.

20. See the comments of Carra de Vaux, *JA*, 9th ser., vol. 14, p. 173.

# XV

## Shahriyār b. al-Ḥasan: A Persian Ismā'īlī *dā'ī* of the Fatimid age

Ever since the rise and expansion of the Ismā'īlī missionary movement throughout the Islamic world in the 3rd/9th century, Iran has been intimately connected with its religious and philosophical thought. The origins of the movement, though much obscured by legendary tale, are commonly sought in western Iran. Investigating its roots, the early critical historian al-Mas'ūdī (d. 345/956) asserted that it was founded in the year 260/874 in Isfahan. Anti-Ismā'īlī polemicists imagined a plot of Persian Shu'ūbīs active in Khūzistān out to destroy Arab Islam. Whilst political success of the movement came in Bahrain, Yemen, and most spectacularly, with the rise of the Fatimid caliphate, in the Maghrib and Egypt, Iran continued to contribute many of the *dā'īs* who profoundly shaped its spiritual identity. As numerous works of early Ismā'īlī literature have become accessible to modern scholarship, the names of Abū Ya'qūb al-Sijistānī, Ḥamīd al-Dīn al-Kirmānī, al-Mu'ayyad fī al-Dīn al-Shīrāzī and Nāṣir-i Khusrau stand out among the chief representatives of Ismā'īlī religious thought.

There were others whose works, although much more modest and conventional, were significant enough to be preserved and treasured by the tradition of the Ismā'īlī *da'wa.* Shahriyār b. al-Ḥasan is known as a *dā'ī* of Fārs and Kirmān, later active in Yemen, in the time of the Fatimid caliph al-Mustanṣir bi Allāh (427-487/1035-1094).[1] Given the lack of concrete data, the story of his life can only vaguely be reconstructed. He was presumably somewhat younger than his illustrious fellow countryman al-Mu'ayyad fī al-Dīn al-Shīrāzī, who was born before 390/1000 and succeeded his own father as head of the Fatimid Ismā'īlī *da'wa* in Fārs. Shahriyār and al-Mu'ayyad must certainly have been known to each other, but there is no evidence of a close relationship between them at that time. In his autobiography al-Mu'ayyad does not mention Shahriyār or any other *dā'ī* in Fārs. It was, no doubt, al-Mu'ayyad fī al-Dīn's fall from grace of the Būyid ruler Abū Kālījār under 'Abbasid pressure and the subsequent persecution of Ismā'īlīs in Fārs which also compelled Shahriyār to leave his homeland after 435/1043. He found a secure refuge in Yemen, where the Ṣulayḥids had recently succeeded in

[1] Brief biographical notes on Shahriyār b. al-Ḥasan are provided by Ḥ. F. al-Hamdānī, *al-Ṣulayḥiyyūn wa al-ḥaraka al-Fāṭimiyya fī al-Yaman* (Cairo, 1955), 266, 272; I. Poonawala, *Biobibliography of Ismā'īlī Literature* (Malibu, 1977), 125-6; and idem, *EI*², s.v.

founding a Fatimid vassal state. Al-Mukarram Aḥmad, the son and successor of the founder, in particular patronized him. An official letter *(sijill)* of the caliph al-Mustanṣir to al-Mukarram dated 15 Ramaḍān 461/8 July 1069 mentions that the latter had made a request in respect to the "faithful" *(wafī)* Shahriyār b. Ḥasan and that the chief *dā'ī*, al-Mu'ayyad fī al-Dīn, would take charge of the matter.[2] On the basis of this note it has been assumed that Shahriyār was actually sent by al-Mukarram with a delegation to Cairo.[3] This seems reasonable, but not certain. It may be that al-Mukarram merely requested a promotion for Shahriyār in the ranks of the *da'wa* in Yemen.

Shahriyār's prestige in the *da'wa* was, in any case, secured by the intervention of al-Mukarram and the chief *dā'ī* in Cairo. Perhaps a decade or two later, he was present at a session of the court of the Queen al-Sayyida Arwā[4] when Abū al-Mundhir 'Āmir b. Sulaymān al-Zawāḥī (d. 492/1099), a dignitary prestigious in the *da'wa* and influential with the queen, put forward a question to the assembled learned men about the Qur'an, verse 68:1: "We have given you a manifest victory, so that God shall forgive you your sin that preceded and that has been delayed." What, he asked, was the sense of the ascription of sin to the Prophet? Are not the prophets impeccable and protected from all sin? All the scholars present, both adherents of the *da'wa* and opponents, offered answers which, on consideration, merely added to the astonishment and confusion of the audience. Finally Shahriyār gave his explanation with words that came to his mind at the moment. His answer was evidently judged to be satisfactory, and he later recorded it in writing and sent it to al-Zawāḥī. Thus it was preserved.

Shahriyār's known works include, besides the letter to al-Zawāḥī, a treatise in refutation of those who deny the spiritual world and a *qaṣīda* poem beginning with the words: "What is love of the world and its people to me?"[5] The poem, which might throw some light on his ascetic world view, unfortunately is not accessible at present. The treatise countering the denial of the spiritual world was included by the Yemenite *dā'ī* Muḥammad b. Ṭāhir al-Ḥārithī in his *Majmū' al-tarbiya,* a popular chrestomathy of basic Ismā'īlī texts chosen for educational purposes.

II

The *Risāla fī al-radd 'alā man yunkir al-'ālam al-rūḥānī* reflects primarily the philosophical cosmology adopted by the Ismā'īlīs. Apart from the reference to the

---

[2] A.M. Mājid (Magued), *al-Sijillāt al-Mustanṣiriyya* (Cairo, 1954), 202.

[3] So both Ḥ. al-Hamdānī, *al-Ṣulayḥiyyūn,* 272, and Poonawala, *Biobibliography,* 125, and *EI*[2], s.v. "Shahriyār b. al-Ḥasan."

[4] The queen is not named in the introduction to Shahriyār's letter to 'Āmir al-Zawāḥī. The use of the feminine pronoun in the formula of blessings, however, indicates that her court is meant.

[5] See Poonawala, Biobibliography, 126.

Prophets, Legatees and Imams as the recipients and transmitters of divine spiritual assistance *(ta'yīd),* little in it is characteristic of Ismāʿīlī gnostic thought. The adversaries are the narrow-minded materialist believers who fail to recognize the spiritual dimension intervening between God and the physical world. The treatise begins with the question of an imaginary interlocutor: "You claim that the world consists of two worlds, the corporeal and the spiritual. The corporeal world we know, and do not deny it. It consists of this immense visible structure of a raised sky, shining stars, complementary elements and successive realms of nature. Beyond that we see or perceive nothing. So prove to us its existence with an irrefutable argument whose truth is witnessed by the hearts."

The author replies by pointing to his and his interlocutor's agreement concerning the corporeal world, its limits and design. From this world, he asserts, the reality of the spiritual world is revealed without difficulty, for whatever is hidden can be deduced from what is apparent. If that were not the case, there would be no way to comprehend what we witness. This visible world may be divided into three domains. The first of them is the world of spheres and stars in which there is no increase or decrease in either its whole or its particulars. If there were any increase, it would have to seek an empty space for itself, but, according to the consensus among the sages, there is absolutely no empty space in the world. Moreover, the celestial world has been observed throughout all ages, yet no spatial expansion or contraction has ever been witnessed. Rather, it is changeless in its sound structure and stable composition, so that corruption has no path to enter it at all. The second domain of this world is the four elements, earth, water, air and fire. They undergo change in their particulars, but not in their collectivity, by mutual exchange and mixture. Whatever enters being by mixture will return to its original state by corruption. Yet if the change in the elements were collective, there would be no stable being upon which to rest for the realms of nature. The third domain consists of the three realms of nature, the minerals, plants and animals. They are subject to change in their collectivity and in their particulars, as each of their bodies goes through its three stages of coming into being, transformation *(istiḥāla),* and corruption.

Shahriyār goes on to affirm that man, being "the first in thought, the last in creation, and the ultimate end of existents," must partake of every genus of the lower world in himself and possess a portion of every substance (*jawhar*) of the upper world. Because of the breadth of his base, the multitude of his powers and the expanse of his margins (*ḥawāshī*), man seeks to attract material (*mādda*) from all of them. As a consequence, opposites meet in him which hold back the material from freely reaching him. He therefore needs to maximize the noble power that the material may reach him in order to progress from the state of potentiality to actuality and from his state of weakness to the state of noble elevation. This noble power becomes fluent in him and aids him to acquire the knowledge and cognition through which he reaches salvation in the abode of the hereafter. As portions of all existents are assembled in him, the whole of creation becomes subservient to him. He rules over it as he puts each thing in its proper place. Thereby he earns permanent being and his transfer from the abode of perdition to the abode of life, which is the Garden of Refuge and the abode of simple substances (*basā'iṭ*), where he is no longer in need of seeking these material benefits as his own substance reaches perfection. All this is lacking in the body since its substance is confined, its basis narrow and its margins close. Thus it draws its material only from whatever is nearby, not from what is remote, and does not deserve to be transferred to the abode of the hereafter and to acquire permanence. It is no equal to man, and any analogy between them is disproportionate.

Increase, decrease, transformation and spatial transfer in bodies are all by nature and compulsion. Yet we may find in them another motion which is not derived from their substance or their kind. That is the motion of choice and will. When bodies are single by themselves, they lack that choice and that motion. The condition for the motion of choice is that the agent has the power to act and to desist. In constrained action, the body by its nature is unable to desist from it. Thus we know that the producer of this motion is not the body.

Among the voluntary acts are those which attract the useful and which ward off harm. The body by itself does not repel defects and is unable to attract benefit. Rather, it is prepared to receive accidentals and the impact of effects, whether they are good or bad. The agent in it thus is able to do with it whatever he wishes. At one time he turns it from its elementary being of earth, water, air and fire into flesh, blood, bones and nerves and all for which the body is prepared. By thus being raised from stage to stage it becomes suited for the purposes of the agent without resistance. At another time he lowers it from its noble state by exposing it to corruption and allows it to disintegrate. The agent thus takes the body for some purpose and when he has reached his aim, discards it and dispenses with it. It then continues to decline until it returns to its original condition from which it began. It remains then unable to lift itself a single degree until another agent utilizes it and does with it as the first one had done. Thus we know that with the body there must be another substance that attracts the useful and wards off the harmful.

This substance, the author proposes, possesses innumerable virtues, but there is a limit to what this chapter of his treatise can contain. Among these virtues is the cognition of things absent in time and space and the expansion of this substance through its information into times past and future. Past and future thus become combined in a single particle (*juz'*) without resistance, while they resist the body, which is unable to control them both. The classes of mankind, however, differ in that respect. There are those who view these two times for the sake of their worldly livelihood. They view in their minds the ways for gaining benefit and the proper moment to reach their aims, scheming to attain them by various means. Rarely a benefit escapes them in most matters. Others look for the governance of others and seek to conquer and rule over their fellow men. They ever employ their minds to set up helpers for those who will tomorrow curb the violence and evil of the enemy and will uproot those expected to assault their kingdom or revolt against it. All this requires proper foresight and understanding of the past in order to plan for the future. The one who is most able to imagine the future will be recognized as the most excellent among them. Is there any physical body which is capable of that? If that ability were founded in the structure of bodies, the excellent and the base, the intelligent and the ignorant would all be equal.

The utmost degree and highest rank of this virtue is attained by the elect of mankind who receive the divine support *(ta'yīd)* through which they tread creation under their feet, yet spread the cover of their kindness and mercy over it. They warn humans about the ultimate outcome in this world and the hereafter, caution them by the prediction of horrific events long before they occur, give them good tidings of bounties and the descent of blessings on them and of good fortune, inform them of where they are going and from where they originated, and explain to them their path between beginning and end. Through their preaching, humans gain knowledge. Those who do this are the veracious prophets, the most noble legatees, and the rightly guided Imams.

Someone may object that this divine support does not depend on any body or anything else. Shahriyār suggests that if the questioner investigated what he said the answer would occur to him from his own words. For this divine support which both he and the questioner acknowledge must be either Creator or created. Since the Creator does not exist in anything created, it must be created. Yet it is obviously part of that spiritual world whose reality Shahriyār is seeking to demonstrate. From that spiritual world everyone receives support in accordance with his capacity, the extent of his substance and the purity of his soul. The one whose substance is most lucid is worthy of being singled out by God for support and revelation *(tanzīl)* and that He should make him an intermediary between Himself and His creation. Through him God thus will lead humans from the darkness of ignorance to the light of knowledge, and through his mediation He will revive them for everlasting life. As for those whose substance is opaque and whose hearts are blind, God indicates to them through the tongue of these intermediaries how to purify their substance, to soften their hearts and to transform their morals, so that if they obey their leaders, they attain what God has prepared for them. God has, furthermore, made His creation dependent on each other, such that each one takes guidance from his companion who is next to him. The chain in which they are suspended and by which they rise up is emanated upon them from the lights of the spiritual world whose reality is denied by the opponent.

The author next argues that the power of each body extends only as far as its limits. If there is any influence by a body on another, it is only by touching it. Otherwise there is absolutely no effect of one body inside another. Yet we find a different substance that reaches to all regions of the earth and to remote places in less than a blink of the eye.

Anyone endowed with a will is able to imagine India or China or any other far-off region without needing to go there, finding them represented in himself. Likewise he may engage the vision of his heart and the thought of his mind in comprehending the structure of the heavens, the stars, their orbits, their elevation relative to others, the power of their influence in ascent and its decline in descent. He is able to imagine all this in the shortest time possible, in which the body is unable to perceive and realize it. He may further employ his mind in imagining the totality of the universe as if it were a ball before him and can quickly penetrate into any part of it and their movements. God has alerted us to this meaning in His words (Qur'an 55:33): "O assembly of Jinn and men, if you are capable of passing through the regions of the heavens and the earth, pass through; but you will not pass through without authority (*sulṭān*)." That authority consists in the simple spiritual powers which attract everything to their essence and substance and hold the corporeal world in their horizon.

We find that a single seed, when sown in the earth, will attract to itself many parts from the elements, and these parts will increase manifold. Then they will bring forth numerous seeds, each one of them endowed with the same shape and power as the first one. If there were not a noble power and an active substance in that seed, it could not have this effect. The same is true of animals and humans as they reproduce themselves innumerably.

We also say, Shahriyār continues, that the spiritual world is not obscure to us because of its intrinsic obscurity, but rather because of our inability to perceive it. In this respect it is like speech composed of letters that contains noble meanings. It escapes children and fools, not because it is obscure in itself, but because of the weakness of their faculties in comprehending it. Similarly, the bat becomes weak in vision when the sun rises. As its sight is darkened, it is unable to fly, and directions are closed to it. Yet when night obscures it, it sets out to fly in search of its food. Likewise, the people who draw least benefit from their spirituality are those who possess least knowledge of it. According to the extent of their recognition of spiritual matters will be their connection with them, their nobility and their capability to seek everlasting life.

Further evidence is that we find the composite body holding together its parts and soundly constructed for some time. Then, as time advances, its parts fall apart and disperse, and it has no power to control itself. If its hold on these parts were by the body itself, it would never break apart. Thus we know that there is something else that is itself hidden and appears to us only by the power of its effect. God has made it a bond for the composite parts and it holds them together and preserves their order. When it departs, the body is unable to hold on to its parts and falls into ruin until it disintegrates.

The treatise ends with an appeal to the denier of the spiritual world to consider and meditate all that in order to realize the power of God in his creation of the world, the subtle as well as the massive, the apparent as well as the concealed. By that he will recognize the unicity of God, as His Messenger has said: "The most cognizant of himself is also the most cognizant of his Lord."

III

Shahriyār's other treatise, on the offenses committed by the prophets, is more specifically Ismāʿīlī in motivation. The Qur'an mentions various offenses of the major prophets and alludes to those of Muḥammad in Sūrat al-Fatḥ (48:1-2). This created a problem for many Muslim theologians who, to various degrees, upheld belief in *'iṣma,* the impeccability of prophets, and much was written to interpret the relevant passages of the Qur'an accordingly. Shahriyār's opponents are here the literalists, the *ahl al-ẓāhir,* who accept the Qur'anic text at face value and concede that the prophets may commit sins like ordinary human beings. For Shahriyār the offenses of the prophets are purely spiritual, a temporary failure to recognize the proper order of ranking in the spiritual hierarchy. This is a theme well known in gnostic thought. One may be reminded of its archetypal representation in the tragic fall of the Third Intellect from its rank in the luminous World of Origination because of its failure to recognize the precedence of the Second Intellect which resulted in the constitution of this physical world of darkness. This mythical representation, so prominent in the literature of the later Yemenite Ismāʿīlī *da'wa,* was probably still unknown. Shahriyār, in any case, does not refer to it.

The treatise opens with due praise to God, who is beyond all comprehension, to His Messenger Muḥammad, to the Legatee 'Alī and to the Imams, the lords of the people of their age and rescuers of their followers from the fire and perdition. The author then affirms that the Qur'an mentions mistakes of all the prophets and Messengers, but this does not lower their ranks and their perfection. Thus God said about Adam (20:121-2): "Adam disobeyed his Lord and went astray; then his Lord chose him and turned to him and gave him guidance." The reason for this was that when Adam recognized the station of the Qā'im (of the era preceding him) and the majesty of his rank, he desired it for himself. This was evidently before Adam reached his own rank as the first Messenger of our present era.

Similarly the Qur'an (11:45) reports that Noah said: "Surely, my son is of my family." This referred to a man from whom Noah had taken the oath of initiation before he was trained by complete and effective breaking (*kasr*) of his false convictions.[6] When Noah pleaded with him (11:42), "O my son, embark with us and do not be with the unbelievers," he answered (11:43), "I will seek refuge on a mountain which will protect me from the water." He meant that he would return to his tutor (*murabbī*) with whom he could attain perfection, and that he had no need of the rank of inspired interpretation

[6] *Kasr* refers to the early stage in the initiation when the false beliefs of the neophyte are "broken" by critical questioning. Among the ranks of the *da'wa* there is mention of the *mukāsir*.

(*ta'wīl*). Noah now realized that the man was not properly trained. When told (XI 46): "Do not ask me that of which you have no knowledge," he thus answered: "Surely, I seek refuge with You lest I should ask You for that of which I have no knowledge. If You do not forgive me and have mercy on me, I will be among the losers."

The literalists (*ahl al-ẓāhir*) understand Qur'an 6:75-79 to mean that Abraham, actually seeing a star, said about it: "This is my Lord", and that he said the same about the moon and the sun. God forbid that Abraham could have been on such a level as they imagine. Rather, the star which he saw was a licentiate (*ma'dhūn*) left over from the cycle of Noah. When Abraham at the beginning of his own cycle met him, he thought he was suited to be his tutor (*murabbī*), but as he found the licentiate deficient in that regard, he turned away from him. He then relied on the one above the *ma'dhūn* in rank, the summoner (*dā'ī*). When he found him also falling short of his expectations, he turned away and sought the help of the proof (*ḥujja*), who was above the *dā'ī*, as the rank of the imamate was empty at the time. When Abraham heard his discourse, however, his heart was not impressed by it. For although Abraham was then merely at the beginning of his mission, his soul was pure and perfect. Then when he had taken in their speech about a religion abrogated by his own mission and he received revelation about his imposition (*taklīf*) of a new law, he addressed his people (6:80): "Will you dispute with me about God when He had guided me?" He meant that revelation had come to him and he had been ordered to impose a religious law. From this day he would command and forbid, dispensing with the people of his time.

As for Moses, he learned before his own mission from Shu'ayb. Then he said to him, "My Lord, let me see You that I look upon You. He said: You shall not see me." The literalists imagine that he asked that God appear to him and show Himself to him so that he would look at Him with his eyes. This would have been the gravest of sins if Moses had asked for it. In reality Moses asked Shu'ayb for permission to manifest his own mission before its proper time. His lord, that is Shu'ayb, told him: "You shall not see me, but look at the mountain. If it rests in its place, you shall see me. When his Lord appeared in his glory to the mountain, He crushed it to dust, and Moses fell down as if thunderstruck. When he recovered, he said: 'Glory be to you, surely, I turn in repentence to you and I am the first of the believers.'" The Qur'an meant by this that Shu'ayb told Moses that the time of his appearance had not yet come. Shu'ayb would, however, extend his protective wing over him. Moses should go to the people of his kingdom, and if he found them submissive, he might give Moses permission to manifest his mission at that time. When Moses asked the king for help and the latter instructed his people accordingly, they refused to obey. They rose up against the king, crushed his kingdom and devastated his lands. Moses realized that what his tutor Shu'ayb had told him was the truth and submitted to his command and prohibition. This is when he said: "Glory be to you, surely I turn in repentance to you and am the first of the believers."

Jesus was at first raised spiritually by his mother, that is his tutor (*murabbī*). With him was a companion in the same state, but Jesus had accumulated more of the rank of perfection than his companion, and he wished to honor his tutor. Therefore he said to his companion, "Do you know that I am stronger than anyone in all our rank?" Yet there was no third one in that rank. The companion told his tutor, "Surely, he has claimed perfection after you and that all the people of your cycle are deficient." The tutor asked Jesus (5:116): "Have you said to the people: Take me and my mother as two gods apart from God?" When the tutor then suggested that all the people of the time had become perplexed about the rank of perfection of the tutor, he answered (5:117): "I did not tell them but what you commanded me: that I worship God, my Lord and Your Lord." He meant that what he had said was merely the word and testimony of the tutor which he repeated.

Similarly the Prophet Muḥammad knew that he inevitably needed a legatee who could take his place during his lifetime and in his absence. Thus he observed the state of his companions and drew close to each of them, testing them and seeking to win over their hearts. He imagined the best in them until revelation came to him and he was told (2:144): "We see you turning your face to heaven. Now we shall appoint for you a *qibla* that will satisfy you. So turn your face in the direction of the Sacred Mosque." That was a hidden indication to the Commander of the Faithful ('Alī). The Prophet realized that his effort to draw close to the other people until that time had been a mistake and he also understood what would occur on their part after him because of this mistake. Thus when the revelation came (48:1-2): "We have granted you a manifest victory, so that God will forgive you your sin which has preceded and that which was delayed," it referred to his undue closeness and intimate familiarity with them. Muḥammad's fault was to draw close to some people of whom God knew that they would deviate, seek the ruler's hat (*qalansuwa*), seize his pulpit and lay their hands on his off-spring. They would thus repudiate God's right of which his legatee, the Commander of the Faithful, was most worthy and after him the Imams of his cycle, al-Ḥasan and al-Ḥusayn and his descendants, until God cleared away their misfortunes.

These then were the acts of the Messengers, which resemble slips and which the literalists imagine to be sins, acts of disobedience and seduction. God forbid that the prophets would commit such violation of the forbidden as the literalists fancy. Since Muḥammad knew what had happened to the former Messengers, he was aware that the like of it would happen in his own cycle, although he could not be certain what exactly might occur in his time.

The most astonishing statement in the discourse of the Qur'an addressed to all the prophets, their legatees, the Imams of their cycles and all their followers is the warning (19:71-2): "There is none among you who shall not reach it (hellfire). That is with your Lord a decided decree. Then We shall save those who feared God and leave the evildoers in it kneeling." If this verse were taken at the literal level, it would mean that prophets, legatees, Imams, their followers and all others would enter the fire. The Qur'an likewise states (11:119): "Certainly I shall fill hell with Jinn and humankind altogether." At the literal level this would also imply that no one escapes hellfire, especially if the term Jinn refers to angels as the exegetes hold. Our Masters of the Family of the Prophet, however, have imparted some of their knowledge to us so that we realize what is satisfactory in that respect and have removed us from the mass of the ignorant who fabricate lies about God, His prophets and His friends. They have told us that in the above verse the fire signifies ignorance in the sense of the absence of all objects of knowledge from the mind. It thus is in consonance with God's word (16:78): "And God has brought you forth from the wombs of your mothers not knowing anything." Thus we understand the verse to signify that the prophets and Imams pass through the stage of bareness of their minds from all knowledge, not that they reach the fire of hell which is the abode of the unbelievers and the hypocrites. Rather, they are the intercessors for the offenders and the guides of the obedient. Through them God raises the ranks of the righteous, the believers and the sincere.

# *Kawn al-ʿĀlam:* The cosmogony of the Ismāʿīlī *dāʿī* Muḥammad b. Aḥmad al-Nasafī

The early Transoxanian *dāʿī* Abu l-Ḥasan al-Nasafī (or al-Nakhshabī, d. 332/943) is generally considered the founder of the Persian school of Ismailism in the Fatimid age, who first introduced Neoplatonic thought into the teaching of the Ismaili *daʿwa*. In his *Kitāb al-Maḥṣūl,* published around the year 300/912, he comprehensively set forth his new vision of the Ismaili worldview. The *Kitāb al-Maḥṣūl,* which contained expositions on theology, cosmology, and hiero-history of prophethood and the Imamate, appears to be lost, although numerous quotations from it have been found in later works. The only work of al-Nasafī known to be extant is a *Kitāb (Kayfiyyat) Kawn al-ʿālam* (Book on the Genesis of the World). Since this book has been inaccessible to the public until recently, it has not yet been properly examined in modern scholarship.[1] A single manuscript of it, however, is now available at the Institute of Ismaili Studies in London.[2] The present preliminary study of it will seek to analyze the basic structure of al-Nasafī's cosmology, while ignoring many of its detailed arguments, comparisons, and quotations of Qur'anic proof texts.

There is a question as to the authenticity of the treatise. In contrast to the *Kitāb al-Maḥṣūl, Kawn al-ʿālam* does not seem to be expressly mentioned in extant early literature and is not listed in the *Fihrist* of Ismaili books by al-Majdūʿ. While the Neoplatonic thought espoused in it substantially agrees with the views that have been ascribed to al-Nasafī, there is a significant exception. The *dāʿī* Abū Ḥātim al-Rāzī (d. 322/933), al-Nasafī's contemporary, critically reviewed the *Kitāb al-Maḥṣūl* in his *Kitāb al-Iṣlāḥ*

[1]See H. Halm, *Kosmologie und Heilslehre der frühen Ismāʿīlīya,* Wiesbaden 1978, p. 173.

[2]See A. Gacek, *Catalogue of Arabic Manuscripts in the Library of the Institute of Ismaili Studies,* vol. I, Montreal 1984, pp. 35–36. The title of the treatise is given there as *Risālat Kawn al-ʿālam ta'līf al-dāʿī Muḥammad b. Aḥmad al-Nakhshabī.* I. Poonawala (*Biobibliography of Ismāʿīlī Literature,* Malibu 1978, p. 43) mentions two manuscripts kept in private libraries.

(Book of Correction), in which he quoted al-Nasafī as stating that rational human souls are parts *(ajzāʾ)* of the First Intellect and that humanity was the fruit *(thamara)* of the benefits that the Universal Soul received from the Intellect. Abū Ḥātim rejected this view and insisted that rational souls were merely imprints or traces *(āthār)* of the First Intellect and that mankind was the fruit of the material world as a whole.[3] Abū Yaʿqūb al-Sijistānī in his *Kitāb al-Nuṣra,* where he defended al-Nasafī's doctrine against Abū Ḥātim's criticism, described human souls as parts of the Universal Soul, not of the Intellect, and argued that the Soul had two sides, a luminous one facing towards the Intellect above it and a partly dark one facing towards nature and the material world below it.[4]

On this basis it has been assumed that al-Nasafī described the human souls as parts of the Universal Soul in *al-Maḥṣūl,* thus embracing the gnostic view of the fall of the Soul into the material world because of its original sin.[5] As is well known, this gnostic belief was widely upheld in Ismaili teaching, most elaborately in post-Fatimid Ṭayyibī *ḥaqāʾiq* treatises. The author of *Kawn al-ʿālam,* however, explicitly describes the rational soul as a trace produced by the Universal Soul in the sensitive animal soul. As such, it is able to survive the death of the body and eventually joins the Universal Soul to become part of it. This view seems entirely consistent with the overall design of the cosmology envisaged by the author. There is nothing to suggest that the Universal Soul, even though it is initially deficient in relation to the First Intellect, has any longing for the material world. Whether Abū Yaʿqūb's theory that human souls are parts of the Universal Soul represented al-Nasafī's thought correctly is thus questionable. Al-Nasafī's description of human souls as parts of the First Intellect as quoted and criticized by Abū Ḥātim was obviously ambiguous and can hardly be understood literally. *Kawn al-ʿālam* may be seen partly as a response by al-Nasafī (who survived Abū Ḥātim by a decade) or one of his early disciples to Abū Ḥātim's *Kitāb al-Iṣlāḥ.* The question of authorship cannot at present be settled definitely, though the authoritative tone of *Kawn al-ʿālam* perhaps speaks for al-Nasafī's being the author. The book will be discussed here as his work.

---

[3] Abū Ḥātim al-Rāzī, *Kitāb al-Iṣlāḥ,* ed. Ḥasan Mīnūchehr and Mehdī Moḥaghegh, Tehran 1998, pp. 32–33.

[4] Ḥamīd al-Dīn al-Kirmānī, *Kitāb al-Riyāḍ,* ed. ʿĀrif Tāmir, Beirut 1960, pp. 111–12.

[5] Halm, *Kosmologie,* p. 112.

At the outset, the author addresses an anonymous questioner who had asked him about the manner *(kayfiyya)* of the genesis of the world. He responds by invoking the succor of the two spiritual parents of the faithful, i.e. the Universal Intellect and Soul, as well as the "Lord of Reason" *(ṣāḥib al-manṭiq),* i.e. the Prophet, who kindles the fire of reason in those who join him in seeking it and longing for eternal life. The questioner evidently expected not a mere description, but rather a rational explanation of the origins of the universe, and al-Nasafī repeatedly points out that his elaborations agree with what can presently be observed in the world. The Muʿtazilī Abu l-Qāsim al-Bustī in his anti-Ismaili polemic noted with apparent distaste that the Bāṭiniyya, and al-Nasafī in particular, tried to assign a cause *(ʿilla)* to everything in their cosmology, although they did not employ the term *ʿilla* for it.[6]

Al-Nasafī's Neoplatonism was superimposed on earlier Ismaili speculation, which remained most apparent in his initial description. He states: the beginning of the world was from nothing by the Command *(amr)* of the singular Originator *(mubdiʿ),* who transcends all originated things. Since the Originator was singular *(fard),* the Command was a single one, the cause *(ʿilla)* of all creation. The first created matter came to be two because it was caused *(maʿlūl),* and whatever is caused requires a cause. We thus call creation a pair *(zawj),* as it is not singular, but is made *(mafʿūl).* The Singular is other than the pair, which exists through It. It cannot be demonstrated, but It must be affirmed on account of the existence of the pair. Since initial creation is a pair, one of the two things must be different than the other; for if they were exactly alike, there would be only a single one. The contrast between the absolute singularity of the Creator and the essential pairedness of all creation evidently reflects pre-Fatimid Ismaili thought as set forth by the early *dāʿī* ʿAbdān in his *Kitāb al-Izdiwāj.*

From here on, Neoplatonic terminology and concepts prevail in al-Nasafī's presentation. The being that is originated *(mubdaʿ)* by the perfect *(tāmm)* Originator through perfect origination must necessarily be perfect. The first originated being by perfect origination thus came to be perfect and a perfecter *(mutammim)* of what issued *(munbaʿith)* from it by the power of origination. When the perfect originated being looked at itself in order to recognize itself, that recognition *(maʿrifa)* became a form, just as our recognition consists of a form in us. Unlike our form of recognition,

[6]See Halm, *Kosmologie* p. 129; Abu l-Qāsim al-Bustī, *Min Kashf asrār al-Bāṭiniyya,* in ʿĀdil Sālim al-ʿAbd al-Jādir, *Al-Ismāʿīliyyūn,* Kuwayt 2002, p. 194.

however, that of the perfect originated being had the power to become a substance. The perfect originated being then was called Intellect, and it was perfect in actuality and potentiality. It was called an intellect because in it the Creator cognized *(ʿaqala)* all creatures of the universe, and also because its essence was fully cognizable *(maʿqūl)* for itself without any need for seeking additional benefits *(fawāʾid)*. The form that issued from it was called Soul, and it was an intellect in potentiality, not in actuality. It is intellect in potentiality because it lacks the action *(fiʿl)* of the First Intellect and is not made out of nothing, but rather issued from something else. Yet it has the latent power to become an intellect in actuality after acquiring the benefits provided by the First Intellect.

Here al-Nasafī notes that his explanation had been based on a concept of temporality. The First Intellect and Soul, however, were not created in time. Time was generated only after them, and it was impermissible to imagine any time between Intellect and Soul or to state that there was a distance between them.[7] Rather, the most appropriate description he could find was based on numerology *(ḥisāb)*. He then sets forth his numerological theory. One is the basis *(aṣl)* of number, not a number itself, since it does not accept any increase or decrease by being squared or by division by itself. The first number rather is two, and one is its base *(aṣl)*. Applied to the genesis of the world, this indicates that the perfect originated being could not be at work *(fi l-ʿamal)*, but that its partner that issued from it came to be at work with the power it received from the former. The world, moreover, can be observed to be permanently revolving in circular motion. This circularity is dependent on two points, as when we draw a circle with a compass. One of the two points marks the center and does not enter into work, like the numeral one, while the other, which corresponds to the number two, moves in circular motion and represents the beginning of work.

After the origination of the first pair, the whole world came into existence. First a second pair appeared opposite the first pair, then from the four there appeared seven, and from the seven twelve. With the twelve the numbers were completed, the states were soundly established, and everything settled in its proper place. This can be deduced from the theory of numerology, for we observe the division of the number two to be two single units that are joined. When the two are further joined with the one, they become three, and when the two are joined with two, the result is four. The three and the

[7] It may be noted here that Abū Ḥātim al-Rāzī considered time as having come into existence together with the Soul. *Al-Iṣlāḥ*, pp. 24–25.

four add up to seven. Next when the three is squared, the result is nine, and when the three is multiplied by the four, they become twelve. Thereafter there is no number, but only repetition *(takrār)*. This is so because the beginning of numbers is two and the square of two is four. When the two is joined by one, they become three, whose square amounts to nine, and nine is the completion of numbers since it is followed by the second of the four bases *(uṣūl)* of number. If the four bases are joined to the nine, they become twelve. By the four bases al-Nasafī means one, ten, hundred, and thousand. Since the first base, one, is already included in the nine, only the other three are in fact added to reach twelve.

Applying this theory to cosmology, we find that from Intellect and Soul, motion and rest are generated, and the third is a substance *(jawhar)* consisting of active heat *(ḥarāra fāʿila)*. We find the four after the three represented by the four natures, i.e. heat, cold, humidity, and dryness, and by the four Mothers *(ummahāt)*, the elements fire, air, water, and earth; we find the seven after the four to consist of the seven celestial spheres and the seven planets. After the seven spheres we find the nine accidents *(aʿrāḍ)*, i.e. the categories enumerated by the ancients, which they said were concomitants of every substance: quantity, quality, relation, place, time, position, state, activity, and passivity, the nine being three times three. After the nine we find the twelve signs of the zodiac and the twelve winds. After these cornerstones *(arkān)* of the world we find nothing but the three well-known stages *(marātib)* whose imprints appear in what is below them. The world thus reached completion with these cornerstones and began to generate the Progeny *(mawālīd)*, the three terrestrial kingdoms.[8] Numbers now increased through different mixtures until they reached their predestined limit. The continuous change of mixtures is brought about by the revolutions of the spheres.

Al-Nasafī's numerological speculation focusing on the qualitative significance of a few essential numerals reflects the Pythagorean philosophical tradition, in contrast to Aristotelian and Neoplatonic thought with its purely quantitative concept of infinite serial numbers. Three centuries later Naṣīr al-Dīn al-Ṭūsī was to note the Pythagorean character of Ismaili philosophical doctrine and to chide al-Shahrastānī for not properly understanding it.[9]

---

[8]The three terrestrial kingdoms, i.e. minerals, plants, and animals, appear to be identical with the three "well-known stages" mentioned before, or to be produced by them.

[9]See P. Walker and W. Madelung, *"The* Kitāb al-Izdiwāj *attributed to ʿAbdān,"* now published in: *Fortresses of the Intellect: Ismaili and other Islamic Studies in Honour of Farhad Daftary*, ed. Omar Ali-de-Unzaga, London 2011, pp. 107–109.

The special significance of the numbers seven and twelve had been firmly established in pre-Fatimid theory about the Imamate and the hierarchy of the *daʿwa,* a subject not broached in *Kawn al-ʿālam.* Al-Nasafī could easily accommodate these numbers in his scheme. Further strengthening the Pythagorean character of his elaborations, he then turns to geometry. The first figures *(ashkāl)* of the sages are the circle, then the triangle, then the square. These figures are similar to the first numbers in numerology. The circle, as previously mentioned, depends on two points. Next the triangle corresponds to the number three after the two, and the square corresponds to the four after the three. If the circle is dissected by a line through its axis and a second line is added tying a knot with it in the middle, four triangles are formed in the circle, and all significant numbers become manifest. The number two is represented by the two lines, the three by the two lines[10] with the circle, the four by the four triangles, and the seven by combining these with the two lines and the point (in the center).[11] The nine is found in the eight extremities of the four triangles together with the axis on which the lines rest, and the twelve is represented by the angles of the four triangles, which add up to twelve.

Al-Nasafī next challenges anyone who might claim that some other number represents the origins more properly than those mentioned by him to present his evidence. Truth and falsehood about the beginnings of the world depend on whether the theory put forward agrees with what men can witness anywhere in the furthest regions and in their own selves, as the Qur'ān (41:53) states: "We shall show them Our signs in the horizons and in themselves so that it will be manifest to them that it is the truth." After discussing a few examples of true and false theories, al-Nasafī polemically turns against the views of some "demented fool" who claimed that creation in the beginning consisted of specters *(ashbāḥ)* that became shadows *(aẓilla),* and who adduced the echo *(ṣawt)* coming from a wall as evidence for the specters and the shape *(ṣanam)* that appears in a mirror as evidence for the shadows. The fool no doubt was a champion of the Mufaḍḍal ideological tradition popular among the extremist Shīʿa, with its mythical gnostic doctrine about specters and shadows that preceded humanity in creation. The Mufaḍḍal ideology must have been widespread among neophytes and potential converts to early Ismaili Shiʿism. Al-Nasafī evidently advocated

[10]The manuscript erroneously reads *al-nuqṭatān* instead of *al-khaṭṭān.*

[11]The text of the manuscript is defective here and reads *wa-ammā al-arbaʿa fa-l-muthallathāt al-arbaʿ maqrūna bi-l-khaṭṭayn wa-l-nuqṭa.*

the adoption of more scientific philosophical thought in the Ismaili *daʿwa* and considered the rival tradition as a serious threat to the sound beliefs of the community. He scornfully offers rational explanations for the apparently strange phenomena cited as evidence by the fool and comments: how can anyone be satisfied with such superstitions *(khurāfāt)* and occupy his mind with the likes of them? Addressing his readers, he suggests that if anyone of them held on to a remnant of such beliefs in his heart, he should write him so that he might explain the absurdity of that belief to him with the help of God and His friends.

Returning to his cosmology, al-Nasafī explains that the Universal Soul, being an intellect in potentiality, inevitably demanded benefits from the First Intellect. This entailed motion, and when motion subsides, it turns into rest. Motion produces heat, as can ever be observed, and rest results in cold. We witness heat to be active and therefore call it male, and we witness cold to be passive and call it female. Heat dissolves solids, thus producing humidity, and ultimately may cause them to rise in order to absorb them. When all humidity had been absorbed in it, the heat turned it into air. Cold solidifies liquid and attracts it downward. When it had solidified all humidity, the cold turned it into earth. The cool air surrounded the earth from all directions and held it in its place, while the earth held on to the air, preventing it from dispersal. The two composites, air and earth, then united to generate two further composites, fire and water, the former being male and the latter female. Fire was the finest of the four composites because the two male parts, the heat from air and the dryness from earth, were combined in it. Because of its fineness and lightness, the fire pierces the earth and air and rises above everything else. Water became more humid than earth because two female parts, the humidity from air and the cold from earth, were united in it. Humidity entered into heat only because, being generated between male heat and female cold and being itself female, it moved toward the male heat to become paired with it. Thus it became a single thing, air, whose form is heat and humidity. Likewise dryness, which is male, inclined to the female, cold, to become earth.

With the four Mothers—earth, water, air and fire—the cornerstones *(arkān)* of the world were complete. Thereafter birth revolved among them, driven by the motion produced by heat, the first substance. First earth and water released their fine matter *(laṭīf)* which spread in all directions from their layers, leaving the coarse matter *(kathīf)* behind. The fine matter that was released in seven pushes consolidated into the seven celestial spheres, beginning with the outermost that was to become the sphere of Jupiter. Each subsequent push released less fine matter, which formed the lower spheres. After the formation of the seven spheres, there were further pushes, causing the remaining fine matter of earth and water to rise as a vapor. This vapor consolidated below the celestial spheres as clouds, but the heat under the earth continually liquefies it, and it descends as rain on the earth.

The celestial spheres at first were like dead bodies without a spirit. The heat then gripped the two substances of fire and air and caused their fine matter, which was luminous and resplendent, to rise. Because of its fineness, this matter pierced the spheres until it reached the outer sphere, where it halted. The spheres were in need of it, as bodies need spirit. The outer sphere thus attracted as much of it as it could, and this assembled light was called Jupiter. The rest of the light descended first to the next sphere, where Saturn was formed from it, and then to the other spheres. The middle sphere was the most powerful one and attracted all the remaining light to itself, which formed the sun. There was, however, a surplus of light in the higher spheres, which then descended to form the planets of Mars, Venus, and Mercury. An abundant surplus of light from the sun formed the moon. The planets thus became the spirits of the seven spheres, which surrounded them as their protective bodies. Some of that fine matter also descended below the celestial spheres and appeared as light in the sky. This light is in reality a star that had dissipated, and it is unable to solidify like the planets because of its deficient fineness. The light we presently observe in the sky consists of the vapor formed by fine matter of air. When this vapor is attracted to the ether *(athīr),* i.e. the layer of fire, it is assimilated to it and lights up.

After the completion of the seven celestial spheres by the luminous planets, the vapor of fine matter ever continues to rise below the sphere of the moon, driven by the action of the substance of heat. As the vapor assembles, it pushes against the sphere of the moon, causing it to revolve. The sphere of the moon in turn pushes the higher spheres to move and revolve. That vapor is capable of pushing the spheres is proved by the observable fact that when it is trapped inside the earth it may explode to cause a fissure in the earth from which it can escape. This phenomenon is called an earthquake. It may even toss up a big rock or a clump of earth, and ignorant people consider this a miraculous event. Moreover, the revolution of the spheres continuously produces two strong winds below and above it, and these cause the stars to revolve in the opposite direction.

The revolution of the spheres around the earth functions like a waterwheel, lifting the coarse matter of the four Mother elements while lowering their fine matter and thus continuously producing their varying mixture. This action generated the Progeny *(mawālīd)*, the terrestrial kingdoms. These evolved, like the celestial spheres, in four stages. First, bodies without a spirit were generated, such as minerals and metals that melt. Then bodies with the single spirit of growth developed, such as plants and trees. These correspond to the celestial spheres combined with their planets. Then bodies with two spirits, the spirit of growth and the spirit of motion, were generated, such as birds, animals and beasts. They correspond to the spheres and planets with their circular motion. Finally, mankind evolved. The human being possesses the spirits of growth and motion and is qualified *(mutahayyiʾa)* to receive the rational spirit *(rūḥ nāṭiqa)*. Man is more perfect than any other creature below the celestial spheres and thus may be likened to the perfected spheres when they reached the stage of permanent circular movement and return *(iʿtiyād)*. Everything from the spheres to the Mother elements and the animals on earth exists only for the sake of the perfection of mankind.

Unlike the other spirits or souls,[12] the rational soul did not evolve out of the material world but is an imprint or trace of the Rational Soul, as the Universal Soul is now termed by al-Nasafī, in the sensitive animal soul. The Rational Soul may be likened to the sun, whose rays penetrate fine matter to affect whatever on earth is receptive to its light, but do not penetrate solid walls. Similarly, the traces of the Rational Soul penetrate the material world to affect the receptive rational souls of humankind. The effects of the Rational Soul—salvational knowledge and wisdom—are conveyed to humanity by the Prophets and their Fundaments *(usus)*.[13] The acquisition of these effects, however, depends on the efforts of the individual. Those who fail to acquire them will suffer severe punishment. The rational souls survive death and greatly benefit from their knowledge in the hereafter. Ultimately, they become parts of the Universal Soul, which in turn will reach its perfection as an intellect and join the First Intellect. This obviously will mean the end of the world.

---

[12] Al-Nasafī uses the two terms *rūḥ* and *nafs* almost interchangeably. He presumably viewed the souls as the seats of their respective spirits.

[13] Reading *wa-ususuhā* for *wa-smuhā* in the manuscript.

# INDEX OF PERSONAL AND TRIBAL NAMES

In order to keep the index within bounds some arbitrary exclusions had to be made. Names of authors quoted as such, both early and modern, have been omitted.

**Abbreviations:**

| | | |
|---|---|---|
| A. – Aḥmad | Ḥu. – Ḥusayn | ʿU. – ʿUmar |
| ʿA. – ʿAlī; | Ibr. – Ibrāhīm | ʿUl. – ʿUbayd Allāh |
| ʿAl - ʿAbd Allāh | Ism. – Ismāʿīl | ʿUth. – ʿUthmān |
| ʿAr. – ʿAbd al-Raḥmān | M. – Muḥammad | Y. – Yūsuf |
| Ḥ – Ḥasan | S. – Sulaymān | |

# INDEX OF GEOGRAPHICAL NAMES